New Perspectives on

Microsoft®
Access 97

COMPREHENSIVE—ENHANCED

The New Perspectives Series

The New Perspectives Series consists of texts and technology that teach computer concepts and microcomputer applications (listed below). You can order these New Perspectives texts in many different lengths, software releases, custom-bound combinations, CourseKits™ and Custom Editions®. Contact your Course Technology sales representative or customer service representative for the most up-to-date details.

The New Perspectives Series

Computer Concepts

Borland® dBASE®

Borland® Paradox®

Corel® Presentations™

Corel® Quattro Pro®

Corel® WordPerfect®

DOS

HTML

Lotus® 1-2-3®

Microsoft® Access

Microsoft® Excel

Microsoft® Internet Explorer

Microsoft® Office Professional

Microsoft® PowerPoint®

Microsoft® Windows® 3.1

Microsoft® Windows® 95

Microsoft® Windows NT® Server 4.0

Microsoft® Windows NT® Workstation 4.0

Microsoft® Word

Microsoft® Works

Netscape Navigator™

Netscape Navigator™ Gold

Microsoft® Visual Basic® 4 and 5

New Perspectives on
Microsoft®
Access 97

COMPREHENSIVE—ENHANCED

Joseph J. Adamski
Grand Valley State University

Charles Hommel
University of Puget Sound

Kathleen T. Finnegan

COURSE
TECHNOLOGY

ONE MAIN STREET, CAMBRIDGE, MA 02142

an International Thomson Publishing company I(T)P®

Cambridge • Albany • Bonn • Boston • Cincinnati • London • Madrid • Melbourne • Mexico City
New York • Paris • San Francisco • Singapore • Tokyo • Toronto • Washington

New Perspectives on Microsoft® Access 97—Comprehensive—Enhanced is published by
Course Technology.

Associate Publisher	Mac Mendelsohn
Series Consulting Editor	Susan Solomon
Acquisitions Editor	Mark Reimold
Developmental Editor	Kathy Finnegan
Production Editor	Roxanne Alexander
Text and Cover Designer	Ella Hanna
Cover Illustrator	Douglas Goodman

© 1998 by Course Technology — I(T)P®

For more information contact:

Course Technology
One Main Street
Cambridge, MA 02142

ITP Europe
Berkshire House 168-173
High Holborn
London WCIV 7AA
England

Nelson ITP, Australia
102 Dodds Street
South Melbourne, 3205
Victoria, Australia

ITP Nelson Canada
1120 Birchmount Road
Scarborough, Ontario
Canada M1K 5G4

International Thomson Editores
Seneca, 53
Colonia Polanco
11560 Mexico D.F. Mexico

ITP GmbH
Königswinterer Strasse 418
53227 Bonn
Germany

ITP Asia
60 Albert Street, #15-01
Albert Complex
Singapore 189969

ITP Japan
Hirakawacho Kyowa Building, 3F
2-2-1 Hirakawacho
Chiyoda-ku, Tokyo 102
Japan

ISBN 0-7600-7309-0

Printed in the United States of America

5 6 7 8 9 10 BM 01 00 99

At Course Technology we have one foot in education and the other in technology. We believe that technology is transforming the way people teach and learn, and we are excited about providing instructors and students with materials that use technology to teach about technology.

Our development process is unparalleled in the higher education publishing industry. Every product we create goes through an exacting process of design, development, review, and testing.

Reviewers give us direction and insight that shape our manuscripts and bring them up to the latest standards. Every manuscript is quality tested. Students whose backgrounds match the intended audience work through every keystroke, carefully checking for clarity and pointing out errors in logic and sequence. Together with our own technical reviewers, these testers help us ensure that everything that carries our name is error-free and easy to use.

We show both how and why technology is critical to solving problems in college and in whatever field you choose to teach or pursue. Our time-tested, step-by-step instructions provide unparalleled clarity. Examples and applications are chosen and crafted to motivate students.

As the New Perspectives Series team at Course Technology, our goal is to produce the most timely, accurate, creative, and technologically sound product in the entire college publishing industry. We strive for consistent high quality. This takes a lot of communication, coordination, and hard work. But we love what we do. We are determined to be the best. Write to us and let us know what you think. You can also e-mail us at *NewPerspectives@course.com*.

The New Perspectives Series Team

Joseph J. Adamski	Jessica Evans	Mac Mendelsohn
Judy Adamski	Marilyn Freedman	William Newman
Roy Ageloff	Kathy Finnegan	Dan Oja
Tim Ashe	Robin Geller	David Paradic
David Auer	Donna Gridley	June Parsons
Daphne Barbas	Kate Habib	Harry Phillips
Dirk Baldwin	Roger Hayen	Sandra Poindexter
Rachel Bunin	Charles Hommel	Mark Reimold
Joan Carey	Cindy Johnson	Ann Shaffer
Patrick Carey	Janice Jutras	Karen Shortill
Sharon Caswell	Chris Kelly	Susan Solomon
Barbara Clemens	Mary Kemper	Susanne Walker
Rachel Crapser	Stacy Klein	John Zeanchock
Kim Crowley	Terry Ann Kremer	Beverly Zimmerman
Michael Ekedahl	John Leschke	Scott Zimmerman

What is the New Perspectives Series?

Course Technology's **New Perspectives Series** is an integrated system of instruction that combines text and technology products to teach computer concepts and microcomputer applications. Users consistently praise this series for innovative pedagogy, creativity, supportive and engaging style, accuracy, and use of interactive technology. The first New Perspectives text was published in January of 1993. Since then, the series has grown to more than 100 titles and has become the best-selling series on computer concepts and microcomputer applications. Others have imitated the New Perspectives features, design, and technologies, but none have replicated its quality and its ability to consistently anticipate and meet the needs of instructors and students.

What is the Integrated System of Instruction?

New Perspectives textbooks are part of a truly Integrated System of Instruction: text, graphics, video, sound, animation, and simulations that are linked and that provide a flexible, unified, and interactive system to help you teach and help your students learn. Specifically, the *New Perspectives Integrated System of Instruction* includes a Course Technology textbook in addition to some or all of the following items: Course Labs, Course Test Manager, Online Companions, and Course Presenter. These components—shown in the graphic on the back cover of this book—have been developed to work together to provide a complete, integrative teaching and learning experience.

How is the New Perspectives Series different from other microcomputer concepts and applications series?

The **New Perspectives Series** distinguishes itself from other series in at least four substantial ways: sound instructional design, consistent quality, innovative technology, and proven pedagogy. The applications texts in this series consist of two or more tutorials, which are based on sound instructional design. Each tutorial is motivated by a realistic case that is meaningful to students. Rather than learn a laundry list of features, students learn the features in the context of solving a problem. This process motivates all concepts and skills by demonstrating to students *why* they would want to know them.

Instructors and students have come to rely on the high quality of the **New Perspectives Series** and to consistently praise its accuracy. This accuracy is a result of Course Technology's unique multi-step quality assurance process that incorporates student testing at at least two stages of development, using hardware and software configurations appropriate to the product. All solutions, test questions, and other supplements are tested using similar procedures. Instructors who adopt this series report that students can work through the tutorials independently with minimum intervention or "damage control" by instructors or staff. This consistent quality has meant that if instructors are pleased with one product from the series, they can rely on the same quality with any other New Perspectives product.

The **New Perspectives Series** also distinguishes itself by its innovative technology. This series innovated Course Labs, truly *interactive* learning applications. These have set the standard for interactive learning.

How do I know that the New Perspectives Series will work?

Some instructors who use this series report a significant difference between how much their students learn and retain with this series as compared to other series. With other series, instructors often find that students can work through the book and do well on homework and tests, but still not demonstrate competency when asked to perform particular tasks outside the context of the text's sample case or project. With the **New Perspectives Series**, however, instructors report that students have a complete, integrative learning experience that stays with them. They credit this high retention and competency to the fact that this series incorporates critical thinking and problem-solving with computer skills mastery.

How does this book I'm holding fit into the New Perspectives Series?

New Perspectives applications books are available in the following categories:

Brief books are typically about 150 pages long, contain two to four tutorials, and are intended to teach the basics of an application.

Introductory books are typically about 300 pages long and consist of four to seven tutorials that go beyond the basics. These books often build out of the Brief editions by providing two or three additional tutorials.

Comprehensive books are typically about 600 pages long and consist of all of the tutorials in the Introductory books, plus a few more tutorials covering higher-level topics. Comprehensive books typically also include two Windows tutorials and three or four Additional Cases. The book you are holding is a Comprehensive book.

Advanced books cover topics similar to those in the Comprehensive books, but go into more depth. Advanced books present the most high-level coverage in the series.

Custom Books The New Perspectives Series offers you two ways to customize a New Perspectives text to fit your course exactly: *CourseKits*™, two or more texts packaged together in a box, and *Custom Editions*®, your choice of books bound together. Custom Editions offer you unparalleled flexibility in designing your concepts and applications courses. You can build your own book by ordering a combination of titles bound together to cover only the topics you want. Your students save because they buy only the materials they need. There is no minimum order, and books are spiral bound. Both CourseKits and Custom Editions offer significant price discounts. Contact your Course Technology sales representative for more information.

New Perspectives Series Microcomputer Applications

Brief Titles or Modules	Introductory Titles or Modules	Intermediate Tutorials	Advanced Titles or Modules	Other Modules

Brief	**Introductory**	**Comprehensive**	**Advanced**	**Custom Editions**
2 to 4 tutorials	6 or 7 tutorials, or Brief + 2 or 3 more tutorials	Introductory + 3 to 6 more tutorials. Includes Brief Windows tutorials and Additional Cases	Quick Review of basics + in-depth, high-level coverage	Choose from any of the above to build your own Custom Editions® or CourseKits™

In what kind of course could I use this book?

This book can be used in any course in which you want students to learn all the most important topics of Microsoft Access, including creating and maintaining database tables; defining table relationships; creating, running, and saving queries; sorting and filtering records; creating and customizing forms and reports; publishing Access objects to the World Wide Web; replicating a database; creating and running macros; creating a switchboard; creating custom toolbars and menu bars; and writing Visual Basic code. It is particularly recommended for a full-semester course on Microsoft Access. This book also includes coverage of basic Windows 95 navigation and file management skills in the Windows 95 Brief tutorials.

Windows 98 Preview Following the Brief Windows 95 tutorials of this text, students are presented with a brief explanation of what to expect with Windows 98. This introductory tour explains some of the new features of the operating system, by comparing them to the Windows 95 system. Students are encouraged to look critically at these new features in order to decide whether to upgrade their systems.

This book has been approved by Microsoft as courseware for the Certified Microsoft Office User (CMOU) program. After completing the tutorials and exercises in this book, students will be prepared to take the Expert level CMOU exam for Microsoft Access 97. By passing the certification exam for a Microsoft software program, students demonstrate proficiency in that program to employers. For more information about certification, please visit the CMOU program World Wide Web site at http://www.microsoft.com/office/train_cert.

How do the Windows 95 editions differ from the Windows 3.1 editions?

Sessions We've divided the tutorials into sessions. Each session is designed to be completed in about 45 minutes to an hour (depending, of course, upon student needs and the speed of your lab equipment). With sessions, learning is broken up into more easily assimilated portions. You can more accurately allocate time in your syllabus, and students can better manage the available lab time. Each session begins with a "session box," which quickly describes the skills students will learn in the session. Furthermore, each session is numbered, which makes it easier for you and your students to navigate and communicate about the tutorial. Look on page A 1.5 for the session box that opens Session 1.1.

Quick Checks Each session concludes with meaningful, conceptual Quick Check questions that test students' understanding of what they learned in the session. Answers to the Quick Check questions in this book are provided on pages A 4.35 through A 4.36, A 7.35 through A 7.36, and A 10.61 through A 10.64.

New Design We have retained the best of the old design to help students differentiate between what they are to *do* and what they are to *read*. The steps are clearly identified by their shaded background and numbered steps. Furthermore, this new design presents steps and screen shots in a larger, easier to read format. Some good examples of our new design are pages A 1.14 and A 1.15.

What features are retained in the Windows 95 editions of the New Perspectives Series?

"Read This Before You Begin" Page This page is consistent with Course Technology's unequaled commitment to helping instructors introduce technology into the classroom. Technical considerations and assumptions about software are listed to help

instructors save time and eliminate unnecessary aggravation. See pages A 1.2, A 5.2, and A 8.2 for the "Read This Before You Begin" pages in this book.

Tutorial Case   Each tutorial begins with a problem presented in a case that is meaningful to students. The problem turns the task of learning how to use an application into a problem-solving process. The problems increase in complexity with each tutorial. These cases touch on multicultural, international, and ethical issues—so important to today's business curriculum. See page A 1.3 for the case that begins Tutorial 1.

Step-by-Step Methodology   This unique Course Technology methodology keeps students on track. They enter data, click buttons, or press keys always within the context of solving the problem posed in the tutorial case. The text constantly guides students, letting them know where they are in the course of solving the problem. In addition, the numerous screen shots include labels that direct students' attention to what they should look at on the screen. On almost every page in this book, you can find an example of how steps, screen shots, and labels work together.

TROUBLE?

TROUBLE? Paragraphs   These paragraphs anticipate the mistakes or problems that students are likely to have and help them recover and continue with the tutorial. By putting these paragraphs in the book, rather than in the Instructor's Manual, we facilitate independent learning and free the instructor to focus on substantive conceptual issues rather than on common procedural errors. Some representative examples of TROUBLE? paragraphs appear on pages A 1.7 and A 1.10.

Reference Windows   Reference Windows appear throughout the text. They are succinct summaries of the most important tasks covered in the tutorials. Reference Windows are specially designed and written so students can refer to them when doing the Tutorial Assignments and Case Problems, and after completing the course. Page A 1.18 contains the Reference Window for Using the Office Assistant.

Task Reference   The Task Reference contains a summary of how to perform common tasks using the most efficient method, as well as references to pages where the task is discussed in more detail. It appears as a table at the end of the book.

Tutorial Assignments, Case Problems, and Lab Assignments   Each tutorial concludes with Tutorial Assignments, which provide students with additional hands-on practice of the skills they learned in the tutorial. See page A 1.23 for examples of Tutorial Assignments. The Tutorial Assignments are followed by four Case Problems that have approximately the same scope as the tutorial case. See page A 1.24 for examples of Case Problems. Finally, if a Course Lab accompanies a tutorial, Lab Assignments are included after the Case Problems. See page A 1.27 for examples of Lab Assignments.

Exploration Exercises   The Windows environment allows students to learn by exploring and discovering what they can do. Exploration Exercises can be Tutorial Assignments or Case Problems that challenge students, encourage them to explore the capabilities of the program they are using, and extend their knowledge using the Help facility and other reference materials. Page A 1.23 contains Exploration Exercises for Tutorial 1.

What supplements are available with this textbook?

Course Labs: Now, Concepts Come to Life Computer skills and concepts come to life with the New Perspectives Course Labs—highly-interactive tutorials that combine illustrations, animations, digital images, and simulations. The Labs guide students step-by-step, present them with Quick Check questions, let them explore on their own, test their comprehension, and provide printed feedback. Lab icons at the beginning of the tutorial and in the tutorial margins indicate when a topic has a corresponding Lab. Lab Assignments are included at the end of each relevant tutorial. The Labs available with this book and the tutorials in which they appear are:

TUTORIAL 1
WINDOWS 95

Using a Keyboard

TUTORIAL 1
WINDOWS 95

Using a Mouse

TUTORIAL 2
WINDOWS 95

Using Files

TUTORIAL 1
ACCESS 97

Databases

Course Test Manager This cutting-edge Windows-based testing software helps instructors design and administer tests and pre-tests. The full-featured online program permits students to take tests at the computer where their grades are computed immediately following the completion of the exam. Automatic statistics collection, student study guides customized to the students' performance, and printed tests are only a few of the features.

Skills Assessment Manager (SAM) This ground-breaking new assessment tool tests students' ability to perform real-world tasks live in the Microsoft Office 97 applications. Designed to be administered over a network, SAM tracks every action students perform in Microsoft Office 97 as they work through an exam. Upon completion of an exam, SAM assesses not only the *results* of students' work, but also the *way* students arrived at each answer and *how efficiently* they worked. Instructors may use SAM to create their own custom exams, or they may select from a library of pre-made exams, including exams that map to the content in this text as well as the Microsoft Office User Specialist certification program. SAM is available for free to test students who have purchased this text. Instructors interested in using SAM to test students out of a course, or to place them into a course, should contact their Course Technology sales representative.

Figures on CD-ROM This lecture presentation tool allows instructors to create electronic slide shows or traditional overhead transparencies using the figure files from the book. Instructors can customize, edit, save, and display figures from the text in order to illustrate key topics or concepts in class.

Online Companions: Dedicated to Keeping You and Your Students Up-To-Date When you use a New Perspectives product, you can access Course Technology's faculty sites and student sites on the World Wide Web. You can browse the password-protected Faculty Online Companions to obtain online Instructor's Manuals, Solution Files, Student Files, and more. Please see your Instructor's Manual or call your Course Technology customer service representative for more information. Student and Faculty Online Companions are accessible by clicking the appropriate links on the Course Technology home page at http://www.course.com.

Instructor's Manual New Perspectives Series Instructor's Manuals contain instructor's notes and printed solutions for each tutorial. Instructor's notes provide tutorial overviews and outlines, technical notes, lecture notes, and extra Case Problems. Printed solutions include solutions to Tutorial Assignments, Case Problems, Additional Cases, and Lab Assignments.

Internet Assignments The Instructor's Manual that accompanies this text includes additional assignments that integrate the World Wide Web with the database skills students learn in the tutorials. To complete these assignments, students will need to search the Web and follow the links from the *New Perspectives on Microsoft Access 97* home page. The Access 97 home page is accessible through the Student Online Companion link found on the Course Technology home page at http:\\www.course.com. Please refer to the Instructor's Manual for more information.

Student Files Student Files contain all of the data that students will use to complete the tutorials, Tutorial Assignments, Case Problems, and Additional Cases. A Readme file includes technical tips for lab management. See the inside covers of this book and the "Read This Before You Begin" pages for more information on Student Files.

Solution Files Solution Files contain every file students are asked to create or modify in the tutorials, Tutorial Assignments, Case Problems, and Additional Cases.

The following supplements are included in the Instructor's Resource Kit that accompanies this textbook:

- electronic Instructor's Manual
- Solution Files
- Student Files
- Course Labs
- Course Test Manager Testbank
- Course Test Manager Engine
- Figures on CD-ROM

Some of the supplements listed above are also available over the World Wide Web through Course Technology's password-protected Faculty Online Companions. Please see your Instructor's Manual or call your Course Technology customer service representative for more information.

Acknowledgments

I would like to thank the dedicated and enthusiastic Course Technology staff, including Joe Dougherty, Mac Mendelsohn, Susan Solomon, and Mark Reimold. Thanks as well to all the Production staff, including everyone from GEX who worked hard to produce this book. And a special thanks to Kathy Finnegan for her talents, verve, and long hours of dedicated work.

Joseph J. Adamski

I want to thank all those who helped in completing this book, including Nancy Acree of University of Puget Sound, and Joyce Strain of Green River Community College, who reviewed the first draft; Course Technology's great team, including Mark Reimold, Donna Gridley, Roxanne Alexander, Jane Pedicini, Greg Bigelow, John McCarthy, Chris Hall, Karen Shortill, and all the others involved in creating this book. Also, my thanks to Kathy Finnegan, whose keen eye greatly improved the book and whose good humor made deadlines seem almost fun. Finally, special thanks to Joan, who tolerated many late nights and lost weekends while I worked, and Anna, who helped with paste-ups and backups when she would have preferred a good game of checkers.

Charles Hommel

I would like to thank the following reviewers for their excellent feedback: Cynthia J. Kachik, Jean Smelewicz of Quinsigamond Community College, and Patricia A Smith, Ph.D., of Temple Junior College. My thanks to all the Course Technology staff, including Mac Mendelsohn, Mark Reimold, Donna Gridley, Rachel Crapser, and Kristen Duerr for their support; Roxanne Alexander for her outstanding management of the production process; Jane Pedicini for her superior copy editing skills; and Greg Bigelow and Brian McCooey for ensuring the accuracy of the text. Thanks, too, to everyone at GEX for their efforts in the composition of this book. Special thanks to Sasha Vodnik for his contributions in developing this text, and to Joe Adamski for his invaluable guidance and encouragement. Finally, thanks to Joe, Connor, and Devon for their support and for interrupting me just enough so that I remembered what the outside of my office looked like.

Kathleen T. Finnegan

Brief Contents

Table of **Contents**

TUTORIAL 6

Customizing Reports and Integrating Access with Other Programs

**Creating a Custom Invoices Report and a
Report with an Embedded Chart and a
Linked Text Document**   **A 6.1**

Reference Windows

New Perspectives on

Microsoft®
Windows® 95

BRIEF

TUTORIALS

Read This **Before You Begin**

STUDENT DISKS

To complete the tutorials and Tutorial Assignments, you need a Student Disk. Your instructor will either provide you with a Student Disk or ask you to make your own.

If you are supposed to make your own Student Disk, you will need a blank, formatted high-density disk. Follow the instructions in the section called "Creating Your Student Disk" in Tutorial 2 to use the Make Student Disk program to create your own Student Disk. See the inside front or inside back cover of this book for more information on Student Disk files, or ask your instructor or technical support person for assistance.

COURSE LABS

This book features three interactive Course Labs to help you understand Windows concepts. There are Lab Assignments at the end of each tutorial that relate to these Labs. To start a Lab, click the Start button on the Windows 95 taskbar, point to Programs, point to CTI Windows 95 Applications, point to Windows 95 New Perspectives Brief, and click the name of the Lab you want to use.

USING YOUR OWN COMPUTER

If you are going to work through this book using your own computer, you need:

■ **Computer System** Windows 95 must be installed on your computer. This book assumes a complete installation of Windows 95.

■ **Student Disk** Ask your instructor or lab manager for details on how to get the Student Disk. You will not be able to complete the tutorials or exercises in this book using your own computer until you have the Student Disk. The student files may also be obtained electronically over the Internet. See the inside front or inside back cover of this book for more details.

■ **Course Labs** See your instructor or technical support person to obtain the Course Lab software for use on your own computer.

To complete the tutorials and Tutorial Assignments in this book, your students must use a set of files on a Student Disk. The Instructor's Resource Kit for this book includes either two Student Files Setup Disks or a CD-ROM containing the student disk setup program. Follow the instructions on the disk label or in the Readme file to install the Make Student Disk program onto your server or standalone computers. Your students can then use the Windows 95 Start menu to run the program that will create their Student Disk. Tutorial 2 contains steps that instruct your students on how to generate student disks.

If you prefer to provide Student Disks rather than letting students generate them, you can run the Make Student Disk program yourself following the instructions in Tutorial 2.

COURSE LAB SOFTWARE

This book features three online, interactive Course Labs that introduce basic Windows concepts. The Instructor's Resource Kit for this book contains the Lab software either on four Course Labs Setup Disks or on a CD-ROM. Follow the instructions on the disk label or in the Readme file to install the Lab software on your server or standalone computers. Refer also to the Readme file for essential technical notes related to running the labs in a multiuser environment.

Once you have installed the Course Lab software, your students can start the Labs from the Windows 95 desktop by clicking the Start button on the Windows 95 taskbar, pointing to Programs, pointing to CTI Windows 95 Applications, pointing to Windows 95 New Perspectives Brief, and then clicking the name of the Lab they want to use.

CT LAB SOFTWARE AND STUDENT FILES

You are granted a license to copy the Student Files and Course Labs to any computer or computer network used by students who have purchased this book.

Exploring the Basics

Investigating the Windows 95 Operating System
in the Computer Lab

OBJECTIVES

In this tutorial you will learn to:

■ Identify the controls on the Windows 95 desktop

■ Use the Windows 95 Start button to run software programs

■ Identify and use the controls in a window

■ Switch between programs using the taskbar

■ Use Windows 95 controls such as menus, toolbars, list boxes, scroll bars, radio buttons, tabs, and check boxes

LABS

 Using a Mouse | Using a Keyboard

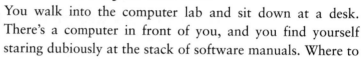

Your First Day in the Lab

CASE You walk into the computer lab and sit down at a desk. There's a computer in front of you, and you find yourself staring dubiously at the stack of software manuals. Where to start? As if in answer to your question, your friend Steve Laslow appears.

Gesturing to the stack of manuals, you tell Steve that you were just wondering where to start.

"You start with the operating system," says Steve. Noticing your slightly puzzled look, Steve explains that the **operating system** is software that helps the computer carry out basic operating tasks such as displaying information on the computer screen and saving data on your disks. Your computer uses the **Microsoft Windows 95** operating system—Windows 95, for short.

Steve tells you that Windows 95 has a "gooey" or **graphical user interface (GUI)**, which uses pictures of familiar objects, such as file folders and documents, to represent a desktop on your screen. Microsoft Windows 95 gets its name from the rectangular-shaped work areas, called "windows," that appear on your screen.

Steve continues to talk as he sorts through the stack of manuals on your desk. He says there are two things he really likes about Windows 95. First, lots of software is available for computers that have the Windows 95 operating system and all this software has a standard graphical user interface. That means once you have learned how to use one Windows software package, such as word-processing software, you are well on your way to understanding how to use other Windows software. Second, Windows 95 lets you use more than one software package at a time, so you can easily switch between your word-processing software and your appointment book software, for example. All in all, Windows 95 makes your computer an effective and easy-to-use productivity tool.

Steve recommends that you get started right away by using some tutorials that will teach you the skills essential for using Microsoft Windows 95. He hands you a book and assures you that everything on your computer system is set up and ready to go.

You mention that last summer you worked in an advertising agency where the employees used something called Windows 3.1. Steve explains that Windows 3.1 is an earlier version of the Windows operating system. Windows 95 and Windows 3.1 are similar, but Windows 95 is more powerful and easier to use. Steve says that as you work through the tutorials you will see notes that point out the important differences between Windows 95 and Windows 3.1.

Steve has a class, but he says he'll check back later to see how you are doing.

Using the Tutorials Effectively

These tutorials will help you learn about Windows 95. The tutorials are designed to be used at a computer. Each tutorial is divided into sessions. Watch for the session headings, such as Session 1.1 and Session 1.2. Each session is designed to be completed in about 45 minutes, but take as much time as you need. It's also a good idea to take a break between sessions.

Before you begin, read the following questions and answers. They are designed to help you use the tutorials effectively.

Where do I start?

Each tutorial begins with a case, which sets the scene for the tutorial and gives you background information to help you understand what you will be doing in the tutorial. Read the case before you go to the lab. In the lab, begin with the first session of the tutorial.

How do I know what to do on the computer?

Each session contains steps that you will perform on the computer to learn how to use Windows 95. Read the text that introduces each series of steps. The steps you need to do at a computer are numbered and are set against a color background. Read each step carefully and completely before you try it.

How do I know if I did the step correctly?

As you work, compare your computer screen with the corresponding figure in the tutorial. Don't worry if your screen display is somewhat different from the figure. The important parts of the screen display are labeled in each figure. Check to make sure these parts are on your screen.

What if I make a mistake?

Don't worry about making mistakes—they are part of the learning process. Paragraphs labeled "**TROUBLE?**" identify common problems and explain how to get back on track. Follow the steps in a **TROUBLE?** paragraph *only* if you are having the problem described. If you run into other problems:

- Carefully consider the current state of your system, the position of the pointer, and any messages on the screen.

- Complete the sentence, "Now I want to...." Be specific, because you are identifying your goal.

- Develop a plan for accomplishing your goal, and put your plan into action.

How do I use the Reference Windows?

Reference Windows summarize the procedures you learn in the tutorial steps. Do not complete the actions in the Reference Windows when you are working through the tutorial. Instead, refer to the Reference Windows while you are working on the assignments at the end of the tutorial.

How can I test my understanding of the material I learned in the tutorial?

At the end of each session, you can answer the Quick Check questions. The answers for the Quick Checks are at the end of the book.

After you have completed the entire tutorial, you should complete the Tutorial Assignments. The Tutorial Assignments are carefully structured so you will review what you have learned and then apply your knowledge to new situations.

What if I can't remember how to do something?

You should refer to the Task Reference at the end of the book; it summarizes how to accomplish commonly performed tasks.

What are the 3.1 Notes?

The 3.1 Notes are helpful if you have used Windows 3.1. The notes point out the key similarities and differences between Windows 3.1 and Windows 95.

What are the Interactive Labs, and how should I use them?

Interactive Labs help you review concepts and practice skills that you learn in the tutorial. Lab icons at the beginning of each tutorial and in the margins of the tutorials indicate topics that have corresponding Labs. The Lab Assignments section includes instructions for how to use each Lab.

Now that you understand how to use the tutorials effectively, you are ready to begin.

SESSION

1.1

In this session, in addition to learning basic Windows terminology, you will learn how to use a mouse, to start and stop a program, and to use more than one program at a time. With the skills you learn in this session, you will be able to use Windows 95 to start software programs.

Using a Keyboard

Starting Windows 95

Windows 95 automatically starts when you turn on the computer. Depending on the way your computer is set up, you might be asked to enter your user name and password. If prompted to do so, type your assigned user name and press the Enter key. Then type your password and press the Enter key to continue.

To start Windows 95:

1. Turn on your computer.

TROUBLE? If the Welcome to Windows 95 box appears on your screen, press the Enter key to close it.

The Windows 95 Desktop

In Windows terminology, the screen represents a **desktop**—a workspace for projects and the tools needed to manipulate those projects. Look at your screen display and locate the objects labeled in Figure 1-1 on the following page.

Because it is easy to customize the Windows environment, your screen might not look exactly the same as Figure 1-1. You should, however, be able to locate objects on your screen similar to those in Figure 1-1.

Icons are small pictures that represent objects such as your computer, your computer network, a specific computer program, or a document. Your desktop probably contains several icons, such as My Computer, Network Neighborhood, and the Recycle Bin. You'll use these icons in later tutorials to work with files stored on your computer or on other computers on the network.

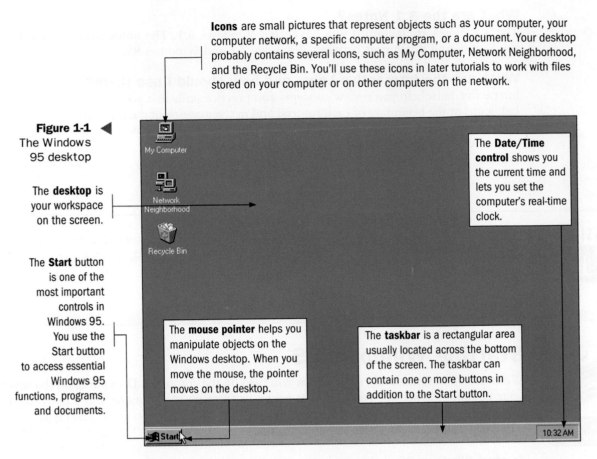

Figure 1-1 ◀
The Windows
95 desktop

The **desktop** is
your workspace
on the screen.

The **Start** button
is one of the
most important
controls in
Windows 95.
You use the
Start button
to access essential
Windows 95
functions, programs,
and documents.

The **Date/Time control** shows you the current time and lets you set the computer's real-time clock.

The **mouse pointer** helps you manipulate objects on the Windows desktop. When you move the mouse, the pointer moves on the desktop.

The **taskbar** is a rectangular area usually located across the bottom of the screen. The taskbar can contain one or more buttons in addition to the Start button.

TROUBLE? If the screen goes blank or starts to display a moving design, press any key to restore the image.

Using the Mouse

Using a Mouse

A **mouse**, like those shown in Figure 1-2, is a pointing device that helps you interact with objects on the screen. In Windows 95 you need to know how to use the mouse to point, click, and drag. In this session you will learn about pointing and clicking. In Session 1.2 you will learn how to use the mouse to drag objects.

You can also interact with objects by using the keyboard; however, the mouse is much more convenient for most tasks, so the tutorials in this book assume you are using one.

Pointing

The **pointer**, or **mouse pointer**, is a small object that moves on the screen when you move the mouse. The pointer is usually shaped like an arrow. As you move the mouse on a flat surface, the pointer on the screen moves in the direction corresponding to the movement of the mouse. The pointer sometimes changes shape depending on where it is on the screen or the action the computer is completing.

Find the arrow-shaped pointer on your screen. If you do not see the pointer, move your mouse until the pointer comes into view.

Figure 1-2 ◀
The mouse

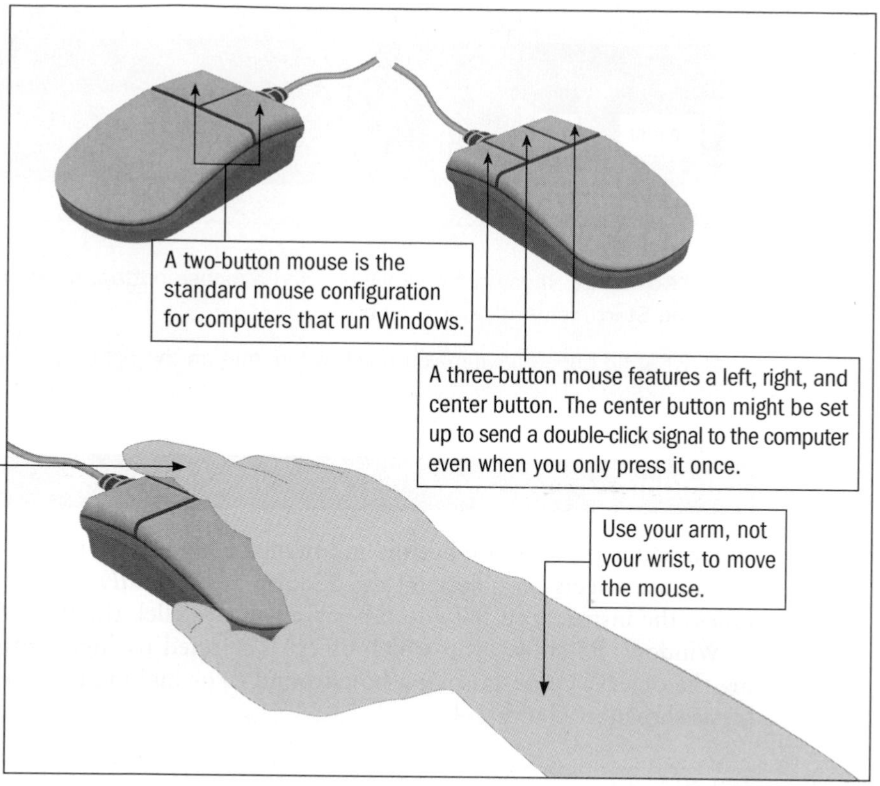

A two-button mouse is the standard mouse configuration for computers that run Windows.

A three-button mouse features a left, right, and center button. The center button might be set up to send a double-click signal to the computer even when you only press it once.

To hold the mouse, place your forefinger over the left mouse button. Place your thumb on the left side of the mouse. Your ring and small fingers should be on the right side of the mouse.

Use your arm, not your wrist, to move the mouse.

Basic "mousing" skills depend on your ability to position the pointer. You begin most Windows operations by positioning the pointer over a specific part of the screen. This is called **pointing**.

To move the pointer:

1. Position your right index finger over the left mouse button, as shown in Figure 1-2. Lightly grasp the sides of the mouse with your thumb and little finger.

   TROUBLE? If you want to use the mouse with your left hand, ask your instructor or technical support person to help you use the Control Panel to change the mouse settings to swap the left and right mouse buttons. Be sure you find out how to change back to the right-handed mouse setting, so you can reset the mouse each time you are finished in the lab.

2. Locate the arrow-shaped pointer on the screen.

3. Move the mouse and watch the movement of the pointer.

If you run out of room to move your mouse, lift the mouse and move it to a clear area on your desk, then place the mouse back on the desk. Notice that the pointer does not move when the mouse is not in contact with the desk.

When you position the mouse pointer over certain objects, such as the objects on the taskbar, a "tip" appears. These "tips" are called **ToolTips**, and they tell you the purpose or function of an object.

To view ToolTips:

1. Use the mouse to point to the **Start** button ⊞Start. After a few seconds, you see the tip "Click here to begin" as shown in Figure 1-3 on the following page.

Figure 1-3 ◀
Viewing ToolTips

Start button ────

pointer   tip

Click here to begin

🔲 Sta

10:33 AM

> **TROUBLE?** If you accidentally pressed a mouse button, press it again to get the Start menu off your screen.
>
> **2.** What tip appears when you point to the date on the right end of the taskbar?

Clicking

When you press a mouse button and immediately release it, it is called **clicking**. Clicking the mouse selects an object on the desktop. *You usually click the left mouse button, so* unless the instructions tell you otherwise, always click the left mouse button.

Windows 95 shows you which object is selected by highlighting it, usually by changing the object's color, putting a box around it, or making the object appear to be pushed in, as shown in Figure 1-4.

Figure 1-4 ◀
Selected objects

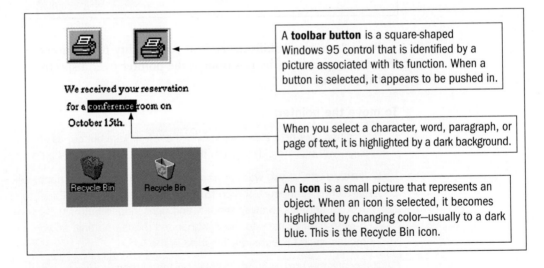

We received your reservation for a conference room on October 15th.

A **toolbar button** is a square-shaped Windows 95 control that is identified by a picture associated with its function. When a button is selected, it appears to be pushed in.

When you select a character, word, paragraph, or page of text, it is highlighted by a dark background.

An **icon** is a small picture that represents an object. When an icon is selected, it becomes highlighted by changing color—usually to a dark blue. This is the Recycle Bin icon.

To select the Recycle Bin icon:

1. Position the pointer over the **Recycle Bin** icon.

2. Click the mouse button and notice how the color of the icon changes to show that it is selected.

Starting and Closing a Program

The software you use is sometimes referred to as a program or an application. To use a program, such as a word-processing program, you must first start it. With Windows 95 you start a program by clicking the Start button. The Start button displays a menu.

A **menu** is a list of options. Windows 95 has a **Start menu** that provides you with access to programs, data, and configuration options. One of the Start menu's most important functions is to let you start a program.

The Reference Window below explains how to start a program. Don't do the steps in the Reference Window now; they are for your later reference.

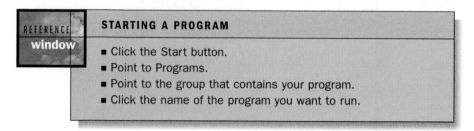

REFERENCE
window

STARTING A PROGRAM

- Click the Start button.
- Point to Programs.
- Point to the group that contains your program.
- Click the name of the program you want to run.

3.1 NOTE

WordPad is similar to Write in Windows 3.1.

Windows 95 includes an easy-to-use word-processing program called WordPad. Suppose you want to start the WordPad program and use it to write a letter or report.

To start the WordPad program from the Start menu:

1. Click the **Start** button 🔲Start as shown in Figure 1-5. A menu appears.

Figure 1-5 ◀
Starting the
WordPad program

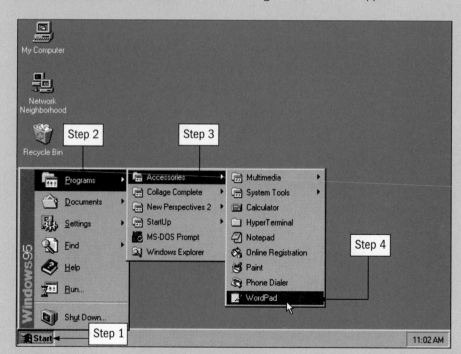

2. Point to **Programs**. After a short pause, the next menu appears.

   TROUBLE? If you don't get the correct menu, go back and point to the correct menu option.

3. Point to **Accessories**. Another menu appears.

4. Click **WordPad**. Make sure you can see the WordPad program as shown in Figure 1-6 on the following page.

Figure 1-6 ◀
The WordPad
program

WordPad program
window

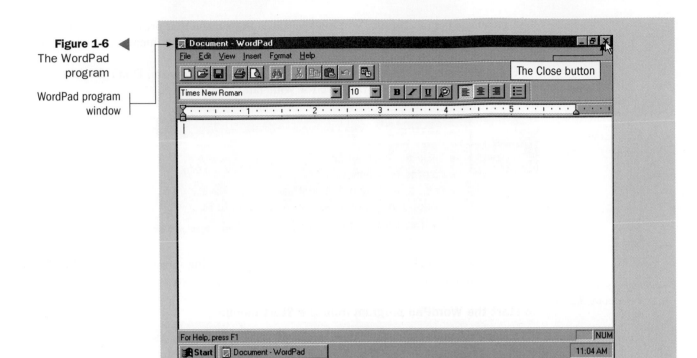

The Close button

TROUBLE? If the WordPad program does not fill the entire screen, click the ⬜ button in the upper right corner.

3.1 NOTE

As with Windows 3.1,
in Windows 95 you
can also exit a
program using the
Exit option from the
File menu.

When you are finished using a program, the easiest way to return to the Windows 95 desktop is to click the Close button ☒.

To exit the WordPad program:

1. Click the **Close** button ☒. See Figure 1-6. You will be returned to the Windows 95 desktop.

Running More than One Program at the Same Time

3.1 NOTE

Paint in Windows 95
is similar to
Paintbrush in
Windows 3.1.

One of the most useful features of Windows 95 is its ability to run multiple programs at the same time. This feature, known as **multi-tasking**, allows you to work on more than one task at a time and to quickly switch between tasks. For example, you can start WordPad and leave it running while you then start the Paint program.

To run WordPad and Paint at the same time:

1. Start WordPad.

    TROUBLE? You learned how to start WordPad earlier in the tutorial: Click the Start button, point to Programs, point to Accessories, and then click WordPad.

2. Now you can start the Paint program. Click the **Start** button 🏁Start again.

3. Point to **Programs**.

4. Point to **Accessories**.

5. Click **Paint**. The Paint program appears as shown in Figure 1-7. Now two programs are running at the same time.

TROUBLE? If the Paint program does not fill the entire screen, click the ▫️ button in the upper right corner.

Figure 1-7
The Paint
Program

Paint program
window

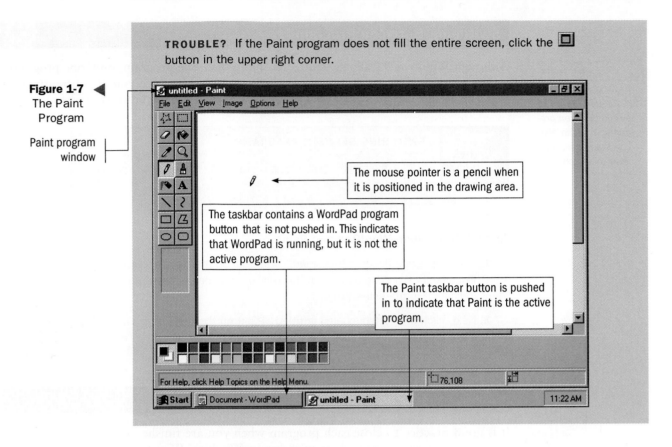

The mouse pointer is a pencil when it is positioned in the drawing area.

The taskbar contains a WordPad program button that is not pushed in. This indicates that WordPad is running, but it is not the active program.

The Paint taskbar button is pushed in to indicate that Paint is the active program.

3.1 NOTE

With Windows 3.1, some users had difficulty finding program windows on the desktop. The buttons on the Windows 95 taskbar make it much easier to keep track of which programs are running.

What happened to WordPad? The WordPad button is still on the taskbar, so even if you can't see it, WordPad is still running. You can imagine that it is stacked behind the Paint program, as shown in Figure 1-8.

Other projects might be hidden under the project you are working on. For example, you might have worked on a letter earlier, but it is now under the picture you are currently drawing.

You might keep other projects handy on your desk. Anytime you want to work with one of them, you bring it to the center of your desk.

Figure 1-8
Programs
stacked on top
of a desk

Think of your screen
as the main work
area of your desk.

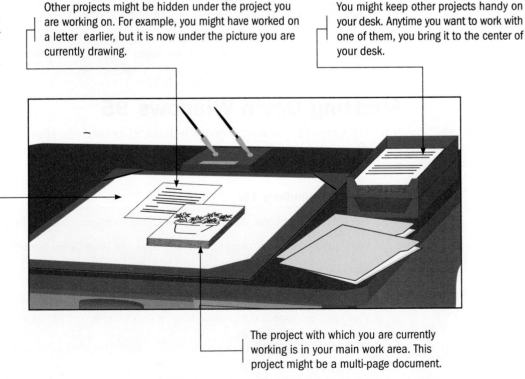

The project with which you are currently working is in your main work area. This project might be a multi-page document.

Switching Between Programs

3.1 NOTE

In Windows 95, you can still use Alt-Tab to switch between programs. You can also click any open window to switch to it.

Although Windows 95 allows you to run more than one program, only one program at a time is active. The **active** program is the program with which you are currently working. The easiest way to switch between programs is to use the buttons on the taskbar.

REFERENCE
window

SWITCHING BETWEEN PROGRAMS

- Click the taskbar button that contains the name of the program to which you want to switch.

To switch between WordPad and Paint:

1. Click the button labeled **Document - WordPad** on the taskbar. The Document - WordPad button now looks like it has been pushed in to indicate it is the active program.

2. Next, click the button labeled **untitled - Paint** on the taskbar to switch to the Paint program.

Closing WordPad and Paint

It is good practice to close each program when you are finished using it. Each program uses computer resources such as memory, so Windows 95 works more efficiently when only the programs you need are open.

To close WordPad and Paint:

1. Click the **Close** button ▣ for the Paint program. The button labeled "untitled - Paint" disappears from the taskbar.

2. Click the **Close** button ▣ for the WordPad program. The WordPad button disappears from the taskbar, and you return to the Windows 95 desktop.

Shutting Down Windows 95

It is very important to shut down Windows 95 before you turn off the computer. If you turn off your computer without correctly shutting down, you might lose data and damage your files.

To shut down Windows 95:

1. Click the **Start** button ▣Start on the taskbar to display the Start menu.

2. Click the **Shut Down** menu option to display the Shut Down Windows dialog box.

3. Make sure the **Shut down the computer?** option is selected.

4. Click the **Yes** button.

5. Wait until you see a message indicating it is safe to turn off your computer, then switch off your computer.

You should typically use the option "Shut down the computer?" when you want to turn off your computer. However, other shut-down options are available. For example, your school might prefer that you select the option to "Close all programs and log on as a different user." This option logs you out of Windows 95, leaves the computer turned on, and allows another user to log on without restarting the computer. Check with your instructor or technical support person for the preferred method for your school's computer lab.

Quick Check

1. Label the components of the Windows 95 desktop in the figure below:

Figure 1-9 ◀
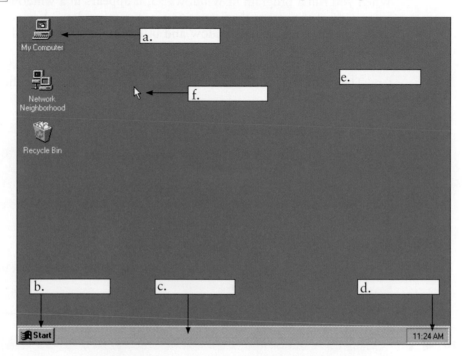

2. The _____ feature of Windows 95 allows you to run more than one program at a time.

3. The _____ is a list of options that provides you with access to programs, data, and configuration options.

4. What should you do if you are trying to move the pointer to the left edge of your screen, but your mouse runs into the keyboard?

5. Windows 95 shows you that an icon is selected by _____ it.

6. Even if you can't see a program, it might be running. How can you tell if a program is running?

7. Why is it good practice to close each program when you are finished using it?

8. Why do you need to shut down Windows 95 before you turn off your computer?

In this session you will learn how to use many of the Windows 95 controls to manipulate windows and programs. You will learn how to change the size and shape of a window and to move a window so that you can customize your screen-based workspace. You will also learn how to use menus, dialog boxes, tabs, buttons, and lists to specify how you want a program to carry out a task.

Anatomy of a Window

When you run a program in Windows 95, it appears in a window. A **window** is a rectangular area of the screen that contains a program or data. A window also contains controls for manipulating the window and using the program. WordPad is a good example of how a window works.

Windows, spelled with an uppercase "W," is the name of the Microsoft operating system. The word "window" with a lowercase "w" refers to one of the rectangular windows on the screen.

To look at window controls:

1. Make sure Windows 95 is running and you are at the Windows 95 desktop screen.

2. Start WordPad.

> **TROUBLE?** To start WordPad, click the Start button, point to Programs, point to Accessories, and then click WordPad.

3. Make sure WordPad takes up the entire screen.

> **TROUBLE?** If WordPad does not take up the entire screen, click the ▢ button in the upper right corner.

4. On your screen, identify the controls labeled in Figure 1-10.

Figure 1-10 ◀
Window
controls

The **menu bar** contains the titles of menus, such as File, Edit, and Help.

The **toolbar** contains buttons that provide you with a shortcut to the commands listed on the menus.

The **status bar** provides you with abbreviated help relevant to the task you are doing.

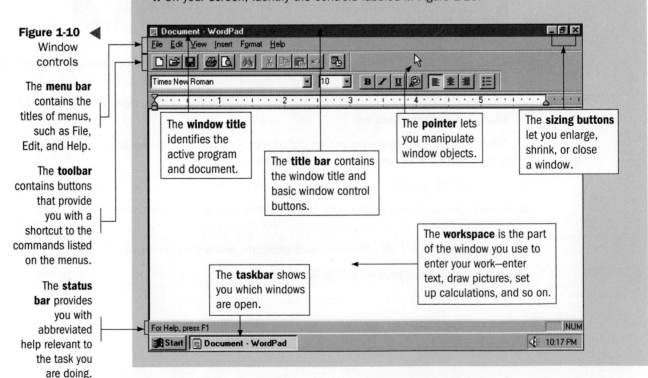

The **window title** identifies the active program and document.

The **title bar** contains the window title and basic window control buttons.

The **pointer** lets you manipulate window objects.

The **sizing buttons** let you enlarge, shrink, or close a window.

The **workspace** is the part of the window you use to enter your work—enter text, draw pictures, set up calculations, and so on.

The **taskbar** shows you which windows are open.

Manipulating a Window

There are three buttons located on the right side of the title bar. You are already familiar with the Close button. The Minimize button hides the window. The other button either maximizes the window or restores it to a predefined size. Figure 1-11 shows how these buttons work.

Figure 1-11 ◀
Minimize,
Maximize and
Restore buttons

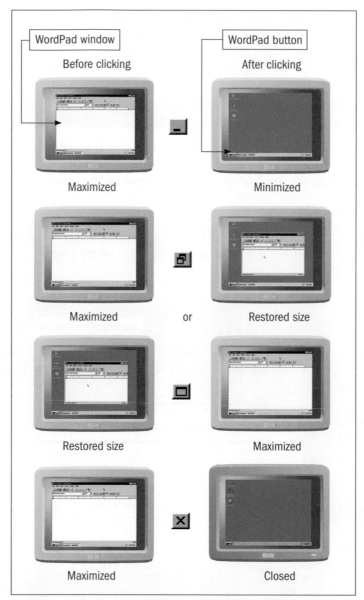

The **Minimize button** 🔲 shrinks the window, so you only see its button on the taskbar.

The middle button appears as a **Restore button** 🗗 or a **Maximize button.** 🔲 When the window is maximized, the Restore button appears. It can be used to reduce the size of the window to a predetermined or "normal" size. When the window does not fill the entire screen, the Maximize button appears. Clicking the Maximize button enlarges the window to fill the screen.

The **Close button** ☒ closes the window and removes its button from the taskbar at the bottom of the screen.

Minimizing a Window

The **Minimize button** 🔲 shrinks the current window so that only the button on the taskbar remains visible. You can use the Minimize button when you want to temporarily hide a window but keep the program running.

To minimize the WordPad window:

1. Click the **Minimize** button 🔲. The WordPad window shrinks so only the Document - WordPad button on the taskbar is visible.

   TROUBLE? If you accidentally clicked the Close button and closed the window, use the Start button to start WordPad again.

Redisplaying a Window

You can redisplay a minimized window by clicking the program's button on the taskbar. When you redisplay a window, it becomes the active window.

To redisplay the WordPad window:

1. Click the **Document - WordPad** button on the taskbar. The WordPad window is restored to its previous size. The Document - WordPad button looks pushed in as a visual clue that it is now the active window.

Restoring a Window

The **Restore** button ⬚ reduces the window so it is smaller than the entire screen. This is useful if you want to see more than one window at a time. Also, because of its small size, you can drag the window to another location on the screen or change its dimensions.

To restore a window:

1. Click the **Restore** button ⬚ on the WordPad title bar. The WordPad window will look similar to Figure 1-12, but the exact size of the window on your screen might be slightly different.

Figure 1-12 ◀
WordPad after
clicking the
Restore button

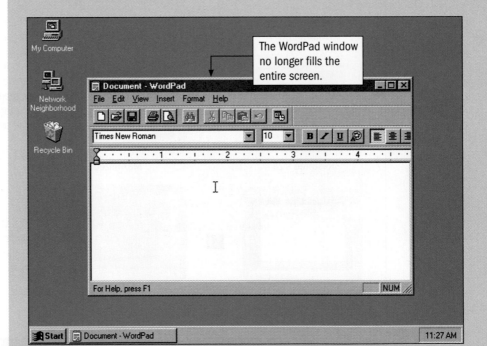

The WordPad window no longer fills the entire screen.

Moving a Window

You can use the mouse to **move** a window to a new position on the screen. When you hold down the mouse button while moving the mouse, it is called **dragging**. You can move objects on the screen by dragging them to a new location. If you want to move a window, you drag its title bar.

To drag the WordPad window to a new location:

1. Position the mouse pointer on the WordPad window title bar.

2. While you hold down the left mouse button, move the mouse to drag the window. A rectangle representing the window moves as you move the mouse.

3. Position the rectangle anywhere on the screen, then release the left mouse button. The WordPad window appears in the new location.

4. Now drag the WordPad window to the upper-left corner of the screen.

Changing the Size of a Window

You can also use the mouse to change the size of a window. Notice the sizing handle at the lower right corner of the window. The **sizing handle** provides a visible control for changing the size of a current window.

To change the size of the WordPad window:

1. Position the pointer over the sizing handle . The pointer changes to a diagonal arrow .

2. While holding down the mouse button, drag the sizing handle down and to the right.

3. Release the mouse button. Now the window is larger.

4. Practice using the sizing handle to make the WordPad window larger or smaller.

Maximizing a Window

The **Maximize button** enlarges a window so that it fills the entire screen. You will probably do most of your work using maximized windows because you can see more of your program and data.

To maximize the WordPad window:

1. Click the **Maximize** button on the WordPad title bar.

Using Program Menus

Most Windows programs use menus to provide an easy way for you to select program commands. The **menu bar** is typically located at the top of the program window and shows the titles of menus such as File, Edit, and Help.

Windows menus are relatively standardized—most Windows programs include similar menu options. It's easy to learn new programs, because you can make a pretty good guess about which menu contains the command you want.

Selecting Commands from a Menu

When you click any menu title, choices for that menu appear below the menu bar. These choices are referred to as **menu options**. To select a menu option, you click it. For example, the File menu is a standard feature in most Windows programs and contains the options related to working with a file: creating, opening, saving, and printing a file or document.

To select Print Preview from the File menu:

1. Click **File** in the WordPad menu bar to display the File menu.

   TROUBLE? If you open a menu but decide not to select any of the menu options, you can close the menu by clicking its title again.

2. Click **Print Preview** to open the preview screen and view your document as it will appear when printed. This document is blank because you didn't enter any text.

3. After examining the screen, click the button labeled "Close" to return to your document.

Not all menu options immediately carry out an action—some show submenus or ask you for more information about what you want to do. The menu gives you hints about what to expect when you select an option. These hints are sometimes referred to as **menu conventions**. Study Figures 1-13a and 1-13b so you will recognize the Windows 95 menu conventions.

Figure 1-13a ◀
Menu
Conventions

Some menu options are toggle switches that can be either "on" or "off." When a feature is turned on, a **check mark** appears next to the menu option. When the feature is turned off, there is no check mark.

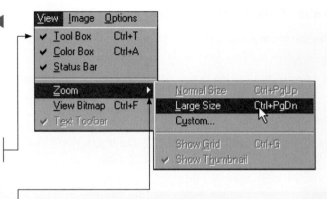

Certain menu selections lead you to an additional menu, called a **submenu**. A triangle on the right side of the menu choice indicates menu options that lead to submenus. When you move the pointer to a menu option with a triangle next to it, the submenu automatically appears.

Figure 1-13b ◀
Menu
conventions
(continued)

Some menu options are followed by a series of three dots, called an **ellipsis**. The dots indicate that you must make additional selections from a dialog box after you select that option. Options without dots do not require additional choices—they take effect as soon a you click them.

Sometimes certain menu options are unavailable. For example, a word-processing program might prevent you from trying to delete text if a document is blank. When a menu option is not available, it is usually **"grayed-out"** to provide you with a visual cue that the function is not available.

A **dialog box** lets you enter specification for how you want a task carried out.

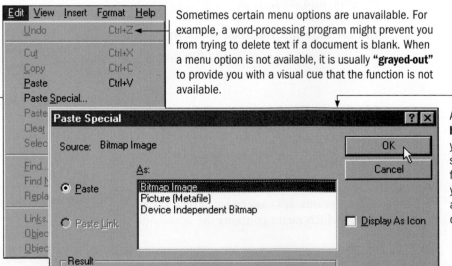

Using Toolbars

A **toolbar** contains buttons that provide quick access to important program commands. Although you can usually perform all program commands using the menus, the toolbar provides convenient one-click access to frequently-used commands. For most Windows 95 functions, there is usually more than one way to accomplish a task. To simplify your introduction to Windows 95 in this tutorial, you will learn only one method for performing a task. As you become more accomplished using Windows 95, you can explore alternative methods.

In Session 1.1 you learned that Windows 95 programs include ToolTips that indicate the purpose and function of a tool. Now is a good time to explore the WordPad toolbar buttons by looking at their ToolTips.

To find out a toolbar button's function:

1. Position the pointer over any button on the toolbar, such as the Print Preview icon ⬚. After a short pause, the name of the button appears in a box and a description of the button appears in the status bar just above the Start button.

2. Move the pointer to each button on the toolbar to see its name and purpose.

You select a toolbar button by clicking it.

To select the Print Preview toolbar button:

1. Click the **Print Preview** button ⬚. The Print Preview dialog box appears. This is the same dialog box that appeared when you selected File, Print Preview from the menu bar.

2. Click ⬚ Close to close the Print Preview dialog box.

Using List Boxes and Scroll Bars

As you might guess from the name, a **list box** displays a list of choices. In WordPad, date and time formats are shown in the Date/Time list box. List box controls include arrow buttons, a scroll bar, and a scroll box, as shown in Figure 1-14.

Figure 1-14 ◄
List box

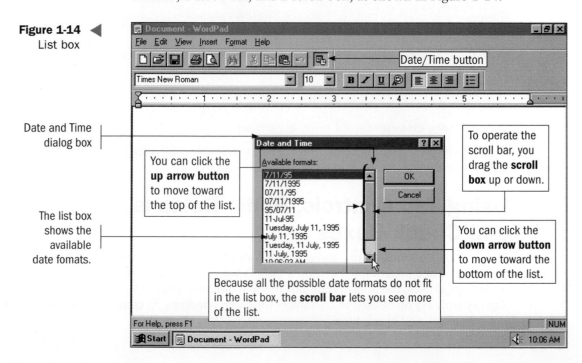

Date and Time dialog box

You can click the **up arrow button** to move toward the top of the list.

The list box shows the available date fomats.

To operate the scroll bar, you drag the **scroll box** up or down.

You can click the **down arrow button** to move toward the bottom of the list.

Because all the possible date formats do not fit in the list box, the **scroll bar** lets you see more of the list.

To use the Date/Time list box:

1. Click the **Date/Time** button 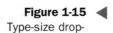 to display the Date and Time dialog box. See Figure 1-14.

2. To scroll down the list, click the **down arrow** button ▼. See Figure 1-14.

3. Find the scroll box on your screen. See Figure 1-14.

4. Drag the **scroll box** to the top of the scroll bar. Notice how the list scrolls back to the beginning.

5. Find a date format similar to "October 2, 1997." Click that date format to select it.

6. Click the **OK** button to close the Date and Time list box. This inserts the current date in your document.

A variation of the list box, called a **drop-down list box**, usually shows only one choice, but can expand down to display additional choices on the list.

To use the Font Size drop-down list:

1. Click the **down arrow** button ▼ shown in Figure 1-15.

Figure 1-15 ◄
Type-size drop-down list box

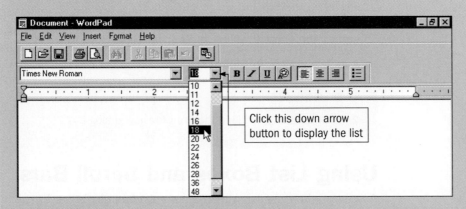

2. Click **18**. The drop-down list disappears and the font size you selected appears at the top of the pull-down list.

3. Type a few characters to test the new font size.

4. Click the **down arrow** button ▼ in the Font Size drop-down list box again.

5. Click **12**.

6. Type a few characters to test this type size.

7. Click the **Close** button ☒ to close WordPad.

8. When you see the message "Save changes to Document?" click the **No** button.

Using Tab Controls, Radio Buttons, and Check Boxes

Dialog boxes often use tabs, radio buttons, or check boxes to collect information about how you want a program to perform a task. A **tab control** is patterned after the tabs on file folders. You click the appropriate tab to view different pages of information or choices. Tab controls are often used as containers for other Windows 95 controls such as list boxes, radio buttons, and check boxes.

Radio buttons, also called **option buttons,** allow you to select a single option from among one or more options. **Check boxes** allow you to select many options at the same time. Figure 1-16 explains how to use these controls.

Figure 1-16 ◀
Tabs, radio buttons, and check boxes

A **tab** indicates an "index card" that contains information or a group of controls, usually with related functions. To look at the functions on an index card, click the tab.

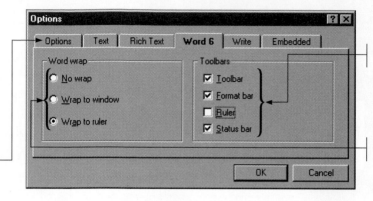

Check boxes allow you to select one or more options from a group. When you click a check box, a check mark appears in it. To remove a check mark from a box, click it again.

Radio buttons are round and usually come in groups of two or more. You can select only one radio button from a group. Your selection is indicated by a black dot.

Using Help

Windows 95 **Help** provides on-screen information about the program you are using. Help for the Windows 95 operating system is available by clicking the Start button on the taskbar, then selecting Help from the Start menu. If you want Help for a program, such as WordPad, you must first start the program, then use the Help menu at the top of the screen.

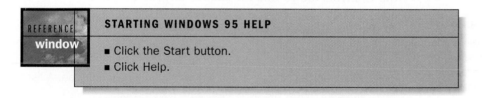

REFERENCE **window**

STARTING WINDOWS 95 HELP

- Click the Start button.
- Click Help.

To start Windows 95 Help:

1. Click the **Start** button.

2. Click **Help.**

Help uses tabs for each section of Help. Windows 95 Help tabs include Contents, Index, and Find as shown in Figure 1-17 on the following page.

Figure 1-17 ◄
Windows 95
Help

Each section of
Help is divided
into "books."
To open a book,
you click the
book, then click
the Open button.

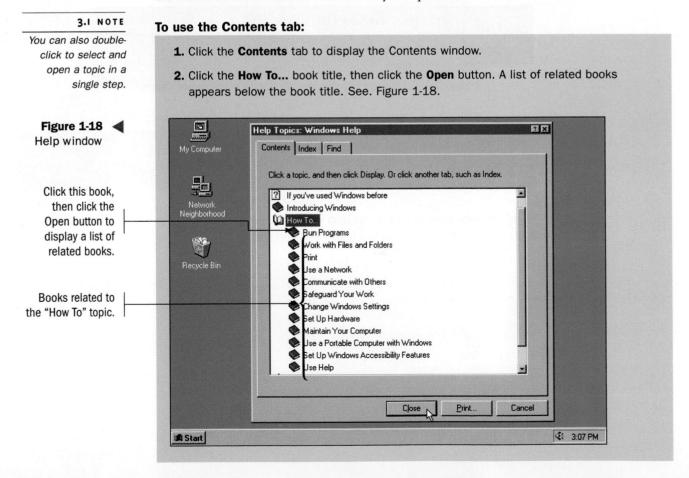

The **Contents tab** groups Help topics into a series of books. You select a book, which then provides you with a list of related topics from which you can choose. The **Index tab** displays an alphabetical list of all the Help topics from which you can choose. The **Find tab** lets you search for any word or phrase in Help.

Suppose you're wondering if there is an alternative way to start programs. You can use the Contents tab to find the answer to your question.

3.1 NOTE

You can also double-click to select and open a topic in a single step.

To use the Contents tab:

1. Click the **Contents** tab to display the Contents window.

2. Click the **How To...** book title, then click the **Open** button. A list of related books appears below the book title. See. Figure 1-18.

Figure 1-18 ◄
Help window

Click this book,
then click the
Open button to
display a list of
related books.

Books related to
the "How To" topic.

3. Click the **Run Programs** book, then click the **Open** button. The table of contents for this Help book is displayed.

4. Click the topic **Starting a Program**, then click the **Display** button. A Help window appears and explains how to start a program.

Help also provides you with definitions of technical terms. You can click any under-lined term to see its definition.

To see a definition of the term "taskbar":

1. Point to the underlined term, **taskbar** until the pointer changes to a hand. Then click.

2. After you have read the definition, click the definition to deselect it.

3. Click the **Close** button ☒ on the Help window.

The **Index tab** allows you to jump to a Help topic by selecting a topic from an indexed list. For example, you can use the Index tab to learn how to arrange the open windows on your desktop.

To find a Help topic using the Index tab:

1. Click the **Start** button.

2. Click **Help**.

3. Click the **Index** tab.

4. A long list of indexed Help topics appears. Drag the scroll box down to view additional topics.

5. You can quickly jump to any part of the list by typing the first few characters of a word or phrase in the line above the Index list. Type **desktop** to display topics related to the Windows 95 desktop.

6. Click the topic **arranging open windows on** in the bottom window.

7. Click the **Display** button as shown in Figure 1-19.

Figure 1-19 ◀
Displaying a
Help Topic

Click here to type
words or phrases.

Index topics are
displayed here.
Click the topic to
select it.

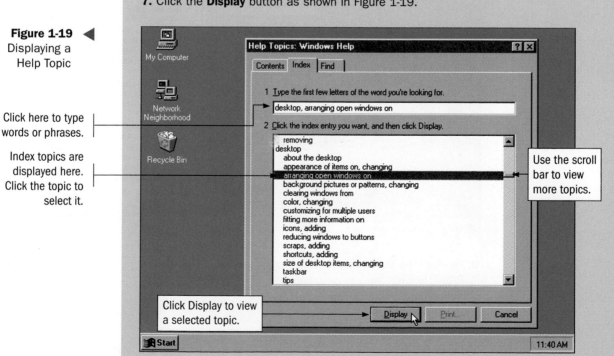

> **8.** Click the **Close** button ☒ to close the Windows Help window.

The **Find tab** contains an index of all words in Windows 95 Help. You can use it to search for Help pages that contain a particular word or phrase. For example, suppose you heard that a screen saver blanks out your screen when you are not using it. You could use the Find tab to find out more about screen savers.

To find a Help topic using the Find tab:

1. Click the **Start** button Start .

2. Click **Help**.

3. Click the **Find** tab.

> **TROUBLE?** If the Find index has not yet been created on your computer, the computer will prompt you through several steps to create the index. Continue with Step 4 below after the Find index is created.

4. Type **screen** to display a list of all topics that start with the letters "screen."

5. Click **screen-saver** in the middle window to display the topics that contain the word "screen-saver."

6. Click **Having your monitor automatically turn off**, then click the **Display** button.

7. Click the **Help window** button shown in Figure 1-20. The screen saver is shown on a simulated monitor.

> **TROUBLE?** If you see an error message, your lab does not allow students to modify screen savers. Click the OK button and go to Step 9.

Figure 1-20 ◀
Clicking a
Button in Help

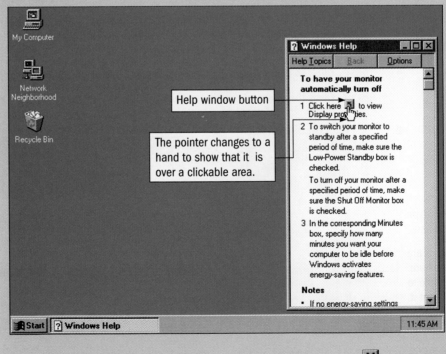

8. To close the Display properties window, click the **Close** button ☒ in the Display Properties window.

9. Click the **Close** button ☒ to close the Help window.

Now that you know how Windows 95 Help works, don't forget to use it! Use Help when you need to perform a new task or when you forget how to complete a procedure.

1 Label the parts of the window shown in Figure 1-21.

Figure 1-21 ◄

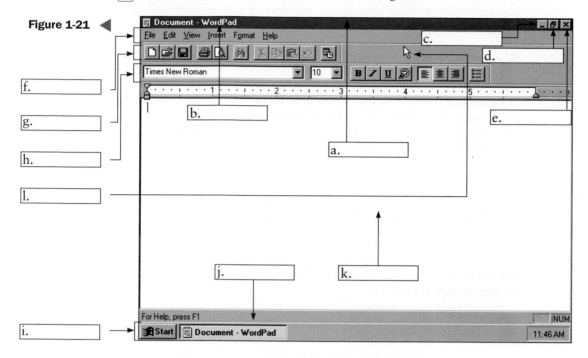

f.

g.

h.

l.

i.

b.

a.

c.

d.

e.

j.

k.

2 Provide the name and purpose of each button:
a.
b.
c.
d.

3 Explain each of the following menu conventions:
a. Ellipsis...
b. Grayed out
c. ▶
d. ✔

4 A(n) _____ consists of a group of buttons, each of which provides one-click access to important program functions.

5 Label each part of the dialog box below:

Figure 1-22 ◄

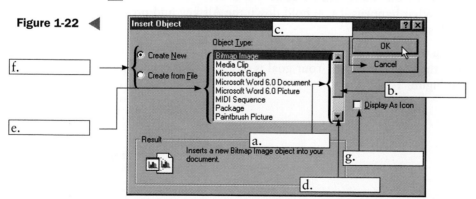

f.

e.

c.

a.

b.

g.

d.

6 Radio buttons allow you to select _____ option(s) at a time, but _____ allow you to select one or more options.

7 It is a good idea to use _____ when you need to learn how to perform new tasks, simplify tedious procedures, and correct actions that did not turn out as you expected.

End Note

You've finished the tutorial, but Steve Laslow still hasn't returned. Take a moment to review what you have learned. You now know how to start a program using the Start button. You can run more than one program at a time and switch between programs using the buttons on the taskbar. You have learned the names and functions of window controls and Windows 95 menu conventions. You can now use toolbar buttons, list boxes, drop-down lists, radio buttons, check boxes, and scroll bars. Finally, you can use the Contents, Index, and Find tabs in Help to extend your knowledge of how to use Windows 95.

Tutorial Assignments

1. Running Two Programs and Switching Between Them In this tutorial you learned how to run more than one program at a time using WordPad and Paint. You can run other programs at the same time, too. Complete the following steps and write out your answers to questions b through f:

    a. Start the computer. Enter your user name and password if prompted to do so.

    b. Click the Start button. How many menu options are on the Start menu?

    c. Run the program Calculator program located on the Programs, Accessories menu. How many buttons are now on the taskbar?

    d. Run the Paint program and maximize the Paint window. How many application programs are running now?

    e. Switch to Calculator. What are the two visual clues that tell you that Calculator is the active program?

    f. Multiply 576 by 1457. What is the result?

    g. Close Calculator, then close Paint.

2. WordPad Help In Tutorial 1 you learned how to use Windows 95 Help. Just about every Windows 95 program has a help feature. Many computer users can learn to use a program just by using Help. To use Help, you would start the program, then click the Help menu at the top of the screen. Try using WordPad Help:

    a. Start WordPad.

    b. Click Help on the WordPad menu bar, then click Help Topics.

    c. Using WordPad help, write out your answers to questions 1 through 3.

        1. How do you create a bulleted list?

        2. How do you set the margins in a document?

        3. What happens if you hold down the Alt key and press the Print Screen key?

    d. Close WordPad.

3. Using Help to Explore Paint In this assignment, you will use the Paint Help to learn how to use the Paint program. Your goal is to create and print a picture that looks like the one in Figure 1-23.

Figure 1-23 ◀

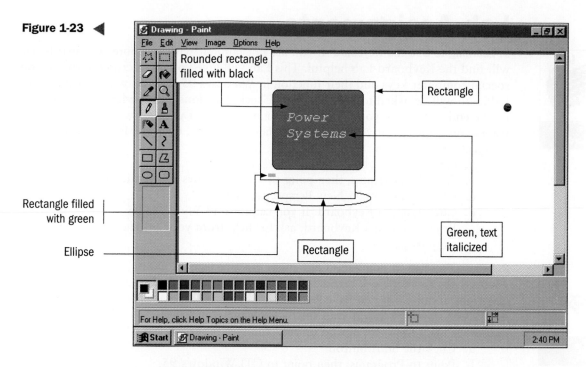

a. Start Paint.

b. Click Help, then click Help Topics.

c. Use Paint Help to learn how to put text in a picture and how to draw rectangles and circles.

d. Draw a picture of a monitor using rectangles, circles, and text as shown in Figure 1-23.

e. Print your picture.

f. Close Paint.

4. The Windows 95 Tutorial Windows 95 includes a five part on-line tutorial. In Tutorial 1 you learned about starting programs, switching windows, and using Help. You can use the on-line Windows 95 Tutorial to review what you learned and pick up some new tips for using Windows 95. Complete the following steps and write out your answers to questions f, g, and h:

a. Click the Start button to display the Start menu.

b. Click Help to display Windows help.

c. Click the Contents tab.

d. From the Contents screen, click Tour: Ten minutes to using Windows.

e. Click the Display button. If an error message appears, the Tour is probably not loaded on your computer. You will not be able to complete this assignment. Click Cancel, then click OK to cancel and check with your instructor or technical support person.

f. Click Starting a Program and complete the tutorial. What are the names of the seven programs on the Accessories menu in the tutorial?

g. Click Switching Windows and complete the on-line tutorial. What does the Minimize button do?

h. Click Using Help and complete the tutorial. What is the purpose of the ? button?

i. Click the Exit button to close the Tour window.

j. Click the Exit Tour button to exit the Tour and return to the Windows 95 desktop.

Lab Assignments

Using a
Keyboard

1. Learning to Use the Keyboard If you are not familiar with computer keyboards, you will find the Keyboard Lab helpful. This Lab will give you a structured introduction to special computer keys and their function in Windows 95. As you work through the Lab, you will be asked to answer Quick Check questions about what you have learned. At the end of the lab, you will see a summary report of your answers. If your instructor wants you to print out your answers to these questions, click the Print button on the summary report screen.

    a. Click the Start button.

    b. Point to Programs, then point to CTI Windows 95 Applications.

    c. Click Windows 95 New Perspectives Brief.

    d. Click Using a Keyboard. If you cannot find Windows 95 New Perspectives Brief or Using a Keyboard, ask for help from your instructor or technical support person.

Using a
Mouse

2. Mouse Practice If you would like more practice using a mouse, you can complete the Mouse Lab. As you work through the Lab, you will be asked to answer Quick Check questions about what you have learned. At the end of the lab, the Quick Check Report shows you how you did. If your instructor wants you to print out your answers to these questions, click the Print button on the summary report screen.

    a. Click the Start button.

    b. Point to Programs, then point to CTI Windows 95.

    c. Point to Windows 95 New Perspectives Brief.

    d. Click Using a Mouse. If you cannot find Windows 95 New Perspectives Brief or Using a Mouse, ask for help from your instructor or technical support person.

Working with Files

LABS
Using Files

CASE

Your First Day in the Lab—Continued

Steve Laslow is back from class, grinning. "I see you're making progress!"

"That's right," you reply. "I know how to run programs, control windows, and use Help. I guess I'm ready to work with my word-processing and spreadsheet software now."

Steve hesitates before he continues, "You could, but there are a few more things about Windows 95 that you should learn first."

Steve explains that most of the software you have on your computer—your word-processing, spreadsheet, scheduling, and graphing software—was created especially for the Windows 95 operating system. This software is referred to as **Windows 95 applications** or **Windows 95 programs**. You can also use software designed for Windows 3.1, but Windows 95 applications give you more flexibility. For example, when you name a document in a Windows 95 application, you can use descriptive filenames with up to 255 characters, whereas in Windows 3.1 you are limited to eight-character names.

You typically use Windows 95 applications to create files. A **file** is a collection of data that has a name and is stored in a computer. You typically create files that contain documents, pictures, and graphs when you use software packages. For example, you might use word-processing software to create a file containing a document. Once you create a file, you can open it, edit its contents, print it, and save it again—usually using the same application program you used to create it.

Another advantage of Windows 95 is that once you know how to save, open, and print files with one Windows 95 application, you can perform those same functions in *any* Windows 95 application. This is because Windows 95 applications have similar controls. For example, your word-processing and spreadsheet software will have identical menu commands to save, open, and print documents. Steve suggests that it would be worth a few minutes of your time to become familiar with these menus in Windows 95 applications.

You agree, but before you can get to work, Steve gives you one final suggestion: you should also learn how to keep track of the files on your disk. For instance, you might need to find a file you have not used for a while or you might want to delete a file if your disk is getting full. You will definitely want to make a backup copy of your disk in case something happens to the original. Steve's advice seems practical, and you're eager to explore these functions so you can get to work!

Tutorial 2 will help you learn how to work with Windows 95 applications and keep track of the files on your disk. When you've completed this tutorial, you'll be ready to tackle all kinds of Windows 95 software!

In Session 2.1 you will learn how to format a disk so it can store files. You will create, save, open, and print a file. You will find out how the insertion point is different from the mouse pointer, and you will learn the basic skills for Windows 95 text entry, such as inserting, deleting, and selecting.

For this tutorial you will need two blank 3 ½-inch disks.

Formatting a Disk

Before you can save files on a disk, the disk must be formatted. When the computer **formats** a disk, the magnetic particles on the disk surface are arranged so data can be stored on the disk. Today, many disks are sold preformatted and can be used right out of the box. However, if you purchase an unformatted disk, or if you have an old disk that you want to completely erase and reuse, you can format the disk using the Windows 95 Format command.

The following steps tell you how to format a 3 ½-inch high-density disk using drive A. Your instructor will tell you how to revise the instructions given in these steps if the procedure is different for your lab equipment.

All data on the disk you format will be erased, so don't perform these steps using a disk that contains important files.

To format a disk:

1. Start Windows 95, if necessary.

2. Write your name on the label of a 3 ½-inch disk.

3. Insert your disk in drive A. See Figure 2-1.

Figure 2-1 ◄
Inserting a
disk into the
disk drive

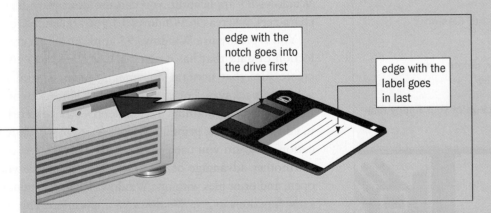

floppy disk drive

edge with the
notch goes into
the drive first

edge with the
label goes
in last

TROUBLE? If your disk does not fit in drive A, put it in drive B and substitute drive B for drive A in all of the steps for the rest of the tutorial.

4. Click the **My Computer** icon to select it, then press the **Enter** key. Make sure you can see the My Computer window. See Figure 2-2.

TROUBLE? If you see a list instead of icons like those in Figure 2-2, click View. Then click Large Icon.

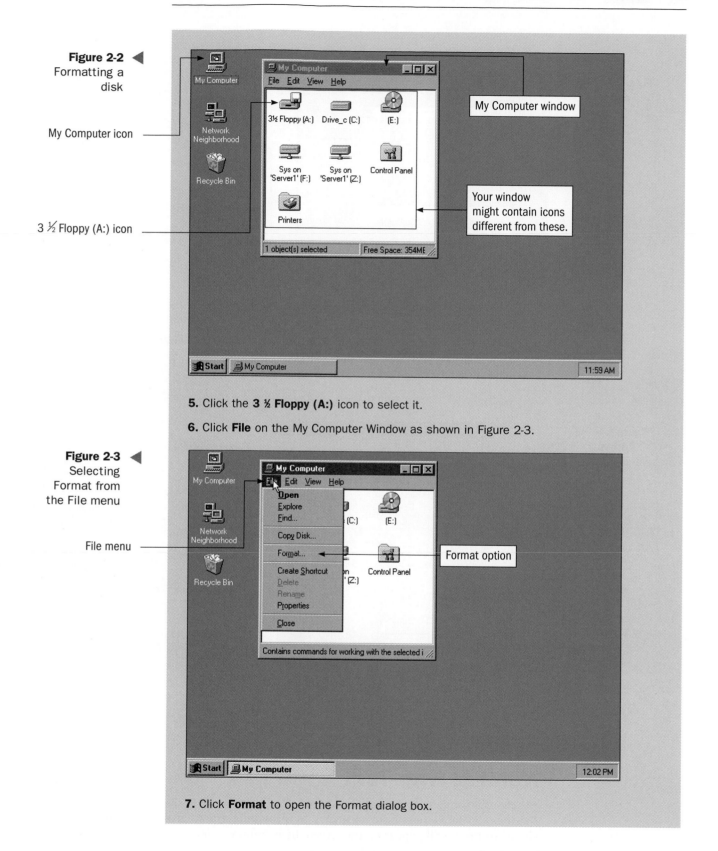

Figure 2-2
Formatting a
disk

My Computer icon

3 ½ Floppy (A:) icon

My Computer window

Your window
might contain icons
different from these.

5. Click the **3 ½ Floppy (A:)** icon to select it.

6. Click **File** on the My Computer Window as shown in Figure 2-3.

Figure 2-3
Selecting
Format from
the File menu

File menu

Format option

7. Click **Format** to open the Format dialog box.

8. Make sure the dialog box settings on your screen match those in Figure 2-4.

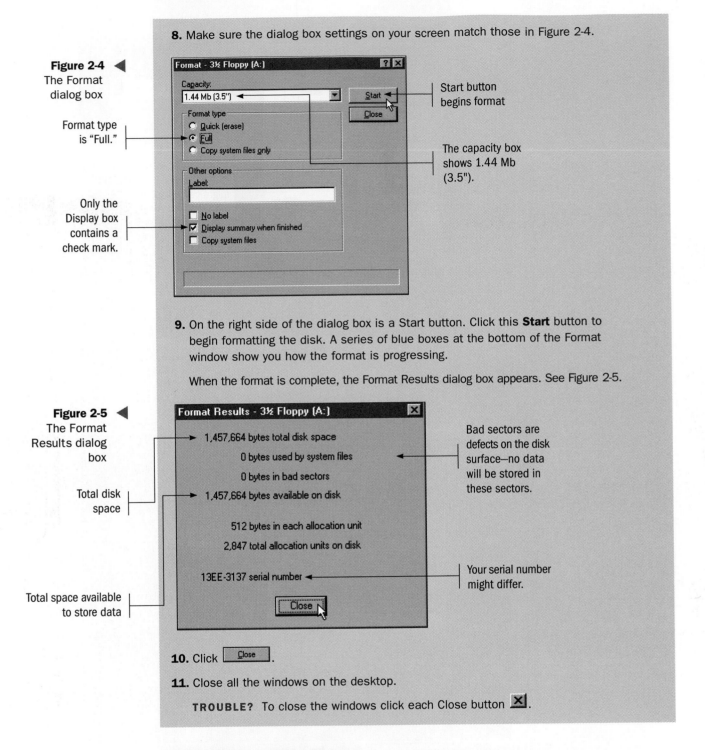

Figure 2-4
The Format
dialog box

Format type
is "Full."

Only the
Display box
contains a
check mark.

Start button
begins format

The capacity box
shows 1.44 Mb
(3.5").

9. On the right side of the dialog box is a Start button. Click this **Start** button to begin formatting the disk. A series of blue boxes at the bottom of the Format window show you how the format is progressing.

When the format is complete, the Format Results dialog box appears. See Figure 2-5.

Figure 2-5
The Format
Results dialog
box

Total disk
space

Total space available
to store data

Bad sectors are
defects on the disk
surface—no data
will be stored in
these sectors.

Your serial number
might differ.

10. Click Close .

11. Close all the windows on the desktop.

TROUBLE? To close the windows click each Close button ☒.

Working with Text

To accomplish many computing tasks, you need to type text in documents and text boxes. Windows 95 facilitates basic text entry by providing a text-entry area, by showing you where your text will appear on the screen, by helping you move around on the screen, and by providing insert and delete functions.

When you type sentences and paragraphs of text, do *not* press the Enter key when you reach the right margin. The software contains a feature called **word wrap** that automatically continues your text on the next line. Therefore, you should press Enter only when you have completed a paragraph.

If you type the wrong character, press the Backspace key to backup and delete the character. You can also use the Delete key. What's the difference between the Backspace and the Delete keys? The Backspace key deletes the character to left. The Delete key deletes the character to the right.

Now you will type some text using WordPad to learn about text entry.

To type text in WordPad:

1. Start WordPad.

   TROUBLE? If the WordPad window does not fill the screen, click the Maximize button ▣.

2. Notice the flashing vertical bar, called the **insertion point**, in the upper-left corner of the document window. The insertion point indicates where the characters you type will appear.

3. Type your name, using the Shift key to type uppercase letters and using the spacebar to type spaces, just like on a typewriter.

4. Press the **Enter** key to end the current paragraph and move the insertion point down to the next line.

5. As you type the following sentences, watch what happens when the insertion point reaches the right edge of the screen:

   This is a sample typed in WordPad. See what happens when the insertion point reaches the right edge of the screen.

   TROUBLE? If you make a mistake, delete the incorrect character(s) by pressing the Backspace key on your keyboard. Then type the correct character(s).

The Insertion Point versus the Pointer

The insertion point is not the same as the mouse pointer. When the mouse pointer is in the text-entry area, it is called the **I-beam pointer** and looks like I. Figure 2-6 explains the difference between the insertion point and the I-beam pointer.

Figure 2-6 ◀
The insertion point vs. the pointer

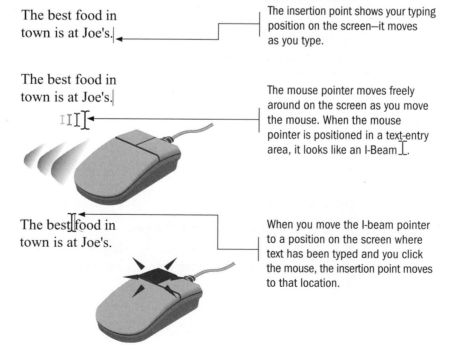

The best food in
town is at Joe's.| ← The insertion point shows your typing position on the screen—it moves as you type.

The best food in
town is at Joe's.| ← The mouse pointer moves freely around on the screen as you move the mouse. When the mouse pointer is positioned in a text-entry area, it looks like an I-Beam I.

The best food in
town is at Joe's. When you move the I-beam pointer to a position on the screen where text has been typed and you click the mouse, the insertion point moves to that location.

To move the insertion point:

1. Check the location of the insertion point and the I-beam pointer. The insertion point should be at the end of the sentence you typed in the last set of steps.

   TROUBLE? If you don't see the I-beam pointer, move your mouse until you see it.

2. Use the mouse to move the I-beam pointer to the word "sample," then click the left mouse button. The insertion point jumps to the location of the I-beam pointer.

3. Move the I-beam pointer to a blank area near the bottom of the work space and click the left mouse button. *Notice that the insertion point does not jump to the location of the I-beam pointer.* Instead the insertion point jumps to the end of the last sentence. The insertion point can move only within existing text. It cannot be moved out of the existing text area.

Selecting Text

Many text operations are performed on a **block** of text, which is one or more consecutive words, sentences, or paragraphs. Once you select a block of text, you can delete it, move it, replace it, underline it, and so on. As you select a block of text, the computer highlights it. If you want to remove the highlighting, just click in the margin of your document.

Suppose you want to replace the phrase "See what happens" with "You can watch word wrap in action." You do not have to delete the text one character at a time. Instead you can highlight the entire phrase and begin to type the replacement text.

To select and replace a block of text:

1. Move the I-beam pointer just to the left of the word "See."

2. While holding down the left mouse button, drag the I-beam pointer over the text to the end of the word "happens." The phrase "See what happens" should now be highlighted. See Figure 2-7.

Figure 2-7 ◄
Highlighting
text

Position the
I-beam pointer here.

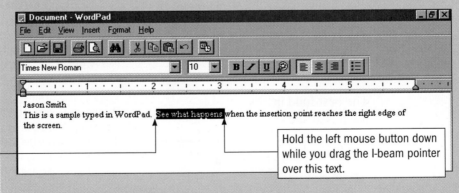

3. Release the left mouse button.

   TROUBLE? If the phrase is not highlighted correctly, repeat Steps 1 through 3.

4. Type: **You can watch word wrap in action**

   The text you typed replaces the highlighted text. Notice that you did not need to delete the highlighted text before you typed the replacement text.

Inserting a Character

Windows 95 programs usually operate in **insert mode**—when you type a new character, all characters to the right of the cursor are pushed over to make room.

Suppose you want to insert the word "sentence" before the word "typed."

To insert characters:

1. Position the I-beam pointer just before the word "typed," then click.

2. Type: **sentence**.

3. Press the **spacebar**.

Notice how the letters in the first line are pushed to the right to make room for the new characters. When a word gets pushed past the right margin, the word-wrap feature pushes it down to the beginning of the next line.

Saving a File

As you type text, it is held temporarily in the computer's memory. For permanent storage, you need to save your work on a disk. In the computer lab, you will probably save your work on a floppy disk in drive A.

When you save a file, you must give it a name. Windows 95 allows you to use filenames containing up to 255 characters, and you may use spaces and punctuation symbols. You cannot use the symbols \ ? : * " < > | in a filename, but other symbols such as &, -, and $ are allowed.

Most filenames have an extension. An **extension** is a suffix of up to three characters that is separated from the filename by a period, as shown in Figure 2-8.

3.1 NOTE

When you save a file with a long filename, Windows 95 also creates an eight-character filename that can be used by Windows 3.1 applications. The eight-character filename is created by using the first six non-space characters from the long filename, then adding a tilde (~) and a number. For example, the filename Car Sales for 1997 would be converted to Carsal~1.

Figure 2-8 ◄
Filename and extension

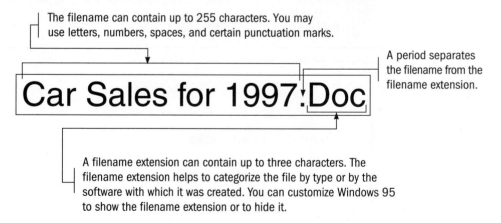

The filename can contain up to 255 characters. You may use letters, numbers, spaces, and certain punctuation marks.

A period separates the filename from the filename extension.

Car Sales for 1997.Doc

A filename extension can contain up to three characters. The filename extension helps to categorize the file by type or by the software with which it was created. You can customize Windows 95 to show the filename extension or to hide it.

The file extension indicates which application you used to create the file. For example, files created with Microsoft Word software have a .Doc extension. In general, you will not add an extension to your filenames, because the application software automatically does this for you.

Windows 95 keeps track of file extensions, but does not always display them. The steps in these tutorials refer to files using the filename, but not its extension. So if you see the filename Sample Text in the steps, but "Sample Text.Doc" on your screen, don't worry—these are the same files.

Now you can save the document you typed.

To save a document:

1. Click the **Save** button 💾 on the toolbar. Figure 2-9 shows the location of this button and the Save As dialog box that appears after you click it.

Figure 2-9 ◀
The Save button

Save button —

Save As
dialog box
appears after
you click the
Save button

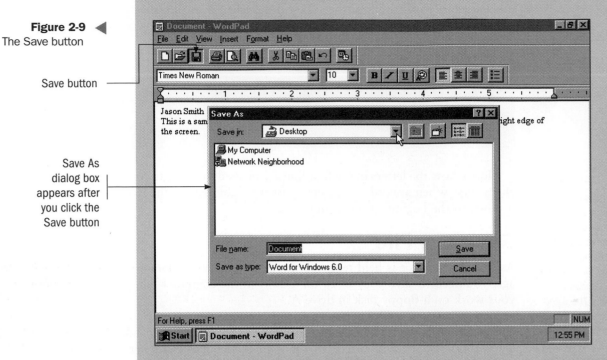

2. Click ▼ on the side of the Save in: box to display a list of drives. See Figure 2-10.

Figure 2-10 ◀
Selecting the
drive

3 ½ Floppy (A:)
drive menu
option

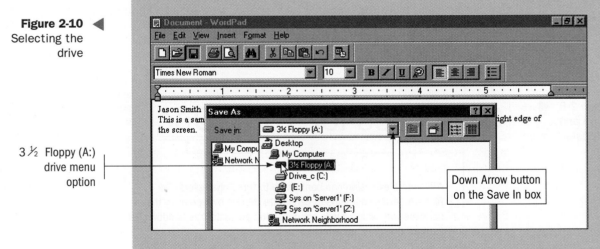

Down Arrow button
on the Save In box

3. Click **3½ Floppy (A:)**.

4. Select the text in the File Name box.

   TROUBLE? To select the text, position the I-beam pointer at the beginning of the word "Document." While you hold down the mouse button, drag the I-beam pointer to the end of the word.

5. Type **Sample Text** in the File Name box.

6. Click the **Save** button. Your file is saved on your Student Disk and the document title, "Sample Text," appears on the WordPad title bar.

What if you tried to close WordPad *before* you saved your file? Windows 95 would display a message—"Save changes to Document?" If you answer "Yes," Windows displays the Save As dialog box so you can give the document a name. If you answer "No," Windows 95 closes WordPad without saving the document.

After you save a file, you can work on another document or close WordPad. Since you have already saved your Sample Text document, you should continue this tutorial by closing WordPad.

To close WordPad:

1. Click the **Close** button ☒ to close the WordPad window.

Opening a File

Suppose you save and close the Sample Text file, then later you want to revise it. To revise a file you must first open it. When you **open** a file, its contents are copied into the computer's memory. If you revise the file, you need to save the changes before you close the application or work on a different file. If you close a revised file without saving your changes, you will lose the revisions.

Typically, you would use one of two methods to open a file. You could select the file from the Documents list or the My Computer window, or you could start an application program and then use the Open button to open the file. Each method has advantages and disadvantages. You will have an opportunity to try both methods.

The first method for opening the Sample Text file simply requires you to select the file from the Documents list or the My Computer window. With this method the document, not the application program, is central to the task; hence this method is sometimes referred to as *document-centric*. You only need to remember the name of your document or file—you do not need to remember which application you used to create the document.

The Documents list contains the names of the last 15 documents used. You access this list from the Start menu. When you have your own computer, the Documents list is very handy. In a computer lab, however, the files other students use quickly replace yours on the list.

If your file is not in the Documents list, you can open the file by selecting it from the My Computer window. Windows 95 starts an application program that you can use to revise the file, then automatically opens the file. The advantage of this method is its simplicity. The disadvantage is that Windows 95 might not start the application you expect. For example, when you select Sample Text, you might expect Windows 95 to start WordPad because you used WordPad to type the text of the document. Depending on the software installed on your computer system, however, Windows 95 might start the Microsoft Word application instead. Usually this is not a problem. Although the application might not be the one you expect, you can still use it to revise your file.

3.1 NOTE

Document-centric features are advertised as an advantage of Windows 95. But you can still successfully use the application-centric approach you used with Windows 3.1 by opening your application, then opening your document.

To open the Sample Text file by selecting it from My Computer:

1. Click the **My Computer** icon. Press the **Enter** key. The My Computer window opens.

2. Click the **3½ Floppy (A:)** icon, then press the **Enter** key. The 3½ Floppy (A:) window opens.

   TROUBLE? If the My Computer window disappears when you open the 3½ floppy (A:) window, click View, click Options, then click the Folder tab, if necessary. Click the radio button labelled "Browse Folders using a separate window for each folder." Then click the OK button.

3. Click the **Sample Text** file icon, then press the **Enter** key. Windows 95 starts an application program, then automatically opens the Sample Text file.

   TROUBLE? If Windows 95 starts Microsoft Word instead of WordPad, don't worry. You can use Microsoft Word to revise the Sample Text document.

Now that Windows 95 has started an application and opened the Sample Text file, you could make revisions to the document. Instead, you should close all the windows on your desktop so you can try the other method for opening files.

To close all the windows on the desktop:

1. Click ⊠ on each of the windows.

   TROUBLE? If you see a message, "Save changes to Document?" click the No button.

The second method for opening the Sample Text file requires you to open WordPad, then use the Open button to select the Sample Text file. The advantage of this method is that you can specify the application program you want to use—WordPad in this case. This method, however, involves more steps than the method you tried previously.

To start WordPad and open the Sample Text file using the Open button:

1. Start WordPad.

2. Click the **Open** button 🖻 on the toolbar. Figure 2-11 shows the location of this button and the dialog box that appears after you click it.

Figure 2-11 ◄
The Open button
and dialog box

Open button

Open dialog box

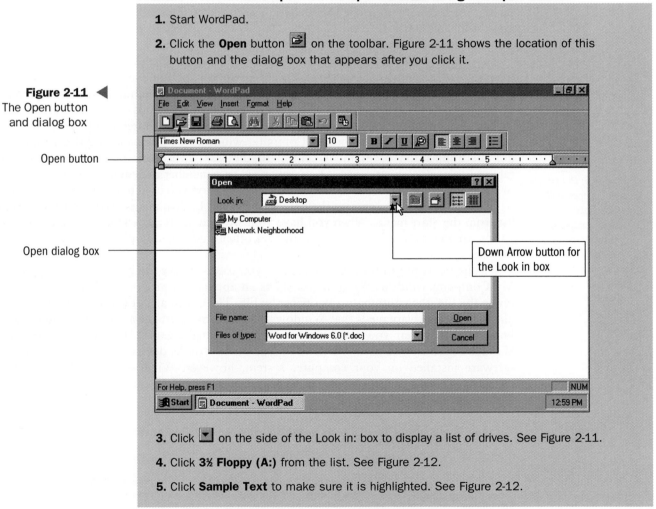

3. Click ▼ on the side of the Look in: box to display a list of drives. See Figure 2-11.

4. Click **3½ Floppy (A:)** from the list. See Figure 2-12.

5. Click **Sample Text** to make sure it is highlighted. See Figure 2-12.

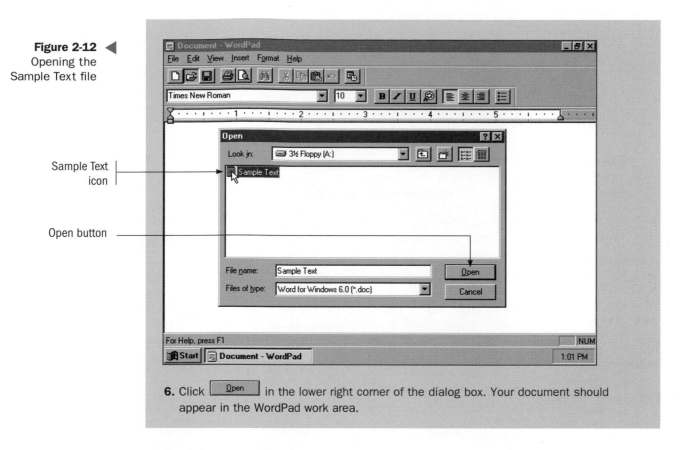

Figure 2-12 ◄
Opening the
Sample Text file

Sample Text
icon

Open button

6. Click [Open] in the lower right corner of the dialog box. Your document should appear in the WordPad work area.

Printing a File

Now that the Sample Text file is open, you can print it. It is a good idea to use Print Preview before you send your document to the printer. **Print Preview** shows on screen exactly how your document will appear on paper. You can check your page layout so you don't waste paper printing a document that is not quite the way you want it. Your instructor or technical support person might supply you with additional instructions for printing in your school's computer lab.

To preview, then print the Sample Text file:

1. Click the **Print Preview** button 🔍 on the toolbar.

2. Look at your print preview. Before you print the document and use paper, you should make sure that the font, margins, and other document features look the way you want them to.

   TROUBLE? If you can't read the document text on screen, click the Zoom In button.

3. Click the **Print** button. A Print dialog box appears.

4. Study Figure 2-13 to familiarize yourself with the controls in the Print dialog box.

This is the name of the printer that Windows 95 will use for this printout. If you are using a network, you might have a choice of printers. If you need to select a different printer, ask your instructor or your technical support person for help.

The Properties button lets you modify the way your printer is set up. Do not change any of the settings on your school printer without the consent of your instructor or technical support person.

When you click this check box, your printout will go on your disk instead of to the printer.

Figure 2-13 ◀
The Print dialog box

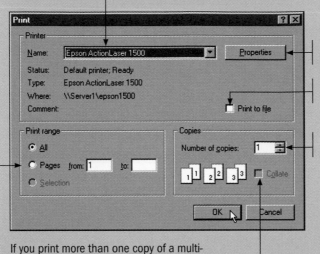

In the Print range box, you specify how much of the document you want to print. If you want to print only part of a document, click the Pages radio button and then enter the starting and ending pages for the printout.

You can specify how many copies you want by typing the number in this box. Alternatively, you can use the arrow buttons to increase or decrease the number in the box.

If you print more than one copy of a multi-page document, you can specify that you want the printout collated, so you don't have to collate the pages manually.

5. Make sure your screen shows the Print range set to "All" and the number of copies set to "1."

6. Click the **OK** button to print your document. If a message appears telling you printing is complete, click the **OK** button.

TROUBLE? If your document does not print, make sure the printer has paper and the printer on-line light is on. If your document still doesn't print, ask your instructor or technical support person for help.

7. Close WordPad.

TROUBLE? If you see the message "Save changes to Document?" click the "No" button.

Quick Check

1 A(n) _____ is a collection of data that has a name and is stored on a disk or other storage medium.

2 _____ erases all the data on a disk and arranges the magnetic particles on the disk surface so the disk can store data.

3 When you are working in a text box, the pointer shape changes to a(n) _____.

4 The _____ shows you where each character you type will appear.

5 _____ automatically moves text down to the beginning of the next line when you reach the right margin.

6 Explain how you select a block of text: _____.

7 Which of these characters are not allowed in Windows 95 file names: \ ? : * " < > | ! @ # $ % ^ & ; + - ( ) /

8   In the filename New Equipment.Doc, .Doc is a(n) _____.

9   Suppose you created a graph using the Harvard Graphics software and then you stored the graph on your floppy disk under the name Projected 1997 Sales - Graph. The next day, you use Harvard Graphics to open the file and change the graph. If you want the new version of the file on your disk, you need to _____.

10   You can save _____ by using the Print Preview feature.

SESSION

2.2

In this session, you will learn how to manage the files on your disk—a skill that can prevent you from losing important documents. You will learn how to list information about the files on your disk; organize the files into folders; and move, delete, copy, and rename files.

Creating Your Student Disk

For this session of the tutorial, you must create a Student Disk that contains some sample files. *You can use the disk you formatted in the previous session.*

If you are using your own computer, the CTI Windows 95 Applications menu selection will not be available. Before you proceed, you must go to your school's computer lab and find a computer that has the CTI Windows 95 Applications installed. Once you have made your own Student Disk, you can use it to complete this tutorial on any computer you choose.

To add the sample files to your Student Disk:

1. Write "Windows 95 Student Disk" on the label of your formatted disk.

2. Place the disk in Drive A.

TROUBLE? If your 3½-inch disk drive is B, place your formatted disk in that drive instead, and for the rest of this session substitute Drive B where ever you see Drive A.

3. Click the **Start** button 🟦**Start**. See Figure 2-14.

Figure 2-14 ◀
Making your
Student Disk

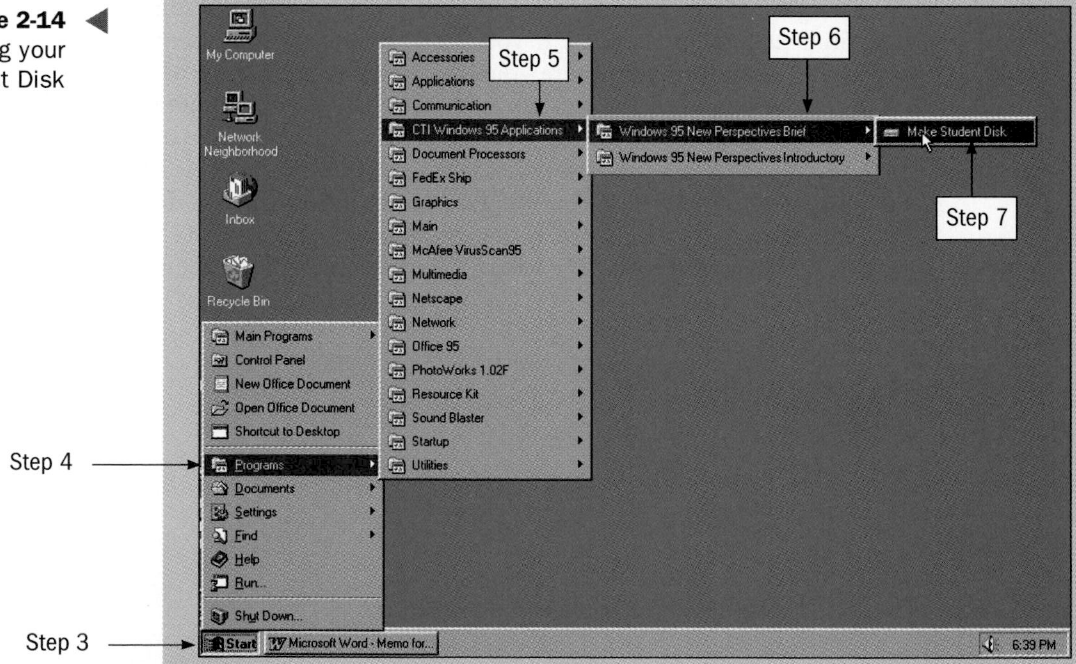

4. Point to **Programs**.

5. Point to **CTI Windows 95 Applications**.

> **TROUBLE?** If CTI Windows 95 Applications is not listed, contact your instructor or technical support person.

6. Point to **Windows 95 New Perspectives Brief**.

7. Select **Make Student Disk**.

> A dialog box opens, asking you to indicate the drive that contains your formatted disk.

8. If it is not already selected, click the Drive radio button that corresponds to the drive containing your student disk.

9. Click the **OK** button.

> The sample files are copied to your formatted disk. A message tells you when all the files have been copied.

10. Click **OK**.

11. If necessary, close all the open windows on your screen.

Your Student Disk now contains sample files that you will use throughout the rest of this tutorial.

My Computer

The **My Computer** icon represents your computer, its storage devices, and its printers. The My Computer icon opens into the My Computer window, which contains an icon for each of the storage devices on your computer. On most computer systems the My Computer window also contains Control Panel and Printers folders, which help you add printers, control peripheral devices, and customize your Windows 95 work environment. Figure 2-15 on the following page explains more about the My Computer window.

You can use the My Computer window to keep track of where your files are stored and to organize your files. In this section of the tutorial you will move and delete files on your Student Disk in drive A. If you use your own computer at home or computer at work, you would probably store your files on drive C, instead of drive A. However, in a school lab environment you usually don't know which computer you will use, so you need to carry your files with you on a floppy disk that you use in drive A. In this session, therefore, you will learn how to work with the files on drive A. Most of what you learn will also work on your home or work computer when you use drive C.

In this session you will work with several icons, including My Computer. As a general procedure, when you want to open an icon, you click it and then press the Enter key.

Figure 2-15 ◀
Information
about My
Computer

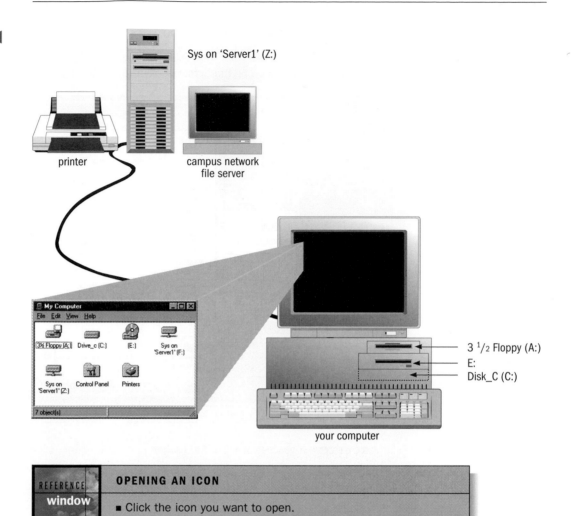

Sys on 'Server1' (Z:)

printer

campus network
file server

3 1/2 Floppy (A:)

E:

Disk_C (C:)

your computer

REFERENCE **window**

OPENING AN ICON

- Click the icon you want to open.
- Press the Enter key.

Now you should open the My Computer icon.

To open the My Computer icon:

1. Click the **My Computer** icon to select it.

2. Press the **Enter** key. The My Computer window opens.

Now that you have opened the My Computer window, you can find out what is on
your Student Disk in drive A.

Figure 2-16 ◄
Contents of
Student Disk

To find out what is on your Student Disk:

1. Open the **3½ Floppy (A:)** icon by clicking it, then pressing the **Enter** key. A window appears showing the contents of drive A:. See Figure 2-16.

Icons show contents
of drive A

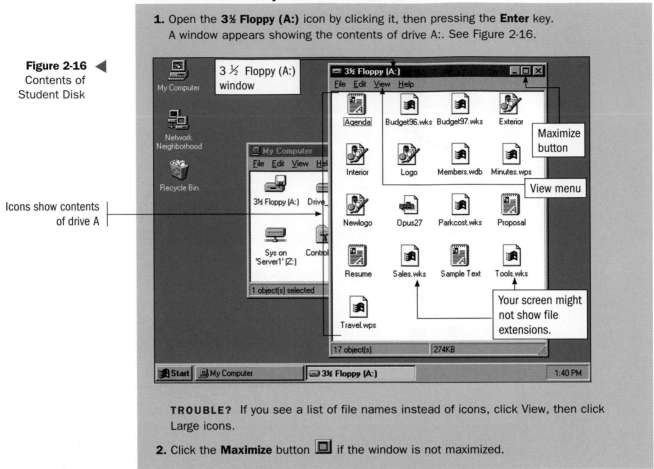

TROUBLE? If you see a list of file names instead of icons, click View, then click Large icons.

2. Click the **Maximize** button 🗖 if the window is not maximized.

Windows 95 provides four ways to view the contents of a disk—large icons, small icons, list, or details. The standard view, shown on your screen, displays a large icon and title for each file. The icon provides a visual cue to the type and contents of the file, as Figure 2-17 illustrates.

Figure 2-17 ◄
Program and
file icons

Text files that you can open and read using the WordPad or NotePad software are represented by notepad icons.	WordPad Document Netlog Exchng32
The icons for Windows programs usually depict an object related to the function of the program. For example, an icon that looks like a calculator signifies the Windows Calc program; an icon that looks like a computer signifies the Windows Explorer program.	Explorer Calc
Many of the files you create are represented by page icons. Here the page icon for the Circles file shows some graphics tools to indicate the file contains a graphic. The Page icon for the Access file contains the Windows logo, indicating that Windows does not know if the file contains a document, graphics, or data base.	Access.mdb Circles
Folders provide a way to group and organize files. A folder icon contains other icons for folders and files. Here, the System folder contains files used by the Windows operating system.	System
Non-Windows programs are represented by this icon of a blank window.	Command

The **Details** view shows more information than the large icon, small icon, and list views. Details view shows the file icon, the filename, the file size, the application you used to create the file, and the date/time the file was created or last modified.

To view a detailed list of files:

1. Click **View** then click **Details** to display details for the files on your disk as shown in Figure 2-18.

Figure 2-18 ◀
Detailed file list

File icon ⟶

Filename ⟶

Your screen might not show file extensions

Total number of files and folders in the window

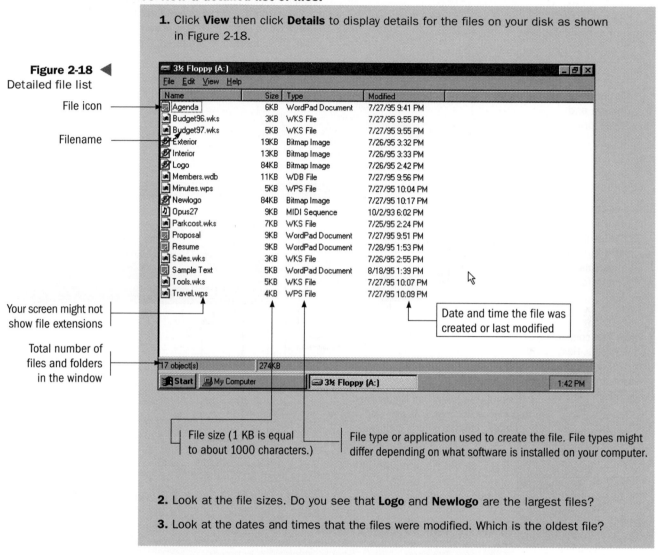

Date and time the file was created or last modified

File size (1 KB is equal to about 1000 characters.)

File type or application used to create the file. File types might differ depending on what software is installed on your computer.

2. Look at the file sizes. Do you see that **Logo** and **Newlogo** are the largest files?

3. Look at the dates and times that the files were modified. Which is the oldest file?

Now that you have looked at the file details, switch back to the large icon view.

To switch to the large icon view:

1. Click **View** then click **Large Icons** to return to the large icon display.

Folders and Directories

A list of files is referred to as a **directory**. The main directory of a disk is sometimes called the **root directory**. The root directory is created when you format a disk and is shown in parentheses at the top of the window. For example, at the top of your screen you should see "3 ½ Floppy (A:)." The root directory is A:. In some situations, the root directory is indicated by a backslash after the drive letter and colon, such as A:\. All of the files on your Student Disk are currently in the root directory.

If too many files are stored in a directory, the directory list becomes very long and difficult to manage. A directory can be divided into **folders** (also called **subdirectories**), into which you group similar files. The directory of files for each folder then becomes much shorter and easier to manage. For example, you might create a folder for all the papers you write for an English 111 class as shown in Figure 2-19.

A folder appears on the screen as a folder icon. When you open the folder icon, the folder is represented by a window. The ENG111 folder appears as the ENG111 window on the screen. The contents of the folder are represented by icons in the window.

Figure 2-19 ◀
Folders and
directories

You create folders
to hold groups
of similar objects,
such as documents,
programs, and
other folders.

A folder can contain
other folders. Here,
the ENG111 folder
contains a folder
called TERM PAPER.

If you open a folder that is contained
in a window, it opens to its own window
and displays the objects it contains.

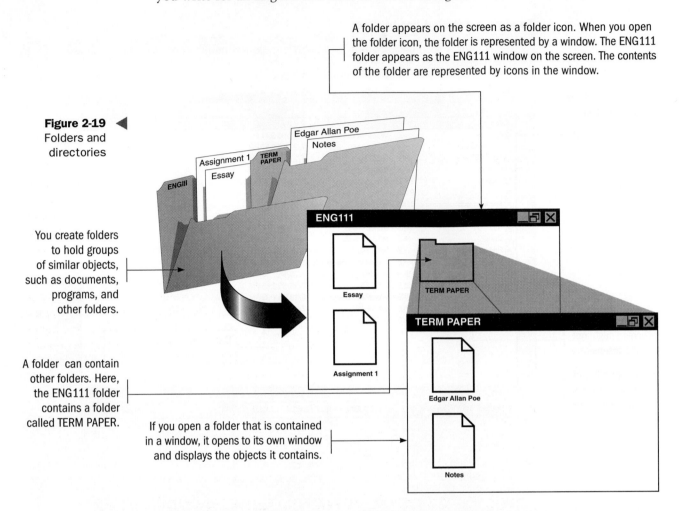

Now, you'll create a folder called My Documents to hold your document files.

To create a My Documents folder:

1. Click **File** then point to **New** to display the submenu.

2. Click **Folder**. A folder icon with the label "New Folder" appears.

3. Type **My Documents** as the name of the folder.

4. Press the **Enter** key.

When you first create a folder, it doesn't contain any files. In the next set of steps you will move a file from the root directory to the My Documents folder.

CREATING A NEW FOLDER

- Open the My Computer icon to display the My Computer window.
- Open the icon for the drive on which you want to create the folder.
- Click File then point to New.
- From the submenu click Folder.
- Type the name for the new folder.
- Press the Enter key.

Moving and Copying a File

You can move a file from one directory to another or from one disk to another. When you move a file it is copied to the new location you specify, then the version in the old location is erased. The move feature is handy for organizing or reorganizing the files on your disk by moving them into appropriate folders. The easiest way to move a file is to hold down the *right* mouse button and drag the file from the old location to the new location. A menu appears and you select Move Here.

You can also copy a file from one directory to another, or from one disk to another. When you copy a file, you create an exact duplicate of an existing file in whatever disk or folder you specify. To copy a file from one folder to another on your floppy disk, you use the same procedure as for moving a file, except that you select Copy Here from the menu.

Suppose you want to move the Minutes file from the root directory to the My Documents folder. Depending on the software applications installed on your computer, this file is either called Minutes or Minutes.wps. In the steps it is referred to simply as Minutes.

To move the Minutes file to the My Documents folder:

1. Click the **Minutes** icon to select it.

2. Press and hold the right mouse button while you drag the **Minutes** icon to the My Documents folder. See Figure 2-20.

Figure 2-20 ◄
Moving a file

Minutes file

My Documents folder

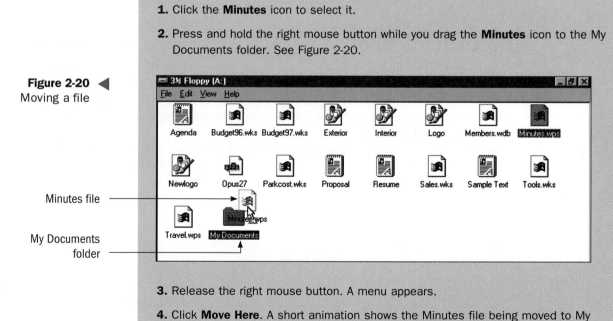

3. Release the right mouse button. A menu appears.

4. Click **Move Here**. A short animation shows the Minutes file being moved to My Documents. The Minutes icon disappears from the window showing the files in the root directory.

MOVING A FILE

- Open the My Computer icon to display the My Computer window.
- If the document you want to move is in a folder, open the folder.
- Hold down the *right* mouse button while you drag the file icon to its new folder or disk location.
- Click Move Here.
- If you want to move more than one file at a time, hold down the Ctrl key while you click the icons for all the files you want to move.

3.1 NOTE

Windows 3.1 users be careful! When you delete or move an icon in the Windows 95 My Computer window you are actually deleting or moving the file. This is quite different from the way the Windows 3.1 Program Manager worked.

Anything you do to an icon in the My Computer window is actually done to the file represented by that icon. If you move an icon, the file is moved; if you delete an icon, the file is deleted.

After you move a file, it is a good idea to make sure it was moved to the correct location. You can easily verify that a file is in its new folder by displaying the folder contents.

To verify that the Minutes file was moved to My Documents:

1. Click the **My Documents** folder, then press **Enter**. The My Documents window appears and it contains one file—Minutes.

2. Click the My Documents window **Close** button ☒.

   TROUBLE? If the My Computer window is no longer visible, click the My Computer icon, then press Enter. You might also need to open the 3 ½ Floppy (A:) icon.

Deleting a File

You delete a file or folder by deleting its icon. However, be careful when you delete a *folder*, because you also delete all the files it contains! When you delete a file from the hard drive, the filename is deleted from the directory but the file contents are held in the Recycle Bin. If you change your mind and want to retrieve the deleted file, you can recover it by clicking the Recycle Bin.

When you delete a file from a floppy disk, it does not go into the Recycle Bin. Instead it is deleted as soon as its icon disappears. Try deleting the file named Agenda from your Student Disk. Because this file is on the floppy disk and not on the hard disk, it will not go into the Recycle Bin.

To delete the file Agenda:

1. Click the icon for the file **Agenda**.

2. Press the **Delete** key.

3. If a message appears asking, "Are sure you want to delete Agenda?", click **Yes**. An animation, which might play too quickly to be seen, shows the file being deleted.

DELETING A FILE

- Click the icon for the file you want to delete.
- Press the Delete key.

Renaming a File

You can easily change the name of a file using the Rename option on the File menu or by using the file's label. Remember that when you choose a filename it can contain up to 255 characters, including spaces, but it cannot contain \ ? : " < > | characters.

Practice using this feature by renaming the Sales file to give it a more descriptive filename.

To rename Sales:

1. Click the **Sales** file to select it.

2. Click the label "Sales". After a short pause a solid box outlines the label and an insertion point appears.

3. Type **Preliminary Sales Summary** as the new filename.

4. Press the **Enter key**.

5. Click the **Close** button to close the 3 ½-inch Floppy (A:) window.

RENAMING A FILE

- Click the icon for the file you want to rename.
- Click the label of the icon.
- Type the new name for the file.
- Press the Enter key.

Copying an Entire Floppy Disk

You can have trouble accessing the data on your floppy disk if the disk gets damaged, exposed to magnetic fields, or picks up a computer virus. If the damaged disk contains important files, you will have to spend many hours to try to reconstruct those files. To avoid losing all your data, it is a good idea to make a copy of your floppy disk. This copy is called a **backup** copy.

If you wanted to make a copy of an audio cassette, your cassette player would need two cassette drives. You might wonder, therefore, how your computer can make a copy of your disk if you have only one disk drive. Figure 2-21 illustrates how the computer uses only one disk drive to make a copy of a disk.

Figure 2-21 ◀
Using one disk
drive to make a
copy of a disk

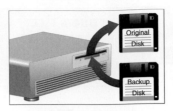

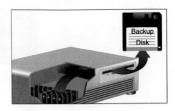

1. First, the computer
copies the data from your
original disk into memory.

2. Once the data is in
memory, you remove your
original disk from the drive
and replace it with your
backup disk.

3. The computer moves the
data from memory onto
your backup disk.

REFERENCE
window

MAKING A BACKUP OF YOUR FLOPPY DISK

- Click My Computer then press the Enter key.
- Insert the disk you want to copy in drive A.
- Click the 3 ½ Floppy (A:) icon   3½ Floppy (A:)   to select it.
- Click File then click Copy Disk to display the Copy Disk dialog box.
- Click Start to begin the copy process.
- When prompted, remove the disk you want to copy. Place your backup disk in drive A.
- Click OK.
- When the copy is complete, close the Copy Disk dialog box.
- Close the My Computer dialog box.

If you have two floppy disks, you can make a backup of your Student Disk now. Make sure you periodically follow the backup procedure, so your backup is up-to-date.

To back up your Student Disk:

1. Write your name and "Backup" on the label of your second disk. This will be your backup disk.

2. Make sure your Student Disk is in drive A.

3. Make sure the My Computer window is open. See Figure 2-22.

Figure 2-22 ◀
The My
Computer
window

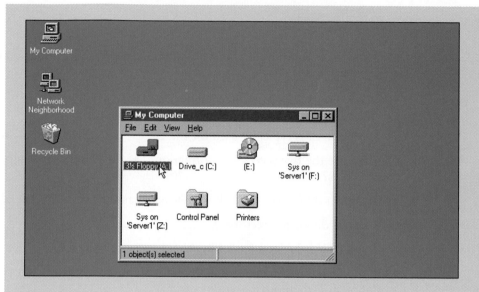

4. Click the **3 ½ Floppy (A:)** icon to select it.

TROUBLE? If you mistakenly open the 3½ Floppy (A:) *window*, click ☒.

5. Click **File**.

6. Click **Copy Disk** to display the Copy Disk dialog box as shown in Figure 2-23.

Figure 2-23 ◀
The Copy Disk
dialog box

7. On the lower right side of the dialog box, you'll see a Start button. Click this **Start** button to begin the copy process.

8. When the message, "Insert the disk you want to copy from (source disk)..." appears, click the **OK** button.

9. When the message, "Insert the disk you want to copy to (destination disk)..." appears, insert your backup disk in drive A.

10. Click the **OK** button. When the copy is complete, you will see the message "Copy completed successfully."

11. After the data is copied to your backup disk, click ☒ on the blue title bar of the Copy Disk dialog box.

12. Click ☒ on the My Computer window to close the My Computer window.

13. Remove your disk from the drive.

Each time you make a backup, the data on your backup disk is erased, and replaced with the data from your updated Student Disk. Now that you know how to copy an entire disk, make a backup whenever you have completed a tutorial or you have spent a long time working on a file.

Quick Check

1 If you want to find out about the storage devices and printers connected to your computer, click the _____ icon.

2 If you have only one floppy disk drive on your computer, it is identified by the letter _____.

3 The letter C: is typically used for the _____ drive of a computer.

4 What are the five pieces of information that the Details view supplies about each of your files?

5 The main directory of a disk is referred to as the _____ directory.

6 You can divide a directory into _____.

7 If you delete the icon for a file, what happens to the file?

8 If you have one floppy disk drive, but you have two disks, can you copy a file from one floppy disk to another?

End Note

Just as you complete the Quick Check for Session 2.2, Steve appears. He asks how you are doing. You summarize what you remember from the tutorial, telling him that you learned how to insert, delete, and select text. You also learned how to work with files using Windows 95 software—you now know how to save, open, revise, and print a document. You tell him that you like the idea that these file operations are the same for almost all Windows 95 software. Steve agrees that this makes work a lot easier.

When Steve asks you if you have a supply of disks, you tell him you do, and that you just learned how to format a disk and view a list of files on your disk. Steve wants you to remember that you can use the Details view to see the filename, size, date, and time. You assure him that you remember that feature—and also how to move, delete, and rename a file.

Steve seems pleased with your progress and agrees that you're now ready to use software applications. But he can't resist giving you one last warning—don't forget to back up your files frequently!

Tutorial Assignments

1. Opening, Editing, and Printing a Document In this tutorial you learned how to create a document using WordPad. You also learned how to save, open, and print a document. Practice these skills by opening the document on your Student Disk called Resume, which is a résumé for Jamie Woods. Make the changes shown in Figure 2-24, and then print the document. After you print, save your revisions.

Figure 2-24 ◀

Change this to your name, address, and phone number. If you don't have an office number delete this.

Change this to the name of your university or college.

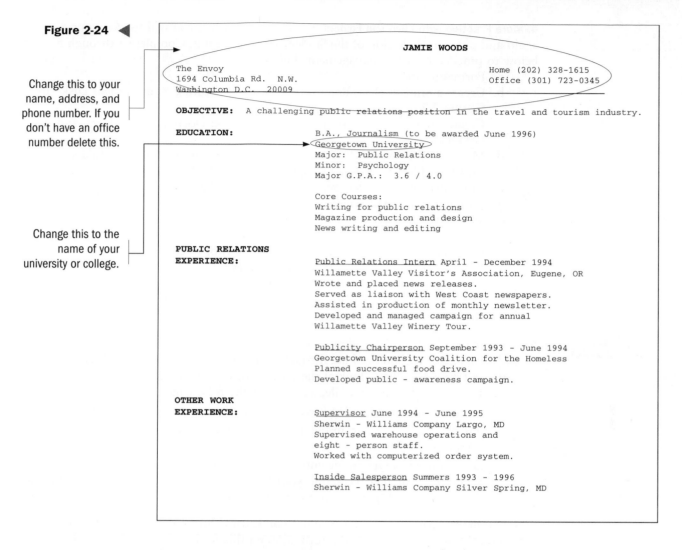

```
                                    JAMIE WOODS

 The Envoy                                      Home (202) 328-1615
 1694 Columbia Rd.  N.W.                        Office (301) 723-0345
 Washington D.C.  20009

 OBJECTIVE:         A challenging public relations position in the travel and tourism industry.

 EDUCATION:                    B.A., Journalism (to be awarded June 1996)
                               Georgetown University
                               Major:  Public Relations
                               Minor:  Psychology
                               Major G.P.A.:  3.6 / 4.0

                               Core Courses:
                               Writing for public relations
                               Magazine production and design
                               News writing and editing

 PUBLIC RELATIONS
 EXPERIENCE:                   Public Relations Intern April - December 1994
                               Willamette Valley Visitor's Association, Eugene, OR
                               Wrote and placed news releases.
                               Served as liaison with West Coast newspapers.
                               Assisted in production of monthly newsletter.
                               Developed and managed campaign for annual
                               Willamette Valley Winery Tour.

                               Publicity Chairperson September 1993 - June 1994
                               Georgetown University Coalition for the Homeless
                               Planned successful food drive.
                               Developed public - awareness campaign.

 OTHER WORK
 EXPERIENCE:                   Supervisor June 1994 - June 1995
                               Sherwin - Williams Company Largo, MD
                               Supervised warehouse operations and
                               eight - person staff.
                               Worked with computerized order system.

                               Inside Salesperson Summers 1993 - 1996
                               Sherwin - Williams Company Silver Spring, MD
```

2. Creating, Saving, and Printing a Letter Use WordPad to write a one-page letter to a relative or a friend. Save the document in the My Documents folder with the name "Letter." Use the Print Preview feature to look at the format of your finished letter, then print it, and be sure you sign it.

3. Managing Files and Folders Earlier in this tutorial you created a folder and moved the file called Minutes into it. Now complete a through g below to practice your file management skills.

a. Create a folder called Spreadsheets on your Student Disk.

b. Move the files ParkCost, Budget96, Budget97, and Sales into the Spreadsheets folder.

c. Create a folder called Park Project.

d. Move the files Proposal, Members, Tools, Logo, and Newlogo into the Park Project folder.

e. Move the ParkCost file from the Spreadsheets folder to the Park Project folder.

f. Delete the file called Travel.

g. Switch to the Details view and answer the following questions:

Write out your answers to questions a through e.

a. What is the largest file in the Park Project folder?

b. What is the newest file in the Spreadsheets folder?

c. How many files are in the root directory?

d. How are the Members and Resume icons different?

e. What is the file with the most recent date on the entire disk?

4. More Practice with Files and Folders For this assignment, you will format your disk again and put a fresh version of the Student Disk files on it. Complete a through h below to practice your file management skills.

    a. Format a disk.
    b. Create a Student Disk. Refer to the section "Creating Your Student Disk" in Session 2.2.
    c. Create three folders on your new Student Disk: Documents, Budgets, and Graphics.
    d. Move the files Interior, Exterior, Logo, and Newlogo to the Graphics folder.
    e. Move the files Travel, Members and Minutes to the Documents folder.
    f. Move Budget96 and Budget97 to the Budgets folder.
    g. Switch to the Details view.

Answer questions a through f.

    a. What is the largest file in the Graphics folder?
    b. How many WordPad documents are in the root directory?
    c. What is the newest file in the root directory?
    d. How many files in all folders are 5KB in size?
    e. How many files in the Documents folder are WKS files?
    f. Do all the files in the Graphics folder have the same icon?

5. Finding a File Microsoft Windows 95 contains an on-line Tour that explains how to find files on a disk without looking through all the folders. Start the Windows 95 Tour (if you don't remember how, look at the instructions for Tutorial Assignment 1 in Tutorial 1), then click Finding a File, and answer the following questions:

    a. To display the Find dialog box, you must click the _____ button, then select _____ from the menu, and finally click _____ from the submenu.
    b. Do you need to type in the entire filename to find the file?
    c. When the computer has found your file, what are the steps you have to follow if you want to display the contents of the file?

6. Help with Files and Folders In Tutorial 2 you learned how to work with Windows 95 files and folders. What additional information on this topic does Windows 95 Help provide? Use the Start button to access Help. Use the Index tab to locate topics related to files and folders. Find at least two tips or procedures for working with files and folders that were not covered in the tutorial. Write out the tip in your own words and indicate the title of the Help screen that contains the information.

Lab Assignments

1. Using Files Lab In Tutorial 2 you learned how to create, save, open, and print files. The Using Files Lab will help you review what happens in the computer when you perform these file tasks. To start the Lab, follow these steps:

    a. Click the Start button.
    b. Point to Programs, then point to CTI Windows 95 Applications.
    c. Point to Windows 95 New Perspectives Brief.
    d. Click Using Files. If you can't find Windows 95 New Perspectives Brief or Using Files, ask for help from your instructor or technical support person.

Answer the Quick Check questions that appear as you work through the Lab. You can print your answers at the end of the Lab.

Using Files

Answers to Quick Check Questions

SESSION 1.1

1 a. icon b. Start button c. taskbar d. Date/Time control e. desktop f. pointer

2 Multitasking

3 Start menu

4 Lift up the mouse, move it to the right, then put it down, and slide it left until the pointer reaches the left edge of the screen.

5 Highlighting

6 If a program is running, its button is displayed on the taskbar.

7 Each program that is running uses system resources, so Windows 95 runs more efficiently when only the programs you are using are open.

8 Answer: If you do not perform the shut down procedure, you might lose data.

SESSION 1.2

1 a. title bar b. program title c. Minimize button d. Restore button e. Close button f. menu bar g. toolbar h. formatting bar i. taskbar j. status bar k. workspace l. pointer

2 a. Minimize button—hides the program so only its button is showing on the taskbar.
b. Maximize button—enlarges the program to fill the entire screen.
c. Restore button—sets the program to a pre-defined size.
d. Close button—stops the program and removes its button from the taskbar.

3 a. Ellipses—indicate a dialog box will appear.
b. Grayed out—the menu option is not currently available.
c. Submenu—indicates a submenu will appear.
d. Check mark—indicates a menu option is currently in effect.

4 Toolbar

5 a. scroll bar b. scroll box c. Cancel button d. down arrow button e. list box f. radio button g. check box

6 one, check boxes

7 On-line Help

SESSION 2.1

1 file

2 formatting

3 I-beam

4 insertion point

5 word wrap

6 You drag the I-beam pointer over
the text to highlight it.

7 \ ? : * < > | "

8 extension

9 save the file again

10 paper

SESSION 2.2

1 My Computer

2 A (or A:)

3 Hard (or hard disk)

4 Filename, file type, file size, date, time

5 Root

6 Folders (or subdirectories)

7 It is deleted from the disk.

8 Yes

Microsoft® Windows® 98
Preview

TUTORIAL

Microsoft Windows 98 Preview

A Brief Comparison of the Windows 95 and Windows 98 Operating Systems

OBJECTIVES

In this tutorial, you will:

- Explore the differences between the Windows 95 and Windows 98 desktop

- Compare the Windows 95 and Windows 98 Start menus

- Compare mouse operations under Windows 95 and Windows 98

- Examine Active Desktop capabilities

- Explore Web view

- Preview additional Windows 98 features

Upgrading to a New Operating System

If you have worked with computers for very long, you already know that computer owners regularly face the decision to upgrade. **Upgrading** is the process of placing a more recent version of a product onto your computer. Upgrades to **hardware**, the physical components of a computer, occur when a computer user decides to purchase a newer computer or computer component that will add features, space, or speed to his or her computer system.

Upgrades to **software**, the set of instructions that make a computer perform a specific task, occur when a user decides to take advantage of improvements in a more recent version of a software product. Software developers produce new versions of software for a variety of reasons. Because hardware is constantly changing as new technology emerges, software developers need to ensure that their software takes full advantage of the latest hardware technology. For example, when it became cheaper and easier to expand the amount of memory on personal computers, many software companies developed their software to take advantage of extra memory. Another important reason for software revisions is usability. Developers are constantly trying to make their software easier to learn and use. For example, when it became clear that people found a graphical interface easy to work with, most software companies provided such an interface to their software. Software revisions also occur when a new software technology emerges. Developers update their products so they can compete against newer products that use newer technology. For example, with the recent explosion in popularity of the World Wide Web, many software companies hastened to include Web features in their products.

Microsoft Corporation's operating system revision from Windows 95 to Windows 98 is a response to these and other trends. For example, hardware now exists that makes it possible for you to run your computer through your television set, so Windows 98 includes a software accessory, TV Viewer, that lets you use this technology if you have the appropriate hardware. Windows 98 features such as automated disk maintenance are a response to the demand for ease of use. To take advantage of emerging software technology, Microsoft designed Windows 98 around features of the World Wide Web.

The decision to upgrade your operating system can be difficult to make. Upgrades can be expensive. To take full advantage of the Windows 98 upgrade, you might need to purchase new hardware, such as an Internet connection via a modem, a TV tuner card, or additional memory. Some revisions don't greatly affect how a software product is used, but other revisions change the interface so significantly that computer owners need to evaluate whether the advantages of upgrading are greater than the disadvantages of having to learn a practically new product. Users also consider the newness of the technology before they upgrade; some like to wait until the dust settles and the technology is tested and proven before they risk using it on their own computers.

In this tutorial, you'll examine how the upgrade to Windows 98 from Windows 95 affects what you see as you use the interface. This tutorial was developed using a prerelease version of Windows 98, so there might be slight differences between what you see in the figures and what you see in the final product. If you want more information about a feature that seems to be operating differently from what you see here, click the Start button and then click Help. Use the online Help system to learn more about the feature.

The Windows 98 Desktop

When you first turn on your computer, you might not notice much difference between the Windows 95 and Windows 98 desktops. Recall that the **desktop** is the workspace on your screen. Because it's easy to customize the desktop, someone might have changed your desktop so that it looks different from the one shown in the figures in this tutorial. You should, however, be able to locate objects similar to those in the figures. Figure 1 shows the Windows 95 desktop. Remember that you might see additional icons, and your screen might show a different background.

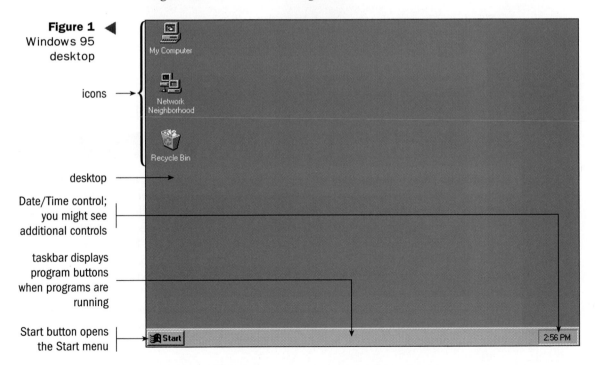

Figure 1 ◄
Windows 95
desktop

icons →

desktop →

Date/Time control;
you might see
additional controls

taskbar displays
program buttons
when programs are
running

Start button opens
the Start menu

Figure 2 shows the Windows 98 desktop. Notice that the Start button, taskbar, Date/Time control, and icons all look the same as their Windows 95 counterparts. Your Windows 98 desktop might show additional objects; you'll learn more about these shortly.

Figure 2
Windows 98 desktop

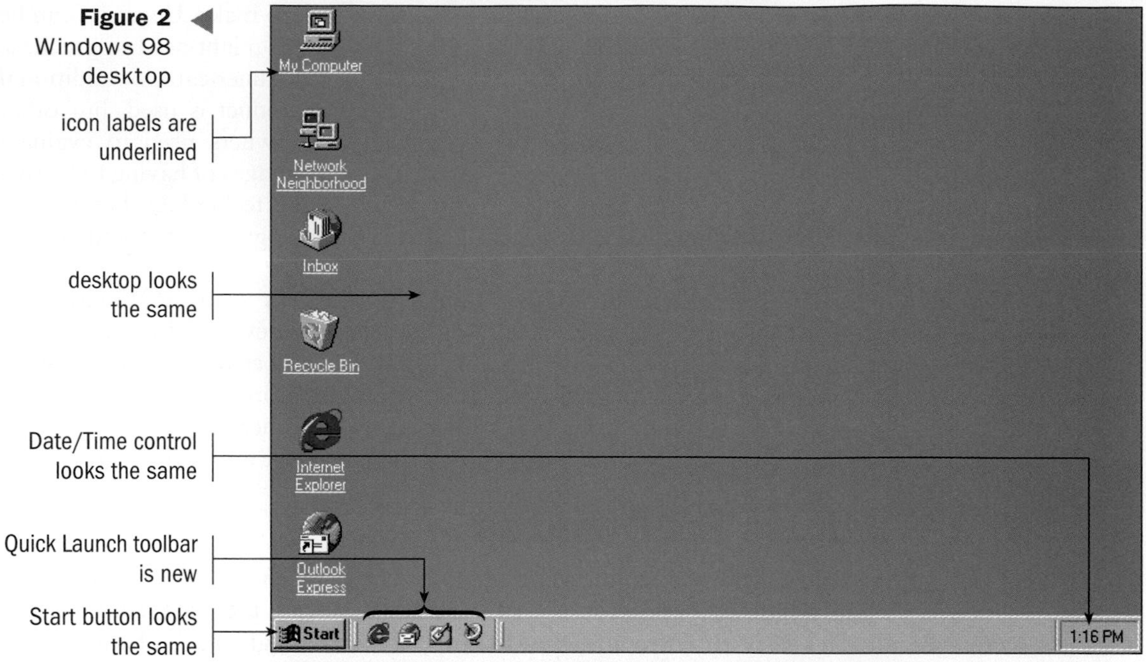
icon labels are underlined
desktop looks the same
Date/Time control looks the same
Quick Launch toolbar is new
Start button looks the same
My Computer
Network Neighborhood
Inbox
Recycle Bin
Internet Explorer
Outlook Express
Start
1:16 PM

There are really only two visible differences between the basic Windows 95 and Windows 98 desktops:

- Windows 98 includes the Quick Launch toolbar.
- In Windows 98, icon names can appear underlined.

If you have access to the Internet and the Web, and if your desktop has been customized, it's possible you'll see additional desktop objects. Windows 98 makes it possible to integrate your Web experience into your desktop, as you'll see shortly.

Underlined Icon Names

The underlined icon names you see are evidence of Microsoft's attempt to make your experience with the Windows 98 desktop more like your experience with the Web. The **World Wide Web**, or just the **Web**, is a service on the Internet that allows you to view documents on computers around the world. Documents on the Web are called **Web pages**. Web pages contain elements known as **links** that you can select, usually by clicking a mouse, to move to another part of the document or another document altogether. A link can be a word, a phrase, or a graphic image. When a link consists of text, the text link usually appears underlined and in a different color.

To view Web pages, you use a program called a **browser**. When you click a link on a Web page in your browser, you jump to a different location—perhaps to a page stored on another computer, as shown in Figure 3.

Figure 3
Clicking Web
page links

Web page on
rock climbing

click this link
to jump to a
different document

this Web page
appears when you
click the Tour link

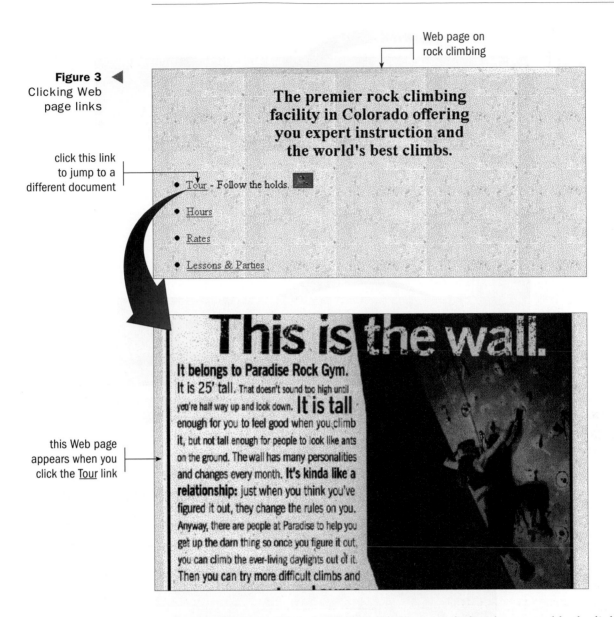

On the Windows 98 desktop, icon labels are underlined to resemble the links you see on Web pages. By attempting to mimic the Web experience, Microsoft is trying to simplify how you interact with your computer. If the actions you take on the desktop are similar to those you take in your browser, you have to learn only one set of techniques.

Thus, when you click one of the icon labels on the Windows 98 desktop, you "jump" to that icon's destination. For example, in Windows 95, to open My Computer, you had to double-click its icon (or click its icon to select it and then press Enter). In Windows 98, however, the My Computer icon label is underlined just like a link. When you point at the icon label, the pointer changes from ⌕ to ⌐, just as it would if you pointed at a link in your browser. When you click the underlined icon label, you "jump" to the My Computer window. The result is the same: The My Computer window opens, but the Windows 98 technique is more like the technique you use on the Web. Figure 4 illustrates this difference.

Figure 4 ◄
Activating an
icon in
Windows 95 vs.
Windows 98

in Windows 95, you
must double-click to
open the My
Computer window

pointer in
Windows 95

pointer in
Windows 98

in Windows 98, you
simply click to open
the My Computer
window

As you work with the Windows 98 operating system, you'll see that underlined text appears not just on the desktop but in numerous places—the My Computer window, the folder windows, and the Windows Explorer window, just to name a few. You can also display Windows 98 icons in the traditional Windows 95 manner: From My Computer, click View, click Folder Options, and then on the General tab, click the Classic style option button.

The Quick Launch Toolbar

The Windows 95 taskbar displays the Start button, buttons that correspond to active programs or open documents, and the tray area that includes the Date/Time control and any other active controls. The Windows 98 taskbar looks the same except for one difference: You can now display toolbars on the taskbar. Figure 5 shows the Windows 95 taskbar, and below it, the Windows 98 taskbar.

Figure 5
Taskbars in
Windows 95
and
Windows 98

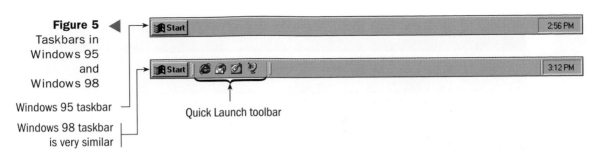

Windows 95 taskbar

Windows 98 taskbar
is very similar

Quick Launch toolbar

Unless a user has customized his or her taskbar, only the Quick Launch toolbar appears on the Windows 98 taskbar, but you can also display three other taskbar toolbars. Like a toolbar in an application, the taskbar toolbars give you single-click access to common operations.

Figure 6 summarizes the Windows 98 taskbar toolbars.

Figure 6
Windows 98
taskbar
toolbars

Toolbar	Description
Address	As in a browser, allows you to select or enter an address, such as a URL, to open the browser to that location.
Links	As in a browser, displays buttons for popular Web pages, such as the Microsoft home page. When you click a button on the Links toolbar, your browser opens and displays the location you clicked.
Desktop	Displays a button for each desktop icon on the taskbar.
Quick Launch	Displays buttons for Internet services and for a direct route to the desktop.

The Quick Launch toolbar is the only toolbar to appear by default; the others you can enable by right-clicking the taskbar, pointing at the Toolbars menu option, and clicking the toolbar you want. Figure 7 shows a Windows 98 taskbar with the Address and Links toolbars visible in addition to the Quick Launch toolbar.

scroll arrow appears
when there are
additional objects
on a toolbar

Figure 7
Windows 98
taskbar with
multiple
toolbars

Quick Launch toolbar

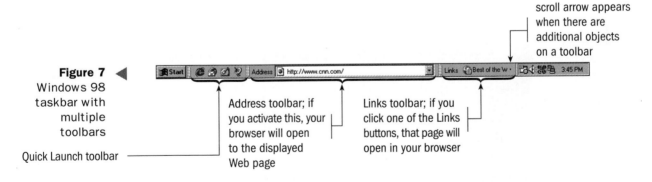

Address toolbar; if
you activate this, your
browser will open
to the displayed
Web page

Links toolbar; if you
click one of the Links
buttons, that page will
open in your browser

Figure 8 describes the default buttons on the Quick Launch toolbar.

Figure 8 ◀
Quick Launch
toolbar buttons

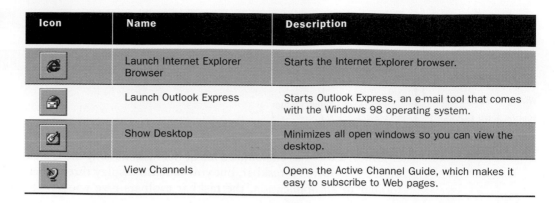

Icon	Name	Description
	Launch Internet Explorer Browser	Starts the Internet Explorer browser.
	Launch Outlook Express	Starts Outlook Express, an e-mail tool that comes with the Windows 98 operating system.
	Show Desktop	Minimizes all open windows so you can view the desktop.
	View Channels	Opens the Active Channel Guide, which makes it easy to subscribe to Web pages.

You can easily customize the taskbar toolbars by adding and removing buttons. Figure 9, for example, shows a taskbar whose Quick Launch toolbar includes buttons for popular applications.

Figure 9 ◀
Quick Launch
toolbar with
application
buttons

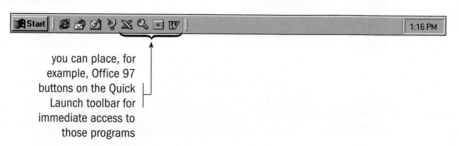

you can place, for
example, Office 97
buttons on the Quick
Launch toolbar for
immediate access to
those programs

To add a button to the Windows 98 Quick Launch toolbar, you simply drag the object you want to the toolbar.

The Start Menu

The Windows 98 Start menu looks similar to the Windows 95 Start menu. The only difference is that the Windows 98 Start menu includes a Favorites folder and a Windows Update link to Microsoft's Web site. Figure 10 shows the two Start menus. Again, since you can customize Start menus, yours might look different.

Figure 10 ◀
Windows 95
and
Windows 98
Start menus

Windows 95 Start
menu

Windows 98 Start
menu

Windows Update
opens the browser to
display the Microsoft
resource site

Favorites folder has
been added to
the Windows 98
Start menu

your Start menu
might include a Log
Off command if you
are on a network

The Favorites folder that Microsoft has added to the Windows 98 Start menu duplicates the Favorites folder in your browser. In your browser, you create a Favorites folder by collecting and saving a list of favorite Web pages. Once a Web page is in your Favorites folder, you can return to it in your browser by simply selecting the page from the folder. By duplicating the browser's list of favorite Web pages on the Windows 98 Start menu, Microsoft allows you to reach your favorite Web pages without having to go through the interim steps of starting your browser and opening the Favorites folder. To view a favorite Web page in Windows 98, you simply click Start, point at the Favorites option, and then click the Web page you want. Your browser launches automatically and connects you directly to that page.

The Windows Update link that appears on the Windows 98 Start menu is a Microsoft resource site on the Web that you connect to by clicking Windows Update on the Start menu. Your browser displays the Windows Update page, which helps you ensure that your system is running the most recent and efficient system software possible.

You might notice one final difference between the Windows 95 and Windows 98 Start menus. If you have more items on your Start menu than can be displayed on the screen, Windows 95 doubles the width of the menu to display the entire list of Start menu objects. Windows 98, however, adds to the bottom of the Start menu an arrow to which you can point to see additional objects.

Mouse Operation

You won't notice a difference between how your mouse operates in Office 97 or your other Windows 95 applications when you run them under the Windows 98 operating system. But if you work with certain Windows 98 windows, such as My Computer or Windows Explorer, be aware that Microsoft has simplified the actions you need to take with the mouse.

You've already seen that the icons on your desktop now behave like links and are, therefore, activated with a single-click rather than a double-click. In fact, in Windows 98, single-clicking completely replaces double-clicking on the desktop. In Windows 95, you generally selected an object by clicking it, but in Windows 98, you select an object by simply pointing to it for a moment. Windows 98 uses the term **hover** to describe pointing to an object, such as an icon, long enough to select it. Passing the pointer over an icon does not select it; you need to hover the pointer over the object long enough for Windows 98 to realize that you mean to select it. Once you've practiced hovering, you'll find it easy. Figure 11 summarizes how mouse functions have changed from Windows 95 to Windows 98.

Figure 11 ◀
Comparing
mouse
functions

Task	Windows 95	Windows 98
Select	Click	Hover
Open or run	Double-click (or click and press Enter)	Click
Select multiple contiguous objects	Shift+click	Shift+hover
Select multiple noncontiguous objects	Ctrl+click	Ctrl+hover

Changes in mouse operation do not affect Windows 98 dialog boxes: They affect only the desktop, My Computer, Windows Explorer, and similar windows.

Active Desktop

In Windows 95, to experience the Web you generally must first start your browser (although new generations of Internet communications software products are now bypassing the browser and placing Web information directly on the desktop even without the Windows 98 operating system). Users with Web access will find Windows 98 **Active Desktop** technology brings Web content directly to the desktop, without requiring extra communications software, allowing your desktop to act like your personal Web page.

You can enable Active Desktop by right-clicking the desktop, pointing to Active Desktop, and then clicking View As Web Page. Active Desktop integrates your Web experience with the Windows 98 desktop in two primary ways: with background wallpaper and with Web components. You can use a Web page as the desktop's background, and you can place Web components (updateable information from the Web) on the desktop.

Using a Web Page as Background Wallpaper

If you've ever worked with the Desktop Properties dialog box in Windows 95 (which you access by right-clicking the desktop and then clicking Properties), you might have experimented with the look of your desktop by changing the color or pattern of the default background wallpaper.

Windows 95 limits you to using image files as your background wallpaper. Trying to create a desktop background that integrated text and images and other objects is impossible. Windows 98, however, extends your control over your desktop's background by allowing you to use Web pages as wallpaper. To write Web pages, you use a language called **HTML**, which stands for Hypertext Markup Language. HTML uses special codes to describe how the page should appear on the screen. A document created using the HTML language is called an **HTML file** and is saved with the htm or html extension.

Because Windows 98 enables you to use an HTML file as your background wallpaper, your Windows 98 desktop background can feature text, images, links, and multimedia objects. You can use Microsoft Word to save a document as an HTML file; also, you can use the HTML editor included with Windows 98, FrontPage Express, to create more complex and sophisticated HTML files. Alternatively, you can use the Internet Explorer browser to save an existing Web page as an HTML file that you can then use as your wallpaper. To use a Web page as your wallpaper, right-click the desktop, click Properties, click the Background tab, click the Browse button, locate and select the HTML file you want to use, then click the OK button.

The added control Windows 98 gives you over background wallpaper makes it possible to make the desktop a launch pad for your most important projects. A corporation, for example, might create an HTML file that contains important company information, an updateable company calendar, links to company documents, a sound clip welcoming new employees to the company, and so on.

Figure 12 shows a sample Windows 98 desktop that might appear on the computers of a gift shop chain's main headquarters.

Figure 12 ◀
Windows 98 desktop with a background HTML file

embedded updateable program

embedded image file

embedded video clip

Windows 98

This company created a wallpaper that includes links to product groups, information about the company, a video clip of a recent company outing, and links to current events, company protocols, and training procedures.

Web Components on the Desktop

In addition to using a Web page as a background, you can also add Web components to the Windows 98 desktop in resizable, movable windows. A **Web component** is an object on the desktop that you can set to update automatically via your Web connection. For example, you might place a weather map, an investor ticker, or a news component on your desktop. You can schedule when each component will update itself and the information will be delivered to your desktop without your having to look for it.

Windows 95 users can purchase separate software that performs a similar function, such as the Internet Explorer 4.0 browser, Netscape Communicator's Netcaster component, or a product such as PointCast. But with Windows 98, the ability to place updateable Web information on the desktop is actually *integrated* into the operating system.

Figure 13 shows a Windows 98 desktop with several such Web components.

Figure 13 ◄
Windows 98 desktop with Web components

CNN news

Wall Street Journal news

weather

investment ticker

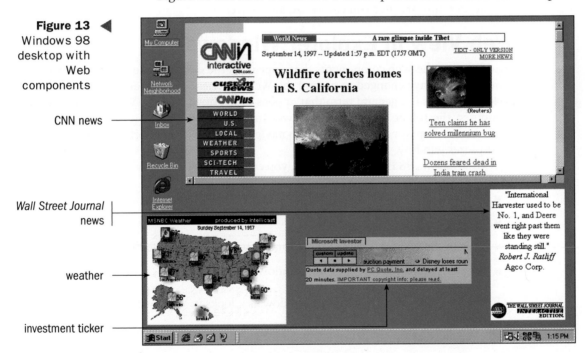

Every morning when this user checks her desktop, each component will have been automatically updated (if, that is, she has set the update schedules that way). The weather map will show the morning's weather instead of weather from the night before, her news service will display the most recent news, and the other Web components will update in a similar fashion. If she wants a more detailed look at, for example, the news, she can select and enlarge one of the Web component windows.

There are three ways to add Web components to the Windows 98 desktop:

- The Active Desktop Gallery offers a small set of useful Web components, including the weather map, investment ticker, clock, and so on. To access the Active Desktop Gallery, right-click the desktop, point to Active Desktop, and then click Customize my Desktop. A list of current Web components appears on the Web tab of the Display Properties dialog box. To add new ones, click the New button and follow the prompts to locate the Active Desktop Gallery.

- The Channel Bar lists companies that have agreements with Microsoft to deliver information directly to the desktops of those who subscribe to the Active Channel service. (A site that offers regularly updated information that can be delivered to the desktop on a predetermined schedule is called a **channel**.) When you subscribe to a channel delivery service, you request that information be "broadcast" to you from that channel at whatever schedule you specify. To add a channel from the Channel Bar, you must first enable the Channel Bar from the Web tab of the Display Properties dialog box. Once you can see the Channel Bar, click the channel you want to add. Follow the prompts to add the channel to your list of channels.

- You can add your own components by connecting to channel sites not necessarily associated with Microsoft and then subscribing to those channels. In most cases, you do this by connecting to the site with your browser. Sites that support channel delivery include a link that asks if you want to subscribe to the site. Click the link and follow the prompts; they vary from site to site.

If any of these components are on your desktop, a rectangular block appears that seems to be a part of the background. When you select that component, however, a window border appears that you can resize and move.

Web View in Explorer Windows

In addition to the Web components that appear on the desktop, the Windows 98 Explorer windows also have changed to extend the Web experience to folder navigation. The term **Explorer windows** is a general term that applies to windows such as Windows Explorer, My Computer, the folder and drive windows, and the Printer window. In other words, any window that displays and allows you to navigate the object hierarchy of your computer is an Explorer window.

With Windows 98 Explorer windows, you can enable **Web view**, which does the following:

- Displays objects on your computer as links

- Allows single-click navigation

- Adds to the window an HTML document with customizable links and information

- Enables you to use the Explorer window as a browser

Figure 14 shows the My Computer window as it looks in Windows 95 and in Windows 98.

Windows 98

Figure 14 ◀
My Computer in
Windows 95
and
Windows 98

Windows 95 My
Computer window

Windows 98
My Computer window

toolbars are different

list of objects is the
same as in Windows
95, except labels are
underlined and
perform like links

Web view HTML
document contains
text and images that
you can customize

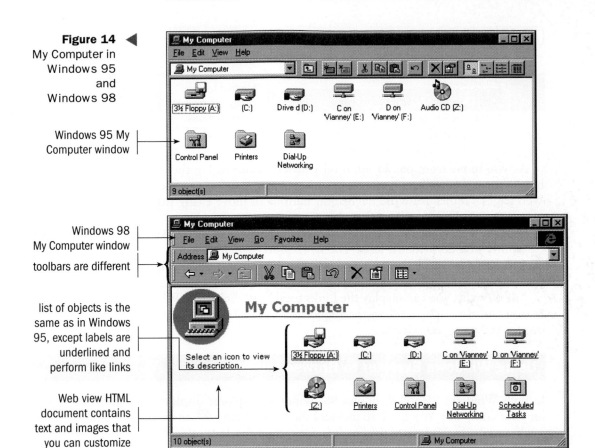

The Windows 95 window shows the familiar object list, but Windows 98 Explorer windows now have HTML documents in the background that you can customize. The ability to customize the Explorer windows by editing their background HTML page makes it easier than ever for you to work efficiently. For example, you could customize a network folder's HTML page so that anyone who accesses that Explorer window sees a description of the folder's contents, links to the most important objects in that window, and links to related objects. You might customize a network folder containing 1999 corporate reports so that it contains links to corporate reports for 1998 and 1997.

The objects that your computer displays look like the links you see on a Web page. As on the desktop, a single click suffices to open the object. For example, if you click the Floppy (A:) icon, the A: window opens. If you are used to thinking of a link as something that targets an object on the Web, you'll have to expand your vision. In Windows 98, links target any object accessible to your computer—not just Web pages, but also local drives, network folders, and files.

Web View Toolbars

In the Explorer windows, the Windows 95 Standard toolbar has been updated to include buttons that enable you to use the Explorer windows as browsers. The Address toolbar looks like the Address bar in a browser, and the Standard toolbar includes buttons that allow you to navigate through the hierarchy of drives and folders just as you would move through pages on the Web in your browser. Figure 15 first shows the Windows 95 Standard toolbar and then the Windows 98 Address and Standard toolbars on separate lines so you can see all the buttons.

Figure 15
My Computer
toolbars in
Windows 95
and
Windows 98

Windows 98 adds the
Address toolbar

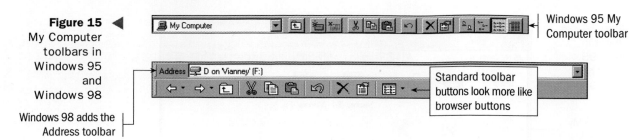

Windows 95 My
Computer toolbar

Standard toolbar
buttons look more like
browser buttons

As you move from one location on your computer to another, Windows 98 "remembers" where you've been, just as in your browser you can move back to previously viewed Web pages. You can use the navigation buttons to move easily through the hierarchy of your computer's objects.

Suppose you want to view the contents of a folder on drive A:. You could open My Computer and click the A: icon. The A: Explorer window would open. Then you could click the folder whose contents you want to view. The folder's Explorer window would open. To return to My Computer, you'd simply click the Back button twice.

Additionally, you can display the Links toolbar in Web view. When you click one of the buttons on the Links toolbar, the Explorer window functions just like your browser to display the page you selected.

Using Windows Explorer to Browse the Web

In both Windows 95 and Windows 98, Windows Explorer displays a hierarchy of objects on your computer. Windows 98 includes the Internet icon as one of those objects. You might recognize this icon as the one that appears on the desktop in Windows 95; if you have an Internet service set up on your computer, double-clicking that icon on the Windows 95 desktop starts your browser. In Windows 98, however, when you click in the Windows Explorer window, your browser's home page appears in the Exploring window. Figure 16 shows Windows Explorer with the object hierarchy on the left and a Web page off the Internet on the right.

Figure 16
Using Windows
Explorer as a
browser

current location is
a Web page

click to connect to
your home page

Explorer toolbars
resemble
browser toolbars

Web page displayed
directly in the
Windows Explorer
window

Notice that when you select a Web page in Windows Explorer, the standard Explorer toolbars and menus are replaced with toolbars and menus that are more browser-oriented. Indeed, you could use Windows Explorer as a Web-browsing tool.

Additional Windows 98 Features

This tutorial has focused primarily on how upgrading to Windows 98 affects the way you interact with the operating system. But Windows 98 offers many other features that replace or expand Windows 95 functions, as well as some completely new features. Figure 17 describes some of the most intriguing updated, expanded, or new features. You might not understand the technology behind all these features, but they should give you an idea of what you can do if you are running Windows 98 with the latest hardware.

Figure 17 ◀
Additional
Windows 98
features

Feature	Description
Digital Versatile Disc (DVD) support	The successor to CD-ROM disks, DVD stores many times the capacity of a CD-ROM, enough to store full-length digitized movies that you can then view on your monitor or TV screen if you have the appropriate hardware.
Disk space	The space available on your hard disk is limited by the type of file system you use. Windows 95 employs the FAT 16 file system. With Windows 98 FAT 32, you can store up to 30 percent more data on your disk, and you can work with drives that are much larger than those available to FAT 16. The FAT 32 converter utility also makes it easy to upgrade your file system.
Internet communications	Windows 98 ships with Internet Explorer, an Internet communications software suite that offers state-of-the-art integrated browsing, e-mail, newsgroup, Web page editing, and conferencing software—and much more!
Internet Connection Wizard	Establishing a connection to the Internet is much easier with this wizard, which works with your Internet service provider to configure your Internet connection properly.
On-line Help	Information about the Windows 98 operating system now appears as a Web page, and is continually updated by Microsoft. You can access the Windows 98 Help Desk to receive online technical support.
Peripheral device support	Windows 98 supports Universal serial bus (USB) technology, a hardware device that plugs into a single port from which you can run multiple peripheral devices.
Power management	If you own a new PC that supports OnNow hardware technology, your PC will start much more quickly, and you will consume less power if you take advantage of power-down features.
Speed	Windows 98 runs your applications faster, saving you time.
Tune-Up Wizard	In an effort to simplify and streamline your computer maintenance program, the Tune-Up Wizard analyzes your system and helps you schedule maintenance tasks such as defragmentation, disk scan, and backup. Most of the maintenance tools have also been improved.
TV Viewer	This accessory brings television to the PC—not just regular TV signals, but also content-rich broadcasts that provide interactivity on your TV. For example, a cooking show might include links to recipes that you could download over your TV satellite or cable connection.
Video playback	ActiveMovie expands the multimedia capabilities of your computer, featuring improved video playback.
Windows Update	Accessed directly from the Windows 98 Start menu, this Microsoft site features a service that scans your system and allows you to update it with the most recent software. This site also helps you troubleshoot problems.

When computer owners consider whether or not to upgrade, they review feature lists and comparisons such as the ones you've seen in this tutorial. They then assess their needs and budget to determine whether to make the upgrade.

Now that you've had a chance to explore how Windows 98 changes the operating system landscape, you can see why users must balance the advantages against the sometimes uncertain world of switching to a new operating system and a new way of working with computers. Many users believe, however, that Windows 98 raises personal computing to new heights, and the benefits far outweigh the challenges.

Tutorial Assignments

1. Based on what you've read in this tutorial, if you were a Windows 95 user, would you make the upgrade to Windows 98? Write a one-page essay that answers this question. In your essay, you'll need to define your computing needs, address how Windows 95 fulfills those needs, and evaluate the degree to which Windows 98 could better meet those needs. Be sure to itemize the features that influence you the most —both pro and con.

2. Using the resources available to you, either online or through your library, locate information about the release of Windows 98. Computing trade magazines, both hard copy and online, are an excellent source of information about software. Read several articles about Windows 98 and then write a one-page essay that discusses the features that seem most important to the people who evaluated the software. If you find reviews of the software, mention the features that reviewers had the strongest reaction to, pro or con.

3. Write a single-page essay defending or refuting the following proposition: "Software developers upgrade their software only to make money."

4. Interview two people you know who are well-informed computer users. Ask them how they decide when to upgrade a software product. If they are using a PC with the Windows 3.X, 95, or 98 operating system, ask them why they did or did not upgrade to Windows 98. Write a single-page essay summarizing what you learned from these interviews about making the decision to upgrade.

5. Based on what you learned about Windows 98 in this tutorial, what Windows 98 features interest you the most? The least? Write two paragraphs describing those features and explaining why you do or do not find them interesting.

6. How has Windows 98 changed the concept of the "home computer"? Research the Windows 98 features that might benefit home users, such as its TV and appliance capabilities, and write two paragraphs summarizing those features and assessing how they could impact home life.

N E W
PERSPECTIVES
S E R I E S

Microsoft®
Access 97

LEVEL I

TUTORIALS

Read This **Before You Begin**

STUDENT DISKS

To complete Access 97 Tutorials 1-4, you need three Student Disks. Your instructor will either provide you with the Student Disks or ask you to make your own.

If you are supposed to make your own Student Disks, you will need three blank, formatted, high-density disks. You will need to copy a set of folders from a file server or standalone computer onto your disks. Your instructor will tell you which computer, drive letter, and folders contain the files you need. The following table shows you which folders go on each of your disks, so that you will have enough disk space to complete all the tutorials, Tutorial Assignments, and Case Problems:

Student Disk	Write this on the disk label	Put these folders on the disk
1	Student Disk 1: Access 97 Tutorials 1-4	Tutorial and TAssign from
	Tutorials and Tutorial Assignments	Disk 1 folder
2	Student Disk 2: Access 97 Tutorials 1-4 Case Problems 1 and 2	Cases from Disk 2 folder
3	Student Disk 3: Access 97 Tutorials 1-4 Case Problems 3 and 4	Cases from Disk 3 folder

When you begin each tutorial, be sure you are using the correct Student Disk. See the inside front or inside back cover of this book for more information on Student Disk files, or ask your instructor or technical support person for assistance.

COURSE LAB

Tutorial 1 features an interactive Course Lab to help you understand database concepts. There are Lab Assignments at the end of the tutorial that relate to this Lab. To start the Lab, click the Start button on the Windows 95 taskbar, point to Programs, point to Course Labs, point to New Perspectives Applications, and click Databases.

USING YOUR OWN COMPUTER

If you are going to work through Tutorials 1-4 using your own computer, you need:

■ **Computer System** Microsoft Windows 95 or Microsoft Windows NT Workstation 4.0 and Microsoft Access 97 must be installed on your computer. Tutorials 1-4 assume a typical installation of Microsoft Access 97.

■ **Student Disks** Ask your instructor or lab manager for details on how to get the Student Disks. You will not be able to complete the tutorials or end-of-tutorial assignments in this book using your own computer until you have the Student Disks. The Student Files may also be obtained electronically over the Internet. See the inside front or inside back cover of this book for more details.

■ **Course Lab** See your instructor or technical support person to obtain the Course Lab software for use on your own computer.

To complete Access 97 Tutorials 1-4, your students must use a set of files on three Student Disks. These files are included in the Instructor's Resource Kit, and they may also be obtained electronically over the Internet. See the inside front or inside back cover of this book for more details. Follow the instructions in the Readme file to copy the files to your server or standalone computer. You can view the Readme file using WordPad. Once the files are copied, you can make Student Disks for the students yourself, or you can tell students where to find the files so they can make their own Student Disks.

COURSE LAB SOFTWARE

The Course Lab software is distributed on a CD-ROM included in the Instructor's Resource Kit. To install the Course Lab software, follow the setup instructions in the Readme file on the CD-ROM. Refer also to the Readme file for essential technical notes related to running the Lab in a multi-user environment. Once you have installed the Course Lab software, your students can start the Lab from the Windows 95 desktop by following the instructions in the Course Lab section above.

COURSE TECHNOLOGY STUDENT FILES AND LAB SOFTWARE

You are granted a license to copy the Student Files and Lab software to any computer or computer network used by students who have purchased this book.

TUTORIAL 1

Introduction to Microsoft Access 97

Viewing and Working with a Table Containing Customer Data

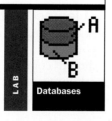

LAB
Databases

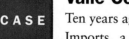

CASE

Valle Coffee

Ten years ago Leonard Valle became the president of Algoman Imports, a small distributor of inexpensive coffee beans to supermarkets in western Michigan. At that time the company's growth had leveled off, so during his first three years Leonard took several dramatic, risky steps in an attempt to increase sales and profits. First, he changed the inexpensive coffee bean varieties that Algoman Imports had been distributing to a selection of gourmet varieties from Central and South America, Africa, and several island nations. Second, he purchased facilities and equipment so that the company could roast, grind, flavor, and package the coffee beans instead of buying them already roasted and packaged whole. Because the company could now control the quality of the finest gourmet coffees, Leonard stopped distributing to supermarkets and shifted sales to restaurants and offices throughout the area.

Within two years, company sales and profits soared; consequently, Leonard took over ownership of the company. He changed the company name to Valle Coffee, continued expanding into other markets and geographic areas (specifically, Ohio and Indiana), and expanded the company's line of coffee flavors and blends.

Part of Valle Coffee's success can be credited to its use of computers in all aspects of its business, including financial management, inventory control, shipping, receiving, production, and sales. Several months ago the company upgraded to Microsoft Windows 95 and **Microsoft Access 97** (or simply **Access**), a computer program used to enter, maintain, and retrieve related data in a format known as a database. Barbara Hennessey, office manager at Valle Coffee, and her staff use Access to maintain company data such as customer orders and billing, coffee supplier orders and payments, and advertising placements and payments. Barbara recently created a database named Restaurant to track the company's restaurant customers, their orders, and related data such as the products they order. She asks for your help in completing and maintaining this database.

Using the Tutorials Effectively

These tutorials are designed to be used at a computer. Each tutorial is divided into sessions. Watch for the session headings, such as "Session 1.1" and "Session 1.2." Each session is designed to be completed in about 45 minutes, but take as much time as you need. When you've completed a session, it's a good idea to exit the program and take a break. You can exit Microsoft Access by clicking the Close button in the top-right corner of the program window.

Before you begin, read the following questions and answers. They are designed to help you use the tutorials effectively.

Where do I start?

Each tutorial begins with a case, which sets the scene for the tutorial and gives you background information to help you understand what you will be doing in the tutorial. Read the case before you go to the lab. In the lab, begin with the first session of the tutorial.

How do I know what to do on the computer?

Each session contains steps that you will perform on the computer to learn how to use Microsoft Access. The steps are numbered and are set against a colored background. Read the text that introduces each series of steps, and read each step carefully and completely before you try it.

How do I know if I did the step correctly?

As you work, compare your computer screen with the corresponding figure in the tutorial. Don't worry if your screen display is somewhat different from the figure. The important parts of the screen display are labeled in each figure. Check to make sure these parts are on your screen.

What if I make a mistake?

Don't worry about making mistakes—they are part of the learning process. Paragraphs labeled **"TROUBLE?"** identify common problems and explain how to get back on track. Follow the steps in a **"TROUBLE?"** paragraph *only* if you are having the problem described. If you run into other problems, carefully consider the current state of your system, the position of the pointer, and any messages on the screen.

How do I use the Reference Windows?

Reference Windows summarize the procedures you learn in the tutorial steps. Do not complete the actions in the Reference Windows when you are working through the tutorial. Instead, refer to the Reference Windows while you are working on the assignments at the end of the tutorial.

How can I test my understanding of the material I learned in the tutorial?

At the end of each session, you can answer the Quick Check questions. If necessary, refer to the Answers to Quick Check Questions to check your work.

After you have completed the entire tutorial, you should complete the Tutorial Assignments and Case Problems. These exercises are carefully structured so you will review what you have learned and then apply your knowledge to new situations.

What if I can't remember how to do something?

You should refer to the Task Reference at the end of the book; it summarizes how to accomplish commonly performed tasks.

What is the Databases Course Lab, and how should I use it?

This interactive Lab helps you review database concepts and practice skills that you learn in Tutorial 1. The Lab Assignments section at the end of Tutorial 1 includes instructions for using the Lab.

Now that you've seen how to use the tutorials effectively, you are ready to begin.

<table>
<tr><td>SESSION
1.1</td><td>In this session you will define key database terms and concepts, start Access and open an existing database, identify components of the Access and Database windows, open and navigate a table, print a table, and exit Access.</td></tr>
</table>

Databases

Introduction to Database Concepts

Before you begin working on Barbara's database and using Access, you need to understand a few key terms and concepts associated with databases.

Organizing Data

Data is a valuable resource to any business. At Valle Coffee, for example, important data includes customers' names and addresses, and order dates and amounts. Organizing, storing, maintaining, retrieving, and sorting this type of data are critical activities that enable a business to find and use information effectively. Before storing data on a computer, however, you first must organize the data.

Your first step in organizing data is to identify the individual fields. A **field** is a single characteristic or attribute of a person, place, object, event, or idea. For example, some of the many fields that Valle Coffee tracks are customer number, customer name, customer address, customer phone number, order number, billing date, and invoice amount.

Next, you group related fields together into tables. A **table** is a collection of fields that describe a person, place, object, event, or idea. Figure 1-1 shows an example of a Customer table consisting of four fields: Customer Number, Customer Name, Customer Address, and Phone Number.

Figure 1-1 ◄
Data organization for a table of customers

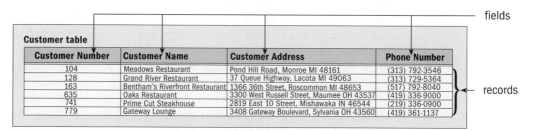

The specific value, or content, of a field is called the **field value**. In Figure 1-1, the first set of field values for Customer Number, Customer Name, Customer Address, and Phone Number are, respectively, 104; Meadows Restaurant; Pond Hill Road, Monroe MI 48161; and (313) 792-3546. This set of field values is called a **record**. In the Customer table, the data for each customer is stored as a separate record. Six records are shown in Figure 1-1; each row of field values is a record.

Databases and Relationships

A collection of related tables is called a **database**, or **relational database**. Valle Coffee's Restaurant database will contain two related tables: the Customer table, which Barbara has already created, and the Order table, which you will create in Tutorial 2. Sometimes you might want information about customers and the orders they placed. To obtain this information you must have a way to connect records in the Customer table to records in the Order table. You connect the records in the separate tables through a **common field** that appears in both tables. In the sample database shown in Figure 1-2, each record in the Customer table has a field named Customer Number, which is also a field in the Order table. For example, Oaks Restaurant is the fourth customer in the Customer table and has a Customer Number of 635. This same Customer Number field value, 635, appears in three records in the Order table. Therefore, Oaks Restaurant is the customer that placed these three orders.

Figure 1-2 ◀
Database
relationship
between tables
for customers
and orders

primary keys

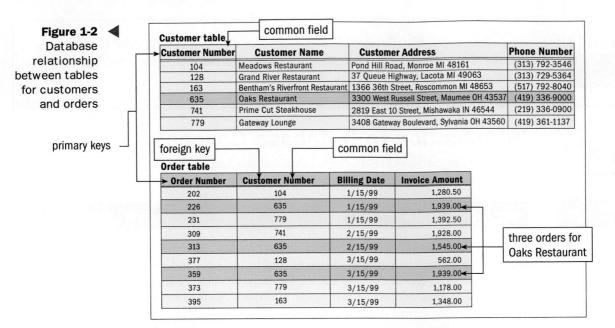

Each Customer Number in the Customer table must be unique, so that you can distinguish one customer from another and identify the customer's specific orders in the Order table. The Customer Number field is referred to as the primary key of the Customer table. A **primary key** is a field, or a collection of fields, whose values uniquely identify each record in a table. In the Order table, Order Number is the primary key.

When you include the primary key from one table as a field in a second table to form a relationship between the two tables, it is called a **foreign key** in the second table, as shown in Figure 1-2. For example, Customer Number is the primary key in the Customer table and a foreign key in the Order table. Although the primary key Customer Number has unique values in the Customer table, the same field as a foreign key in the Order table does not have unique values. The Customer Number value 635, for example, appears three times in the Order table, because the Oaks Restaurant placed three orders. Each foreign key value, however, must match one of the field values for the primary key in the other table. In the example in Figure 1-2, each Customer Number value in the Order table must match a Customer Number value in the Customer table. The two tables are related, enabling users to tie together the facts about customers with the facts about orders.

Relational Database Management Systems

To manage its databases, a company purchases a database management system. A **database management system (DBMS)** is a software program that lets you create databases and then manipulate data in the databases. Most of today's database management systems, including Access, are called relational database management systems. In a **relational database management system**, data is organized as a collection of tables. As stated earlier, a relationship between two tables in a relational DBMS is formed through a common field.

A relational DBMS controls the storage of databases on disk by carrying out data creation and manipulation requests. Specifically, a relational DBMS provides the following functions, which are illustrated in Figure 1-3:

- It allows you to create database structures containing fields, tables, and table relationships.

- It lets you easily add new records, change field values in existing records, and delete records.

- It contains a built-in query language, which lets you obtain immediate answers to the questions you ask about your data.

- It contains a built-in report generator, which lets you produce professional-looking, formatted reports from your data.

- It provides protection of databases through security, control, and recovery facilities.

Figure 1-3 ◀
A relational
database
management
system

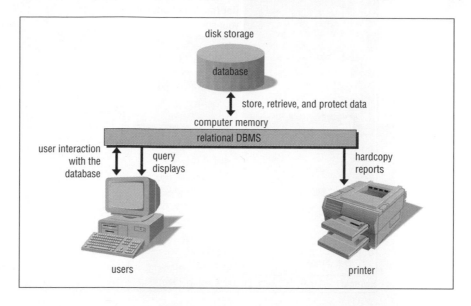

A company like Valle Coffee benefits from a relational DBMS because it allows several users working in different departments to share the same data. More than one user can enter data into a database, and more than one user can retrieve and analyze data that was entered by others. For example, Valle Coffee will keep only one copy of the Customer table, and all employees will be able to use it to meet their specific needs for customer information.

Finally, unlike other software programs, such as spreadsheets, a DBMS can handle massive amounts of data and can easily form relationships among multiple tables. Each Access database, for example, can be up to 1 gigabyte in size and can contain up to 32,768 objects (tables, queries, and so on).

Now that you've learned some database terms and concepts, you're ready to start Access and open the Restaurant database.

Starting Access

You start Access in the same way that you start other Windows 95 programs—using the Start button on the taskbar.

To start Access:

1. Make sure Windows 95 is running on your computer and the Windows 95 desktop appears on your screen.

   TROUBLE? If you're running Windows NT Workstation 4.0 (or a later version) on your computer or network, don't worry. Although the figures in this book were created while running Windows 95, Windows NT 4.0 and Windows 95 share the same interface, and Access 97 runs equally well under either operating system.

2. Click the **Start** button on the taskbar to display the Start menu, and then point to **Programs** to display the Programs menu.

3. Point to **Microsoft Access** on the Programs menu. See Figure 1-4.

Figure 1-4 ◀
Starting
Microsoft
Access

Programs menu
option

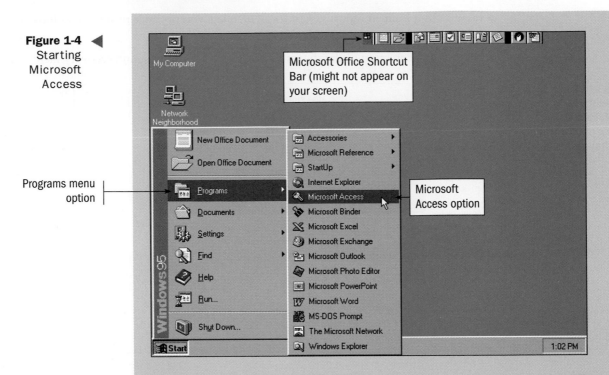

TROUBLE? If you don't see the Microsoft Access option on the Programs menu, ask your instructor or technical support person for help.

TROUBLE? The Office Shortcut Bar, which appears along the top of the desktop in Figure 1-4, might look different on your screen or it might not appear at all, depending on how your system is set up. The steps in these tutorials do not require that you use the Office Shortcut Bar; therefore, the remaining figures do not display the Office Shortcut Bar.

4. Click **Microsoft Access** to start Access. After a short pause, the Access copyright information appears in a message box and remains on the screen until the Access window is displayed. See Figure 1-5.

Figure 1-5 ◀
The Microsoft
Access window

toolbar

initial dialog box

status bar

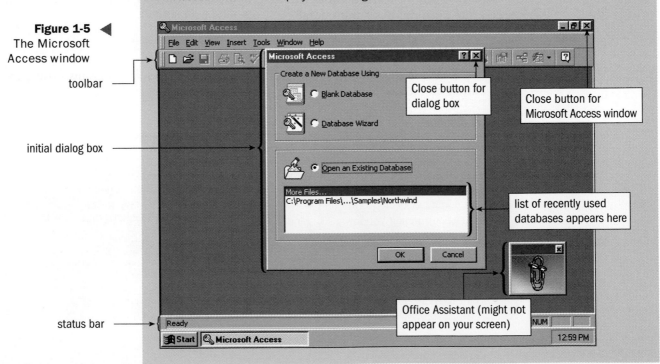

> **TROUBLE?** Depending on how your system is set up, the Office Assistant (see Figure 1-5) might open when you start Access. For now, click the Close button ☒ on the Office Assistant window to close it; you'll learn more about this feature later in this tutorial. If you've started Access immediately after installing it, you'll need to click the Start Using Microsoft Access option, which the Office Assistant displays, before closing the Office Assistant window.

When you start Access, the Access window contains a dialog box that allows you to create a new database or open an existing database. You can choose either the Blank Database option to create a new database on your own, or you can choose the Database Wizard option and let the wizard guide you through the steps for creating a database. In this case, you need to open an existing database.

Opening an Existing Database

To open an existing database, you can select the name of a database in the list of recently opened databases (if the list appears), or you can choose the More Files option to open a database not listed. You need to open an existing database—the Restaurant database on your Student Disk.

To open the Restaurant database:

1. Make sure you have created your copy of the Access Student Disk, and then place your Student Disk in the appropriate disk drive.

   TROUBLE? If you don't have a Student Disk, you need to get one before you can proceed. Your instructor will either give you one or ask you to make your own. (See your instructor for information.) In either case, be sure you have made a copy of your Student Disk before you begin; in this way, the original Student Disk files will be available on the copied disk in case you need to start over because of an error or problem.

2. In the Microsoft Access dialog box, make sure the **Open an Existing Database** option button is selected. Also, if your dialog box contains a list of files, make sure the **More Files** option is selected.

3. Click the **OK** button to display the Open dialog box. See Figure 1-6.

Figure 1-6 ◄
Open dialog
box

Look in list box

list of folders and
database files in
current folder

click to display the list
of available drives
and folders

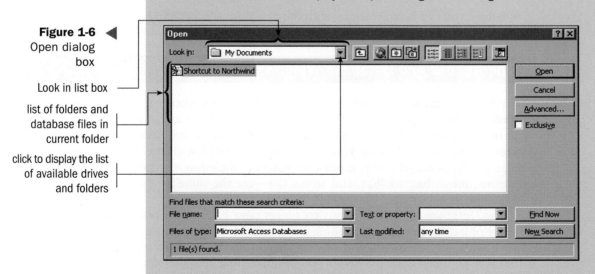

TROUBLE? The list of folders and files on your screen might be different from the list in Figure 1-6.

4. Click the **Look in** list arrow, and then click the drive that contains your Student Disk.

5. Click **Tutorial** in the list box (if necessary), and then click the **Open** button to display a list of the files in the Tutorial folder.

6. Click **Restaurant** in the list box, and then click the **Open** button. The Restaurant database is displayed in the Access window. See Figure 1-7.

Figure 1-7 ◄
Access and Database windows

Access window title bar

Database window menu bar

Database toolbar

Tables list box

Database window

object tabs

command buttons

Database window title bar

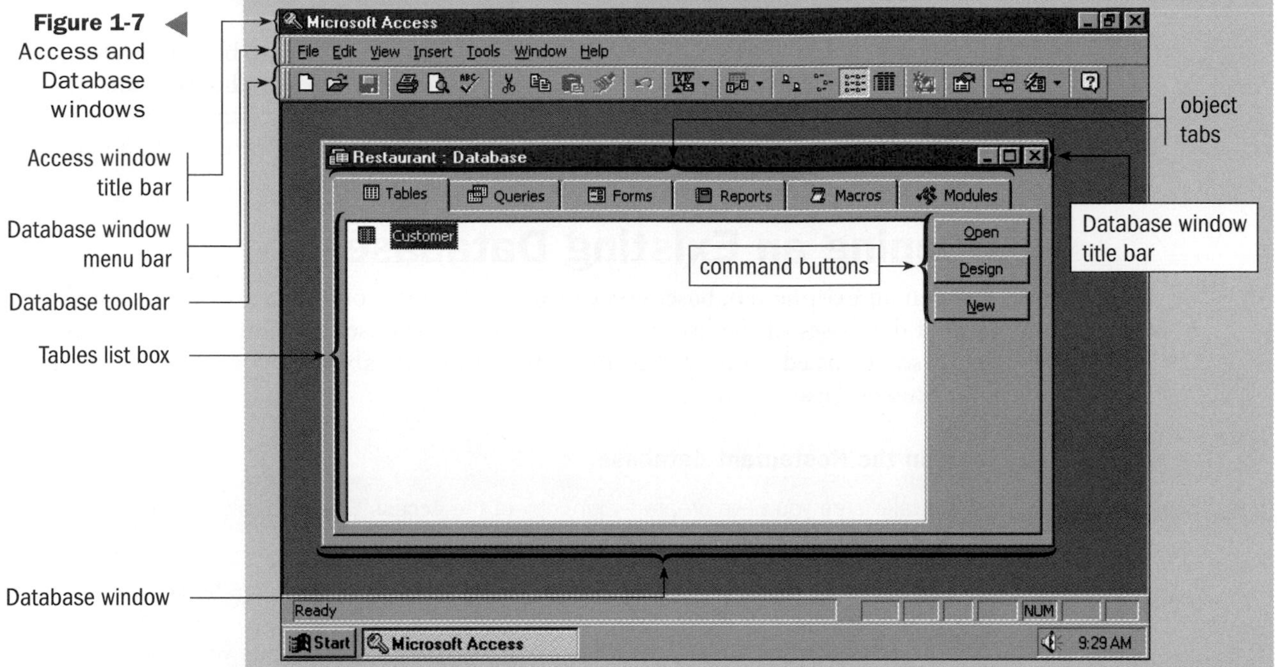

TROUBLE? The filename on your screen might be Restaurant.mdb instead of Restaurant, depending on the default settings on your computer. The extension "mdb" identifies the file as an Access database.

TROUBLE? If the Tables tab is not selected in the Database window, click it to display the list of tables in the database.

Before you can begin working with the database, you need to become familiar with the components of the Access and Database windows.

The Access and Database Windows

The **Access window** is the program window that appears when you start the program. The **Database window** appears when you open a database; this window is the main control center for working with an open Access database. Except for the Access window title bar, all screen components now on your screen are associated with the Database window (see Figure 1-7). Most of these screen components—including the title bars, window sizing buttons, menu bar, toolbar, and status bar—are the same as the components in other Windows 95 programs.

The Database window contains six object tabs. Each **object tab** controls one of the six major object groups, such as tables, in an Access database. (In addition to tables, you'll work with queries, forms, and reports later in this book; macros and modules are used for more complex database design and programming and, therefore, are outside the scope of this text.)

Barbara has already created the Customer table in the Restaurant database. She suggests that you open the Customer table and view its contents.

Opening an Access Table

As noted earlier, tables contain all the data in a database. Tables are the fundamental objects for your work in Access. To view, add, change, or delete data in a table, you first must open the table. You can open any Access object by using the Open button in the Database window.

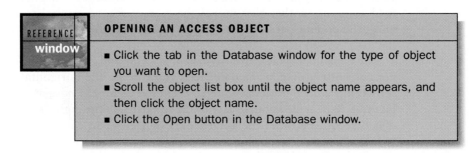

REFERENCE window	**OPENING AN ACCESS OBJECT**
	■ Click the tab in the Database window for the type of object you want to open.
	■ Scroll the object list box until the object name appears, and then click the object name.
	■ Click the Open button in the Database window.

You need to open the Customer table, which is the only table currently in the Restaurant database.

To open the Customer table:

1. If the Customer table is not highlighted, click **Customer** to select it.

2. Click the **Open** button in the Database window. The Customer table opens in Datasheet view on top of the Database and Access windows. See Figure 1-8.

Figure 1-8 ◀
Table displayed in Datasheet view

field selector for CustomerName field

table name

current record symbol

record selector for second record

field name

total number of records in the table

Specific Record box

navigation buttons

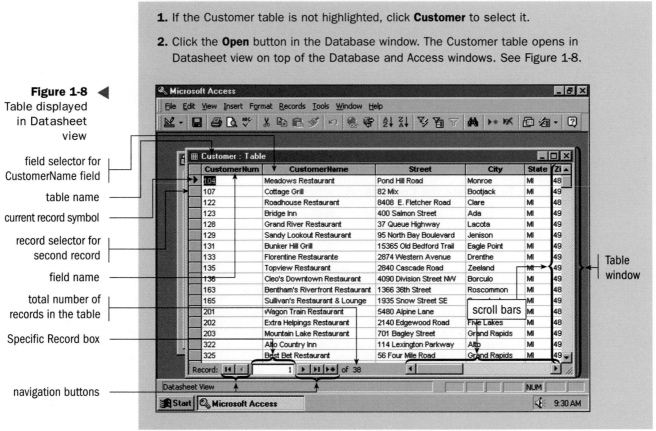

Table window

scroll bars

Datasheet view shows a table's contents as a **datasheet** in rows and columns, similar to a table or spreadsheet. Each row is a separate record in the table, and each column contains the field values for one field in the table. Each column is headed by a field name inside a field selector, and each row has a record selector to its left. Clicking a **field selector** or a **record selector** selects that entire column or row (respectively), which you can then manipulate. A field selector is also called a **column selector**, and a record selector is also called a **row selector**.

Navigating an Access Datasheet

When you first open a datasheet, Access selects the first field value in the first record. Notice that this field value is highlighted and that a darkened triangle symbol, called the current record symbol, appears in the record selector to the left of the first record. The **current record symbol** identifies the currently selected record. Clicking a record selector or field value in another row moves the current record symbol to that row. You can also move the pointer over the data on the screen and click one of the field values to position the insertion point.

The Customer table currently has nine fields and 38 records. To view fields or records not currently visible in the datasheet, you can use the horizontal and vertical scroll bars shown in Figure 1-8 to navigate through the data. The **navigation buttons**, also shown in Figure 1-8, provide another way to move vertically through the records. Figure 1-9 shows which record becomes the current record when you click each navigation button. The **Specific Record box**, which appears between the two sets of navigation buttons, displays the current record number; and the total number of records in the table appears to the right of the navigation buttons.

Figure 1-9 ◄
Navigation
buttons

Navigation Button	Record Selected	Navigation Button	Record Selected
◄◄	First Record	►►	Last Record
◄	Previous Record	►*	New Record
►	Next Record		

Barbara suggests that you use the various navigation techniques to move through the Customer table and become familiar with its contents.

To navigate the Customer datasheet:

1. Click the right arrow button in the horizontal scroll bar a few times to scroll to the right and view the remaining fields in the Customer table.

2. Drag the scroll box in the horizontal scroll bar back to the left to return to the previous display of the datasheet.

3. Click the **Next Record** navigation button ►. The second record is now the current record, as indicated by the current record symbol in the second record selector. Also, notice that the second record's value for the CustomerNum field is highlighted, and "2" (for record number 2) appears in the Specific Record box.

4. Click the **Last Record** navigation button ►►. The last record in the table, record 38, is now the current record.

5. Click the **Previous Record** navigation button ◄. Record 37 is now the current record.

6. Click the **First Record** navigation button ◄◄. The first record is now the current record.

Next, Barbara asks you to print the Customer table so that you can refer to it as you continue working with the Restaurant database.

Printing a Table

In Access you can print a table using either the Print command on the File menu or the Print button on the toolbar. The Print command displays a dialog box in which you can specify print settings. The Print button prints the table using the current settings. You'll use the Print button to print the Customer table.

To print the Customer table:

1. Click the **Print** button 🖨 on the Table Datasheet toolbar. Because all of the fields can't fit across one page, the table prints on two pages. You'll learn how to specify different print settings in later tutorials.

Now that you've viewed and printed the Customer table, you can exit Access.

Exiting Access

To exit Access, you simply click the Close button on the Access window title bar. When exiting, Access closes any open tables and the open database before closing the program.

To exit Access:

1. Click the **Close** button ✕ on the Access window title bar. The Customer table and the Restaurant database close, Access closes, and you return to the Windows 95 desktop.

Quick Check

1. A(n) _____ is a single characteristic of a person, place, object, event, or idea.

2. You connect the records in two separate tables through a(n) _____ that appears in both tables.

3. The _____, whose values uniquely identify each record in a table, is called a _____ when it is placed in a second table to form a relationship between the two tables.

4. In a table, the rows are called _____ and the columns are called _____.

5. The _____ identifies the selected record in an Access table.

6. Describe the two methods for navigating through a table.

Now that you've become familiar with Access and the Restaurant database, you're ready to work with the data stored in the database.

SESSION

1.2

In this session you will create and print a query; create and print a form; use the Help system; and create, preview, and print a report.

Kim Carpenter, the director of marketing at Valle Coffee, wants a list of all restaurant customers so that her staff can call customers to check on their satisfaction with Valle

Coffee's services and products. She doesn't want the list to include all the fields in the Customer table (such as Street and ZipCode). To produce this list for Kim, you need to create a query using the Customer table.

Creating and Printing a Query

A **query** is a question you ask about the data stored in a database. In response to a query, Access displays the specific records and fields that answer your question. When you create a query, you tell Access which fields you need and what criteria Access should use to select the records. Access then displays only the information you want, so you don't have to scan through the entire database for the information.

You can design your own queries or use an Access **Query Wizard**, which guides you through the steps to create a query. The Simple Query Wizard allows you to select records and fields quickly, and is an appropriate choice for producing the customer list Kim wants.

To start the Simple Query Wizard:

1. Insert your Student Disk in the appropriate disk drive.

2. Start Access, make sure the **Open an Existing Database** option button is selected and the **More Files** option is selected, and then click the **OK** button to display the Open dialog box.

3. Click the **Look in** list arrow, click the drive that contains your Student Disk, click **Tutorial** in the list box, and then click the **Open** button to display the list of files in the Tutorial folder.

4. Click **Restaurant** in the list box, and then click the **Open** button.

5. Click the **Queries** tab in the Database window to display the Queries list. The Queries list box is empty because you haven't defined any queries yet.

6. Click the **New** button to open the New Query dialog box.

7. Click **Simple Query Wizard** and then click the **OK** button. The first Simple Query Wizard dialog box opens. See Figure 1-10.

Figure 1-10 ◀
First Simple
Query Wizard
dialog box

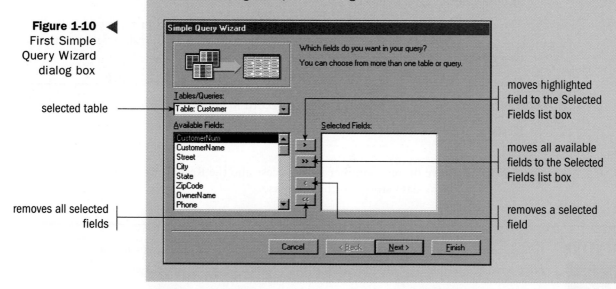

Because Customer is the only object currently in the Restaurant database, it is listed in the Tables/Queries box. You could click the Tables/Queries list arrow to choose another table or a query on which to base the query you're creating. The Available Fields box lists the fields in the selected table (in this case, Customer). You need to select fields from this list to include them in the query. To select fields one at a time, click a field and then click the ▶ button. The selected field moves from the Available Fields list box on the left to the Selected Fields list box on the right. To select all the fields, click the [>>] button. If you change your mind or make a mistake, you can remove a field by clicking it in the Selected Fields list box and then clicking the [<] button. To remove all selected fields, click the [<<] button.

Each wizard dialog box contains buttons on the bottom that allow you to move to the previous dialog box (Back button), the next dialog box (Next button), or to cancel the creation process (Cancel button) and return to the Database window. You can also finish creating the object (Finish button) and accept the wizard's defaults for the remaining options.

Kim wants her list to include data from only the following fields: CustomerNum, CustomerName, City, State, OwnerName, and Phone. You need to select these fields to be included in the query.

To create the query using the Simple Query Wizard:

1. Click **CustomerNum** in the Available Fields list box (if necessary), and then click the [>] button. The CustomerNum field moves to the Selected Fields list box.

2. Repeat Step 1 for the fields **CustomerName**, **City**, **State**, **OwnerName**, and **Phone**, and then click the **Next** button. The second, and final, Simple Query Wizard dialog box opens and asks you to choose a name for your query. This name will appear in the Queries list in the Database window. You'll change the suggested name (Customer Query) to "Customer List."

3. Click at the end of the highlighted name, use the Backspace key to delete the word "Query," and then type **List**. You can now view the query results.

4. Click the **Finish** button to complete the query. Access displays the query results in Datasheet view.

5. Click the **Maximize** button [□] on the Query window to maximize the window. See Figure 1-11.

Figure 1-11 ◄
Query results

selected fields
displayed

all 38 records are
included in the results

CustomerNum	CustomerName	City	State	OwnerName	Phone
104	Meadows Restaurant	Monroe	MI	Mr. Ray Suchecki	(313) 792-3546
107	Cottage Grill	Bootjack	MI	Ms. Doris Reaume	(616) 643-8821
122	Roadhouse Restaurant	Clare	MI	Ms. Shirley Woodruff	(517) 966-8651
123	Bridge Inn	Ada	MI	Mr. Wayne Bouwman	(616) 888-9827
128	Grand River Restaurant	Lacota	MI	Mr. John Rohrs	(313) 729-5364
129	Sandy Lookout Restaurant	Jenison	MI	Ms. Michele Yasenak	(616) 111-9148
131	Bunker Hill Grill	Eagle Point	MI	Mr. Ronald Kooienga	(906) 895-2041
133	Florentine Restaurante	Drenthe	MI	Mr. Donald Bench	(616) 111-3260
135	Topview Restaurant	Zeeland	MI	Ms. Janice Stapleton	(616) 643-4635
136	Cleo's Downtown Restaurant	Borculo	MI	Ms. Joan Hoffman	(616) 888-2046
163	Bentham's Riverfront Restaurant	Roscommon	MI	Mr. Joe Markovicz	(517) 792-8040
165	Sullivan's Restaurant & Lounge	Saugatuck	MI	Ms. Dawn Parker	(616) 575-6731
201	Wagon Train Restaurant	Selkirk	MI	Mr. Carl Seaver	(517) 111-5545
202	Extra Helpings Restaurant	Five Lakes	MI	Ms. Deborah Wolfe	(517) 889-6003
203	Mountain Lake Restaurant	Grand Rapids	MI	Mr. Donald MacPherson	(616) 532-4499
322	Alto Country Inn	Alto	MI	Mr. James Cowan	(616) 888-7111
325	Best Bet Restaurant	Grand Rapids	MI	Ms. Rebecca Van Singel	(616) 415-7294
407	Jean's Country Restaurant	Mattawan	MI	Ms. Jean Brooks	(517) 620-4431
423	Bay Pointe Restaurant	Shelbyville	MI	Mr. Janosfi Petofi	(616) 679-5681
515	Cheshire Restaurant	Burlington	MI	Mr. Jeffrey Hersha	(517) 717-9855

Record: [◄][◄] 1 [►][►I][►*] of 38

Datasheet View   NUM

Start   Microsoft Access - [C...   9:35 AM

The datasheet displays the six selected fields for each record in the Customer table. The fields are shown in the order you selected them, from left to right.

The records are currently listed in order by the primary key field (CustomerNum). Kim prefers the records to be listed in order by state so that her staff members can focus on all the customers in a particular state. To display the records in the order Kim wants, you need to sort the query results by the State field.

To sort the query results:

1. Click to position the insertion point anywhere in the State column. This establishes the State column as the current field.

2. Click the **Sort Ascending** button ▼ on the Query Datasheet toolbar. The records are now sorted in ascending alphabetical order by the values in the State field. All the records for Indiana are listed first, followed by the records for Michigan and then Ohio.

Kim asks for a printed copy of the query results so that she can bring the customer list to a meeting with her staff members. To print the query results, you can use the Print button on the Query Datasheet toolbar.

To print the query results:

1. Click the **Print** button 🖨 on the Query Datasheet toolbar to print one copy of the query results with the current settings.

2. Click the **Close** button ✖ on the menu bar to close the query.

   A dialog box opens asking if you want to save changes to the design of the query. This box appears because you changed the sort order of the query results.

3. Click the **Yes** button to save the changed query design and return to the Database window. Notice that the Customer List query is now shown in the Queries list box. In addition, because you had maximized the Query window, the Database window is also now maximized. You need to restore the window.

4. Click the **Restore** button 🗗 on the menu bar to restore the Database window.

The results of the query are not stored with the database; however, the query design is stored as part of the database with the name you specify. You can then re-create the query results at any time by running the query again. You'll learn more about creating and running queries in Tutorial 3.

After Kim leaves for her staff meeting, Barbara asks you to create a form for the Customer table so that her staff members can use the form to enter and work with data easily in the table.

Creating and Printing a Form

A **form** is an object you use to maintain, view, and print records in a database. Although you can perform these same functions with tables and queries, forms can present data in customized and useful ways.

In Access, you can design your own forms or use a Form Wizard to create forms for you automatically. A **Form Wizard** is an Access tool that asks you a series of questions, then creates a form based on your answers. The quickest way to create a form is to use an **AutoForm Wizard**, which places all the fields from a selected table (or query) on a form automatically, without asking you any questions, and then displays the form on the screen.

Barbara wants a form for the Customer table that will show all the fields for one record at a time, with fields listed one below another. This type of form will make it easier for her staff to focus on all the data for a particular customer. You'll use the AutoForm: Columnar Wizard to create the form.

To create the form using an AutoForm Wizard:

1. Click the **Forms** tab in the Database window to display the Forms list. The Forms list box is currently empty because you haven't created any forms yet.

2. Click the **New** button to open the New Form dialog box. See Figure 1-12.

Figure 1-12 ◀
New Form
dialog box

click to design your
own form

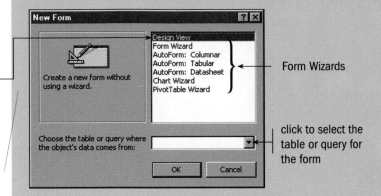

Form Wizards

click to select the
table or query for
the form

The top list box provides options for designing your own form or creating a form using one of the Form Wizards. In the bottom list box, you choose the table or query that will supply the data for the form.

3. Click **AutoForm: Columnar** to select this AutoForm Wizard.

4. Click the list arrow for choosing the table or query on which to base the form, and then click **Customer**.

5. Click the **OK** button. The AutoForm Wizard creates the form and displays it in Form view. See Figure 1-13.

Figure 1-13 ◀
Form created
by the
AutoForm:
Columnar
Wizard

The form displays one record at a time in the Customer table. Access displays the field values for the first record in the table and selects the first field value (CustomerNum). Each field name appears on a separate line and on the same line as its field value, which appears in a box. The widths of the boxes are different to accommodate the different sizes of the displayed field values; for example, compare the small box for the State field's value with the larger box for the CustomerName field's value. The AutoForm: Columnar Wizard automatically placed the field names and values on the form and supplied the background style.

Also, notice that the Form window contains navigation buttons, similar to those available in Datasheet view, which you can use to move to different records in the table.

Barbara asks you to print the data for the Embers Restaurant, which is the last record in the table. After printing this record in the form, you'll save the form with the name "Customer Data" in the Restaurant database. The form will then be available for later use. You'll learn more about creating and customizing forms in Tutorial 4.

To print the form with data for the last record, and then save and close the form:

1. Click the **Last Record** navigation button . The last record in the table, record 38 for Embers Restaurant, is now the current record.

2. Click **File** on the menu bar, and then click **Print**. The Print dialog box opens.

3. Click the **Selected Record(s)** option button, and then click the **OK** button to print only the current record in the form.

4. Click the **Save** button 🖫 on the Form View toolbar. The Save As dialog box opens.

5. In the Form Name text box, click at the end of the highlighted word "Customer," press the **spacebar**, type **Data**, and then press the **Enter** key. Access saves the form as Customer Data in your Restaurant database and closes the dialog box.

6. Click the **Close** button ☒ on the Form window title bar to close the form and return to the Database window. Note that the Customer Data form is now listed in the Forms list box.

Kim returns from her staff meeting with another request. She wants the same customer list you produced earlier when you created the Customer List query, but she'd like the information presented in a more readable format. She suggests you use the Access Help system to learn about formatting data in reports.

Getting Help

The Access Help system provides the same options as the Help system in other Windows programs—the Help Contents, the Help Index, and the Find Feature, which are available on the Help menu. The Access Help system also provides additional ways to get help as you work—the Office Assistant and the What's This? command. You'll learn how to use the Office Assistant next in this section. The What's This? ▯ command provides context-sensitive Help information. When you choose this command from the Help menu, the pointer changes to the Help pointer, which you can then use to click any object or option on the screen to see a description of the object.

Finding Information with the Office Assistant

The Office Assistant is an interactive guide to finding information in the Help system. You can ask the Office Assistant a question, and it will look through the Help system to find an answer.

REFERENCE window	**USING THE OFFICE ASSISTANT**
	■ Click the Office Assistant button on any toolbar (or choose Microsoft Access Help from the Help menu).
	■ Click in the text box, type your question, and then click the Search button.
	■ Choose a topic from the list of topics displayed by the Office Assistant. Click additional topics, as necessary.
	■ When finished, close the Help window and the Office Assistant.

You'll use the Office Assistant to get Help about creating reports in Access.

To get Help about reports:

1. Click the **Office Assistant** button ▯ on the Database toolbar. The Office Assistant appears and displays a dialog box with several options. See Figure 1-14.

Figure 1-14 ◀
Office
Assistant

list of topics

type your question
in this text box

click to have Office
Assistant search
for an answer

Office
Assistant
window

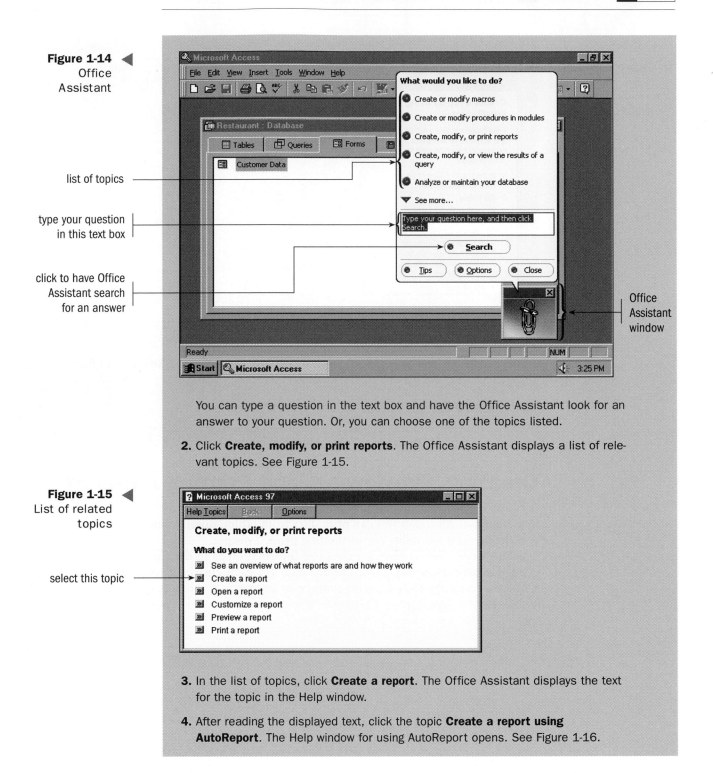

You can type a question in the text box and have the Office Assistant look for an answer to your question. Or, you can choose one of the topics listed.

2. Click **Create, modify, or print reports**. The Office Assistant displays a list of relevant topics. See Figure 1-15.

Figure 1-15 ◀
List of related
topics

select this topic

3. In the list of topics, click **Create a report**. The Office Assistant displays the text for the topic in the Help window.

4. After reading the displayed text, click the topic **Create a report using AutoReport**. The Help window for using AutoReport opens. See Figure 1-16.

Figure 1-16 ◀
Help
information on
AutoReport

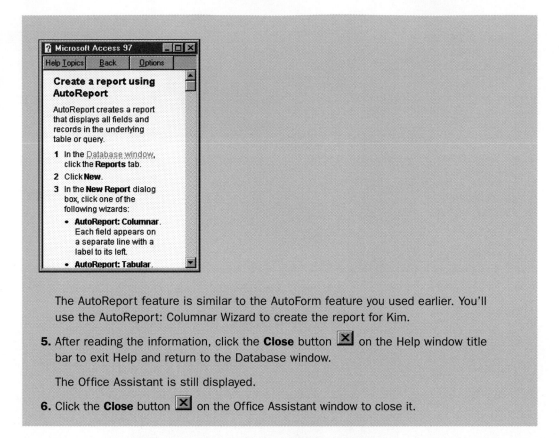

The AutoReport feature is similar to the AutoForm feature you used earlier. You'll use the AutoReport: Columnar Wizard to create the report for Kim.

5. After reading the information, click the **Close** button ▣ on the Help window title bar to exit Help and return to the Database window.

The Office Assistant is still displayed.

6. Click the **Close** button ▣ on the Office Assistant window to close it.

Creating, Previewing, and Printing a Report

A **report** is a formatted printout (or screen display) of the contents of one or more tables in a database. Although you can print data from tables, queries, and forms, reports allow you the greatest flexibility for formatting printed output.

Kim wants a report showing the same information as in the Customer List query you created earlier. However, she'd like the data for each customer to be grouped together, with one customer record below another, as shown in the report sketch in Figure 1-17. You'll use the AutoReport: Columnar Wizard to produce the report for Kim.

Figure 1-17 ◀
Sketch of
Kim's report

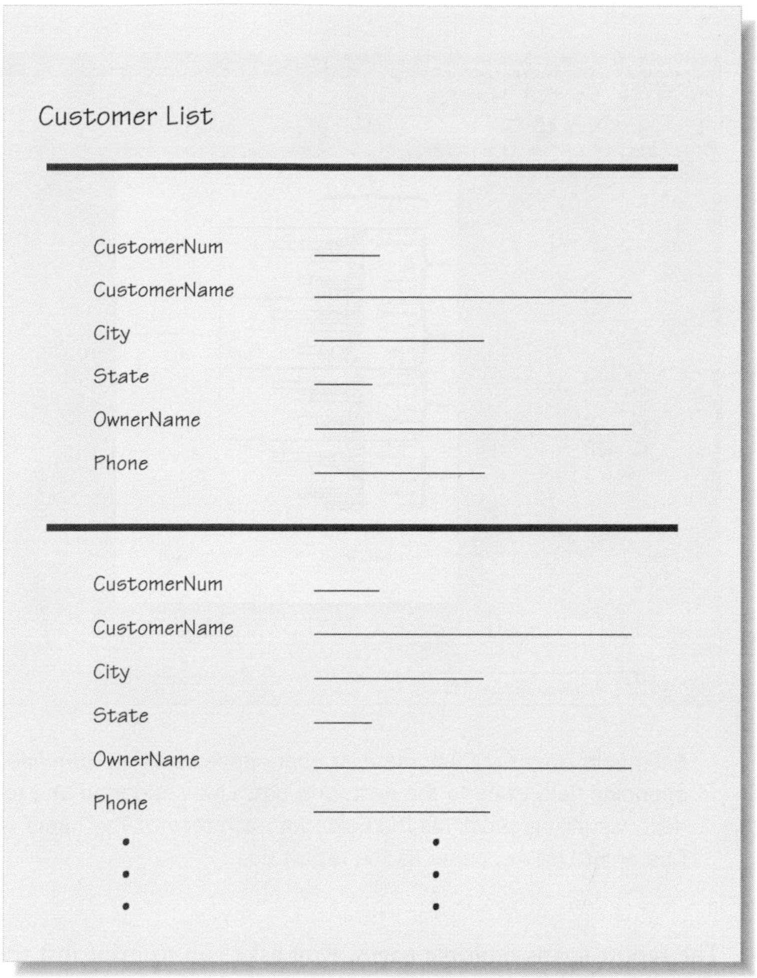

Customer List

_____

    CustomerNum   _____

    CustomerName   _____

    City   _____

    State   _____

    OwnerName   _____

    Phone   _____

_____

    CustomerNum   _____

    CustomerName   _____

    City   _____

    State   _____

    OwnerName   _____

    Phone   _____

      •   •

      •   •

      •   •

To create the report using the AutoReport: Columnar Wizard:

1. Click the **Reports** tab in the Database window, and then click the **New** button to open the New Report dialog box. This dialog box is similar to the New Form dialog box you saw earlier.

2. Click **AutoReport: Columnar** to select this wizard for creating the report.

   Because Kim wants the same data as in the Customer List query, you need to choose that query as the basis for the report.

3. Click the list arrow for choosing the table or query on which to base the report, and then click **Customer List**.

4. Click the **OK** button. The AutoReport Wizard creates the report and displays it in Print Preview, which shows exactly how the report will look when printed.

   To better view the report, you'll maximize the window and change the Zoom setting so that you can see the entire page.

5. Click the **Maximize** button ▢ on the Report window, click the **Zoom** list arrow (next to the value 100%) on the Print Preview toolbar, and then click **Fit**. The entire first page of the report is displayed in the window. See Figure 1-18.

Figure 1-18 ◀
First page of
the report in
Print Preview

report title taken from
query name

fields grouped for
each record

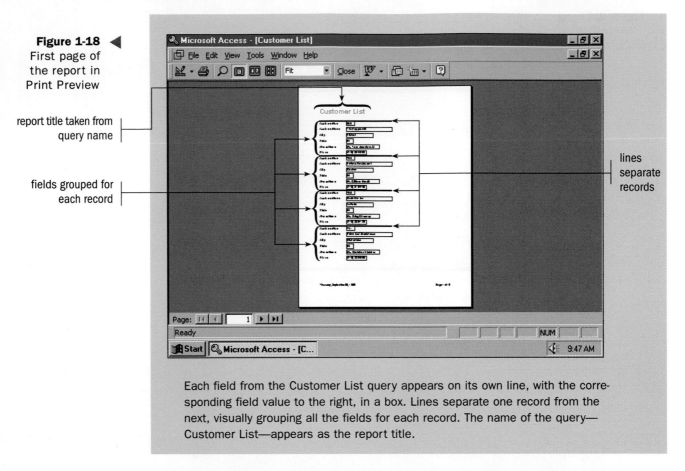

lines
separate
records

Each field from the Customer List query appears on its own line, with the corresponding field value to the right, in a box. Lines separate one record from the next, visually grouping all the fields for each record. The name of the query—Customer List—appears as the report title.

The report spans multiple pages. Kim asks you to print just the first page of the report so that she can review its format. After printing the report page, you'll close the report without saving it, because you can easily re-create it at any time. In general, it's best to save an object—report, form, or query—only if you anticipate using the object frequently or if it is time-consuming to create, because these objects can take up considerable storage space on your disk. You'll learn more about creating and customizing reports in Tutorial 4.

To print the first report page, and then close the report and exit Access:

1. Click **File** on the menu bar, and then click **Print**. The Print dialog box opens. You need to change the print settings so that only the first page of the report is printed.

2. In the Print Range section, click the **Pages** option button, type **1** in the From text box, press the **Tab** key, and then type **1** in the To text box.

3. Click the **OK** button to print the first page of the report. Now you can close the report.

4. Click the **Close** button ⊠ on the menu bar. *Do not* click the Close button on the Print Preview toolbar.

   TROUBLE? If you clicked the Close button on the Print Preview toolbar, you switched to Design view. Simply click the Close button ⊠ on the menu bar, and then continue with the tutorial.

   A dialog box opens asking if you want to save the changes to the report design.

5. Click the **No** button to close the report without saving it. Now you can exit Access.

6. Click the **Close** button ⊠ on the Access window title bar to exit Access.

Quick Check

1   A(n) _____ is a question you ask about the data stored in a database.

2   Unless you specify otherwise, the records resulting from a query are listed in order by the _____.

3   The quickest way to create a form is to use a(n) _____.

4   Describe the form created by the AutoForm: Columnar Wizard.

5   Describe how you use the Office Assistant to get Help.

6   After creating a report, the AutoReport Wizard displays the report in _____.

With the Customer table in place, Barbara can continue to build the Restaurant database and use it to store, manipulate, and retrieve important data for Valle Coffee. In the following tutorials, you'll help Barbara complete and maintain the database, and you'll use it to meet the specific information needs of other Valle Coffee employees.

Tutorial Assignments

In the Tutorial Assignments, you'll work with the Customer database, which is similar to the database you worked with in the tutorial. Complete the following:

1. Make sure your Student Disk is in the disk drive.

2. Start Access and open the Customer database, which is located in the TAssign folder on your Student Disk.

3. Choose the Contents and Index command from the Help menu, and then select the Contents tab. Open the topic "Introduction to Microsoft Access 97" and then open the topic "Databases: What they are and how they work." Read the displayed information, and then click the >> button at the top of the window to move through the remaining screens for the topic. When finished, click the Help Topics button at the top of the window to return to the Contents tab. Repeat this procedure for the similarly worded topics for tables, queries, forms, and reports. On any screen that contains boxed items, click each item and read the information displayed in the pop-up window. When finished reading all the topics, close the Help window.

4. Use the Office Assistant to ask the following question: "How do I rename a table?" Choose the topic "Rename a table, query, form, report, macro, or module" and read the displayed information. Close the Help window and the Office Assistant. Then, in the Customer database, rename the Table1 table as Customers.

5. Open the Customers table.

6. Choose the Contents and Index command from the Help menu, and then select the Index tab. Look up the word "landscape," and then choose the topic "landscape page orientation." Choose the subtopic "Set margins, page orientation, and other page setup options." Read the displayed information, and then close the Help window. Print the Customers table datasheet in landscape orientation. Close the Customers table.

7. Use the Simple Query Wizard to create a query that includes the CustomerName, OwnerName, and Phone fields from the Customers table. Name the query Customer Phone List. Sort the query results in ascending order by CustomerName. Print the query results, and then close and save the query.

8. Use the AutoForm: Columnar Wizard to create a form for the Customers table.

9. Use context-sensitive Help to find out how to move to a particular record and display it in the form. Choose the What's This? command from the Help menu, and then use the Help pointer to click the number 1 in the Specific Record box at the bottom of the form. Read the displayed information. Click to close the Help box, and then use the Specific Record box to move to record 20 (for Cheshire Restaurant) in the Customers table.

10. Print the form for the current record (20), save the form as Customer Info, and then close the form.

11. Use the AutoReport: Tabular Wizard to create a report based on the Customers table. Print the first page of the report, and then close the report without saving it.

12. Exit Access.

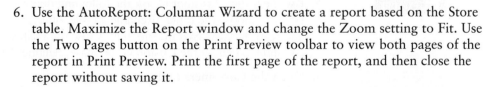

Case Problems

1. Ashbrook Mall Information Desk Ashbrook Mall is a large, modern mall located in Phoenix, Arizona. The Mall Operations Office is responsible for everything that happens within the mall and anything that affects the mall's operation. Among the independent operations that report to the Mall Operations Office are the Maintenance Group, the Mall Security Office, and the Information Desk. You will be helping the personnel at the Information Desk.

One important service provided by the Information Desk is to maintain a catalog of current job openings at stores within the mall. Sam Bullard, the director of the Mall Operations Office, recently created an Access database named MallJobs to store this information. You'll help Sam complete and maintain this database. Complete the following:

1. Make sure your Student Disk is in the disk drive.

2. Start Access and open the MallJobs database, which is located in the Cases folder on your Student Disk.

3. Open the Store table, print the table datasheet, and then close the table.

4. Use the Simple Query Wizard to create a query that includes the StoreName, Contact, and Extension fields from the Store table. Name the query Contact Phone List. Print the query results, and then close the query.

5. Use the AutoForm: Tabular Wizard to create a form for the Store table. Print the form, and then close it without saving it.

6. Use the AutoReport: Columnar Wizard to create a report based on the Store table. Maximize the Report window and change the Zoom setting to Fit. Use the Two Pages button on the Print Preview toolbar to view both pages of the report in Print Preview. Print the first page of the report, and then close the report without saving it.

7. Exit Access.

2. Professional Litigation User Services Professional Litigation User Services (PLUS) is a company that creates all types of visual aids for judicial proceedings. Clients are usually private law firms, although the District Attorney's office has occasionally contracted for their services. PLUS creates graphs, maps, timetables, and charts, both for computerized presentations and in large-size form for presentation to juries. PLUS also creates videos, animations, presentation packages, slide shows—in short, anything of a visual nature that can be used in a judicial proceeding to make, clarify, or support a point.

Raj Jawahir, a new employee at PLUS, is responsible for tracking the daily payments received from the firm's clients. He created an Access database named Payments, and needs your help in working with this database. Complete the following:

1. Make sure your Student Disk is in the disk drive.

2. Start Access and open the Payments database, which is located in the Cases folder on your Student Disk.

3. Open the Firm table, print the table datasheet, and then close the table.

4. Use the Simple Query Wizard to create a query that includes the FirmName, PLUSAcctRep, and Extension fields from the Firm table. Name the query Rep List. Sort the results in ascending order by the PLUSAcctRep field.

 5. Use the Office Assistant to ask the following question: "How do I select multiple records?" Choose the topic "Selecting fields and records in Datasheet view," read the displayed information, and then close the Help window and the Office Assistant. Then select the first 11 records in the datasheet (all the records with the value "Abelson, David" in the PLUSAcctRep field), and then print just the selected records. Close the query, saving the changes to the design.

6. Use the AutoForm: Columnar Wizard to create a form for the Firm table. Move to record 31, and then print the form for the current record only. Close the form without saving it.

7. Use the AutoReport: Columnar Wizard to create a report based on the Firm table. Maximize the Report window and change the Zoom setting to Fit.

 8. Use the View menu to view all eight pages of the report at the same time in Print Preview.

9. Print just the first page of the report, and then close the report without saving it.

10. Exit Access.

3. Best Friends Best Friends is a not-for-profit organization that trains hearing and service dogs for people with disabilities. Established in 1989 in Boise, Idaho, by Noah and Sheila Warnick, Best Friends is modeled after Paws With A Cause®, the original and largest provider of hearing and service dogs in the United States. Like Paws With A Cause® and other such organizations, Best Friends strives to provide "Dignity Through Independence."

To raise funds for Best Friends, Noah and Sheila periodically conduct Walk-A-Thons. The events have become so popular, Noah and Sheila created an Access database named Walks to track walker and pledge data. You'll help them complete and maintain the Walks database. Complete the following:

1. Make sure your Student Disk is in the disk drive.

2. Start Access and open the Walks database, which is located in the Cases folder on your Student Disk.

3. Open the Walker table, print the table datasheet, and then close the table.

 4. Use the Simple Query Wizard to create a query that includes all the fields in the Walker table *except* the Phone field. (*Hint:* Use the >> and < buttons to select the necessary fields.) In the second Simple Query Wizard dialog box, make sure the Detail option button is selected. (This second dialog box appears because the table contains numeric values.) Name the query "Walker Distance." Sort the results in ascending order by the LastName field. Print the query results, and then close and save the query.

5. Use the AutoForm: Columnar Wizard to create a form for the Walker table. Move to record 25, and then print the form for the current record only. Close the form without saving it.

6. Use the AutoReport: Columnar Wizard to create a report based on the Walker table. Maximize the Report window and change the Zoom setting to Fit.

7. Use the View menu to view all six pages of the report at the same time in Print Preview.

8. Print just the first page of the report, and then close the report without saving it.

9. Exit Access.

4. Lopez Lexus Dealerships Maria and Hector Lopez own a chain of Lexus dealerships throughout Texas. They have used a computer in their business for several years to handle payroll and typical accounting functions. Because of their phenomenal expansion, both in the number of car locations and the number of cars handled, they created an Access database named Lexus to track their car inventory. You'll help them work with and maintain this database. Complete the following:

1. Make sure your Student Disk is in the disk drive.

2. Start Access and open the Lexus database, which is located in the Cases folder on your Student Disk.

3. Open the Cars table.

4. Print the Cars table datasheet in landscape orientation, and then close the table.

5. Use the Simple Query Wizard to create a query that includes the Model, Year, LocationCode, Cost, and SellingPrice fields from the Cars table. In the second Simple Query Wizard dialog box, make sure the Detail option button is selected. (This second dialog box appears because the table contains numeric values.) Name the query "Cost vs Selling."

6. Sort the query results in descending order by SellingPrice. (*Hint:* Use a toolbar button.)

7. Print the query results, and then close and save the query.

8. Use the AutoForm: Columnar Wizard to create a form for the Cars table. Move to record 11, and then print the form for the current record only. Close the form without saving it.

9. Use the AutoReport: Tabular Wizard to create a report based on the Cars table. Maximize the Report window and change the Zoom setting to Fit. Use the Two Pages button on the Print Preview toolbar to view both pages of the report in Print Preview. Print the first page of the report, and then close the report without saving it.

10. Exit Access.

Lab Assignments

These Lab Assignments are designed to accompany the interactive Course Lab called Databases. To start the Databases Lab, click the Start button on the Windows 95 taskbar, point to Programs, point to Course Labs, point to New Perspectives Applications, and click Databases. If you do not see Course Labs on your Programs menu, see your instructor or technical support person.

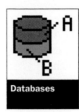

Databases

Databases This Databases Lab demonstrates the essential concepts of file and database management systems. You will use the Lab to search, sort, and report the data contained in a file of classic books.

1. Click the Steps button to review basic database terminology and to learn how to manipulate the classic books database. As you proceed through the Steps, answer all of the Quick Check questions that appear. After you complete the Steps, you will see a Quick Check summary report. Follow the instructions on the screen to print this report.

2. Click the Explore button. Make sure you can apply basic database terminology to describe the classic books database by answering the following questions:
   a. How many records does the file contain?
   b. How many fields does each record contain?
   c. What are the contents of the Catalog # field for the book written by Margaret Mitchell?
   d. What are the contents of the Title field for the record with Thoreau in the Author field?
   e. Which field has been used to sort the records?

3. In Explore, manipulate the database as necessary to answer the following questions:
   a. When the books are sorted by title, what is the first record in the file?
   b. Use the Search button to search for all the books in the West location. How many do you find?
   c. Use the Search button to search for all the books in the Main location that are checked in. What do you find?

4. Use the Report button to print out a report that groups the books by Status and sorts them by Title. On your report, circle the four field names. Draw a box around the summary statistics showing which books are currently checked in and which books are currently checked out.

TUTORIAL 2

Maintaining a Database

Creating, Modifying, and Updating an Order Table

In this tutorial you will:

■ Learn the guidelines for designing databases and Access tables

■ Create and save a table

■ Define fields and specify the primary key

■ Add records to a table

■ Modify the structure of a table

■ Delete, move, and add fields

■ Change field properties

■ Copy records from another Access database

■ Delete and change records

CASE

Valle Coffee

The Restaurant database currently contains only one table—the Customer table—which stores data about Valle Coffee's restaurant customers. Barbara also wants to track information about each order placed by each restaurant customer. This information includes the order's billing date and invoice amount. Barbara asks you to create a second table in the Restaurant database, named Order, in which to store the order data.

Some of the order data Barbara needs is already stored in another Valle Coffee database. After creating the Order table and adding some records to it, you'll copy the records from the other database into the Order table. Then you'll maintain the Order table by modifying it and updating it to meet Barbara's specific data requirements.

SESSION

2.1

In this session you will learn the guidelines for designing databases and Access tables. You'll also learn how to create a table, define the fields for a table, select the primary key for a table, save the table structure, and add records to a table datasheet.

Guidelines for Designing Databases

A database management system can be a useful tool, but only if you first carefully design the database so that it meets the needs of those who will use it. In database design, you determine the fields, tables, and relationships needed to satisfy the data and processing requirements. When you design a database, you should follow these guidelines:

- **Identify all the fields needed to produce the required information.** For example, Barbara needs information about customers and orders. Figure 2-1 shows the fields that satisfy those information requirements.

Figure 2-1 ◀
Barbara's data
requirements

CustomerName	BillingDate
OrderNum	OwnerName
Street	InvoiceAmt
City	PlacedBy
State	Phone
ZipCode	FirstContact
CustomerNum	

- **Group related fields into tables.** For example, Barbara grouped the fields relating to customers into the Customer table. The other fields are grouped logically into the Order table, which you will create, as shown in Figure 2-2.

Figure 2-2 ◀
Barbara's fields
grouped into
Customer and
Order tables

<u>Customer table</u>	<u>Order table</u>
CustomerNum	OrderNum
CustomerName	BillingDate
Street	PlacedBy
City	InvoiceAmt
State	
ZipCode	
OwnerName	
Phone	
FirstContact	

- **Determine each table's primary key.** Recall that a primary key uniquely identifies each record in a table. Although a primary key is not mandatory in Access, it's usually a good idea to include one in each table. Without a primary key, selecting the exact record you want can be a problem. For some tables, one of the fields, such as a Social Security number or credit card number, naturally serves the function of a primary key. For other tables, two or more fields might be needed to function as the primary key. In these cases, the primary key is referred to as a **composite key**. For example, a school grade table would use a combination of student number and course code to serve as the primary key. For a third category of tables, no single field or combination of fields can uniquely identify a record in a table. In these cases, you need to add a field whose sole purpose is to serve as the primary key.

For Barbara's tables, CustomerNum is the primary key for the Customer table, and OrderNum will be the primary key for the Order table.

- **Include a common field in related tables.** You use the common field to connect one table logically with another table. For example, Barbara's Customer and Order tables will include the CustomerNum field as a common field. Recall that when you include the primary key from one table as a field in a second table to form a relationship, the field is called a foreign key in the second table; therefore, the CustomerNum field will be a foreign key in the Order table. With this common field, Barbara can find all orders placed by a customer; she can use the CustomerNum value for a customer and search the Order table for all orders with that CustomerNum value. Likewise, she can determine which customer placed a particular order by searching the Customer table to find the one record with the same CustomerNum value as the corresponding value in the Order table.

- **Avoid data redundancy.** Data redundancy occurs when you store the same data in more than one place. With the exception of common fields to connect tables, you should avoid redundancy because it wastes storage space and can cause inconsistencies, if, for instance, you type a field value one way in one table and a different way in the same table or in a second table. Figure 2-3 shows an example of incorrect database design that illustrates data redundancy in the Order table; the Customer Name field is redundant and one value was entered incorrectly, in three different ways.

Figure 2-3 ◄
Incorrect
database
design with
data
redundancy

inconsistent data ——

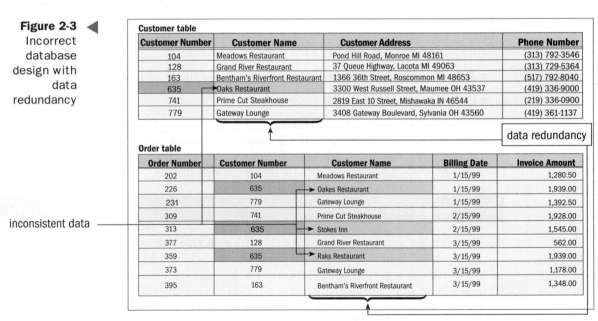

Customer table

Customer Number	Customer Name	Customer Address	Phone Number
104	Meadows Restaurant	Pond Hill Road, Monroe MI 48161	(313) 792-3546
128	Grand River Restaurant	37 Queue Highway, Lacota MI 49063	(313) 729-5364
163	Bentham's Riverfront Restaurant	1366 36th Street, Roscommon MI 48653	(517) 792-8040
635	Oaks Restaurant	3300 West Russell Street, Maumee OH 43537	(419) 336-9000
741	Prime Cut Steakhouse	2819 East 10 Street, Mishawaka IN 46544	(219) 336-0900
779	Gateway Lounge	3408 Gateway Boulevard, Sylvania OH 43560	(419) 361-1137

data redundancy

Order table

Order Number	Customer Number	Customer Name	Billing Date	Invoice Amount
202	104	Meadows Restaurant	1/15/99	1,280.50
226	635	Oakes Restaurant	1/15/99	1,939.00
231	779	Gateway Lounge	1/15/99	1,392.50
309	741	Prime Cut Steakhouse	2/15/99	1,928.00
313	635	Stokes Inn	2/15/99	1,545.00
377	128	Grand River Restaurant	3/15/99	562.00
359	635	Raks Restaurant	3/15/99	1,939.00
373	779	Gateway Lounge	3/15/99	1,178.00
395	163	Bentham's Riverfront Restaurant	3/15/99	1,348.00

- **Determine the properties of each field.** You need to identify the **properties**, or characteristics, of each field so that the DBMS knows how to store, display, and process the field. These properties include the field name, the field's maximum number of characters or digits, the field's description, the field's valid values, and other field characteristics. You will learn more about field properties later in this tutorial.

The Order table you need to create will contain the fields shown in Figure 2-2. Before you create the table, you first need to learn some guidelines for designing Access tables.

Guidelines for Designing Access Tables

As just noted, the last step of database design is to determine the properties, such as the name and data type, of each field. Access has rules for naming fields, choosing data types, and defining other properties for fields.

Naming Fields and Objects

You must name each field, table, and other object in an Access database. Access then stores these items in the database using the names you supply. It's best to choose a field or object name that describes the purpose or contents of the field or object, so that later you can easily remember what the name represents. For example, the two tables in the Restaurant database will be named Customer and Order, because these names suggest their contents.

The following rules apply to naming fields and objects:

- A name can be up to 64 characters long.

- A name can contain letters, numbers, spaces, and special characters except a period (.), exclamation mark (!), accent grave (`), and square brackets ([ ]).

- A name cannot start with a space.

- A table or query name must be unique within a database. A field name must be unique within a table, but it can be used again in another table.

In addition, experienced users of databases have the following tips for naming fields and objects:

- Capitalize the first letter of each word in the name.

- Avoid extremely long names because they are difficult to remember and refer to.

- Use standard abbreviations such as Num for Number, Amt for Amount, and Qty for Quantity.

- Do not use spaces in field names because these names will appear in column headings on datasheets and labels on forms and reports. By not using spaces you'll be able to show more fields on these objects at one time.

Assigning Field Data Types

You must assign a data type for each field. The **data type** determines what field values you can enter for the field and what other properties the field will have. For example, the Order table will include a BillingDate field, so you will assign the date/time data type to this field because it will store date values. Access will allow you to enter only dates or times as values for the field and will allow you to manipulate a value only as a date or time.

Figure 2-4 lists the ten data types available in Access, describes the field values allowed with each data type, explains when each data type should be used, and indicates the field size of each data type.

Figure 2-4 ◀
Data types
for fields

Data Type	Description	Field Size
Text	Allows field values containing letters, digits, spaces, and special characters. Use for names, addresses, descriptions, and fields containing digits that are not used in calculations.	1 to 255 characters; 50 characters default
Memo	Allows field values containing letters, digits, spaces, and special characters. Use for long comments and explanations.	1 to 64,000 characters; exact size is determined by entry
Number	Allows positive and negative numbers as field values. Numbers can contain digits, a decimal point, commas, a plus sign, and a minus sign. Use for fields that you will use in calculations, except calculations involving money.	1 to 15 digits
Date/Time	Allows field values containing valid dates and times from January 1, 100 to December 31, 9999. Dates can be entered in mm/dd/yy (month, day, year) format, several other date formats, or a variety of time formats such as 10:35 PM. You can perform calculations on dates and times and you can sort them. For example, you can determine the number of days between two dates.	8 digits
Currency	Allows field values similar to those for the number data type. Unlike calculations with number data type decimal values, calculations performed using the currency data type are not subject to round-off error.	15 digits
AutoNumber	Consists of integers with values controlled by Access. Access automatically inserts a value in the field as each new record is created. You can specify sequential numbering or random numbering. This guarantees a unique field value, so that such a field can serve as a table's primary key.	9 digits
Yes/No	Limits field values to yes and no, or true and false. Use for fields that indicate the presence or absence of a condition, such as whether an order has been filled, or if an employee is eligible for the company dental plan.	1 character
OLE Object	Allows field values that are created in other programs as objects, such as photographs, video images, graphics, drawings, sound recordings, voice-mail messages, spreadsheets, and word-processing documents. These objects can be linked or embedded.	1 gigabyte maximum; exact size depends on object size
Hyperlink	Consists of text or combinations of text and numbers stored as text and used as a hyperlink address. A hyperlink address can have up to three parts: the text that appears in a field or control; the path to a file or page; and a location within the file or page. Hyperlinks help you to connect your application easily to the Internet or an intranet.	Up to 2048 characters for each of the three parts of a hyperlink data type
Lookup Wizard	Creates a field that lets you look up a value in another table or in a predefined list of values.	Same size as the primary key field used to perform the lookup

Assigning Field Sizes

The **field size** property defines a field value's maximum storage size for text and number fields only. The other data types have no field size property, because their storage size is either a fixed, predetermined amount or is determined automatically by the field value itself, as shown in Figure 2-4. A text field has a default field size of 50 characters. You set its field size by entering a number in the range 1 to 255. For example, the OrderNum and CustomerNum fields in the Order table will be text fields with sizes of 3 each.

Barbara documented the design for the Order table by listing each field's name, data type, size (if applicable), and description, as shown in Figure 2-5. OrderNum, the table's primary key, CustomerNum, a foreign key to the Customer table, and PlacedBy will each be assigned the text data type. BillingDate will have the date/time data type, and InvoiceAmt will have the currency data type.

Figure 2-5 ◀
Design for the
Order table

Field Name	Data Type	Field Size	Description
OrderNum	Text	3	primary key
CustomerNum	Text	3	foreign key
BillingDate	Date/Time		
PlacedBy	Text	25	person who placed order
InvoiceAmt	Currency		

With Barbara's design, you are ready to create the Order table.

Creating a Table

Creating a table consists of naming the fields and defining the properties for the fields, specifying a primary key (and a foreign key, if applicable) for the table, and then saving the table structure. You will use Barbara's design (Figure 2-5) as a guide to creating the Order table. First, you need to open the Restaurant database.

To open the Restaurant database:

1. Place your Student Disk in the appropriate disk drive.

2. Start Access. The Access window opens with the initial dialog box.

3. Make sure the **Open an Existing Database** option button and the **More Files** option are selected, and then click the **OK** button to display the Open dialog box.

4. Click the **Look in** list arrow, and then click the drive that contains your Student Disk.

5. Click **Tutorial** in the list box, and then click the **Open** button to display a list of the files in the Tutorial folder.

6. Click **Restaurant** in the list box, and then click the **Open** button. The Restaurant database is displayed in the Access window.

7. Make sure the Tables tab is selected in the Database window.

The Customer table is listed in the Tables list box. Now you'll create the Order table in the Restaurant database.

To begin creating the Order table:

1. Click the **New** button in the Database window. The New Table dialog box opens. See Figure 2-6.

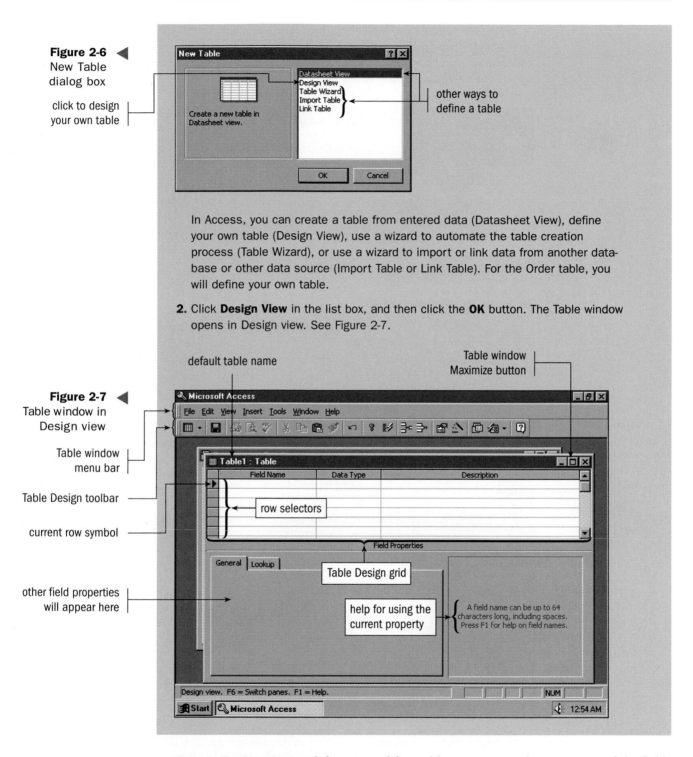

Figure 2-6 ◀
New Table
dialog box

click to design
your own table

other ways to
define a table

In Access, you can create a table from entered data (Datasheet View), define
your own table (Design View), use a wizard to automate the table creation
process (Table Wizard), or use a wizard to import or link data from another database or other data source (Import Table or Link Table). For the Order table, you
will define your own table.

2. Click **Design View** in the list box, and then click the **OK** button. The Table window
opens in Design view. See Figure 2-7.

default table name

Table window
Maximize button

Figure 2-7 ◀
Table window in
Design view

Table window
menu bar

Table Design toolbar

current row symbol

other field properties
will appear here

row selectors

Table Design grid

help for using the
current property

You use Design view to define or modify a table structure or the properties of the fields
in a table. If you create a table without using a wizard, you enter the fields and their properties for your table directly in this window.

Defining Fields

Initially, the default table name, Table1, appears in the Table window title bar, the current row symbol is positioned in the first row selector of the Table Design grid, and the
insertion point is located in the first row's Field Name box. The purpose or characteristics of the current property (Field Name, in this case) appear in the lower-right of the
Table window. You can display more complete information about the current property by
pressing the F1 key.

You enter values for the Field Name, Data Type, and Description field properties in the upper-half of the Table window. You select values for all other field properties, most of which are optional, in the lower-half of the window. These other properties will appear when you move to the first row's Data Type text box.

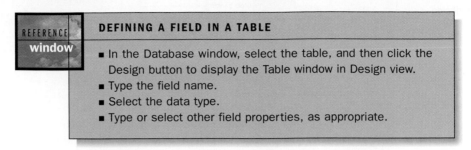

REFERENCE window

DEFINING A FIELD IN A TABLE

- In the Database window, select the table, and then click the Design button to display the Table window in Design view.
- Type the field name.
- Select the data type.
- Type or select other field properties, as appropriate.

The first field you need to define is OrderNum.

To define the OrderNum field:

1. Type **OrderNum** in the first row's Field Name text box, and then press the **Tab** key (or press the **Enter** key) to advance to the Data Type text box. The default data type, Text, appears highlighted in the Data Type text box, which now also contains a list arrow, and field properties for a text field appear in the lower-half of the window. See Figure 2-8.

Figure 2-8
Table window after entering the first field name

field name

default data type

properties for a text field

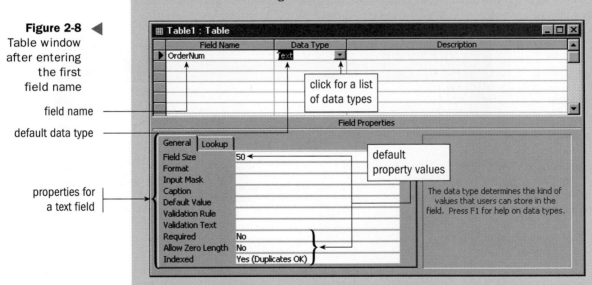

Notice that the lower-right of the window now provides an explanation for the current property, Data Type.

TROUBLE? If you make a typing error, you can correct it by clicking the mouse to position the insertion point, and then using either the Backspace key to delete characters to the left of the insertion point or the Delete key to delete characters to the right of the insertion point. Then type the correct text.

Because order numbers will not be used for calculations, you will assign the text data type to it instead of the number data type, and then enter the Description property value as "primary key." You can use the Description property to enter an optional description for a field to explain its purpose or usage. A field's Description property can be up to 255 characters long, and its value appears in the status bar when you view the table datasheet.

2. Press the **Tab** key to accept Text as the field's data type and move to the Description text box, and then type **primary key** in the Description text box.

The Field Size property has a default value of 50, which you will change to a value of 3, because order numbers at Valle Coffee contain 3 digits. The Required property has a default value of No, which means that a value does not need to be entered for the field. Because Barbara doesn't want an order entered without an order number, you will change the Required property to Yes. The Allow Zero Length property has a value of No, meaning that a value *must* be entered for the field, as is appropriate for the OrderNum field. Finally, the Indexed property has a value of "Yes (Duplicates OK)," which means that a list of index entries will be created to speed up operations using the OrderNum field.

3. Select **50** in the Field Size text box either by dragging the pointer or double-clicking the mouse, and then type **3**.

4. Click the **Required** text box to position the insertion point there. A list arrow appears on the right side of the Required text box.

5. Click the **Required** list arrow. Access displays the Required list box. See Figure 2-9.

Figure 2-9 ◀
Defining the
OrderNum field

changed from
default value of 50

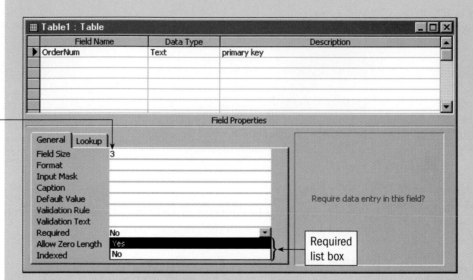

When you position the insertion point or select text in many Access text boxes, Access displays a list arrow, which you can click to display a list box with options. You can display the list arrow *and* the list box simultaneously if you click the text box near its right side.

6. Click **Yes** in the list box. The list box closes, and Yes is now the value for the Required property. The definition of the first field is complete.

Barbara's Order table design shows CustomerNum as the second field. You will define CustomerNum as a text field with a Description of "foreign key" and a Field Size of 3, because customer numbers at Valle Coffee contain 3 digits. Because it's possible that a record for an order might need to be entered for a customer not yet added to the database, Barbara asks you to leave the Required property at its default value of No and to change the Allow Zero Length property value to Yes.

To define the CustomerNum field:

1. Place the insertion point in the second row's Field Name text box, type **CustomerNum** in the text box, and then press the **Tab** key to advance to the Data Type text box.

Customer numbers are not used in calculations, so you'll assign the text data type to the field, and then enter its Description value as "foreign key."

2. Press the **Tab** key to accept Text as the field's data type and move to the Description text box, and then type **foreign key** in the Description text box.

   Finally, change the Field Size property to 3 and the Allow Zero Length property to Yes.

3. Select **50** in the Field Size text box, type **3**, click the right side of the Allow Zero Length text box, and then click **Yes**. You have completed the definition of the second field. See Figure 2-10.

Figure 2-10 ◀
Table window
after defining
the first
two fields

current field

property values for
the current field

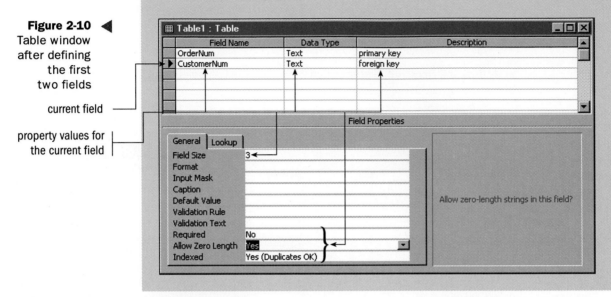

Using Barbara's Order table design in Figure 2-5, you can now complete the remaining field definitions: BillingDate with the date/time data type, PlacedBy with the text data type, and InvoiceAmt with the currency data type.

To define the BillingDate, PlacedBy, and InvoiceAmt fields:

1. Place the insertion point in the third row's Field Name text box, type **BillingDate** in the text box, and then press the **Tab** key to advance to the Data Type text box.

2. Click the **Data Type** list arrow, click **Date/Time** in the list box, and then press the **Tab** key to advance to the Description text box.

   If you've assigned a descriptive field name and the field does not fulfill a special function (for example, primary key), you usually do not enter a value for the optional Description property. BillingDate is a field that does not require a value for its Description property.

   Barbara does not want to require that a value be entered for the BillingDate field, nor does she want an index for the field. So, you do not need to change any of the default property values for the BillingDate field. Neither do you need to enter any new property values. Because you have finished defining the BillingDate field, you can now define the PlacedBy field.

3. Press the **Tab** key to advance to the fourth row's Field Name text box.

4. Type **PlacedBy** in the Field Name text box, and then press the **Tab** key to advance to the Data Type text box.

This field will contain names, so you'll assign the text data type to it. Also, Barbara wants to include the description "person who placed order" to clarify the contents of the field.

5. Press the **Tab** key to accept Text as the field's data type and move to the Description text box, and then type **person who placed order** in the Description text box.

Next, you'll change the Field Size property's default value of 50 to 25, which should be long enough to accommodate all names. Also, Barbara does not want to require that a value be entered for the field.

6. Select **50** in the Field Size text box, type **25**, click the right side of the Allow Zero Length text box, and then click **Yes**.

The definition of the PlacedBy field is complete. Next, you'll define the fifth and final field, InvoiceAmt. This field will contain dollar amounts so you'll assign the currency data type to it.

7. Place the insertion point in the fifth row's Field Name text box.

8. Type **InvoiceAmt** in the Field Name text box, and then press the **Tab** key to advance to the Data Type text box.

You can select a value from the Data Type list box as you did for the BillingDate field. Alternatively, you can type the property value in the text box or type just the first character of the property value.

9. Type **c**. The value in the fifth row's Data Type text box changes to "currency," with the letters "urrency" highlighted. See Figure 2-11.

Figure 2-11 ◀
Selecting a
value for the
Data Type
property

"c" typed ──────

"urrency"
automatically added
and highlighted

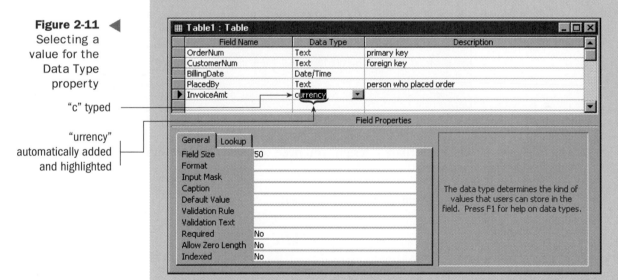

10. Press the **Tab** key to advance to the Description text box. Access changes the value for the Data Type property to Currency.

In the Field Properties section, notice the default values for the Format and Decimal Places properties. For a field with a Format property value of Currency, two decimal places are provided when the Decimal Places property value is Auto. This is the format Barbara wants for the InvoiceAmt field, so you have finished defining the fields for the Order table.

Next, you need to specify the primary key for the Order table.

Specifying the Primary Key

Although Access does not require a table to have a primary key, including a primary key offers several advantages:

- A primary key uniquely identifies each record in a table.

- Access does not allow duplicate values in the primary key field. If a record already exists with an OrderNum value of 143, for example, Access prevents you from adding another record with this same value in the OrderNum field. Preventing duplicate values ensures the uniqueness of the primary key field and helps to avoid data redundancy.

- Access forces you to enter a value for the primary key field in every record in the table. This is known as **entity integrity**. If you do not enter a value for a field, you have actually given the field what is known as a **null value**. You cannot give a null value to the primary key field because entity integrity prevents Access from accepting and processing that record.

- Access stores records on disk in the same order as you enter them but displays them in order by the field values of the primary key. If you enter records in no specific order, you are ensured that you will later be able to work with them in a more meaningful, primary key sequence.

- Access responds faster to your requests for specific records based on the primary key.

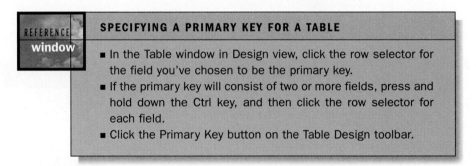

REFERENCE window

SPECIFYING A PRIMARY KEY FOR A TABLE

- In the Table window in Design view, click the row selector for the field you've chosen to be the primary key.
- If the primary key will consist of two or more fields, press and hold down the Ctrl key, and then click the row selector for each field.
- Click the Primary Key button on the Table Design toolbar.

According to Barbara's design, you need to specify OrderNum as the primary key for the Order table.

To specify OrderNum as the primary key:

1. Position the pointer on the row selector for the OrderNum field until the pointer changes to ➡ . See Figure 2-12.

Figure 2-12 ◀
Specifying
OrderNum as
the primary key

pointer ————

row selector ————

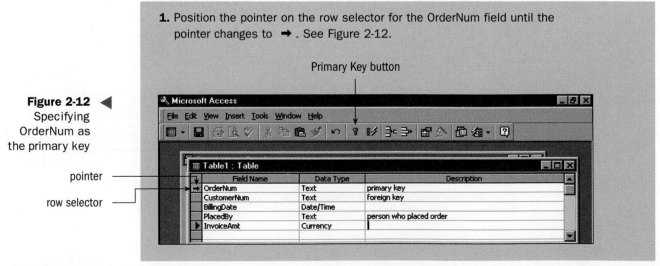

2. Click the mouse button. The entire first row of the Table Design grid is highlighted.

3. Click the **Primary Key** button 🔑 on the Table Design toolbar, and then click to the right of InvoiceAmt in the fifth row's Field Name text box to deselect the first row. A key symbol appears in the row selector for the first row, indicating that the OrderNum field is the table's primary key. See Figure 2-13.

Figure 2-13 ◀
OrderNum
selected as the
primary key

key symbol indicating
the primary key

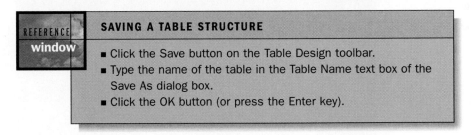

Field Name	Data Type	Description
OrderNum	Text	primary key
CustomerNum	Text	foreign key
BillingDate	Date/Time	
PlacedBy	Text	person who placed order
InvoiceAmt	Currency	

You've defined the fields for the Order table and specified its primary key, so you can now save the table structure.

Saving the Table Structure

The last step in creating a table is to name the table and save the table's structure on disk. Once the table is saved, you can use it to enter data in the table.

> **REFERENCE window**
>
> **SAVING A TABLE STRUCTURE**
>
> - Click the Save button on the Table Design toolbar.
> - Type the name of the table in the Table Name text box of the Save As dialog box.
> - Click the OK button (or press the Enter key).

You need to save the table you've defined as "Order."

To name and save the Order table:

1. Click the **Save** button 💾 on the Table Design toolbar. The Save As dialog box opens.

2. Type **Order** in the Table Name text box, and then press the **Enter** key. Access saves the table with the name Order in the Restaurant database on your Student Disk. Notice that Order appears instead of Table1 in the Table window title bar.

Next, Barbara asks you to add two records, shown in Figure 2-14, to the Order table. These two records contain data for orders that were recently placed with Valle Coffee.

Figure 2-14 ◀
Records to be
added to the
Order table

OrderNum	CustomerNum	BillingDate	PlacedBy	InvoiceAmt
323	624	2/15/99	Isabelle Rouy	$1,986.00
201	107	1/15/99	Matt Gellman	$854.00

Adding Records to a Table

You can add records to an Access table in several ways. A table datasheet provides a simple way for you to add records. As you learned in Tutorial 1, a datasheet shows a table's contents in rows and columns, similar to a table or worksheet. Each row is a separate record in the table, and each column contains the field values for one field in the table. To view a table datasheet, you first must change from Design view to Datasheet view.

You'll switch to Datasheet view and add the two records in the Order table datasheet.

To add the records in the Order table datasheet:

1. Click the **View** button for Datasheet view 🔲 on the Table Design toolbar. The Table window opens in Datasheet view. See Figure 2-15.

Figure 2-15 ◀
Table window in
Datasheet view

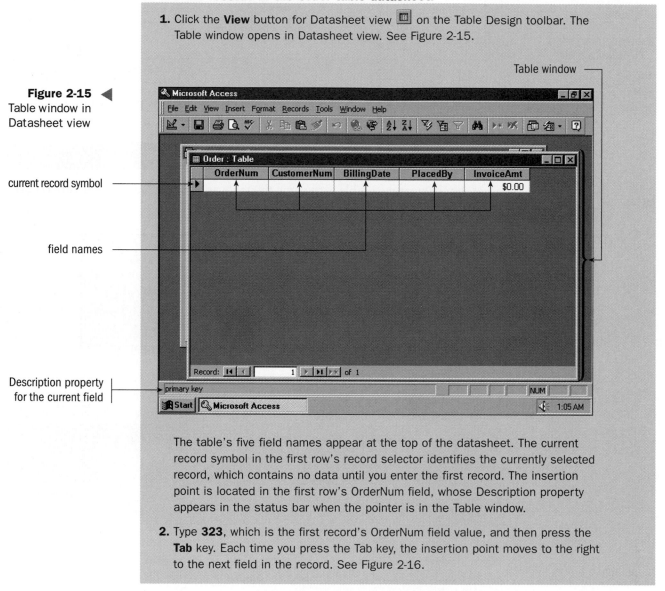

The table's five field names appear at the top of the datasheet. The current record symbol in the first row's record selector identifies the currently selected record, which contains no data until you enter the first record. The insertion point is located in the first row's OrderNum field, whose Description property appears in the status bar when the pointer is in the Table window.

2. Type **323**, which is the first record's OrderNum field value, and then press the **Tab** key. Each time you press the Tab key, the insertion point moves to the right to the next field in the record. See Figure 2-16.

Figure 2-16 ◀
Datasheet for
Order table
after entering
the first
field value

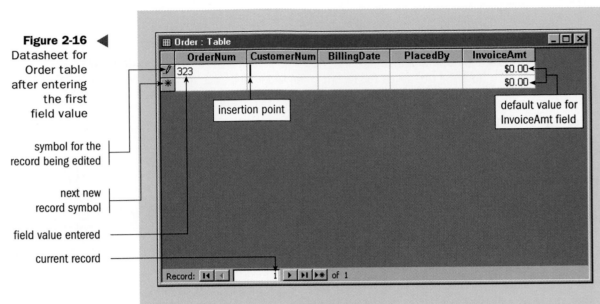

symbol for the
record being edited

next new
record symbol

field value entered

current record

TROUBLE? If you make a mistake when typing a value, use the Backspace key to delete characters to the left of the insertion point or the Delete key to delete characters to the right of the insertion point. Then type the correct text. If you want to correct a value by replacing it entirely, double-click the value to select it, and then type the correct value.

The pencil symbol in the first row's record selector indicates that the record is being edited. The star symbol in the second row's record selector identifies the second row as the next one available for a new record. The InvoiceAmt column displays "$0.00," the default value for the field.

3. Type **624** and then press the **Tab** key. The insertion point moves to the right side of the BillingDate field.

4. Type **2/15/99** and then press the **Tab** key. The insertion point moves to the PlacedBy field.

5. Type **Isabelle Rouy** and then press the **Tab** key. The insertion point moves to the InvoiceAmt field, whose field value is highlighted.

   Notice that field values for text fields are left-aligned in their boxes and field values for date/time and currency fields are right-aligned in their boxes. If the default value of $0.00 is correct for the InvoiceAmt field, you can press the Tab key to accept the value and advance to the beginning of the next record. Otherwise, type the field value for the InvoiceAmt field. You do not need to type the dollar sign, commas, or decimal point (for whole dollar amounts) because Access adds these symbols automatically for you.

6. Type **1986** and then press the **Tab** key. Access displays $1,986.00 for the InvoiceAmt field, stores the first completed record in the Order table, removes the pencil symbol from the first row's record selector, advances the insertion point to the second row's OrderNum text box, and places the current record symbol in the second row's record selector.

   Now you can enter the values for the second record.

7. Type **201** in the OrderNum field, press the **Tab** key to move to the CustomerNum field, type **107** in the CustomerNum field, and then press the **Tab** key. The insertion point moves to the right side of the BillingDate field.

8. Type **1/15/99** and then press the **Tab** key. The insertion point moves to the PlacedBy field.

9. Type **Matt Gellman** and then press the **Tab** key. The value in the InvoiceAmt field is now highlighted.

10. Type **854** and then press the **Tab** key. Access changes the InvoiceAmt field value to $854.00, saves the record in the Order table, and moves the insertion point to the beginning of the third row. See Figure 2-17.

Figure 2-17 ◀
Order table
datasheet after
entering the
second record

two added records ─

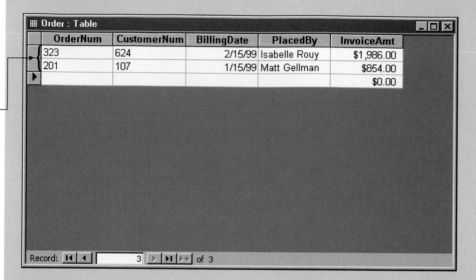

OrderNum	CustomerNum	BillingDate	PlacedBy	InvoiceAmt
323	624	2/15/99	Isabelle Rouy	$1,986.00
201	107	1/15/99	Matt Gellman	$854.00
				$0.00

Record: 3 of 3

Notice that "Record 3 of 3" appears around the navigation buttons even though the table contains only two records. Access is anticipating that you will enter a new record, which would be the third of three records in the table. If you move the insertion point to the second record, the display would change to "Record 2 of 2."

Even though the Order table contains only two records, Barbara asks you to print the table datasheet so that she can bring it with her to a staff meeting. She wants to show the table design to her staff members to make sure that it will meet their needs for tracking order data.

You'll use the Print button on the Table Datasheet toolbar to print one copy of the Order table with the current settings.

To print the Order table:

1. Click the **Print** button 🖨 on the Table Datasheet toolbar.

Notice that the two records are currently listed in the order in which you entered them. However, once you close the table or change to another view, and then redisplay the table datasheet, the records will be listed in primary key order by the values in the OrderNum field.

You have created the Order table in the Restaurant database and added two records to the table, which Access saved automatically to the database on your Student Disk.

Saving a Database

Notice the Save button on the Table Datasheet toolbar. This Save button, unlike the Save buttons in other Windows programs, does not save the active document (database) to your disk. Instead, you use the Save button to save the design of a table, query, form, or report, or to save datasheet format changes. Access does not have a button or option you can use to save the active database.

Access saves the active database to your disk automatically, both on a periodic basis and whenever you close the database. This means that if your database is stored on a disk in drive A or drive B, you should never remove the disk while the database file is open. If you do remove the disk, Access will encounter problems when it tries to save the database; this might damage the database.

Quick Check

1. What guidelines should you follow when you design a database?

2. What is the purpose of the data type property for a field?

3. For which two types of fields do you assign a field size?

4. Why did you define the OrderNum field as a text field instead of a number field?

5. A(n) _____ value, which results when you do not enter a value for a field, is not permitted for a primary key.

6. What does a pencil symbol in a datasheet's row selector represent? A star symbol?

The Order table is now complete. In Session 2.2, you'll continue to work with the Order table by modifying its structure and entering and maintaining data in the table.

SESSION 2.2

In this session you will modify the structure of a table by deleting, moving, and adding fields and changing field properties; copy records from another Access database; and update a database by deleting and changing records.

Modifying the Structure of an Access Table

Even a well-designed table might need to be modified. For example, the government at all levels and the competition place demands on a company to track more data and to modify the data it already tracks. Access allows you to modify a table's structure in Design view: you can add and delete fields, change the order of fields, and change the properties of the fields.

After meeting with her staff members and reviewing the structure of the Order table and the format of the field values in the datasheet, Barbara has several changes she wants you to make to the table. First, she has decided that it's not necessary to keep track of the name of the person who placed a particular order, so she wants you to delete the PlacedBy field. Also, she thinks that the InvoiceAmt field should remain a currency field, but she wants the dollar signs removed from the displayed field values in the datasheet. She also wants the BillingDate field moved to the end of the table. Finally, she wants you to add a yes/no field, named Paid, to the table to indicate whether the invoice has been paid for the order. The Paid field will be inserted between the CustomerNum and InvoiceAmt fields. Figure 2-18 shows Barbara's modified design for the Order table.

Figure 2-18 ◀
Modified design for the Order table

Field Name	Data Type	Field Size	Description
OrderNum	Text	3	primary key
CustomerNum	Text	3	foreign key
Paid	Yes/No		
InvoiceAmt	Currency		
BillingDate	Date/Time		

You'll begin modifying the table by deleting the PlacedBy field.

Deleting a Field

After you've defined a table structure and added records to the table, you can delete a field from the table structure. When you delete a field, you also delete all the values for the field from the table. Therefore, you should make sure that you need to delete a field and that you delete the correct field.

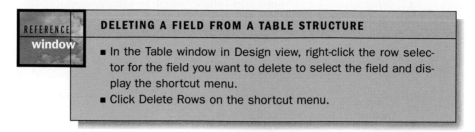

REFERENCE window	DELETING A FIELD FROM A TABLE STRUCTURE
	■ In the Table window in Design view, right-click the row selector for the field you want to delete to select the field and display the shortcut menu.
	■ Click Delete Rows on the shortcut menu.

You need to delete the PlacedBy field from the Order table structure.

To delete the PlacedBy field:

1. If you took a break after the previous session, make sure that Access is running and that the Order table of the Restaurant database is open.

2. Click the **View** button for Design view 🔍 on the Table Datasheet toolbar. The Table window for the Order table opens in Design view.

3. Position the pointer on the row selector for the PlacedBy field until the pointer changes to ➡ .

4. Right-click to select the entire row for the field and display the shortcut menu, and then click **Delete Rows**.

   A dialog box opens asking you to confirm the deletion.

5. Click the **Yes** button to close the dialog box and to delete the field and its values from the table. See Figure 2-19.

Figure 2-19 ◀
Table structure
after deleting
PlacedBy field

field deleted here ——

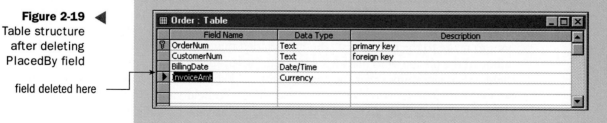

You have deleted the PlacedBy field in the Table window, but the change doesn't take place in the table on disk until you save the table structure. Because you have other modifications to make to the table, you'll wait until you finish them all before saving the modified table structure to disk.

Moving a Field

To move a field, you use the mouse to drag it to a new location in the Table window in Design view. Your next modification to the Order table structure is to move the BillingDate field to the end of the table, as Barbara requested.

To move the BillingDate field:

1. Click the **row selector** for the BillingDate field to select the entire row.

2. Place the pointer in the row selector for the BillingDate field, click the pointer
   ⬎ , and then drag the pointer ⬎ to the row selector below the InvoiceAmt row
   selector. See Figure 2-20.

Figure 2-20 ◀
Moving a field
in the table
structure

selected field

position the move
pointer in this
row selector

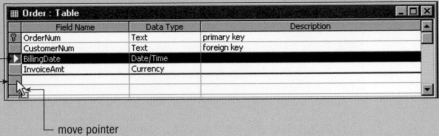

move pointer

3. Release the mouse button. Access moves the BillingDate field below the
   InvoiceAmt field in the table structure.

   TROUBLE? If the BillingDate field did not move, repeat Steps 1 through 3, making sure you firmly hold down the mouse button during the drag operation.

Adding a Field

Next, you need to add the Paid field to the table structure between the CustomerNum and
InvoiceAmt fields. To add a new field between existing fields, you must insert a row. You
begin by selecting the field that will be below the new field you want to insert.

ADDING A FIELD BETWEEN TWO EXISTING FIELDS

- In the Table window in Design view, right-click the row selector for the row above which you want to add a new field to
  select the field and display the shortcut menu.
- Click Insert Rows on the shortcut menu.
- Define the new field by entering the field name, data type,
  description (optional), and any property specifications.

To add the Paid field to the Order table:

1. Right-click the **row selector** for the InvoiceAmt field to select this field and
   display the shortcut menu, and then click **Insert Rows**. Access adds a new,
   blank row between the CustomerNum and InvoiceAmt fields. See Figure 2-21.

Figure 2-21 ◀
After inserting
a row in the
table structure

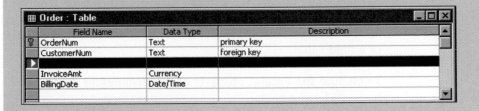

You'll define the Paid field in the new row for the Order table. Access will add this new field to the Order table structure between the CustomerNum and InvoiceAmt fields.

2. Click the **Field Name** text box for the new row, type **Paid**, and then press the **Tab** key.

The Paid field will be a yes/no field that will specify whether an invoice has been paid.

3. Type **y**. Access completes the data type as "yes/No."

4. Press the **Tab** key to select the yes/no data type and move to the Description text box.

Notice that Access changes the value in the Data Type text box from "yes/No" to "Yes/No." Barbara wants the Paid field to have a Default Value property value of "no." When you select or enter a value for a property, you *set* the property.

5. In the Field Properties section, click the **Default Value** text box, type **no**, and then click the **Description** text box for the Paid field. Notice that Access changes the Default Value property value from "no" to "No." See Figure 2-22.

Figure 2-22 ◀
Paid field
added to the
Order table

new field ———

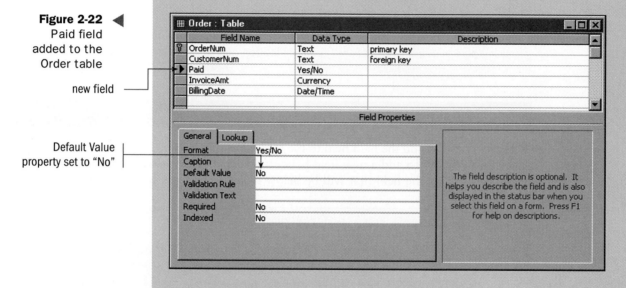

Default Value
property set to "No"

Because its field name clearly indicates its purpose, you do not need to enter a description for the Paid field.

You've completed adding the Paid field to the Order table in Design view. As with the other changes you've made, however, the Paid field is not added to the Order table in the Restaurant database until you save the changes to the table structure.

Changing Field Properties

Barbara's last modification to the table structure is to remove the dollar signs from the InvoiceAmt field values displayed in the datasheet, because repeated dollar signs are unnecessary and clutter the datasheet. You use the **Format property** to control the display of a field value.

To change the Format property of the InvoiceAmt field:

1. Click the **Description** text box for the InvoiceAmt field. The InvoiceAmt field is now the current field.

2. Click the **Format** text box in the Field Properties section, and then click the **Format** list arrow to display the Format list box. See Figure 2-23.

Figure 2-23 ◄
Format list box

Format property
options

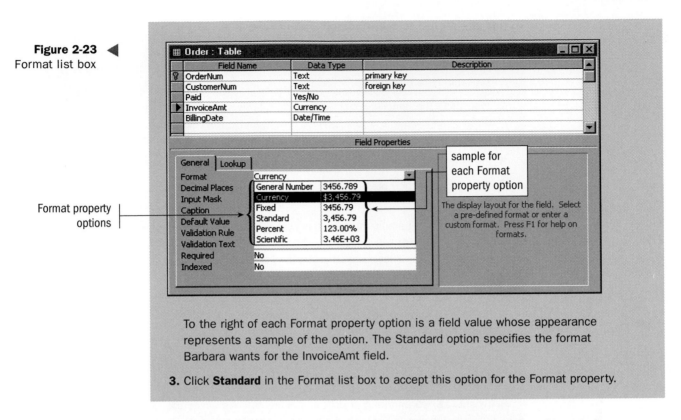

To the right of each Format property option is a field value whose appearance represents a sample of the option. The Standard option specifies the format Barbara wants for the InvoiceAmt field.

3. Click **Standard** in the Format list box to accept this option for the Format property.

Barbara wants you to add a third record to the Order table datasheet. Before you can add the record, you must save the modified table structure, and then switch to the Order table datasheet.

To save the modified table structure, and then switch to the datasheet:

1. Click the **Save** button 🖫 on the Table Design toolbar. The modified table structure for the Order table is stored in the Restaurant database.

2. Click the **View** button for Datasheet view 🏢 on the Table Design toolbar. The Order table datasheet opens. See Figure 2-24.

Figure 2-24 ◄
Datasheet for
the modified
Order table

records in primary
key order

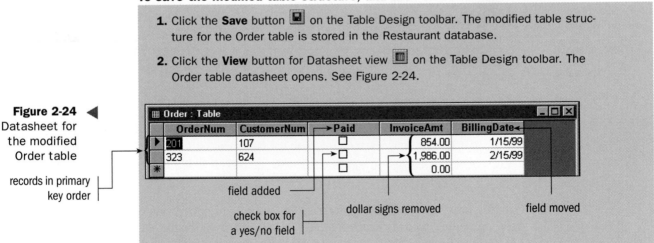

field added

check box for
a yes/no field

dollar signs removed

field moved

Notice that the PlacedBy field no longer appears in the datasheet, the BillingDate field is now the rightmost column, the InvoiceAmt field values do not contain dollar signs, and the Paid field appears between the CustomerNum and InvoiceAmt fields. The Paid column contains check boxes to represent the yes/no field values. Empty check boxes signify "No," which is the default value you assigned to the Paid field. A "Yes" value is indicated by a check mark in the check box. Also notice that the records appear in ascending order based on the value in the OrderNum field, the Order table's primary key, even though you did not enter the records in this order.

Barbara asks you to add a third record to the table. This record is for an order that has been paid.

To add the record to the modified Order table:

1. Click the **New Record** button ▶* on the Table Datasheet toolbar. The insertion point is located in the OrderNum field for the third row, which is the next row available for a new record.

2. Type **211**. The pencil symbol appears in the row selector for the third row, and the star appears in the row selector for the fourth row. Recall that these symbols represent a record being edited and the next available record, respectively.

3. Press the **Tab** key. The insertion point moves to the CustomerNum field.

4. Type **201** and then press the **Tab** key. The insertion point moves to the Paid field.

   Recall that the default value for this field is "No," which means the check box is initially empty. For yes/no fields with check boxes, you press the Tab key to leave the check box unchecked; you press the spacebar or click the check box to add or remove a check mark in the check box. Because the invoice for this order has been paid, you need to insert a check mark in the check box.

5. Press the **spacebar**. A check mark appears in the check box.

6. Press the **Tab** key. The value in the InvoiceAmt field is now highlighted.

7. Type **703.5** and then press the **Tab** key. The insertion point moves to the BillingDate field.

8. Type **1/15/99** and then press the **Tab** key. Access saves the record in the Order table and moves the insertion point to the beginning of the fourth row. See Figure 2-25.

Figure 2-25 ◀
Order table
datasheet
with third
record added

record added ───

"Yes" value ───

"No" values ───

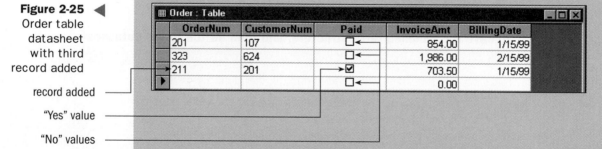

As you add records, Access places them at the end of the datasheet. If you switch to Design view then return to the datasheet or if you close the table then open the datasheet, Access will display the records in primary key sequence.

You have modified the Order table structure and added one record. Instead of typing the remaining records in the Order table, Barbara suggests that you copy them from a table that already exists in another database, and then paste them into the Order table.

Copying Records from Another Access Database

You can copy and paste records from a table in the same database or in a different database, but only if the tables have the same table structure. Barbara's Valle database in the Tutorial folder on your Student Disk has a table named Restaurant Order, which has the same table structure as the Order table. The records in the Restaurant Order table are the records Barbara wants you to copy into the Order table.

Other programs, such as Microsoft Word and Microsoft Excel, allow you to have two or more documents open at a time. However, you can have only one Access database open at a time. Therefore, you need to close the Restaurant database, open the Restaurant Order table in the Valle database, select and copy the table records, close the Valle database, reopen the Order table in the Restaurant database, and then paste the copied records.

To copy the records from the Restaurant Order table:

1. Click the **Close** button ⊠ on the Table window title bar to close the Order table, and then click the **Close** button ⊠ on the Database window title bar to close the Restaurant database.

2. Click the **Open Database** button 🖻 on the Database toolbar. The Open dialog box opens.

3. If necessary, display the list of files on your Student Disk, and then open the **Tutorial** folder.

4. Open the file named **Valle**. The Database window opens, showing the tables for the Valle database.

   Notice that the Valle database contains two tables: the Restaurant Customer table and the Restaurant Order table. The Restaurant Order table contains the records you need to copy.

5. Click **Restaurant Order** in the Tables list box, and then click the **Open** button. The datasheet for the Restaurant Order table opens. See Figure 2-26. Note that this table contains a total of 102 records.

Figure 2-26 ◄
Datasheet for the Valle database's Restaurant Order table

click here to select all records

OrderNum	CustomerNum	Paid	InvoiceAmt	BillingDate
200	135	☑	871.35	1/15/99
202	104	☑	1,280.50	1/15/99
203	122	☑	1,190.00	1/15/99
204	123	☑	1,055.00	1/15/99
205	128	☑	654.50	1/15/99
206	129	☑	1,392.50	1/15/99
207	131	☑	1,604.50	1/15/99
208	133	☑	1,784.00	1/15/99
209	136	☐	1,106.00	1/15/99
210	163	☑	1,223.00	1/15/99
212	203	☑	1,220.50	1/15/99
213	325	☑	1,426.50	1/15/99
214	407	☐	1,070.50	1/15/99
215	741	☑	1,852.00	1/15/99
216	515	☑	1,309.50	1/15/99

Record: ⏮ ◄ [1] ► ⏭ ►* of 102

total number of records in the table

Barbara wants you to copy all the records in the Restaurant Order table. You can select all records by clicking the row selector for the field name row.

6. Click the **row selector** for the field name row (see Figure 2-26). All the records in the table are now highlighted, which means that Access has selected all of them.

7. Click the **Copy** button 🖺 on the Table Datasheet toolbar. All the records are copied to the Clipboard.

8. Click the **Close** button ⊠ on the Table window title bar. A dialog box opens asking if you want to save the data you copied on the Clipboard.

9. Click the **Yes** button in the dialog box. The dialog box closes and then the table closes.

10. Click the **Close** button ⊠ on the Database window title bar to close the Valle database.

To finish copying and pasting the records, you must open the Order table and paste the copied records into the table.

To paste the copied records into the Order table:

1. Click **File** on the menu bar, and then click **Restaurant** in the list of recently opened databases. The Database window opens, showing the tables for the Restaurant database.

2. In the Tables list box, click **Order** and then click the **Open** button. The datasheet for the Order table opens.

   You must paste the records at the end of the table.

3. Click the **row selector** for row four, which is the next row available for a new record.

4. Click the **Paste** button 📋 on the Table Datasheet toolbar. All the records are pasted from the Clipboard, and a dialog box appears, asking if you are sure you want to paste the records.

5. Click the **Yes** button. The pasted records remain highlighted. See Figure 2-27. Notice that the table now contains a total of 105 records—the three original records plus the 102 copied records.

Figure 2-27 ◀
Table after copying and pasting records

original records (3)

pasted records (102)

table now contains a total of 105 records

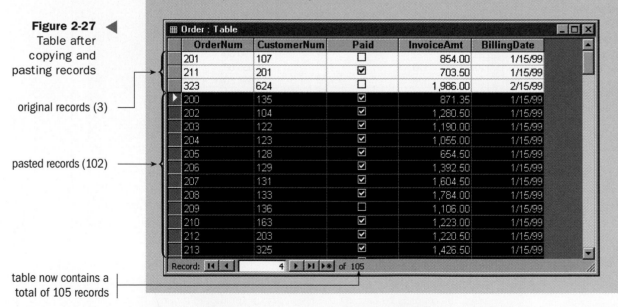

You've completed copying and pasting the records between the two tables. Now that you have all the records in the Order table, Barbara examines the records to make sure they are correct. She finds one record that she wants you to delete and another record that needs changes to its field values.

Updating a Database

Updating, or **maintaining,** a database is the process of adding, changing, and deleting records in database tables to keep them current and accurate. You've already added records to the Order table. Now Barbara wants you to delete and change records.

Deleting Records

To delete a record, you need to select the record in Datasheet view, and then delete it using the Delete Record button on the Table Datasheet toolbar or the Delete Record option on the shortcut menu.

REFERENCE window	**DELETING A RECORD**
	■ In the Table window in Datasheet view, click the row selector for the record you want to delete and then click the Delete Record button on the Table Datasheet toolbar (or right-click the row selector for the record, and then click Delete Record on the shortcut menu). ■ In the dialog box asking you to confirm the deletion, click the Yes button.

Barbara asks you to delete the record whose OrderNum is 200 because this record was entered in error; it represents an order from an office customer, not a restaurant customer, and therefore does not belong in the Restaurant database. The fourth record in the table has an OrderNum value of 200. This is the record you need to delete.

To delete the record:

1. Right-click the **row selector** for row four. Access selects the fourth record and displays the shortcut menu. See Figure 2-28.

Figure 2-28 ◀
Deleting
a record

selected record ⎯⎯⎯⎯⎯⎯

click to delete the
selected record

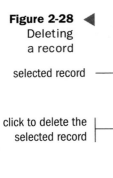

	OrderNum	CustomerNum	Paid	InvoiceAmt	BillingDate
	201	107	☐	854.00	1/15/99
	211	201	☑	703.50	1/15/99
	323	624	☐	1,986.00	2/15/99
	200	135	☑	871.35	1/15/99
		04	☑	1,280.50	1/15/99
		22	☑	1,190.00	1/15/99
		23	☑	1,055.00	1/15/99
		28	☑	654.50	1/15/99
		29	☑	1,392.50	1/15/99
		31	☑	1,604.50	1/15/99
		33	☑	1,784.00	1/15/99
	209	136	☐	1,106.00	1/15/99
	210	163	☑	1,223.00	1/15/99
	212	203	☑	1,220.50	1/15/99
	213	325	☑	1,426.50	1/15/99

Shortcut menu (overlapping the table):
- ▶* New Record
- ▶✖ Delete Record
- ✂ Cut
- 🗐 Copy
- 📋 Paste
- ‡☐ Row Height...

Order : Table window, Record: ◀◀ ◀ 4 ▶ ▶◀ ▶* of 105

2. Click **Delete Record** on the shortcut menu. Access deletes the record and opens a dialog box asking you to confirm the deletion.

TROUBLE? If you selected the wrong record for deletion, click the No button. Access ends the deletion process and redisplays the deleted record. Repeat Steps 1 and 2 to delete the correct record.

3. Click the **Yes** button to confirm the deletion and close the dialog box.

Barbara's final update to the Order table involves changes to field values in one of the records.

Changing Records

To change the field values in a record, you first must make the record the current record. Then you position the insertion point in the field value to make minor changes or select the field value to replace it entirely. In Tutorial 1, you used the mouse with the scroll bars and the navigation buttons to navigate through the records in a datasheet. You can also use keystroke combinations and the F2 key to navigate a datasheet and to select field values.

The **F2 key** is a toggle that you use to switch between navigation mode and editing mode:

- In **navigation mode**, Access selects an entire field value. If you type while you are in navigation mode, your typed entry replaces the highlighted field value.

- In **editing mode**, you can insert or delete characters in a field value based on the location of the insertion point.

The navigation mode and editing mode keystroke techniques are shown in Figure 2-29.

Figure 2-29 ◀
Navigation
mode and
editing mode
keystroke
techniques

Press	To Move the Selection in Navigation Mode	To Move the Insertion Point in Editing Mode
←	Left one field value at a time	Left one character at a time
→	Right one field value at a time	Right one character at a time
Home	Left to the first field value in the record	To the left of the first character in the field value
End	Right to the last field value in the record	To the right of the last character in the field value
↑ or ↓	Up or down one record at a time	Up or down one record at a time and switch to navigation mode
Tab or Enter	Right one field value at a time	Right one field value at a time and switch to navigation mode
Ctrl + Home	To the first field value in the first record	To the left of the first character in the field value
Ctrl + End	To the last field value in the last record	To the right of the last character in the field value

The record Barbara wants you to change has an OrderNum field value of 397. Some of the values were entered incorrectly for this record, and you need to enter the correct values.

To modify the record:

1. Make sure the OrderNum field value for the fourth record is still highlighted, indicating that the table is in navigation mode.

2. Press **Ctrl + End**. Access displays records from the end of the table and selects the last field value in the last record. This field value is for the BillingDate field.

3. Press the **Home** key. The first field value in the record is now selected. This field value is for the OrderNum field.

4. Press the ↑ key. The OrderNum field value for the previous record is selected. This is the record you need to change.

Barbara wants you to change these field values in the record: OrderNum to 398, CustomerNum to 165, Paid to "Yes" (checked), and InvoiceAmt to 1426.50. The BillingDate does not need to be changed.

5. Type **398**, press the **Tab** key, type **165**, press the **Tab** key, press the **spacebar** to insert a check mark in the Paid check box, press the **Tab** key, and then type **1426.5**. This completes the changes to the record.

6. Press the ↓ key to save the changes to the record and make the next record the current record. See Figure 2-30.

Figure 2-30 ◄
Table after
changing field
values in
a record

field values changed ——

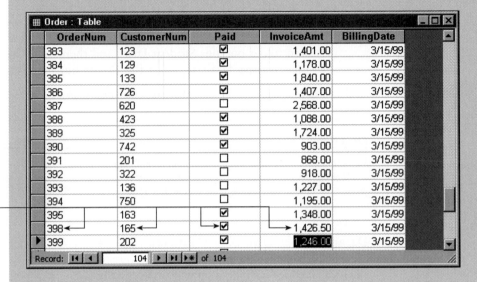

You've completed all of Barbara's updates to the Order table. Barbara asks you to print just the first page of data from the Order table datasheet so that she can show the revised table structure to her staff members. After you print the page, you can exit Access.

To print the first page of Order table data, and then exit Access:

1. Click **File** on the menu bar, and then click **Print** to display the Print dialog box.

2. In the Print Range section, click the **Pages** option button, type **1** in the From text box, press the **Tab** key, and then type **1** in the To text box.

3. Click the **OK** button to print the first page of data.

Now you can exit Access.

4. Click the **Close** button ☒ on the Access window title bar to close the Order table and the Restaurant database and to exit Access.

Quick Check

1 What is the effect of deleting a field from a table structure?

2 How do you insert a field between existing fields in a table structure?

3 A field with the _____ data type can appear in the table datasheet as a check box.

4 Which property do you use to control the display appearance of a field value?

5 Why must you close an open database when you want to copy records to it from a table in another database?

6 What is the difference between navigation mode and editing mode?

Barbara and her staff members approve of the revised table structure for the Order table. They are confident that the table will allow them to easily track order data for Valle Coffee's restaurant customers.

Tutorial Assignments

Barbara needs a database to track the coffee products offered by Valle Coffee. She asks you to create the database by completing the following:

1. Make sure your Student Disk is in the disk drive, and then start Access.

2. In the initial Access dialog box, click the Blank Database option button, and then click the OK button. In the File New Database dialog box, select the TAssign folder on your Student Disk, and then enter the filename Valle Products for the database. Click the Create button to create the new database.

3. Create a table using the table design shown in Figure 2-31.

Figure 2-31 ◀

Field Name	Data Type	Description	Field Size	Other Properties
ProductCode	Text	primary key	4	
CoffeeCode	Text	foreign key	4	
Price	Currency	price for this product		Format: Fixed Decimal Places: 2
Decaf	Text	D if decaf, Null if regular	1	Default Value: D
BackOrdered	Yes/No	back-ordered from supplier?		

4. Specify ProductCode as the primary key, and then save the table as Product.

5. Add the product records shown in Figure 2-32 to the Product table.

Figure 2-32 ◀

ProductCode	CoffeeCode	Price	Decaf	BackOrdered
2316	JRUM	8.99		Yes
9754	HAZL	40.00	D	No
9309	COCO	9.99	D	No

6. Make the following changes to the structure of the Product table:
   a. Add a new field between the CoffeeCode and Price fields, using these properties:
   Field Name: WeightCode
   Data Type: Text
   Description: foreign key
   Field Size: 1
   b. Move the BackOrdered field so that it appears between the WeightCode and Price fields.
   c. Save the revised table structure.

7. Use the Product datasheet to update the database as follows:
   a. Enter these WeightCode values for the three records: A for ProductCode 2316, A for ProductCode 9309, and E for ProductCode 9754.

b. Add a record to the Product datasheet with these field values:

ProductCode: 9729
CoffeeCode: COLS
WeightCode: E
BackOrdered: No
Price: 37.50
Decaf: D

8. Barbara created a database with her name as the database name. The Coffee Product table in that database has the same format as the Product table you created. Copy all the records from the Coffee Product table in the Barbara database (located in the TAssign folder on your Student Disk) to the end of your Product table.

9. Close the Product table, and then reopen it so that the records are displayed in primary key order by ProductCode. Then delete the record with the ProductCode 2333 from the Product table.

10. Delete the BackOrdered field from the Product table structure.

11. Use the Access Help system to learn how to resize datasheet columns to fit the data, and then resize all columns in the datasheet for the Product table so that each column fits its data. Scroll the datasheet to make sure all field values are fully displayed. For any field values that are not fully displayed, make sure the field values are visible on the screen, and then resize the appropriate columns again.

12. Print the first page of data from the Product table datasheet, and then save and close the table.

13. Create a table named Weight based on the data shown in Figure 2-33.

Figure 2-33 ◀

WeightCode	Weight/Size
A	1 lb pkg
B	6 lb case
C	24 ct 1.5 oz pkg
D	44 ct 1.25 oz pkg
E	44 ct 1.5 oz pkg
F	88 ct 1.25 oz pkg
G	88 ct 1.5 oz pkg

a. Select the Datasheet View option in the New Table dialog box.
b. Enter the seven records shown in Figure 2-33. (Do *not* enter the field names at this point.)
c. Switch to Design view, supply the table name, and then answer No if asked if you want to create a primary key.
d. Type the following field names and set the following properties:
   WeightCode
   Description: primary key
   Field Size: 1

   Weight/Size
   Description: weight in pounds or size in packages
                   (number and weight) per case
   Field Size: 17
e. Specify the primary key, save the table structure changes, and then switch back to Datasheet view. If you receive any warning messages, answer Yes to continue.

f. Resize both datasheet columns to fit the data (use Access Help to learn how to resize datasheet columns, if necessary); then save, print, and close the datasheet.

EXPLORE

14. Create a table named Coffee using the Import Table Wizard. The table you need to import is named Coffee.dbf and is located in the TAssign folder on your Student Disk. This table has a dBASE 5 file type. (You'll need to change the entry in the Files of type list box to display the file in the list.) After importing the table, complete the following:
   a. Change all field names to use the Valle Coffee convention of uppercase and lowercase letters, and then enter the following Description property values:
   CoffeeCode: primary key
   Decaf: Is decaf available for this coffee?
   b. Change the Format property of the Decaf field to Yes/No.
   c. Specify the primary key, and then save the table structure changes.
   d. Switch to Datasheet view, and then resize all columns in the datasheet to fit the data. (Use Access Help to learn how to resize datasheet columns, if necessary.) Be sure to scroll through the table to make sure that all field values are fully displayed.
   e. Save, print, and then close the datasheet. Close the Valle Products database.

Case Problems

1. Ashbrook Mall Information Desk Sam Bullard, the director of the Mall Operations Office at Ashbrook Mall, uses the MallJobs database to maintain information about current job openings at stores in the mall. Sam asks you to help him maintain the database by completing the following:

1. Make sure your Student Disk is in the disk drive.

2. Start Access and open the MallJobs database located in the Cases folder on your Student Disk.

3. Create a table using the table design shown in Figure 2-34.

Figure 2-34 ◄

Field Name	Data Type	Description	Field Size
Job	Text	primary key	5
Store	Text	foreign key	3
Hours/Week	Text		20
Position	Text		35
ExperienceReq	Yes/No		

4. Specify Job as the primary key, and then save the table as Job.

5. Add the job records shown in Figure 2-35 to the Job table.

Figure 2-35 ◄

Job	Store	Hours/Week	Position	ExperienceReq
10037	WT	negotiable	Salesclerk	No
10053	BR	14-24	Server Assistant	No
10022	JP	35-45	Assistant Manager	Yes

6. Sam created a database named Openings that contains a table with job data named Current Jobs. The Job table you created has the same format as the Current Jobs table. Copy all the records from the Current Jobs table in the Openings database (located in the Cases folder on your Student Disk) to the end of your Job table.

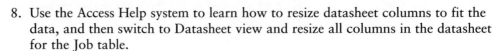

7. Modify the structure of the Job table by completing the following:
   a. Delete the ExperienceReq field.
   b. Move the Hours/Week field so that it follows the Position field.

8. Use the Access Help system to learn how to resize datasheet columns to fit the data, and then switch to Datasheet view and resize all columns in the datasheet for the Job table.

9. Use the Job datasheet to update the database as follows:
   a. For Job 10046, change the Position value to Clerk, and change the Hours/Week value to 20-30.
   b. Add a record to the Job datasheet with the following field values:
      Job: 10034
      Store: JP
      Position: Salesclerk
      Hours/Week: negotiable
   c. Delete the record for Job 10029.

10. Switch to Design view, and then switch back to Datasheet view so that the records are displayed in primary key sequence by Job.

11. Print the Job table datasheet, and then save and close the table. Close the MallJobs database.

2. Professional Litigation User Services Raj Jawahir is responsible for tracking the daily payments received from PLUS clients. You'll help him maintain the Payments database by completing the following:

1. Make sure your Student Disk is in the disk drive.

2. Start Access and open the Payments database located in the Cases folder on your Student Disk.

3. Create a table named Payment using the table design shown in Figure 2-36.

Figure 2-36 ◀

Field Name	Data Type	Description	Field Size	Other Properties
Payment#	Text	primary key	5	
Firm#	Text	foreign key	4	
DatePaid	Date/Time			Format: Medium Date
AmtPaid	Currency			Format: Standard
				Decimal Places: 2
				Default Value: 0

4. Add the payment records shown in Figure 2-37 to the Payment table.

Figure 2-37 ◀

Payment#	Firm#	DatePaid	AmtPaid
10031	1147	6/3/99	2435.00
10002	1100	6/1/99	1300.00
10015	1142	6/1/99	2000.00

5. Modify the structure of the Payment table by completing the following:
   a. Add a new field between the Payment# and Firm# fields, using these properties:
      Field Name: Deposit#
      Data Type: Text
      Field Size: 3
   b. Move the DatePaid field so that it follows the AmtPaid field.

6. Use the Payment datasheet to update the database as follows:
   a. Enter these Deposit# values for the three records: 100 for Payment# 10002, 101 for Payment# 10015, and 103 for Payment# 10031.
   b. Add a record to the Payment datasheet with these field values:
      Payment#:   10105
      Deposit#:   117
      Firm#:   1103
      AmtPaid: 2,500.00
      DatePaid: 6/20/99

7. Raj created a database named PlusPays that contains recent payments in the Payment Records table. The Payment table you created has the same format as the Payment Records table. Copy all the records from the Payment Records table in the PlusPays database (located in the Cases folder on your Student Disk) to the end of your Payment table.

8. Use the Access Help system to learn how to resize datasheet columns to fit the data, and then resize all columns in the datasheet for the Payment table.

9. For Payment# 10002, change the AmtPaid value to 1100.00.

10. Delete the record for Payment# 10101.

11. Print the first page of data from the Payment table datasheet, and then save and close the table. Close the Payments database.

3. Best Friends Noah and Sheila Warnick continue to track information about participants in the Walk-A-Thons held to benefit Best Friends. Help them maintain the Walks database by completing the following:

1. Make sure your Student Disk is in the disk drive.

2. Start Access and open the Walks database located in the Cases folder on your Student Disk.

3. Create a table named Pledge using the Import Table Wizard. The table you need to import is named Pledge.dbf and is located in the Cases folder on your Student Disk. This table has a Microsoft FoxPro file type. (You'll need to change the entry in the Files of type list box to display the file in the list. Make sure you choose the Microsoft FoxPro file type, not the Microsoft FoxPro 3.0 file type.) After importing the table, complete the following:
   a. Change all field names to use uppercase and lowercase letters, as appropriate, and then enter the following Description property values:
      PledgeNo: primary key
      WalkerID: foreign key
      PerMile: amount pledged per mile
   b. Specify the primary key, and then save the table structure changes.
   c. Switch to Datasheet view, and then resize all columns in the datasheet to fit the data. (Use Access Help to learn how to resize datasheet columns, if necessary.)

4. Modify the structure of the Pledge table by completing the following:
   a. Add a new field between the PaidAmt and PerMile fields, using these properties:
      Field Name: DatePaid
      Data Type: Date/Time
      Format: Medium Date
   b. Change the Data Type of both the PledgeAmt field and the PaidAmt field to Currency. For each of these fields, choose the Fixed format.

5. Use the Pledge datasheet to update the database as follows:
   a. Enter these DatePaid values for the five records: 9/15/99 for PledgeNo 1, 9/1/99 for PledgeNo 2, 8/27/99 for PledgeNo 3, 9/20/99 for PledgeNo 4, and 8/30/99 for PledgeNo 5. Resize the DataPaid column to fit the data.
   b. Add a record to the Pledge datasheet with these field values:
PledgeNo:	6
Pledger:	Fernando Carazana
WalkerID:	138
PledgeAmt:	25
PaidAmt:	25
DatePaid:	9/18/99
PerMile:	0
   c. Enter the value 183 in the WalkerID field for PledgeNo 1.
   d. Change both the PledgeAmt value and the PaidAmt value for PledgeNo 3 to 10.00.
   e. Change the WalkerID value for PledgeNo 5 to 187.

6. Print the Pledge table datasheet, and then save and close the table. Close the Walks database.

4. Lopez Lexus Dealerships Maria and Hector Lopez use the Lexus database to track the car inventory in the chain of Lexus dealerships they own. You'll help them maintain the Lexus database by completing the following:

1. Make sure your Student Disk is in the disk drive.

2. Start Access and open the Lexus database located in the Cases folder on your Student Disk.

3. Use the Import Spreadsheet Wizard to create a new table named Locations. The data you need to import is contained in the Lopez workbook, which is a Microsoft Excel file located in the Cases folder on your Student Disk.
   a. Select the Import Table option in the New Table dialog box.
   b. Change the entry in the Files of type list box to display the list of Excel workbook files in the Cases folder.
   c. Select the Lopez file and then click the Import button.
   d. In the Import Spreadsheet Wizard dialog boxes, choose the option for using column headings as field names; select the option for choosing your own primary key and specify LocationCode as the primary key; and enter the table name (Locations). Otherwise, accept the wizard's choices for all other options for the imported data.

4. Use the Access Help system to learn how to resize datasheet columns to fit the data, and then open the Locations table and resize all columns in the datasheet.

5. Modify the structure of the Locations table by completing the following:
   a. For the LocationCode field, enter a Description property of "primary key," change the Field Size to 2, and change the Required property to Yes.
   b. For the LocationName field, change the Field Size to 20.
   c. For the ManagerName field, change the Field Size to 30.
   d. Save the table. If you receive any warning messages about lost data or integrity rules, click the Yes button.

6. Use the Locations datasheet to update the database as follows:
    a. For LocationCode A2, change the ManagerName value to Curran, Leo.
    b. Add a record to the Locations datasheet with these field values:
    LocationCode: H2
    LocationName: Houston
    ManagerName: Cohen, Sandra
    c. Delete the record for LocationCode L2.

7. Print the Locations table datasheet, and then close the table and the Lexus database.

Querying a Database

Retrieving Information About Restaurant Customers and Their Orders

OBJECTIVES

In this tutorial you will:

- Learn how to use the Query window in Design view

- Create, run, and save queries

- Define a relationship between two tables

- Sort data in a query

- Filter data in a query

- Specify an exact match condition in a query

- Change a datasheet's appearance

- Use a comparison operator to match a range of values

- Use the And and Or logical operators

- Perform calculations in a query using calculated fields, aggregate functions, and record group calculations

Valle Coffee

CASE At a recent company meeting, Leonard Valle and other Valle Coffee employees discussed the importance of regularly monitoring the business activity of the company's restaurant customers. For example, Kim Carpenter and her marketing staff track customer activity to develop new strategies for promoting Valle Coffee products. Barbara Hennessey and her office staff need to track information about all the orders for which bills were sent out on a specific date so that they can determine whether the bills have been paid. In addition, Leonard is interested in analyzing the payment history of restaurant customers to determine which customers pay their invoices in a timely manner, which customers have higher invoice amounts, and so on. All of these informational needs can be satisfied by queries that retrieve information from the Restaurant database.

SESSION

3.1

In this session you will use the Query window in Design view to create, run, and save queries; define a one-to-many relationship between two tables; sort data with a tool-bar button and in Design view; and filter data in a query datasheet.

Introduction to Queries

As you learned in Tutorial 1, a query is a question you ask about data stored in a database. For example, Kim might create a query to find records in the Customer table for only those customers in a specific state. When you create a query, you tell Access which fields you need and what criteria Access should use to select the records.

Access provides powerful query capabilities that allow you to:

- display selected fields and records from a table

- sort records

- perform calculations

- generate data for forms, reports, and other queries

- update data in the tables in a database

- find and display data from two or more tables

Most questions about data are generalized queries in which you specify the fields and records you want Access to select. These common requests for information, such as "Which customers have unpaid bills?" or "Which type of coffee sells best in Ohio?" are called **select queries**. The answer to a select query is returned in the form of a datasheet.

More specialized, technical queries, such as finding duplicate records in a table, are best formulated through a Query Wizard. A Query Wizard prompts you for information through a set of questions and then creates the appropriate query based on your answers. In Tutorial 1, you used the Simple Query Wizard to display only some of the fields in the Customer table; Access provides other Query Wizards for more complex queries. For common, informational queries, it is easier for you to design your own query rather than use a Query Wizard.

Kim wants you to create a query to display the customer number, customer name, city, owner name, and first contact information for each record in the Customer table. She needs this information for a market analysis her staff is completing on Valle Coffee's restaurant customers. You'll open the Query window to create the query for Kim.

The Query Window

You use the Query window in Design view to create a query. In Design view you specify the data you want to view by constructing a query by example. Using **query by example (QBE)**, you give Access an example of the information you are requesting. Access then retrieves the information that precisely matches your example.

For Kim's query, you need to display data from the Customer table. You'll begin by starting Access, opening the Restaurant database, and displaying the Query window in Design view.

To start Access, open the Restaurant database, and open the Query window in Design view:

1. Place your Student Disk in the appropriate disk drive.

2. Start Access and open the Restaurant database located in the Tutorial folder on your Student Disk. The Restaurant database is displayed in the Access window.

3. Click the **Queries** tab in the Database window, and then click the **New** button. The New Query dialog box opens. See Figure 3-1.

Figure 3-1 ◄
New Query
dialog box

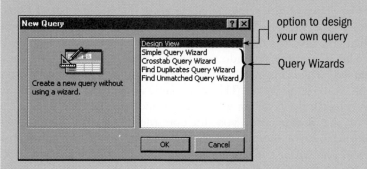

option to design
your own query

Query Wizards

You'll design your own query instead of using a Query Wizard.

4. If necessary, click **Design View** in the list box.

5. Click the **OK** button. Access opens the Show Table dialog box on top of the Query window. Notice that the title bar of the window shows that you are creating a select query.

   The query you are creating will retrieve data from the Customer table, so you need to add this table to the Select Query window.

6. Click **Customer** in the Tables list box (if necessary), click the **Add** button, and then click the **Close** button. Access places the Customer table field list in the Select Query window and closes the dialog box.

   To display more of the fields you'll be using for creating queries, you'll maximize the Select Query window.

7. Click the **Maximize** button ▢ on the Select Query window title bar. See Figure 3-2.

Query Type button
shows select query

Run button

Figure 3-2 ◄
Select Query
window in
Design view

View button for
Datasheet view

field list

design grid

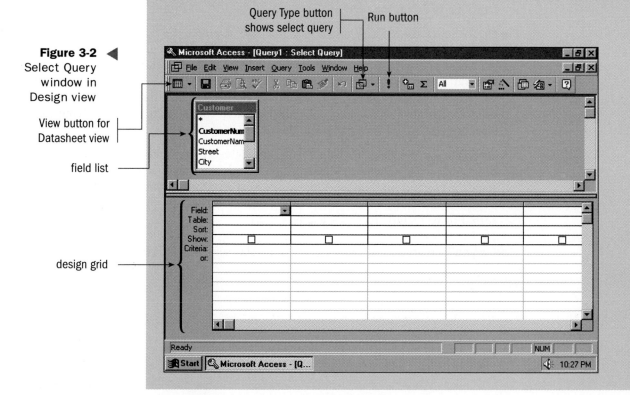

In Design view, the Select Query window contains the standard title bar, menu bar, toolbar, and status bar. On the toolbar, the Query Type button shows a select query; the icon on this button changes according to the type of query you are creating. The title bar on the Select Query window displays the query type, Select Query, and the default query name, Query1. You'll change the default query name to a more meaningful one later when you save the query.

The Select Query window in Design view contains a field list and the design grid. The **field list**, which appears in the upper-left area of the window, contains the fields for the table you are querying. The table name appears at the top of the list box, and the fields are listed in the order in which they appear in the table.

In the **design grid**, you include the fields and record selection criteria for the information you want to see. Each column in the design grid contains specifications about a field you will use in the query. You can choose a single field for your query by dragging its name from the field list to the design grid in the lower portion of the window. Alternatively, you can double-click a field name to place it in the next available column in the design grid.

When you are constructing a query, you can see the query results at any time by clicking the View button or the Run button on the Query Design toolbar. In response, Access displays the datasheet, which contains the set of fields and records that result from answering, or **running**, the query. The order of the fields in the datasheet is the same as the order of the fields in the design grid. Although the datasheet looks just like a table datasheet and appears in Datasheet view, a query datasheet is temporary and its contents are based on the criteria you establish in the design grid. In contrast, a table datasheet shows the permanent data in a table. However, you can update data while viewing a query datasheet, just as you can when working in a table datasheet or a form.

If the query you are creating includes all the fields from the specified table, you could use one of the following three methods to transfer all the fields from the field list to the design grid:

- Click and drag each field individually from the field list to the design grid. Use this method if you want the fields in your query to appear in an order that is different from the order in the field list.

- Double-click the asterisk in the field list. Access places the table name followed by a period and an asterisk (as in "Customer.*") in the design grid. This signifies that the order of the fields will be the same in the query as it is in the field list. Use this method if the query does not need to be sorted or to have conditions for the records you want to select. The advantage of using this method is that you do not need to change the query if you add or delete fields from the underlying table structure. They will all appear automatically in the query.

- Double-click the field list title bar to highlight all the fields, and then click and drag one of the highlighted fields to the design grid. Access places each field in a separate column and arranges the fields in the order in which they appear in the field list. Use this method rather than the previous one if your query needs to be sorted or to include record selection criteria.

Now you'll create and run Kim's query to display selected fields from the Customer table.

Creating and Running a Query

A table datasheet displays all the fields in the table, in the same order as they appear in the table. In contrast, a query datasheet can display selected fields from a table, and the order of the fields can be different from that of the table.

Kim wants the CustomerNum, CustomerName, City, OwnerName, and FirstContact fields to appear in the query results. You'll add each of these fields to the design grid.

To select the fields for the query, and then run the query:

1. Drag **CustomerNum** from the Customer field list to the design grid's first column Field text box, and then release the mouse button. See Figure 3-3.

Figure 3-3 ◀
Field added to
the design grid

drag field from here ——

release mouse
button here

indicates that the
field will appear
in the datasheet

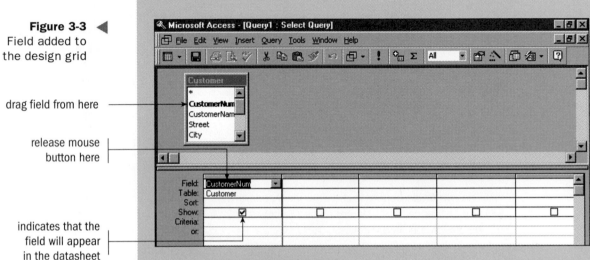

In the design grid's first column, the field name CustomerNum appears in the Field text box, the table name Customer appears in the Table text box, and the check mark in the Show check box indicates that the field will be displayed in the datasheet when you run the query. There are times when you might choose not to display a field and its values in the query results. For example, if you are creating a query to show all the customers located in Michigan, and you assign the name "Customers in Michigan" to the query, you would not need to include the State field value for each record in the query results. Even if you choose not to include a field in the display of the query results, you can still use the field as part of the query to select specific records or to specify a particular sequence for the records in the datasheet.

2. Double-click **CustomerName** in the Customer field list. Access adds this field to the second column of the design grid.

3. Scrolling the Customer field list as necessary, repeat Step 2 for the **City**, **OwnerName**, and **FirstContact** fields to add these fields to the design grid in that order.

Having selected the fields for Kim's query, you can now run the query.

4. Click the **Run** button ⏷ on the Query Design toolbar. Access runs the query and displays the results in Datasheet view. See Figure 3-4.

Figure 3-4
Datasheet
displayed
after running
the query

selected
fields displayed

38 records selected

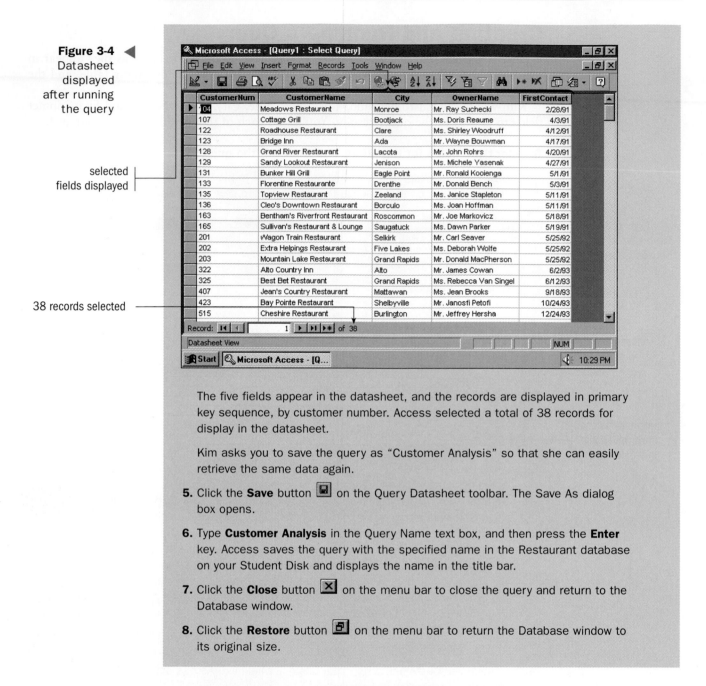

The five fields appear in the datasheet, and the records are displayed in primary key sequence, by customer number. Access selected a total of 38 records for display in the datasheet.

Kim asks you to save the query as "Customer Analysis" so that she can easily retrieve the same data again.

5. Click the **Save** button 🖫 on the Query Datasheet toolbar. The Save As dialog box opens.

6. Type **Customer Analysis** in the Query Name text box, and then press the **Enter** key. Access saves the query with the specified name in the Restaurant database on your Student Disk and displays the name in the title bar.

7. Click the **Close** button ☒ on the menu bar to close the query and return to the Database window.

8. Click the **Restore** button 🗗 on the menu bar to return the Database window to its original size.

Barbara also wants to view specific information in the Restaurant database. However, she needs to see data from both the Customer table and the Order table at the same time. To accomplish this, you need to define a relationship between the two tables.

Defining Table Relationships

One of the most powerful features of a relational database management system is its ability to define relationships between tables. You use a common field to relate one table to another. The process of relating tables is often called performing a **join**. When you join tables that have a common field, you can extract data from them as if they were one larger table. For example, you can join the Customer and Order tables by using the CustomerNum field in both tables as the common field. You then can use a query, form, or report to extract selected data from each table, even though the data is contained in two separate tables, as shown in Figure 3-5. In the Orders query shown in Figure 3-5, the OrderNum, Paid, and InvoiceAmt columns are fields from the Order table; and the CustomerName and State columns are fields from the Customer table. The joining of records is based on the common field of CustomerNum. The Customer and Order tables have a type of relationship called a one-to-many relationship.

Figure 3-5 ◀
One-to-many
relationship
and sample
query

primary table

fields from Order
table

query that joins fields
from the Customer
and Order tables

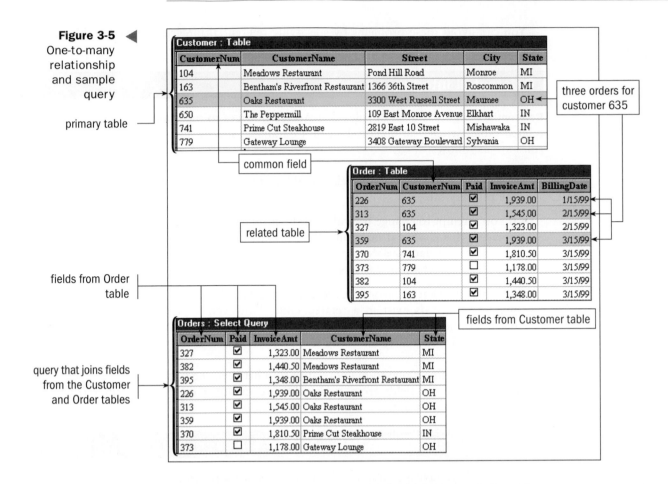

One-to-Many Relationships

A **one-to-many relationship** exists between two tables when one record in the first table matches zero, one, or many records in the second table, and when one record in the second table matches exactly one record in the first table. For example, as shown in Figure 3-5, customer 635 has three orders, customer 650 has zero orders, customers 163, 741, and 779 each have one order, and customer 104 has two orders. Every order has a single matching customer.

Access refers to the two tables that form a relationship as the primary table and the related table. The **primary table** is the "one" table in a one-to-many relationship; in Figure 3-5, the Customer table is the primary table because there is only one customer for each order. The **related table** is the "many" table; in Figure 3-5, the Order table is the related table because there can be many orders for each customer.

Because related data is stored in two tables, inconsistencies between the tables can occur. Consider the following scenarios:

- Barbara adds an order to the Order table for customer 107, Cottage Grill. This order does not have a matching record in the Customer table. The data is inconsistent, and the order record is considered to be an **orphaned** record.

- Barbara changes Oaks Restaurant from customer number 635 to 997 in the Customer table. Three orphaned records for customer 635 now exist in the Order table, and the database is inconsistent.

- Barbara deletes the record for Meadows Restaurant, customer 104, in the Customer table because this customer is no longer a Valle Coffee customer. The database is again inconsistent; two records for customer 104 in the Order table have no matching record in the Customer table.

You can avoid these problems by specifying referential integrity between tables when you define their relationships.

Referential Integrity

Referential integrity is a set of rules that Access enforces to maintain consistency between related tables when you update data in a database. Specifically, the referential integrity rules are as follows:

- When you add a record to a related table, a matching record must already exist in the primary table.

- If you attempt to change the value of the primary key in the primary table, Access prevents this change if matching records exist in a related table. However, if you choose the **cascade updates** option, Access permits the change in value to the primary key and changes the appropriate foreign key values in the related table.

- When you delete a record in the primary table, Access prevents the deletion if matching records exist in a related table. However, if you choose the **cascade deletes** option, Access deletes the record in the primary table and all records in related tables that have matching foreign key values.

Now you'll define a one-to-many relationship between the Customer and Order tables so that you can use fields from both tables to create a query that will retrieve the information Barbara wants.

Defining a Relationship Between Two Tables

When two tables have a common field, you can define a relationship between them in the Relationships window. The **Relationships window** illustrates the relationships among a database's tables. In this window you can view or change existing relationships, define new relationships between tables, and rearrange the layout of the tables.

You need to open the Relationships window and define the relationship between the Customer and Order tables. You'll define a one-to-many relationship between the two tables, with Customer as the primary table and Order as the related table, and with CustomerNum as the common field (the primary key in the Customer table and a foreign key in the Order table).

To define a one-to-many relationship between the two tables:

1. Click the **Relationships** button 🔲 on the Database toolbar. Access displays the Show Table dialog box on top of the Relationships window. See Figure 3-6.

Figure 3-6 ◄
Show Table
dialog box

add both tables

Relationships window

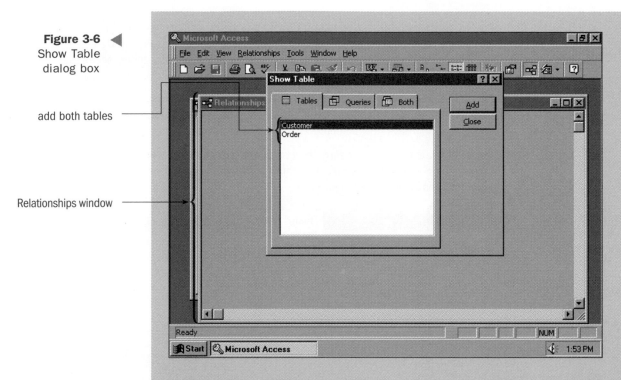

Each table participating in a relationship must be added to the Relationships window.

2. Click **Customer** (if necessary) and then click the **Add** button. The Customer table is added to the Relationships window.

3. Click **Order** and then click the **Add** button. The Order table is added to the Relationships window.

4. Click the **Close** button in the Show Table dialog box. Access closes the dialog box and reveals the entire Relationships window.

To form the relationship between the two tables, you drag the common field of CustomerNum from the primary table to the related table. Access then opens the Relationships dialog box in which you select the relationship options for the two tables.

5. Click **CustomerNum** in the Customer table list, and drag it to **CustomerNum** in the Order table list. When you release the mouse button, Access opens the Relationships dialog box. See Figure 3-7.

Figure 3-7 ◄
Relationships
dialog box

primary table

common field

referential
integrity option

cascade options

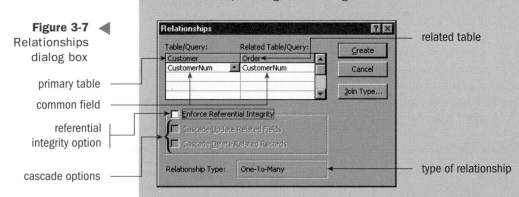

related table

type of relationship

The primary table, related table, and common field appear at the top of the dialog box. The type of relationship, one-to-many, appears at the bottom of the dialog box. When you click the Enforce Referential Integrity check box, the two cascade options become available. With the Cascade Update Related Fields option,

Access will change the appropriate foreign key values in the related table when you change a primary key value in the primary table. With the Cascade Delete Related Records option, when you delete a record in the primary table, Access will delete all records in the related table that have a matching foreign key value.

6. Click the **Enforce Referential Integrity** check box, click the **Cascade Update Related Fields** check box, and then click the **Cascade Delete Related Records** check box. You have now selected all the necessary relationship options.

7. Click the **Create** button to define the one-to-many relationship between the two tables and close the dialog box. The completed relationship appears in the Relationships window. See Figure 3-8.

Figure 3-8 ◄
Defined relationship in the Relationships window

"one" side of the relationship

join line

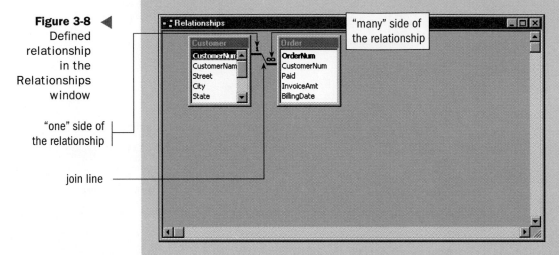

The *join line* connects the CustomerNum fields, which are common to the two tables. The common field joins the two tables, which have a one-to-many relationship. The join line is thick at both ends; this signifies that you have chosen the option to enforce referential integrity. If you do not select this option, the join line is thin at both ends. The "one" side of the relationship has the digit 1 at its end, and the "many" side of the relationship has the infinity symbol ∞ at its end. The two tables are still separate tables, but you can use the data in them as if they were one table.

8. Click the **Save** button 🖫 on the Relationship toolbar to save the layout in the Relationships window.

9. Click the **Close** button ✖ on the Relationships window title bar. Access closes the Relationships window and returns you to the Database window.

Now that you have joined the Customer and Order tables, you can create a query to produce the information Barbara wants. As part of her tracking of payments received from restaurant customers, Barbara needs a query that displays the CustomerName, City, and State fields from the Customer table and the BillingDate, InvoiceAmt, and Paid fields from the Order table.

To create, run, and save the query using the Customer and Order tables:

1. From the Queries tab in the Database window, click the **New** button to open the New Query dialog box, click **Design View** in the dialog box, and then click the **OK** button. Access opens the Show Table dialog box on top of the Query window in Design view.

You need to add both tables to the Query window.

2. Click **Customer** in the Tables list box (if necessary), click the **Add** button, click **Order**, click the **Add** button, and then click the **Close** button. Access places the

Customer and Order field lists in the Query window and closes the Show Table dialog box. Note that the one-to-many relationship that exists between the two tables is shown in the Query window.

You need to place the CustomerName, City, and State fields from the Customer field list into the design grid, and then place the BillingDate, InvoiceAmt, and Paid fields from the Order field list into the design grid.

3. Double-click **CustomerName** in the Customer field list. Access places CustomerName in the design grid's first column Field text box.

4. Repeat Step 3 to add the **City** and **State** fields from the Customer table, and then add the **BillingDate**, **InvoiceAmt**, and **Paid** fields (in that order) from the Order table, so that these fields are placed in the second through sixth columns of the design grid.

The query specifications are complete, so you can now run the query.

5. Click the **Run** button ⬚ on the Query Design toolbar. Access runs the query and displays the results in the datasheet.

6. Click the **Maximize** button ⬚ on the Query window. See Figure 3-9.

Figure 3-9 ◀
Datasheet for the query based on the Customer and Order tables

fields from the Customer table

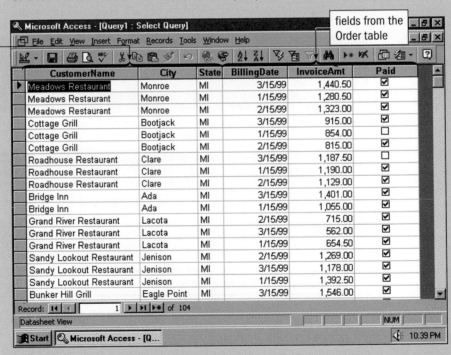

Only the six selected fields from the Customer and Order tables appear in the datasheet. The records are displayed in order according to the values in the primary key field, CustomerNum, even though this field is not included in the query datasheet.

Barbara plans on tracking the data retrieved by the query frequently, so she asks you to save the query as "Customer Orders."

7. Click the **Save** button ⬚ on the Query Datasheet toolbar. The Save As dialog box opens.

8. Type **Customer Orders** in the Query Name text box, and then press the **Enter** key. Access saves the query with the specified name and displays the name in the Query window title bar.

Barbara decides she wants the records displayed in alphabetical order by customer name. Because your query displays data in order by the field value of CustomerNum, the primary key for the Customer table, you need to sort the records by CustomerName to display the data in the order Barbara wants.

Sorting Data in a Query

Sorting is the process of rearranging records in a specified order or sequence. Often you need to sort data before displaying or printing it to meet a specific request. For example, Barbara might want to review order information arranged by the Paid field because she is interested in which orders are still unpaid. On the other hand, Leonard might want to view order information arranged by the InvoiceAmt totals for each customer because he tracks company sales.

When you sort data in a database, Access does not change the sequence of the records in the underlying tables. Only the records in the query datasheet are rearranged according to your specifications.

To sort records, you must select the **sort key**, which is the field used to determine the order of records in the datasheet. In this case, Barbara wants the data sorted by the customer name, so you need to specify the CustomerName field as the sort key. Sort keys can be text, number, date/time, currency, AutoNumber, or yes/no fields, but not memo, OLE object, or hyperlink fields. You sort records in either ascending (increasing) or descending (decreasing) order. Figure 3-10 shows the results of each type of sort for different data types.

Figure 3-10
Sorting results
for different
data types

Data Type	Ascending Sort Results	Descending Sort Results
Text	A to Z	Z to A
Number	lowest to highest numeric value	highest to lowest numeric value
Date/Time	oldest to most recent date	most recent to oldest date
Currency	lowest to highest numeric value	highest to lowest numeric value
AutoNumber	lowest to highest numeric value	highest to lowest numeric value
Yes/No	yes (check mark in check box) then no values	no then yes values

Access provides several methods for sorting data in a table or query datasheet and in a form. One method, clicking the toolbar sort buttons, lets you quickly sort the displayed records.

Using a Toolbar Button to Sort Data

The **Sort Ascending** and **Sort Descending** buttons on the toolbar allow you to sort records immediately, based on the selected field. First you select the column on which you want to base the sort, and then click the appropriate sort button on the toolbar to rearrange the records in either ascending or descending order. Unless you save the datasheet or form after you've sorted the records, the rearrangement of records is temporary.

Recall that in Tutorial 1 you used the Sort Ascending button to sort query results by the State field. You'll use this same button to sort the Customer Orders query results by the CustomerName field.

To sort the records using a toolbar sort button:

1. Click any visible CustomerName field value to establish this field as the current field.

2. Click the **Sort Ascending** button 🔼 on the Query Datasheet toolbar. Access rearranges the records in ascending order by customer name. See Figure 3-11.

Figure 3-11 ◀
Sorting records
on a single field
in a datasheet

Sort Ascending
button

Sort Descending
button

records sorted in
ascending order by
CustomerName

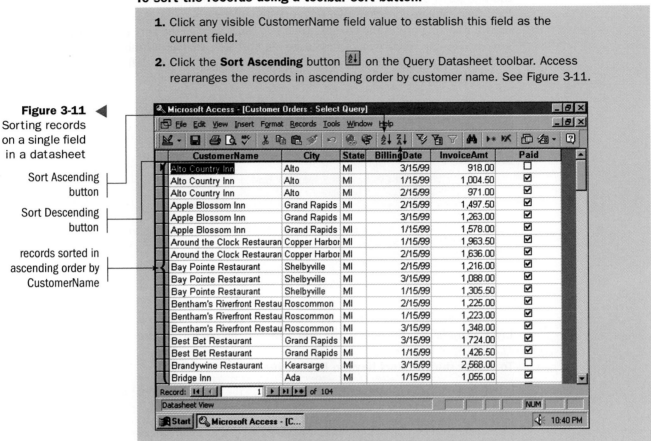

After viewing the query results, Barbara decides that she'd prefer the records to be arranged by the value in the Paid field so that she can determine more easily which invoices have been paid. She wants to view all the unpaid invoices before the paid invoices (descending order for the Paid field, which is a yes/no field); plus, she wants to display the records within each group in decreasing value of the InvoiceAmt field. To do this you need to sort using two fields.

Sorting Multiple Fields in Design View

Sort keys can be unique or nonunique. A sort key is **unique** if the value of the sort key field for each record is different. The CustomerNum field in the Customer table is an example of a unique sort key because each customer record has a different value in this field. A sort key is **nonunique** if more than one record can have the same value for the sort key field. The Paid field in the Order table is a nonunique sort key because more than one record has the same Paid value.

When the sort key is nonunique, records with the same sort key value are grouped together, but they are not in a specific order within the group. To arrange these grouped records in a specific order, you can specify a **secondary sort key**, which is a second sort key field. The first sort key field is called the **primary sort key**. Note that the primary sort key is not the same as a table's primary key field. A table has at most one primary key, which must be unique, whereas any field in a table can serve as a primary sort key.

Access lets you select up to 10 different sort keys. When you use the toolbar sort buttons, the sort key fields must be in adjacent columns in the datasheet. You highlight the columns, and Access sorts first by the first column and then by each other highlighted column in order from left to right.

Barbara wants the records sorted first by the Paid field and then by the InvoiceAmt field. Although the two fields are adjacent, they are in the wrong order. If you used a toolbar sort button, the InvoiceAmt field would be the primary sort key instead of the Paid field. When you have two or more nonadjacent sort keys or when the fields to be used for sorting are in the wrong order, you must specify the sort keys in the Query window in Design view. Access first uses the sort key that is leftmost in the design grid. Therefore, you must arrange the fields you want to sort from left to right in the design grid with the primary sort key being the leftmost sort key field.

REFERENCE window

SORTING A QUERY DATASHEET

- In the query datasheet, select the field or adjacent fields on which you want to sort.
- Click the Sort Ascending button or the Sort Descending button on the Query Datasheet toolbar.
or
- In Design view, position the fields serving as sort keys from left (primary sort key) to right, and then select the sort order for each sort key.

To achieve the results Barbara wants, you need to switch to Design view, move the InvoiceAmt field to the right of the Paid field, and then specify the sort order for the two fields.

To select the two sort keys in Design view:

1. Click the **View** button for Design view ☒ on the Query Datasheet toolbar. Access closes the window and opens the query in Design view.

   First, you'll move the InvoiceAmt field to the right of the Paid field.

2. If necessary, click the right arrow in the design grid's horizontal scroll bar to scroll to the right until both the InvoiceAmt and Paid fields are visible.

3. Position the pointer above the InvoiceAmt field name until the pointer changes to ↓ , and then click to select the field. See Figure 3-12.

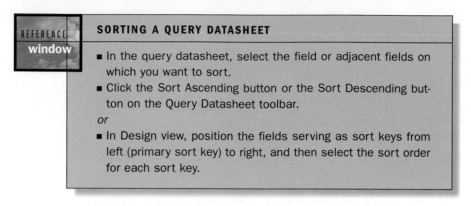

field selector

Figure 3-12 ◄
Selected
InvoiceAmt
field

entire column is highlighted

4. Position the pointer in the field selector at the top of the highlighted column, and then click and drag the pointer ⬚ to the right until the vertical line on the right of the Paid field is highlighted. See Figure 3-13.

Figure 3-13 ◄
Dragging the
field in the
design grid

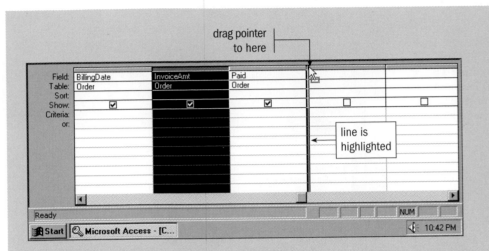

5. Release the mouse button. Access places the InvoiceAmt field to the right of the
   Paid field.

   The fields are now in the correct order for the sort. Now you need to specify a
   descending sort order for each of the two fields.

6. Click the **Paid Sort** text box, click the **Sort** list arrow, and then click **Descending**.
   You've selected a descending sort order for the Paid field, which will be the primary sort key. The Paid field is a yes/no field, and a descending sort order for
   this type of field displays all the no (unpaid) values before the yes (paid) values.

7. Click the **InvoiceAmt Sort** text box, click the **Sort** list arrow, click **Descending**,
   and then click in the Criteria text box for the InvoiceAmt field. You've selected a
   descending sort order for the InvoiceAmt field, which will be the secondary sort
   key. See Figure 3-14.

Figure 3-14 ◄
Selecting two
sort keys in
Design view

primary sort key ———————————————

secondary sort key ———————————————

Field:	BillingDate	Paid	InvoiceAmt		
Table:	Order	Order	Order		
Sort:		Descending	Descending		
Show:	☑	☑	☑	☐	☐
Criteria:					
or:					

Ready

Start Microsoft Access - [C...   10:44 PM

You have finished your query changes, so now you can run the query and then
save the modified query with the same query name.

8. Click the **Run** button 🔘 on the Query Design toolbar. Access runs the query and
   displays the query datasheet. The records appear in descending order, based on
   the values of the Paid field. Within groups of records with the same Paid field
   value, the records appear in descending order by the values of the InvoiceAmt
   field. See Figure 3-15.

Figure 3-15 ◀
Datasheet
sorted on
two fields

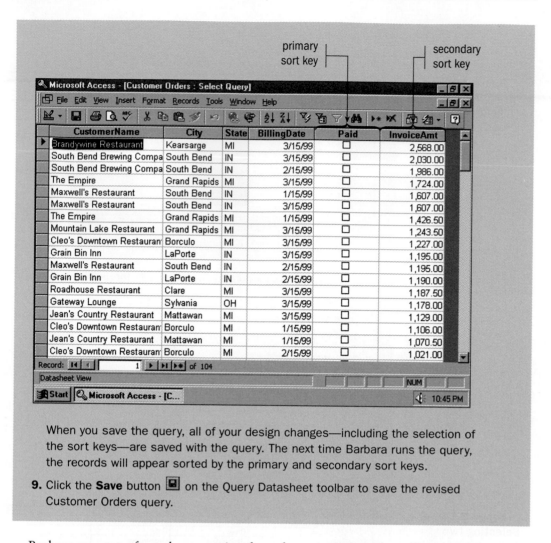

When you save the query, all of your design changes—including the selection of the sort keys—are saved with the query. The next time Barbara runs the query, the records will appear sorted by the primary and secondary sort keys.

9. Click the **Save** button 🖫 on the Query Datasheet toolbar to save the revised Customer Orders query.

Barbara wants to focus her attention for a few minutes on the orders in the datasheet that are unpaid. Because selecting only the unpaid orders is a temporary change Barbara wants in the datasheet, you do not need to switch to Design view and change the query. Instead, you can apply a filter.

Filtering Data

A **filter** is a set of restrictions you place on the records in an open datasheet or form to *temporarily* isolate a subset of the records. A filter lets you view different subsets of displayed records so you can focus on only the data you need. Unless you save a query or form with a filter applied, an applied filter is not available the next time you run the query or open the form. The simplest technique for filtering records is Filter By Selection. **Filter By Selection** lets you select all or part of a field value in a datasheet or form, and then display only those records that contain the selected value in the field.

REFERENCE window

USING FILTER BY SELECTION

- In the datasheet or form, select all or part of the field value that will be the basis for the filter.
- Click the Filter By Selection button on the toolbar.

For Barbara's request, you need to select an unchecked box in the Paid field, which represents an unpaid order, and then use Filter By Selection to display only those query records with this value.

Access

To display the records using Filter By Selection:

1. Click any check box that is unchecked in the Paid column. When you click the check box, you select the field value, but you also change the check box from unchecked to checked. Because you've changed an unpaid order to a paid order, you need to click the same check box a second time.

2. Click the same check box a second time. The field value changes back to unchecked, which is now the selected field value.

3. Click the **Filter By Selection** button on the Query Datasheet toolbar. Access displays the filtered results. Only the 25 query records that have an unchecked Paid field value appear in the datasheet; these records are the unpaid order records. Note that the status bar display and the selected Remove Filter button on the toolbar both indicate that records have been filtered. See Figure 3-16.

Filter By
Selection button

Remove Filter
button

Figure 3-16 ◀
Using Filter
By Selection

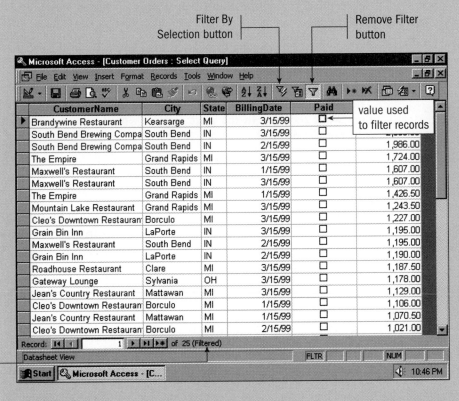

indicates records
have been filtered

Barbara asks you to print the current datasheet so that she can give the printout to a staff member who is tracking unpaid orders.

4. Click the **Print** button on the Query Datasheet toolbar. Access prints the datasheet.

Now you can redisplay all the query records by clicking the Remove Filter button; this button works as a toggle to switch between the filtered and nonfiltered displays.

5. Click the **Remove Filter** button on the Query Datasheet toolbar. Access redisplays all the records in the query datasheet.

6. Click the **Save** button on the Query Datasheet toolbar, and then click the **Close** button on the menu bar to save and close the query and return to the Database window.

7. Click the **Restore** button on the menu bar to return the Database window to its original size.

Quick Check

1. What is a select query?

2. Describe the field list and the design grid in the Query window in Design view.

3. How are a table datasheet and a query datasheet similar? How are they different?

4. The _____ is the "one" table in a one-to-many relationship, and the _____ is the "many" table in the relationship.

5. _____ is a set of rules that Access enforces to maintain consistency between related tables when you update data in a database.

6. For a date/time field, what is ascending sort order?

7. When must you define multiple sort keys in Design view instead of in the query datasheet?

8. A(n) _____ is a set of restrictions you place on the records in an open datasheet or form to temporarily isolate a subset of records.

The queries you've created will help Valle Coffee employees retrieve just the information they want to view. In the next session, you'll continue to create queries to meet their information needs.

SESSION 3.2

In this session you will specify an exact match condition in a query, change a datasheet's appearance, use a comparison operator to match a range of values, use the And and Or logical operators to define multiple selection criteria for queries, and perform calculations in queries.

Barbara wants to display customer and order information for all orders billed on 1/15/99 so she can see which orders have been paid. For this request, you need to create a query that displays selected fields from the Order and Customer tables and selected records that satisfy a condition.

Defining Record Selection Criteria for Queries

Just as you can display selected fields from a table in a query datasheet, you can display selected records. To tell Access which records you want to select, you must specify a condition as part of the query. A **condition** is a criterion, or rule, that determines which records are selected. To define a condition for a field, you place the condition in the field's Criteria text box in the design grid.

A condition usually consists of an operator, often a comparison operator, and a value. A **comparison operator** asks Access to compare the values of a database field to the condition value and to select all the records for which the relationship is true. For example, the condition >1000.00 for the InvoiceAmt field selects all records in the Order table having InvoiceAmt field values greater than 1000.00. The Access comparison operators are shown in Figure 3-17.

Access

Figure 3-17 ◀
Access
comparison
operators

Operator	Meaning	Example
=	equal to (optional, default operator)	="Hall"
<	less than	<#1/1/94#
<=	less than or equal to	<=100
>	greater than	>"C400"
>=	greater than or equal to	>=18.75
<>	not equal to	<>"Hall"
Between ... And...	between two values (inclusive)	Between 50 And 325
In ()	in a list of values	In ("Hall", "Seeger")
Like	matches a pattern that includes wildcards	Like "706*"

Specifying an Exact Match

For Barbara's request, you need to create a query that will display only those records in the Order table with the value 1/15/99 in the BillingDate field. This type of condition is called an **exact match** because the value in the specified field must match the condition exactly in order for the record to be included in the query results. You'll use the Simple Query Wizard to create the query, and then you'll specify the exact match condition.

To create the query using the Simple Query Wizard:

1. If you took a break after the previous session, make sure that Access is running, the Restaurant database is open, and the Queries tab is displayed in the Database window, and then click the **New** button.

2. Click **Simple Query Wizard** and then click the **OK** button. Access opens the first Simple Query Wizard dialog box, in which you select the tables and fields for the query.

3. Click the **Tables/Queries** list arrow, and then click **Table: Order**. The fields in the Order table appear in the Available Fields list box. See Figure 3-18.

Figure 3-18 ◀
First Simple
Query Wizard
dialog box

selected table ——→

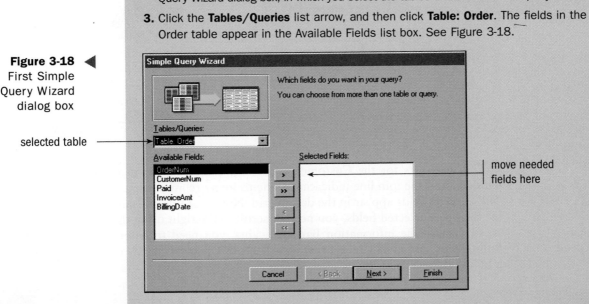

move needed
fields here

Except for the CustomerNum field, you will include all fields from the Order table in the query.

4. Click the ⟫ button. Access removes all the fields from the Available Fields list box and places them in the same order in the Selected Fields list box.

5. Click **CustomerNum** in the Selected Fields list box, click the ‹ button to move the CustomerNum field back to the Available Fields list box, and then click **BillingDate** in the Selected Fields list box.

Barbara also wants certain information from the Customer table included in the query results.

6. Click the **Tables/Queries** list arrow, and then click **Table: Customer**. The fields in the Customer table now appear in the Available Fields list box.

7. Click **CustomerName** in the Available Fields list box, and then click the › button to move CustomerName to the Selected Fields list box.

8. Repeat Step 7 for the **State**, **OwnerName**, and **Phone** fields.

9. Click the **Next** button to open the second Simple Query Wizard dialog box, in which you choose whether the query will display records from the selected tables or a summary of those records. Barbara wants to view the details for the records, not a summary.

10. Make sure the **Detail** option button is selected, and then click the **Next** button to open the last Simple Query Wizard dialog box, in which you choose a name for the query and complete the wizard. You need to enter a condition for the query, so you'll want to modify the query's design.

11. Type **January Orders**, click the **Modify the query design** option button, and then click the **Finish** button. Access saves the query as January Orders and opens the query in Design view. See Figure 3-19.

Figure 3-19 ◄
Query in
Design view

field lists ——

indicates a one-to-
many relationship

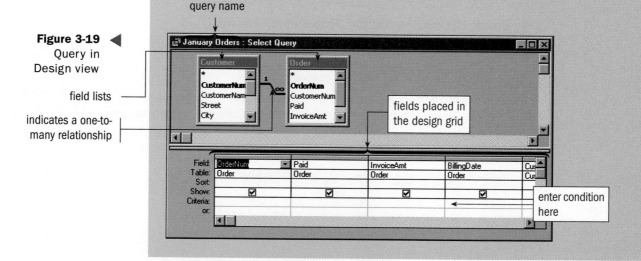

The field lists for the Customer and Order tables appear in the top portion of the window, and the join line indicating a one-to-many relationship connects the two tables. The selected fields appear in the design grid. Not all of the fields are visible in the grid; to see the other selected fields, you need to scroll to the right using the horizontal scroll bar.

To display the information Barbara wants, you need to enter the condition for the BillingDate field in its Criteria text box. Barbara wants to display only those records with a billing date of 1/15/99.

To enter the exact match condition, and then run the query:

1. Click the **BillingDate Criteria** text box, type **1/15/99**, and then press the **Enter** key. Access changes the condition to #1/15/99#.

   Access automatically placed number signs (#) before and after the condition. You must place date and time values inside number signs when using these values as selection criteria. If you omit the number signs, however, Access will include them automatically.

2. Click the **Run** button [!] on the Query Design toolbar. Access runs the query and displays the selected field values for only those records with a BillingDate field value of 1/15/99. A total of 36 records are selected and displayed in the datasheet. See Figure 3-20.

only records with a
BillingDate value
of 1/15/99
are selected

Figure 3-20 ◄
Datasheet
displaying
selected fields
and records

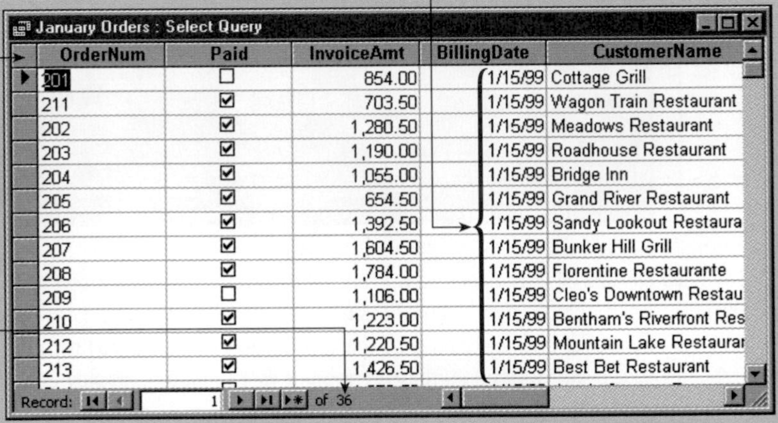

click here to
select all records

36 records selected

OrderNum	Paid	InvoiceAmt	BillingDate	CustomerName
201	☐	854.00	1/15/99	Cottage Grill
211	☑	703.50	1/15/99	Wagon Train Restaurant
202	☑	1,280.50	1/15/99	Meadows Restaurant
203	☑	1,190.00	1/15/99	Roadhouse Restaurant
204	☑	1,055.00	1/15/99	Bridge Inn
205	☑	654.50	1/15/99	Grand River Restaurant
206	☑	1,392.50	1/15/99	Sandy Lookout Restaura
207	☑	1,604.50	1/15/99	Bunker Hill Grill
208	☑	1,784.00	1/15/99	Florentine Restaurante
209	☐	1,106.00	1/15/99	Cleo's Downtown Restau
210	☑	1,223.00	1/15/99	Bentham's Riverfront Res
212	☑	1,220.50	1/15/99	Mountain Lake Restaurar
213	☑	1,426.50	1/15/99	Best Bet Restaurant

January Orders : Select Query

Record: I◄ ◄ 1 ► ►I ►* of 36

Barbara would like to see more fields and records on the screen at one time. She asks you to maximize the datasheet, change the datasheet's font size, and resize all the columns to their best fit.

Changing a Datasheet's Appearance

You can change the characteristics of a datasheet, including the font type and size of text in the datasheet, to improve its appearance or readability. You can also resize the datasheet columns to view more columns on the screen at the same time.

You'll maximize the datasheet, change the font size from the default 10 to 8, and then resize the datasheet columns.

To change the font size and resize columns in the datasheet:

1. Click the **Maximize** button [□] on the Query window title bar.

2. Click the **record selector** to the left of the field names at the top of the datasheet (see Figure 3-20). The entire datasheet is selected.

3. Click **Format** on the menu bar, and then click **Font** to open the Font dialog box.

4. Scroll the Size list box, click **8**, and then click the **OK** button. The font size for the entire datasheet changes to 8.

   Next you need to resize the columns to their best fit—that is, so each column is just wide enough to fit the longest value in the column.

5. Position the pointer in the OrderNum field selector. When the pointer changes to ↓ , click to select the entire column.

6. Click the horizontal scroll right arrow until the Phone field is fully visible, and position the pointer in the Phone field selector until the pointer changes to ↓ .

7. Press and hold the **Shift** key, and then click the mouse button. All the columns are selected. Now you can resize all of them at once.

8. Position the pointer at the right edge of the Phone field selector until the pointer changes to ↔ . See Figure 3-21.

Figure 3-21 ◄
Preparing to
resize all
columns to
their best fit

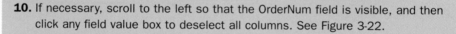
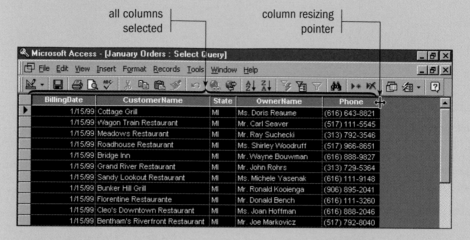

9. Double-click the mouse button. All columns are resized to their best fit, which makes each column just large enough to fit the longest *visible* field value in the column, including the field name at the top of the column. Scroll through the datasheet and resize individual columns as needed to completely display all field values.

10. If necessary, scroll to the left so that the OrderNum field is visible, and then click any field value box to deselect all columns. See Figure 3-22.

Figure 3-22 ◄
Datasheet
after changing
font size and
column widths

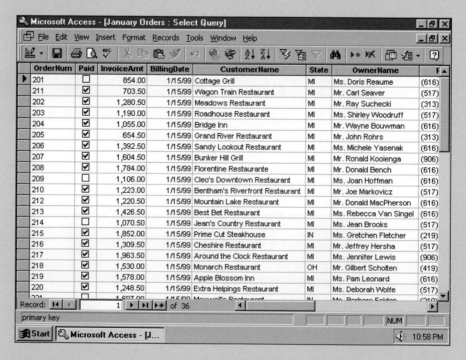

TROUBLE? Your screen might show more or fewer columns depending on the monitor you are using.

11. Click the **Save** button 🔲 on the Query Datasheet toolbar, and then click the **Close** button ⊠ on the menu bar. Access saves and closes the query, and you return to the Database window.

After viewing the query results, Barbara decides that she would like to see the same fields but only for those records whose InvoiceAmt exceeds $2,000. She wants to note this information and pass it along to her staff members so that they can contact those customers with higher outstanding invoices. To create the query needed to produce these results, you need to use a comparison operator to match a range of values—in this case, any InvoiceAmt value greater than $2,000.

Using a Comparison Operator to Match a Range of Values

Once you create and save a query, you can click the Open button to run it again, or you can click the Design button to change its design. Because the design of the query you need to create next is similar to the January Orders query, you will change its design, run the query to test it, and then save the query with a new name, keeping the January Orders query intact.

To change the January Orders query design to create a new query:

1. With the January Orders query selected in the Database window, click the **Design** button. Access opens the January Orders query in Design view.

2. Click the **InvoiceAmt Criteria** text box, type **>2000**, and then press the **Tab** key. See Figure 3-23.

Figure 3-23 ◄
Changing a
query's design
to create
a new query

new condition ——

condition to delete ——

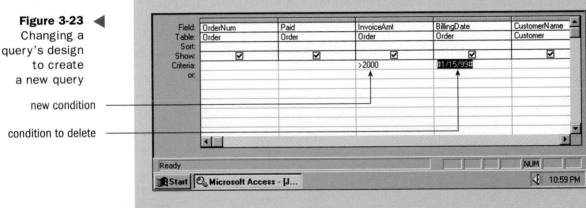

The new condition specifies that a record will be selected only if its InvoiceAmt field value exceeds 2000. Before you run the query, you need to delete the condition for the BillingDate field.

3. With the BillingDate field condition highlighted, press the **Delete** key. Access deletes the selected condition for the BillingDate field.

4. Click the **Run** button 🔘 on the Query Design toolbar. Access runs the query and displays the selected fields for only those records with an InvoiceAmt field value greater than 2000. A total of four records are selected. See Figure 3-24.

Figure 3-24 ◄
Running the
modified query

only records with an
InvoiceAmt value
greater than 2,000
are selected

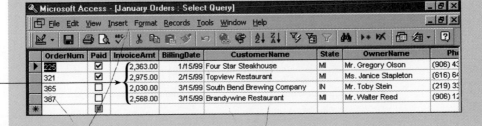

Of the records retrieved, Barbara notes that order numbers 365 and 387 have not yet been paid and the amount of each. She gives this information to her staff.

So that Barbara can display this information again, as necessary, you'll save the query as High Invoice Amounts.

5. Click **File** on the menu bar, and then click **Save As/Export** to open the Save As dialog box.

6. Type **High Invoice Amounts** in the New Name text box, and then press the **Enter** key. Access saves the query using the new query name and displays the new query name in the datasheet window title bar.

7. Click the **Close** button ❌ on the menu bar. The Database window becomes the active window.

Leonard asks Barbara for a list of the orders billed on 1/15/99 that are still unpaid. He wants to know which customers are slow in paying their invoices. To produce this data, you need to create a query containing two conditions.

Defining Multiple Selection Criteria for Queries

Multiple conditions require you to use **logical operators** to combine two or more conditions. When you want a record selected only if two or more conditions are met, you need to use the **And logical operator**. In this case, Leonard wants to see only those records with a BillingDate field value of 1/15/99 *and* a Paid field value of No. If you place conditions in separate fields in the *same* Criteria row of the design grid, all the conditions in that row must be met in order for a record to be included in the query results. However, if you place conditions in *different* Criteria rows, Access selects a record if at least one of the conditions is met. If none of the conditions is met, then Access does not select the record. This is known as the **Or logical operator**. The difference between these two logical operators is illustrated in Figure 3-25.

Figure 3-25 ◀
Logical operators And and Or for multiple selection criteria

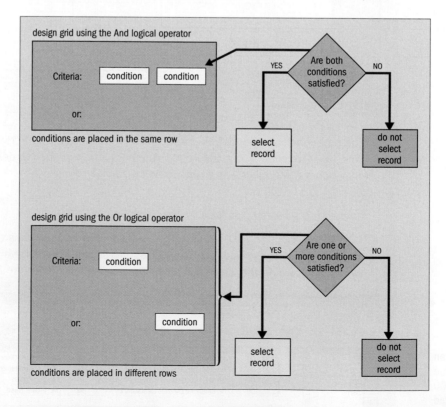

The And Logical Operator

To create the query, you need to modify the existing January Orders query to show only the unpaid orders billed on 1/15/99. For the modified query, you must add a second condition in the same Criteria row. The condition #1/15/99# for the BillingDate field finds records billed on the specified date, and the condition "No" in the Paid field finds records whose invoices have not been paid. Because the conditions appear in the same Criteria row, Access selects records only if both conditions are met.

After modifying the query, you'll save it and rename it as "Unpaid January Orders," overwriting the January Orders query, which Barbara no longer needs.

To modify the January Orders query and use the And logical operator:

1. In the Queries tab of the Database window, click **January Orders** and then click the **Design** button to open the query in Design view.

2. Click the **Paid Criteria** text box, type **no**, and then press the **Tab** key. See Figure 3-26.

Figure 3-26 ◀
Query to
find unpaid
January orders

And logical operator:
conditions entered
in the same row

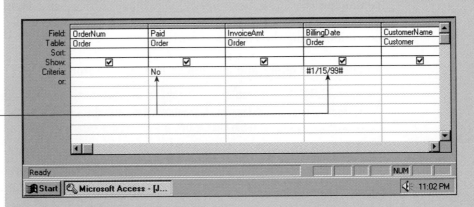

The condition for the BillingDate field is already entered, so you can run the query.

3. Click the **Run** button on the Query Design toolbar. Access runs the query and displays in the datasheet only those records that meet both conditions: a BillingDate field value of 1/15/99 and a Paid field value of No. A total of six records are selected. See Figure 3-27.

Figure 3-27 ◀
Results of
query using the
And logical
operator

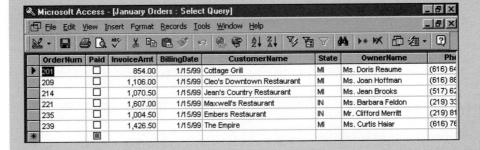

Now you can save the changes to the query and rename it.

4. Click the **Save** button on the Query Datasheet toolbar, and then click the **Close** button on the menu bar.

5. Right-click **January Orders** in the Queries list box, and then click **Rename** on the shortcut menu.

6. Click to position the insertion point to the left of the word "January," type **Unpaid**, press the **spacebar**, and then press the **Enter** key. The query name is now Unpaid January Orders.

Leonard also wants to determine which restaurant customers are most valuable to Valle Coffee. Specifically, he wants to see a list of those customers who have been placing orders for many years or who place orders for a substantial amount of money. He needs this information so that he can call the customers personally and thank them for their business. To create this query, you need to use the Or logical operator.

The Or Logical Operator

For Leonard's request, you need a query that selects records when either one of two conditions is satisfied or when both conditions are satisfied. That is, a record is selected if the FirstContact field value is less than 1/1/92 (to find those customers who have been doing business with Valle Coffee the longest) *or* if the InvoiceAmt field value is greater than 2000 (to find those customers who spend more money). You will enter the condition for the FirstContact field in one Criteria row and the condition for the InvoiceAmt field in another Criteria row.

To display the information Leonard wants to view, you'll create a new query containing the CustomerName, OwnerName, Phone, and FirstContact fields from the Customer table and the InvoiceAmt field from the Order table. Then you'll specify the conditions using the Or logical operator.

To create the query and use the Or logical operator:

1. From the Queries tab of the Database window, click the **New** button to open the New Query dialog box, click **Design View**, and then click the **OK** button. Access opens the Show Table dialog box on top of the Query window in Design view.

2. Click **Customer** in the Tables list box (if necessary), click the **Add** button, click **Order**, click the **Add** button, and then click the **Close** button. Access places the Customer and Order field lists in the Query window and closes the Show Table dialog box.

3. Double-click **CustomerName** in the Customer field list. Access places CustomerName in the design grid's first column Field text box.

4. Repeat Step 3 to add the **OwnerName**, **Phone**, and **FirstContact** fields from the Customer table, and then add the **InvoiceAmt** field from the Order table.

   Now you need to specify the first condition, <1/1/92, in the FirstContact field.

5. Click the **FirstContact Criteria** text box, type **<1/1/92** and then press the **Tab** key.

   Because you want records selected if either of the conditions for the FirstContact or InvoiceAmt fields is satisfied, you must enter the condition for the InvoiceAmt field in the "or" row of the design grid.

6. Press the ↓ key, and then type **>2000**. See Figure 3-28.

Figure 3-28 ◀
Query window
with the Or
logical operator

Or logical operator:
conditions entered
in different rows

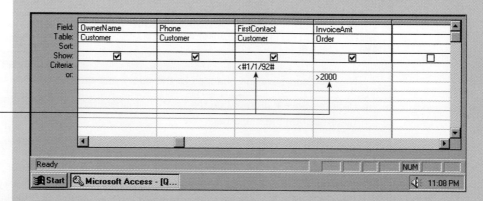

The query specifications are complete, so you can now run the query.

Access

7. Click the **Run** button ⚡ on the Query Design toolbar. Access runs the query and displays only those records that meet either condition: a FirstContact field value less than 1/1/92 or an InvoiceAmt field value greater than 2000. A total of 35 records are selected.

Leonard wants the list displayed in alphabetical order by CustomerName.

8. Click any visible CustomerName field value to establish this field as the current field, and then click the **Sort Ascending** button ⬇ on the Query Datasheet toolbar.

9. Resize all datasheet columns to their best fit. Be sure to scroll through the entire datasheet to make sure that all values are completely displayed. See Figure 3-29.

records with
InvoiceAmt values
greater than 2,000

Figure 3-29 ◀
Results of
query using the
Or logical
operator

records with
FirstContact values
earlier than 1/1/92

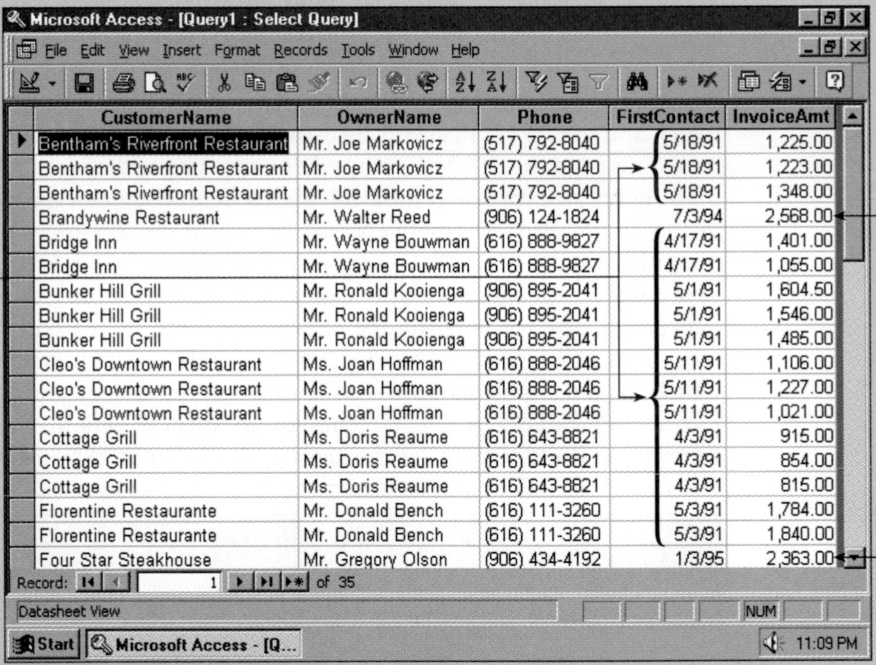

CustomerName	OwnerName	Phone	FirstContact	InvoiceAmt
Bentham's Riverfront Restaurant	Mr. Joe Markovicz	(517) 792-8040	5/18/91	1,225.00
Bentham's Riverfront Restaurant	Mr. Joe Markovicz	(517) 792-8040	5/18/91	1,223.00
Bentham's Riverfront Restaurant	Mr. Joe Markovicz	(517) 792-8040	5/18/91	1,348.00
Brandywine Restaurant	Mr. Walter Reed	(906) 124-1824	7/3/94	2,568.00
Bridge Inn	Mr. Wayne Bouwman	(616) 888-9827	4/17/91	1,401.00
Bridge Inn	Mr. Wayne Bouwman	(616) 888-9827	4/17/91	1,055.00
Bunker Hill Grill	Mr. Ronald Kooienga	(906) 895-2041	5/1/91	1,604.50
Bunker Hill Grill	Mr. Ronald Kooienga	(906) 895-2041	5/1/91	1,546.00
Bunker Hill Grill	Mr. Ronald Kooienga	(906) 895-2041	5/1/91	1,485.00
Cleo's Downtown Restaurant	Ms. Joan Hoffman	(616) 888-2046	5/11/91	1,106.00
Cleo's Downtown Restaurant	Ms. Joan Hoffman	(616) 888-2046	5/11/91	1,227.00
Cleo's Downtown Restaurant	Ms. Joan Hoffman	(616) 888-2046	5/11/91	1,021.00
Cottage Grill	Ms. Doris Reaume	(616) 643-8821	4/3/91	915.00
Cottage Grill	Ms. Doris Reaume	(616) 643-8821	4/3/91	854.00
Cottage Grill	Ms. Doris Reaume	(616) 643-8821	4/3/91	815.00
Florentine Restaurante	Mr. Donald Bench	(616) 111-3260	5/3/91	1,784.00
Florentine Restaurante	Mr. Donald Bench	(616) 111-3260	5/3/91	1,840.00
Four Star Steakhouse	Mr. Gregory Olson	(906) 434-4192	1/3/95	2,363.00

Record: 1 of 35

Datasheet View

Start   Microsoft Access - [Q...   11:09 PM

Now you'll save the query as Top Customers, print the query results, and then close the query.

10. Click the **Save** button 🖫 on the Query Datasheet toolbar, type **Top Customers** in the Query Name text box, and then press the **Enter** key. Access saves the query with the specified name in the Restaurant database.

11. Click the **Print** button 🖨 on the Query Datasheet toolbar to print the query results, and then click the **Close** button ⊠ on the menu bar to close the query and return to the Database window.

Next, Leonard asks Barbara if the Restaurant database can be used to perform calculations. He is considering adding a 2% late charge to the unpaid invoices billed in January, and he wants to know exactly what these charges would be.

Performing Calculations

In addition to using queries to retrieve, sort, and filter data in a database, you can use a query to perform calculations. To perform a calculation, you define an **expression** containing a combination of database fields, constants, and operators. For numeric expressions, the data types of the database fields must be number, currency, or date/time; the constants are numbers such as .02 (for the 2% late charge); and the operators can be arithmetic operators (+ – * /) or other specialized operators. In complex expressions you can use parentheses ( ) to indicate which calculation should be performed first. In expressions without parentheses, Access calculates in the following order of precedence: multiplication and division before addition and subtraction. Access calculates operators that have equal precedence in order from left to right.

To perform a calculation in a query, you add a calculated field to the query. A **calculated field** is a field that displays the results of an expression. A calculated field appears in a query datasheet but does not exist in a database. When you run a query that contains a calculated field, Access evaluates the expression defined by the calculated field and displays the resulting value in the datasheet.

Creating a Calculated Field

To produce the information Leonard wants, you need to open the Unpaid January Orders query and create a calculated field that will multiply each InvoiceAmt field value by .02 to account for the 2% late charge Leonard is considering.

To enter an expression for a calculated field, you can type it directly in a Field text box in the design grid. Alternatively, you can open the Zoom box or Expression Builder and use either one to enter the expression. The **Zoom box** is a large text box for entering text, expressions, or other values. **Expression Builder** is an Access tool that contains an expression box for entering the expression, buttons for common operators, and one or more lists of expression elements, such as table and field names. Unlike a Field text box, which is too small to show an entire expression at one time, the Zoom box and Expression Builder are large enough to display lengthy expressions. In most cases Expression Builder provides the easiest way to enter expressions.

REFERENCE window

USING EXPRESSION BUILDER

- Display the query in Design view.
- In the design grid, position the insertion point in the Field text box of the field for which you want to create an expression.
- Click the Build button on the Query Design toolbar.
- Use the expression elements and common operators to build the expression.
- Click the OK button.

You'll begin by opening the Unpaid January Orders query in Design view and modifying it to show only the information Leonard wants to view.

To modify the Unpaid January Orders query:

1. In the Queries tab, click **Unpaid January Orders**, and then click the **Design** button.

   Leonard wants to see only the OrderNum, CustomerName, and InvoiceAmt fields. So, you'll first delete the unnecessary fields, and then uncheck the Show boxes for the Paid and BillingDate fields. You need to keep these two fields in the query because they specify the conditions for the query; however, they do not have to be included in the query results.

Access

2. Scroll the design grid to the right until the last three fields—State, OwnerName, and Phone—are visible.

3. Position the pointer on the State field until the pointer changes to **↓**, click and hold down the mouse button, drag the mouse to the right to highlight the State, OwnerName, and Phone fields, and then release the mouse button.

4. Press the **Delete** key to delete the three selected fields.

5. Scroll the design grid back to the left, click the **Show** check box for the Paid field to remove the check mark, and then click the **Show** check box for the BillingDate field to remove the check mark.

   Next, you'll move the InvoiceAmt field to the right of the CustomerName field so that the InvoiceAmt values will appear next to the calculated field values in the query results.

6. Make sure both the InvoiceAmt field and the empty field to the right of the CustomerName field are visible in the design grid.

7. Select the InvoiceAmt field, and then use the pointer ⌖ to drag the field to the right of the CustomerName field.

8. If necessary, scroll the design grid so that the empty field to the right of InvoiceAmt is visible, and then click anywhere in the design grid to deselect the InvoiceAmt field. See Figure 3-30.

Figure 3-30 ◀
Modified query
before adding
the calculated
field

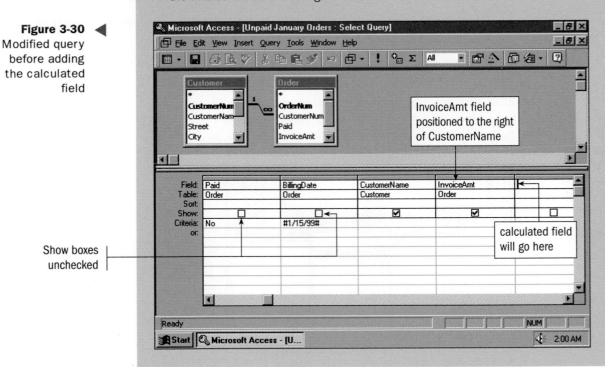

Now you're ready to use Expression Builder to enter the calculated field in the Unpaid January Orders query.

To add the calculated field to the Unpaid January Orders query:

1. Position the insertion point in the Field text box to the right of the InvoiceAmt field, and then click the **Build** button ▦ on the Query Design toolbar. The Expression Builder dialog box opens. See Figure 3-31.

Figure 3-31 ◄
Initial
Expression
Builder dialog
box

expression box ——

expression elements ——

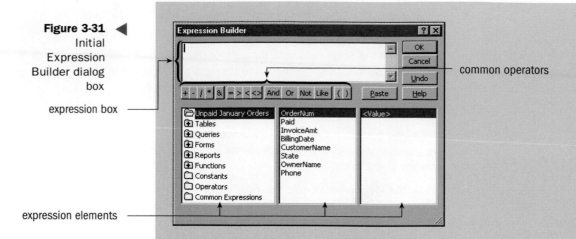

common operators

You use the common operators and expression elements to help you build an expression. Note that the Unpaid January Orders query is already selected in the list box on the bottom left; the fields included in the query are listed in the center box.

The expression for the calculated field will multiply the InvoiceAmt field values by the numeric constant .02 (which represents a 2% late charge). To include a field in the expression, you select the field and then click the Paste button. To include a numeric constant, you simply type the constant in the expression.

2. Click **InvoiceAmt** and then click the **Paste** button. Access places [InvoiceAmt] in the expression box.

To include the multiplication operator in the expression, you click the asterisk (*) button.

3. Click the * button in the row of common operators, and then type **.02**. You have completed the entry of the expression. See Figure 3-32.

Figure 3-32 ◄
Completed
expression for
the calculated
field

expression ——

4. Click the **OK** button. Access closes the Expression Builder dialog box and adds the expression to the design grid.

Next, you need to specify a name for the calculated field as it will appear in the query results.

5. Press the **Home** key to position the insertion point to the left of the expression.

You'll enter the name LateCharge, which is descriptive of the field's contents; then you'll run the query.

6. Type **LateCharge:** Make sure you include the colon following the field name. The colon is used to separate the field name from its expression.

Now you can run the query.

7. Click the **Run** button [!] on the Query Design toolbar. Access runs the query and displays the query datasheet, which contains the three specified fields and the calculated field. See Figure 3-33.

Figure 3-33 ◀
Datasheet displaying the calculated field

specified name for calculated field

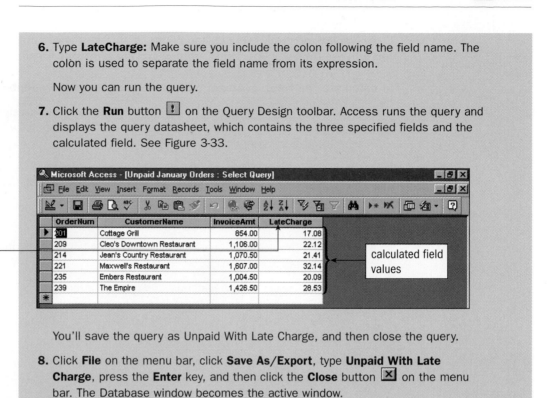

You'll save the query as Unpaid With Late Charge, and then close the query.

8. Click **File** on the menu bar, click **Save As/Export**, type **Unpaid With Late Charge**, press the **Enter** key, and then click the **Close** button ☒ on the menu bar. The Database window becomes the active window.

Barbara prepares a report of Valle Coffee's restaurant business for Leonard on a regular basis. The information in the report includes a summary of the restaurant orders. Barbara lists the total invoice amount for all orders, the average invoice amount, and the total number of orders. She asks you to create a query to determine these statistics from data in the Order table.

Using Aggregate Functions

You can calculate statistical information, such as totals and averages, on the records selected in a query. To do this, you use the Access aggregate functions. **Aggregate functions** perform arithmetic operations on selected records in a database. Figure 3-34 lists the most frequently used aggregate functions. Aggregate functions operate on the records that meet a query's selection criteria. You specify an aggregate function for a specific field, and the appropriate operation applies to that field's values for the selected records.

Figure 3-34 ◀
Frequently used aggregate functions

Aggregate Function	Determines	Data Types Supported
Avg	Average of the field values for the selected records	AutoNumber, Currency, Date/Time, Number
Count	Number of records selected	AutoNumber, Currency, Date/Time, Memo, Number, OLE Object, Text, Yes/No
Max	Highest field value for the selected records	AutoNumber, Currency, Date/Time, Number, Text
Min	Lowest field value for the selected records	AutoNumber, Currency, Date/Time, Number, Text
Sum	Total of the field values for the selected records	AutoNumber, Currency, Date/TIme, Number

To display the total, average, and count of all the invoice amounts in the Order table, you will use the Sum, Avg, and Count aggregate functions for the InvoiceAmt field.

To calculate the total, average, and count of all invoice amounts:

1. Click the **New** button to open the New Query dialog box, click **Design View** (if necessary), and then click the **OK** button. Access opens the Show Table dialog box on top of the Query window in Design view.

2. Click **Order**, click the **Add** button, and then click the **Close** button. Access adds the Order field list to the top of the Query window and closes the dialog box.

   To perform the three calculations on the InvoiceAmt field, you need to add the field three times to the design grid.

3. Double-click **InvoiceAmt** in the Order field list three times to add three copies of the field to the design grid.

   You need to select an aggregate function for each InvoiceAmt field. When you click the Totals button on the Query Design toolbar, Access adds a row labeled "Total" to the design grid. The Total row provides a list of the aggregate functions that can be selected.

4. Click the **Totals** button ∑ on the Query Design toolbar. Access inserts a row labeled "Total" between the Table and Sort rows in the design grid. See Figure 3-35.

Figure 3-35 ◀
Total row
inserted in the
design grid

Total row ───────→

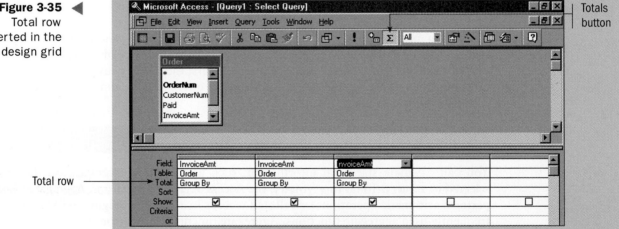

In the Total row, you specify the aggregate function you want to use for a field.

5. Click the right side of the first column's **Total** text box, and then click **Sum**. This field will calculate the total of all the InvoiceAmt field values.

   Access automatically assigns a datasheet column name of "SumOfInvoice Amount" for this field. You can change the datasheet column name to a more descriptive or readable name by entering the name you want in the Field text box. However, you must also keep InvoiceAmt in the Field text box because it identifies the field whose values will be summed. The Field text box will contain the datasheet column name you specify followed by the field name (InvoiceAmt) with a colon separating the two names.

6. Position the insertion point to the left of InvoiceAmt in the first column's Field text box, and then type **Total of Invoices:**. Be sure you include the colon at the end.

7. Click the right side of the second column's **Total** text box, and then click **Avg**. This field will calculate the average of all the InvoiceAmt field values.

8. Position the insertion point to the left of InvoiceAmt in the second column's Field text box, and then type **Average of Invoices:**.

9. Click the right side of the third column's **Total** text box, and then click **Count**. This field will calculate the total number of invoices (orders).

10. Position the insertion point to the left of InvoiceAmt in the third column's Field text box, and then type **Number of Invoices:**.

The query design is complete, so you can run the query.

11. Click the **Run** button [!] on the Query Design toolbar. Access runs the query and displays one record containing the three aggregate function values. The one row of summary statistics represents calculations based on the 104 records selected in the query.

You need to resize the three columns to their best fit to see the column names.

12. Resize each column by double-clicking the ⟷ on the right edge of each column's field selector; then position the insertion point at the start of the field value in the first column. See Figure 3-36.

Figure 3-36 ◄
Results of the query using aggregate functions

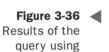

Total of Invoices	Average of Invoices	Number of Invoices
$136,715.00	$1,314.57	104

You'll save the query as Invoice Statistics.

13. Click the **Save** button [💾] on the Query Datasheet toolbar, type **Invoice Statistics**, and then press the **Enter** key.

Barbara's report to Leonard also includes the same invoice statistics (total, average, and count) for each month. Because Valle Coffee sends invoices to their restaurant customers once a month, each invoice in a month has the same billing date. Barbara asks you to display the invoice statistics for each different billing date in the Order table.

Using Record Group Calculations

In addition to calculating statistical information on all or selected records in selected tables, you can calculate statistics for groups of records. For example, you can determine the number of customers in each state or the total invoice amounts by billing date.

To create a query for Barbara's latest request, you can modify the current query by adding the BillingDate field and assigning the Group By operator to it. The **Group By operator** divides the selected records into groups based on the values in the specified field. Those records with the same value for the field are grouped together, and the datasheet displays one record for each group. Aggregate functions, which appear in the other columns of the design grid, provide statistical information for each group.

You need to modify the current query to add the Group By operator for the BillingDate field. This will display the statistical information grouped by billing date for the 104 selected records in the query.

To add the BillingDate field with the Group By operator, and then run the query:

1. Click the **View** button for Design view [📐] on the Query Datasheet toolbar to switch to Design view.

2. Scroll the Order field list, if necessary, and then double-click **BillingDate** to add the field to the design grid. Group By, which is the default option in the Total row, appears for the BillingDate field.

You've completed the query changes, so you can run the query.

3. Click the **Run** button ⚠ on the Query Design toolbar. Access runs the query and displays three records, one for each BillingDate group. Each record contains the three aggregate function values and the BillingDate field value for the group. Again, the summary statistics represent calculations based on the 104 records selected in the query. See Figure 3-37.

Figure 3-37 ◄
Aggregate
functions
grouped by
BillingDate

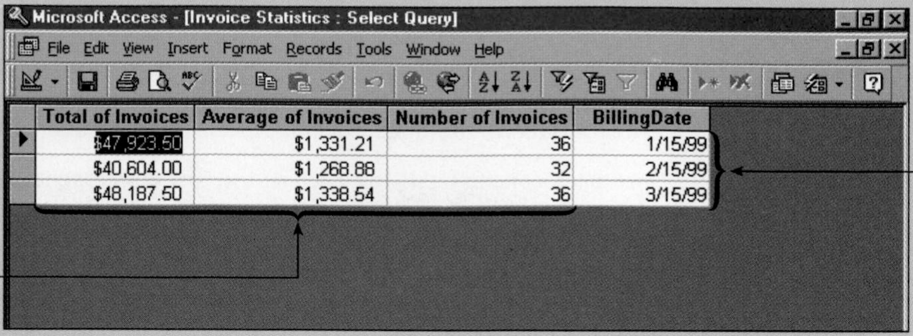

Total of Invoices	Average of Invoices	Number of Invoices	BillingDate
$47,923.50	$1,331.21	36	1/15/99
$40,604.00	$1,268.88	32	2/15/99
$48,187.50	$1,338.54	36	3/15/99

aggregate function results

record groups

You'll save the query as Invoice Statistics by Billing Date, and then close the query.

4. Click **File** on the menu bar, and then click **Save As/Export**.

5. Position the insertion point to the right of the last character in the New Name text box, press the **spacebar**, type **by Billing Date**, and then press the **Enter** key.

6. Click the **Close** button ☒ on the menu bar. The Database window becomes the active window.

7. Click the **Close** button ☒ on the Access window title bar to close the Restaurant database and to exit Access.

Quick Check

1 A(n) _____ is a criterion, or rule, that determines which records are selected for a query datasheet.

2 In the design grid, where do you place the conditions for two different fields when you use the And logical operator? The Or logical operator?

3 To perform a calculation in a query, you define a(n) _____ containing a combination of database fields, constants, and operators.

4 How does a calculated field differ from a table field?

5 What is an aggregate function?

6 The _____ operator divides selected records into groups based on the values in a field.

The queries you've created and saved will help Leonard, Barbara, Kim, and other employees monitor and analyze the business activity of Valle Coffee's restaurant customers. The queries can be run at any time, modified as needed, or used as the basis for designing new queries to meet additional information requirements.

Access

Tutorial Assignments

Barbara needs information from the Valle Products database, and she asks you to query the database by completing the following:

1. Make sure your Student Disk is in the disk drive, start Access, and then open the Valle Products database located in the TAssign folder on your Student Disk.

2. Create a select query based on the Product table. Display the ProductCode, WeightCode, and Price fields in the query results; sort in descending order based on the Price field values; and select only those records whose CoffeeCode value equals COLA. (*Hint:* Do not display the CoffeeCode field values in the query results.) Save the query as COLA Coffee, run the query, print the query datasheet, and then close the query.

3. Define a one-to-many relationship between the primary Coffee table and the related Product table, and then define a one-to-many relationship between the primary Weight table and the related Product table. (*Hint:* Add all three tables to the Relationships window, and then define the two relationships.) Select the referential integrity option and both cascade options for both relationships.

4. Create a select query based on the Coffee, Product, and Weight tables. Display the CoffeeType, CoffeeName, ProductCode, Price, and Weight/Size fields in that order. Sort in ascending order based on the CoffeeName field values. Select only those records whose CoffeeType equals "Special Import." Save the query as Special Imports, and then run the query. Resize all columns in the datasheet to fit the data. Print the datasheet and then close the query.

5. Create a query based on the Product table that shows all products that do not have a WeightCode field value of B, and whose Price field value is less than 30; display all fields except Decaf from the Product table. Save the query as Pricing, and then run the query.

6. Open the Pricing query in Design view. Create a calculated field named NewPrice that displays the results of increasing the Price values by 4%. Display the results in descending order by NewPrice. Save the query as New Prices, run the query, print the query datasheet, and then close the query.

7. Open the Special Imports query in Design view. Modify the query to display only those records with a CoffeeType field value of Special Import or with a Price field value greater than 50. Run the query, and then resize all columns in the datasheet to fit the data. Save the query as Special Imports Plus Higher Priced, print the query datasheet, and then close the query.

8. Create a new query based on the Product table. Use the Min and Max aggregate functions to find the lowest and highest values in the Price field. Name the two aggregate fields Lowest Price and Highest Price, respectively. Save the query as Lowest And Highest Prices, run the query, and then print the query datasheet.

9. Open the Lowest And Highest Prices query in Design view. Use the Show Table button on the Query Design toolbar to display the Show Table dialog box; then add the Weight table to the query. Modify the query so that the records are grouped by the Weight/Size field. Save the query as Lowest And Highest Prices By Weight/Size, run the query, print the query datasheet, and then close the query. Close the Valle Products database.

Case Problems

1. Ashbrook Mall Information Desk Sam Bullard wants to view specific information about jobs available at the Ashbrook Mall. He asks you to query the MallJobs database by completing the following:

1. Make sure your Student Disk is in the disk drive, start Access, and then open the MallJobs database located in the Cases folder on your Student Disk.

2. Define a one-to-many relationship between the primary Store table and the related Job table. Select the referential integrity option and both cascade options for the relationship.

3. Create a select query based on the Store and Job tables. Display the StoreName, Location, Position, and Hours/Week fields, in that order. Sort in ascending order based on the StoreName field values. Run the query, save the query as Store Jobs, and then print the datasheet.

4. Use Filter By Selection to temporarily display only those records with a Location field value of D1 in the Store Jobs query datasheet. Print the datasheet and then remove the filter.

5. Open the Store Jobs query in Design view. Modify the query to display only those records with a Position value of Clerk. Run the query, save the query as Clerk Jobs, and then print the datasheet.

6. Open the Clerk Jobs query in Design view. Modify the query to display only those records with a Position value of Clerk and with an Hours/Week value of 20-30. Run the query, save it with the same name, print the datasheet, and then close the query. Close the MallJobs database.

2. Professional Litigation User Services Raj Jawahir is completing an analysis of the payment history of PLUS clients. To help him find the information he needs, you'll query the Payments database by completing the following:

1. Make sure your Student Disk is in the disk drive, start Access, and then open the Payments database located in the Cases folder on your Student Disk.

2. Define a one-to-many relationship between the primary Firm table and the related Payment table. Select the referential integrity option and both cascade options for the relationship.

3. Create a select query based on the Firm and Payment tables. Display the Firm#, FirmName, AmtPaid, and DatePaid fields, in that order. Sort in descending order based on the AmtPaid field values. Select only those records whose AmtPaid is greater than 2,400.00. Save the query as Large Payments, and then run the query. Print the datasheet and then close the query.

4. For all payments on 6/2/99, display the Payment#, AmtPaid, DatePaid, and FirmName fields. Save the query as June 2 Payments, and then run the query. Switch to Design view, modify the query so that the DatePaid values do not appear in the query results, and then save the modified query. Run the query, print the query results, and then close the query.

5. For all firms that have Nancy Martinez as a PLUS account representative, display the FirmName, FirmContact, AmtPaid, and DatePaid fields. Save the query as Martinez Accounts, run the query, print the query results, and then close the query.

6. For all payments made on 6/11/99 or 6/12/99, display the DatePaid, AmtPaid, FirmName, and Firm# fields. Display the results in ascending order by DatePaid and then in descending order by AmtPaid. Save the query as Selected Dates, run the query, print the query datasheet, and then close the query.

7. Use the Payment table to display the highest, lowest, total, average, and count of the AmtPaid field for all payments. Then do the following:
   a. Specify column names of HighestPayment, LowestPayment, TotalPayments, AveragePayment, and #Payments. Save the query as Payment Statistics, and then run the query. Resize all datasheet columns to their best fit, and then print the query results.
   b. Change the query to display the same statistics by DatePaid. Save the query as Payment Statistics By Date, run the query, and then print the query results.
   c. Change the Payment Statistics By Date query to display the same statistics by DatePaid then by Deposit#. Save the query as Payment Statistics By Date By Deposit, print the query results using landscape orientation, and then close the query. Close the Payments database.

3. Best Friends Noah and Sheila Warnick want to find specific information about the Walk-A-Thons they conduct for Best Friends. You'll help them find the information in the Walks database by completing the following:

1. Make sure your Student Disk is in the disk drive, start Access, and then open the Walks database located in the Cases folder on your Student Disk.

2. Define a one-to-many relationship between the primary Walker table and the related Pledge table. Select the referential integrity option and both cascade options for the relationship.

3. For all walkers with a PledgeAmt field value of greater than 20, display the WalkerID, LastName, PledgeNo, and PledgeAmt fields. Sort the query in descending order by PledgeAmt. Save the query as Large Pledges, run the query, print the query datasheet, and then close the query.

4. For all walkers who pledged less than $10 or who pledged $5 per mile, display the Pledger, PledgeAmt, PerMile, LastName, and FirstName fields. Save the query as Pledged Or Per Mile, run the query, and then print the query datasheet. Change the query to select all walkers who pledged less than $10 and who pledged $5 per mile. Save the query as Pledged And Per Mile, and then run the query. Describe the results. Close the query.

5. For all pledges, display the Pledger, Distance, PerMile, and PledgeAmt fields. Save the query as Difference. Create a calculated field named CalcPledgeAmt that displays the results of multiplying the Distance and PerMile fields; then save the query. Create a second calculated field named Difference that displays the results of subtracting the CalcPledgeAmt field from the PledgeAmt field. Format the calculated fields as fixed with two decimal places. (*Hint:* Choose the Properties option on the shortcut menu for the selected fields.) Display the results in ascending order by PledgeAmt. Save the modified query, and then run the query. Resize all datasheet columns to their best fit, print the query results, and then close the query.

6. Use the Pledge table to display the total, average, and count of the PledgeAmt field for all pledges. Then do the following:
   a. Specify column names of TotalPledge, AveragePledge, and #Pledges.

   b. Change properties so that the values in the TotalPledge and AveragePledge columns display two decimal places and the fixed format. (*Hint:* Choose the Properties option on the shortcut menu for the selected field.)
   c. Save the query as Pledge Statistics, run the query, resize all datasheet columns to their best fit, and then print the query datasheet.

   d. Change the query to display the sum, average, and count of the PledgeAmt field for all pledges by LastName. (*Hint:* Use the Show Table button on the Query Design toolbar to add the Walker table to the query.) Save the query as Pledge Statistics By Walker, run the query, print the query datasheet, and then close the query. Close the Walks database.

4. Lopez Lexus Dealerships Maria and Hector Lopez want to analyze data about the cars and different locations for their Lexus dealerships. Help them query the Lexus database by completing the following:

1. Make sure your Student Disk is in the disk drive, start Access, and then open the Lexus database located in the Cases folder on your Student Disk.

2. Define a one-to-many relationship between the primary Locations table and the related Cars table. Select the referential integrity option and both cascade options for the relationship.

3. For all vehicles, display the Model, Year, LocationCode, and SellingPrice fields. Save the query as Car Info, and then run the query. Resize all datasheet columns to their best fit. In Datasheet view, sort the query results in ascending order by the SellingPrice field. Print the query datasheet, and then save and close the query.

4. For all vehicles manufactured in 1998, display the Model, Year, Cost, SellingPrice, and LocationName fields. Sort the query in descending order by Cost. Save the query as 1998 Cars, and then run the query. Modify the query to remove the display of the Year field values from the query results. Save the modified query, run the query, print the query datasheet, and then close the query.

5. For all vehicles located in Houston or with a transmission of A4, display the Model, Year, Cost, SellingPrice, Transmission, LocationCode, and LocationName fields. Save the query as Location Or Trans, run the query, and then print the query datasheet using landscape orientation. Change the query to select all vehicles located in Houston and with a transmission of A4. Save the query as Location And Trans, run the query, print the query datasheet in landscape orientation, and then close the query.

6. For all vehicles, display the Model, Year, Cost, and SellingPrice fields. Save the query as Profit. Then create a calculated field named Profit that displays the difference between the vehicle's selling price and cost. Display the results in descending order by Profit. Save the query, run the query, print the query datasheet, and then close the query.

7. Use the Cars table to determine the total cost, average cost, total selling price, and average selling price of all vehicles. Use the Index tab in online Help to look up the word "caption"; then choose the topic "Change a field name in a query." Read the displayed information, and then choose and read the subtopic "Display new field names by changing the Caption property." Close the Help window. Set the Caption property of the four fields to Total Cost, Average Cost, Total Selling Price, and Average Selling Price, respectively. Save the query as Car Statistics, run the query, resize all datasheet columns to their best fit, and then print the query datasheet. Revise the query to show the car statistics by LocationName. (*Hint:* Use the Show Table button on the Query Design toolbar to display the Show Table dialog box.) Set the Caption property of the LocationName field to Location. Save the revised query as Car Statistics By Location, run the query, print the query datasheet, and then close the query.

8. Use the Office Assistant to ask the following question: "How do I create a Top Values query?" Choose the topic "Display only the highest or lowest values in the query's results." Read the displayed information, and then close the Help window and the Office Assistant. Open the Profit query in Design view, and then modify the query to display only the top five values for the Profit field. Save the query as Top Profit, run the query, print the query datasheet, and then close the query. Close the Lexus database.

Creating Forms and Reports

Creating an Order Data Form, a Customer Orders Form, and a Customers and Orders Report

CASE

Valle Coffee

Barbara Hennessey wants to continue to enhance the Restaurant database to make it easier for her office staff members and other Valle Coffee employees to find and maintain data. In particular, she wants the database to include a form for the Order table, similar to the Customer Data form, which is based on the Customer table. She also wants a form that shows data from both the Customer and Order tables at the same time, so that all the order information for each customer appears with the corresponding customer data, giving a complete picture of the restaurant customers and their orders.

In addition, Kim Carpenter would like a report showing customer and order data so that her marketing staff members have printed output to refer to when completing market analyses and planning strategies for selling to restaurant customers. She wants the information to be formatted attractively, perhaps including the Valle Coffee cup logo on the report for visual interest.

In this session you will create a form using the Form Wizard, change a form's AutoFormat, navigate a form, find data using a form, print selected form records, and maintain table data using a form.

Creating a Form Using the Form Wizard

As you learned in Tutorial 1, a form is an object you use to maintain, view, and print records in a database. In Access, you can design your own forms or use Form Wizards to create them for you automatically.

Barbara asks you to create a new form her staff can use to view and maintain data in the Order table. In Tutorial 1, you used the AutoForm Wizard, which creates a form automatically using all the fields in the selected table or query, to create the Customer Data form. To create the form for the Order table, you'll use the Form Wizard. The **Form Wizard** allows you to choose some or all of the fields in the selected table or query, choose fields from other tables and queries, and display the chosen fields in any order on the form. You can also choose a style for the form.

To open the Restaurant database and activate the Form Wizard:

1. Place your Student Disk in the appropriate disk drive.

2. Start Access and open the Restaurant database located in the Tutorial folder on your Student Disk. The Restaurant database is displayed in the Access window.

3. Click the **Forms** tab in the Database window to select the tab. The Forms list includes the Customer Data form you created in Tutorial 1.

4. Click the **New** button in the Database window. The New Form dialog box opens.

5. Click **Form Wizard**, click the list arrow for choosing a table or query, click **Order** to select this table as the source for the form, and then click the **OK** button. The first Form Wizard dialog box opens. See Figure 4-1.

Figure 4-1 ◀
First Form
Wizard
dialog box

selected table ——▶

fields in the
selected table ——▶

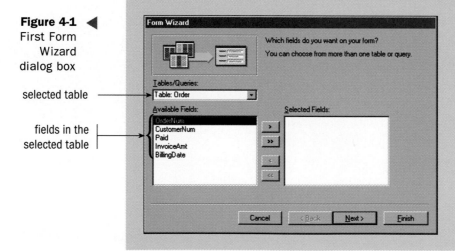

Barbara wants the form to display all the fields in the Order table, but in a different order. She would like the Paid field to be placed at the bottom of the form so that it stands out more, making it easier to determine if an order has been paid.

To finish creating the form using the Form Wizard:

1. Click **OrderNum** in the Available Fields list box (if necessary), and then click the
[>] button to move the field to the Selected Fields list box.

2. Repeat Step 1 to select the **CustomerNum**, **InvoiceAmt**, **BillingDate**, and **Paid** fields, in that order.

3. Click the **Next** button to display the second Form Wizard dialog box, in which you select a layout for the form. See Figure 4-2.

Figure 4-2 ◄
Choosing a
layout for
the form

sample of the
selected layout

selected layout

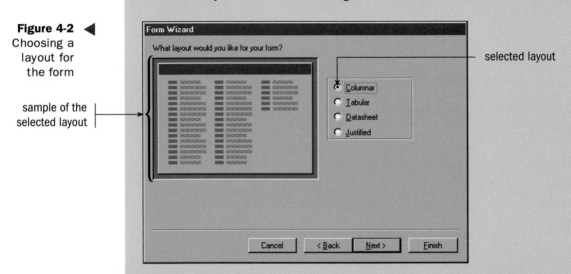

The layout choices are columnar, tabular, datasheet, and justified. A sample of the selected layout appears on the left side of the dialog box.

4. Click each of the option buttons and review the corresponding sample layout.

The tabular and datasheet layouts display the fields from multiple records at one time, whereas the columnar and justified layouts display the fields from one record at a time. Barbara thinks the columnar layout is the appropriate arrangement for displaying and updating data in the table, so you'll choose this layout.

5. Click the **Columnar** option button (if necessary), and then click the **Next** button. Access displays the third Form Wizard dialog box, in which you choose a style for the form. See Figure 4-3.

Figure 4-3 ◄
Choosing a
style for
the form

sample of the
selected style

Form Wizard
styles

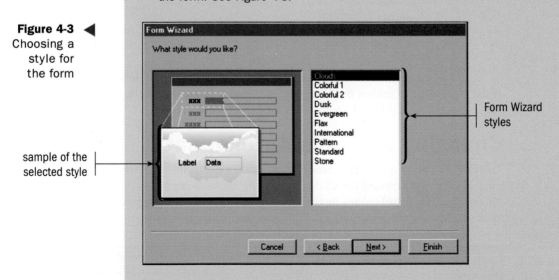

A sample of the selected style appears in the box on the left. If you choose a style, which is called an *AutoFormat*, and decide you'd prefer a different one after the form is created, you can change it.

6. Click each of the styles and review the corresponding sample.

Barbara likes the Evergreen style and asks you to use it for the form.

7. Click **Evergreen** and then click the **Next** button. Access displays the final Form Wizard dialog box and shows the table name as the default for the form name and for the title that will appear in the form title bar. See Figure 4-4.

Figure 4-4 ◀
Final Form
Wizard
dialog box

option to
display the form

option to change
the form's design

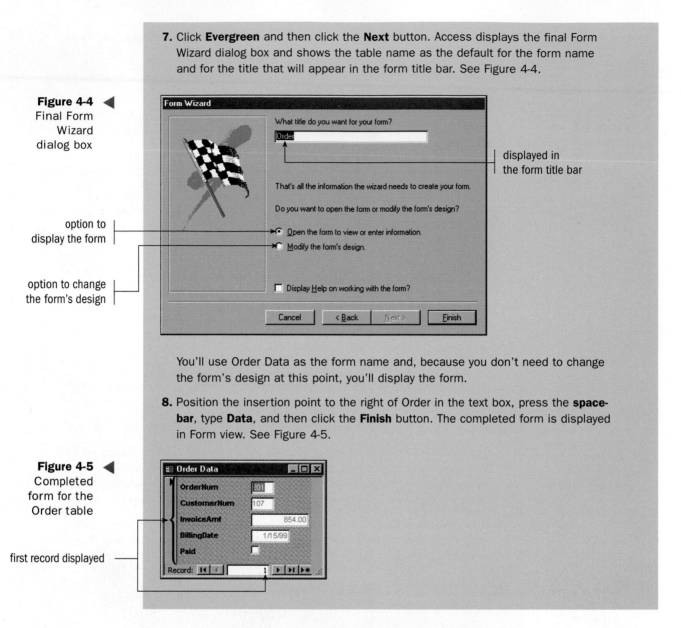

displayed in
the form title bar

You'll use Order Data as the form name and, because you don't need to change the form's design at this point, you'll display the form.

8. Position the insertion point to the right of Order in the text box, press the **spacebar**, type **Data**, and then click the **Finish** button. The completed form is displayed in Form view. See Figure 4-5.

Figure 4-5 ◀
Completed
form for the
Order table

first record displayed

After viewing the form, Barbara decides that she doesn't like the form's style—the green background makes the field names difficult to read and the green type for the field values is too light. She asks you to change the form's style.

Changing a Form's AutoFormat

You can change a form's appearance by choosing a different AutoFormat for the form. As you learned when you created the Order Data form, an **AutoFormat** is a predefined style for a form (or report). The AutoFormats available for a form are the ones you saw when you selected the form's style using the Form Wizard. To change an AutoFormat, you must switch to Design view.

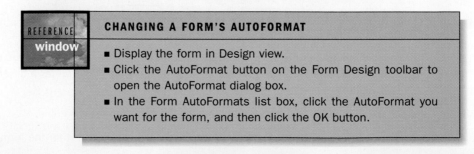

REFERENCE
window

CHANGING A FORM'S AUTOFORMAT

- Display the form in Design view.
- Click the AutoFormat button on the Form Design toolbar to open the AutoFormat dialog box.
- In the Form AutoFormats list box, click the AutoFormat you want for the form, and then click the OK button.

Access

To change the AutoFormat for the Order Data form:

1. Click the **View** button for Design view 🖾 on the Form View toolbar. The form is displayed in Design view. See Figure 4-6.

Figure 4-6 ◀
Form displayed in Design view

Form window ⎯⎯⎯⎯

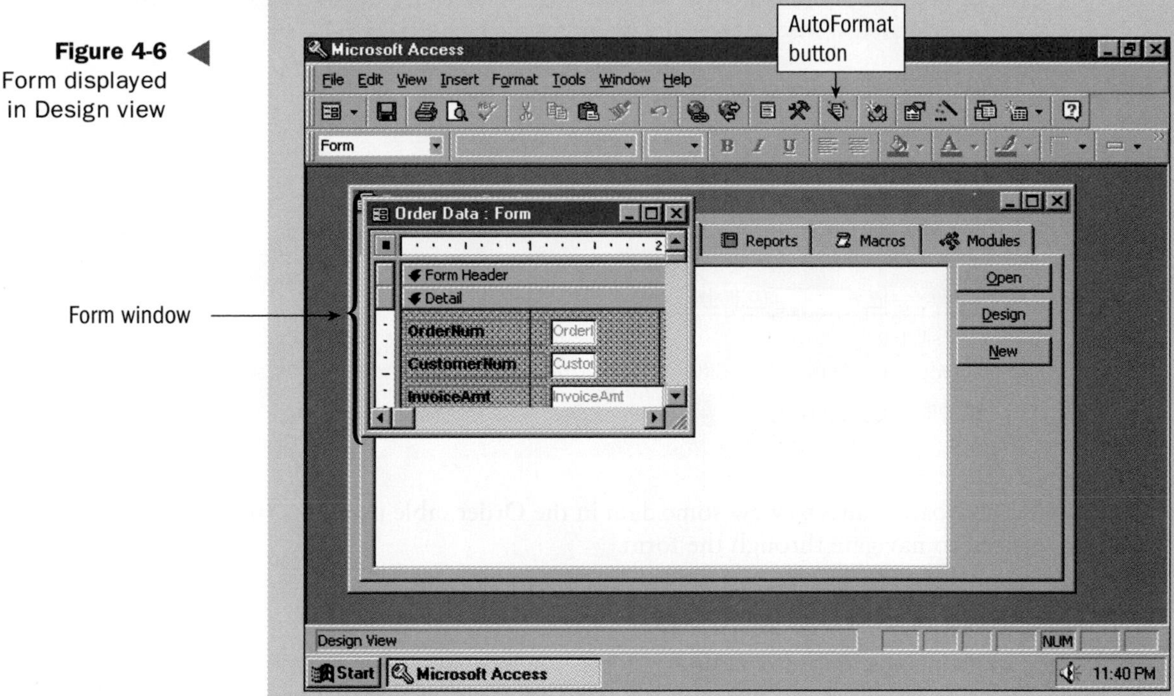

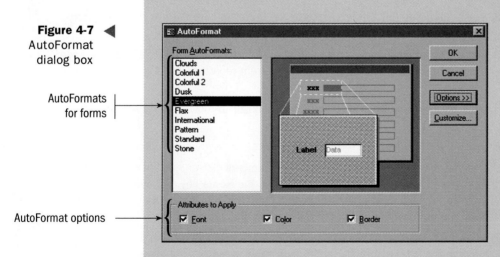

TROUBLE? If your screen displays any other windows than those shown in Figure 4-6, click the Close button ⊠ on the particular window's title bar to close it.

You use Design view to modify an existing form or to create a form from scratch. In this case, you need to change the AutoFormat for the Order Data form.

2. Click the **AutoFormat** button 🔯 on the Form Design toolbar. The AutoFormat dialog box opens.

3. Click the **Options** button to display the AutoFormat options. See Figure 4-7.

Figure 4-7 ◀
AutoFormat dialog box

AutoFormats for forms ⎯⎯⎯⎯

AutoFormat options ⎯⎯⎯⎯➤

A sample of the selected AutoFormat appears to the right of the Form AutoFormats list box. The options at the bottom of the dialog box allow you to apply the selected AutoFormat or just its font, color, or border.

Barbara decides that she prefers the Standard AutoFormat, because its field names and field values are easy to read.

4. Click **Standard** in the Form AutoFormats list box, and then click the **OK** button. The AutoFormat dialog box closes, the AutoFormat is applied to the form, and the Form window in Design view becomes the active window.

5. Click the **View** button for Form view 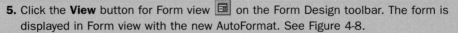 on the Form Design toolbar. The form is displayed in Form view with the new AutoFormat. See Figure 4-8.

Figure 4-8 ◄
Form displayed
with the new
AutoFormat

You have finished modifying the format of the form and can now save it.

6. Click the **Save** button 🖫 on the Form View toolbar to save the modified form.

Barbara wants to view some data in the Order table using the form. To view data, you need to navigate through the form.

Navigating a Form

To maintain and view data using a form, you must know how to move from field to field and from record to record. The mouse movement, selection, and placement techniques to navigate a form are the same techniques you've used to navigate a table datasheet and the Customer Data form you created in Tutorial 1. Also, the navigation mode and editing mode keystroke techniques are the same as those you used previously for datasheets (see Figure 2-29).

To navigate through the form:

1. Press the **Tab** key to move to the CustomerNum field value, and then press the **End** key to move to the Paid field. Because the Paid field is a yes/no field, its value is not highlighted; instead, a dashed box appears around the field name to indicate it is the current field.

2. Press the **Home** key to move back to the OrderNum field value. The first record in the Order table still appears in the form.

3. Press **Ctrl + End** to move to the Paid field in record 104, which is the last record in the table. The record number for the current record appears between the navigation buttons at the bottom of the form.

4. Click the **Previous Record** navigation button ◄ to move to the Paid field in record 103.

5. Press the ↑ key twice to move to the InvoiceAmt field value in record 103.

6. Position the insertion point between the numbers "2" and "6" in the InvoiceAmt field value to switch to editing mode, press the **Home** key to move the insertion point to the beginning of the field value, and then press the **End** key to move the insertion point to the end of the field value.

7. Click the **First Record** navigation button ◄◄ to move to the InvoiceAmt field value in the first record. The entire field value is highlighted because you have switched from editing mode to navigation mode.

8. Click the **Next Record** navigation button ► to move to the InvoiceAmt field value in record 2, which is the next record.

Barbara asks you to display the records for Jean's Country Restaurant, whose customer number is 407, because she wants to review the orders for this customer.

Finding Data Using a Form

The **Find** command allows you to search the data in a form and to display only those records you want to view. You choose a field to serve as the basis for the search by making that field the current field; then you enter the value you want Access to match in the Find in field dialog box. You can use the Find command for a form or datasheet, and you can activate the command from the Edit menu or by clicking the toolbar Find button.

REFERENCE window	**FINDING DATA**
	■ On a form or datasheet, click anywhere in the field value you want to search.
	■ Click the Find button on the toolbar to open the Find in field dialog box.
	■ In the Find What text box, type the field value you want to find.
	■ Complete the remaining options, as necessary, to specify the type of search you want Access to perform.
	■ Click the Find First button to have Access begin the search at the beginning of the table, or click the Find Next button to begin the search at the current record.
	■ Click the Find Next button to continue the search for the next match.
	■ Click the Close button to stop the search operation.

You need to find all records in the Order table for Jean's Country Restaurant, whose customer number is 407.

To find the records using the Order Data form:

1. Position the insertion point in the CustomerNum field value box. This is the field for which you will find matching values.

2. Click the **Find** button on the Form View toolbar to open the Find in field dialog box. Note that the title bar of the dialog box specifies the name of the field that Access will search, in this case, the CustomerNum field.

3. If the Find in field dialog box covers any part of the form, move the dialog box by dragging its title bar. See Figure 4-9.

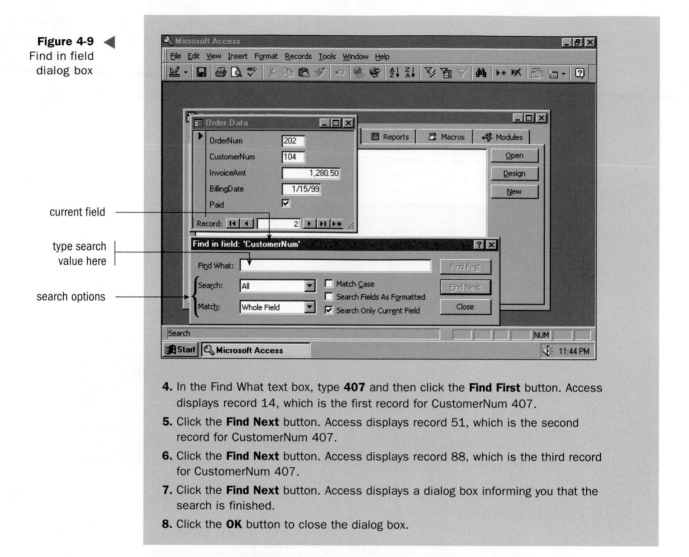

Figure 4-9 ◀
Find in field
dialog box

current field

type search
value here

search options

4. In the Find What text box, type **407** and then click the **Find First** button. Access displays record 14, which is the first record for CustomerNum 407.

5. Click the **Find Next** button. Access displays record 51, which is the second record for CustomerNum 407.

6. Click the **Find Next** button. Access displays record 88, which is the third record for CustomerNum 407.

7. Click the **Find Next** button. Access displays a dialog box informing you that the search is finished.

8. Click the **OK** button to close the dialog box.

The search value you enter can be an exact value, such as the customer number 407 you just entered, or it can include wildcard characters. A **wildcard character** is a placeholder you use when you know only part of a value or when you want to start or end with a specific character or match a certain pattern. Figure 4-10 shows the wildcard characters you can use when finding data.

Figure 4-10 ◀
Wildcard
characters

Wildcard Character	Purpose	Example
*	Match any number of characters. It can be used as the first and/or last character in the character string.	th* finds *the, that, this, therefore,* and so on
?	Match any single alphabetic character.	a?t finds *act, aft, ant,* and *art*
[ ]	Match any single character within the brackets.	a[fr]t finds *aft* and *art* but not *act* and *ant*
!	Match any character not within brackets.	a[!fr]t finds *act* and *ant* but not *aft* and *art*
-	Match any one of a range of characters. The range must be in ascending order (a to z, not z to a).	a[d-p]t finds aft and ant but not act and art
#	Match any single numeric character.	#72 finds *072, 172, 272, 372,* and so on

To check if their orders have been paid, Barbara wants to view the order records for two customers: Cheshire Restaurant (CustomerNum 515) and Around the Clock Restaurant (CustomerNum 597). You'll use the * wildcard character to search for these customers' orders.

To find the records using the * wildcard character:

1. Double-click **407** in the Find What text box to select the entire value, and then type **5***.

   Access will match any field value in the CustomerNum field that starts with the digit 5.

2. Click the **Find First** button. Access displays record 16, which is the first record for CustomerNum 515. Note that the Paid field value is checked, indicating that this order has been paid.

3. Click the **Find Next** button. Access displays record 17, which is the first record for CustomerNum 597.

4. Click the **Find Next** button. Access displays record 39, which is the second record for CustomerNum 597.

5. Click the **Find Next** button. Access displays record 68, which is the second record for CustomerNum 515.

6. Click the **Find Next** button. Access displays record 82, which is the third record for CustomerNum 515.

7. Click the **Find Next** button. Access displays a dialog box informing you that the search is finished.

8. Click the **OK** button to close the dialog box.

9. Click the **Close** button to close the Find in field dialog box.

All five orders have been paid, but Barbara wants to make sure Valle Coffee has a record of payment for order number 375. She asks you to print the data displayed on the form for record 82, which is for order number 375, so she can ask a staff member to look for the payment record for this order.

Previewing and Printing Selected Form Records

Access prints as many form records as can fit on a printed page. If only part of a form record fits on the bottom of a page, the remainder of the record prints on the next page. Access allows you to print all pages or a range of pages. In addition, you can print the currently selected form record.

Before printing record 82, you'll preview the form record to see how it will look when printed.

To preview the form and print the data for record 82:

1. Make sure record 82 is the current record in the Order Data form.

2. Click the **Print Preview** button 🔍 on the Form View toolbar. The Print Preview window opens, showing the form records for the Order table in miniature.

3. Click the **Maximize** button 🔲 on the form title bar.

4. Click the **Zoom** button 🔍 on the Print Preview toolbar, and then use the vertical scroll bar to view the contents of the window. See Figure 4-11.

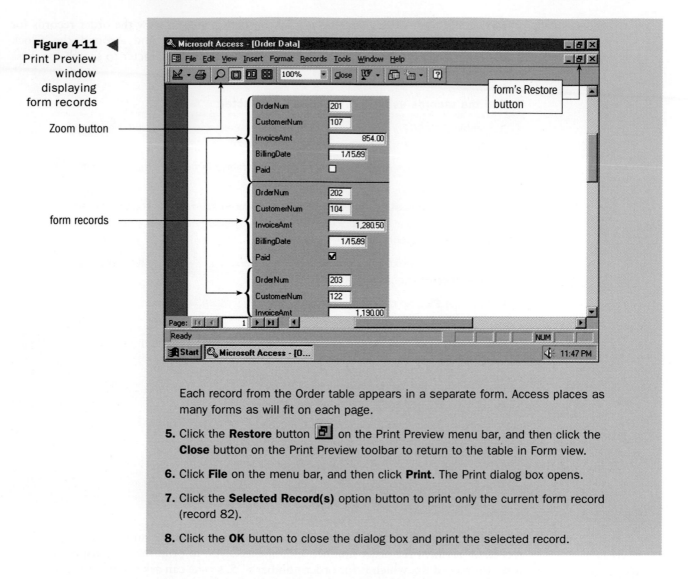

Figure 4-11
Print Preview
window
displaying
form records

Zoom button

form records

Each record from the Order table appears in a separate form. Access places as many forms as will fit on each page.

5. Click the **Restore** button on the Print Preview menu bar, and then click the **Close** button on the Print Preview toolbar to return to the table in Form view.

6. Click **File** on the menu bar, and then click **Print**. The Print dialog box opens.

7. Click the **Selected Record(s)** option button to print only the current form record (record 82).

8. Click the **OK** button to close the dialog box and print the selected record.

Barbara has identified several updates she wants you to make to the Order table using the Order Data form, as shown in Figure 4-12.

Figure 4-12
Updates to the
Order table

Order Number	Update Action
319	Change InvoiceAmt to 1,175.00 Change Paid to Yes
392	Delete record
400	Add new record for CustomerNum 135, InvoiceAmt of 1,350.00, BillingDate of 3/15/99, and Paid status of No

Access

Maintaining Table Data Using a Form

Maintaining data using a form is often easier than using a datasheet, because you can concentrate on all the changes required to a single record at a time. You already know how to navigate a form and find specific records. Now you'll make the changes Barbara requested to the Order table using the Order Data form.

First, you'll update the record for OrderNum 319.

To change the record using the Order Data form:

1. Make sure the Order Data form is displayed in Form view.

   The current record number appears between the sets of navigation buttons at the bottom of the form. If you know the number of the record you want to change, you can type the number and press the Enter key to go directly to the record. When she reviewed the order data to identify possible corrections, Barbara noted that 48 is the record number for order number 319.

2. Select the number 82 that appears between the navigation buttons, type **48**, and then press the **Enter** key. Record 48 is now the current record.

   You need to change the InvoiceAmt field value to 1,175.00 and the Paid field value to Yes for this record.

3. Position the insertion point between the numbers 9 and 5 in the InvoiceAmt field value, press the **Backspace** key, and then type **7**. Note that the pencil symbol appears in the top left of the form, indicating that the form is in editing mode.

4. Press the **Tab** key twice to move to the Paid field value, and then press the **spacebar** to insert a check mark in the check box. See Figure 4-13.

Figure 4-13 ◀
Order record after changing field values

indicates editing mode

field values changed

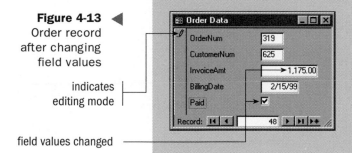

You have completed the changes for order number 319. Barbara's next update is to delete the record for order number 392. The customer who placed this order canceled it before the order was filled and processed.

To delete the record using the Order Data form:

1. Click anywhere in the OrderNum field value to make it the current field.

2. Click the **Find** button 🔍 on the Form View toolbar. The Find in field dialog box opens.

3. Type **392** in the Find What text box, click the **Find First** button, and then click the **Close** button. The record for order number 392 is now the current record.

   To delete the record, you first need to select the entire record by clicking anywhere in the large rectangular area surrounding the record selector.

4. Click the **record selector** in the top left of the form to select the entire record. See Figure 4-14.

Figure 4-14 ◀
Entire record
selected

click to select
the entire record

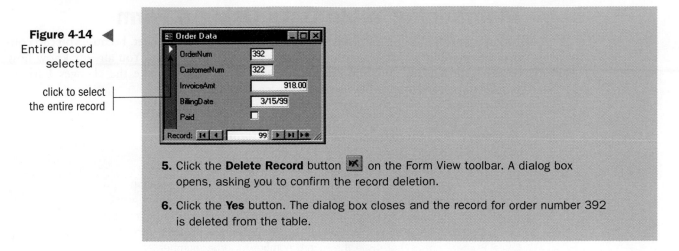

5. Click the **Delete Record** button [X] on the Form View toolbar. A dialog box opens, asking you to confirm the record deletion.

6. Click the **Yes** button. The dialog box closes and the record for order number 392 is deleted from the table.

Barbara's final maintenance change is to add a record for a new order placed by Topview Restaurant.

To add the new record using the Order Data form:

1. Click the **New Record** button [▶*] on the Form View toolbar. Record 104, the next record available for a new record, becomes the current record. All field value boxes are empty, and the insertion point is positioned at the beginning of the field value for OrderNum.

2. Refer to Figure 4-15 and enter the value shown for each field, pressing the Tab key to move from field to field.

Figure 4-15 ◀
Completed
form for the
new record

TROUBLE? Compare your screen with Figure 4-15. If any field value is wrong, correct it now using the methods described earlier for editing field values.

3. After entering the value for BillingDate, press the **Tab** key twice (if necessary). Record 105, the next record available for a new record, becomes the current record, and the record for order number 400 is saved in the Order table.

You've completed Barbara's changes to the Order table, so you can close the Order Data form.

4. Click the **Close** button [X] on the form title bar. The form closes and you return to the Database window. Notice that the Order Data form is listed in the Forms list box.

 **Check**

1 Describe the difference between creating a form using the AutoForm Wizard and creating a form using the Form Wizard.

2 What is an AutoFormat, and how do you change one for an existing form?

3 Which table record is displayed in a form when you press Ctrl + End?

4 You can use the Find command to search for data in a form or _____.

5 Which wildcard character matches any single alphabetic character?

6 How many form records does Access print by default on a page?

7 How do you select an entire form record?

The Order Data form will enable Barbara and her staff to enter and maintain data easily in the Order table. In the next session, you'll create another form for working with data in both the Order and Customer tables at the same time. You'll also create a report showing data from both tables.

SESSION 4.2

In this session you will create a form with a main form and a subform, create a report using the Report Wizard, insert a picture on a report, preview and print a report, and compact a database.

Barbara would like you to create a form so that she can view the data for each customer and all the orders for the customer at the same time. The type of form you need to create will include a main form and a subform.

Creating a Form with a Main Form and a Subform

To create a form based on two tables, you must first define a relationship between the two tables. In Tutorial 3, you defined a one-to-many relationship between the Customer (primary) and Order (related) tables, so you are ready to create the form based on both tables.

When you create a form containing data from two tables that have a one-to-many relationship, you actually create a main form for data from the primary table and a subform for data from the related table. Access uses the defined relationship between the tables to automatically join the tables through the common field that exists in both tables.

Barbara and her staff will use the form when contacting customers about the status of their order payments. Consequently, the main form will contain the customer number and name, owner name, and phone number; the subform will contain the order number, paid status, invoice amount, and billing date.

You'll use the Form Wizard to create the form.

To activate the Form Wizard to create the form:

1. If you took a break after the previous session, make sure that Access is running, the Restaurant database is open, and the Forms tab is displayed in the Database window, and then click the **New** button. The New Form dialog box opens.

   When creating a form based on two tables, you first choose the primary table and select the fields you want to include in the main form; then you choose the related table and select fields from it for the subform.

2. Click **Form Wizard**, click the list arrow for choosing a table or query, click **Customer** to select this table as the source for the main form, and then click the **OK** button. The first Form Wizard dialog box opens, in which you select fields in the order you want them to appear on the main form.

   Barbara wants the form to include only the CustomerNum, CustomerName, OwnerName, and Phone fields from the Customer table.

3. Click **CustomerNum** in the Available Fields list box (if necessary), and then click the [>] button to move the field to the Selected Fields list box.

4. Repeat Step 3 for the **CustomerName**, **OwnerName**, and **Phone** fields.

   The CustomerNum field will appear in the main form, so you do not have to include it in the subform. Otherwise, Barbara wants the subform to include all the fields from the Order table.

5. Click the **Tables/Queries** list arrow, and then click **Table: Order**. The fields from the Order table appear in the Available Fields list box. The quickest way to add the fields you want to include is to move all the fields to the Selected Fields list box, and then remove only the field you don't want to include (CustomerNum).

6. Click the [>>] button to move all the fields from the Order table to the Selected Fields list box.

7. Click **Order.CustomerNum** in the Selected Fields list box, and then click the [<] button to move the field back to the Available Fields list box. Note that the table name (Order) is included in the field name to distinguish it from the same field (CustomerNum) in the Customer table.

8. Click the **Next** button. The next Form Wizard dialog box opens. See Figure 4-16.

Figure 4-16 ◄
Choosing a
main/subform
format

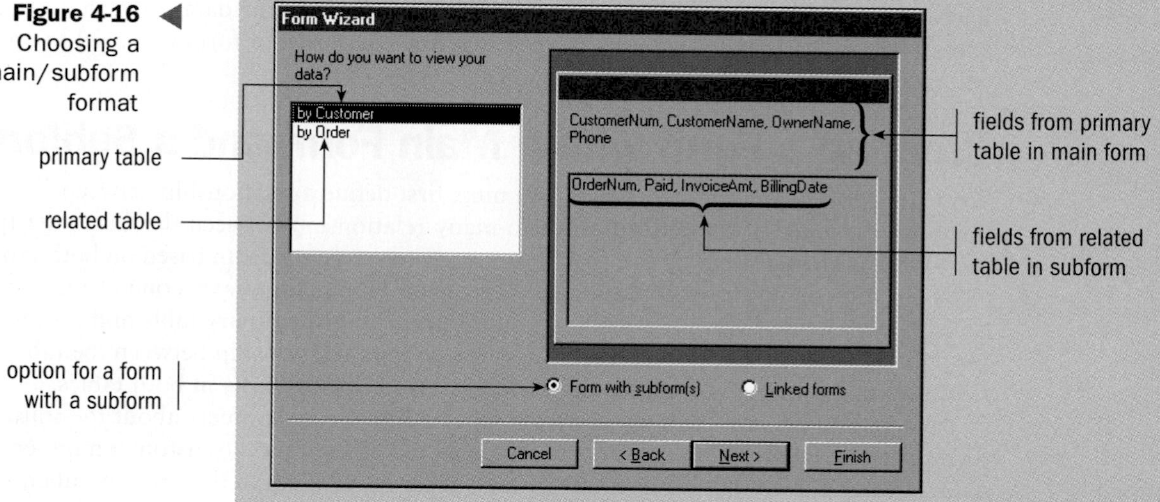

primary table

related table

option for a form
with a subform

fields from primary
table in main form

fields from related
table in subform

In this dialog box, the list box on the left shows the order in which you will view the selected data: first by data from the Customer table (primary table), then by data from the Order table (related table). The form will be displayed as shown in the right side of the dialog box, with the fields from the Customer table at the top in the main form, and the fields from the Order table at the bottom in the subform. The selected option button specifies a main form with a subform.

The default options shown in Figure 4-16 are correct for creating a form with Customer data in the main form and Order data in the subform.

To finish creating the form:

1. Click the **Next** button. The next Form Wizard dialog box opens, in which you choose the subform layout.

   The tabular layout displays subform fields as a table, whereas the datasheet layout displays subform fields as a table datasheet. The layout choice is a matter of personal preference. You'll use the datasheet layout.

2. Click the **Datasheet** option button (if necessary), and then click the **Next** button. The next Form Wizard dialog box opens, in which you choose the form's AutoFormat.

   Barbara wants all forms to have the same style, so you will choose the Standard AutoFormat, which is the same AutoFormat you used to create the Order Data form earlier.

3. Click **Standard** (if necessary) and then click the **Next** button. The next Form Wizard dialog box opens, in which you choose names for the main form and the subform.

   You will use Customer Orders as the main form name and Order Subform as the subform name.

4. Position the insertion point to the right of the last letter in the Form text box, press the **spacebar**, and then type **Orders**. The main form name is now Customer Orders. Note that the default subform name, Order Subform, is the name you want, so you don't need to change it.

   You have answered all the Form Wizard questions.

5. Click the **Finish** button. The completed form is displayed in Form view.

   Notice that some columns in the subform are not wide enough to display the field names entirely. You need to resize the columns to their best fit.

6. Double-click the pointer ✛ at the right edge of each column in the subform. The columns are resized to their best fit and all field names are fully displayed. See Figure 4-17.

Figure 4-17 ◄
Completed
form

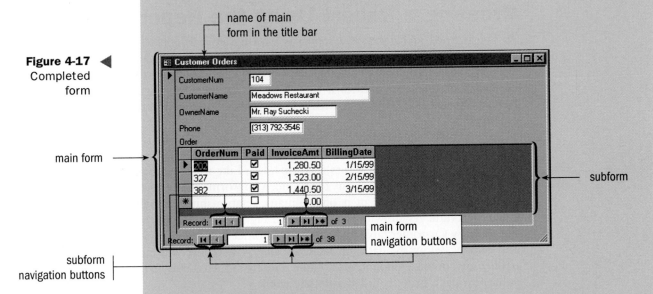

In the main form, Access displays the fields from the first record in the Customer table in columnar format. The records in the main form appear in primary key sequence by customer number. Customer 104 has three related records in the Order table; these records are shown at the bottom in a datasheet format. The form shows that Meadows Restaurant has placed three orders with Valle Coffee, and each order has been paid.

Two sets of navigation buttons appear near the bottom of the form. You use the top set of navigation buttons to select records from the related table in the subform and the bottom set to select records from the primary table in the main form.

You'll use the navigation buttons to view different records.

To navigate to different main form and subform records:

1. Click the **Last Record** navigation button ⏭ in the main form. Record 38 in the Customer table for Embers Restaurant becomes the current record in the main form. The subform shows that this customer placed three orders with Valle Coffee, all of which are unpaid.

2. Click the **Last Record** navigation button ⏭ in the subform. Record 3 in the Order table becomes the current record in the subform.

3. Click the **Previous Record** navigation button ◀ in the main form. Record 37 in the Customer table for The Empire becomes the current record in the main form. This customer has placed two orders, both of which are unpaid.

   You have finished your work with the form, so you can close it.

4. Click the **Close** button ✕ on the form title bar. The form closes, and you return to the Database window. Notice that both the main form, Customer Orders, and the subform, Order Subform, appear in the Forms list box.

Kim would like a report showing data from both the Customer and Order tables so that all the pertinent information about restaurant customers and their orders is available in one place.

Creating a Report Using the Report Wizard

As you learned in Tutorial 1, a report is a formatted hardcopy of the contents of one or more tables in a database. In Access, you can create your own reports or use the Report Wizard to create them for you. Like the Form Wizard, the **Report Wizard** asks you a series of questions and then creates a report based on your answers. Whether you use the Report Wizard or design your own report, you can change the report's design after you create it.

Kim wants you to create a report that includes selected customer data from the Customer table and all the orders from the Order table for each customer. Kim sketched a design of the report she wants (Figure 4-18). Like the Customer Orders form you just created, which includes a main form and a subform, the report will be based on both tables, which are joined in a one-to-many relationship through the common field of CustomerNum. As shown in the sketch in Figure 4-18, the selected customer data from the primary Customer table includes the customer number, name, city, state, owner name, and phone. Below the data for each customer, the report will include the order number, paid status, invoice amount, and billing date from the related Order table. The set of field values for each order is called a **detail record**.

Figure 4-18
Report sketch
for the
Customers and
Orders report

fields from Customer
table: primary table

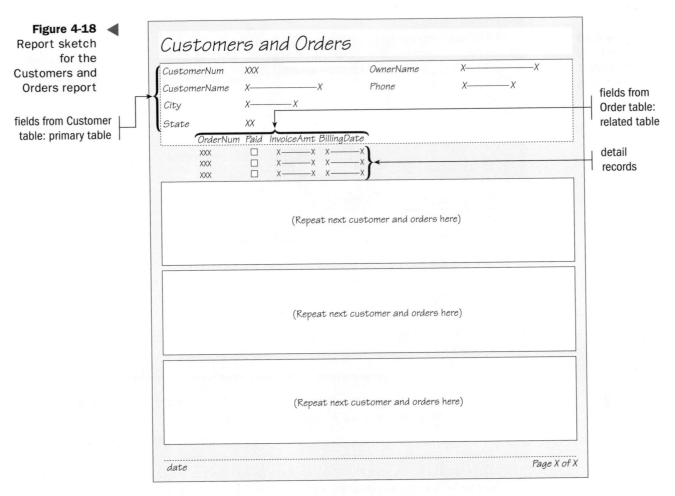

You'll use the Report Wizard to create the report according to the design in Kim's sketch.

To activate the Report Wizard and select the fields to include in the report:

1. Click the **Reports** tab in the Database window to display the Reports list box. You have not created and saved any reports, so the list box is empty.

2. Click the **New** button in the Database window. The New Report dialog box opens.

   Although the data for the report exists in two tables (Customer and Order), you can choose only one table or query to be the data source for the report in the New Report dialog box. However, in the Report Wizard dialog boxes you can include data from other tables. You will select the primary Customer table in the New Report dialog box.

3. Click **Report Wizard**, click the list arrow for choosing a table or query, and then click **Customer**. See Figure 4-19.

Figure 4-19 ◀
Completed
New Report
dialog box

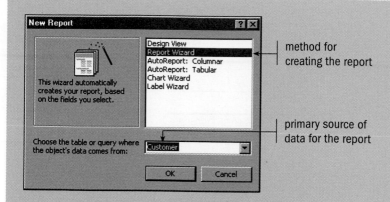

method for
creating the report

primary source of
data for the report

4. Click the **OK** button. The first Report Wizard dialog box opens.

In the first Report Wizard dialog box, you select fields in the order you want them to appear on the report. Kim wants the CustomerNum, CustomerName, City, State, OwnerName, and Phone fields from the Customer table to appear on the report.

5. Click **CustomerNum** in the Available Fields list box, and then click the ⟩ button. The field moves to the Selected Fields list box.

6. Repeat Step 5 for **CustomerName**, **City**, **State**, **OwnerName**, and **Phone**.

7. Click the **Tables/Queries** list arrow, and then click **Table: Order**. The fields from the Order table appear in the Available Fields list box.

The CustomerNum field will appear on the report with the customer data, so you do not have to include it in the detail records for each order. Otherwise, Kim wants all the fields from the Order table to be included in the report. The easiest way to include the necessary fields is to add all the Order table fields to the Selected Fields list box and then to remove the only field you don't want to include—CustomerNum.

8. Click the ⟩⟩ button to move all the fields from the Available Fields list box to the Selected Fields list box.

9. Click **Order.CustomerNum** in the Selected Fields list box, click the ⟨ button to move the selected field back to the Available Fields list box, and then click the **Next** button. The second Report Wizard dialog box opens. See Figure 4-20.

Figure 4-20 ◀
Choosing a
grouped or
ungrouped
report

grouped by table

click to display
tips and examples

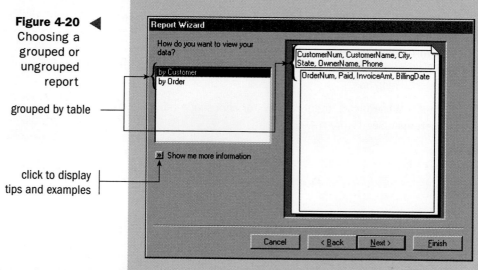

You can choose to arrange the selected data grouped by table, which is the default, or ungrouped. For a grouped report, the data from a record in the primary table appears as a group, followed by the joined records from the related table. For the report you are creating, data from a record in the Customer table appears in a group, followed by the records for the customer from the Order table. An example of an ungrouped report would be a report of records from the Customer and Order tables in order by OrderNum. Each order and its associated customer data would appear together; the data would not be grouped by table.

You can display tips and examples for the choices in the Report Wizard dialog box by clicking the ⟫ button ("Show me more information").

To display tips about the options in the Report Wizard dialog box:

1. Click the ⟫ button. The Report Wizard Tips dialog box opens. Read the displayed information in the dialog box.

   You can display examples of different grouping methods by clicking the ⟫ button ("Show me examples").

2. Click the ⟫ button. The Report Wizard Examples dialog box opens. See Figure 4-21.

Figure 4-21 ◀
Report Wizard
Examples
dialog box

click to
display examples

click to return to
Report Wizard Tips
dialog box

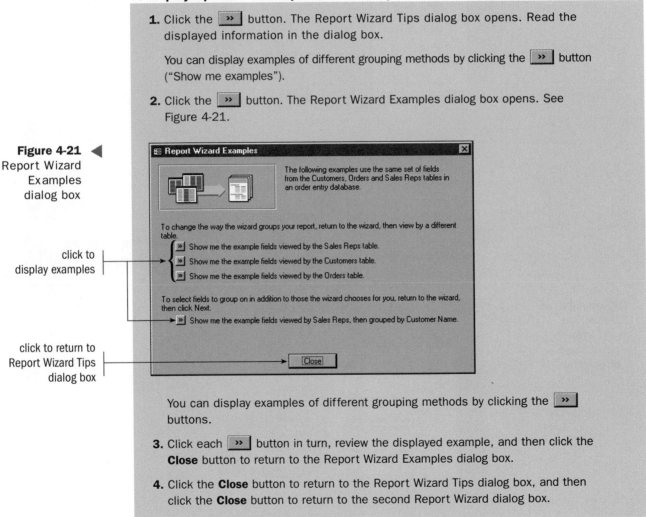

You can display examples of different grouping methods by clicking the ⟫ buttons.

3. Click each ⟫ button in turn, review the displayed example, and then click the **Close** button to return to the Report Wizard Examples dialog box.

4. Click the **Close** button to return to the Report Wizard Tips dialog box, and then click the **Close** button to return to the second Report Wizard dialog box.

The default options shown on your screen are correct for the report Kim wants, so you can continue responding to the Report Wizard questions.

To finish creating the report using the Report Wizard:

1. Click the **Next** button. The next Report Wizard dialog box opens, in which you choose additional grouping levels.

Two grouping levels are shown: one for each customer's data, the other for a customer's orders. Grouping levels are useful for reports with multiple levels, such as those containing month, quarter, and annual totals; or containing city and country groups. Kim's report contains no further grouping levels, so you can accept the default options.

2. Click the **Next** button. The next Report Wizard dialog box opens, in which you choose the sort order for the detail records. See Figure 4-22.

Figure 4-22 ◄
Choosing the sort order for detail records

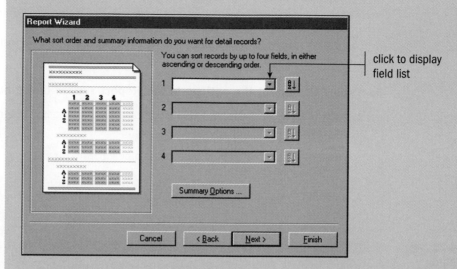

click to display field list

The records from the Order table for a customer represent the detail records for Kim's report. She wants these records to appear in increasing, or ascending, order by the value in the OrderNum field.

3. Click the **1** list arrow, click **OrderNum**, and then click the **Next** button. The next Report Wizard dialog box opens, in which you choose a layout and page orientation for the report. See Figure 4-23.

Figure 4-23 ◄
Choosing the report layout and page orientation

layout sample ──

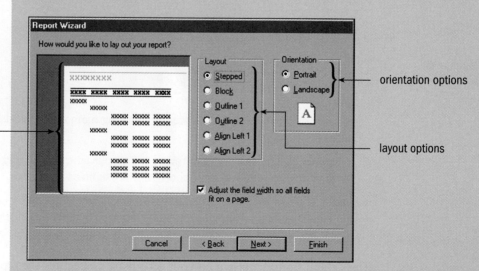

orientation options

layout options

A sample of each layout appears in the box on the left.

4. Click each layout option and examine each sample that appears. You'll use the Outline 2 layout option because it resembles the layout shown in Kim's sketch of the report.

5. Click the **Outline 2** option button, and then click the **Next** button. The next Report Wizard dialog box opens, in which you choose a style for the report.

A sample of the selected style, or AutoFormat, appears in the box on the left. You can always choose a different AutoFormat after you create the report, just as you could when creating a form. Kim likes the appearance of the Corporate AutoFormat, so you'll choose this one for your report.

6. Click **Corporate** and then click the **Next** button. The last Report Wizard dialog box opens, in which you choose a report name, which also serves as the printed title on the report.

   According to Kim's sketch, the report title you need to specify is "Customers and Orders."

7. Type **Customers and Orders** and then click the **Finish** button. The Report Wizard creates the report based on your answers and saves it to your Student Disk. Then Access opens the Customers and Orders report in Print Preview.

   To better view the report, you need to maximize the report window.

8. Click the **Maximize** button 🔲 on the Customers and Orders title bar.

   To view the entire page, you need to change the Zoom setting.

9. Click the **Zoom** list arrow on the Print Preview toolbar, and then click **Fit**. The first page of the report is displayed in Print Preview. See Figure 4-24.

Figure 4-24 ◀
Report
displayed in
Print Preview

Zoom list arrow

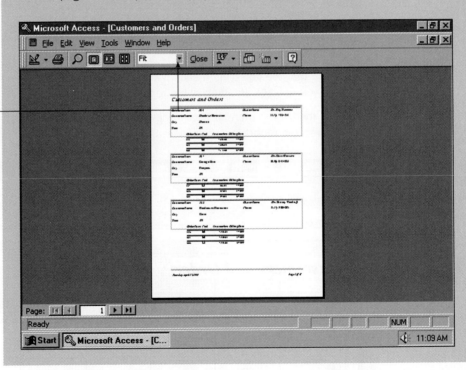

When a report is displayed in Print Preview, you can use the pointer to toggle between a full-page display and a close-up display of the report. Kim asks you to check the report to see if any adjustments need to be made. To do so, you need to view a close-up display of the report.

To view a close-up display of the report and make any necessary corrections:

1. Click the pointer ⊕ at the top center of the report. The display changes to show the report close up. See Figure 4-25.

Figure 4-25 ◀
Close-up view
of the report

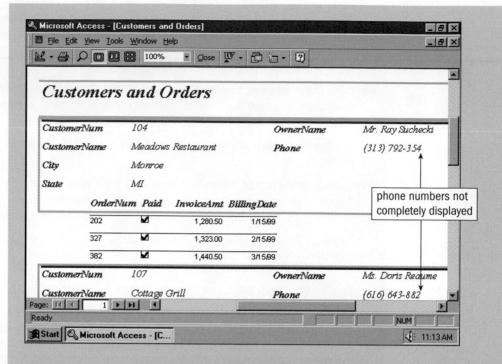

TROUBLE? Scroll your screen as necessary so that it matches the screen in Figure 4-25.

Notice that the last digit in each phone number is not visible in the report. To fix this, you need to first display the report in Design view.

2. Click the **View** button for Design view ⬛ on the Print Preview toolbar. Access displays the report in Design view. See Figure 4-26.

Figure 4-26 ◀
Report
displayed in
Design view

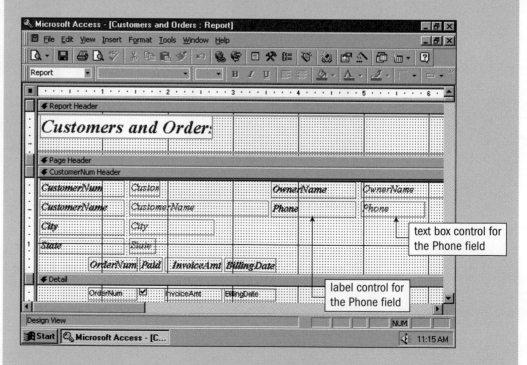

TROUBLE? If the Toolbox is displayed on your screen, close it by clicking its Close button ✕.

You use the Report window in Design view to modify existing reports and to create custom reports.

Each item on a report in Design view is called a *control*. For example, the Phone field consists of two controls: the label "Phone," which appears on the report to identify the field value, and the Phone text box in which the actual field value appears. You need to widen the text box control for the Phone field so that the entire field value is visible in the report.

3. Click the text box control for the Phone field to select it. Notice that small black boxes appear on the border around the control. These boxes, which are called *handles*, indicate that the control is selected and can be manipulated.

4. Position the pointer on the center right handle of the Phone text box control until the pointer changes to ↔. See Figure 4-27.

Figure 4-27 ◀
Resizing the
Phone text box
control

drag this pointer
to the right

handles indicate
control is selected

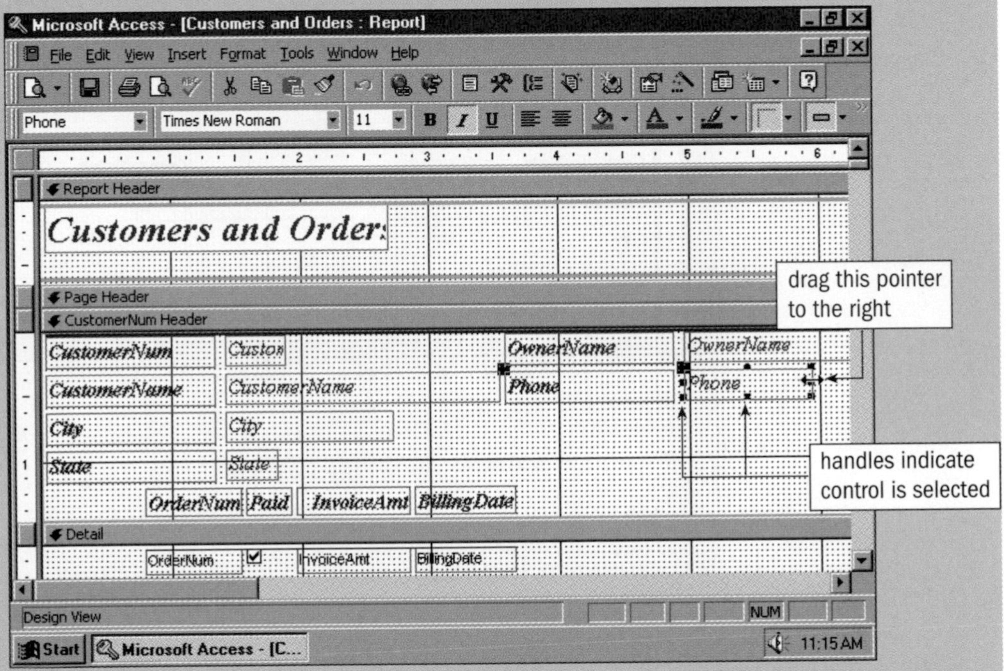

5. Click and drag the pointer to the right until the right edge of the control is aligned with the 6-inch mark on the horizontal ruler, and then release the mouse button.

Now you need to switch back to Print Preview and make sure that the complete value for the Phone field is visible.

6. Click the **View** button for Print Preview 🔍 on the Report Design toolbar. The report appears in Print Preview. Notice that the Phone field values are now completely displayed.

7. Click **File** on the menu bar, and then click **Save** to save the modified report.

Kim decides that she wants the report to include the Valle Coffee cup logo to the right of the report title, for visual interest. You can add the logo to the report by inserting a picture of the coffee cup.

Inserting a Picture on a Report

In Access, you can insert a picture or other graphic image on a report or form to enhance the appearance of the report or form. Sources of graphic images include Microsoft Paint, other drawing programs, and scanners. The file containing the picture you need to insert is named ValleCup, and is located in the Tutorial folder on your Student Disk.

To insert the picture on the report:

1. Click the **Close** button on the Print Preview toolbar to display the report in Design view. See Figure 4-28.

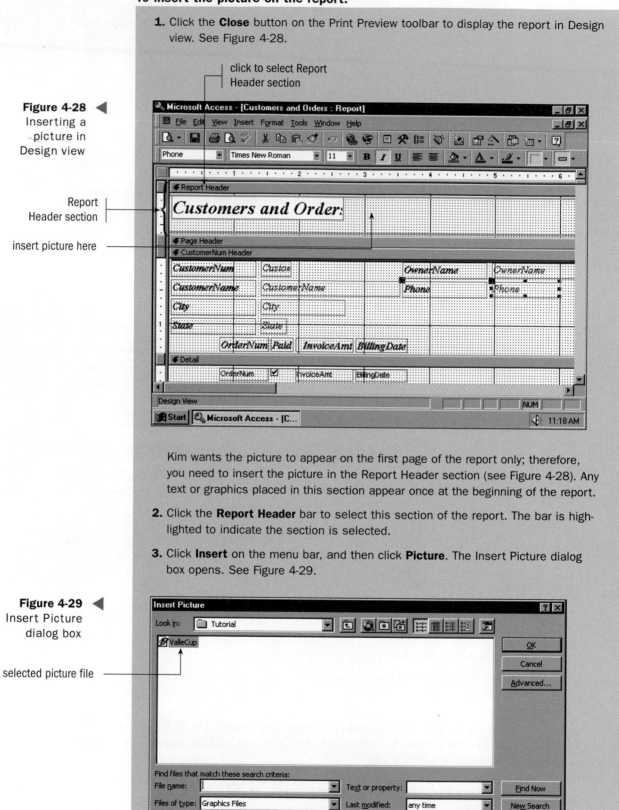

click to select Report Header section

Figure 4-28 ◀
Inserting a picture in Design view

Report Header section

insert picture here

Kim wants the picture to appear on the first page of the report only; therefore, you need to insert the picture in the Report Header section (see Figure 4-28). Any text or graphics placed in this section appear once at the beginning of the report.

2. Click the **Report Header** bar to select this section of the report. The bar is highlighted to indicate the section is selected.

3. Click **Insert** on the menu bar, and then click **Picture**. The Insert Picture dialog box opens. See Figure 4-29.

Figure 4-29 ◀
Insert Picture dialog box

selected picture file

4. Make sure Tutorial appears in the Look in text box, click **ValleCup** to select the picture of the Valle Coffee cup, and then click the **OK** button. The picture is inserted at the far left of the Report Header section, covering some of the report title text. See Figure 4-30.

top border
line of report

Figure 4-30 ◄
Picture
inserted
in report

inserted picture ——

move picture
to here

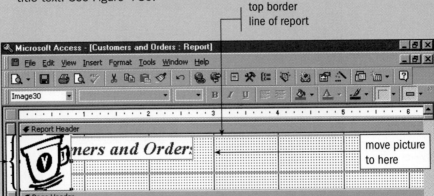

Notice that handles appear on the border around the picture, indicating that the picture is selected and can be manipulated.

Kim wants the picture to appear to the right of the report title, so you need to move the picture using the mouse.

5. Position the pointer on the picture until the pointer changes to 🖑, and then click and drag the mouse to move the picture to the right so that its left edge aligns with the 3-inch mark on the horizontal ruler and its top edge is just below the top border line above the report title (see Figure 4-30).

6. Release the mouse button. The picture appears in the new position. See Figure 4-31.

Figure 4-31 ◄
Repositioned
picture in
the report

TROUBLE? If your picture is in a different location from the one shown in Figure 4-31, use the pointer 🖑 to reposition the picture until it is in approximately the same position shown in the figure. Be sure that the top edge of the picture is below the top border line of the report.

7. Click the **View** button for Print Preview 🔍 on the Report Design toolbar to view the report in Print Preview. The report now includes the inserted picture. If necessary, click the **Zoom** button 🔍 on the Print Preview toolbar to display the entire report page. See Figure 4-32.

Figure 4-32 ◀
Print Preview
of report
with picture

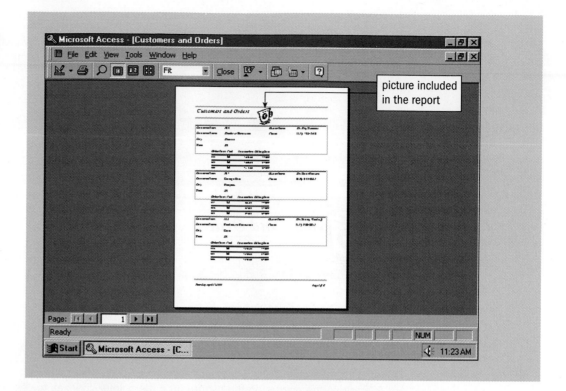

The report is now complete. You'll print a hardcopy of just the first page of the report so that Kim can review the report layout and the inserted picture.

To print page 1 of the report:

1. Click **File** on the menu bar, and then click **Print**. The Print dialog box opens.

2. In the Print Range section, click the **Pages** option button. The insertion point now appears in the From text box so that you can specify the range of pages to print.

3. Type **1** in the From text box, press the **Tab** key to move to the To text box, and then type **1**. These settings specify that only page 1 of the report will be printed.

4. Click the **OK** button. The Print dialog box closes and the first page of the report is printed. See Figure 4-33.

Figure 4-33 ◀
First page
of the
Customers and
Orders report

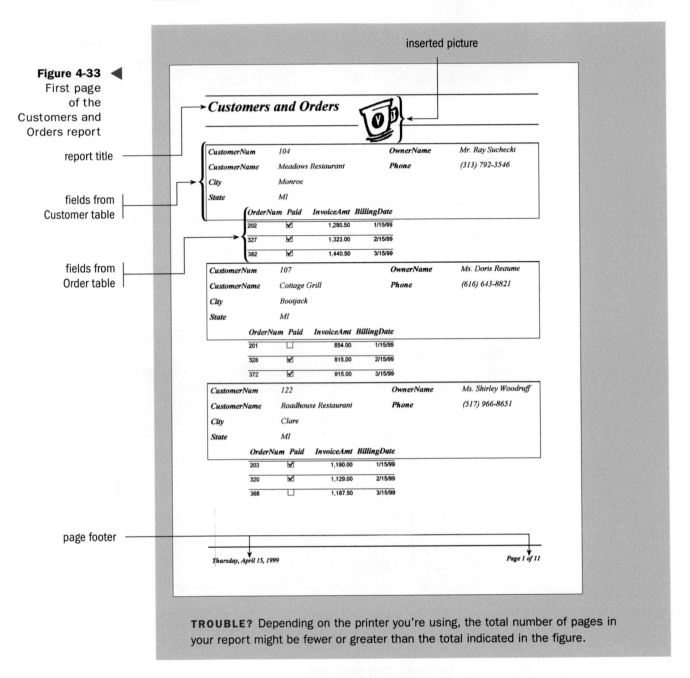

inserted picture

Customers and Orders

report title

fields from
Customer table

fields from
Order table

page footer

TROUBLE? Depending on the printer you're using, the total number of pages in your report might be fewer or greater than the total indicated in the figure.

Kim approves of the report layout and contents, so you can close and save the report.

To close and save the report:

1. Click the **Close** button ☒ on the menu bar.

> **TROUBLE?** If you click the Close button on the Print Preview toolbar by mistake, Access redisplays the report in Design view. Click the Close button ☒ on the menu bar.

Access displays a dialog box asking if you want to save the changes to the design of your report.

2. Click the **Yes** button to save and close the report and return to the Database window.

You no longer need to have the Database window maximized, so you can restore it now.

3. Click the **Restore** button on the Database window.

Before you exit Access, you'll compact the Restaurant database to free up disk space.

Compacting a Database

When you delete records in an Access table, the space occupied by the deleted records on disk does not become available for other records. The same is true if you delete an object, such as a table, query, or form. To make the space available, you must compact the database. **Compacting** a database rearranges the data and objects in a database and creates a smaller copy of the database. Unlike making a copy of a database file, which you do to protect your database against loss or damage, you compact the database to make it smaller, thereby making more space available on your disk. Before compacting a database, you must close it.

REFERENCE window

COMPACTING A DATABASE

- Make sure the database you want to compact is closed.
- In the Access window, click Tools on the menu bar, point to Database Utilities, and then click Compact Database to open the Database to Compact From dialog box.
- In the Look in box, select the drive and directory containing the database you want to compact; in the File name box, select the database you want to compact.
- Click the Compact button. Access opens the Compact Database Into dialog box.
- In the Save in box, select the drive and directory for the location of the compacted database; in the File name text box, type the name you want to assign to the compacted database.
- Click the Save button.

You'll compact the Restaurant database, delete the original (uncompacted) database file, and then rename the compacted file.

To compact the Restaurant database:

1. Click the **Close** button ☒ on the Database window title bar.

2. Click **Tools** on the menu bar, point to **Database Utilities**, and then click **Compact Database**. Access opens the Database to Compact From dialog box, in which you select the database you want to compact.

3. Make sure Tutorial appears in the Look in list box, click **Restaurant** in the list box, and then click the **Compact** button. Access opens the Compact Database Into dialog box, in which you enter the filename for the compacted copy of the database and select its drive and folder location.

Usually you would make a backup copy of the database as a safeguard before compacting. Here, you'll save the compacted database with a different name, delete the original database file, and then rename the compacted database to the original database name.

4. Type **Compacted Restaurant** in the File name text box, make sure Tutorial appears in the Save in list box, and then click the **Save** button. Access compacts the Restaurant database, creating the copied file named Compacted Restaurant, and returns you to the Access window.

Now you need to exit Access, delete the original Restaurant database, and then rename the compacted database as Restaurant. To delete and rename the necessary files, you'll open the Exploring window from the desktop.

To open the Exploring window and delete and rename the database files:

1. Click the **Close** button ☒ on the Access window title bar. Access closes and you return to the Windows 95 desktop.

2. Using the right mouse button, click the **Start** button on the taskbar, and then click **Explore**. The Exploring window opens.

3. Scrolling as necessary, click the plus symbol to the left of the drive that contains your Student Disk in the All Folders list box, and then click **Tutorial**. The list of files in the Tutorial folder on your Student Disk appears in the Contents of 'Tutorial' list box. See Figure 4-34.

Figure 4-34 ◀
Original and compacted database files in Exploring window

original database file

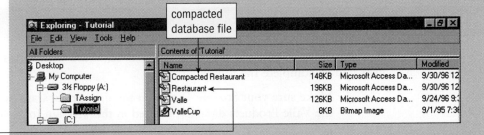

Verify that both database files—the original Restaurant database and the Compacted Restaurant database—are included in the window. Note the difference in size of the two files.

TROUBLE? The size of your files might be different from those in the figure.

Now you need to delete the original (uncompacted) database file and then rename the compacted file.

4. Click **Restaurant** in the list box, click **File** on the menu bar, and then click **Delete**. The Confirm File Delete dialog box opens and asks you to confirm the deletion.

5. Click the **Yes** button to delete the file.

6. Click **Compacted Restaurant** in the list box, click **File** on the menu bar, and then click **Rename**. The filename appears highlighted inside a box to indicate it is selected for editing.

7. Position the insertion point to the left of the word "Compacted," and then use the **Delete** key to delete the word "Compacted" and the space following it.

8. Press the **Enter** key. The filename of the compacted file is now Restaurant.

9. Click the **Close** button ☒ on the Exploring title bar to close the Exploring window and return to the desktop.

Quick Check

1 How are a related table and a primary table associated with a form that contains a main form and a subform?

2 Describe how you use the navigation buttons to move through a form containing a main form and a subform.

3 When you use the Report Wizard, the report name is also used as the _____.

4 To insert a picture on a report, the report must be displayed in _____.

5 Any text or graphics placed in the _____ section of a report appear only on the first page of the report.

6 What is the purpose of compacting a database?

Barbara is satisfied that both forms—the Order Data form and the Customer Orders form—will make it easier to enter, view, and update data in the Restaurant database. The Customers and Orders report presents important information about Valle Coffee's restaurant customers in an attractive, professional format, which will help Kim and her staff in their sales and marketing efforts.

Tutorial Assignments

Barbara wants to enhance the Valle Products database with forms and reports, and she asks you to complete the following:

1. Make sure your Student Disk is in the disk drive, start Access, and then open the Valle Products database located in the TAssign folder on your Student Disk.

2. Use the Form Wizard to create a form based on the Product table. Select all fields for the form, the Columnar layout, the Stone style, and the title name of Product Data.

3. Using the form you created in the previous step, print the fifth form record, change the AutoFormat to Standard, save the changed form, and then print the fifth form record again.

4. Use the Product Data form to update the Product table as follows:
   a. Navigate to the record with the ProductCode 2310. Change the field values for WeightCode to A, Price to 8.99, and Decaf to Null for this record.
   b. Use the Find command to move to the record with the ProductCode 4306, and then delete the record.
   c. Add a new record with the following field values:
   ProductCode: 2306
   CoffeeCode: AMAR
   WeightCode: A
   Price: 8.99
   Decaf: Null
   Print only this form record, and then save and close the form.

5. Use the Form Wizard to create a form containing a main form and a subform. Select the CoffeeName and CoffeeType fields from the Coffee table for the main form, and select all fields except CoffeeCode from the Product table for the subform. Use the Tabular layout and the Standard style. Specify the title Coffee Products for the main form and the title Product Subform for the subform. Print the fourth main form record and its subform records.

Access

6. Use the Report Wizard to create a report based on the primary Coffee table and the related Product table. Select all fields from the Coffee table except Decaf, and select all fields from the Product table except CoffeeCode. In the third Report Wizard dialog box, specify the CoffeeType field as an additional grouping level. Sort the detail records by ProductCode. Choose the Align Left 1 layout and the Casual style for the report. Specify the title Valle Coffee Products for the report.

7. Insert the ValleCup picture, which is located in the TAssign folder on your Student Disk, in the Report Header section of the Valle Coffee Products report. Position the picture so that its left edge aligns with the 4-inch mark on the horizontal ruler and its top edge is just below the top border line of the report.

8. Print only the first page of the report, and then close and save the modified report.

9. Compact the Valle Products database; name the copy of the database Compacted Valle Products. After the compacting process is complete, delete the original Valle Products database, and then rename the Compacted Valle Products file as Valle Products.

Case Problems

1. Ashbrook Mall Information Desk Sam Bullard wants the MallJobs database to include forms and reports that will help him track and distribute information about jobs available at the Ashbrook Mall. You'll create the necessary forms and reports by completing the following:

1. Make sure your Student Disk is in the disk drive, start Access, and then open the MallJobs database located in the Cases folder on your Student Disk.

2. Use the Form Wizard to create a form based on the Store table. Select all fields for the form, the Columnar layout, and the Clouds style. Specify the title Store Data for the form.

3. Change the AutoFormat for the Store Data form to Flax.

4. Use the Find command to move to the record with the Store value of TC, and then change the Contact field value for this record to Sarah Pedicini.

5. Use the Store Data form to add a new record with the following field values:
   Store: PW
   StoreName: Pet World
   Location: B2
   Contact: Killian McElroy
   Extension: 2750
   Print only this form record, and then save and close the form.

6. Use the Form Wizard to create a form containing a main form and a subform. Select all the fields from the Store table for the main form, and select all fields except Store from the Job table for the subform. Use the Tabular layout and the Flax style. Specify the title Jobs By Store for the main form and the title Job Subform for the subform.

7. Display the Jobs By Store form in Design view. To improve the appearance of the form, you need to reduce the width of the subform so that it does not block out the Flax background. Maximize the Form window, if necessary. Click the subform to select it; handles will appear around the subform to indicate it is selected. Position the pointer on the right middle handle until the pointer changes to ↔, click and drag the mouse to the left until the right edge

of the subform aligns with the 4-inch mark on the horizontal ruler, and then release the mouse button. Restore the Form window and then display the form in Form view.

8. Print the eighth main form record and its subform records, and then save and close the Jobs By Store form.

9. Use the Report Wizard to create a report based on the primary Store table and the related Job table. Select all fields from the Store table, and select all fields from the Job table except Store. Sort the detail records by Job. Choose the Block layout and Landscape orientation for the report. Choose the Bold style. Specify the title Available Jobs for the report, and then print and close the report.

10. Compact the MallJobs database; name the copy of the database Compacted MallJobs. After the compacting process is complete, delete the original MallJobs database, and then rename the Compacted MallJobs file as MallJobs.

2. Professional Litigation User Services Raj Jawahir continues his work with the Payments database to track and analyze the payment history of PLUS clients. To help him, you'll enhance the Payments database by completing the following:

1. Make sure your Student Disk is in the disk drive, start Access, and then open the Payments database located in the Cases folder on your Student Disk.

2. Use the Form Wizard to create a form containing a main form and a subform. Select the Firm# and FirmName fields from the Firm table for the main form, and select all fields except Firm# from the Payment table for the subform. Use the Datasheet layout and the Dusk style. Specify the title Firm Payments for the main form and the title Payment Subform for the subform. Resize all columns in the subform to their best fit. Print the first main form record and its displayed subform records.

3. For the form you just created, change the AutoFormat to Colorful 2, save the changed form, and then print the first main form record and its displayed subform records.

4. Navigate to the third record in the subform for the first main record, and then change the AmtPaid field value to 1,500.00.

5. Use the Find command to move to the record with the Firm# 1136, and delete the record. Answer Yes to any warning messages about deleting the record.

6. Use the appropriate wildcard character to find all records with the abbreviation "DA" (for District Attorney) in the firm name. (*Hint:* You must enter the wildcard character before and after the text you are searching for.) How many records did you find?

7. Use the Report Wizard to create a report based on the primary Firm table and the related Payment table. Select all fields from the Firm table except Extension, and select all fields from the Payment table except Firm#. In the third Report Wizard dialog box, specify the PLUSAcctRep field as an additional grouping level. Sort the detail records by AmtPaid in *descending* order. Choose the Outline 1 layout and the Formal style for the report. Specify the title Payments By Firms for the report.

8. Insert the Plus picture, which is located in the Cases folder on your Student Disk, in the Report Header section of the Payments By Firms report. Leave the picture in its original position at the left edge of the report header.

9. Use the Office Assistant to ask the following question: "How do I move an object behind another?" Choose the topic "Move a control in front of or behind other controls." Read the information and then close the Help window. Make sure the Plus picture is still selected, and then move it behind the Payments By Firms title.

10. Use the Office Assistant to ask the following question: "How do I change the background color of an object?" Choose the topic "Change the background color of a control or section." Read the information and then close the Help window and the Office Assistant. Select the Payments By Firms title object, and then change its background color to Transparent. Select each of the two horizontal lines in the Report Header section that cut through the middle of the Plus picture, and then use the Delete key to delete each line.

11. Display the report in Print Preview. Print just the first page of the report, and then close and save the report.

12. Compact the Payments database; name the copy of the database Compacted Payments. After the compacting process is complete, delete the original Payments database, and then rename the Compacted Payments file as Payments.

3. Best Friends Noah and Sheila Warnick want to create forms and reports for the Walks database. You'll help them create these database objects by completing the following:

1. Make sure your Student Disk is in the disk drive, start Access, and then open the Walks database located in the Cases folder on your Student Disk.

2. Use the Form Wizard to create a form based on the Walker table. Select all fields for the form, the Columnar layout, and the Colorful 1 style. Specify the title Walker Data for the form.

3. Use the Walker Data form to update the Walker table as follows:
   a. For the record with the WalkerID 223, change the LastName to Hoban and the Distance to 0.
   b. Add a new record with the following values:
      WalkerID: 225
      LastName: DelFavero
      FirstName: Cindi
      Phone: 711-1275
      Distance: 2.0
      Print just this form record.
   c. Delete the record with the WalkerID field value of 123.

4. Change the AutoFormat of the Walker Data form to Pattern, save the changed form, and then use the form to print the last record in the Walker table. Close the form.

5. Use the Form Wizard to create a form containing a main form and a subform. Select all the fields from the Walker table for the main form, and select the PledgeAmt, PaidAmt, and DatePaid fields from the Pledge table for the subform. Use the Tabular layout and the Standard style. Specify the title Walkers And Pledges for the main form and the title Pledge Subform for the subform. Use the navigation buttons to find the first main form record that contains values in the subform. Print this main form record and its subform records.

6. Use the Report Wizard to create a report based on the primary Walker table and the related Pledge table. Select all fields from the Walker table, and select all fields from the Pledge table except WalkerID. Sort the detail records by PledgeNo. Choose the Align Left 2 layout and Landscape orientation for the report. Choose the Soft Gray style. Specify the title Walk-A-Thon Walkers And Pledges for the report.

7. View both pages of the report in Print Preview. (*Hint:* Use a toolbar button.) Notice that the pledge data for the third record appears at the top of the second page. You need to decrease the size of the bottom margin so that the pledge data will appear with its corresponding walker data. Use the Office Assistant to ask the question, "How do I change the margins in a report?" Choose the topic "Set margins, page orientation, and other page setup options" and then read the displayed Help information. Use the Page Setup command to change the bottom margin of the report to .5".

8. Print the entire report.

9. Compact the Walks database; name the copy of the database "Compacted Walks." After the compacting process is complete, delete the original Walks database, and then rename the Compacted Walks file as Walks.

4. Lopez Lexus Dealerships Maria and Hector Lopez want to create forms and reports that will help them track and analyze data about the cars and different locations for their Lexus dealerships. Help them enhance the Lexus database by completing the following:

1. Make sure your Student Disk is in the disk drive, start Access, and then open the Lexus database located in the Cases folder on your Student Disk.

2. Use the Form Wizard to create a form containing a main form and a subform. Select all the fields from the Locations table for the main form, and select the VehicleID, Model, Class, Year, Cost, and SellingPrice fields from the Cars table for the subform. Use the Datasheet layout and the International style. Specify the title Locations And Cars for the main form and the title Cars Subform for the subform. Resize all columns in the subform to their best fit. Print the first main form record and its displayed subform records.

3. For the form you just created, change the AutoFormat to Standard, save the changed form, and then print the first main form record and its displayed subform records.

4. Navigate to the second record in the subform for the fifth main record, and then change the SellingPrice field value to $42,175.00.

5. Use the Find command to move to the record with the LocationCode P1, and delete the record. Answer Yes to any warning messages about deleting the record.

6. Use the appropriate wildcard character to find all records with a LocationCode value that begins with the letter "A." How many records did you find?

7. Use the Report Wizard to create a report based on the primary Locations table and the related Cars table. Select all fields from the Locations table, and select all fields from the Cars table except Manufacturer and LocationCode. Specify two sort fields for the detail records: first, the VehicleID field in ascending order, then the Cost field in descending order. Choose the Align Left 1 layout and Landscape orientation for the report. Choose the Compact style. Specify the title Dealership Locations And Cars for the report, and then print just the first page of the report.

8. Compact the Lexus database; name the copy of the database Compacted Lexus. After the compacting process is complete, delete the original Lexus database, and then rename the Compacted Lexus file as Lexus.

Questions

5   cur...

6   Use the hor... ...ical scroll bars to view fields or records not currently visible in the datasheet; use the navigatio... ...s to move vertically through the records.

SESSION 1.2

1   query

2   primary key

3   AutoForm Wizard

4   The form displays each field name on a separate line to the left of its field value, which appears in a box; the widths of the boxes represent the size of the fields.

5   Click the Office Assistant button on any toolbar, type a question in the text box, click the Search button, and then choose a topic from the list displayed.

6   Print Preview

SESSION 2.1

1   Identify all the fields needed to produce the required information; group related fields into tables; determine each table's primary key; include a common field in related tables; avoid data redundancy; and determine the properties of each field.

2   The data type determines what field values you can enter for the field and what other properties the field will have.

3   text fields and number fields

4   Order numbers will not be used for calculations.

5   null

6   the record being edited; the next row available for a new record

SESSION 2.2

1   The field and all its values are removed from the table.

2   In Design view, right-click the row selector for the row above which you want to insert the field, click Insert Rows on the shortcut menu, and then define the new field.

3   yes/no

4   Format property

5   Access allows you to have only one database open at a time.

6   In navigation mode, the entire field value is selected and anything you type replaces the field value; in editing mode, you can insert or delete characters in a field value based on the location of the insertion point.

SESSION 3.1

1 a general query in which you specify the fields and records you want Access to select

2 The field list contains the table name at the top of the list box and the table's fields listed in the order in which they appear in the table; the design grid displays columns that contain specifications about a field you will use in the query.

3 A table datasheet and a query datasheet look the same, appearing in Datasheet view, and can be used to update data in a database. A table datasheet shows the permanent data in a table, whereas a query datasheet is temporary and its contents are based on the criteria you establish in the design grid.

4 primary table; related table

5 referential integrity

6 oldest to most recent date

7 when you have two or more nonadjacent sort keys or when the fields to be used for sorting are in the wrong order

8 filter

SESSION 3.2

1 condition

2 in the same Criteria row; in different Criteria rows

3 expression

4 A calculated field appears in a query datasheet but does not exist in a database, as does a table field.

5 a function that performs an arithmetic operation on selected records in a database

6 Group By

SESSION 4.1

1 The AutoForm Wizard creates a form automatically using all the fields in the selected table or query; the Form Wizard allows you to choose some or all of the fields in the selected table or query, choose fields from other tables and queries, and display fields in any order on the form.

2 An AutoFormat is a predefined style for a form (or report). To change a form's AutoFormat, display the form in Design view, click the AutoFormat button on the Form Design toolbar, click the new AutoFormat in the Form AutoFormats list box, and then click OK.

3 the last record in the table

4 datasheet

5 the question mark (?)

6 as many form records as can fit on a printed page

7 Click the record selector in the top left of the form.

SESSION 4.2

1 The main form displays the data from the primary table and the subform displays the data from the related table.

2 You use the top set of navigation buttons to select and move through records from the related table in the subform and the bottom set to select and move through records from the primary table in the main form.

3 report title

4 Design view

5 Report Header

6 to make the database smaller and make more space available on your disk

NEW
PERSPECTIVES
SERIES

Microsoft®
Access 97

LEVEL II

TUTORIALS

STUDENT DISKS

To complete Access 97 Tutorials 5–7, you need three Student Disks. Your instructor will either provide you with Student Disks or ask you to make your own.

If you are supposed to make your own Student Disks, you will need three blank, formatted, high-density disks. You will need to copy a set of folders from a file server or standalone computer onto your disks. Your instructor will tell you which computer, drive letter, and folders contain the files you need. The following table shows you which folders go on each of your disks, so that you will have enough disk space to complete all the tutorials, Tutorial Assignments, and Case Problems:

Student Disk	Write this on the disk label	Put these folders on the disk
1	Student Disk 1: Access 97 Tutorials 5–7 Tutorials and Tutorial Assignments	Tutorial and TAssign from Disk 1 folder
2	Student Disk 2: Access 97 Case Problems 1 and 2	Cases from Disk 2 folder
3	Student Disk 3: Access 97 Case Problems 3 and 4	Cases from Disk 3 folder

When you begin each tutorial, be sure you are using the correct Student Disk. See the inside front or inside back cover of this book for more information on Student Disk files, or ask your instructor or technical support person for assistance.

USING YOUR OWN COMPUTER

If you are going to work through this book using your own computer, you need:

■ **Computer System** Microsoft Windows 95 or Microsoft Windows NT Workstation 4.0 (or a later version) and Microsoft Access 97 must be installed on your computer. This book assumes a typical installation of Microsoft Access 97.

■ **Student Disks** Ask your instructor or technical support person for details on how to get the Student Disks. You will not be able to complete the tutorials or end-of-tutorial assignments in this book using your own computer until you have Student Disks. The Student Files may also be obtained electronically over the Internet. See the inside front or inside back cover of this book for more details.

TO THE INSTRUCTOR

To complete Access 97 Tutorials 5–7, your students must use a set of files on three Student Disks. These files are included in the Instructor's Resource Kit, and they may also be obtained electronically over the Internet. See the inside front or inside back cover of this book for more details. Follow the instructions in the Readme file to copy the files to your server or standalone computer. You can view the Readme file using WordPad. Once the files are copied, you can make Student Disks for the students yourself, or you can tell students where to find the files so they can make their own Student Disks.

COURSE TECHNOLOGY STUDENT FILES

You are granted a license to copy the Student Files to any computer or computer network used by students who have purchased this book.

Creating More Advanced Queries and Custom Forms

Making the Restaurant Database Easier to Use

Valle Coffee

CASE Ten years ago Leonard Valle became president of Algoman Imports, a small distributor of inexpensive coffee beans to supermarkets in western Michigan. Since that time, Leonard has transformed the company into a popular distributor of gourmet coffees to restaurants and offices. He took over company ownership, changed the company name to Valle Coffee, and expanded its market area to include Indiana and Ohio.

Leonard has incorporated the use of computers in all aspects of the business, including financial management, inventory, production, and sales. The company has developed the Restaurant database of customer information and uses **Microsoft Access 97** (or simply **Access**) to manage it.

The Restaurant database contains tables, queries, forms, and reports that Barbara Hennessey, office manager, and Kim Carpenter, director of marketing, use to keep track of customer orders and billing and marketing information.

Leonard, Kim, and Barbara are pleased with the information they are able to get from the Restaurant database. They are interested in taking better advantage of the power of Access to make the database easier to use and to create more sophisticated queries and custom forms. For example, Kim wants to obtain lists of customers in certain area codes and Barbara needs a list of unpaid invoices for customers in Indiana or Ohio. Barbara also wants to make a change to the design of the Order table to make it easier to enter the CustomerNum value for an Order record. In this tutorial, you'll make the necessary modifications and customizations to the Restaurant database.

SESSION

5.1

In this session you will change the CustomerNum field in the Order table to a Lookup Wizard field. You will also create a pattern match query, a list-of-values query, and a query selecting non-matching values. Finally, you will construct complex selection criteria using And with Or, and you'll create a parameter query.

Creating a Lookup Wizard Field

The Order table in the Restaurant database contains information about orders placed by Valle Coffee's customers. Barbara wants to make it easier for her staff members to enter data in the table. In particular, it would be easier for them if they did not have to remember the correct customer number of the customer who placed the order. So, Barbara wants to change the CustomerNum field in the Order table to a Lookup Wizard field. A **Lookup Wizard field** allows the user to select a value from a list of possible values. For the CustomerNum field, the user will be able to select from the list of customer names in the Customer table rather than having to remember the correct customer number. The CustomerNum field in the Order table will store the customer number, but the customer name will appear in Datasheet view. This makes it easier for the user and guarantees that the customer number entered is valid.

Barbara asks you to change the CustomerNum field in the Order table to a Lookup Wizard field. You begin by opening the Order table in Design view.

To open the Order table in Design view:

1. Make sure you have created your copy of the Access Student Disk, and then place your Student Disk in the appropriate disk drive.

   TROUBLE? If you don't have a Student Disk, you need to get one before you can proceed. Your instructor will either give you one or ask you to make your own. (See your instructor for information.) In either case, be sure you have made a copy of your Student Disk before you begin; in this way, the original Student Disk files will be available on the copied disk in case you need to start over because of an error or problem.

2. Start Access and open the Restaurant database located in the Tutorial folder on your Student Disk. The Restaurant database is displayed in the Access window.

3. Click the **Tables** tab (if necessary), click **Order**, and then click the **Design** button to display the Order table in Design view. See Figure 5-1.

Figure 5-1 ◄
Order table in
Design view

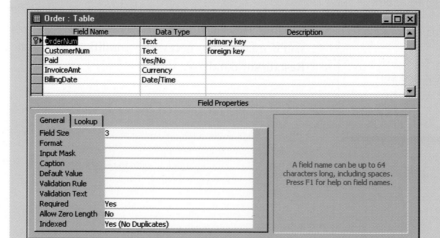

Now you can change the data type of the CustomerNum field to Lookup Wizard.

To change the CustomerNum field to a Lookup Wizard field:

1. Click the **Data Type** text box for the CustomerNum field, click the **Data Type** list arrow, and then click **Lookup Wizard**. Access displays the first Lookup Wizard dialog box. See Figure 5-2.

Figure 5-2 ◄
First Lookup
Wizard dialog
box

make sure this option
is selected

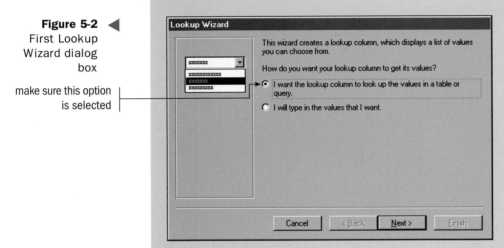

This dialog box allows you to specify a list of values that are allowed for the CustomerNum value in a record in the Order table. You can specify a table or query from which the value is selected or you can enter a new list of values. You want the CustomerNum value to come from the Customer table.

2. Make sure the option for looking up the values in a table or query is selected, and then click the **Next** button to display the next Lookup Wizard dialog box.

3. Make sure **Customer** is selected, and then click the **Next** button. See Figure 5-3.

Figure 5-3 ◄
Selecting the
Customer table
fields

select these two
fields

click to select
highlighted field

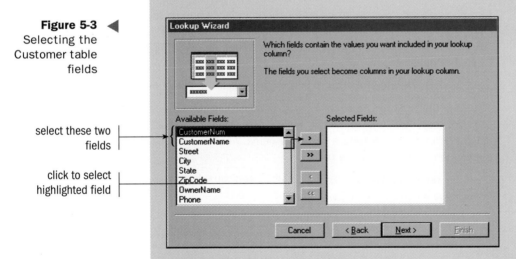

This dialog box allows you to select the necessary fields from the Customer table. You need to select the CustomerNum field because it is the common field that links the Customer and Order tables. You also must select the CustomerName field because Barbara wants the user to be able to select from a list of customer names when entering a new order record.

4. Click the ⟩ button to select the CustomerNum field from the Customer table to be included in the lookup column. Click the ⟩ button to select the CustomerName field, and then click the **Next** button. See Figure 5-4.

Figure 5-4 ◀
Adjusting the
width of the
lookup column

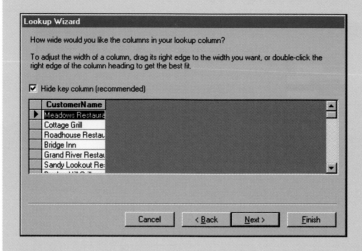

In this dialog box you can adjust the width of the CustomerName column. This column will appear when a user enters a CustomerNum for the order in the Order table. The user can select a CustomerName and Access will enter the correct CustomerNum. The selected "Hide key column" option means that the list of CustomerNum values will not appear in the datasheet.

5. Place the pointer on the right edge of the CustomerName field column heading. When the pointer changes to ✛, double-click to resize the column to fit the data, and then click the **Next** button.

In this dialog box you can specify the caption that will appear for the field in Datasheet view. The default value is the field name, CustomerNum. Because the field will show customer names in Datasheet view, you will change the caption to CustomerName.

6. Type **CustomerName** in the text box, and then click the **Finish** button.

To create the Lookup Wizard field, Access must save the table design and create the necessary relationship so that Access can enter the correct CustomerNum value when the user selects a customer name. Access displays a dialog box asking you to confirm saving the table.

7. Click the **Yes** button. Access creates the Lookup Wizard field and returns to the Order table in Design view. See Figure 5-5.

Figure 5-5 ◀
Lookup Wizard
field defined

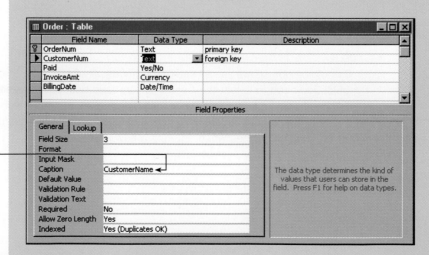

new caption

The Data Type value for the CustomerNum field still says Text, because this field contains text data. However, Access will now use the CustomerNum field value to look up and display customer names from the Customer table.

8. Click the **Save** button 🖫 on the Table Design toolbar to save the changes to the table design.

Barbara asks you to enter a new record in the Order table (Figure 5-6). To do so you need to switch to Datasheet view.

Figure 5-6 ◄
The new Order
table record

OrderNum	CustomerName	Paid	InvoiceAmt	BillingDate
401	Roadhouse Restaurant	No	1,100.00	3/15/99

To enter the new order record:

1. Click the **View** button for Datasheet view 🖩 on the Table Design toolbar to display the Order table in Datasheet view. Notice that the customer names instead of the customer numbers now appear in the second column, as specified by the Lookup Wizard field.

   You need to widen the CustomerName column to display the complete field values.

2. Place the pointer on the right edge of the CustomerName column heading. When the pointer changes to ↔, double-click to resize the column to fit the data.

3. Click the **New Record** button ▶* on the Table Datasheet toolbar. Access displays a new blank record (number 105).

4. In the OrderNum field, type **401** and then press the **Tab** key to move to the CustomerNum field, which has the caption CustomerName. Access displays a list arrow at the right of the CustomerNum field text box.

5. Click the list arrow. Access displays the list of CustomerName field values from the Customer table. See Figure 5-7.

Figure 5-7 ◄
List of
CustomerName
field values

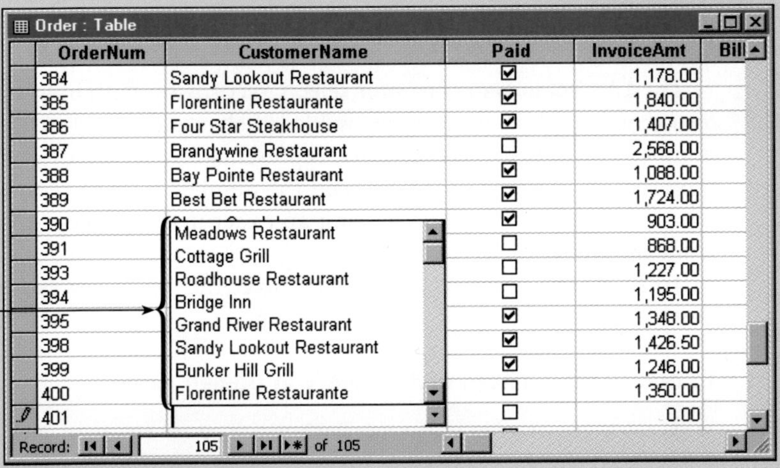

OrderNum	CustomerName	Paid	InvoiceAmt	Bill ▲
384	Sandy Lookout Restaurant	☑	1,178.00	
385	Florentine Restaurante	☑	1,840.00	
386	Four Star Steakhouse	☑	1,407.00	
387	Brandywine Restaurant	☐	2,568.00	
388	Bay Pointe Restaurant	☑	1,088.00	
389	Best Bet Restaurant	☑	1,724.00	
390	Meadows Restaurant	☑	903.00	
391	Cottage Grill	☐	868.00	
393	Roadhouse Restaurant	☐	1,227.00	
394	Bridge Inn	☐	1,195.00	
395	Grand River Restaurant	☑	1,348.00	
398	Sandy Lookout Restaurant	☑	1,426.50	
399	Bunker Hill Grill	☑	1,246.00	
400	Florentine Restaurante	☐	1,350.00	
401		☐	0.00	

Lookup Wizard
list box

Record: ◄◄ ◄ | 105 | ► ►◄ ►* of 105

6. Click **Roadhouse Restaurant** to select this field value. Access closes the list box and displays Roadhouse Restaurant in the CustomerNum field text box. Access also stores the value 122, the CustomerNum for Roadhouse Restaurant, in the CustomerNum field for this order.

7. Refer to Figure 5-6 and enter the remaining field values for the new order record.

8. Click the **Close** button ☒ on the Table window title bar to close the Order table.

9. Click the **Yes** button when Access asks if you want to save changes.

You are now ready to create the queries that Barbara and Kim have requested. You are already familiar with queries that use an exact match or a range of values (using the > comparison operator) to select records. Access provides many other operators for creating select queries. These operators allow you to create more complicated queries that are difficult or impossible to create with exact match or range of values selection criteria.

Barbara and Kim have created a list of questions they want to answer using the Restaurant database:

- What customers are located in the 313 area code?

- What is the customer information for customers 123, 135, and 202?

- What is the customer information for all customers *except* customers 123, 135, and 202?

- What are the customer numbers, customer names, order numbers, and invoice amounts for unpaid invoices for customers in Indiana or Ohio?

- What are the customer names, amounts overdue, and potential late charges for customers with overdue January invoices in a particular state? For this query, the user specifies the state.

You will create the necessary queries to answer these questions. To do so you'll use the Query window in Design view.

Using a Pattern Match in a Query

Kim wants to view the records for all customers in the 313 area code. She will be travelling in that area next week and wants to contact those customers. To answer Kim's question, you can create a query that uses a pattern match. A **pattern match** selects records that have a value for the selected field matching the pattern of the simple condition value, in this case, to select customers with 313 area codes. You do this using the Like comparison operator.

The **Like comparison operator** selects records by matching field values to a specific pattern that includes one or more wildcard characters—asterisk (*), question mark (?), and number symbol (#). The asterisk represents any string of characters, the question mark represents any single character, and the number symbol represents any single digit. Using a pattern match is similar to using an exact match, except that a pattern match includes wildcard characters.

To create the query, you must first place the Customer table field list in the Query window in Design view.

To create the pattern match query in Design view:

1. Click the **Queries** tab in the Database window, and then click the **New** button. The New Query dialog box opens.

2. Click **Design View** in the list box (if necessary), and then click the **OK** button. Access opens the Show Table dialog box on top of the Query window.

3. Click **Customer** in the Tables list box, click the **Add** button, and then click the **Close** button. Access places the Customer table field list in the Query window.

4. Double-click the title bar of the Customer field list to highlight all the fields, click and drag one of the highlighted fields to the design grid, and then release the mouse button. Access places each field in a separate column in the design grid, in the same order that the fields appear in the table. See Figure 5-8.

Figure 5-8 ◄
Adding the
fields for the
query

all Customer table
fields in the design
grid

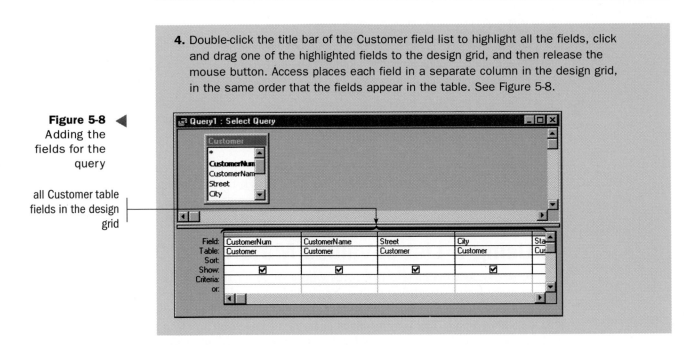

You will now enter the pattern match condition Like "(313)*" for the Phone field. Access will select records that have a Phone field value containing (313) in positions one through five. The asterisk (*) wildcard character specifies that any characters can appear in the remaining positions of the field value.

To select records that match the specified pattern:

1. Scroll the design grid until the Phone field is visible.

2. Click the **Phone Criteria** text box, and then type **Like "(313)*"**. See Figure 5-9. (Note that if you omit the operator Like, Access will automatically add it when you run the query.)

Figure 5-9 ◄
Record
selection based
on matching a
specific pattern

pattern match
selection criterion

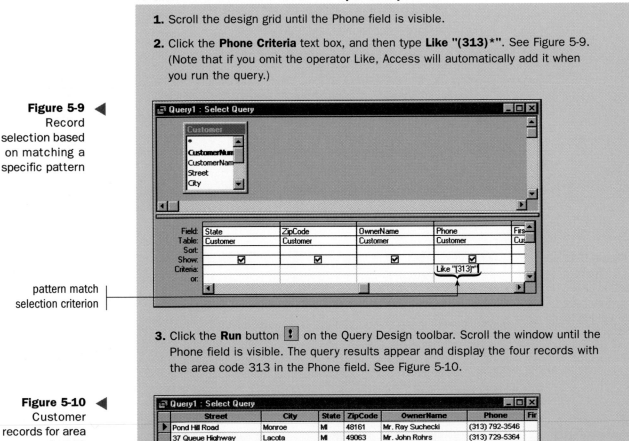

3. Click the **Run** button [!] on the Query Design toolbar. Scroll the window until the Phone field is visible. The query results appear and display the four records with the area code 313 in the Phone field. See Figure 5-10.

Figure 5-10 ◄
Customer
records for area
code 313

Street	City	State	ZipCode	OwnerName	Phone	Fir
Pond Hill Road	Monroe	MI	48161	Mr. Ray Suchecki	(313) 792-3546	
37 Queue Highway	Lacota	MI	49063	Mr. John Rohrs	(313) 729-5364	
2890 Canyonside Way	Romulus	MI	48174	Ms. Nancy Mills	(313) 888-7778	
3509 Garfield Avenue	Romulus	MI	48174	Mr. Shannon Petree	(313) 461-8899	

> Now you can save the query.
>
> 4. Click the **Save** button 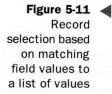 on the Query Datasheet toolbar. The Save As dialog box opens.
>
> 5. Type **313 Area Code** in the Query Name text box, and then press the **Enter** key. Access saves the query in the Restaurant database on your Student Disk.

Next, Kim asks you to create a query that will display the customer information for customers 123, 135, and 202. She wants to assign these customers to a particular salesperson, and she would like a printout of the customer data to give to the salesperson. To produce the results Kim wants, you'll create a query using a list-of-values match.

Using a List-of-Values Match in a Query

A **list-of-values match** selects records whose value for the selected field matches one of two or more simple condition values. You could accomplish this by including several Or conditions in the design grid, but Access also provides the In comparison operator that works as a shorthand. The **In comparison operator** allows you to define a condition with two or more values. If a record's field value matches at least one value from the list of values, Access selects that record for inclusion in the query results.

To display the information Kim requested, you want records selected if the CustomerNum field value is equal to 123, 135, or 202. These are the values you will use with the In comparison operator.

To create the query using a list-of-values match:

> 1. Click the **View** button for Design view 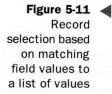 on the Query Datasheet toolbar to display the Query window in Design view.
>
> First you need to delete the condition for the previous query you created.
>
> 2. Click the **Phone Criteria** text box, press the **F2** key to highlight the entire condition, and then press the **Delete** key to remove the condition.
>
> Now you can enter the criteria for the new query using the In comparison operator. When you use this operator, the list of values you want to match must be enclosed within parentheses. Each value must also be surrounded by quotation marks and separated by a comma.
>
> 3. Scroll the design grid to the left to display the CustomerNum column, click the **CustomerNum Criteria** text box, and then type **In ("123","135","202")**. See Figure 5-11.

Figure 5-11 ◀
Record selection based on matching field values to a list of values

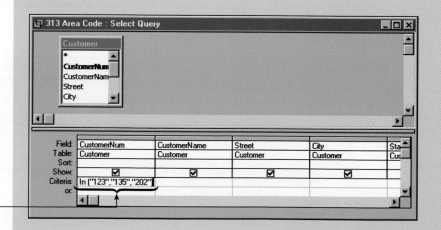

list-of-values selection criterion

4. Click the **Run** button ⏩ on the Query Design toolbar. Access runs the query and displays the results, which show the three records with 123, 135, or 202 in the CustomerNum field.

   Now you can print the query results for Kim. Also, because Kim won't need to display this information again, you don't have to save this query.

5. Click the **Print** button 🖨 on the Query Datasheet toolbar. Access prints the query results.

Kim wants to assign the remaining customers to other salespersons in her group. She needs a list of all the customers except customers 123, 135, and 202 to help her plan the assignments. You can create this query by modifying the previous one to include a non-matching value.

Using a Non-Matching Value in a Query

A **non-matching value** selects records whose value for the selected field does not match the simple condition value. You create the selection criterion using the Not logical operator. The **Not logical operator** negates a criterion. For example, if you enter Not = "MI" in the Criteria text box for the State field in the Customer table, the query results will show the records for which the State field value is not MI; that is, all customers not located in Michigan.

To create Kim's query, you will combine the Not operator with the In operator to select customer records whose CustomerNum field value is not in the list ("123","135","202").

To create the query using a non-matching value:

1. Click the **View** button for Design view 🔲 on the Query Datasheet toolbar to switch back to Design view.

2. If necessary, position the insertion point immediately to the left of the word "In" in the Criteria text box for the CustomerNum field.

3. Type **Not** and then press the **spacebar**. Access will select a record only if the CustomerNum field value is not in the list ("123","135","202"). See Figure 5-12.

Figure 5-12 ◀
Record
selection
based on not
matching a list
of values

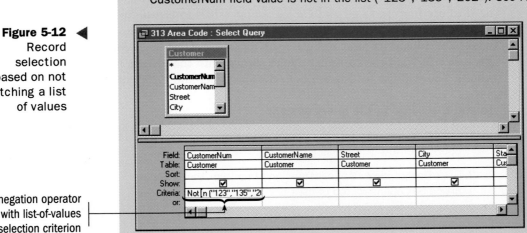

negation operator
with list-of-values
selection criterion

4. Click the **Run** button [⚡] on the Query Design toolbar. Access runs the query and displays only those records with a CustomerNum field value that is not 123, 135, or 202. A total of 35 records are included in the query results. See Figure 5-13.

Figure 5-13 ◀
Results of
query using
non-matching
values

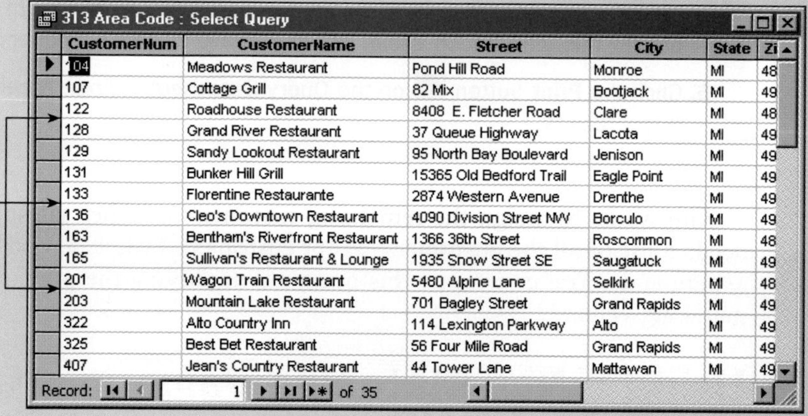

customers 123, 135,
and 202 not selected

CustomerNum	CustomerName	Street	City	State	Zi
104	Meadows Restaurant	Pond Hill Road	Monroe	MI	48
107	Cottage Grill	82 Mix	Bootjack	MI	49
122	Roadhouse Restaurant	8408 E. Fletcher Road	Clare	MI	48
128	Grand River Restaurant	37 Queue Highway	Lacota	MI	49
129	Sandy Lookout Restaurant	95 North Bay Boulevard	Jenison	MI	49
131	Bunker Hill Grill	15365 Old Bedford Trail	Eagle Point	MI	49
133	Florentine Restaurante	2874 Western Avenue	Drenthe	MI	49
136	Cleo's Downtown Restaurant	4090 Division Street NW	Borculo	MI	49
163	Bentham's Riverfront Restaurant	1366 36th Street	Roscommon	MI	48
165	Sullivan's Restaurant & Lounge	1935 Snow Street SE	Saugatuck	MI	49
201	Wagon Train Restaurant	5480 Alpine Lane	Selkirk	MI	48
203	Mountain Lake Restaurant	701 Bagley Street	Grand Rapids	MI	49
322	Alto Country Inn	114 Lexington Parkway	Alto	MI	49
325	Best Bet Restaurant	56 Four Mile Road	Grand Rapids	MI	49
407	Jean's Country Restaurant	44 Tower Lane	Mattawan	MI	49

313 Area Code : Select Query

Record: |◀ ◀| 1 |▶ ▶| ▶*| of 35

5. Click the **Print** button [🖶] on the Query Datasheet toolbar to print the query results.

Now you can close the query without saving it, because Kim will not need to run this query again.

6. Click the **Close** button [✕] on the Query window to close it, and then click the **No** button when Access asks if you want to save the query.

You are now ready to create the query to answer Barbara's question about unpaid invoices in Indiana or Ohio.

Using Both the And and Or Operators in the Same Query

Barbara wants to see the customer numbers, customer names, order numbers, and invoice amounts for unpaid invoices for customers in Indiana or Ohio. To create this query, you need to use both the And and Or logical operators to create two compound conditions. That is, you will create conditions that select records for customers located in Indiana *and* who have unpaid invoices *or* customers located in Ohio *and* who have unpaid invoices. Because you want the customer names shown with the invoice information in the query results, you will use fields from both the Customer and Order tables.

To add the fields to the query design:

1. From the Queries tab of the Database window, click the **New** button. Access opens the New Query dialog box.

2. Click **Design View** (if necessary), and then click the **OK** button. The Show Table dialog box opens on top of the Query window in Design view.

3. Double-click **Customer** to add the Customer table to the Query window.

4. Double-click **Order** to add the Order table to the Query window, and then click the **Close** button to close the Show Table dialog box.

5. Double-click **CustomerNum**, double-click **CustomerName**, and then double-click **State** in the Customer field list to add these fields to the design grid.

6. Double-click **OrderNum**, double-click **Paid**, and then double-click **InvoiceAmt** in the Order field list to add these fields to the design grid.

You've selected all the fields to include in the query. Now you're ready to add the selection criteria, which will include both the And and Or logical operators.

To specify the criteria using the And logical operator with the Or logical operator:

1. Click the **State Criteria** text box, and then type **="IN"**.

   Kim wants to view data for customers in Indiana or Ohio, so you need to enter the Or condition for the State field.

2. Press the ↓ key and then type **="OH"**.

   Now, for each of the existing conditions, you need to enter the And condition that selects only those records for customers who have not paid their invoices.

3. Scroll right to display the Paid field, click the **Paid Criteria** text box, and then type **=No**.

4. Press the ↓ key and then type **=No**.

   When you save this query, you'll specify a name that indicates the data is for unpaid invoices. Therefore, you don't have to display the Paid field values in the query results.

5. Click the **Show** check box for the Paid field to remove the check mark. The query definition is now complete. See Figure 5-14.

Figure 5-14 ◀
And and Or
conditions in
the design grid

one-to-many
relationship

first And condition

or row for Or
condition

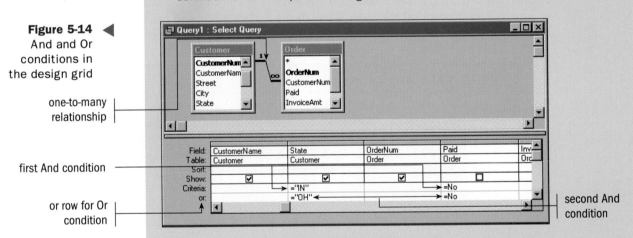

second And
condition

6. Click the **Run** button 🔢 on the Query Design toolbar. Access runs the query and displays the results. See Figure 5-15.

Figure 5-15 ◀
Results of
query using
And with Or

Indiana customers
selected

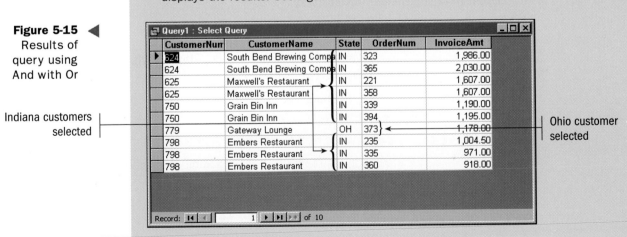

Ohio customer
selected

The query results show the records for customers in Indiana or Ohio that have unpaid invoices. Because you unchecked the Show box for the Paid field, it does not appear in the query results. Next, you'll save the query with a name indicating that the query selects unpaid invoices.

7. Click the **Save** button 🖫 on the Query Datasheet toolbar, type **IN and OH Unpaid Invoices** in the Query Name text box, and then press the **Enter** key to save the query.

8. Click the **Close** button ⊠ on the Query window.

Creating a Parameter Query

Barbara's final query asks for the customer name, amount overdue, and late charge for customers with overdue January invoices in a particular state. For this query, she wants to be able to specify the state, such as MI (Michigan), IN (Indiana), or OH (Ohio).

To create this query, you will modify the existing Unpaid With Late Charge query. You could create a simple condition using an exact match for the State field, which you would need to change in Design view every time you run the query. Instead, you will create a parameter query. A **parameter query** is a query that prompts you for information when the query runs. In this case, you want to create a query that prompts you for the state of the customers to select from the table. You enter the prompt in the Criteria text box for the State field.

When Access runs the query, it will display a dialog box and prompt you to enter the state. Access then creates the query results just as if you had changed the criteria in Design view.

REFERENCE window

CREATING A PARAMETER QUERY

- Create a select query that includes all the fields that will appear in the query results. Also choose the sort keys and set the criteria that do not change when you run the query.
- Decide on the fields that will have prompts when you run the query. In the Criteria text box for each of these fields, type the prompt you want to appear in a message box when you run the query, and enclose the prompt in brackets.

Now you can open the Unpaid With Late Charge query in Design view and change its design to create the parameter query.

To create the parameter query based on an existing query:

1. From the Queries tab of the Database window, click **Unpaid With Late Charge**, and then click the **Design** button to display the query in Design view.

   Now you need to add the State field to the query design and enter a prompt in the Criteria box for the State field.

2. Scroll the design grid to the right to display the first blank column.

3. Double-click **State** in the Customer field list to add this field in the next available column in the design grid.

   Next you must enter the criteria for the parameter query. In this case, Kim wants the query to prompt users to enter the state for the customer information they want to view. So, you need to enter the prompt in the Criteria text box for the State field. The text of the prompt must be enclosed within brackets.

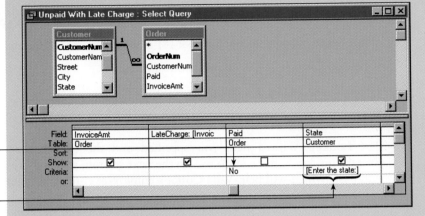

4. Scroll right to display the State field, click the **State Criteria** text box, and then type **[Enter the state:]**. See Figure 5-16.

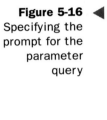

Figure 5-16 ◀
Specifying the prompt for the parameter query

specifies unpaid invoices

prompt

5. Click the **Run** button ⏸ on the Query Design toolbar. Access runs the query and displays a dialog box prompting you for the name of the state. See Figure 5-17.

Figure 5-17 ◀
Enter Parameter Value dialog box

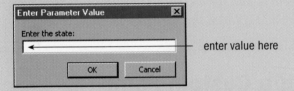

enter value here

The text you specified in the Criteria text box of the State field appears above a text box, in which you must type a State field value. You must enter the value exactly as it appears in the table.

6. To see the January unpaid invoices for customers in Indiana, type **IN**, and then click the **OK** button. Access displays the data for the customers in Indiana who have unpaid January invoices (in this case, only two customers). See Figure 5-18.

Figure 5-18 ◀
Results of the parameter query

	OrderNum	BillingDate	CustomerName	InvoiceAmt	LateCharge	State
▶	321	1/15/99	Maxwell's Restaurant	1,607.00	32.14	IN
	235	1/15/99	Embers Restaurant	1,004.50	20.09	IN
✱						

Indiana customers selected

Barbara plans on running this query frequently to monitor the payment activity of the restaurant customers, so she asks you to save it with a new name (to keep the original query intact).

7. Click **File** on the menu bar, and then click **Save As/Export**. The Save As dialog box opens.

8. Position the insertion point immediately to the right of the "e" in Charge, press the **spacebar**, type **Parameter**, and then press the **Enter** key.

9. Click the **Close** button ✖ on the Query window.

Access

Quick Check

1. What is a Lookup Wizard field?

2. What comparison operator is used to select records based on a specific pattern?

3. What is the purpose of the asterisk (*) in a pattern match query?

4. When do you use the In comparison operator?

5. How do you negate a selection criterion?

6. When do you use a parameter query?

The Lookup Wizard field you specified and the queries you created will make the Restaurant database easier to use. In the next session, you will create a custom form for the database, which will help Valle Coffee's employees enter and maintain data more easily.

SESSION

5.2

In this session, you will create a custom form for customer information. You will work in Design view to add form controls, create a form header with a title and a graphic image, and add color to the background of the form.

Creating a Custom Form

Barbara has been using the Customer Orders form to enter and view information about Valle Coffee's customers and their orders. She likes having all the information on a single form, but she would like to have the fields rearranged and a graphic image added to the form. To make the form easier to read, she wants to have the customer and order information on separate pages, like the tabs in a dialog box. She asks you to create a new form to display the information in this way. Because this form is significantly different from the Customer Orders form, you will create a new custom form.

To create a custom form, you can modify an existing form or design and create a form from scratch. In either case, you create a custom form working in the Form window in Design view. A custom form can be designed to match a paper form, to display some fields side by side and others top to bottom, to highlight certain sections with color, or to add special buttons and list boxes. A multi-page form displays the form on more than one page on a single screen. Each page is labeled with a tab like the tabs in the Database window. By clicking a tab, you can display the information on that page.

Designing a Custom Form

Whether the custom form you want to create is a simple or complex form, it is always best to plan the form's content and appearance first. Figure 5-19 shows Barbara's design for the custom form that she wants you to create.

Figure 5-19 ◄
Barbara's design for the multi-page custom form

title label

picture created by drawing application software

first page of form

second page of form

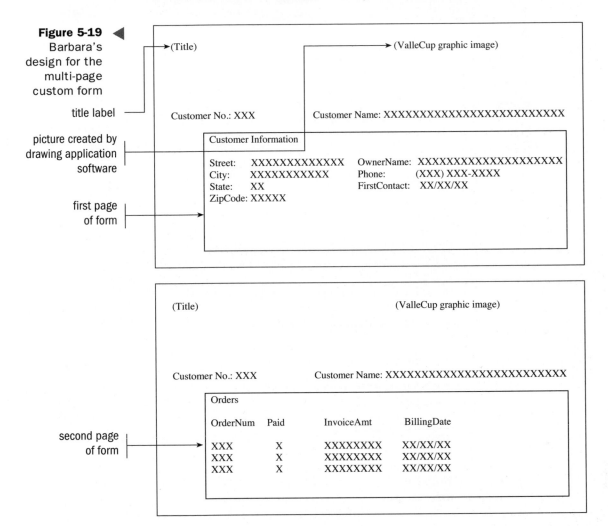

Notice that the top of the form displays a title and graphic image. Below these are the CustomerNum and CustomerName fields. Also, notice that Barbara's form contains two pages. The first page, labeled "Customer Information," displays the address and contact information for the customer. The second page, labeled "Orders," displays order information for the customer. Each field value from the Customer table will appear in a text box and will be preceded by a label. The label will be the value of the field's Caption property (if any) or the field name. The locations and lengths of each field value are indicated by a series of Xs in Barbara's form design. For example, the three Xs that follow the CustomerNum field label indicate that the field value will be three characters long. The Order table fields appear in a subform on the second page.

   With the design for the custom form in place, you are ready to create it. You could use an AutoForm Wizard or the Form Wizard to create a basic form and then customize it in Design view. However, you would need to make many modifications to a basic form to create the form Barbara wants, so you will design the entire form directly in Design view.

The Form Window in Design View

You use the Form window in Design view to create and modify forms. To create Barbara's custom form, you'll create a blank form based on the Customer table and then add the Order table fields in a subform.

REFERENCE
window

CREATING A FORM IN DESIGN VIEW

- In the Database window, click the Forms tab to display the Forms list.
- Click the New button to display the New Form dialog box, and then click Design View.
- Select the table or query on which the form will be based, and then click the OK button.
- Place the necessary controls in the Form window in Design view. Modify the size, position, and other properties of the controls as necessary.
- Click the Save button on the Form Design toolbar, and then enter a name for the form.

To create a blank form in Design view:

1. If you took a break after the previous session, make sure that Access is running and the Restaurant database from the Tutorial folder on your Student Disk is open.

2. Click the **Forms** tab to display the Forms list in the Database window, and then click the **New** button. The New Form dialog box opens.

3. Click **Design View** (if necessary), click the list arrow for choosing a table or query, click **Customer**, and then click the **OK** button. Access displays the Form window in Design view.

4. Click the **Maximize** button ⬜ on the Form window to maximize the window. See Figure 5-20.

Figure 5-20 ◄
Form window in
Design view

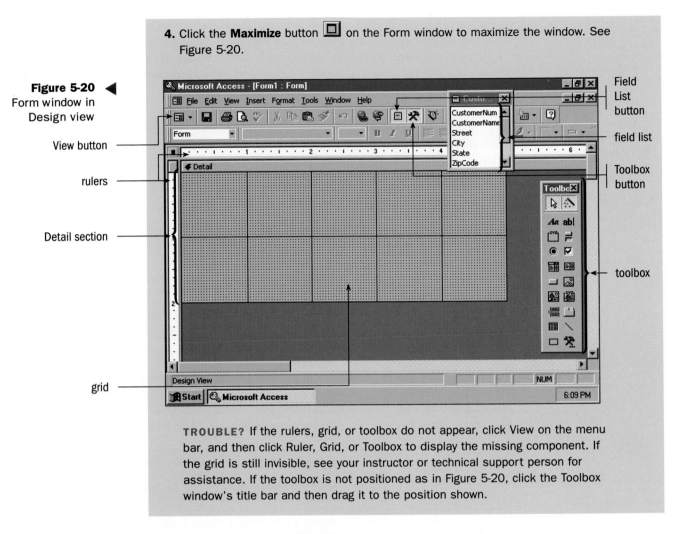

View button

rulers

Detail section

grid

Field List button

field list

Toolbox button

toolbox

TROUBLE? If the rulers, grid, or toolbox do not appear, click View on the menu bar, and then click Ruler, Grid, or Toolbox to display the missing component. If the grid is still invisible, see your instructor or technical support person for assistance. If the toolbox is not positioned as in Figure 5-20, click the Toolbox window's title bar and then drag it to the position shown.

The Form window in Design view contains the tools necessary to create a custom form. You create the form by placing objects on the blank form in the window. Each object—such as a text box, list box, rectangle, or command button—that you place on a form is called a **control**. There are three kinds of controls that you can place on a form:

- A **bound control** is linked, or bound, to a field in the underlying table or query. You use a bound control to display table field values.

- An **unbound control** is not linked to a field in the underlying table or query. You use an unbound control to display text, such as a form title or instructions, or to display graphics and pictures from other software programs. An unbound control that displays text is called a **label**.

- A **calculated control** displays a value calculated from data from one or more fields.

To create a bound control, you use the Field List button on the Form Design toolbar to display a list of fields available from the underlying table or query. Then you drag fields from the field list box to the Form window and place the bound controls where you want them to appear on the form.

To place other controls on a form, you use the tools on the toolbox. The **toolbox** is a specialized toolbar containing buttons that represent the tools you use to place controls on a form or a report. ScreenTips are available for each tool. If you want to show or hide the toolbox, click the Toolbox button on the Form Design toolbar. The tools available on the toolbox are described in Figure 5-21.

Figure 5-21 ◀
Summary of tools available in the toolbox for a form or report

Button	Tool Name	Purpose on a Form or a Report	Control Wizard Available
	Select Objects	Select, move, size, and edit controls	No
	Control Wizards	Activate Control Wizards for certain other toolbox tools	No
	Label	Display text, such as title or instructions; an unbound control	No
	Text Box	Display a label attached to a text box that contains a bound control or a calculated control	No
	Option Group	Display a group frame containing toggle buttons, option buttons, or check boxes	Yes
	Toggle Button	Display a toggle button control bound to a Yes/No field	Yes
	Option Button	Display an option button control bound to a Yes/No field	Yes
	Check Box	Display a check box control bound to a Yes/No field	Yes
	Combo Box	Display a control that combines the features of a list box and a text box; you can type in the text box or select an entry in the list box to add a value to an underlying field	Yes
	List Box	Display a control that contains a scrollable list of values	Yes
	Command Button	Display a control button you can use to link to an action, such as finding a record, printing a record, or applying a form filter	Yes
	Image	Display a graphic image	Yes
	Unbound Object Frame	Display a frame for enclosing an unbound OLE object, such as a Microsoft Excel spreadsheet	Yes
	Bound Object Frame	Display a frame for enclosing an bound OLE object stored in an Access database table	Yes
	Page Break	Begin a new screen on a form or a new page on a report	No
	Tab Control	Display a tab control with multiple pages	No
	Subform/ Subreport	Display data from more than one table	Yes
	Line	Display a line	No
	Rectangle	Display a rectangle	No
	More Controls	Display a list of all available controls	No

The Form window in Design view also contains a Detail section, which appears as a light gray rectangle, in which you place the fields, labels, and values for your form. You can change the size of the Detail section size by dragging its edges. The grid consists of the dots that appear in the Detail section to help you position controls precisely on a form.

The rulers at the top and at the left edge of the Detail section define the horizontal and vertical dimensions of the form and serve as a guide to the placement of controls on the form.

Your first task is to add bound controls to the Detail section for the CustomerNum and CustomerName fields from the Customer table.

Adding Fields to a Form

When you add a bound control to a form, Access adds a field-value text box and, to its left, a label. The text box displays the field values from the table or query, and the label identifies the values. To create a bound control, you display the field list by clicking the Field List button. Then you select one or more fields from the field list box and drag them to the form. You select a single field by clicking the field. You select two or more fields by holding down the Ctrl key and clicking each field; and you select all fields by double-clicking the field list title bar.

You will add bound controls to the Detail section for two of the fields in the field list. Because you will not need the toolbox for a while, you can close it.

To add bound controls for the CustomerNum and CustomerName fields:

1. Click the **Close** button ☒ on the toolbox to close it.

2. If necessary, click the **Field List** button 🖻 on the Form Design toolbar to display the field list.

3. Click **CustomerNum** in the field list, press and hold the **Ctrl** key, and then click **CustomerName** in the field list. Both fields are selected.

4. Click the highlighted fields and then drag them to the form's Detail section. Release the mouse button when the pointer ▱ is positioned at the 1-inch mark on the horizontal ruler and just below the top of the Detail section. Access adds two bound controls—one for the CustomerNum field and one for the CustomerName field—in the Detail section of the form. See Figure 5-22.

Figure 5-22 ◄
Adding text boxes and attached labels as bound controls to the form

two attached labels

position the pointer here

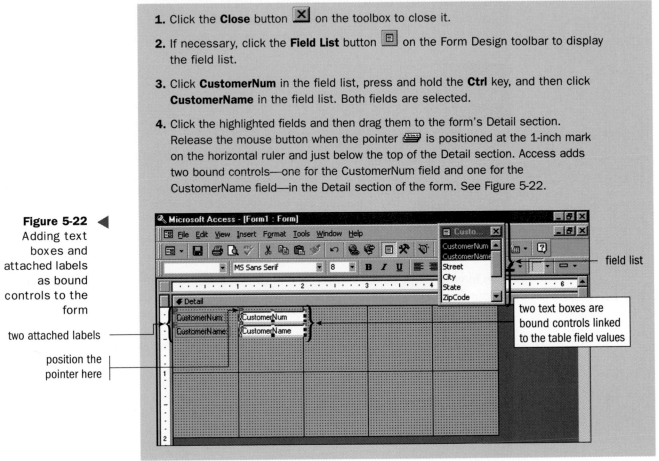

field list

two text boxes are bound controls linked to the table field values

TROUBLE? Your controls do not have to be in the exact same position as the controls in Figure 5-22. However, they should be in approximately the same position. If you did not position the bound controls properly in the Detail section, click the Undo button 🔄 on the Form Design toolbar to delete the text boxes and labels from the Detail section. Then repeat Steps 3 and 4 to add the bound controls.

4. Click the **Close** button ❌ on the field list to close it.

Working on a form in Design view might seem awkward at first. With practice you will become comfortable with creating a custom form. Remember that you can always click the Undo button immediately after you make an error or undesired form adjustment.

Comparing the form's Detail section with Barbara's design, notice that you need to arrange the text boxes so that they appear next to each other. To do so you must select and move the controls.

Selecting and Moving Controls

Two text boxes now appear in the form's Detail section, one below the other. Each text box is a bound control linked to a field in the underlying table and has a label box attached to its left. This means that if you move the text box, the label will move with it. Each text box and each label is an object on the form and appears with square boxes on the corners and edges. These boxes are called **handles**. Handles appear around an object when it is selected and they allow you to move or resize the control.

REFERENCE window	**SELECTING AND MOVING CONTROLS**
	■ Click the control to select it. To select several controls at once, press and hold the Shift key while clicking each control. Handles appear around all selected controls.
	■ To move a single selected control, click the control's move handle and drag it to its new position.
	■ To move a group of selected controls, click any selected control (but do not click its move handle) and then drag the group of selected controls to its new position.

To move a single bound control, you must first select just that control. All the controls on your form are currently selected and will move together if you move any one of them. You first need to deselect all of the bound controls and then select the CustomerName control to move it to the right of the CustomerNum control. The CustomerName control consists of the CustomerName field-value text box and the corresponding label to its left.

To select the CustomerName bound control:

1. Click the gray area outside the Detail section to deselect the selected controls.

2. Click the **CustomerName field-value text box** to select it. Move handles, which are the larger handles, appear on the upper-left corner of the field-value text box and its attached label box. Sizing handles appear but only on the field-value text box. See Figure 5-23.

Figure 5-23 ◄
Selecting a
single bound
control

label boxes

move handles

sizing handles

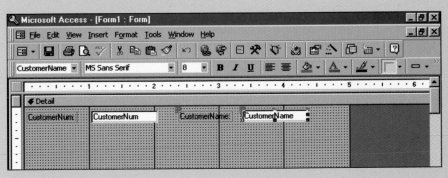

You can move a field-value text box and its attached label box together. To move them, place the pointer anywhere on the border of the field-value text box, but not on a move handle or a sizing handle. When the pointer changes to 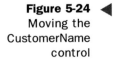, you can drag the field-value text box and its attached label box to the new location. As you move the boxes, their outline moves to show you the changing position.

You can also move either the field-value text box or its label box individually. If you want to move the field-value text box but not its label box, for example, place the pointer on the text box's move handle. When the pointer changes to ✋, drag the field-value text box to the new location. You use the label box's move handle in a similar way to move just the label box.

To arrange the text boxes to match Barbara's design, you must move the CustomerName control up and to the right.

To move the CustomerName control:

1. Place the pointer on the CustomerName control, but not on a move handle or a sizing handle. When the pointer changes to ✋, click and drag the control up and to the right. An outline of the control appears as you change its position to guide you in the move operation. Use the grid dots in the Detail section to help you position the control as shown in Figure 5-24.

Figure 5-24 ◄
Moving the
CustomerName
control

> **TROUBLE?** Your control does not have to be in the exact same position as the control in Figure 5-24. However, it should be in approximately the same position, and it should be aligned with the CustomerNum control. If you did not place the control correctly, click the Undo button on the Form Design toolbar, and then repeat Step 1.

According to Barbara's design, the labels for the two controls should be "Customer No.:" and "Customer Name:" (respectively). To modify the text of the labels, you need to change each label's caption.

Changing a Label's Caption

The text in a label is defined by the field name or by the field's Caption property. By default, a label displays the field name as it exists in the underlying table or query. If you want the label to display different text, you need to change the label's Caption property value.

REFERENCE window	**CHANGING A LABEL'S CAPTION**
	▪ Click the label to select it.
	▪ Click the right mouse button to display the shortcut menu, and then click Properties to display the property sheet.
	▪ If necessary, click the Format tab to display the Format page of the property sheet.
	▪ Edit the existing label in the Caption text box, or double-click the Caption text box to select the current value, and then type a new caption.
	▪ Click the property sheet Close button to close it.

You need to change the Caption property of the two labels on your form to "Customer No.:" and "Customer Name:" (respectively).

To change the Caption property value for the two labels:

1. Click the **CustomerNum label box** to select it.

2. Click the right mouse button to display the shortcut menu, and then click **Properties**. The property sheet for the CustomerNum label opens.

3. If necessary, click the property sheet title bar and drag the property sheet down until the CustomerNum and CustomerName label boxes are visible.

4. If necessary, click the **Format** tab to display the Format page of the property sheet.

5. Position the insertion point between the "r" and the "N" in CustomerNum, and then press the **spacebar**.

6. Position the insertion point between the "m" in Num and the colon following it, press the **Backspace** key twice, and then type **o.** (including the period). The value should now be Customer No.:. See Figure 5-25.

Figure 5-25 ◄
Changing the
Caption
property for
the label

property sheet

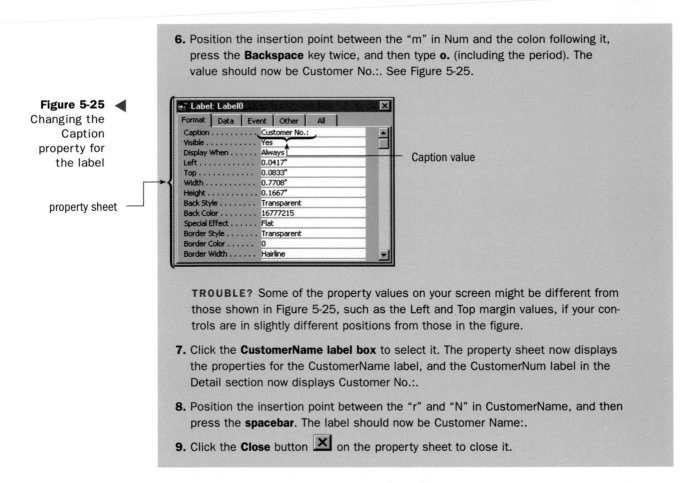

Caption value

TROUBLE? Some of the property values on your screen might be different from those shown in Figure 5-25, such as the Left and Top margin values, if your controls are in slightly different positions from those in the figure.

7. Click the **CustomerName label box** to select it. The property sheet now displays the properties for the CustomerName label, and the CustomerNum label in the Detail section now displays Customer No.:.

8. Position the insertion point between the "r" and "N" in CustomerName, and then press the **spacebar**. The label should now be Customer Name:.

9. Click the **Close** button ☒ on the property sheet to close it.

When you create a form, you should periodically check your progress by displaying the form in Form view. You might see adjustments you want to make on your form in Design view. Next, you'll save the current form design and then view the form in Form view.

To save the form and switch to Form view:

1. Click the **Save** button 🖫 on the Form Design toolbar. The Save As dialog box opens.

2. Type **Customer Information Multi-page**, and then press the **Enter** key. Access saves the form design.

3. Click the **View** button for Form view 🖽 on the Form Design toolbar. Access closes the Form window in Design view and displays the form in Form view. See Figure 5-26.

Figure 5-26 ◄
Form window in
Form view

record displayed in
custom form

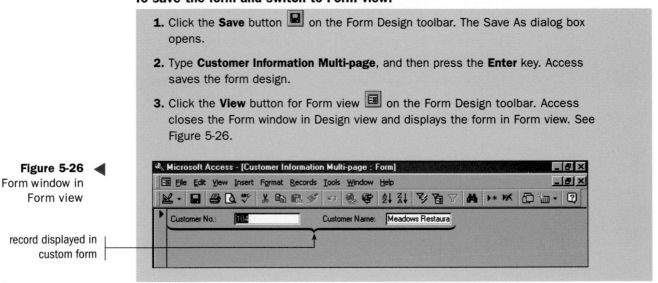

Access displays the CustomerNum and CustomerName field values for the first record in the Customer table (Meadows Restaurant). You can use the navigation buttons to view other records from the table in the form.

The form displayed in Form view reveals some adjustments you need to make to the form design. The CustomerNum field-value text box is too large for the field value, and the CustomerName field-value text box is too small for the field value. So you will resize both of the text boxes.

Resizing Controls

A selected object displays seven sizing handles, one on each side of the object and one at each corner except the upper-left corner. The upper-left corner displays the move handle. Positioning the pointer over a sizing handle changes the pointer to a two-headed arrow; the direction in which the arrows are pointing indicates the direction in which you can resize the selected object. When you drag a sizing handle, you resize the control. Thin lines appear, which guide you as you resize the control.

REFERENCE window

RESIZING A CONTROL

- Click the control to select it and display the sizing handles.
- Place the pointer over the sizing handle you want, and then click and drag the edge of the object until it is the size you want.

You'll begin by resizing the CustomerNum text box, which is much larger than necessary to display the three-digit customer number. Then you'll resize the CustomerName text box to make it large enough to display the complete customer name.

To resize the two text boxes:

1. Click the **View** button for Design view 🖼 on the Form View toolbar to return to the Form window in Design view.

2. Click the **CustomerNum text box** to select it.

3. Place the pointer on the middle right handle. When the pointer changes to ↔, click and drag the right border horizontally to the left until the text box is approximately the size of the text box shown in Figure 5-27.

   TROUBLE? If you change the vertical size of the box by mistake, just click the Undo button 🔙 on the Form Design toolbar and then repeat Step 3.

   Now you will move the CustomerName control to its correct position, and then resize the CustomerName text box.

4. Click the **CustomerName text box** to select the bound control. Place the pointer on the CustomerName text box, but not on a move handle or a sizing handle. When the pointer changes to ✋, click and drag the control to the left until its left edge is at the 2-inch mark on the horizontal ruler. Release the mouse button.

Access

5. Place the pointer on the middle right handle of the control. When the pointer changes to ↔, click and drag the right border horizontally to the right until the right edge of the text box is at the 4¾-inch mark on the horizontal ruler. Release the mouse button. See Figure 5-27.

Figure 5-27 ◄
CustomerNum
and
CustomerName
text boxes
moved and
resized

CustomerNum text
box resized

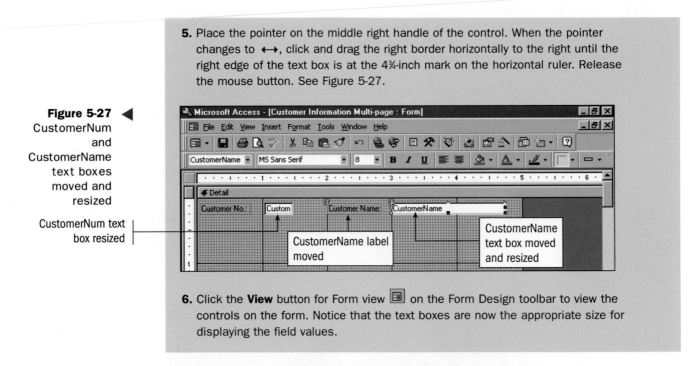

6. Click the **View** button for Form view 🔲 on the Form Design toolbar to view the controls on the form. Notice that the text boxes are now the appropriate size for displaying the field values.

Now you will add the title and picture to the top of the form.

Using Form Headers and Form Footers

The Form Header and Form Footer sections allow you to add titles, instructions, command buttons, and other information to the top and bottom of your form, respectively. Controls placed in the Form Header or Form Footer sections remain on the screen whenever the form is displayed; they do not change when the contents of the Detail section change. To add either a header or footer to your form, you must first add both the Form Header and Form Footer sections as a pair to the Form window in Design view. If your form needs one of these sections but not the other, you can remove a section by setting its height to zero, which is the method you would use to remove any section on a form.

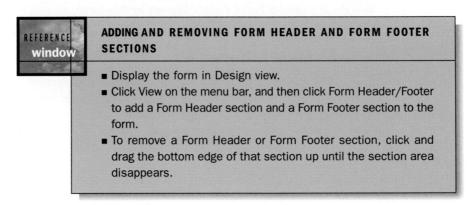

REFERENCE
window

ADDING AND REMOVING FORM HEADER AND FORM FOOTER SECTIONS

■ Display the form in Design view.
■ Click View on the menu bar, and then click Form Header/Footer to add a Form Header section and a Form Footer section to the form.
■ To remove a Form Header or Form Footer section, click and drag the bottom edge of that section up until the section area disappears.

According to Barbara's design, your form must include a Form Header section that will contain the form title and a picture of the Valle Coffee cup logo. You need to add this section to your form.

To add Form Header and Form Footer sections to the form:

1. Click the **View** button for Design view ⊠ on the Form View toolbar to switch to Design view.

2. Click **View** on the menu bar, and then click **Form Header/Footer**. Access inserts a Form Header section above the Detail section and a Form Footer section below the Detail section. See Figure 5-28.

Figure 5-28 ◀
Adding the
Form Header
and Form
Footer sections

Form Header section

Form Footer section

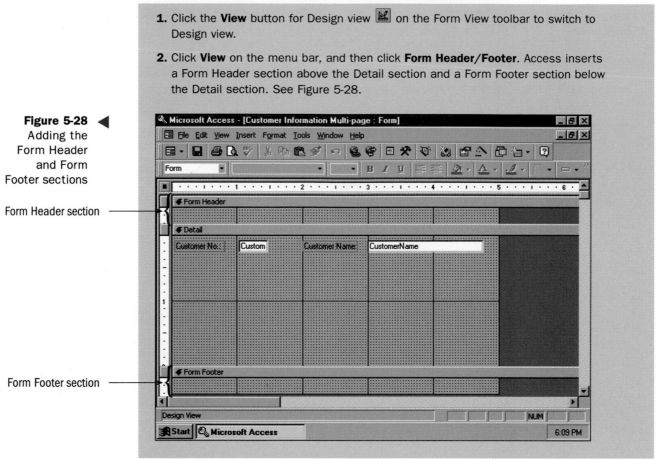

You do not need a Form Footer section in this form, so you'll remove it by making its height zero.

To remove the Form Footer section:

1. Place the pointer at the bottom edge of the Form Footer section. When the pointer changes to ✛, click and drag the bottom edge of the section up until it disappears. Even though the words Form Footer remain, the area defining the section is set to zero, and the section will not appear in the form.

You can now add the title to the Form Header section with the Label tool on the toolbox.

Adding a Label to a Form

The form design shows a title at the top of the form. You can add a title or other text to a form by using the Label tool on the toolbox.

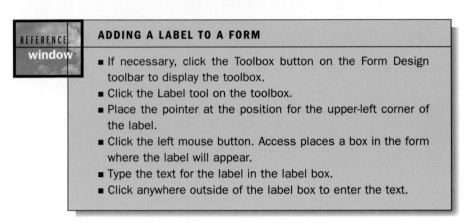

REFERENCE window	ADDING A LABEL TO A FORM
	■ If necessary, click the Toolbox button on the Form Design toolbar to display the toolbox.
	■ Click the Label tool on the toolbox.
	■ Place the pointer at the position for the upper-left corner of the label.
	■ Click the left mouse button. Access places a box in the form where the label will appear.
	■ Type the text for the label in the label box.
	■ Click anywhere outside of the label box to enter the text.

You'll begin by placing a label box for the title in the Form Header section.

To place a label on the form:

1. Click the **Toolbox** button [⚒] on the Form Design toolbar to display the toolbox.

2. Click the **Label** tool [Aa] on the toolbox.

3. Move the pointer to the Form Header section. The pointer changes to ^{+}A.

4. Place the pointer in the upper-left corner of the Form Header section. This will be the upper-left corner of the label.

5. Click the left mouse button. Access inserts a small label box in the Form Header section and places the insertion point in the label box.

6. Type **Valle Coffee Customer Information** in the label box, and then click anywhere outside of the label box to deselect the label box and enter the text. See Figure 5-29.

Figure 5-29 ◄
Label placed
in the Form
Header
section

label added —

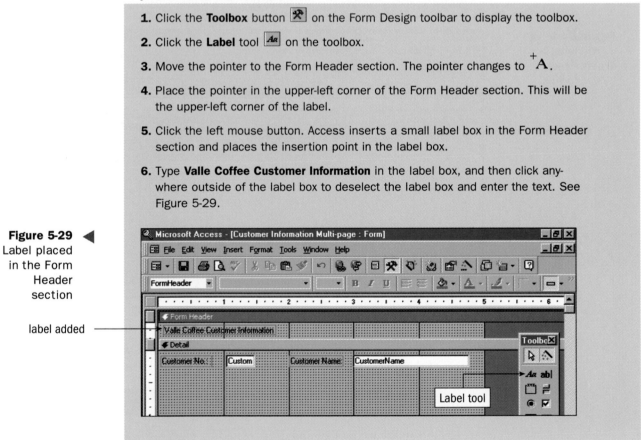

Barbara wants the title to be prominent on the form, so you will change the format of the text in the label to increase its font size and change the font weight to bold. You do this by using the buttons on the Formatting toolbar.

To change the font size and weight for the title:

1. Click the **title label control** to select it.

2. Click the **Font Size** list arrow on the Formatting toolbar, and then click **14**.

3. Click the **Bold** button [B] on the Formatting toolbar. See Figure 5-30.

Figure 5-30 ◄
Setting the
properties for
the title label
control

label font size and
weight changed

Bold
button

click to
select
font
size

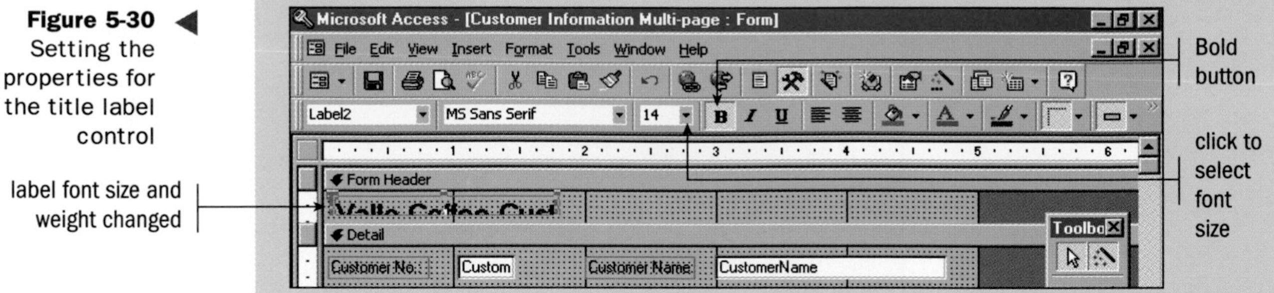

The label control now displays the title in 14-point bold. However, the label control is not large enough to display the entire title. You need to resize the label control so that it is large enough to display all the text.

4. Click **Format** on the menu bar, point to **Size**, and then click **To Fit**. The label control is resized to display the entire title. The Form Header automatically increases in size to accommodate the new label size. See Figure 5-31.

Figure 5-31 ◄
Title label
control resized
to fit

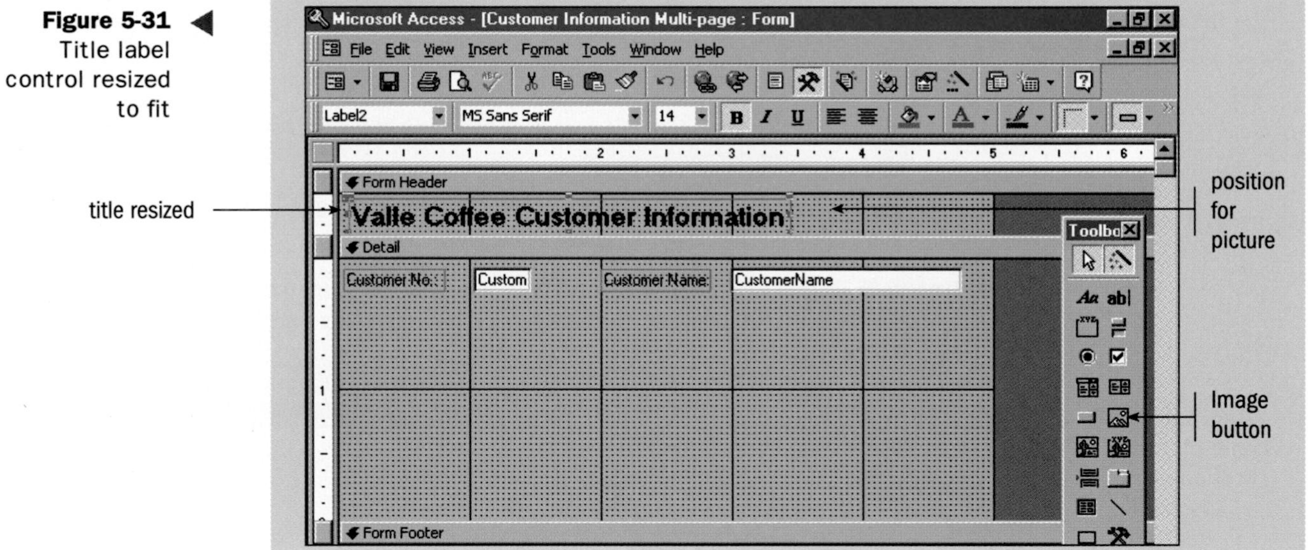

title resized

position
for
picture

Image
button

Barbara also wants the Valle Coffee logo, which is a picture of a coffee cup, to appear at the top of the form. You will now add the picture to the Form Header section.

Adding a Picture to a Form

Access has the ability to use files and data created by other software programs. To enhance the appearance of a form or report, for example, you can include a picture or other graphic image on the form or report. To do so you use the Image tool on the toolbox.

ADDING A PICTURE TO A FORM

- Display the form in Design view.
- If necessary, click the Toolbox button on the Form Design toolbar to display the toolbox.
- Click the Image tool on the toolbox.
- Place the pointer at the position for the upper-left corner of the picture.
- Click the left mouse button. Access places an outline in the form and opens the Insert Picture dialog box.
- If necessary, use the Look in list box to locate the picture file you want.
- Click the name of the picture file, and then click the OK button.

In this case, the Valle Coffee logo was created in a drawing program and saved in a file named ValleCup. Now you'll add this picture to the top right of the form.

To place the picture on the form:

1. Click the **Image** tool ⊞ on the toolbox.

2. Move the pointer to the Form Header section. The pointer changes to ⁺⊞.

3. Using the ruler as a guide, place the pointer slightly below the top of the Form Header section, approximately ¼-inch from the right edge of the title label control. (See Figure 5-31 for the correct position.) This will be the upper-left corner of the picture.

4. Click the left mouse button. Access places an outline in the Form Header section and opens the Insert Picture dialog box. See Figure 5-32.

Figure 5-32 ◀
Insert Picture
dialog box

place this picture
in form

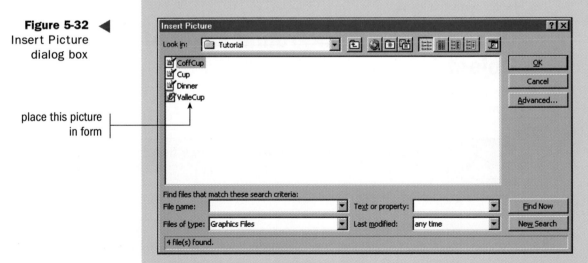

5. Make sure Tutorial appears in the Look in list box, click **ValleCup** to select the picture file, and then click the **OK** button.

Access closes the Insert Picture dialog box and inserts the picture. The Form Header section automatically enlarges to accommodate the size of the image.

Now view the form with the new header.

6. Click the **View** button for Form view 🖽 on the Form Design toolbar to view the form. See Figure 5-33.

Figure 5-33 ◀
Viewing the
form with the
new header

Form Header section ──▶

Detail section ──▶

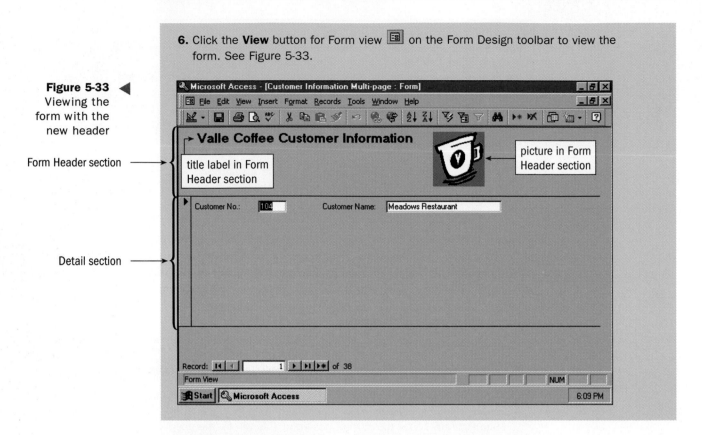

Barbara views the form and confirms that the title and picture are correctly placed, formatted, and sized. However, she would like the background color of the form to be dark gray to match the background color of the picture, so that the picture will blend in better with the form.

Changing the Background Color of a Form Object

You can change the background color of a form or of a specific section or object on the form by using tools available in Design view.

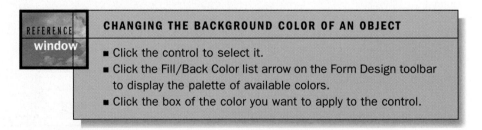

REFERENCE window

CHANGING THE BACKGROUND COLOR OF AN OBJECT

■ Click the control to select it.
■ Click the Fill/Back Color list arrow on the Form Design toolbar to display the palette of available colors.
■ Click the box of the color you want to apply to the control.

You need to change the background color of the Form Header section and the Detail section of the form to match the background color of the picture. This will cause the picture to blend in with the form.

To change the background color of the Detail and Form Header sections:

1. Click the **View** button for Design view on the Form View toolbar to switch to Design view.

2. Click an empty area of the Detail section. This makes the Detail section the selected control.

3. Click the list arrow for the **Fill/Back Color** button on the Form Design toolbar. Access displays the palette of available colors. See Figure 5-34.

Figure 5-34 ◀
Changing the background color of the form sections

Fill/Back Color button

Fill/Back Color palette

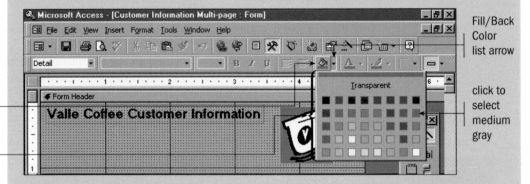

Fill/Back Color list arrow

click to select medium gray

4. Click the medium gray box in the color palette at the right end of the second row (see Figure 5-34). The background of the Detail section changes to the medium gray color.

Now you need to apply the same color to the Form Header section. To do so, you do not have to redisplay the color palette; once you select a color from the palette, it remains in effect so that you can apply the color to other objects by simply clicking the Fill/Back Color button.

5. Click an empty area of the Form Header section. This makes the Form Header section the selected control.

6. Click the **Fill/Back Color** button (not the list arrow) on the Form Design toolbar. The Form Header section now appears with the medium gray background.

Now you can save the form and view your changes in Form View.

7. Click the **Save** button on the Form Design toolbar to save the form.

8. Click the **View** button for Form view on the Form Design toolbar to view the form. See Figure 5-35.

Figure 5-35 ◀
Form with new background color

medium gray background color applied

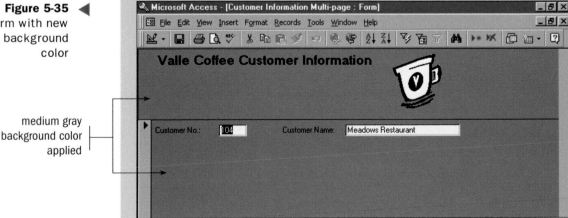

Quick Check

1 What is the difference between a bound control and an unbound control?

2 How do you move a control and its label together?

3 How do you change a label name?

4 How do you resize a control?

5 What is the Form Header section?

6 How do you insert a picture, created using another software program, in a form?

You are now ready to add the two pages to the form to display the customer address and contact information on one page and the order information on another.

SESSION 5.3

In this session, you will create a multi-page form and use Control Wizards to add a subform. You will also use the custom form to filter the data and save the filter as a query.

Creating a Multi-page Form Using Tab Controls

You can create a multi-page form in two ways: by inserting a page break control in the form or by using a tab control. If you insert a page break control in a form, the user can move between pages using the Page Up and Page Down keys on the keyboard. If you use a tab control, the control appears with tabs at the top, one tab for each page. The user can switch between pages by clicking the tabs.

Barbara wants to include a tab control with two pages on the Valle Coffee Customer Information form. The first page of the tab control will contain customer information, such as the customer name, address, and other fields from the Customer table. The second page of the tab control will contain a subform with order information for that customer.

First you will resize the Detail section of the form to make room for the tab control.

To resize the Detail section:

1. If you took a break after the previous session, make sure that Access is running, that the Restaurant database from the Tutorial folder on your Student Disk is open, and that the Customer Information Multi-page form is open and the window is maximized.

2. Click the **View** button for Design view 🖉 on the Form View toolbar to display the form in Design view.

3. Place the pointer on the right edge of the Detail section. When the pointer changes to ↔, click and drag the edge to the right until it is at the 5½-inch mark on the horizontal ruler. Release the mouse button.

Now you can place the tab control on the form.

To place the tab control on the form:

1. Click the **Tab Control** tool 🖼 on the toolbox.

2. Place the pointer at the left edge of the Detail section, approximately ½-inch below the top of the Detail section, and then click the left mouse button. (Refer to Figure 5-36 for the correct position for the tab control.) Access places a tab control in the Detail section.

   Now you will resize the tab control so that it is large enough to display the remaining fields for the form.

3. Scroll down the Form window until the tab control is completely visible, click the right middle handle of the tab control, and then drag it to the right until it is three grid dots from the right edge of the form. Release the mouse button. See Figure 5-36.

Figure 5-36 ◄
Tab control
placed in the
Detail section
and resized

tab for second page
of tab control

tab for first page of
tab control

tab control in form

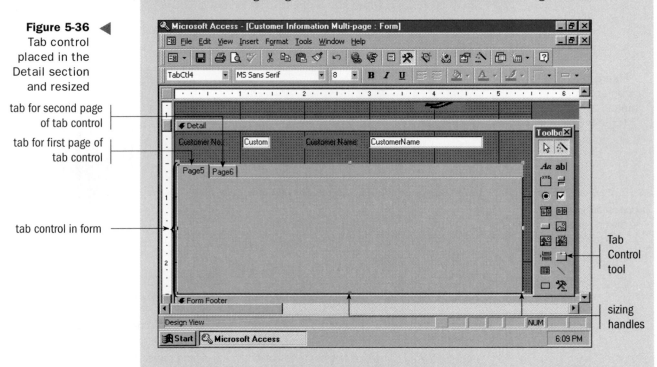

Tab
Control
tool

sizing
handles

TROUBLE? The page tabs on your screen might show different page numbers in the labels, depending on how you completed the previous steps. This will not affect the form. Just continue with the tutorial.

The top of the tab control displays two tabs. Each tab indicates a separate page on the form. On the first page, you will place the controls for the fields from the Customer table. On the second page, you will place a subform displaying the fields from the Order table for that customer. The user can move between the two pages by clicking the tabs.

To add the fields to the tab control:

1. Click the **Field List** button 🖼 on the Form Design toolbar to display the field list.

2. Click the **Street** field in the field list, scroll to the end of the field list, press and hold the **Shift** key, and then click the **FirstContact** field. All the fields in the list, except CustomerNum and CustomerName, should be selected.

3. Drag the selected fields to the tab control and release the mouse button when the pointer is approximately at the 1-inch mark on the horizontal ruler.

4. Click the **Close** button ☒ on the field list to close it.

5. Click a blank area of the tab control to deselect the text boxes and their labels.

   Now you need to move and resize the text boxes to match Barbara's form design.

6. Click the **Street text box** to select it, and then place the pointer on its move handle in the upper-left corner. When the pointer changes to 👆 , click and drag the Street text box to the left to the ¾-inch mark (approximately) on the horizontal ruler. Refer to Figure 5-37 to help you position the text box.

7. Place the pointer on the middle right handle of the Street text box. When the pointer changes to ↔, click and drag the right border to the right until the text box is approximately the size of the text box shown in Figure 5-37.

8. Move and resize the text boxes for the remaining fields. Use Figure 5-37 as a guide for positioning and sizing the text boxes.

Figure 5-37 ◀
Customer fields placed in the tab control

bound controls added to the first page of the tab control

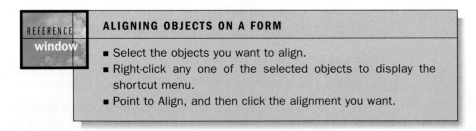

TROUBLE? Your controls do not have to be in the exact same position as the controls in Figure 5-37. However, they should be in approximately the same position. If you did not place the controls correctly, move and resize them now.

Notice that the label boxes on the form are left-justified; that is, they are aligned on their left edges. Barbara thinks that the form will look better if these labels are right-justified, or aligned on their right edges. To align them, you will select all of the labels and use the shortcut menu.

REFERENCE window	**ALIGNING OBJECTS ON A FORM**
	■ Select the objects you want to align.
	■ Right-click any one of the selected objects to display the shortcut menu.
	■ Point to Align, and then click the alignment you want.

To select and align all the label boxes on the right:

1. Click the **Street label box** to select it.

2. Press and hold the **Shift** key while you click each of the remaining label boxes below the Street label so that all four are selected, and then release the Shift key.

3. Right-click any one of the selected label boxes to display the shortcut menu.

4. Point to **Align**, and then click **Right**. Access aligns the label boxes on their right edges. See Figure 5-38.

Figure 5-38 ◀
Aligning the
label boxes

label boxes
right-aligned

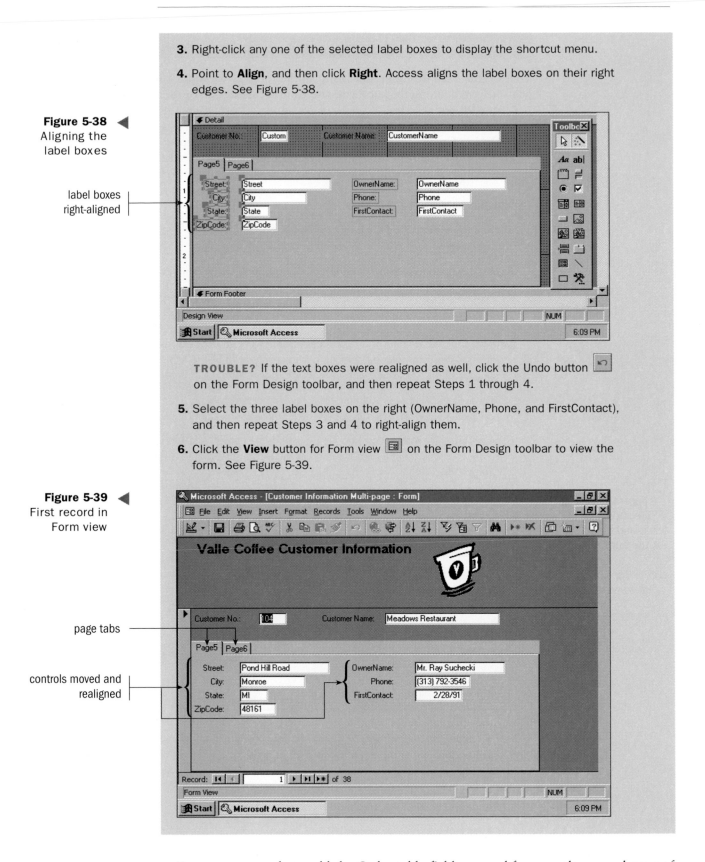

TROUBLE? If the text boxes were realigned as well, click the Undo button ↺ on the Form Design toolbar, and then repeat Steps 1 through 4.

5. Select the three label boxes on the right (OwnerName, Phone, and FirstContact), and then repeat Steps 3 and 4 to right-align them.

6. Click the **View** button for Form view ⊞ on the Form Design toolbar to view the form. See Figure 5-39.

Figure 5-39 ◀
First record in
Form view

page tabs

controls moved and
realigned

You are now ready to add the Order table fields as a subform on the second page of the form.

Adding a Subform Using Control Wizards

You use the Subform/Subreport tool on the toolbox to add a subform to a form. If you want help in defining the subform, you can first select one of the Access Control Wizards. A **Control Wizard** asks you a series of questions and then creates a control on a form or report based on your answers. Access offers Control Wizards for the Combo Box, List Box, Option Group, Command Button, and Subform/Subreport tools, among others.

You will use the Subform/Subreport Wizard to add the subform for the Order table records. This subform will appear on the second page of the form.

To add the subform to the form:

1. Click the **View** button for Design view 📐 on the Form View toolbar to switch to Design view.

2. Make sure the **Control Wizards** tool 🔲 on the toolbox is selected.

3. Click the tab for the second page (the tab on the right) to select that page.

4. Click the **Subform/Subreport** tool 📇 on the toolbox.

5. Place the pointer near the upper-left corner of the tab control, and then click the left mouse button. Access places a subform control in the tab control and displays the first Subform/Subreport Wizard dialog box.

   This dialog box allows you to create a new subform based on a table or query, or use an existing subform. You will use the Order table as the basis for a new subform.

6. Make sure the **Table/Query** option button is selected, and then click the **Next** button. Access displays the next Subform/Subreport Wizard dialog box. See Figure 5-40.

Figure 5-40 ◀
Selecting the
table and fields
for the subform

click to display list of
tables and queries

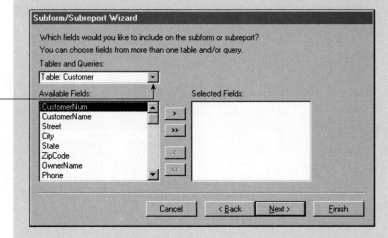

This dialog box allows you to select the table or query on which the subform is based and to select the fields from that table or query.

Access

7. Click the **Tables and Queries** list arrow to display the list of tables and queries in the Restaurant database, and then click **Table: Order**. The Available Fields list box shows the fields in the Order table.

8. Click the ⌐»⌐ button to move all available fields to the Selected Fields list box, and then click the **Next** button. See Figure 5-41.

Figure 5-41 ◄
Selecting the
linking field

make sure this option
is selected

make sure this link
is selected

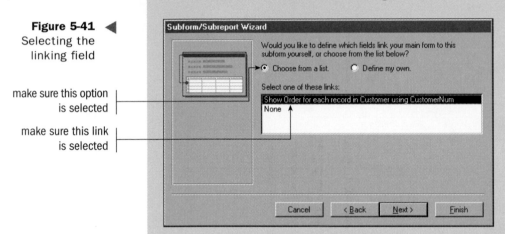

This dialog box allows you to select the link between the Customer table and the Order table.

9. Make sure the **Choose from a list** option button is selected and that the first link is highlighted, and then click the **Next** button. The next Subform/Subreport Wizard dialog box allows you to specify a name for the subform.

10. Type **Customer Information Subform** and then click the **Finish** button. Access inserts a subform object in the tab control where the Order records will appear.

11. Click the **View** button for Form view ⌐⊞⌐ on the Form Design toolbar to view the form. See Figure 5-42.

Figure 5-42 ◄
Viewing the
form with the
tab control

click to display
second page

first page of
tab control

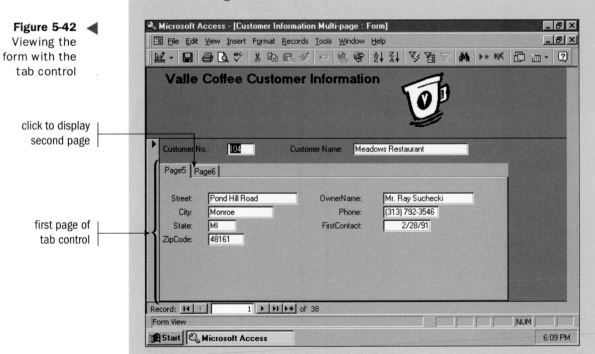

The tab control shows the customer information on the current page. You can view the order information for the customer by clicking the second page.

12. Click the page tab on the right to display the order information. See Figure 5-43.

Figure 5-43 ◀
Viewing the
subform on the
tab control

second page of
tab control

Order records for
Meadows Restaurant
in subform

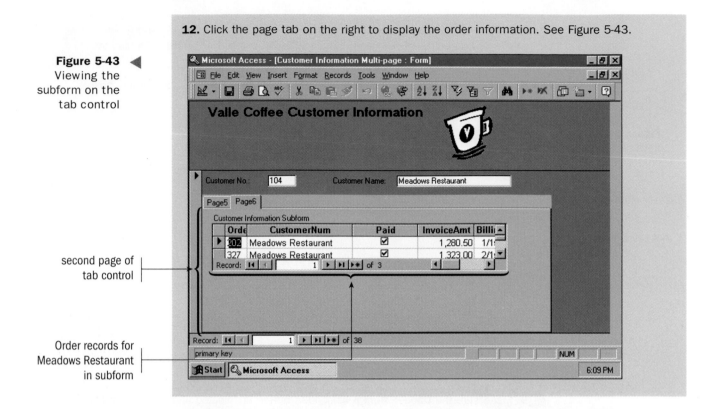

After viewing the form, Barbara identifies several modifications she'd like you to make. The subform is not properly sized and the field values in the subform are not displayed completely. She wants you to resize the subform and the field values so that the entire field values are visible. She also wants you to delete the CustomerNum field from the subform, because the labels at the top of the form already provide both the customer number and the customer name. Finally, she asks you to delete the Customer Information Subform label and edit the labels for the tabs in the tab control so that they indicate the contents of each page.

You can resize the subform, edit the labels, and delete the CustomerNum field from the subform in Design view. Then you can resize the Order columns in Form view. You will begin by resizing the subform, deleting its labels, and editing the labels for the tabs.

To resize the subform, delete its label, and edit the labels for the tabs:

1. Click the **View** button for Design view ⊠ on the Form View toolbar.

2. Scroll down until the bottom of the subform is visible. If necessary, click the subform to select it. Place the pointer on the middle right sizing handle of the subform. When the pointer changes to ↔, click and drag the edge of the sub-form to the right to the 5¼-inch mark on the horizontal ruler.

3. Place the pointer on the middle bottom sizing handle of the subform. When the pointer changes to ↕, click and drag the edge of the subform down to the 2¼-inch mark on the vertical ruler.

4. Right-click the label for the subform control, and then click **Cut** on the shortcut menu. See Figure 5-44.

Figure 5-44 ◀
Subform resized and label deleted

label deleted

subform resized

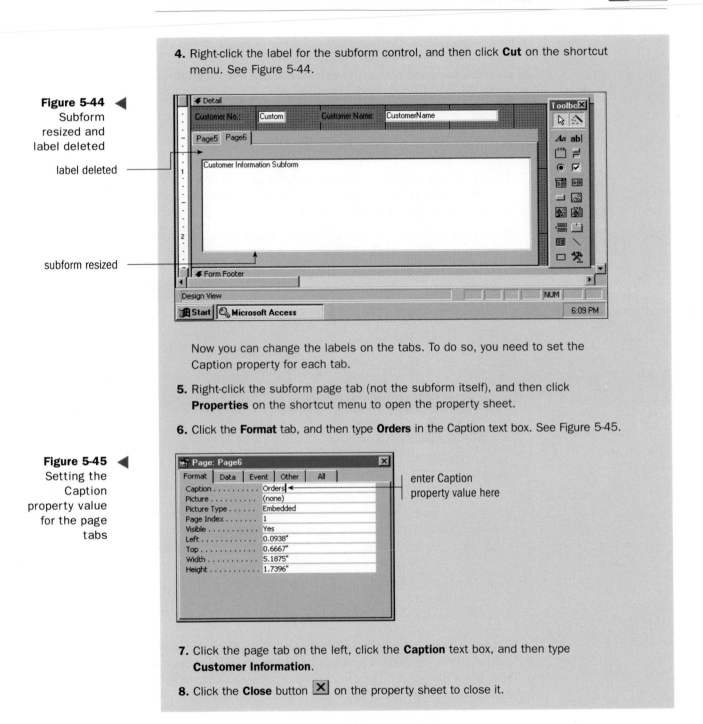

Now you can change the labels on the tabs. To do so, you need to set the Caption property for each tab.

5. Right-click the subform page tab (not the subform itself), and then click **Properties** on the shortcut menu to open the property sheet.

6. Click the **Format** tab, and then type **Orders** in the Caption text box. See Figure 5-45.

Figure 5-45 ◀
Setting the Caption property value for the page tabs

enter Caption property value here

7. Click the page tab on the left, click the **Caption** text box, and then type **Customer Information**.

8. Click the **Close** button ☒ on the property sheet to close it.

Next you'll delete the CustomerNum field from the subform. To do so, you need to open the subform in Design view.

To delete the CustomerNum field from the subform:

1. Click the **Orders** tab to display the subform.

2. Double-click the subform. Access opens the subform in Design view.

3. Right-click the **CustomerNum label**, and then click **Cut** on the shortcut menu.

4. Right-click the **CustomerNum text box**, and then click **Cut** on the shortcut menu.

5. Click the **Close** button ☒ on the Form window in Design view for the subform, and then click the **Yes** button to save the changes to the subform.

Now you can view the form and resize the columns in the Orders subform.

To view the form and resize the columns in the Orders subform:

1. Click the **View** button for Form view 🖼 on the Form Design toolbar. Access displays the first customer record, for Meadows Restaurant, in the form.

2. Click the **Orders** tab. The second page of the multi-page form displays the Order records for Meadows Restaurant.

3. Place the pointer on the column heading for the OrderNum field in the subform. When the pointer changes to ↓, click and drag the pointer to the right to highlight all of the columns in the subform.

4. Place the pointer on the line between any two columns. When the pointer changes to ↔, double-click to resize all the columns. See Figure 5-46.

Figure 5-46 ◀
Order fields
after resizing

resized fields ——

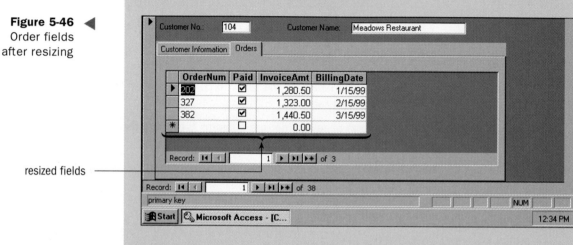

5. Practice navigating through the Customer and Order table records using the form. When you are finished, click the **Customer Information** tab, and then click the **First Record** button 🖼 to display the customer information for Meadows Restaurant.

Now you can save the completed form.

6. Click the **Save** button 🖫 on the Form Design toolbar.

Kim has a new request. She wants to see information for all of the new customers in Indiana or Ohio. She defines a new customer as one whose first contact date was in 1996 or later. She'd like to view this information using the Customer Information Multi-page form. To produce the results she wants, you need to use a filter with the form.

Using a Filter with a Form

Recall that a **filter** is a set of criteria that describes the records you want to see in a datasheet or a form and their sequence. A filter is like a query, but it applies only to the current datasheet or form. If you want to use a filter at another time, you can save the filter as a query.

Access provides three filter tools that allow you to specify and apply filters: Filter By Selection, Filter By Form, and Advanced Filter/Sort. With Filter By Selection and Filter By Form, you specify the record selection criteria directly in the form. Filter By Selection finds records that match a particular field value. Filter By Form finds records that match multiple selection criteria using the same Access logical and comparison operators that you use in queries. After applying a filter by selection or by form, you can rearrange the records using the Sort Ascending or Sort Descending toolbar buttons, if necessary.

Advance Filter/Sort allows you to specify multiple selection criteria and to specify a sort order for the selected records in the Advanced Filter/Sort window, in the same way you specify record selection criteria and sort orders for a query in Design view.

To produce the results Kim wants, you'll use Filter By Form.

Using Filter By Form

Because the Customer Information Multi-page form already shows all of the customer information, you can use Filter By Form to display information for only the new customers in Indiana or Ohio.

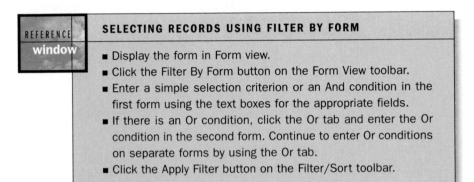

REFERENCE window

SELECTING RECORDS USING FILTER BY FORM

- Display the form in Form view.
- Click the Filter By Form button on the Form View toolbar.
- Enter a simple selection criterion or an And condition in the first form using the text boxes for the appropriate fields.
- If there is an Or condition, click the Or tab and enter the Or condition in the second form. Continue to enter Or conditions on separate forms by using the Or tab.
- Click the Apply Filter button on the Filter/Sort toolbar.

The multiple selection criteria you will enter are: Indiana *and* first contact after 12/31/95 *or* Ohio *and* first contact after 12/31/95.

To select the records using Filter By Form:

1. Click the **Filter By Form** button on the Form View toolbar. Access displays a blank form. See Figure 5-47.

Figure 5-47 ◄
Blank form for
Filter By Form

Clear Grid button

enter selection criteria
for first And condition
on blank form

Or tab

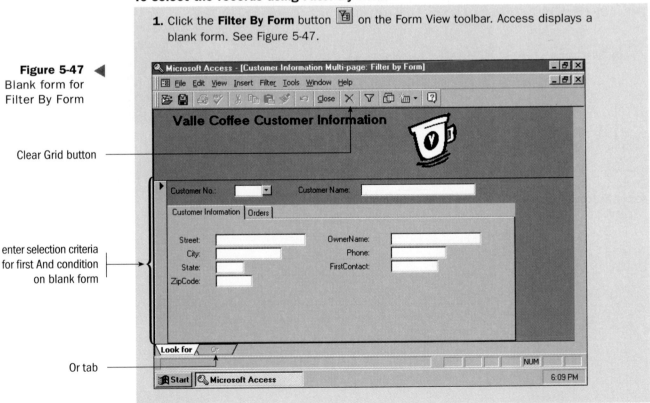

In this blank form, you specify multiple selection criteria by entering conditions in the text boxes for the fields in a record. If you enter criteria in more than one field, you create the equivalent of an And condition: Access will select any record that matches all of the criteria. To create an Or condition, you enter the criteria for the first part of the condition in the field on the first (Look for) blank form, and then click the Or tab to display a new blank form. You enter the criteria for the second part of the condition in the same field on this new blank form. Access selects any record that matches all the criteria on the Look for form *or* all the criteria on the Or form.

2. Click the **State** text box, click the list arrow, and then click **IN**.

3. Click the **FirstContact** text box, and then type **>#12/31/95#**. The number signs (#) indicate a date. If you omit them, Access adds them automatically.

   You have now specified the logical operator (And) and the comparison operator (>) for the condition Indiana *and* after 12/31/95. To add the rest of the criteria, you need to display the Or form.

4. Click the **Or** tab to display a second blank form. The insertion point is in the text box for the FirstContact field. Also, notice that a third tab, which is also labeled "Or," is now available in case you need to specify another Or condition.

5. Click the **State** text box, click the list arrow, and then click **OH**.

6. Click the **FirstContact** text box, and then type **>#12/31/95#**. The form now contains the equivalent of the second And condition: Ohio *and* after 12/31/95. See Figure 5-48.

Figure 5-48 ◀
Completed
Filter By Form

Apply Filter button ——

second And condition
entered on Or tab ——

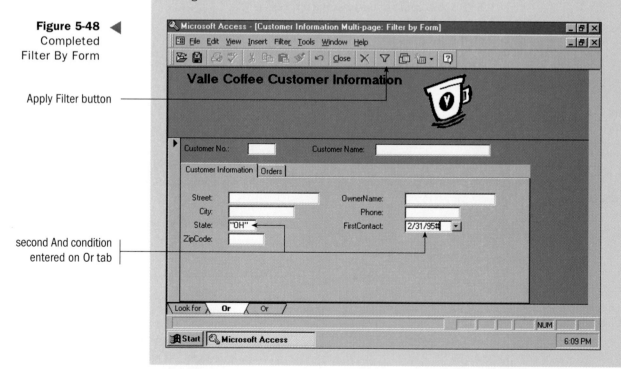

Combined with the Look for form, you now have the Or condition, and the Filter By Form conditions are complete.

7. Click the **Apply Filter** button ![icon] on the Filter/Sort toolbar. Access applies the filter and displays the first record that matches the selection criteria (the Gateway Lounge in Ohio, first contacted on 3/5/96). The bottom of the screen shows that 2 records were selected. See Figure 5-49.

Figure 5-49 ◀
First record that matches the selection criteria

Remove Filter button ——

indicates filter applied

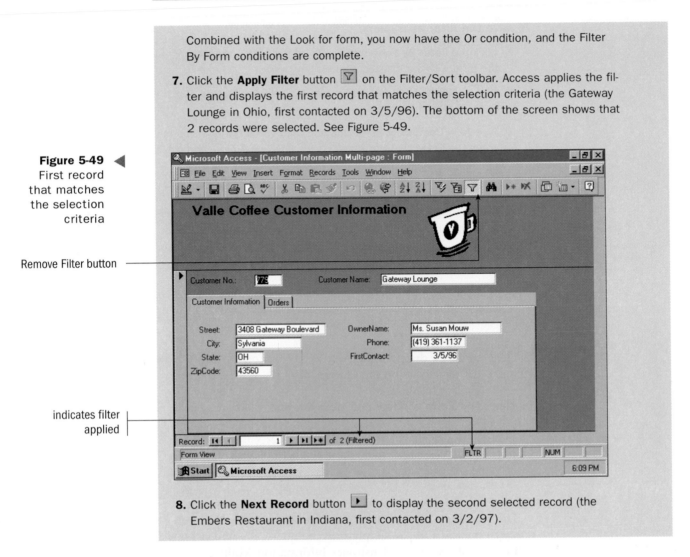

8. Click the **Next Record** button ![icon] to display the second selected record (the Embers Restaurant in Indiana, first contacted on 3/2/97).

Now that you have defined the filter, you can save it as a query, so that Kim can easily view this information again in the future.

Saving a Filter as a Query

By saving a filter as a query, you can reuse the filter in the future by opening the saved query.

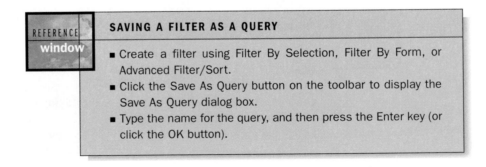

REFERENCE
window

SAVING A FILTER AS A QUERY

- Create a filter using Filter By Selection, Filter By Form, or Advanced Filter/Sort.
- Click the Save As Query button on the toolbar to display the Save As Query dialog box.
- Type the name for the query, and then press the Enter key (or click the OK button).

You'll save the filter you just created as a query named "New Customers in Indiana and Ohio."

To save the filter as a query:

1. Click the **Filter By Form** button ⊞ on the Form View toolbar. Access displays the form with the selection criteria.

2. Click the **Save As Query** button ⊞ on the Filter/Sort toolbar. The Save As Query dialog box opens.

3. Type **New Customers in Indiana and Ohio** in the Query Name text box, and then press the **Enter** key. Access saves the filter as a query and closes the dialog box.

   Now you can clear the selection criteria, close the filter window, and return to Form view.

4. Click the **Clear Grid** button ⊠ on the Filter/Sort toolbar. Access removes the selection criteria from the forms.

5. Click the **Close** button ⊠ to close the filter window and return to Form view. The filter is still in effect in this window, so you need to remove it.

6. Click the **Remove Filter** button ▽ on the Form View toolbar. The bottom of the screen shows that there are 38 available records.

Next, to check that the filter was saved as a query, you'll close the Form window and view the list of queries on the Queries tab.

To close the Form window and view the query list:

1. Click the **Close** button ⊠ on the Form View toolbar.

2. Click the **Queries** tab to display the Queries list box. The query "New Customers in Indiana and Ohio" is now listed.

The next time Kim wants to view the records selected by this query, she can apply the query to the form. If she simply runs the query, she will see the selected records, but they will not be shown in the Customer Information Multi-page form. Instead, she can open the form and apply the saved query to select the records she wants to view in the form.

Applying a Filter that Was Saved as a Query

To see how to apply a query as a filter to a form, you will open the Customer Information Multi-page form and apply the New Customers in Indiana and Ohio query as a filter.

REFERENCE window	**APPLYING A FILTER THAT WAS SAVED AS A QUERY**
	■ Open the form to which you want to apply the filter.
	■ Click the Filter By Form button on the Form View toolbar.
	■ Click the Load from Query button on the Filter/Sort toolbar.
	■ Select the query you want to apply. Access loads the saved query into the Filter grid.
	■ Click the Apply Filter button on the Filter/Sort toolbar.

Access

To apply the filter that you saved as a query:

1. Click the **Forms** tab in the Database window, and then double-click **Customer Information Multi-page** to display this form in Form view.

2. Click the **Filter By Form** button 🔠 on the Form View toolbar.

3. Click the **Load from Query** button 🖼 on the Filter/Sort toolbar. Access displays the Applicable Filter dialog box. See Figure 5-50.

Figure 5-50 ◀
Applicable
Filter dialog
box

click to select filter
saved as query

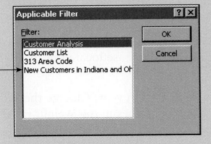

4. Click **New Customers in Indiana and Ohio** in the Filter list box, and then click the **OK** button. Access loads the saved query into the Filter grid.

5. Click the **Apply Filter** button 🔽 on the Filter/Sort toolbar. Access applies the filter and displays the first record in the form.

6. Click the **Close** button ⊠ on the Form window to close it and return to the Database window.

You can now close the Restaurant database and exit Access.

7. Click the **Close** button ⊠ on the Access window to close the database and exit Access.

Quick Check

1. Describe how you would use a Control Wizard to add a tab control to a form.

2. How do you right-align a group of labels?

3. How do you open a subform in Design view to edit it?

4. What is the purpose of Filter By Form?

5. How do you reuse a filter in the future?

6. What is the difference between opening a query and applying a query to a form?

The new queries and forms that you created will make it much easier for Leonard, Barbara, and Kim to enter, retrieve, and view information in the Restaurant database.

Tutorial Assignments

The Products database in the TAssign folder on your Student Disk contains information about Valle Coffee products. The Coffee table in the database contains records of the various types of coffee that Valle Coffee sells. The Product table contains pricing information and the Weight table contains packaging information. The database contains several other objects including queries, forms, and reports. Barbara wants you to make a change to the design of the Product table, create some new queries, and create a custom form. Complete the following:

1. Make sure your Student Disk is in the appropriate disk drive, start Access, and then open the Products database located in the TAssign folder on your Student Disk.

2. Open the Product table in Design view. Change the WeightCode field data type to Lookup Wizard. Look up values in the Weight table, select all fields from the Weight table, and accept all other Lookup Wizard default choices.

3. Create a query to find all records in the Coffee table where the CoffeeName field begins with "Colombian." Include all fields in the query results. Run the query, save it as Colombian Coffees, and then close the query.

4. Create a query to find all records in the Product table where the WeightCode value is A, B, or G. Use a list-of-values match for the selection criterion. Include all fields in the query results. Print the query results. Keep the query open, but do not save the query.

5. Modify the previous query to find all records in the Product table where the WeightCode is not A, B, or G. Print the query results, and then close the query without saving it.

6. Create a query to select all the records from the Coffee table for Decaffeinated coffees that are African or Special Import. Display the CoffeeName and CoffeeType fields in the query results. Print the query results, and then close the query without saving it.

7. Create a parameter query to select the Product table records for a WeightCode that the user specifies. Include all fields in the query results. Save the query as Weight Code Parameter. Run the query and enter the WeightCode A. Print the query results, and then close the query.

8. Create a custom form based on the Special Imports query. Use the design in Figure 5-51 as a guide. Save the form as Special Imports. Open the form and print the first record.

Figure 5-51 ◀

Valle Coffee Special Imports

Coffee Name: XXXXXXXXXXX   Price: $XXX.XX

Product Code: XXXX   Weight/Size: XXXXXXX

9. Use Filter By Form with the Special Imports form to select all records where the CoffeeName field value starts with "Hawaiian" or "Yemen" and the price is over $50.00. Apply the filter. How many records are selected? Print the first selected record. Save the filter as a query named Expensive Hawaiian And Yemen Products.

10. Using Figure 5-52 as a guide, create a multi-page form based on the Coffee and Product tables.

Figure 5-52 ◀

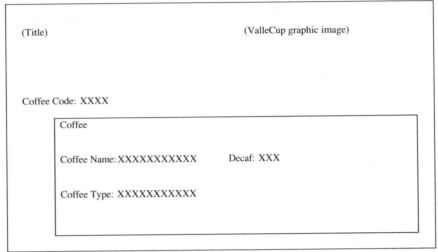

a. Place the CoffeeCode field at the top of the Detail section. Change the caption for the CoffeeCode control to Coffee Code:.

b. Insert a Form Header section in the form. Place a title label in the Form Header section. Enter the title Valle Coffee Products.

c. Place the ValleCup picture in the Form Header section to the right of the title. The file containing this picture is located in the TAssign folder on your Student Disk.

d. Place a tab control below the Coffee Code label in the Detail section. On the first page of the tab control, place the remaining fields from the Coffee table.

e. On the second page of the tab control, place a subform based on the Product table.

f. Change the Caption property for each tab and for the necessary fields on the first page. Then change the Caption property for the necessary fields on the subform.

g. Save the form as Coffee Multi-page.

h. View the form, print both pages for the last record, and then close the form.

11. Open the Coffee Multi-page form and then save it as Enhanced Coffee Multi-page. Make the following changes to the form design and save the changes:

a. Use the Font/Fore Color button to change the color of the text in the title label to red.

    b. Add a Form Footer section. In the center of the Form Footer section, place a label with the text "Valle Gourmet Coffees are the Midwest's favorite." Change the font to 12-point italic and make the color of the text red.

    c. Print both pages for the first record, and then close the form.

12. Close the Products database.

Case Problems

1. Ashbrook Mall Information Desk The Mall Operations Office is responsible for everything that happens in the Ashbrook Mall in Phoenix, Arizona. To maintain a catalog of job openings at the mall stores, Sam Bullard, director of the Mall Operations Office, has created an Access database called MallJobs. Sam asks you to create several new queries and a new form for this database. You'll do so by completing the following:

1. Make sure your Student Disk is in the appropriate disk drive, start Access, and then open the MallJobs database located in the Cases folder on your Student Disk.

2. Open the Job table in Design view. Change the Store field data type to Lookup Wizard. Look up values in the Store table, select the Store and Store Name fields from the Store table, and accept all other Lookup Wizard default choices.

3. Create a query to find all records in the Store table where the Location field begins with "B." Include all fields from the Store table in the query results. Print the query results. Save the query as B Locations, and then close the query.

4. Create a query to find all records in the Job table where the Position value is Clerk, Salesclerk, or Stock Clerk. Use a list-of-values match for the selection criterion. Display the Position and Hours/Week fields in the query results. Print the query results. Keep the query open, but do not save the query.

5. Modify the previous query to find all records in the Job table where the Position value is not Clerk, Salesclerk, or Stock Clerk. Print the query results. Close the query without saving it.

6. Create a query to select all the records for jobs where the Position value is Clerk and the Location value is A3 or B5. Display the Job, StoreName, and Contact fields in the query results. Print the query results, and then close the query without saving it.

7. Create a parameter query to select the Job table records for a Location that the user specifies. Include all the fields in the query results. Save the query as Job Location Parameter. Run the query and enter the Location B5. Print the query results, and then close the query.

8. Create a custom form based on the Store Jobs query. Display all fields in the form. Use your own design for the form. Save the form as Store Jobs. Open the form and print the first record.

9. Use Filter By Form with the Store Jobs form to select all records where the Position value is Clerk or the StoreName value is Pinson Shoes. Apply the filter. How many records are selected? Print the first record. Save the filter as a query named Clerks Or Shoe Stores.

10. Create a multi-page custom form based on the Job and Store tables by completing the following:

    a. Place the Position field in the Detail section of the form.

    b. On the first page of the tab control, display the fields from the Job table.

    c. On the second page of the tab control, display the Store information in a subform.

    d. Insert a Form Header section in the form. Place a title label in the Form Header section. Enter the title Ashbrook Mall Jobs.

EXPLORE

    e. Select the title and use the Special Effect button on the Form Design toolbar to apply the raised special effect to the title.

    f. View the form, and then print both pages for the first record.

11. Close the form and save it as Job Information Multi-page.

12. Close the MallJobs database.

2. Professional Litigation User Services Professional Litigation User Services (PLUS) creates all types of visual aids for judicial proceedings. To track daily payments received from the firm's clients, Raj Jawahir has created the Payments database. To make the database easier to use, Raj wants several new queries and forms created, which you'll do by completing the following:

1. Make sure your Student Disk is in the appropriate disk drive, start Access, and then open the Payments database located in the Cases folder on your Student Disk.

2. Open the Payment table in Design view. Change the Firm# field data type to Lookup Wizard. Look up values in the Firm table, select the Firm# and FirmName fields from the Firm table, and accept all other Lookup Wizard default choices.

3. Create a query to find all records in the Firm table where the PLUSAcctRep field begins with "Tyler." Display all fields in the query results. Print the query results. Save the query as Tyler Accounts, and then close the query.

4. Create a query to find all records in the Payment table where the Firm# value is 1111, 1115, or 1152. Use a list-of-values match for the selection criterion. Display the Payment#, Firm#, AmountPaid, and DatePaid fields in the query results. Print the query results. Keep the query open, but do not save the query.

5. Modify the previous query to find all records in the Payment table where the Firm# value is not 1111, 1115, or 1152. Print the query results, and then close the query without saving it.

6. Modify the June 2 Payments query to select all the records where the PLUSAcctRep field is Abelson, David or Martinez, Nancy. Display all the fields in the query results. Print the query results, and then close the query without saving it.

7. Create a parameter query to select the Payment table records for a Deposit# that the user specifies. Select only records where the AmountPaid is greater than $1,000.00. Include all the fields in the query results. Save the query as Deposits Parameter. Run the query and enter the Deposit# 102. Print the query results, and then close the query.

8. Create a custom form based on the Payment Statistics by Date query. Display all fields in the form. Use your own design for the form. Save the form as Payment Statistics by Date. Open the form, print the first record, and then close the form.

EXPLORE

9. Create a custom form based on the Payment Statistics by Date by Deposit query. Display all fields in the form. Use your own design for the form. Change the Deposit# label and text box format so that the label and field value are displayed with 12-point bold text on a red background. Open the form and print the first record. Save the form as Payment Statistics by Date by Deposit.

10. Use Filter By Form with the Payment Statistics by Date by Deposit form to select all deposits made after June 10 where the Highest Payment was greater than $1800.00 or the Average Payment was greater than $1200.00. Apply the filter. How many records are selected? Print the first selected record. Do not save the filter as a query.

11. Create a multi-page custom form based on the Firm and Payment tables by completing the following:

   a. Place the Firm# and FirmName fields in the Detail section of the form.

   b. On the first page of the tab control, display the other fields from the Firm table.

   c. On the second page of the tab control, display the Payment information in a subform.

   d. Change the Firm# and FirmName label and text box formats so that the label and field values are displayed with 12-point bold text in red letters.

   e. Save the form as Firm Multi-page.

   f. View the form, print both pages for the first record, and then close the form.

12. Open the Firm Multi-page form and save it as Enhanced Firm Multi-page. Make the following changes to the form design and save the changes:

   a. Change the background color of all sections of the form (except the subform) to light blue.

   b. Use the Line/Border Width button to place a border (weight 2) around the Title label. Change the font size and weight for the Title label so that it stands out more on the form. Resize the label control, if necessary.

   c. Use the Font/Fore Color button to change the color of the Title value to red.

   d. Print both pages of the finished form for the first record.

13. Close the Payments database.

3. Best Friends Best Friends is a not-for-profit organization that trains hearing and service dogs for people with disabilities. To raise funds, Best Friends periodically sponsors Walk-A-Thons. These fundraisers have been so popular that Noah and Sheila Warnick, the founders of Best Friends, have created the Walks database to keep track of walkers and their pledges. The Walks database has been a useful tool for Noah and Sheila. Now, they need several new queries and new forms to provide them with better information. You'll help them create these queries and forms by completing the following:

1. Make sure your Student Disk is in the appropriate disk drive, start Access, and then open the Walks database located in the Cases folder on your Student Disk.

2. Open the Pledge table in Design view. Change the WalkerID field data type to Lookup Wizard. Look up values in the Walker table, select the WalkerID, LastName, and FirstName fields from the Walker table, and accept all other Lookup Wizard default choices.

3. Create a query to find all records in the Walker table where the Distance value is 2.4, 2.7, or 2.8. Use a list-of-values match for the selection criterion. Display all fields in the query results. Print the query results. Keep the query open, but do not save the query.

4. Modify the previous query to find all records in the Walker table where the Distance value is not 2.4, 2.7, or 2.8. Print the query results, and then close the query without saving it.

5. Modify the Pledge Statistics by Walker query to select all records where the TotalPledge is greater than 20 and the AveragePledge is greater than 10 or the #Pledges is greater than 1. Display all the fields in the query results. Print the query results, and then close the query without saving it.

6. Create a parameter query to select the Walker table records for a Distance that the user specifies. Display the LastName, FirstName, and Distance fields in the query results. Save the query as Distance Parameter. Run the query and enter the Distance 2.3. Print the query results, and then close the query.

7. Create a custom form based on the Walker table. Display all fields in the form. Use your own design for the form. Save the form as Walker. Open the form, print the first record, and then close the form.

8. Create a custom form based on the Difference query. Display all fields in the form. Use your own design for the form. Change the Pledger label and text box format so that the label and field value are displayed with 12-point bold text on a yellow background. Save the form as Difference.

9. Use Filter By Form with the Difference form to select all records where the PledgeAmt is less than $10.00. Apply the filter. How many records are selected? Print the first selected record. Save the filter as a query named Small Pledges.

10. Create a multi-page custom form based on the Walker and Pledge tables by completing the following:
   a. Place the WalkerID, LastName, and FirstName fields in the Detail section of the form.
   b. On the first page, display the other fields from the Walker table.
   c. On the second page, display the Pledge information in a subform.
   d. Save the form as Walker Information Multi-page.
   e. View the form, print both pages for the first record, and then close the form.

11. Open the Walker Information Multi-page form and save it as Enhanced Walker Information Multi-page. Make the following changes to the form design and save the changes:
   a. Change the background color of all sections of the form (except the subform) to light yellow.
   b. Use the Line/Border Width button to place a border (weight 2) around the WalkerID, LastName, and FirstName text boxes. Change the font size and weight for these labels and text boxes so that they stand out more on the form. Resize the label and text box controls, if necessary.
   c. Use the Font/Fore Color button to change the color of the LastName and FirstName values to red.
   d. Use the Special Effect button on the Form Design toolbar to display the Pledge subform with a shadow.
   e. Print the finished form for the first record.

12. Close the Walks database.

4. Lopez Lexus Dealerships Maria and Hector Lopez own a chain of Lexus dealerships throughout Texas. To keep track of the cars at their various dealerships, they have created the Lexus database. Maria and Hector want you to create several queries and forms to make the Lexus database easier to use. To create the queries and forms, complete the following:

1. Make sure your Student Disk is in the appropriate disk drive, start Access, and then open the Lexus database located in the Cases folder on your Student Disk.

2. Open the Cars table in Design view. Change the LocationCode field data type to Lookup Wizard. Look up values in the Locations table, select the LocationCode and LocationName fields from the Locations table, and accept all other Lookup Wizard default choices.

3. Create a query to find all records in the Cars table where the Class value is S1, S3, or S4. Use a list-of-values match for the selection criterion. Display all fields in the query results. Print the query results. Keep the query open, but do not save the query.

4. Modify the previous query to find all records in the Cars table where the Class value is not S1, S3, or S4. Print the query results, and then close the query without saving it.

5. Create a query to select all Cars records for cars with 5-speed manual transmissions (Transmission field value M5) in Location E1 or L1. Display the Model, Class, Year, and Selling Price fields in the query results. Print the query results, and then close the query without saving it.

6. Create a parameter query to select the Cars table records for a Transmission that the user specifies. Save the query as Transmission Parameter. Run the query and enter the Transmission A4. Print the query results, and then close the query.

7. Create a custom form based on the Cars table. Display all fields in the form. Use your own design for the form. Save the form as Car Data. Open the form, print the first record, and then close the form.

8. Create a custom form based on the 1998 Cars query. Display all fields in the form. Use your own design for the form, but place the title "1998 Lexus Automobiles" in the Form Header section. Change the Model label and text box format so that the label and field value are displayed with 12-point bold text on a light blue background. Save the form as 1998 Cars, and then close it.

9. Use Filter By Form with the 1998 Cars form to select all records for cars over $50,000 in price or located in Houston. Apply the filter. Print the first record. How many records are selected? Do not save the filter as a query.

10. Create a multi-page custom form based on the Cars and Locations tables by completing the following:
    a. Place the LocationName field in the Detail section of the form.
    b. On the first page, display the other fields from the Locations table.
    c. On the second page, display the Cars information in a subform.
    d. Save the form as Locations Information Multi-page.
    e. View the form, print both pages for the first record, and then close the form.

11. Open the Locations Information Multi-page form and save it as Enhanced Locations Information Multi-page. Make the following changes to the form design and save the changes:
    a. Change the background color of all sections of the form (except the subform) to light blue.
    b. Use the Line/Border Width button to place a border (weight 2) around the LocationName text box. Change the font size and weight for this label and text box so that they stand out more on the form. Resize the label and text box controls, if necessary.
    c. Use the Font/Fore Color button to change the color of the ManagerName value to red.
    d. Use the Raised Special Effect button on the Form Design toolbar to change the display of the Cars subform.
    e. Print the finished form for the first record.

12. Close the Lexus database.

TUTORIAL 6

Customizing Reports and Integrating Access with Other Programs

Creating a Custom Invoices Report and a Report with an Embedded Chart and a Linked Text Document

CASE

Valle Coffee

At a recent staff meeting, Leonard indicated that he would like new reports created for the Restaurant database. In the first report, he wants to see a printed list of all orders placed by Valle Coffee customers. He also wants monthly subtotals of billing amounts and a grand total for all billing amounts. The second report Leonard would like is a customer report with an embedded chart that graphically summarizes monthly billing activity. He can use both of these reports to monitor customer orders and monthly billing.

In this tutorial, you will create the reports for Leonard. In building the reports, you will use many of the Access report customization features—such as grouping data, calculating totals, and adding lines to separate report sections. These features enhance a report and make it easier to read.

You will also integrate Access with other programs to include the chart that Leonard requested to graphically summarize monthly billing activity. Finally, you will link a report to a word-processing document that describes the report's contents, and you'll export the records from an Access table to a spreadsheet for further analysis.

OBJECTIVES

In this tutorial you will:

- Design and create a custom report
- Modify report controls and properties
- Sort and group data
- Calculate group and overall totals
- Hide duplicate values
- Embed and link objects in a report
- Export Access data to other programs

SESSION

6.1

In this session you will create a custom report. You will add and modify fields in the report; create a page header with a page number and date; sort and group data; and calculate group and report totals.

Creating a Custom Report

A **report** is a formatted hardcopy of the contents of one or more tables from a database. Although you can format and print data using datasheets, queries, and forms, reports allow you greater flexibility and provide a more professional, custom appearance. Reports can be used, for example, to print billing statements and mailing labels.

An Access report is divided into sections. Each report can have seven different sections, which are described in Figure 6-1.

Figure 6-1 ◀
Descriptions of
Access report
sections

Report Section	Description
Report Header	Appears once at the beginning of a report. Use it for report titles, company logos, report introductions, and cover pages.
Page Header	Appears at the top of each page of a report. Use it for column headings, report titles, page numbers, and report dates. If your report has a Report Header section, it precedes the first Page Header section.
Group Header	Appears once at the beginning of a new group of records. Use it to print the group name and the field value that all records in the group have in common. A report can have up to 10 grouping levels.
Detail	Appears once for each record in the underlying table or query. Use it to print selected fields from the table or query and to print calculated values.
Group Footer	Appears once at the end of a group of records. It is usually used to print totals for the group.
Report Footer	Appears once at the end of the report. Use it for report totals and other summary information.
Page Footer	Appears at the bottom of each page of a report. Use it for page numbers and brief explanations of symbols or abbreviations. If your report has a Report Footer section, it precedes the Page Footer section on the last page of the report.

You don't have to include all seven sections in a report. When you design your report, you determine which sections to include and what information to place in each section. Figure 6-2 shows a sample report produced from the Restaurant database.

Figure 6-2 ◄
Sample report
showing the
seven sections
of a report

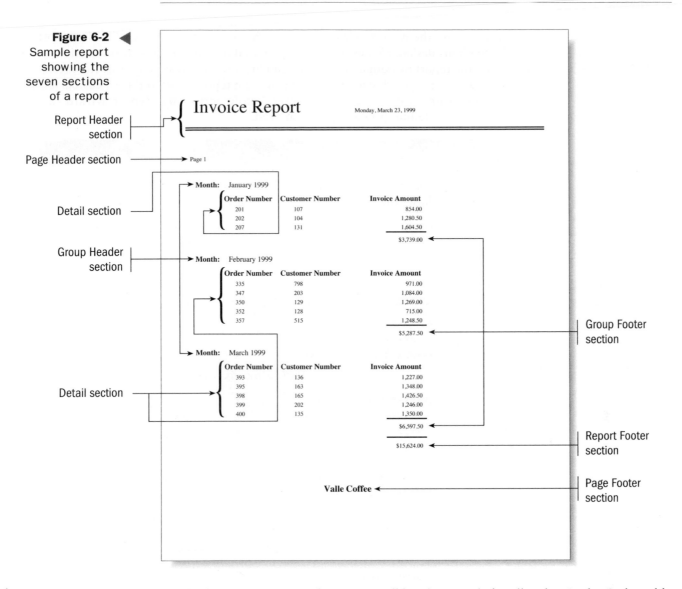

The first report you need to create will list the records for all orders in the Order table. Leonard wants the report to group the invoices by the value in the BillingDate field. The report should also contain the following five sections:

- A Report Header section will contain the report title.

- A Page Header section will show the current date, page number, and column headings for each field.

- A Detail section will list the billing date, order number, customer name, invoice amount, and whether the invoice has been paid. Records in each group will appear in ascending order by customer name.

- A Group Footer section will print subtotals of the InvoiceAmt field for each BillingDate group.

- A Report Footer section will print the grand total of the InvoiceAmt field.

From your work with AutoReport and the Report Wizard, you know that, by default, Access places the report title in the Report Header section and the date and page number in the Page Footer section. Leonard prefers the date and page number to appear at the top of each page, so you need to place this information in the Page Header section.

You could use the Report Wizard to create the report, and then modify the report to match the report design. However, because you need to make several customizations, you will create the report in Design view. If you modify a report created by AutoReport or the Report Wizard, or if you design and create your own report, you produce a **custom report**. You should create a custom report whenever AutoReport or the Report Wizard cannot automatically create the specific report you need.

Designing a Custom Report

Before you create a custom report, you should first plan the report's contents and appearance. Figure 6-3 shows the design of the report you will create for Leonard.

Figure 6-3
Design for the
custom report

Report Header
section

Page Header section

Detail section

Group Footer
section

Report Footer
section

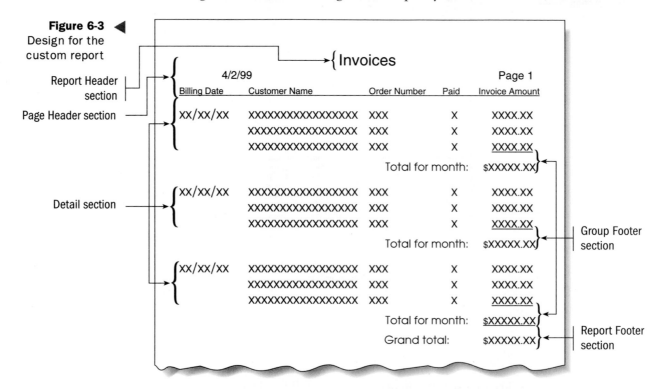

The Report Header section contains the report title, Invoices. Descriptive column headings appear at the bottom of the Page Header section, which also contains the current date and page number.

In the Detail section, the locations and lengths of the field values are indicated by a series of Xs. For example, the three Xs below the Order Number field indicate that the field value will be three characters long.

The subtotals for each group will appear in the Group Footer section, and an overall total will appear in the Report Footer section. The Invoice Amount field is the only field for which totals will appear.

The data for a report can come from either a single table or from a query based on one or more tables. Your report will contain data from the Customer and Order tables. The High Invoice Amounts query contains the fields you need. You will modify the query by removing the selection criterion and deleting unnecessary fields; then you'll use the query as the basis for your report.

To modify the query:

1. Place your Student Disk in the appropriate disk drive.

2. Start Access and then open the Restaurant database located in the Tutorial folder on your Student Disk.

3. Click the **Queries** tab, click **High Invoice Amounts**, and then click the **Design** button. The query is displayed in Design view. See Figure 6-4.

Figure 6-4 ◀
Query in Design
view

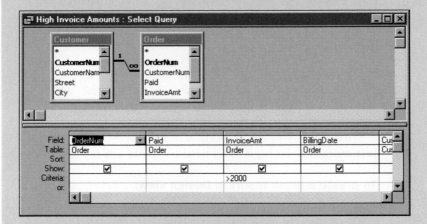

TROUBLE? If you do not see the High Invoice Amounts query in the Queries list box, you might need to scroll the Queries list box to the left.

4. Click the **InvoiceAmt Criteria** text box, press the **F2** key to select the criterion, and then press the **Delete** key.

    The query design also contains the State, OwnerName and Phone fields, which you do not need for this query, so you can delete them.

5. Scroll the design grid to the right until the State, OwnerName, and Phone fields are visible.

6. Position the pointer on the State field until the pointer changes to ↓, click and drag the mouse to the right until all three fields—State, OwnerName, and Phone—are selected, and then release the mouse button.

7. Click the **Cut** button ✂ on the Query Design toolbar to remove the three fields.

    The query now selects the OrderNum, Paid, InvoiceAmt, BillingDate, and CustomerName fields for all records in the Customer and Order tables. To keep the original query intact, you'll save this query as "Invoice Amounts."

8. Click **File** on the menu bar, and then click **Save As/Export**. The Save As dialog box opens.

9. Position the insertion point to the left of the query name, use the Delete key to delete the word "High" and the space following it, and then click the **OK** button. Access saves the modified query.

10. Click the **Close** button ✕ on the Query window to close it and return to the Database window.

You are now ready to create the report. To do so, you need to display the report in Design view.

Report Window in Design View

The Report window in Design view is similar to the Form window in Design view, which you used in the previous tutorial to customize forms.

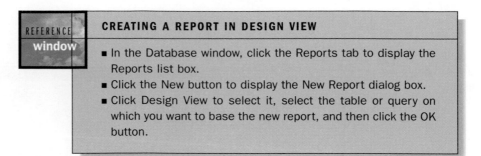

REFERENCE window

CREATING A REPORT IN DESIGN VIEW

- In the Database window, click the Reports tab to display the Reports list box.
- Click the New button to display the New Report dialog box.
- Click Design View to select it, select the table or query on which you want to base the new report, and then click the OK button.

The report you are creating will be based on the Invoice Amounts query, which you just modified. To begin, you need to create a blank report in Design view.

To create a blank report in Design view:

1. Click the **Reports** tab to display the Reports list box, and then click the **New** button to open the New Report dialog box.

2. Click **Design View** (if necessary), and then click the list arrow to display the list of tables and queries in the Restaurant database.

3. Click **Invoice Amounts** to select this query as the basis for your report, and then click the **OK** button. Access displays the Report window in Design view.

4. Click the **Maximize** button 🔲 on the Report window. See Figure 6-5.

Figure 6-5 ◄
Report window in Design view

Toolbox button

Field List button

Page Header section

Detail section

Page Footer section

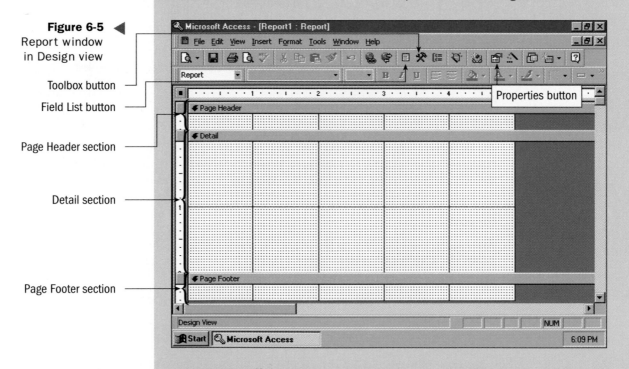

TROUBLE? If the rulers or grid do not appear, click View on the menu bar, and then click Ruler or Grid to display the missing component. A check mark appears to the left of these components when they are displayed in the Report window. If the grid is still not displayed, see your instructor or technical support person for assistance. If the toolbox is open, click the Close button 🗙 on the toolbox to close it.

Notice that the Report window in Design view has many of the same components as the Form window in Design view. For example, the Report Design toolbar includes a Properties button, a Field List button, and a Toolbox button. Both windows also have horizontal and vertical rulers, a grid, and a Formatting toolbar.

Unlike the Form window in Design view, which initially displays only the Detail section on a blank form, the Report window also displays a Page Header section and a Page Footer section. Reports often contain these sections, so Access automatically includes them in a blank report.

Adding Fields to a Report

Your first task is to add bound controls to the Detail section for all the fields from the Invoice Amounts query. Recall that a bound control displays field values from the table or query on which a form or report is based. You add bound controls to a report in the same way that you add them to a form.

REFERENCE window

ADDING FIELDS TO A REPORT

- Display the report in Design view.
- Click the Field List button on the Report Design toolbar to display the field list.
- To place all fields in the report, double-click the field list title bar to highlight all the fields. Then click anywhere in the highlighted area of the field list and drag the fields to the report. Release the mouse button when the pointer is correctly positioned.
- To place a single field in the report, position the pointer on the field name in the field list, and then click and drag the field name to the report. Release the mouse button when the pointer is correctly positioned.

You need to add a bound control for each field in the Invoice Amounts query. You can add all of these bound controls at once by dragging them as a group from the field list to the Detail section.

To add bound controls for all the fields in the field list:

1. Click the **Field List** button  on the Report Design toolbar. The field list box opens. See Figure 6-6.

Figure 6-6 ◀
Field list box

2. Double-click the field list title bar to highlight all the fields in the Invoice Amounts field list.

3. Click anywhere in the highlighted area of the field list (but not on the title bar), and then drag the fields to the Detail section. Release the mouse button when the pointer ⬚ is positioned at the top of the Detail section and at the 1¼-inch mark on the horizontal ruler. Access adds bound controls for the five selected fields. Each bound control consists of a text box and an attached label. The attached labels are positioned to the left of the text boxes, except for the label for the Paid check box. See Figure 6-7. Notice that the text boxes are aligned at the 1¼-inch mark.

Figure 6-7 ◀
Adding bound
controls to
the report

one check box

attached labels

four text boxes

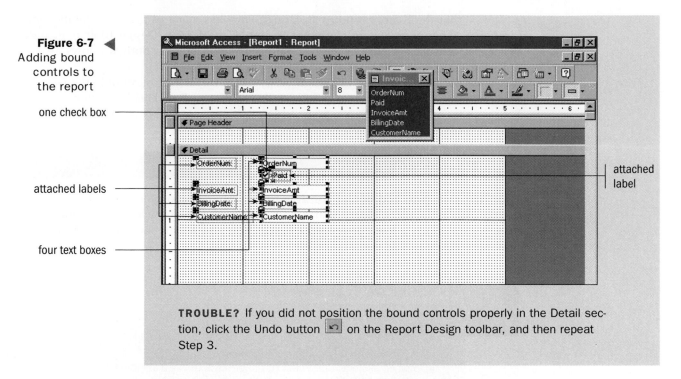

attached
label

TROUBLE? If you did not position the bound controls properly in the Detail section, click the Undo button ↶ on the Report Design toolbar, and then repeat Step 3.

Performing operations in the Report window in Design view will become easier with practice. Remember, you can always click the Undo button immediately after you make a report design change that produces unsatisfactory results. You can also click the Print Preview button at any time to view your progress on the report.

Working with Controls

Four text boxes and one check box now appear in a column in the Detail section. Each of these boxes is a bound control linked to a field in the underlying query and has an attached label box. The label boxes appear to the left of the text boxes and to the right of the check box. The labels identify the contents of the text boxes and the check box, which will display the field values from the database. According to Leonard's plan for the report (see Figure 6-3), you need to move all the label boxes to the Page Header section, where they will serve as column headings for the field values. You then need to reposition the label boxes, text boxes, and the check box so that they are aligned properly. Before you begin working with the controls in the Report window, you'll close the field list because you no longer need it.

To close the field list and then move all the label boxes to the Page Header section:

1. Click the **Close** button ☒ on the field list box to close it.

2. Click anywhere in the Page Header section to deselect the four text boxes, the check box, and their attached label boxes.

3. While pressing and holding down the **Shift** key, click each of the five label boxes in the Detail section, and then release the Shift key. This action selects all the label boxes in preparation for cutting them from the Detail section and pasting them in the Page Header section.

4. Position the pointer in any one of the selected label boxes. The pointer changes to 🖑 .

5. Click the right mouse button to display the shortcut menu.

6. Click **Cut** on the shortcut menu to delete the label boxes from the Detail section. See Figure 6-8.

Figure 6-8
Label boxes
cut from the
Detail section

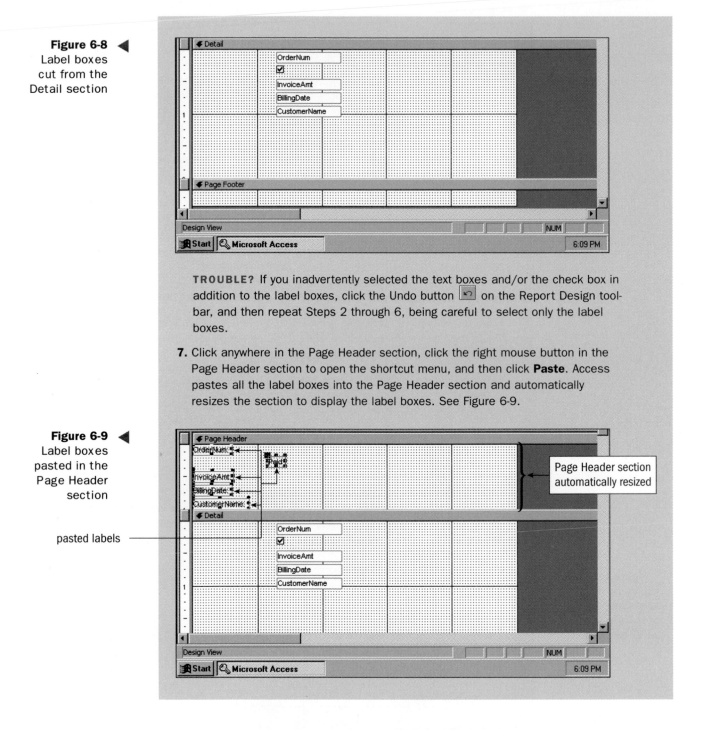

Figure 6-9
Label boxes
pasted in the
Page Header
section

pasted labels

TROUBLE? If you inadvertently selected the text boxes and/or the check box in addition to the label boxes, click the Undo button on the Report Design tool-bar, and then repeat Steps 2 through 6, being careful to select only the label boxes.

7. Click anywhere in the Page Header section, click the right mouse button in the Page Header section to open the shortcut menu, and then click **Paste**. Access pastes all the label boxes into the Page Header section and automatically resizes the section to display the label boxes. See Figure 6-9.

Cutting and pasting the label boxes has unlinked them from their attached text boxes and check box. You can now select and move either a label box or a text box (or check box), but not both at once.

Moving and Resizing Controls

You can move or resize any individual control or multiple selected controls in the Report window. When you select a control, a move handle appears in the top-left corner of the control. This is the handle you use to reposition the control. A selected control also displays sizing handles around its border, which you can use to resize a control in different directions.

> REFERENCE
> window
>
> **MOVING AND RESIZING CONTROLS**
>
> ■ In Design view, click the control to select it.
> ■ To move a control, position the pointer on the control's move handle, click and drag the control to its new location, and then release the mouse button.
> ■ To resize a control, position the pointer on one of the control's sizing handles, click and drag the sizing handle until the control is the proper size, and then release the mouse button.

You need to reposition the text boxes, check box, and label boxes to match the report's design. You'll begin by repositioning the text boxes and check box in the Detail section, which should appear in a row beginning with the BillingDate field. You will also resize the text boxes so the contents will be displayed completely.

To move the text boxes and check box and resize the text boxes:

1. Click the **BillingDate text box** in the Detail section, position the pointer on the move handle in the upper-left corner of the text box, and then click and drag the text box to the upper-left corner of the Detail section.

   Now you will resize the BillingDate text box so it is just large enough to display a date.

2. Position the pointer on the middle right sizing handle of the BillingDate text box. When the pointer changes to ↔, click and drag the right border to the left, to the ½-inch mark (approximately) on the horizontal ruler.

3. Refer to Figure 6-10 and use the procedures noted in Steps 1 and 2 to move the other four controls and resize the remaining text boxes in the Detail section to match the figure as closely as possible. Note that you need to increase the size of the CustomerName text box and decrease the size of both the OrderNum and InvoiceAmt text boxes. See Figure 6-10.

Figure 6-10 ◀
After moving and resizing the controls in the Detail section

check box moved

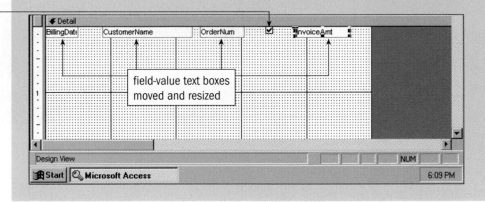

The Detail section is now much taller than necessary to display these controls. The extra space below the text boxes and check box will show as white space between records in the printed report. The report will be more readable and require fewer pages if the records in the Detail section are printed without a large space between them. You can resize the Detail section so that the records will be printed without spacing between them.

Access

To resize the Detail section:

1. If necessary, scroll down to display the bottom edge of the Detail section.

2. Position the pointer on the bottom edge of the Detail section. When the pointer changes to ╪, click and drag the bottom edge up to align with the bottom of the controls. If necessary, scroll up to display the top of the report. See Figure 6-11.

Figure 6-11 ◄
After resizing
the Detail
section

Detail section resized ——————

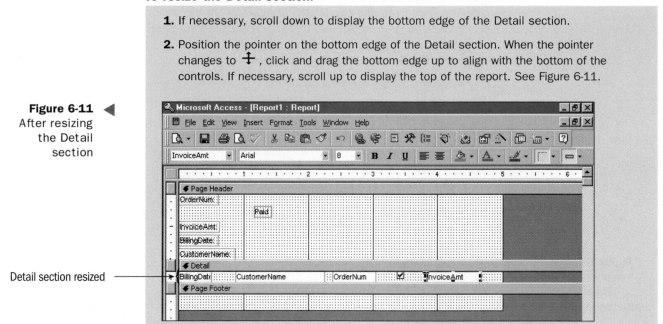

You've made many modifications to the report design and should save the report before proceeding.

To save the report design:

1. Click the **Save** button 🖫 on the Report Design toolbar. The Save As dialog box opens.

2. Type **Invoices** in the Report Name text box, and then press the **Enter** key. The dialog box closes and Access saves the report in the Restaurant database.

The report design shows column headings different from the text currently displayed in the label boxes in the Page Header section. Next, you need to change the text of the labels by changing each label's Caption property.

Changing the Caption Property

Each label has a Caption property that controls the text displayed in the label. The default Caption property value for a bound control is the field name followed by a colon. Other controls, such as buttons and tab controls, have Caption properties as well. You can change the value of a Caption property for an object by using the property sheet for that object. You should change the Caption property value for an object if the default value is difficult to read or understand.

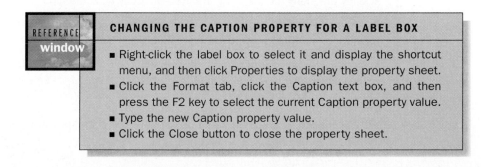

REFERENCE window	**CHANGING THE CAPTION PROPERTY FOR A LABEL BOX**
	■ Right-click the label box to select it and display the shortcut menu, and then click Properties to display the property sheet.
	■ Click the Format tab, click the Caption text box, and then press the F2 key to select the current Caption property value.
	■ Type the new Caption property value.
	■ Click the Close button to close the property sheet.

The default Caption property values for the labels in the report do not match Leonard's report design. For example, the label BillingDate: should be Billing Date. You need to change the Caption property for each label except the Paid label.

To change the Caption property for the labels:

1. Right-click the **BillingDate label box** in the Page Header section, and then click **Properties** to display the property sheet for the BillingDate label.

2. If necessary, click the **Format** tab to display the Format page of the property sheet. The current Caption property value, BillingDate:, is selected. You simply need to insert a space between the words "Billing" and "Date" and delete the colon following the text.

3. Position the insertion point to the right of the letter "g," press the **spacebar**, position the insertion point to the right of the colon, and then press the **Backspace** key to delete it. See Figure 6-12.

Figure 6-12 ◄
Changing the
Caption
property value

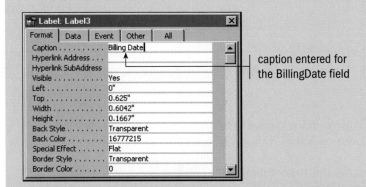

caption entered for
the BillingDate field

4. If necessary, drag the property sheet to the right until the OrderNum label box is visible. Click the **OrderNum label box** to select it. The property sheet changes to show the properties for the OrderNum label.

5. Edit the text of the Caption property so that it displays the value **Order Number**.

6. Click the **InvoiceAmt label box** to select it, and then edit the text of the Caption property so that it displays the value **Invoice Amount**.

7. Click the **CustomerName label box** to select it, and then edit the text of the Caption property so that it displays the value **Customer Name**.

8. Click the **Close** button [X] on the property sheet to close it.

Next, you need to resize the Order Number and Invoice Amount label boxes so that the captions fit. You can resize both boxes at the same time.

To resize the label boxes:

1. Click an empty area of the grid to deselect any selected label boxes.

2. While pressing and holding down the **Shift** key, click the **Order Number label box** and then click the **Invoice Amount label box** to select both of them.

3. Click **Format** on the menu bar, point to **Size**, and then click **To Fit**. Access resizes the two label boxes to fit the captions.

Now you need to align the label boxes with the corresponding text boxes in the Detail section.

Access

Aligning Controls

You can align controls in a report or form using the **Align** command. This command provides options for aligning controls in different ways. For example, if you select objects in a column, you can use the Align Left option to align the left edges of the objects. Similarly, if you select objects in a row, you can use the Align Top option to align the top edges of the objects. The Align Right and Align Bottom options work in the same way. A fifth option, Align To Grid, aligns selected objects with the grid dots in the Report window. You will use the Align Right and Align Top options to align the labels in the Page Header section with their corresponding text boxes in the Detail section. Recall that the labels will serve as column headings in the report, so they must be aligned correctly with the text boxes, which will display the field values from the database.

To align the labels in the Page Header section with the text boxes in the Detail section:

1. Click the **Customer Name label** to select it. Position the pointer on the Customer Name label. When the pointer changes to 🖐, click and drag the Customer Name label to the right above the CustomerName text box.

2. Press and hold down the **Shift** key, and then click the **CustomerName text box** to select it. Both the label box and the text box are selected. You can now align them on their left edges.

3. Click **Format** on the menu bar, point to **Align**, and then click **Left** to left-align the label with the text box. See Figure 6-13.

Figure 6-13 ◀
After aligning the Customer Name label and CustomerName text box

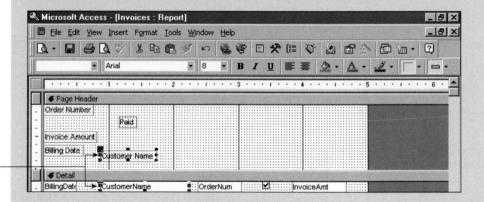

label and text box
are left-aligned

4. Repeat Steps 1 through 3 to left-align the remaining labels with their respective text boxes.

   Now you can align the tops of all the labels. This will ensure that the column headings in the report appear in a straight row.

5. Click an empty area of the Page Header section to deselect all objects, click the **Billing Date label** to select it, press and hold down the **Shift** key, and then click the remaining labels. All of the labels are now selected.

6. Click **Format** on the menu bar, point to **Align**, and then click **Top** to top-align the labels.

7. Position the pointer on any of the selected labels. When the pointer changes to 🖐, click and drag the labels up or down as necessary until they are positioned like the labels in Figure 6-14. Leave two lines of grid dots visible below the labels to visually separate the labels from the field values when the report is printed.

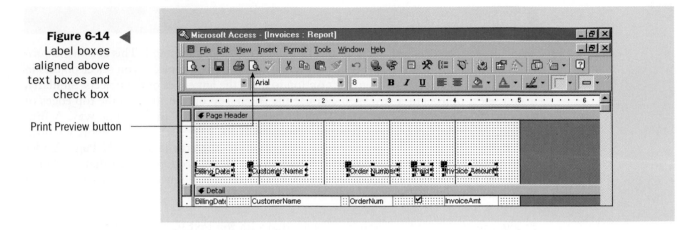

Now you'll save the modified report and preview it to see what it will look like when printed.

To save and preview the report:

1. Click the **Save** button 🖫 on the Report Design toolbar.

2. Click the **Print Preview** button 🔍 on the Report Design toolbar. Access displays the report in Print Preview.

3. Scroll the Print Preview window so that you can see more of the report on the screen. See Figure 6-15.

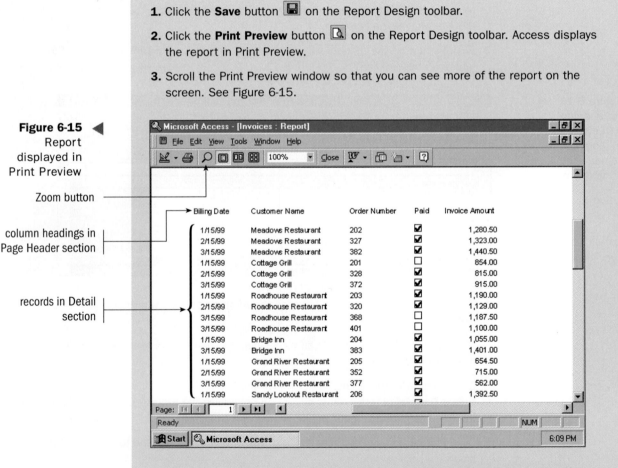

TROUBLE? If your report shows a larger gap between the records in the Detail section, you need to reduce the height of the Detail section. The bottom of the Detail section should align with the bottom of the text boxes in that section. Click the Close button on the Print Preview toolbar to return to Design view, and then drag the bottom of the Detail section up until it aligns with the bottom of the text boxes in that section. Then redisplay the report in Print Preview.

You can use the Zoom button to view the entire page on the screen. This will give you a sense of how the final printed page will look.

4. Click the **Zoom** button 🔍 on the Print Preview toolbar. Access displays the full report page on the screen. See Figure 6-16.

Figure 6-16 ◀
Full report page
displayed

Print Preview
Close button

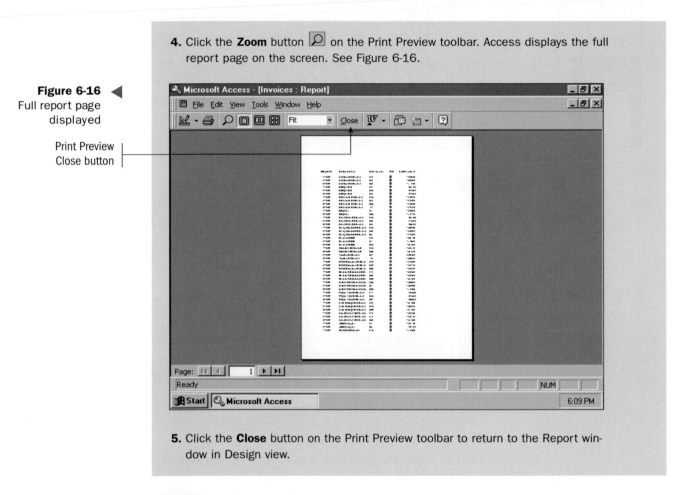

5. Click the **Close** button on the Print Preview toolbar to return to the Report window in Design view.

Quick Check

1. Describe the seven sections in an Access report.

2. What is a custom report?

3. What does the Report window in Design view have in common with the Form window in Design view? How do the two windows differ?

4. What is the Caption property for an object and when would you change it?

5. How do you left-align objects in a column?

6. What is the purpose of the Zoom button in Print Preview?

You have completed the Detail section of the report and started to work on the Page Header section. In the next session, you will complete the report according to Leonard's design.

SESSION 6.2

In this session, you will complete the Invoices report. You will insert the date and page number and a line in the Page Header section, and place a title in the Report Header section. You will also add Group Header and Group Footer sections and specify the grouping and sorting fields for the records. Finally, you will add group subtotals to the Group Footer section and a grand total to the Report Footer section.

Adding the Date to a Report

According to Leonard's design, the report must include the date in the Page Header section. To add the date to a report, you insert the Date function in a text box. The **Date function** is a type of calculated control that prints the current date on a report. The format of the Date function is =Date(). The equals sign (=) indicates that this is a calculated control; Date is the name of the function; and the parentheses () indicate a function rather than simple text.

REFERENCE window

ADDING THE DATE TO A REPORT

- Display the Report in Design view.
- Click the Text Box tool on the toolbox.
- Position the pointer where you want the date to appear, and then click to place the text box in the report.
- Click the text box, type =Date(), and then press the Enter key.

You need to insert the Date function in the Page Header section so that the current date will be printed on each page of the report.

To add the Date function to the Page Header section:

1. If you took a break after the previous session, make sure your Student Disk is in the appropriate drive. Open the Restaurant database and then open the Invoices report in Design view. If necessary, maximize the Report window.
2. If necessary, click the **Toolbox** button on the Report Design toolbar to display the toolbox.

   TROUBLE? If the toolbox is in the way of your report design, drag the toolbox to the far right side of the Report window.
3. Click the **Text Box** tool on the toolbox.
4. Position the pointer in the Page Header section. The pointer changes to +abl.
5. When the pointer's plus symbol (+) is positioned at the top of the Page Header section at approximately the ¾-inch mark on the horizontal ruler (see Figure 6-17), click the mouse button. Access adds a text box with an attached label box to its left. Inside the text box is the description Unbound. Recall that an unbound control is a control that is not linked to a database table field.
6. Click the **Unbound text box** to position the insertion point and remove the word "Unbound," type **=Date()**, and then press the **Enter** key. See Figure 6-17.

Access

Figure 6-17 ◀
Adding the
current date to
the report

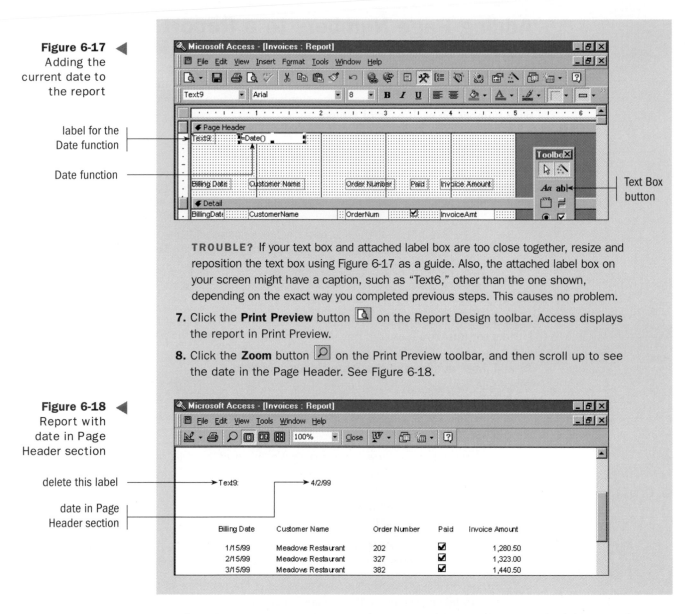

label for the
Date function

Date function

Text Box
button

TROUBLE? If your text box and attached label box are too close together, resize and reposition the text box using Figure 6-17 as a guide. Also, the attached label box on your screen might have a caption, such as "Text6," other than the one shown, depending on the exact way you completed previous steps. This causes no problem.

7. Click the **Print Preview** button on the Report Design toolbar. Access displays the report in Print Preview.

8. Click the **Zoom** button on the Print Preview toolbar, and then scroll up to see the date in the Page Header. See Figure 6-18.

Figure 6-18 ◀
Report with
date in Page
Header section

delete this label

date in Page
Header section

When Access prints your report, the current date appears instead of the Date function you entered in the Unbound text box. Notice that the label for the date is unnecessary, so you can delete the label box. To make the date more prominent in the Page Header, you'll increase the font size of text in the Date text box to 10 and then move the text box to the upper-left corner of the Page Header section.

To delete the Date label box and modify the Date text box:

1. Click the **Close** button on the Print Preview toolbar to return to Design view.

2. Position the pointer on the Date label box, which is located in the upper-left corner of the Page Header section.

3. Click the right mouse button to select the label box and open the shortcut menu, and then click **Cut** to delete the label.

4. Click the **Date text box**, and then drag its move handle to the upper-left corner of the Page Header section.

5. Click the **Font Size** list arrow on the Formatting toolbar, and then click **10** to change the font size of the Date text box.

You are now ready to complete the report's Page Header section by adding page numbers.

Adding Page Numbers to a Report

You can instruct Access to print the page number in a report by including an expression in the Page Header or Page Footer section. You can type the expression in an unbound control, just as you did for the Date function, or you can use the Page Numbers option on the Insert menu. The inserted page number expression automatically prints the correct page number on each page of a report.

REFERENCE window	**ADDING PAGE NUMBERS TO A REPORT**
	■ Display the report in Design view.
	■ Click the section where you want to place the page numbers.
	■ Click Insert on the menu bar, and then click Page Numbers.
	■ Select the formatting, position, and alignment options you want.
	■ Click the OK button to place the page number expression in the report.

Leonard wants the page number to be printed in the upper-right corner of the Page Header section. You'll use the Page Numbers option to insert the page number in the report.

To add page numbers in the Page Header section:

1. Click an empty area of the Page Header section to deselect the Date text box.

2. Click **Insert** on the menu bar, and then click **Page Numbers**. The Page Numbers dialog box opens.

    The Format options allow you to specify the format of the page number. Leonard wants the page numbers to appear as Page 1, Page 2, etc. This is the Page N format option. The Position options allow you to place the page numbers at the top of the page in the Page Header section or at the bottom of the page in the Page Footer section. Leonard's design shows the page numbers at the top of the page.

3. Make sure that the **Page N** option button is selected in the Format section and that the **Top of Page [Header]** option button is selected in the Position section.

    The report design shows the page numbers at the right side of the page. You can specify this placement in the Alignment list box.

4. Click the **Alignment** list arrow, and then click **Right**.

5. Make sure that the **Show Number on First Page** check box is checked so that Access prints the page number on the first page as well as all other pages. See Figure 6-19.

Figure 6-19 ◀
Completed
Page Numbers
dialog box

click to select format

click to select
position on page

indicates page
number will be
printed on all pages

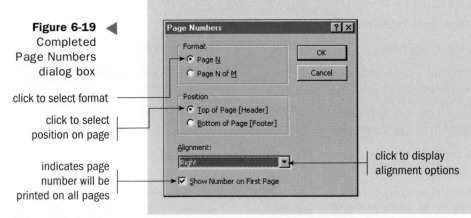

click to display
alignment options

6. Click the **OK** button. Access adds a text box in the upper-right corner of the Page Header section. See Figure 6-20. The expression ="Page" & [Page] in the text box means that the report will show the word "Page" followed by the page number when the report is printed.

Figure 6-20 ◄
Page number
expression
added to the
Report window

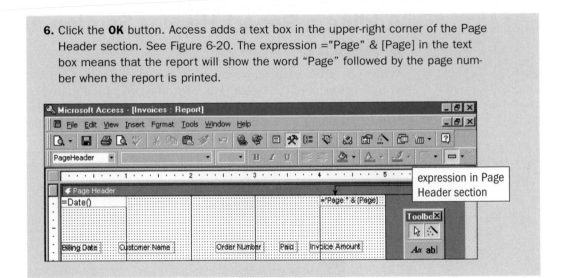

expression in Page
Header section

Leonard wants the text of the page number to be the same size as the text of the date. So, you need to change the font size of the Page Number text box to 10. To duplicate the formatting of the Date text box, you can use the Format Painter. The **Format Painter** allows you to copy the format of an object to other objects in the report. This makes it easy to create several objects with the same font style and size, the same color, and the same special effect applied.

To use the Format Painter to format the Page Number text box:

1. Click the **Date text box** to select it.

2. Click the **Format Painter** button on the Report Design toolbar.

3. Click the **Page Number text box**. The Format Painter automatically formats the Page Number text box like the Date text box (with a font size of 10). The label ="Page" & [Page] is larger than the text box. Also, notice that the letter "g" in the word "Page" is not completely visible, so you need to resize the text box to fit.

4. Click the **Page Number text box**, click **Format** on the menu bar, point to **Size**, and then click **To Fit**. Access resizes the text box, and the "g" in Page is now visible. The page number expression still does not fit the text box, but the actual page number will fit when the report is printed.

5. Click the **Print Preview** button on the Report Design toolbar. Access displays the report in Print Preview. See Figure 6-21.

Figure 6-21 ◄
Completed
Page Header
section

date ────────────► 4/2/99   ► Page 1

page number ──────

Billing Date   Customer Name   Order Number   Paid   Invoice Amount

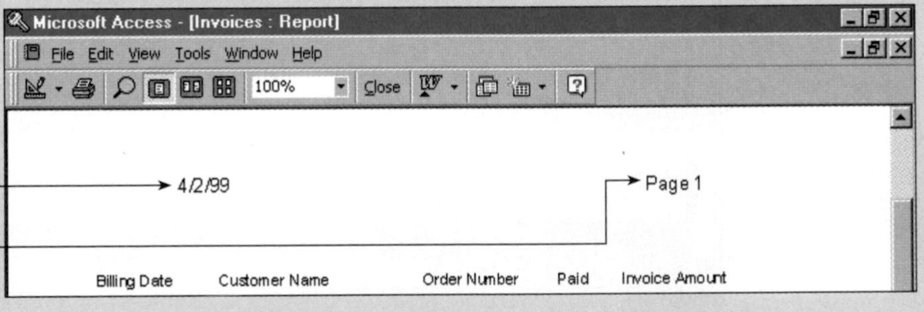

Now that you have completed the Page Header section of the report, you are ready to add the title in the Report Header section.

Adding a Report Header Section and a Title to a Report

When you print a report, anything contained in the Report Header section appears once at the beginning of the report. This section is often used to display the report title or other identifying information. To include information in the Report Header, you must first add both a Report Header section and a Report Footer section to the report.

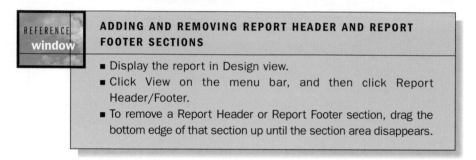

REFERENCE window

ADDING AND REMOVING REPORT HEADER AND REPORT FOOTER SECTIONS

- Display the report in Design view.
- Click View on the menu bar, and then click Report Header/Footer.
- To remove a Report Header or Report Footer section, drag the bottom edge of that section up until the section area disappears.

The report design includes the title Invoices, which you'll add to the Report Header section. To make the report title stand out, Leonard asks you to increase the report title font size from 8, the default, to 14. You'll begin by adding Report Header and Report Footer sections to the report.

To add Report Header and Report Footer sections and then add the title:

1. Click the **Close** button on the Print Preview toolbar to return to Design view.

2. Click **View** on the menu bar, and then click **Report Header/Footer**. Access places a Report Header section at the top of the Report window and a Report Footer section at the bottom. See Figure 6-22.

Figure 6-22 ◄
Report Header and Report Footer sections added

Report Header section

Report Footer section

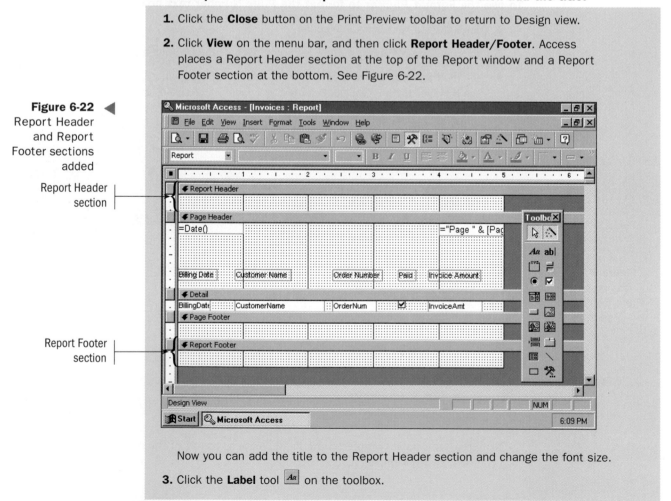

Now you can add the title to the Report Header section and change the font size.

3. Click the **Label** tool Aa on the toolbox.

4. Position the pointer in the Report Header section. The pointer changes to $^+$A.

5. Click the left mouse button when the pointer's plus symbol (+) is positioned at the top of the Report Header section at the 2-inch mark on the horizontal ruler. Access places a very narrow text box in the Page Header section. When you start typing in this text box, it will expand to accommodate the text.

6. Type **Invoices** and then press the **Enter** key. See Figure 6-23.

Figure 6-23 ◀
Adding a label
for the report
title

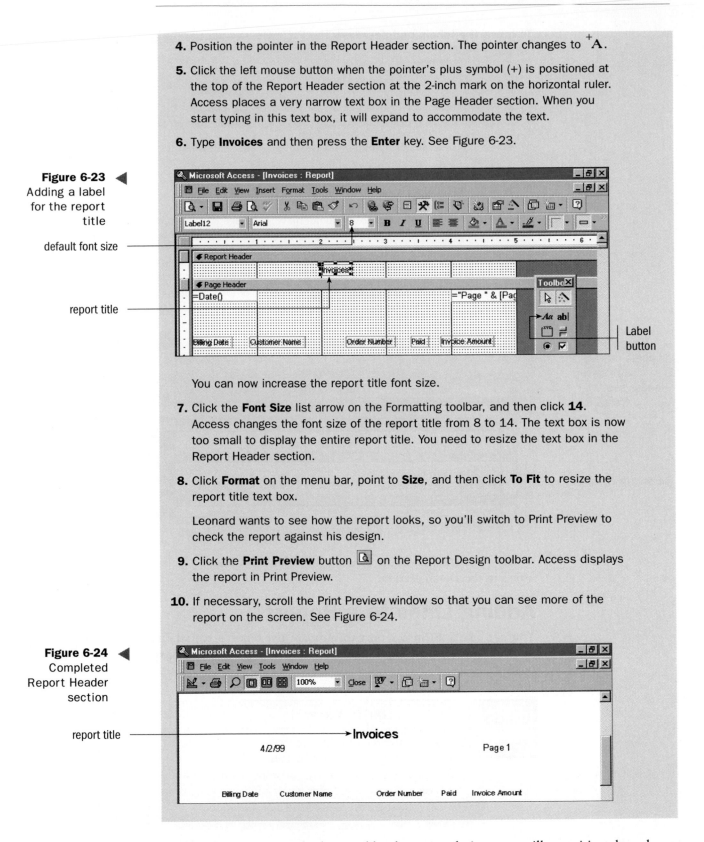

You can now increase the report title font size.

7. Click the **Font Size** list arrow on the Formatting toolbar, and then click **14**. Access changes the font size of the report title from 8 to 14. The text box is now too small to display the entire report title. You need to resize the text box in the Report Header section.

8. Click **Format** on the menu bar, point to **Size**, and then click **To Fit** to resize the report title text box.

   Leonard wants to see how the report looks, so you'll switch to Print Preview to check the report against his design.

9. Click the **Print Preview** button 🔍 on the Report Design toolbar. Access displays the report in Print Preview.

10. If necessary, scroll the Print Preview window so that you can see more of the report on the screen. See Figure 6-24.

Figure 6-24 ◀
Completed
Report Header
section

To make your report look more like the report design, you will reposition the column heading labels to just below the date and page number, and you'll decrease the height of the Page Header section to reduce the white space around it.

To move the labels and decrease the Page Header section height:

1. Click the **Close** button on the Print Preview toolbar to return to Design view.

2. Click an empty area of the Page Header section to deselect any selected objects.

3. While pressing and holding down the **Shift** key, click each of the five label boxes (for the report's column headings) in the Page Header section to select them.

4. Position the pointer on one of the selected labels, and when the pointer changes to ✋, click and drag the label boxes up so that they are positioned just below the date and page number. Release the mouse button when the labels are positioned one row of grid dots below the date and page number (see Figure 6-25).

   TROUBLE? If the label boxes do not move, the Page Number text box or Date text box is probably selected along with the label boxes. Repeat Steps 2 through 4.

5. Position the pointer at the bottom edge of the Page Header section. When the pointer changes to ↕, click and drag the bottom edge up to reduce the height of the Page Header section. Align the bottom edge of the section at approximately the ½-inch mark on the vertical ruler. See Figure 6-25.

Figure 6-25 ◀
Labels moved
and Page
Header section
resized

labels in new position ────

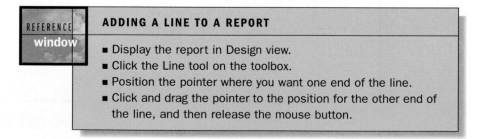

Page
Header
section
is now
smaller

Now you can add a line beneath the column headings to separate them from the text boxes in the Detail section.

Adding Lines to a Report

You can use lines in a report to improve the report's readability and to group related information together. The Line tool on the toolbox allows you to add a line to a report or form.

REFERENCE
window

ADDING A LINE TO A REPORT

- Display the report in Design view.
- Click the Line tool on the toolbox.
- Position the pointer where you want one end of the line.
- Click and drag the pointer to the position for the other end of the line, and then release the mouse button.

You will add a horizontal line to the bottom of the Page Header section to visually separate it from the Detail section when the report is printed.

To add a line to the report:

1. Click the **Line** tool ⬚ on the toolbox.

2. Position the pointer in the Page Header section. The pointer changes to ⁺＼.

3. Position the pointer's plus symbol (+) at the left edge of the Page Header section, just below the column headings.

4. Click and drag a horizontal line from left to right, ending at the right edge of the Page Header section, and then release the mouse button.

   TROUBLE? If the line is not straight, click the Undo button ↶ on the Report Design toolbar, and then repeat Steps 1 through 4.

   Leonard wants the line to stand out more, so he asks you to increase the line's thickness.

5. Click the **Properties** button 🖻 on the Report Design toolbar to display the property sheet. The Border Width property controls the width, or thickness, of lines in a report.

6. Click the right side of the **Border Width** text box in the property sheet to display the list of border width options, and then click **3 pt**. The line's width increases. See Figure 6-26.

Figure 6-26 ◀
Changing
the width of
the line

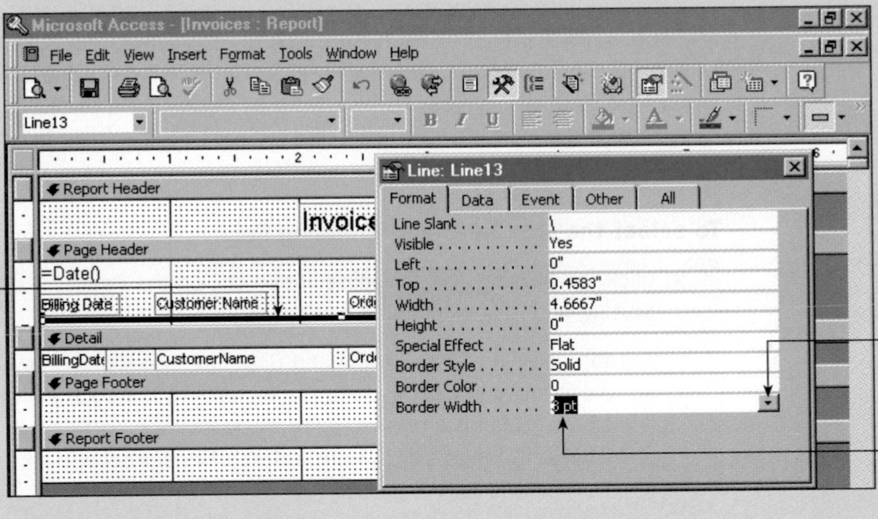

thicker line —

click to
display
list of
options

new line
width

7. Click the **Close** button ☒ on the property sheet to close it.

8. Click the **Save** button 🖫 on the Report Design toolbar to save your changes to the report.

Leonard would like the report to print records in ascending order based on the BillingDate field and to print subtotals for each set of BillingDate field values. He also wants the records for each BillingDate group to be printed with the unpaid invoices first and in descending order by InvoiceAmt. That way, he can review the monthly billings more easily and monitor the invoices that have not been paid. To make these changes, you need to sort and group data in the report.

Sorting and Grouping Data in a Report

Access allows you to organize the records in a report by sorting the records using one or more sort keys. Each sort key can also be a grouping field. If you specify a sort key as a grouping field, you can include a Group Header section and a Group Footer section for the group. A Group Header section will typically include the name of the group, and a Group Footer section will typically include a count or subtotal for records in that group.

You use the Sorting and Grouping button on the Report Design toolbar to select sort keys and grouping fields for a report. Each report can have up to 10 sort fields, and any of the sort fields can also be grouping fields.

REFERENCE window	**SORTING AND GROUPING DATA IN A REPORT**
	▪ Display the report in Design view. ▪ Click the Sorting and Grouping button on the Report Design toolbar. ▪ Click the first Field/Expression list arrow in the Sorting and Grouping dialog box, and select the field to use as the primary sort key. In the Sort Order text box, select the sort order. ▪ Repeat the previous step to select subsorting keys and their sort orders. ▪ To group data, click the field in the Field/Expression text box by which you want to group records. In the Group Properties section, select the grouping option for the field. ▪ Click the Close button on the Sorting and Grouping dialog box to close it.

Because Leonard wants records listed in ascending order based on the BillingDate field and subtotals printed for each BillingDate group, you need to specify the BillingDate field as both the primary sort key and the grouping field. Leonard also wants unpaid invoices listed first and all invoices to be sorted in descending order by InvoiceAmt. So, you need to specify the Paid field as the secondary sort key and the InvoiceAmt field as the tertiary (third) sort key.

To select the sort keys and grouping field:

1. Click the **Sorting and Grouping** button [≣] on the Report Design toolbar. The Sorting and Grouping dialog box opens.

   The top section of the Sorting and Grouping dialog box allows you to specify the sort keys for the records in the Detail section. For each sort key, the bottom section of the dialog box allows you to designate the sort key as a grouping field and to specify whether you want a Group Header section, a Group Footer section, or other options for the group.

2. Click the list arrow in the first **Field/Expression** text box to display the list of available fields, and then click **BillingDate**. Ascending is the default sort order in the Sort Order text box, so you do not need to change this setting.

   You can now designate BillingDate as a grouping field and specify that you want a Group Footer section for this group. This section will contain the subtotals for the invoices by BillingDate.

3. Click the right side of the **Group Footer** text box, and then click **Yes**. Access adds a Group Footer section called BillingDate Footer to the Report window. See Figure 6-27.

Figure 6-27 ◄
Adding a Group
Footer section

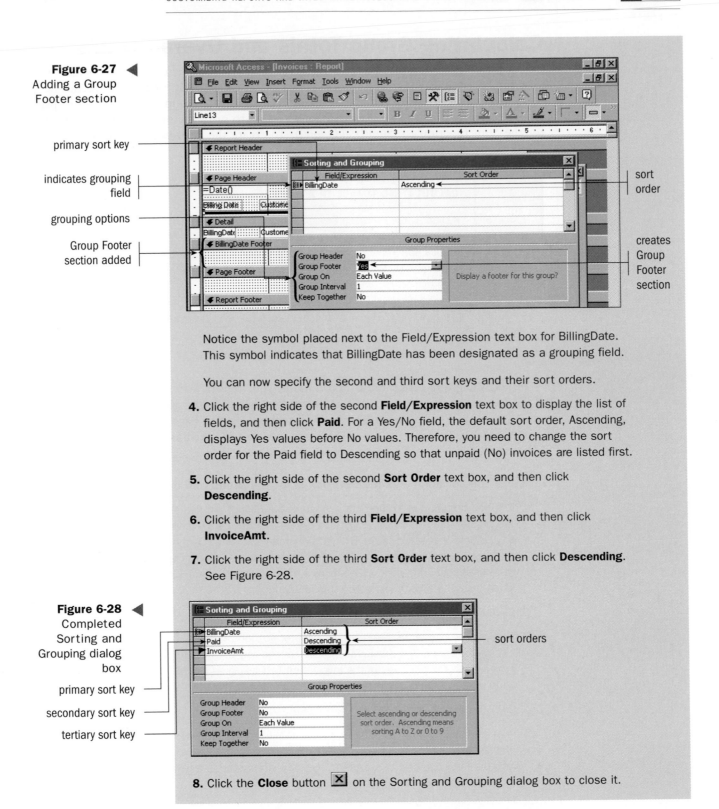

Notice the symbol placed next to the Field/Expression text box for BillingDate. This symbol indicates that BillingDate has been designated as a grouping field.

You can now specify the second and third sort keys and their sort orders.

4. Click the right side of the second **Field/Expression** text box to display the list of fields, and then click **Paid**. For a Yes/No field, the default sort order, Ascending, displays Yes values before No values. Therefore, you need to change the sort order for the Paid field to Descending so that unpaid (No) invoices are listed first.

5. Click the right side of the second **Sort Order** text box, and then click **Descending**.

6. Click the right side of the third **Field/Expression** text box, and then click **InvoiceAmt**.

7. Click the right side of the third **Sort Order** text box, and then click **Descending**. See Figure 6-28.

Figure 6-28 ◄
Completed
Sorting and
Grouping dialog
box

8. Click the **Close** button ⊠ on the Sorting and Grouping dialog box to close it.

You are now ready to calculate the group totals and overall totals for the InvoiceAmt field values.

Calculating Group Totals and Overall Totals

Leonard wants the report to print subtotals for each BillingDate group, as well as an overall total, based on the InvoiceAmt field. To calculate these totals for the InvoiceAmt field, you use the **Sum function**. You place the Sum function in a Group Footer section to print each group's total and in the Report Footer section to print the overall total. The format for the Sum function is =Sum([*fieldname*]). To create the appropriate text boxes in the footer sections, you use the Text Box tool on the toolbox.

REFERENCE window

CALCULATING TOTALS IN A REPORT

- Display the report in Design view.
- Click the Text Box tool on the toolbox.
- Click the report section for the total—Group Footer for a group total, Page Footer for a page total, or Report Footer for an overall report total.
- In the displayed text box, type =Sum([*fieldname*]) where *fieldname* is the name of the field to total, and then press the Enter key.

To add the group totals and overall total to your report, you need to increase the size of the BillingDate Footer and Report Footer sections to make room for the control that will contain the Sum function. Because you will not use the Page Footer section, you can also decrease its size to zero now. Then you need to add text boxes for the Sum function in both the BillingDate Footer section and the Report Footer section.

To resize the sections and add text boxes for the group and overall totals:

1. Position the pointer on the bottom edge of the BillingDate Footer section. When the pointer changes to ✛ , click and drag the bottom edge down until six rows of grid dots are visible in the BillingDate Footer section. Use the same procedure to decrease the height of the Page Footer section to 0, and increase the height of the Report Footer section to six rows of grid dots. These heights will allow sufficient room to place the totals in these sections.

2. Click the **Text Box** tool abl on the toolbox.

3. Position the pointer in the BillingDate Footer section, and click when the pointer's plus symbol (+) is positioned in the second row of grid dots and vertically aligned with the left edge of the InvoiceAmt text box (see Figure 6-29). Access adds a text box with an attached label box to its left.

4. Click the **Text Box** tool abl on the toolbox.

5. Position the pointer in the Report Footer section, and click when the pointer's plus symbol (+) is positioned in the second row of grid dots and vertically aligned with the left edge of the InvoiceAmt text box. Access adds a text box with an attached label box to its left. See Figure 6-29.

Figure 6-29 ◄
Adding text
boxes in the
footer sections

sections resized ──

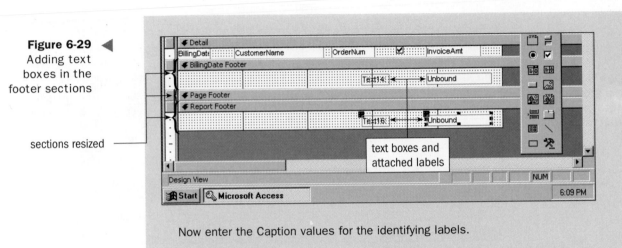

text boxes and
attached labels

Now enter the Caption values for the identifying labels.

6. Right-click the label box in the BillingDate Footer section, and then click **Properties** on the shortcut menu to display the property sheet. The Format tab is selected and the Caption text box is highlighted.

7. Type **Total for month:**.

8. Click the label box in the Report Footer section.

9. Click the **Caption** text box, press the **F2** key to select the existing caption, and then type **Grand total:**.

10. Click the **Close** button ☒ on the property sheet to close it.

The text box labels are not big enough to display the label values, so you need to resize them now.

To resize the text box labels:

1. Press and hold down the **Shift** key and click the label box in the BillingDate Footer section. Both total label boxes are now selected.

2. Click **Format** on the menu bar, point to **Size**, and then click **To Fit**. Access resizes the label boxes to display the entire labels.

You can now add the Sum function to the two footer section text boxes. Leonard wants the totals displayed as currency, with dollar signs and two digits after the decimal point. You can specify this format in the Format property for the text boxes.

To add the Sum function to calculate group and overall totals:

1. Click the text box in the BillingDate Footer section to select it, click the text box again to position the insertion point, type **=Sum([InvoiceAmt])**, and then press the **Enter** key.

You can now resize the text box so that the total will line up with the InvoiceAmt values in the printed report.

2. Click the middle right sizing handle of the text box and drag it to the left until the right edge of the box is slightly to the right of the InvoiceAmt text box in the Detail section. Refer to Figure 6-30 to help you position the right edge.

3. Click the text box in the Report Footer section to select it, click the text box again to position the insertion point, type **=Sum([InvoiceAmt])**, and then press the **Enter** key.

4. Resize the text box in the Report Footer section so that its right edge is slightly to the right of the InvoiceAmt text box in the Detail section. See Figure 6-30.

Figure 6-30 ◄
Adding a group
total and
overall total

labels

overall total

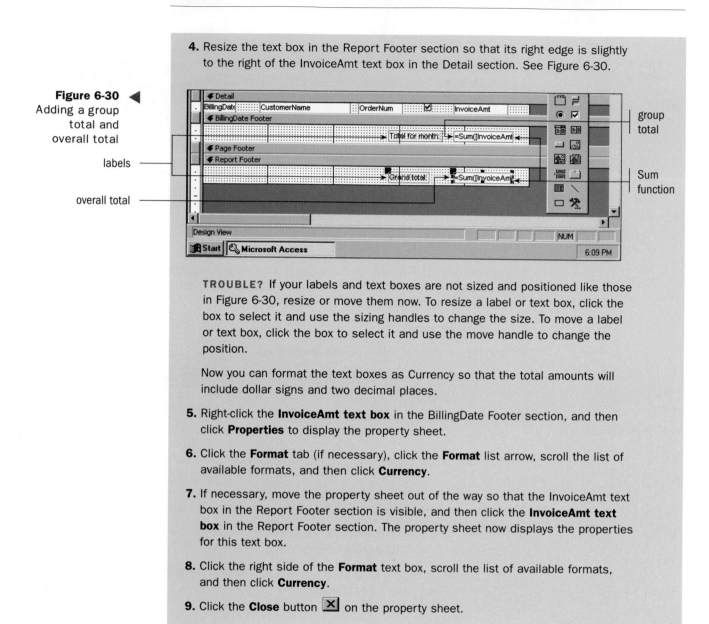

group
total

Sum
function

TROUBLE? If your labels and text boxes are not sized and positioned like those in Figure 6-30, resize or move them now. To resize a label or text box, click the box to select it and use the sizing handles to change the size. To move a label or text box, click the box to select it and use the move handle to change the position.

Now you can format the text boxes as Currency so that the total amounts will include dollar signs and two decimal places.

5. Right-click the **InvoiceAmt text box** in the BillingDate Footer section, and then click **Properties** to display the property sheet.

6. Click the **Format** tab (if necessary), click the **Format** list arrow, scroll the list of available formats, and then click **Currency**.

7. If necessary, move the property sheet out of the way so that the InvoiceAmt text box in the Report Footer section is visible, and then click the **InvoiceAmt text box** in the Report Footer section. The property sheet now displays the properties for this text box.

8. Click the right side of the **Format** text box, scroll the list of available formats, and then click **Currency**.

9. Click the **Close** button ⊠ on the property sheet.

Leonard wants lines above both the group total and the overall total to visually separate the total amounts from the values in the Detail section. So, you'll add lines above each Sum function.

To add lines above the totals:

1. Click the **Line** tool ◻ on the toolbox.

2. Position the pointer in the BillingDate Footer section. The pointer changes to ⁺�.

3. Position the pointer's plus symbol (+) in the first row of grid dots and vertically align it with the left edge of the InvoiceAmt text box in the Detail section above.

4. Click and drag the pointer to the right until the right end of the horizontal line is approximately above the right edge of the Sum text box (see Figure 6-31).

5. Repeat Steps 1 through 4 to add a line above the Sum function in the Report Footer section. See Figure 6-31.

Access

Figure 6-31 ◀
Adding lines
above the
group and
overall totals

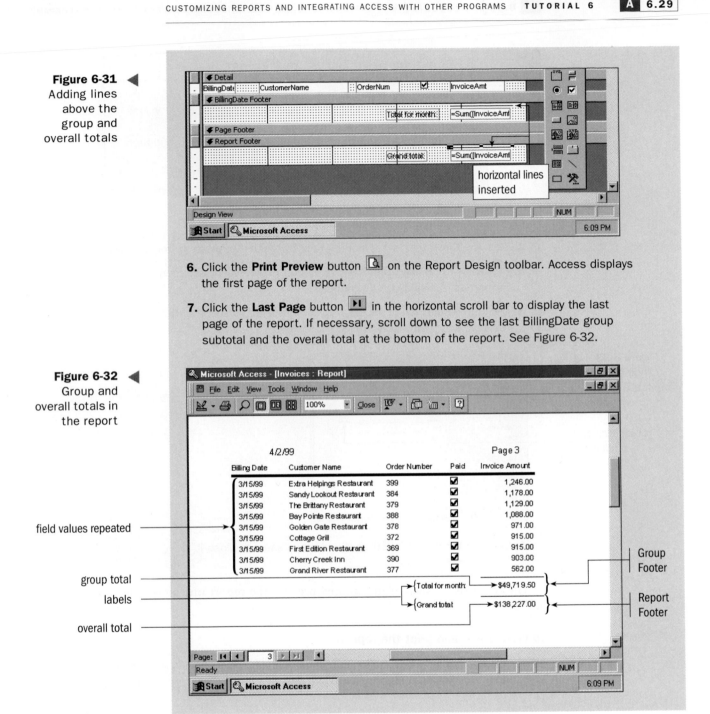

6. Click the **Print Preview** button 🔍 on the Report Design toolbar. Access displays the first page of the report.

7. Click the **Last Page** button ▶❘ in the horizontal scroll bar to display the last page of the report. If necessary, scroll down to see the last BillingDate group subtotal and the overall total at the bottom of the report. See Figure 6-32.

Figure 6-32 ◀
Group and
overall totals in
the report

After viewing the report, Leonard decides that the Detail section would be more readable if the BillingDate was printed only once for each group.

Hiding Duplicate Values in a Report

Your next change is to display the BillingDate value only in the first record in a group. Within a group, all BillingDate field values are the same, so if you display only the first one, you simplify the report and make it easier to read.

HIDING DUPLICATE VALUES IN A REPORT

- Display the report in Design view.
- Right-click the text box for the field whose duplicate values you want to hide, and then click Properties.
- Click the right side of the Hide Duplicates text box, and then click Yes.
- Click the Close button on the property sheet to close it.

To hide the duplicate BillingDate values:

1. Click the **Close** button on the Print Preview toolbar to return to Design view.

2. Right-click the **BillingDate text box** in the Detail section, and then click **Properties** to display the property sheet.

3. Click the **Format** tab (if necessary), click the right side of the **Hide Duplicates** text box, and then click **Yes**. See Figure 6-33.

Figure 6-33 ◄
Hiding the
duplicate field
values

click to display
options

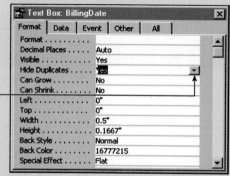

4. Click the **Close** button ☒ on the property sheet to close it.

The report is finished. You can now preview the report one more time, and then save and print the report.

To view, save, and print the report:

1. Click the **Print Preview** button 🔍 on the Report Design toolbar. Access displays the first page of the report. See Figure 6-34.

Figure 6-34 ◀
The beginning
of the report in
Print Preview

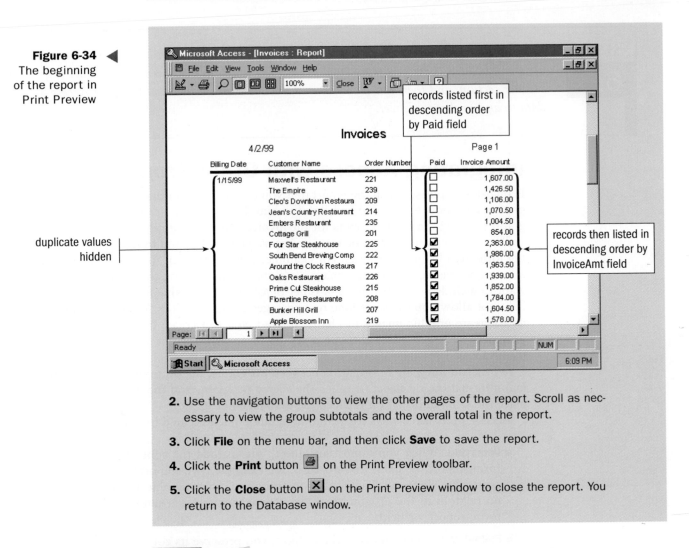

2. Use the navigation buttons to view the other pages of the report. Scroll as necessary to view the group subtotals and the overall total in the report.

3. Click **File** on the menu bar, and then click **Save** to save the report.

4. Click the **Print** button 🖨 on the Print Preview toolbar.

5. Click the **Close** button ✕ on the Print Preview window to close the report. You return to the Database window.

Quick Check

1 What is a grouping field?

2 When do you use the Text Box tool?

3 What do you type in a text box to tell Access to print the current date?

4 How do you insert a page number in a Page Header section?

5 What is the function of the Sorting and Grouping button?

6 How do you calculate group totals and overall totals?

7 Why might you want to hide duplicate values in a report that includes groups?

Leonard is very pleased with the report and feels that it will help him keep better track of outstanding invoices. In the next session, you'll use integration techniques to create another report for Leonard.

SESSION 6.3

In this session, you will integrate Access with other Windows programs. You will create an embedded chart in a report and place a linked Word document in a Report Header section, and then edit the chart and the document. Then you'll export Access data to an Excel spreadsheet.

Integrating Access with Other Programs

Leonard is so pleased with the report that you created for him that he immediately thinks of another report that would be helpful to him. He asks if you can create a report with a graph showing the total amounts for the invoices for each month.

When you create a report or form in Access, you might want to include more than just the formatted listing of records. For example, you might want to include objects such as a long text passage, a graphic image, or a chart summarizing the data. You also might want to include a graphic image or other object as a field value in a table record. Access does not allow you to create long text passages easily, nor does Access have the capability to create graphic images or charts. Instead, you can create these objects using other programs and then place them in a report or form using the appropriate integration method.

When you integrate information between programs, the program containing the original information, or **object**, is called the **source** program, and the program in which you place the same information is called the **destination** program.

Access offers three ways for you to integrate objects created by other programs:

- **Importing.** When you import an object, you include the contents of a file in the form, report, or field. In Tutorial 5, for example, you imported a graphic image created in Microsoft Paint, a drawing program. Once an object is imported, it has no relation to the program in which it was created; it is simply an object in the form, report, or field.

- **Embedding.** When you embed an object, you preserve its connection to the source program, which enables you to edit the object, if necessary, using the features of the source program. You can edit the object by double-clicking it, which starts the source program. Any changes you make to the object are reflected *only* in the form, report, or field in which it is embedded; the changes do not affect the original object in the file from which it was embedded. Likewise, if you start the source program outside of Access and make any changes to the original object, these changes are not reflected in the embedded object.

- **Linking.** When you link an object to a form, report, or field, you preserve its connection to the original file. You can edit a linked object by double-clicking it, which starts the source program. Any changes you make to the object are reflected in both the original file created in the source program and the linked file in the destination program. You can also start the source program outside of Access and edit the object's original file. These changes would also be reflected in the original file and in the linked object in the Access form, report, or field.

In general, you would import an object when you simply want a copy of the object in your form, report, or field and you don't intend to make any changes to the object. You would embed or link an object when you want a copy of the object in your form, report, or field and you intend to edit the object. You embed the object if you do not want your edits to affect any other copies of the object in other programs. You link the object when you want your edits to be reflected in both the original object and the linked object.

Integrating objects among programs is made possible through the features of **Object Linking and Embedding (OLE)**. Not all programs support OLE, although most do. If you have difficulty linking or embedding objects between programs, it is possible that the program you are using does not support OLE.

The design for Leonard's report, shown in Figure 6-35, includes an embedded chart showing the totals of invoices in the report by month, and a linked text document in the Detail section. To include the chart you will use the Access Chart Wizard. The text document is a Microsoft Word file, which you will link to the report. In that way, any changes made to the original Word document will appear in the report.

Figure 6-35 ◀
Design for the
Invoice Totals
by Month
report

embedded chart

linked text document

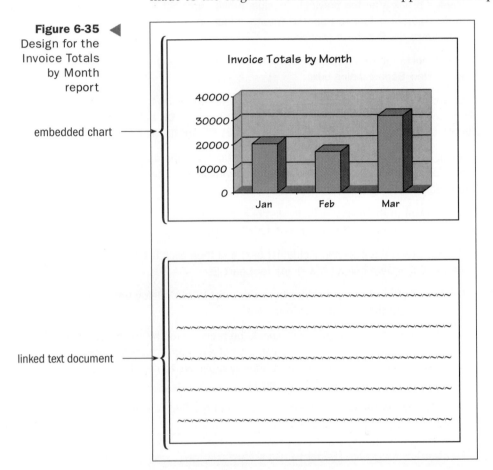

Embedding a Chart in a Report

Access provides the Chart Wizard to assist you in embedding a chart in a form or report. The chart itself is actually created by another program, Microsoft Graph, and automatically embedded by the Chart Wizard. After embedding a chart in a report, you can edit it using the Microsoft Graph program.

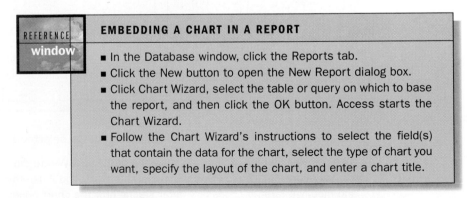

REFERENCE
window

EMBEDDING A CHART IN A REPORT

- In the Database window, click the Reports tab.
- Click the New button to open the New Report dialog box.
- Click Chart Wizard, select the table or query on which to base the report, and then click the OK button. Access starts the Chart Wizard.
- Follow the Chart Wizard's instructions to select the field(s) that contain the data for the chart, select the type of chart you want, specify the layout of the chart, and enter a chart title.

The Order table in the Restaurant database contains all the information necessary for the chart Leonard wants to include in his report, so you will base the report on the Order table.

To create a report with an embedded chart:

1. If you took a break after the previous session, make sure that Access is running and the Restaurant database from the Tutorial folder on your Student Disk is open. Maximize the Database window.

2. Click the **Reports** tab of the Database window, and then click the **New** button to display the New Report dialog box.

3. Click **Chart Wizard** to select it, click the list arrow for choosing the table or query on which to base the report, click **Order**, and then click the **OK** button. Access starts the Chart Wizard and displays the first Chart Wizard dialog box.

   This dialog box allows you to select the fields that contain the data for the chart. Leonard wants the chart to show the totals of the InvoiceAmt field by BillingDate, so you need to select these two fields.

4. Click **InvoiceAmt** in the Available Fields list box, and then click the ⟩ button to move the InvoiceAmt field to the Fields for Chart list.

5. Click **BillingDate** in the Available Fields list box, and then click the ⟩ button to move the BillingDate field to the Fields for Chart list.

6. Click the **Next** button. Access displays the next Chart Wizard dialog box, which allows you to select the type of chart you want.

   According to Leonard's design, the data should be represented by columns. A column chart is appropriate for showing the variation of a quantity (total of invoices) over a period of time (month). A 3-D chart adds perspective to the chart. So, you'll select a 3-D Column Chart for the report.

7. Click the **3-D Column Chart** button (second button in the first row) to select the 3-D Column Chart type. See Figure 6-36.

Figure 6-36 ◀
Selecting the type of chart

click to select 3-D Column Chart type

chart type description

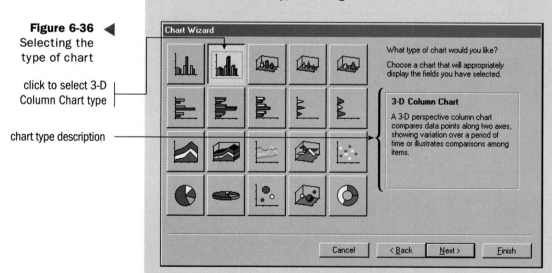

The box on the right displays a brief description of the selected chart type.

8. Click the **Next** button. Access displays the next Chart Wizard dialog box. This dialog box allows you to modify the layout of the chart. You'll use the default layout and modify it later, if necessary, after seeing how the chart appears in the report.

9. Click the **Next** button to display the final dialog box, in which you enter the title that will appear at the top of the chart.

10. Type **Invoice Totals by Month** in the text box, make sure the options for displaying a legend and opening the report are selected and that the option for displaying help is not, and then click the **Finish** button. Access creates the report and displays it, with the embedded chart, in the Print Preview window.

11. Scroll the window until the entire chart is visible. See Figure 6-37.

Figure 6-37 ◀
Completed
chart in Print
Preview

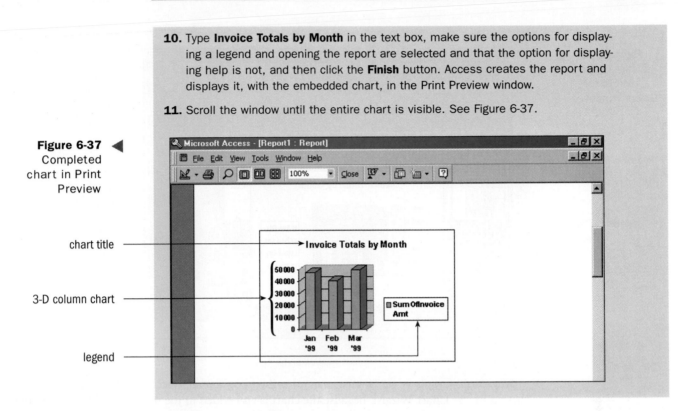

chart title

3-D column chart

legend

After viewing the chart, Leonard decides that it needs some modification. He'd like the chart to be larger and centered on the page. Also, he thinks that the legend is unnecessary, because the chart title is descriptive enough, and can be deleted. You can make these changes by switching to Design view and starting Microsoft Graph so that you can edit the chart.

To switch to Design view and start Microsoft Graph:

1. Click the **Close** button on the Print Preview toolbar to display the Report window in Design view. The chart appears in the Detail section of the report.

TROUBLE? If the chart appears with the incorrect legend and different columns, this is a minor Access display error and will not affect the final chart in the printed report.

2. Double-click the chart object. Microsoft Graph starts and displays the chart. See Figure 6-38.

Figure 6-38 ◀
Chart in the
Microsoft
Graph window

Report - Datasheet
window

Report - Chart
window

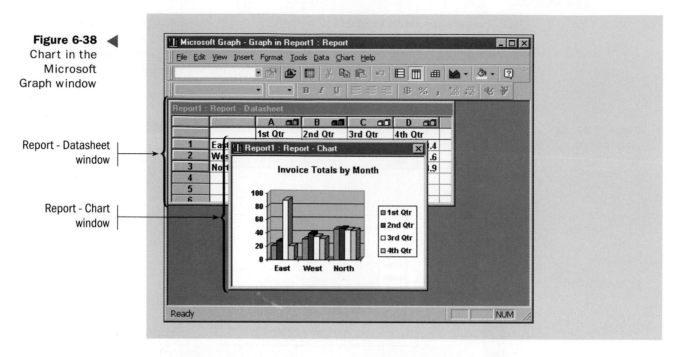

Microsoft Graph is the source program, the program in which the original chart was created by the Chart Wizard. Because the chart is embedded in the report, double-clicking the chart object starts Graph and allows you to edit the chart. The Graph window contains two smaller windows: Report - Datasheet and Report - Chart. The Report - Datasheet window displays the data on which the chart is based. The Report - Chart window displays the chart itself. All of your changes will be made in the Report - Chart window.

First, you need to enlarge the chart. Then you'll delete the legend.

To enlarge the chart and delete the legend:

1. Click the title bar of the Report - Chart window and drag the window up and to the right until it is positioned as shown in Figure 6-39. Release the mouse button.

2. Position the pointer on the lower-right corner of the Report - Chart window. When the pointer changes to ↘, click and drag the lower-right corner down and to the right until the window is the size shown in Figure 6-39. Release the mouse button.

Figure 6-39 ◄
Chart after
repositioning
and resizing
the window

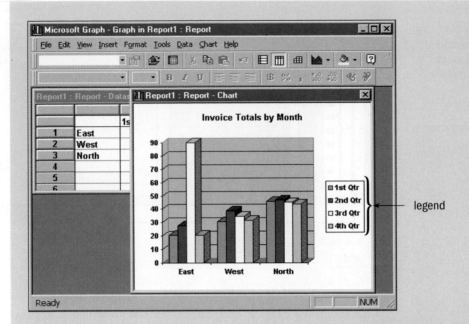

Now you can delete the legend from the chart.

3. Position the pointer on the legend object, right-click to display the shortcut menu, and then click **Clear** to remove the legend from the chart. See Figure 6-40.

Figure 6-40 ◄
Modified chart

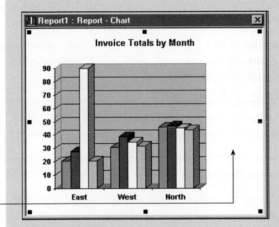

legend deleted

Finally, you'll return to the Report window in Design view and center the chart on the report page.

4. Click **File** on the menu bar, and then click **Exit & Return to Report1 : Report**. Microsoft Graph closes and the edited chart appears in the Report window. See Figure 6-41.

Figure 6-41 ◀
Edited chart in
the Report
window

resized chart

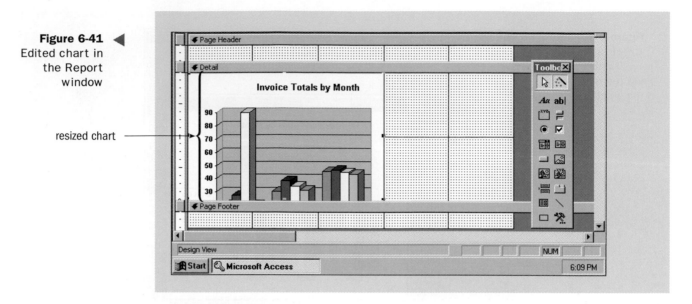

Although the chart is now larger, the box in which it appears in the Detail section is still its original size. Only a portion of the enlarged chart would show on the printed report page. So, you need to enlarge the box and center the chart in the report page.

To enlarge and center the chart in the report page:

1. Click the **Close** button ⊠ on the toolbox to close it. This will give you more room for enlarging the box containing the chart.

2. Position the pointer on the chart object. When the pointer changes to 🖑, click and drag the chart object to the right until its left edge is at the 1½-inch mark on the horizontal ruler, and then release the mouse button.

3. Position the pointer on the middle right sizing handle of the chart object. When the pointer changes to ↔, click and drag the right edge of the chart object to the 5-inch mark on the horizontal ruler, and then release the mouse button.

   Now you can make the chart object taller to accommodate the height of the resized chart. First you need to increase the height of the Detail section.

4. Move the pointer to the bottom of the Detail section. When the pointer changes to ↨, click and drag the bottom of the Detail section down a few inches, and then release the mouse button. Then adjust the bottom of the Detail section so that it is at the 3½-inch mark on the vertical ruler. Notice that the report design automatically scrolls when the pointer reaches the bottom of the screen. Use Figure 6-42 as a guide for placing the bottom of the Detail section.

   TROUBLE? If you did not position the bottom of the Detail section correctly, simply click and drag the bottom of the Detail section up or down as necessary. Then continue with the steps.

   Now you can increase the height of the chart object in the Detail section.

5. If necessary, scroll up until the bottom of the chart object is visible, click the chart object to select it, and then position the pointer on the middle bottom sizing handle of the chart object. When the pointer changes to ↕, click and drag the bottom of the chart object to the bottom of the Detail section. See Figure 6-42.

Figure 6-42 ◄
Chart object
and Detail
section resized

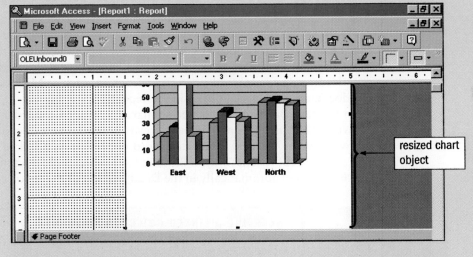

6. Click the **Print Preview** button 🔍 on the Report Design toolbar. Access displays the first page of the report. Notice that the correct chart is displayed. Scroll to see more of the chart. See Figure 6-43.

Figure 6-43 ◄
Chart report in
Print Preview

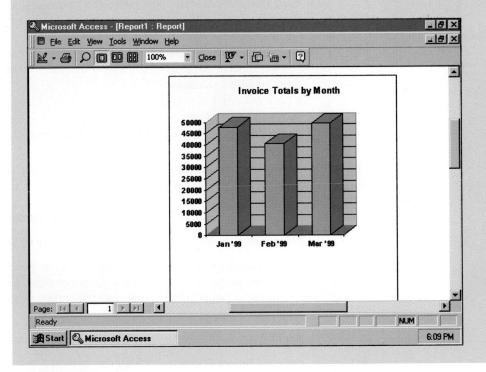

Now that the chart is properly positioned on the report page, you are ready to place the text document in the Detail section. Because you've made many changes to the report design, you'll save it first.

To save the report:

1. Click **File** on the menu bar, and then click **Save**. The Save As dialog box opens.

2. Type **Invoice Totals by Month**, and then press the **Enter** key. Access saves the report on your Student Disk.

Linking a Word Document in a Report

The report design in Figure 6-35 shows some text below the chart. This text explains the contents of the chart. You can add text to an Access report by creating a label control, but a label control is not designed to hold a large amount of text. It is inconvenient to enter and edit more than a short label in a label control. Instead, you can create a larger text document using a word-processing program, such as Microsoft Word, and then insert the document as a linked object in the report.

In the past, Barbara has created similar reports for Leonard using Microsoft Word and drawing the chart by hand. She has already created a text document that you can include in your report. You will insert this Word document as a linked object in the Detail section of your report. That way, if Barbara later changes the document in Word, the changes will be reflected automatically in the Detail section of the Invoice Totals by Month report.

REFERENCE window	**INSERTING A LINKED OBJECT IN A REPORT**
	■ Display the report in Design view.
	■ Click the Unbound Object Frame button on the toolbox.
	■ Position the pointer at the upper-left corner for the linked object, click and drag the pointer to the lower-right corner for the linked object, and then release the mouse button.
	■ Click the Create from File option button in the Insert Object dialog box.
	■ In the File text box, enter the name of the file containing the object; or click the Browse button and use the Browse dialog box to locate and select the file.
	■ Click the Link check box to select it.
	■ Click the OK button.

The Word document contains several lines of text. To make room for it in the Detail section, you need to resize the Detail section; then you'll insert the linked document.

To resize the Detail section and insert the linked text document:

1. Click the **Close** button on the Print Preview toolbar to return to Design view.

2. Scroll down until the bottom of the Detail section is visible. Position the pointer at the bottom of the Detail section. When the pointer changes to ✛, click and drag the bottom of the Detail section down until the bottom is at the 5-inch mark on the vertical ruler. Release the mouse button.

3. Click the **Toolbox** button 🛠 on the Report Design toolbar to display the toolbox.

4. Click the **Unbound Object Frame** tool 🖼 on the toolbox.

5. Position the pointer at the 3¾-inch mark on the vertical ruler and the 1½-inch mark on the horizontal ruler. Click and drag the pointer to the bottom of the Detail section (the 5-inch mark on the vertical ruler) and the 5-inch mark on the horizontal ruler. Release the mouse button. Access inserts an unbound object frame in the Detail section and opens the Insert Object dialog box.

   The Word document is a file stored on your Student Disk, so you need to create the linked object from a file.

6. Click the **Create from File** option button to select it. The dialog box changes to display the File text box, the Browse button, and the Link check box. See Figure 6-44.

Figure 6-44 ◀
Insert Object
dialog box

click to create an
object from a file

click to locate the file

click to create a link

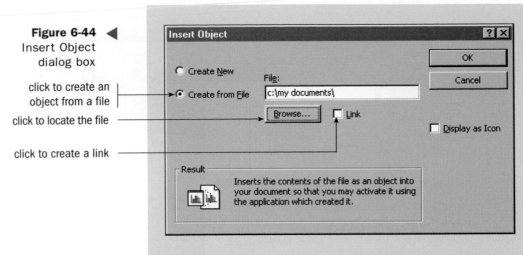

7. Click the **Browse** button to display the Browse dialog box. If necessary, use the Drives and Directories list boxes to display the contents of the Tutorial folder on your Student Disk.

8. In the files list box, click **ChartTxt.doc** to select the Word document file, and then click the **Open** button. The Browse dialog box closes.

Next, you must indicate that you want to link to the document file rather than embed it in the report.

9. Click the **Link** check box to select it, and then click the **OK** button. The Insert Object dialog box closes, and the text document is placed in the Detail section. See Figure 6-45.

Figure 6-45 ◀
Linked text
document in
the Detail
section

linked text document

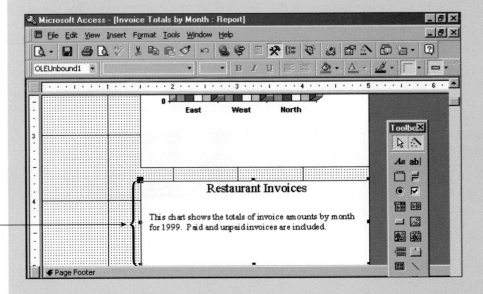

10. Click the **Print Preview** button [icon] on the Report Design toolbar, and then click the **Zoom** button [icon] on the Print Preview toolbar to view the entire report page. See Figure 6-46.

Figure 6-46 ◀
Completed
report in Print
Preview

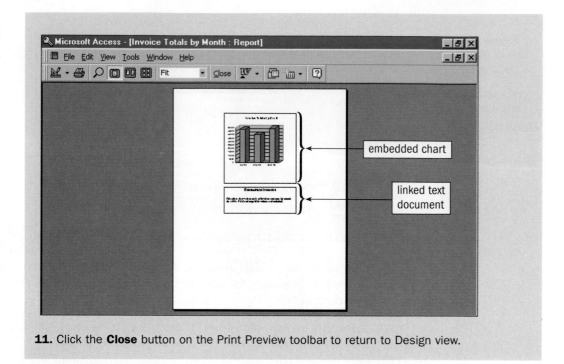

11. Click the **Close** button on the Print Preview toolbar to return to Design view.

Because you checked the Link check box, the text document is *linked* to the original Word document. Any changes made to the original document will be reflected automatically in the text document in your Access report. If you had not checked the Link check box, the text document would be *embedded*.

Barbara wants to make a change to the ChartTxt document. She wants to add a sentence indicating that the chart is updated monthly. Because the report object is linked to the Word document, you'll make this change to the original document using the Word program, and then view the results in the Report window in Access.

To edit the original document in Word:

1. Click the **Start** button on the taskbar, point to **Programs**, and then click **Microsoft Word**. The Word 97 program starts and the Word window opens. See Figure 6-47.

Figure 6-47 ◀
Word window

Open button

Save button

TROUBLE? If you cannot locate Word on the Programs menu, it might be located in another program group on your computer. Try looking through program groups to find it. If you cannot locate Word anywhere, ask your instructor or technical support person for assistance. If the Word program is not installed on your computer, click the Access window to close the Programs menu and then skip Steps 2 through 7.

2. Click the **Open** button 🖼 on the Standard toolbar to display the Open dialog box. Use the Look in list box to open the Tutorial folder on your Student Disk, and then double-click **ChartTxt** in the file list to open the document file.

You'll add the new sentence in its own paragraph, below the existing text.

3. Click at the end of the last sentence in the text, and then press the **Enter** key to start a new paragraph.

4. Type **This chart is updated monthly.** (Include the period.) See Figure 6-48.

Figure 6-48 ◀
Modified Word
document

new sentence added ⎯⎯

TROUBLE? If you make a typing error, use the Backspace key to erase the incorrect text and then retype the text correctly.

5. Click the **Save** button 🖫 on the Standard toolbar to save the modified document, and then click the **Close** button ☒ on the Word window title bar to exit Word. The Word window closes, and the Access Report window in Design view becomes active.

6. If necessary, scroll down to see the text object.

The text object in the Detail section does not yet reflect the change you made in the original Word document. If you were to close the Report window and return to the Database window and then reopen the report, Access would update the link and the report would show the new sentence you added. Access automatically updates any links to linked objects whenever a form or report is opened. However, you can also update a link manually to see a change reflected.

To update the link manually:

1. Click **Edit** on the menu bar, and then click **OLE/DDE Links** to display the Links dialog box. This dialog box allows you to select the linked object or objects to be updated.

2. Click **charttxt** in the Links list box to select this file. See Figure 6-49.

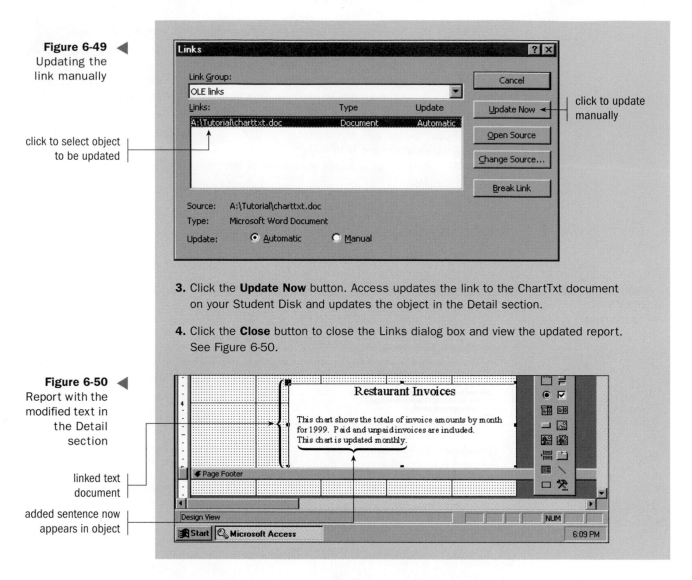

Figure 6-49 ◄
Updating the
link manually

click to select object
to be updated

click to update
manually

3. Click the **Update Now** button. Access updates the link to the ChartTxt document on your Student Disk and updates the object in the Detail section.

4. Click the **Close** button to close the Links dialog box and view the updated report. See Figure 6-50.

Figure 6-50 ◄
Report with the
modified text in
the Detail
section

linked text
document

added sentence now
appears in object

The report is now complete. You can save the report design, print the report for Leonard, and then close the Report window.

To save, print, and close the report:

1. Click the **Save** button 🖫 on the Report Design toolbar.

2. Click the **Print** button 🖨 on the Report Design toolbar to print the report.

3. Click the **Close** button ☒ on the Report window to close it and return to the Database window.

Leonard views the printed report and is pleased with the results. Being able to integrate Access data with other programs, Graph and Word in this instance, makes it easier to analyze the data. Leonard has one more integration task for you to complete. He wants to perform some more detailed analysis on invoice data. To do so, he wants to work with the data in a Microsoft Excel worksheet.

Exporting an Access Table as an Excel Worksheet

A spreadsheet program, such as Microsoft Excel, is designed to assist you in analyzing data. Although a database management program provides some data analysis capabilities, it is primarily designed for storing and retrieving records. A spreadsheet program has many more powerful tools for analyzing data to create budgets, projections, and models.

You can export the contents of most Access objects, including tables, forms, and reports, to other Windows programs, including Excel.

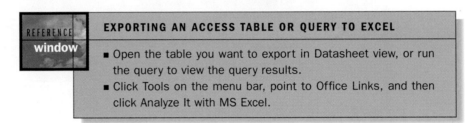

REFERENCE window	EXPORTING AN ACCESS TABLE OR QUERY TO EXCEL
	■ Open the table you want to export in Datasheet view, or run the query to view the query results.
	■ Click Tools on the menu bar, point to Office Links, and then click Analyze It with MS Excel.

Like many business managers, Leonard uses a spreadsheet program as a planning and budgeting tool for his business. He would like to use the invoice information from past months to help him project future sales. He asks you to transfer the results of the Invoice Statistics by Billing Date query to an Excel worksheet so that he can use the results to create the necessary projections. Recall that when Access runs a query, the query results are a temporary display of the records in a table. After you run the Invoice Statistics by Billing Date query, you can export the query results, just as you would any other table, directly to Excel.

To open and run the query, and then export the query results to Excel:

1. Click the **Queries** tab in the Database window to display the queries list.

2. Click **Invoice Statistics by Billing Date**, and then click the **Open** button to run the query. Access displays the query results.

3. Click **Tools** on the menu bar, point to **Office Links**, and then click **Analyze It with MS Excel**. Access automatically starts Excel and places the query results in the worksheet. See Figure 6-51.

Figure 6-51 ◄
Query results in the Excel worksheet

cell A4 ———►

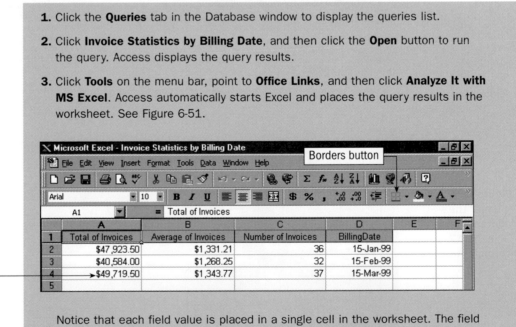

Notice that each field value is placed in a single cell in the worksheet. The field names are entered in the first row of cells in the worksheet. You can now use this data just as you would any other data in an Excel worksheet.

Leonard wants to see the total of the invoice amounts, so he asks you to create a grand total for the data in column A. You'll first create a line to separate the grand total amount from the other invoice amounts.

To create the grand total amount:

1. Click cell **A4** to select the first cell in the last row of data in column A (see Figure 6-51).

2. Click the list arrow for the **Borders** button on the Formatting toolbar to display the list of border options, and then click the heavy bottom border (the second choice in row two). See Figure 6-52. Access places a heavy border on the bottom of cell A4.

Figure 6-52 ◀
Adding a
bottom border
to the cell

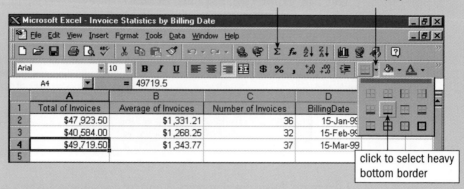

3. Click cell **A5** to select it, and then click the **AutoSum** button Σ on the Standard toolbar. Excel automatically creates the formula to sum the contents of the cells above cell A5. See Figure 6-53.

Figure 6-53 ◀
Formula to sum
the contents of
cells A2
through A4

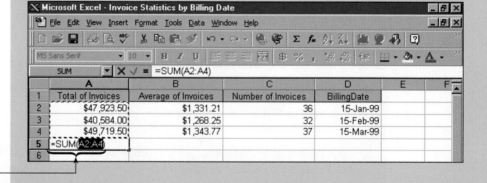

formula created
by AutoSum

4. Press the **Enter** key to enter the formula. Excel displays the sum of the contents of cells A2 through A4 in cell A5. See Figure 6-54.

Figure 6-54 ◀
Sum of the
contents of
cells A2
through A4

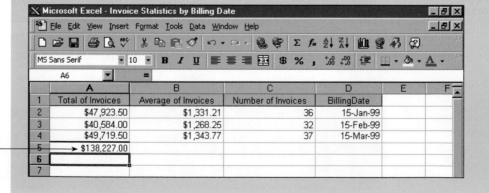

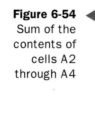

total invoice amount

Leonard plans on doing more work with the data in Excel later. For now, you can save the worksheet, close Excel, and return to the Database window in Access.

Saving the Worksheet and Exiting Excel

When you exported the Invoice Statistics by Billing Date query results to Excel, the worksheet was automatically saved with the name Invoice Statistics by Billing Date. Because you have made changes to the worksheet, you need to save them now before exiting Excel. Then you can exit Access.

To save the worksheet, exit Excel, and then exit Access:

1. Click the **Save** button 🖫 on the Standard toolbar. Excel saves the modified worksheet.

   TROUBLE? If Excel displays a dialog box indicating that this worksheet was created by a previous version, click the Yes button to save the worksheet.

2. Click the **Close** button ☒ on the Excel window title bar to exit Excel and return to the Database window in Access.

3. Click the **Close** button ☒ on the Access window to close Access. You return to the Windows 95 desktop.

When you exported the query results to Excel, Access placed a copy of the query results in the worksheet. The query results are not linked or embedded in the Excel worksheet, so any later changes made to the Access data will not be reflected in the Excel worksheet. Similarly, any changes made in the worksheet will not affect the Access data.

Quick Check

1. Why might you want to embed or link an object in an Access report?

2. What is the difference between embedding and linking?

3. What is OLE?

4. When you insert an object in a report or form using the Insert Object dialog box, how do you specify that the object is to be linked rather than embedded?

5. If you modify a linked object, in what program do you make the changes?

6. What are two ways to update links to linked objects in a report?

7. How do you export a table or the results of a query to Excel?

Leonard is very pleased with the new reports and the Excel worksheet you created. The reports and the integrated data will help him monitor and analyze the invoice activity of Valle Coffee's restaurant customers more easily.

Tutorial Assignments

Barbara wants you to make several changes to the Products database. She asks you to create a report based on the Coffee table. The report will contain Report Header, Page Header, Detail, Page Footer, and Report Footer sections. Barbara wants the records to be grouped on the value in the CoffeeType field, and she wants you to add a CoffeeType Header section. Barbara would also like you to embed a chart in a new report. The chart should be a pie chart showing the distribution of CoffeeType values. Finally, Barbara asks you to create an Excel worksheet based on the query results from the Pricing query.

1. Make sure your Student Disk is in the appropriate disk drive, start Access, and then open the Products database located in the TAssign folder on your Student Disk.

2. Create a new report based on the Coffee table. Figure 6-55 shows the completed report. Refer to the figure as a guide as you complete Steps 3 through 11.

Figure 6-55 ◀

14-point, bold, italic

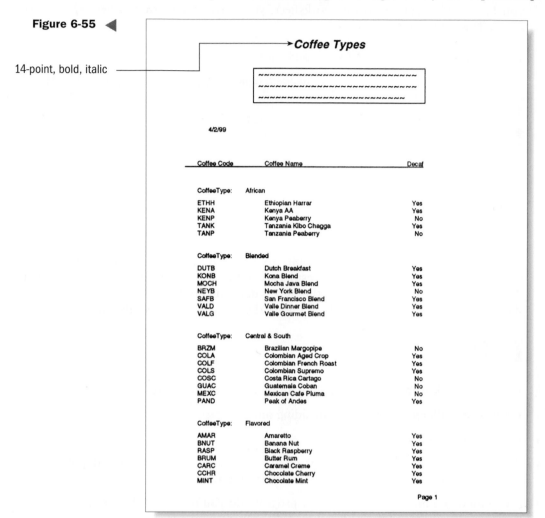

3. Include the following sections in your report: Report Header, Page Header, Detail, and Page Footer.

4. At the top of the Report Header section, enter and format the report title. In the Page Header section, enter the current date. Position the column heading labels below the date. Add a single line below the column headings and change the necessary captions to match the figure.

5. Specify CoffeeType as the grouping field. Sort the records in ascending order by CoffeeName.

 6. Create a Group Header section for the CoffeeType grouping field. Place the CoffeeType field value in the CoffeeType Header section.

7. In the Detail section, include all other field values from the Coffee table.

8. In the Page Footer section, include a right-aligned page number.

 9. Use a word-processing program to create a short document describing the contents of the report. Save the document as Coffee Report Description. Link the document to your report, placing it in the Report Header section.

10. When you finish creating the report, save it as Coffee Types.

11. Print the entire report.

12. Use the Chart Wizard to create a report based on the Coffee table. Create a column chart showing the distribution of CoffeeType values. Select CoffeeType as the only field in the chart and select the Column Chart chart type. Save the report as CoffeeType Chart, and then print the report.

13. Run the Pricing query and export the query results to Excel. Save the Excel worksheet, print the worksheet, and then exit Excel.

14. Close the Products database, and then exit Access.

Case Problems

1. Ashbrook Mall Information Desk Sam Bullard needs a custom report for the MallJobs database and he wants to export the data in the Store table to an Excel worksheet. You will create the necessary report and worksheet by completing the following:

1. Make sure your Student Disk is in the appropriate disk drive, start Access, and then open the MallJobs database located in the Cases folder on your Student Disk.

2. Create a custom report based on the Store Jobs query. Figure 6-56 shows the completed report. Refer to the figure as you complete Steps 3 through 11.

Figure 6-56 ◀

12-point, bold ⎯⎯⎯⎯⎯⎯⎯→ **Job Types**

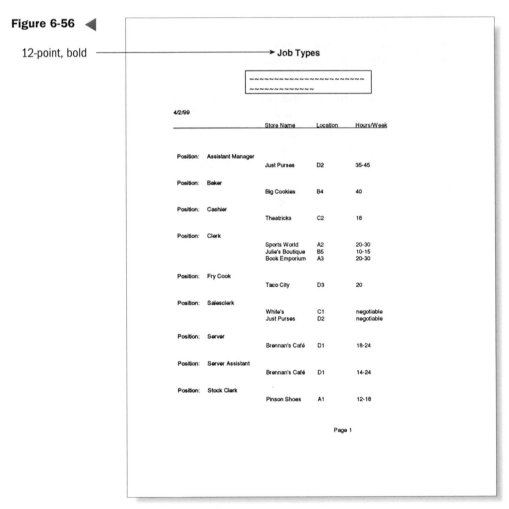

3. Include the following sections in your report: Report Header, Page Header, Detail, and Page Footer.

4. At the top of the Report Header section, enter and format the report title. At the top of the Page Header section, enter the current date. Position the column heading labels below the date. Add a single line below the column headings and change the necessary captions to match the figure.

5. Specify Position as the grouping field. There is no sorting field. Create a Position Group Header section and include the Position field value in the section.

6. In the Detail section, include all other field values from the Store Jobs query.

7. In the Page Footer section, include a page number centered at the bottom of the page.

8. Use a word-processing program, such as Word, WordPad, or NotePad, to create a short document describing the contents of the report. Save the document as Store Jobs Report Description. Link the document to your report, placing it in the Report Header section.

9. Use the Special Effect button on the Report Design toolbar to create a Shadowed special effect for the report title in the Report Header section.

10. When you finish creating the report, save it as Store Jobs.

11. Print the report.

12. Export the Store table data to Excel. Save the Excel worksheet, print the worksheet, and then exit Excel.

13. Close the MallJobs database, and then exit Access.

2. Professional Litigation User Services Raj Jawahir wants you to create a custom report for the Payments database. The report will be based on the results of a query you will create using the Firm and Payments tables. Raj also asks you to export the Payments data to Excel for analysis. You will create the query, report, and worksheet by completing the following:

1. Make sure your Student Disk is in the disk drive, start Access, and then open the Payments database located in the Cases folder on your Student Disk.

2. Create a query based on the Firm and Payments tables. Select the Firm#, FirmName and PLUSAcctRep fields from the Firm table and all fields except Firm# from the Payments table. Save the query as Account Representatives.

3. Create a custom report based on the Account Representatives query. Figure 6-57 shows the completed report. Refer to the figure as a guide as you complete Steps 4 through 15.

Figure 6-57 ◀

14-point, bold ————————————————————▶

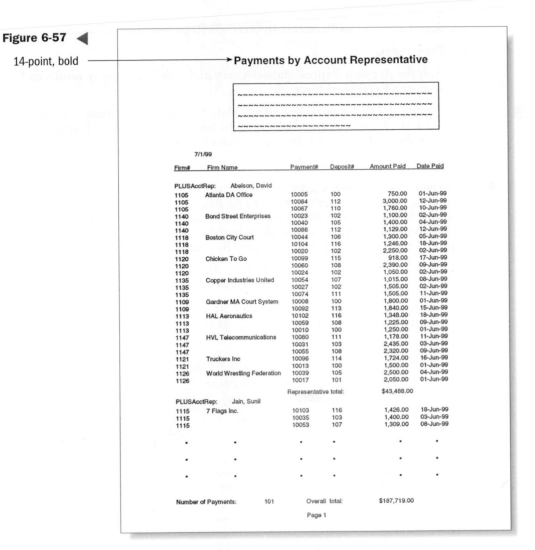

Payments by Account Representative

7/1/99					
Firm#	**Firm Name**	**Payment#**	**Deposit#**	**Amount Paid**	**Date Paid**
PLUSAcctRep:	Abelson, David				
1105	Atlanta DA Office	10005	100	750.00	01-Jun-99
1105		10084	112	3,000.00	12-Jun-99
1105		10067	110	1,760.00	10-Jun-99
1140	Bond Street Enterprises	10023	102	1,100.00	02-Jun-99
1140		10040	105	1,400.00	04-Jun-99
1140		10086	112	1,129.00	12-Jun-99
1118	Boston City Court	10044	106	1,300.00	05-Jun-99
1118		10104	116	1,246.00	18-Jun-99
1118		10020	102	2,250.00	02-Jun-99
1120	Chicken To Go	10099	115	918.00	17-Jun-99
1120		10060	108	2,390.00	09-Jun-99
1120		10024	102	1,050.00	02-Jun-99
1135	Copper Industries United	10054	107	1,015.00	08-Jun-99
1135		10027	102	1,505.00	02-Jun-99
1135		10074	111	1,505.00	11-Jun-99
1109	Gardner MA Court System	10008	100	1,800.00	01-Jun-99
1109		10092	113	1,840.00	15-Jun-99
1113	HAL Aeronautics	10102	116	1,348.00	18-Jun-99
1113		10059	108	1,225.00	09-Jun-99
1113		10010	100	1,250.00	01-Jun-99
1147	HVL Telecommunications	10080	111	1,178.00	11-Jun-99
1147		10031	103	2,435.00	03-Jun-99
1147		10055	108	2,320.00	09-Jun-99
1121	Truckers Inc	10096	114	1,724.00	16-Jun-99
1121		10013	100	1,500.00	01-Jun-99
1126	World Wrestling Federation	10039	105	2,500.00	04-Jun-99
1126		10017	101	2,050.00	01-Jun-99
		Representative total:		$43,488.00	
PLUSAcctRep:	Jain, Sunil				
1115	7 Flags Inc.	10103	116	1,426.00	18-Jun-99
1115		10035	103	1,400.00	03-Jun-99
1115		10053	107	1,309.00	08-Jun-99
Number of Payments:	101	Overall total:		$187,719.00	
		Page 1			

4. Include the following sections in your report: Report Header, Page Header, Detail, Page Footer, and Report Footer.

5. In the Report Header section, enter and format the report title.

6. At the top of the Page Header section, enter the current date. Position the column headings below the date. Add a single line below the column headings and change the necessary captions to match the figure.

 7. Specify PLUSAcctRep as the grouping field. Sort the records in ascending order by FirmName. Create a PLUSAcctRep Group Header section and a PLUSAcctRep Group Footer section. In the PLUSAcctRep Header section, include the PLUSAcctRep field value.

8. In the Detail section, include all other field values from the Account Representatives query. Hide duplicate values for the Firm# and FirmName fields.

9. In the Page Footer section, include a centered page number.

10. In the PLUSAcctRep Footer section, include a subtotal of the AmtPaid field values.

11. In the Report Footer section, include a grand total of the AmtPaid field values.

 12. In the Report Footer section, include a count of the Payment# values. Use the expression =Count([Payment#]) and enter the label shown in the figure.

 13. Use a word-processing program, such as Word, WordPad, or NotePad, to create a short document describing the contents of the report. Save the document as Account Representatives Report Description. Link the document to your report, placing it in the Report Header section.

14. Save the report as Payments By Account Representative.

15. Print the report.

16. Run the Account Representatives query and export the query results to Excel. Print the Excel worksheet.

17. Modify the Excel worksheet to calculate the average payment amount. (*Hint:* Click the Paste Function button on the toolbar.) Label the cell appropriately. Save the modified worksheet, and then exit Excel.

18. Close the Payments database, and then exit Access.

3. Best Friends Noah Warnick asks you to create a custom report for the Walks database so that he can keep better track of the participants in their Walk-A-Thons. The report will be based on the Walker table. Also, Sheila Warnick needs to analyze the pledges and asks you to create a worksheet based on the Pledge Statistics by Walker query. You'll create the report and worksheet by completing the following:

1. Make sure your Student Disk is in the disk drive, start Access, and then open the Walks database located in the Cases folder on your Student Disk.

2. Create a report based on the Walker table. Figure 6-58 shows the completed report. Refer to the figure as a guide as you complete Steps 3 through 12.

Figure 6-58 ◀

16-point, bold

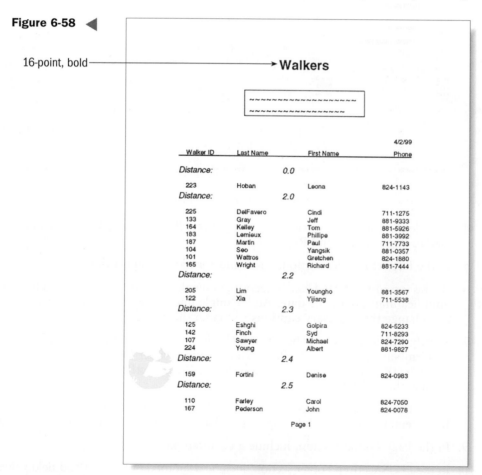

3. Include the following sections in your report: Report Header, Page Header, Detail, and Page Footer.

4. At the top of the Report Header section, enter and format the report title.

5. Use the Special Effect button on the Report Design toolbar to apply the Raised special effect to the title label in the Report Header section.

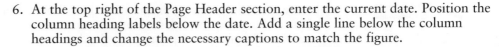

6. At the top right of the Page Header section, enter the current date. Position the column heading labels below the date. Add a single line below the column headings and change the necessary captions to match the figure.

7. Specify Distance as the grouping field. Sort the records in ascending order by LastName. Add the Distance Group Header section and include the Distance field value and the label "Distance:" in the section. Format the Distance field value and label as 10-point italic.

8. In the Detail section, include all other field values from the Walker table.

9. In the Page Footer section, include a page number at the center of the page.

10. Use a word-processing program to create a short document describing the contents of the report. Save the document as Walkers Report Description. Link the document to your report, placing it in the Report Header section.

11. When you finish creating the report, save it as Walkers.

12. Print the report.

13. Run the Pledge Statistics by Walker query and export the query results to Excel. Save the Excel worksheet, print the worksheet, and then exit Excel.

14. Close the Walks database, and then exit Access.

4. Lopez Lexus Dealerships Maria and Hector Lopez need two new custom reports for the Lexus database. Hector asks you to create a report based on the Cars table by modifying a report you will create using the Report Wizard. Maria asks you to create a custom report based on the Cars table. The Cars records will be grouped by Model and you will include subtotals and totals for the Cost and SellingPrice fields. They also ask you to create an Excel chart based on the query results from the Cost vs Selling query. Complete the following:

1. Make sure your Student Disk is in the disk drive, start Access, and then open the Lexus database located in the Cases folder on your Student Disk.

2. Use the Report Wizard to create a report in the Corporate style based on the Cars table. Select all the fields from the table in the order in which they are stored in the table. Do not select a grouping field, use the tabular layout, and enter Cars by Year as the report title. Save the report as Cars By Year.

3. Move the day/date (Now()) and page number text fields to the Report Header section. Adjust the font size and widths in the column headings so that the entire labels are visible.

4. Preview and then print the entire report.

5. Save the report, and then return to the Database window.

6. Create a blank report based on the Cars table.

7. Sketch a design for the report based on the requirements described in Steps 8 through 13, and then create the report following these steps.

8. Include the following sections in your report: Page Header, Detail, Group Footer, and Report Footer.

9. At the top of the Page Header section, enter the report title Cars by Model and Year. Enter the current date and the page number in appropriate locations in this section. Below these elements, add a row of column headings with these labels: Manufacturer, Model, Year, Cost, and Selling Price. Add a single horizontal line below the column headings.

10. In the Detail section, include the field values for Manufacturer, Model, Year, Cost, and Selling Price. Hide duplicate values for the Manufacturer field.

11. In the Group Footer section, print the group total for the Cost and Selling Price fields. Select Model as the primary sort key and as the grouping field. Select Year as the secondary sort key, but do not use it as a grouping field. Choose ascending sort order for the sort keys.

12. Use a word-processing program, such as Word, WordPad, or NotePad, to create a short document describing the contents of the report. Save the document as Cars Report Description. Link the document to your report, placing it in the Report Header section.

13. In the Report Footer section, print the overall totals for the Cost and Selling Price fields.

14. When you finish creating the report, save it as Cars By Model And Year.

15. Print the entire report.

16. Use the Chart Wizard to create a pie chart report based on the Model field in the Cars table. Each wedge in the pie should represent the count of cars of each model. Insert percents as labels for each wedge. Save the report as Model Pie Chart. Print the report.

17. Run the Cost vs Selling query and export the query results to Excel. Print the Excel worksheet.

18. Use Excel's Chart Wizard to create a chart based on the Cost vs Selling query. Create an X-Y chart with Cost on the x-axis and Selling on the y-axis. Print the worksheet with the chart. Save the worksheet, and then exit Excel.

19. Hector has pictures of some of the cars available for sale. He asks you to include these pictures with the appropriate records in the Cars table. You'll embed the pictures as OLE objects in a new field by doing the following:
    a. Open the Cars table in Design view.
    b. Create a new field named Picture. Select OLE Object as the data type for the new field.
    c. Save the table design and switch to Datasheet view.
    d. Click the Picture field for the record for VehicleID 3N4TA (record 1). Click Insert on the menu bar, and then click Object to display the Insert Object dialog box.
    e. Click the Create from File option button, and then click the Browse button. Open the file 3N4TA.bmp. Click the OK button in the Insert Object dialog box to insert the object in the field. Notice that the value Bitmap Image appears in the Picture field for the first record.
    f. Repeat Steps d and e to enter field values for VehicleID 79XBF (record 3) and VehicleID AAEAF (record 6). The filenames are 79XBF.bmp and AAEAF.bmp, respectively.
    g. Double-click the Picture field value for the first record to view the picture. Access automatically opens the Paint application to display the picture. When you are done viewing the picture, close the Paint window.
    h. Repeat Step g to view the picture for record 3 and then for record 6.
    i. Close the Cars table.

20. Close the Lexus database, and then exit Access.

Using the World Wide Web and Hyperlink Fields

Creating Hypertext Documents for Valle Coffee

Valle Coffee

CASE

Leonard, Barbara, and Kim are pleased with the design and contents of the Restaurant database. Their work has been made much easier because they are able to obtain the information they need from the database quickly. Barbara feels that others in the company would benefit from access to the Restaurant database. Leonard asks whether the database can be made available to employees over the company network. That way, employees could obtain company information through their desktop computers rather than through paper forms.

Kim mentions that most employees, such as the customer representatives in the Marketing Department, do not need access to the entire database nor should they be able to make changes to the database objects. She proposes publishing the necessary Access data on the company's internal network as World Wide Web documents.

In this tutorial you will use the Access tools for publishing data to the World Wide Web to publish objects in the Restaurant database.

SESSION

7.1

In this session, you will save an Access table and an Access report in HTML format using the Publish to the Web Wizard. You will view the HTML files using a Web browser. You will also use templates to enhance the appearance of the HTML files and save your Publish to the Web Wizard choices in a profile. Then, you'll use the saved profile to create updated HTML files. Finally, you will import data from an HTML file into an Access table.

Using the World Wide Web

The **World Wide Web** (also called **WWW** or simply the **Web**) is a vast collection of linked documents that reside on computers around the world. These computers are linked together in a public worldwide network called the **Internet**. A computer that publishes documents on the World Wide Web must be running special server software. A computer running server software is called a **Web server** and it has an Internet address called a **Uniform Resource Locator (URL)**. If your computer has a telephone connection, such as a modem, and you have an account with an Internet service provider, you can connect your computer to any Web server and view the World Wide Web documents published there. You view the documents using a program called a **Web browser**. Popular Web browsers, like Microsoft Internet Explorer and Netscape Navigator, are often bundled with other application software.

A World Wide Web document contains the necessary instructions for your Web browser to display text and graphics. These instructions, called **tags**, describe how text is formatted, where graphic images are displayed, the background color, and other visual characteristics of the Web page. Certain tags, called **hyperlinks**, link one Web document to another. When you click hyperlink text, the linked document is displayed. Hyperlinks connect Web documents throughout the Internet and these connections form the World Wide Web. Hyperlinks are the primary means of navigation in the World Wide Web.

You can create a World Wide Web page by typing the necessary instructions, using the **HyperText Markup Language (HTML)**, into a word-processing document and saving the document on a disk. Some programs, such as Access, have built-in tools to convert objects to HTML documents for viewing on the Web. Figure 7-1 illustrates the process of creating a Web page using Access and viewing it with a Web browser.

Figure 7-1 ◀
Creating and
viewing a Web
page

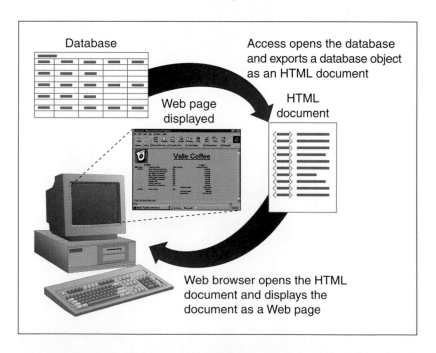

Database

Access opens the database
and exports a database object
as an HTML document

HTML
document

Web page
displayed

Web browser opens the HTML
document and displays the
document as a Web page

Figure 7-2 shows a Web page and the HTML document that creates it.

Figure 7-2 ◀
A World Wide
Web page

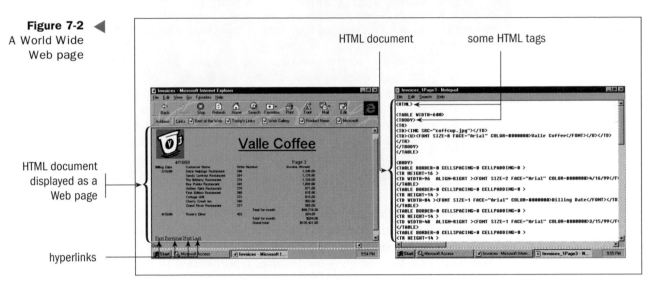

The HTML document in Figure 7-2 contains the necessary information to create a Web page that displays one page of the Invoices report. The words enclosed in angle brackets (<>) are HTML tags. The Web page shows how this document looks when you view it using a Web browser. Notice the words First, Previous, Next, and Last at the bottom of the Web page. These are hyperlinks to other Web pages, in this case to other pages of the Invoices report. Hyperlinks are usually displayed in a different color from other text on a Web page and are often underlined to indicate that they are hyperlinks.

Web pages that are created from an Access database can be either static or dynamic. A **static** page reflects the state of the database when the page is created. Subsequent changes to the database records are not reflected in the Web page. A **dynamic** page is updated automatically each time the page is viewed and reflects the current state of the database at that time.

To publish information in the Restaurant database to the World Wide Web, you must convert Access objects to HTML format. When you have created the HTML documents, you can place them on the company Web server where they can be viewed on any computer on the network using a Web browser. Of course, Valle Coffee does not want its private database to be available worldwide, so your documents will be placed on a Web server dedicated to the company's private network. Private networks, called **intranets**, are common in companies, schools, and other organizations. Data can be shared on an intranet in much the same way as on the Internet, but access is restricted to members of the organization.

Saving Access Objects in an HTML File

Leonard has asked you to create HTML documents for the Customer table and the Invoices report. He wants this data to be available to customer representatives working outside the office. The customer representatives will access the company's intranet from laptop computers connected to telephone lines. Leonard wants these Web pages to be static, because the customer representatives need to view them only once a month, when completing their monthly status reports. The pages will be updated monthly by Barbara. Also, Leonard decides that the Web pages don't need to include the Paid field, so he asks you to remove the Paid field from the Invoices report.

Creating the necessary HTML documents is not as difficult as it might appear at first. You will use the Publish to the Web Wizard, which can automatically convert database objects to HTML files.

SAVING ACCESS OBJECTS IN AN HTML FILE

REFERENCE
window

- Open the database that contains the objects you want to save in an HTML file.
- Click File on the menu bar, and then click Save As HTML. Access opens the Publish to the Web Wizard.
- Complete the wizard dialog boxes to select the objects you want to save as HTML files, select any templates to use, specify which objects will be static and which will be dynamic, select a folder in which to store the HTML files, and indicate whether you want to create a home page.

To complete the following steps, you need a Web browser in addition to Access. The steps in this tutorial are written for Internet Explorer, the Web browser used at Valle Coffee. If you use the Netscape Navigator browser, the steps you need to complete will be slightly different.

You will begin by modifying the Invoices report design to remove the Paid field from the report.

To remove the Paid field from the Invoices report:

1. Place your Student Disk in the appropriate disk drive.

2. Start Access and open the Restaurant database located in the Tutorial folder on your Student Disk.

3. Click the **Reports** tab to display the Reports list, click **Invoices**, and then click the **Design** button. Access opens the Invoices report in Design view. See Figure 7-3.

Figure 7-3 ◄
Invoices report
in Design view

delete Paid label ———

delete Paid
check box ——

Invoices : Report						

◄ Report Header

Invoices

◄ Page Header
=Date()   ="Page " & [
Billing Date   Customer Name   Order Number   Paid   Invoice Amount

◄ Detail
BillingDate   CustomerName   OrderNum   ☑   InvoiceAmt

◄ BillingDate Footer
Total for month: =Sum([InvoiceAmt

◄ Page Footer
◄ Report Footer
Grand total   =Sum([InvoiceAmt

Toolbox

4. Right-click the **Paid** label in the Page Header section, and then click **Cut** on the shortcut menu.

5. Right-click the **Paid** check box in the Detail section, and then click **Cut** on the shortcut menu.

6. Click the **Save** button 🖫 on the Report Design toolbar to save the changes, and then click the **Close** button ☒ on the Report window to close it and return to the Database window.

You can now use the Publish to the Web Wizard to save the Customer table and the Invoices report as HTML files.

To save the Customer table and the Invoices report as HTML files:

1. Click **File** on the menu bar, and then click **Save As HTML**. The Publish to the Web Wizard opens and displays the introductory page. See Figure 7-4.

Figure 7-4 ◄
Publish to the
Web Wizard
introductory
page

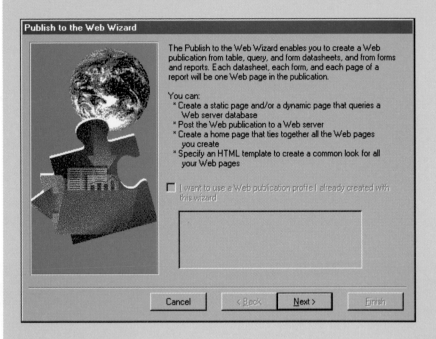

2. Click the **Next** button. The wizard displays the list of tables in the Restaurant database. Click the check box next to the **Customer** table to select it.

3. Click the **Reports** tab, and then click the check box next to the **Invoices** report to select it. See Figure 7-5.

Figure 7-5 ◄
Selecting the
database
objects to
publish

click to select object ⟶

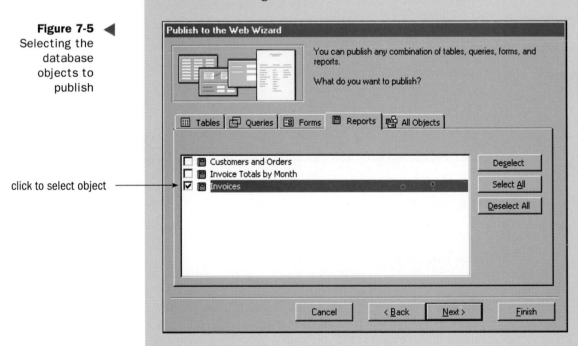

4. Click the **Next** button. This dialog box allows you to select a template for the HTML pages that will be created. For now, you don't want to select a template.

5. Click the **Next** button. This dialog box allows you to specify which objects will be displayed in static pages and which will be in dynamic pages. Make sure the **Static HTML** option button is selected, because Leonard wants the pages to be static, not dynamic.

6. Click the **Next** button. This dialog box allows you to select the folder in which the HTML files will be stored for later viewing. Make sure the text box displays the Tutorial folder on your Student Disk.

7. Click the **Next** button. This dialog box allows you to create a home page that will contain hyperlinks to each of the HTML pages created by the wizard. Click the check box for creating a home page.

   The home page will be the starting point for viewing the Customer table page and the Invoices report page. Users will be able to click either of the hyperlinks and then view the selected page.

8. Click the file name text box, select the current file name (Default), and then type **Valle Home Page**. Access will create a home page file with the name Valle Home Page.html. See Figure 7-6.

Figure 7-6 ◄
Selecting the
home page
option

click to create
a home page

name of home
page file

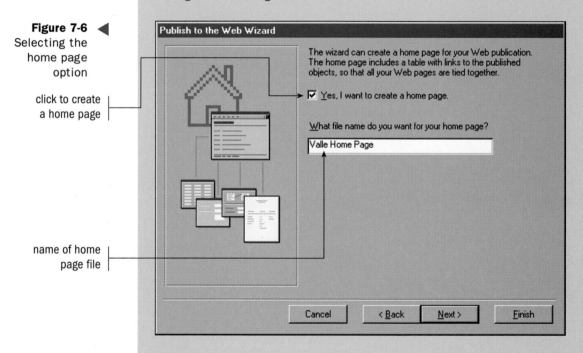

9. Click the **Next** button. The next Publish to the Web Wizard dialog box allows you to save your choices in a profile. You do not want to save a profile now; you'll learn about profiles later in the tutorial.

10. Click the **Finish** button. The Publish to the Web Wizard dialog box closes, and the wizard creates the HTML files you requested.

The Publish to the Web Wizard now has all the information necessary to create the home page and the HTML files for the Customer table and the Invoices report. The wizard creates a home page HTML file called Valle Home Page and an HTML file for the Customer table data, called Customer_1. The wizard also creates three HTML files for the Invoices report—one file for each page of the report. These files are named Invoices_1, Invoices_1Page2, and Invoices_1Page3. All of the HTML files are stored in the Tutorial folder on your Student Disk and can be viewed using the Web browser on your computer.

Viewing the HTML Files Using Internet Explorer

Leonard asks to see the Web pages you have created. The HTML files created by the Publish to the Web Wizard can be viewed using any Web browser software. You'll view these files using Microsoft Internet Explorer.

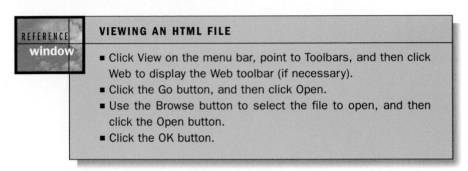

REFERENCE window	**VIEWING AN HTML FILE**
	▪ Click View on the menu bar, point to Toolbars, and then click Web to display the Web toolbar (if necessary).
	▪ Click the Go button, and then click Open.
	▪ Use the Browse button to select the file to open, and then click the Open button.
	▪ Click the OK button.

You'll begin by viewing the Valle Home Page file.

To view the Valle Home Page HTML file:

1. Click **View** on the menu bar, point to **Toolbars**, and then click **Web**. Access displays the Web toolbar. See Figure 7-7.

Figure 7-7 ◀
Displaying the
Web toolbar

Web toolbar —

Go button —

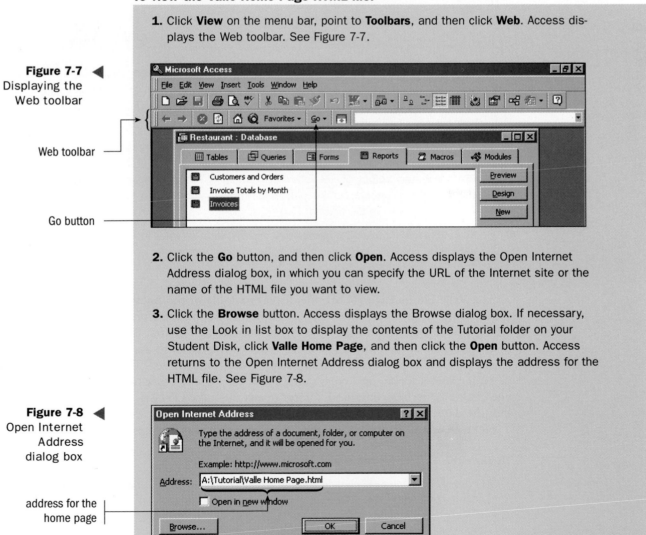

2. Click the **Go** button, and then click **Open**. Access displays the Open Internet Address dialog box, in which you can specify the URL of the Internet site or the name of the HTML file you want to view.

3. Click the **Browse** button. Access displays the Browse dialog box. If necessary, use the Look in list box to display the contents of the Tutorial folder on your Student Disk, click **Valle Home Page**, and then click the **Open** button. Access returns to the Open Internet Address dialog box and displays the address for the HTML file. See Figure 7-8.

Figure 7-8 ◀
Open Internet
Address
dialog box

address for the
home page

4. Click the **OK** button. Access opens the Internet Explorer and displays the Valle Home Page HTML file. See Figure 7-9.

Figure 7-9 ◄
Internet
Explorer
displaying the
Valle Home
Page HTML file

page title

hyperlinks to other
HTML files

Web page

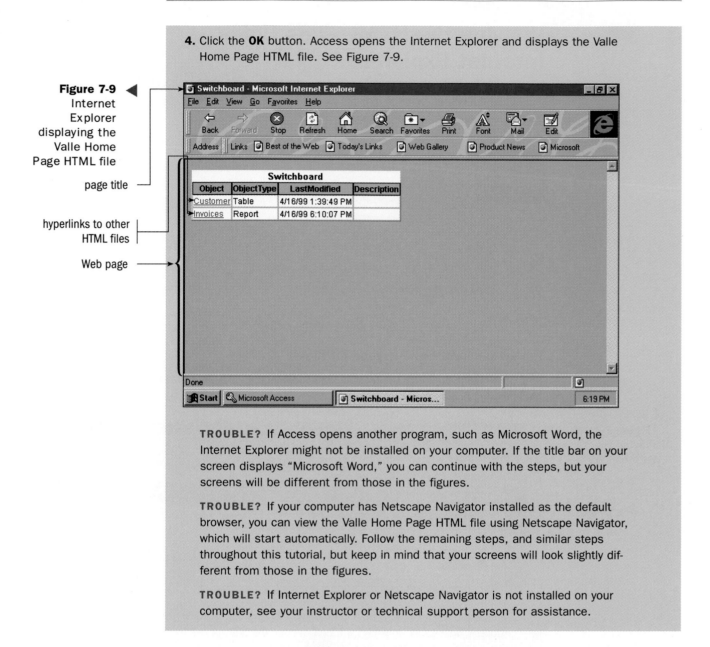

Object	ObjectType	LastModified	Description
Customer	Table	4/16/99 1:39:49 PM	
Invoices	Report	4/16/99 6:10:07 PM	

TROUBLE? If Access opens another program, such as Microsoft Word, the Internet Explorer might not be installed on your computer. If the title bar on your screen displays "Microsoft Word," you can continue with the steps, but your screens will be different from those in the figures.

TROUBLE? If your computer has Netscape Navigator installed as the default browser, you can view the Valle Home Page HTML file using Netscape Navigator, which will start automatically. Follow the remaining steps, and similar steps throughout this tutorial, but keep in mind that your screens will look slightly different from those in the figures.

TROUBLE? If Internet Explorer or Netscape Navigator is not installed on your computer, see your instructor or technical support person for assistance.

The Valle Home Page HTML file displays a table of the Access objects that you published to the Web. This table is called a **switchboard**, and it serves as a home page from which you can view all of the objects you published. The first column of the table contains the name of the object. The name is also a hyperlink to another HTML file, which is why each name appears in a different color and is underlined. The linked document can be an Internet address, an Access table, a text file, or any other object. In this case, when you click a hyperlink, Internet Explorer opens the linked HTML file for the object. Note that the dates in the Last Modified column will be different on your screen.

Next, Leonard wants to view the Customer table and Invoices report pages.

To view the Customer table and Invoices report pages:

1. Click the **Customer** hyperlink. Internet Explorer displays the Customer_1 HTML file showing the records in the Customer table. See Figure 7-10.

Figure 7-10 ◀
Customer table
in the Internet
Explorer

records from the
Customer table

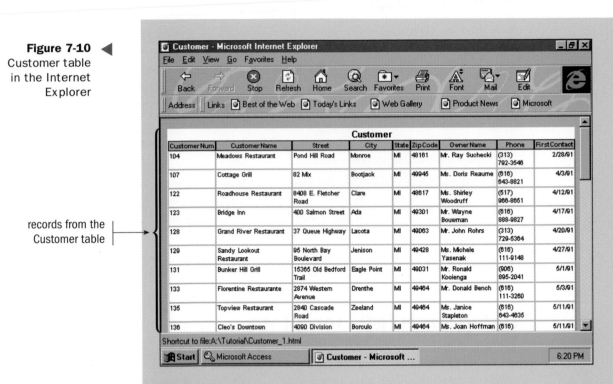

2. Click the **Back** button on the toolbar. Internet Explorer returns to the switchboard page.

3. Click the **Invoices** hyperlink. Internet Explorer displays the Invoices_1 HTML file, the first page of the Invoices report.

4. Scroll to the bottom of the report page. Because the report has more than one page, Access automatically included hyperlinks to the other pages of the report. These hyperlinks are named First, Previous, Next, and Last, and they are linked with the first, previous, next, and last pages of the report, respectively. Because you are viewing the first page of the report, the First and Previous hyperlinks are inactive and appear in a different color from the Next and Last hyperlinks. See Figure 7-11.

Figure 7-11 ◀
Viewing the
report page

report page

hyperlinks to other
report pages

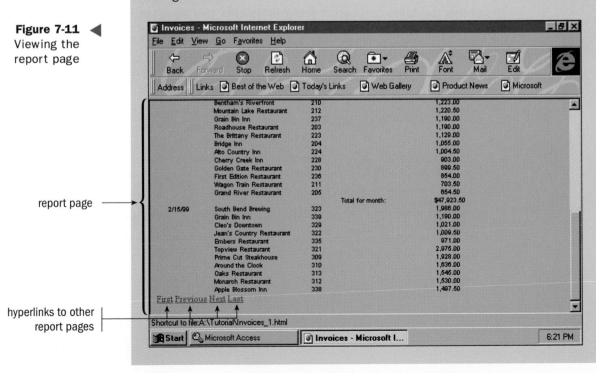

5. Click the **Next** hyperlink. Internet Explorer displays the second page of the report, contained in the Invoices_1Page2 HTML file. Notice that the Address text box displays the address for this page.

6. Scroll to the bottom of the report page, and then click the **Last** hyperlink. Internet Explorer displays the third and last page of the report, contained in the Invoices_1Page3 HTML file.

7. Click the **First** hyperlink at the bottom of the report page. Internet Explorer displays the first page of the report.

8. Click the **Close** button ⊠ on the Internet Explorer window to close it.

9. Click the **Microsoft Access** button on the taskbar to return to Access.

Barbara stops by to see the Web pages you have created. She likes the pages but suggests that they would look better with a title and graphic image at the top to identify them as Valle Coffee's pages.

Using an HTML Template

You can include text, graphics, and other information in the pages created by the Publish to the Web Wizard by using a template. A **template** is a file that contains HTML instructions for creating a Web page together with special instructions that tell Access where to place the Access data on the page. Barbara has created two templates using Microsoft Word. She saved the templates in two files, Valletbl and Vallerpt. The Valletbl template includes instructions for a title and the Valle Coffee cup logo at the top of the page. You can use the Valletbl template to create an HTML file for a table (or query results). The Vallerpt template is similar, but it also contains the necessary instructions to include the First, Previous, Next, and Last hyperlinks. You can use the Vallerpt template to create an HTML file for a report.

Barbara will need to recreate these Web pages periodically as the data in the Restaurant database changes. To save her time later on, you can instruct the Publish to the Web Wizard to record your choices and save them as a **profile**. In this way, Barbara can recreate the Web pages by telling the Publish to the Web Wizard to use the saved profile.

To publish the table and report using templates and save your choices in a profile:

1. Click **File** on the menu bar, and then click **Save As HTML**. Access opens the Publish to the Web Wizard.

2. Click the **Next** button. The wizard displays the list of tables in the Restaurant database. Click the check box next to the **Customer** table to select it.

3. Click the **Reports** tab, and then click the check box next to the **Invoices** report to select it.

4. Click the **Next** button. This dialog box allows you to select a template for the HTML pages that will be created. Because you need to use different templates for each of the selected objects, click the check box for using different templates.

5. Click the **Next** button. Access displays a dialog box listing the selected objects.

6. Make sure the **Table:Customer** table is highlighted, and then click the **Browse** button. Access opens the Select an HTML Template dialog box.

   Because Customer is a table, you will use the Valletbl template that Barbara created to create the HTML file.

7. Use the Look in list box to display the contents of the Tutorial folder on your Student Disk, click **Valletbl**, and then click the **Select** button.

8. Click **Report: Invoices** to highlight it, click the **Browse** button, click **Vallerpt** to select the template for a report, and then click the **Select** button to return to the Publish to the Web Wizard. See Figure 7-12.

Figure 7-12 ◀
Selecting templates for the objects to be published

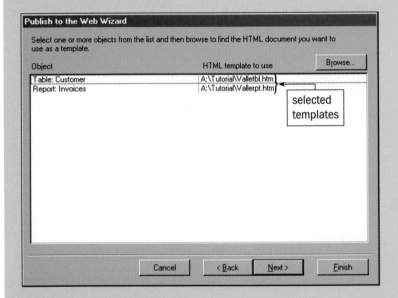

9. Click the **Next** button to display the next dialog box. Make sure the **Static HTML** option button is selected, and then click the **Next** button.

10. Click the **Next** button to place your Web publication in the Tutorial folder on your Student Disk. Click the check box for creating a home page, click the file name text box, select the Default name, and then type **Valle Home Page**. Click the **Next** button. The next dialog box allows you to save your choices in a profile.

11. Click the check box for saving your choices in a profile, click the **Profile Name** text box, select the current name, and then type **Valle Profile**. Your Web page choices will be saved in a profile named Valle Profile. See Figure 7-13.

Figure 7-13 ◀
Creating the Web publication profile

click to save choices in a profile

enter profile name here

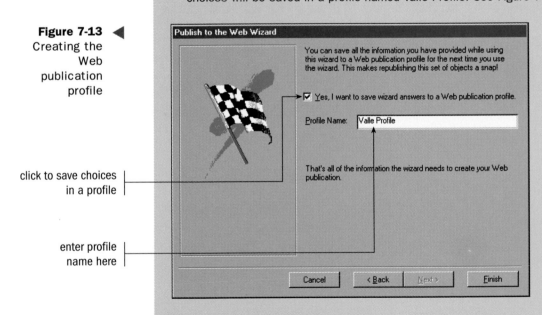

12. Click the **Finish** button. The Publish to the Web Wizard creates the HTML files according to the profile and saves them in the Tutorial folder on your Student Disk.

When the Publish to the Web Wizard creates the new Web pages, it overwrites the pages you created before. When these pages need to be updated in the future, you can simply use the profile you saved rather than having to complete all the Publish to the Web Wizard steps again.

Barbara asks to see the new HTML files created with the templates, which display the Valle Coffee title and coffee cup logo.

To view the new HTML files:

1. Click the **Go** button on the Web toolbar, and then click **Open**.

2. Click the **Browse** button, click **Valle Home Page** in the Tutorial folder on your Student Disk, and then click the **Open** button to return to the Open Internet Address dialog box.

3. Click the **OK** button. Access opens the Internet Explorer and displays the Valle Home Page HTML file.

4. Click the **Customer** hyperlink. Internet Explorer displays the Customer_1 HTML file showing the records in the Customer table. Because you used the Valletbl template to create this page, it displays both the Valle Coffee title and coffee cup logo. See Figure 7-14.

Figure 7-14 ◀
Customer table
with title
and logo

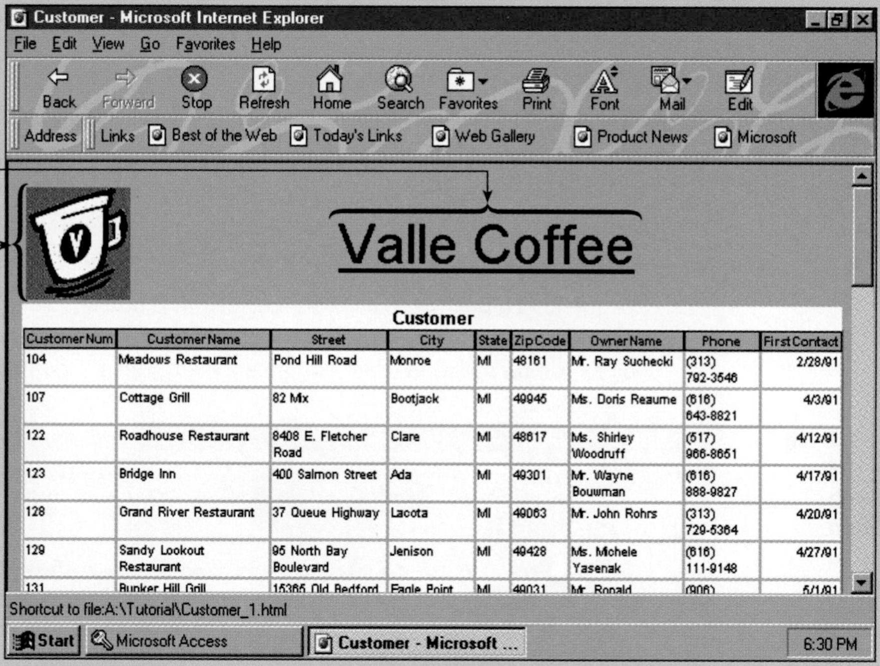

added title ———

added picture (logo) ———

5. Click the **Back** button on the toolbar. Internet Explorer returns to the switchboard page.

6. Click the **Invoices** hyperlink. Internet Explorer displays the Invoices_1 HTML file, the first page of the Invoices report. Because you used the Vallerpt template to create this page, it displays both the Valle Coffee title and coffee cup logo.

7. Use the First, Previous, Next, and Last hyperlinks to view the other pages of the report. When you are finished, click the **Close** button ☒ on the Internet Explorer window to close it.

8. Click the **Microsoft Access** button on the taskbar to return to Access.

Barbara likes the new HTML files much better. She mentions that Valle Coffee has received an order from a new customer. The customer and order information must be entered in the Restaurant database. The new information must be put in the HTML files as well. She asks you to do this now.

Updating a Web Page

The HTML files created by the Publish to the Web Wizard are static—that is, they reflect the state of the database at the time they were created. Changes to the database are not automatically reflected in the HTML files. If database records are changed, the HTML files must be created again so that they are up to date. Because you saved a profile when you created the HTML files, you can update the HTML files easily by instructing the Publish to the Web Wizard to use the profile to recreate the files.

Figure 7-15 shows the two new records, one for the Customer table and one for the Order table.

Figure 7-15 ◀
New records for
the Restaurant
database

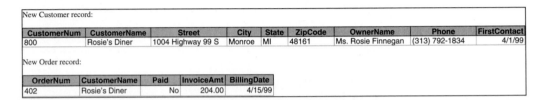

New Customer record:

CustomerNum	CustomerName	Street	City	State	ZipCode	OwnerName	Phone	FirstContact
800	Rosie's Diner	1004 Highway 99 S	Monroe	MI	48161	Ms. Rosie Finnegan	(313) 792-1834	4/1/99

New Order record:

OrderNum	CustomerName	Paid	InvoiceAmt	BillingDate
402	Rosie's Diner	No	204.00	4/15/99

First you'll enter the new records in the Restaurant database.

To enter the new records:

1. If necessary click the **Tables** tab to display the tables list in the Database window, click **Customer** to select it, and then click the **Open** button to open the table.

2. Click the **New Record** button ▶* on the Table Datasheet toolbar, and then enter the data for the new Customer record, as shown in Figure 7-15.

3. Click the **Close** button ☒ on the Table window to close the Customer table datasheet.

4. Click **Order**, and then click the **Open** button to open the Order table.

5. Click the **New Record** button ▶* on the Table Datasheet toolbar, and then enter the data for the new Order record, as shown in Figure 7-15.

6. Click the **Close** button ☒ on the Table window to close the Order table datasheet.

Now you can create the HTML files again using the profile you saved earlier.

To create the HTML files using the saved profile:

1. Click **File** on the menu bar, and then click **Save As HTML**. Access starts the Publish to the Web Wizard. The first dialog box shows the Valle Profile in the profiles list. See Figure 7-16.

Figure 7-16 ◄
Selecting
the profile

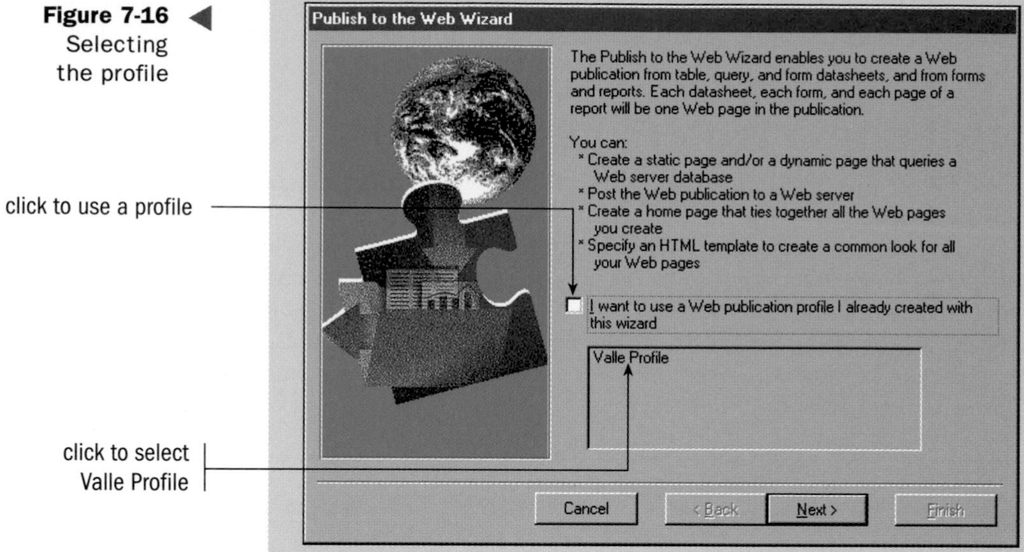

click to use a profile ———

click to select
Valle Profile

2. Click the check box for using an existing profile.

3. Click **Valle Profile** to select the profile. Because you don't need to change any of the choices you made before, you are finished with the wizard.

4. Click the **Finish** button. The Publish to the Web Wizard creates a Valle Home Page HTML file and HTML files for the Customer table and the Invoices report. The new files include the information in the new records you just added.

5. Click the **Go** button on the Web toolbar, and then click **Open**.

6. Click the **Browse** button, click the **Valle Home Page** file in the Tutorial folder on your Student Disk, and then click the **Open** button to return to the Open Internet Address dialog box.

7. Click the **OK** button. Access opens the Internet Explorer and displays the Valle Home Page HTML file.

8. Click the **Customer** hyperlink. Internet Explorer displays the Customer_1 HTML file showing the records in the Customer table. Scroll down to see that the new customer record, CustomerNum 800, has been added to the customer list. See Figure 7-17.

Figure 7-17
Customer table
with the new
customer
record

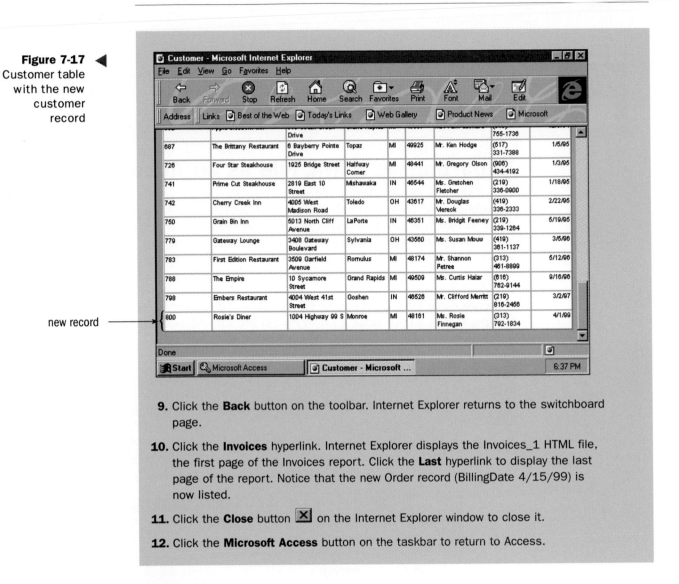

new record

9. Click the **Back** button on the toolbar. Internet Explorer returns to the switchboard page.

10. Click the **Invoices** hyperlink. Internet Explorer displays the Invoices_1 HTML file, the first page of the Invoices report. Click the **Last** hyperlink to display the last page of the report. Notice that the new Order record (BillingDate 4/15/99) is now listed.

11. Click the **Close** button ☒ on the Internet Explorer window to close it.

12. Click the **Microsoft Access** button on the taskbar to return to Access.

Quick Check

1. What is HTML?

2. What is the World Wide Web?

3. What is the purpose of a Web browser?

4. What is a hyperlink?

5. What is an HTML template?

6. What is the purpose of saving a profile for the Publish to the Web Wizard?

Leonard and Barbara are pleased with the HTML files that you created. The files will make it easy to distribute important Restaurant database information on the company's intranet. In the next session, you will continue to work with HTML files to further enhance the database.

SESSION

7.2

In this session you will import data from an HTML file into an Access table. You will add a hyperlink field to a table and enter hyperlink values that link records to bookmarks in a Word document. You will also add a hyperlink field to a table and enter hyperlink values that link records to HTML files.

Importing an HTML File as an Access Table

Kim Carpenter, the marketing manager, is an active user of the World Wide Web. She recently discovered a site published by the Upper Midwest Tourism Office. One of the pages at that site lists restaurants that have opened recently in Valle Coffee's customer area. Each of these new restaurants is a potential customer for Valle Coffee. Kim asks whether you can import the restaurant information from that page into an Access table. With the data in an Access table, she will be able to create queries, forms, and reports based on the data.

Access can import data from an HTML file as a database object. Provided that the data is formatted as a table or as a list in the HTML file, Access can import it directly into a database table.

REFERENCE
window

IMPORTING AN HTML FILE AS AN ACCESS TABLE

- Click File on the menu bar, point to Get External Data, and then click Import.
- Click the Files of type list arrow, and then click HTML Documents.
- Use the Look in list box to select the HTML file to import.
- Click the Import button. Access displays the first Import HTML Wizard dialog box.
- Complete the wizard dialog boxes to specify whether the first row of data should be used for column headings; specify whether records should be imported to a new table or appended to an existing table; specify the field names, data types, and indexing options for the fields; specify a primary key; and enter the table name.
- Click the OK button to confirm that the data has been imported.

The HTML file containing the information Kim wants is stored in the Tutorial folder on your Student Disk with the name NewRest. You will use the Access Import HTML Wizard to import the data into a new table in the Restaurant database. First, you'll begin by viewing the HTML file using Internet Explorer.

To view the NewRest HTML file:

1. If you took a break after the previous session, make sure that Access is running and the Restaurant database from the Tutorial folder on your Student Disk is open.

2. Click the **Go** button on the Web toolbar, and then click **Open**.

3. Click the **Browse** button.

4. Make sure the Look in list box displays the Tutorial folder on your Student Disk, click **NewRest**, and then click the **Open** button to select the file and return to the Open Internet Address dialog box.

5. Click the **OK** button. Access opens the Internet Explorer and displays the NewRest HTML file. See Figure 7-18.

Figure 7-18
NewRest
HTML file

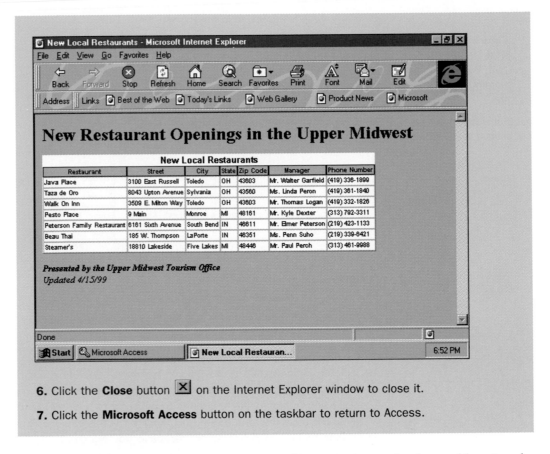

6. Click the **Close** button [X] on the Internet Explorer window to close it.

7. Click the **Microsoft Access** button on the taskbar to return to Access.

Now you will import the NewRest HTML file as an Access database table using the Import HTML Wizard.

To import the HTML file as an Access table:

1. Click **File** on the menu bar, point to **Get External Data**, and then click **Import**. The Import dialog box opens.

2. Click the **Files of type** list arrow, and then click **HTML Documents**.

3. Make sure the Look in list box displays the Tutorial folder on your Student Disk, and then click **NewRest** to select the HTML file.

4. Click the **Import** button. Access displays the first Import HTML Wizard dialog box. This dialog box displays the first few rows of data read from the HTML file. See Figure 7-19.

Figure 7-19 ◄
First Import
HTML Wizard
dialog box

click to select first row
as column headings

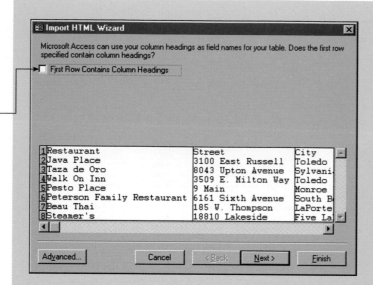

Access allows you to specify that the first row of data contains column headings (field names). Because the first row of this data contains column headings, you will specify that the first row should be used as field names in the new table.

5. Click the **First Row Contains Column Headings** check box, and then click the **Next** button. Access displays the next Import HTML Wizard dialog box, which allows you to import the records to a new table or append them to an existing table. Because the structure of this table is not the same as the structure of any existing tables in the Restaurant database, you will create a new table.

6. Make sure the **In a New Table** option button is selected, and then click the **Next** button to display the next dialog box. See Figure 7-20.

Figure 7-20 ◄
Specifying field
names, data
types, and
indexing
options

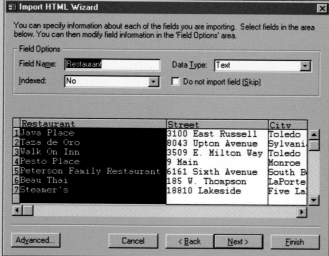

In this dialog box you can change the field name, data type, and indexing option for each of the fields in the new table. If you do not make any choices, Access will assign an appropriate field name, data type, and indexing option for each field. You can also choose not to import selected fields. You will change the name of the Zip Code field to ZipCode and the name of the Phone Number field to PhoneNumber to be consistent with the field naming style in other Restaurant database tables.

7. Scroll the field list to the right to display the Zip Code and Phone Number fields. Click the **Zip Code** field to select it, and then delete the space between Zip and Code in the Field Name text box.

8. Click the **Phone Number** field to select it, and then delete the space between Phone and Number in the Field Name text box. See Figure 7-21.

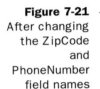

Figure 7-21 ◄
After changing the ZipCode and PhoneNumber field names

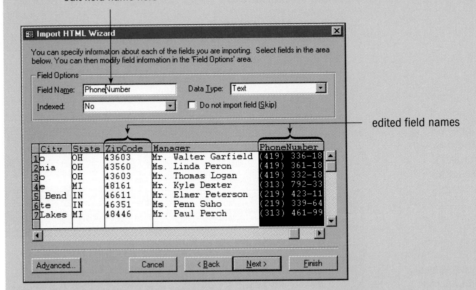

9. Click the **Next** button. The next dialog box allows you to specify a primary key field for the table or let Access add an AutoNumber field as a primary key field. See Figure 7-22.

Figure 7-22 ◄
Specifying the primary key field

indicates that Access will create an AutoNumber field as the primary key

column for AutoNumber field

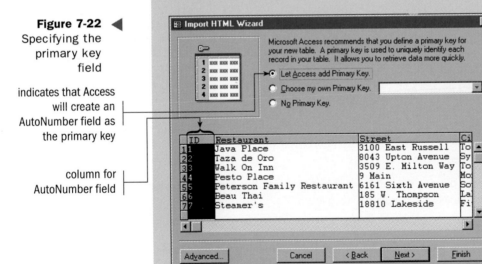

Because the table does not contain a field that would be appropriate as a primary key, you'll let Access assign a primary key field. Access will create a field with the AutoNumber data type as the primary key field for the new table.

10. Make sure the **Let Access add Primary Key** option button is selected, and then click the **Next** button. This dialog box allows you to enter the name of the new table.

11. In the Import to Table text box, type **Potential Customers**, and then click the **Finish** button. Access imports the HTML file and saves the data in a table called Potential Customers. When the wizard is finished creating the file, it displays a dialog box confirming that it has finished.

12. Click the **OK** button to end the importing process and return to the Database window.

The HTML file has been imported and the data has been saved in a new table called Potential Customers. This table is now listed on the Tables tab of the Database window. Kim asks you to view the data and then print a copy of the records for her.

To view the Potential Customers table and print the records:

1. Click **Potential Customers** in the tables list (if necessary), and then click the **Open** button. Access opens the Potential Customers table in Datasheet view. See Figure 7-23.

Figure 7-23 ◄
The new Potential Customers table

primary key values added by Access

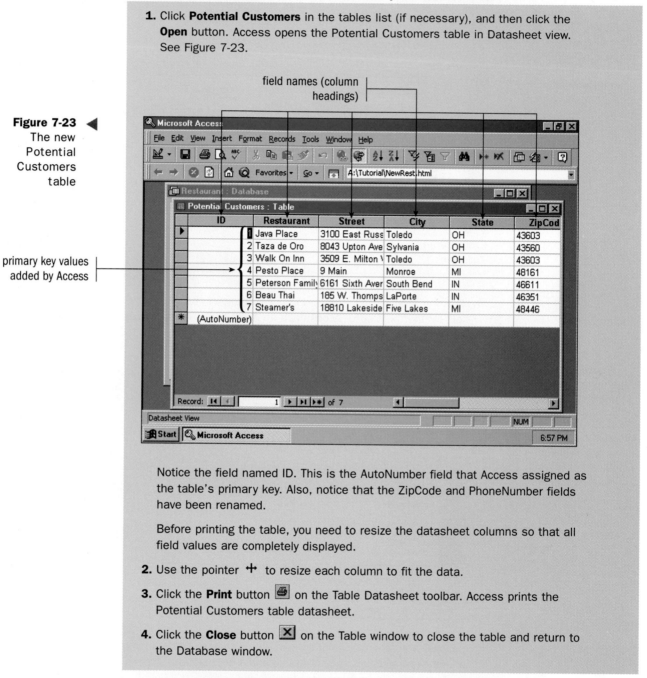

Notice the field named ID. This is the AutoNumber field that Access assigned as the table's primary key. Also, notice that the ZipCode and PhoneNumber fields have been renamed.

Before printing the table, you need to resize the datasheet columns so that all field values are completely displayed.

2. Use the pointer ✛ to resize each column to fit the data.

3. Click the **Print** button 🖨 on the Table Datasheet toolbar. Access prints the Potential Customers table datasheet.

4. Click the **Close** button ☒ on the Table window to close the table and return to the Database window.

Kim reviews and approves the printed output. In the future, when the Upper Midwest Tourism Office publishes new lists of recently opened restaurants, she can add them to the Potential Customers table.

Creating Hyperlinks to Documents in Other Office 97 Programs

Kim has used the Potential Customers list to set up meetings with the new restaurants' managers. She visited several of the restaurants and returned with notes about the visits. Kim saved her field notes in a Word document named Fldnotes. Now she would like some way of connecting these notes with the corresponding records in the Potential Customers table. This would allow her to review her notes when she views the records in the table.

Each restaurant's set of notes in the Fldnotes file is identified with a bookmark. A **bookmark** is a section of text in a Word document that is identified with a name. For example, Kim has placed a bookmark named Java to mark her notes on the new Java Place restaurant. Similarly, her notes on Taza de Oro are marked with the bookmark Taza, and the bookmark for Peterson Family Restaurant is named Peterson. To connect Kim's notes with the corresponding records in the Potential Customers table, you need to create a hyperlink field in the table.

Creating a Hyperlink Field

Access allows you to create a hyperlink field in a table. The field value in a hyperlink field is a hyperlink to another object. These objects can be database objects (such as tables or forms), a bookmark in a Word document, a named range in an Excel worksheet, or even a World Wide Web page. When you click a hyperlink field value, Access starts the associated program and opens the linked object.

REFERENCE window	**CREATING A HYPERLINK FIELD**
	▪ Display the table in Design view.
	▪ In a blank Field Name text box, type the name of the new field, and then press the Tab key.
	▪ Click the Data Type list arrow, and then click Hyperlink.

You will create a hyperlink field in the Potential Customers table. The hyperlink field value will be a hyperlink to a bookmark in Kim's Fldnotes document. When Kim clicks a hyperlink, Access will start Word and display the bookmarked text.

To add a hyperlink field to the table:

1. In the Database window tables list, click **Potential Customers** (if necessary), and then click the **Design** button. The table is displayed in Design view.

2. Scroll down the field list to display a blank row, click the Field Name text box, type **FieldNotes**, and then press the **Tab** key.

3. Click the **Data Type** list arrow, and then click **Hyperlink**. See Figure 7-24.

Figure 7-24 ◀
Adding a
hyperlink field

new field ——

selected data type ——

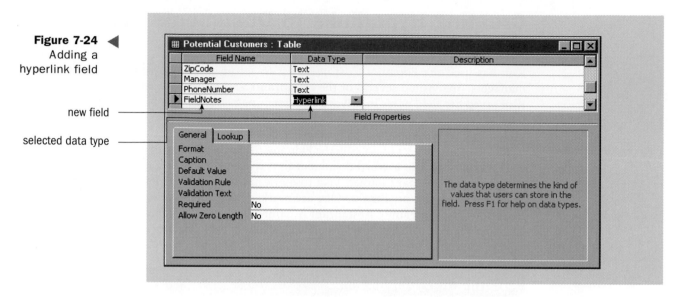

Now you can add the hyperlink field values to the Potential Customers table. These field values will be hyperlinks to the bookmarked text in the Fldnotes document.

Entering a Hyperlink Field Value

When you add a field value in a hyperlink field, you can enter the name of an object, such as a table, form, worksheet or document, or a URL. You can type the field value directly into the field or you can use the Insert Hyperlink dialog box to enter it. If you use the Insert Hyperlink dialog box, you can also specify a named location in the object. For example, in a Word document, a named location is any bookmark. If you are hyperlinking to an Access database, a named location could be a table, query, form, or any other database object.

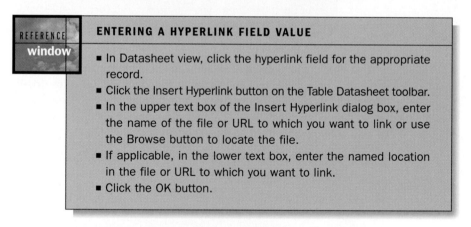

REFERENCE
window

ENTERING A HYPERLINK FIELD VALUE

- In Datasheet view, click the hyperlink field for the appropriate record.
- Click the Insert Hyperlink button on the Table Datasheet toolbar.
- In the upper text box of the Insert Hyperlink dialog box, enter the name of the file or URL to which you want to link or use the Browse button to locate the file.
- If applicable, in the lower text box, enter the named location in the file or URL to which you want to link.
- Click the OK button.

You will use the Insert Hyperlink dialog box to enter the necessary hyperlink field values and specify the relevant bookmarks in the Fldnotes document.

To enter field values in the hyperlink field:

1. Click the **View** button for Datasheet view 🖿 on the Table Design toolbar. Access opens a dialog box asking if you want to save the table.

2. Click the **Yes** button. The table is displayed in Datasheet view.

3. Scroll right until the FieldNotes field is visible, and then click the **FieldNotes** text box for the Java Place record (record 1).

4. Click the **Insert Hyperlink** button 🔗 on the Table Datasheet toolbar. The Insert Hyperlink dialog box opens. See Figure 7-25.

Figure 7-25 ◄
Insert
Hyperlink
dialog box

enter bookmark
name here

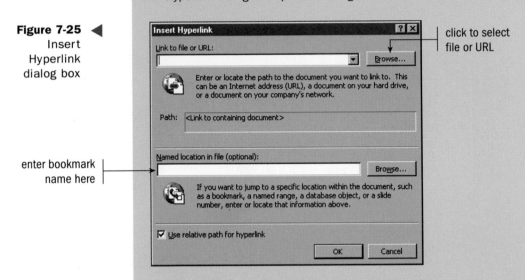

click to select
file or URL

The Insert Hyperlink dialog box contains two text boxes. The upper text box allows you to enter the name of the file or URL to which you want to link, and the lower text box allows you to enter the named location in that file or URL to which you want to link (if applicable). Notice that the insertion point is already in the Link to file or URL text box.

5. Click the **Browse** button. The Link to File dialog box opens.

6. Make sure the Look in list box displays the contents of the Tutorial folder on your Student Disk, click **Fldnotes**, and then click the **OK** button. The Link to File dialog box closes and the name of the Fldnotes file appears in the Link to file or URL text box.

The named location for Kim's notes on the Java Place restaurant is a bookmark called Java. You will specify the bookmark as a named location in the Fldnotes file, so that Access will display the text at this location when the user clicks the hyperlink field value.

7. Click the **Named location in file** text box, and then type **Java**. See Figure 7-26.

Figure 7-26 ◄
Entering a
hyperlink field
value and
named location

hyperlinked file

bookmark in
Word document

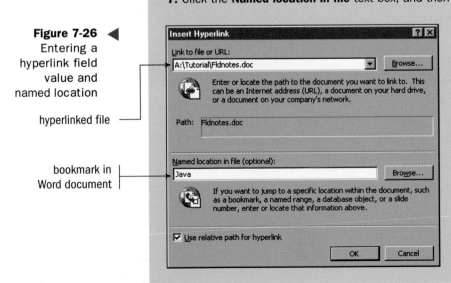

TROUBLE? The Fldnotes filename on your screen might be displayed in all uppercase letters or some other variation of uppercase and lowercase letters. This will not affect the final results; simply proceed with the steps.

8. Click the **OK** button to close the Insert Hyperlink dialog box. The hyperlink field value appears in the FieldNotes field for the first record. See Figure 7-27.

Figure 7-27 ◀
Hyperlink field
value entered

hyperlink field

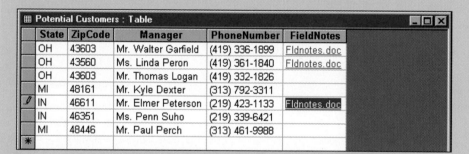

hyperlink
field value

	State	ZipCode	Manager	PhoneNumber	FieldNotes
	OH	43603	Mr. Walter Garfield	(419) 336-1899	Fldnotes.doc
	OH	43560	Ms. Linda Peron	(419) 361-1840	
	OH	43603	Mr. Thomas Logan	(419) 332-1826	
	MI	48161	Mr. Kyle Dexter	(313) 792-3311	
	IN	46611	Mr. Elmer Peterson	(219) 423-1133	
	IN	46351	Ms. Penn Suho	(219) 339-6421	
	MI	48446	Mr. Paul Perch	(313) 461-9988	

9. Use the same procedure to enter hyperlink field values for the records for Taza de Oro (record 2) and Peterson Family Restaurant (record 5). Enter **Taza** as the named location in the Fldnotes file for the Taza de Oro record and **Peterson** as the named location in the Fldnotes file for the Peterson record. When you are finished, the Datasheet window should look like Figure 7-28.

Figure 7-28 ◀
Hyperlink field
values entered
for the three
records

Potential Customers : Table

	State	ZipCode	Manager	PhoneNumber	FieldNotes
	OH	43603	Mr. Walter Garfield	(419) 336-1899	Fldnotes.doc
	OH	43560	Ms. Linda Peron	(419) 361-1840	Fldnotes.doc
	OH	43603	Mr. Thomas Logan	(419) 332-1826	
	MI	48161	Mr. Kyle Dexter	(313) 792-3311	
	IN	46611	Mr. Elmer Peterson	(219) 423-1133	Fldnotes.doc
	IN	46351	Ms. Penn Suho	(219) 339-6421	
	MI	48446	Mr. Paul Perch	(313) 461-9988	

Notice that the hyperlink field values have a different appearance from the other field values. The hyperlink field values are shown in a different color and are underlined. This indicates that they are hyperlinks.

Kim wants to test the new hyperlink field in the Potential Customers table. You'll use the hyperlinks to view the corresponding notes.

Using a Hyperlink

When you click a hyperlink field value, Access starts the associated program and displays the linked object. When you click a value in the FieldNotes field, for example, Access will start Word, open the Fldnotes document, and place the cursor at the appropriate bookmark.

To use a hyperlink to open the Word document:

1. Click the **Peterson Family Restaurant FieldNotes** hyperlink. Access starts Word, opens the Fldnotes document, and positions the cursor at the Peterson bookmark at the beginning of the field notes for Peterson Family Restaurant. See Figure 7-29.

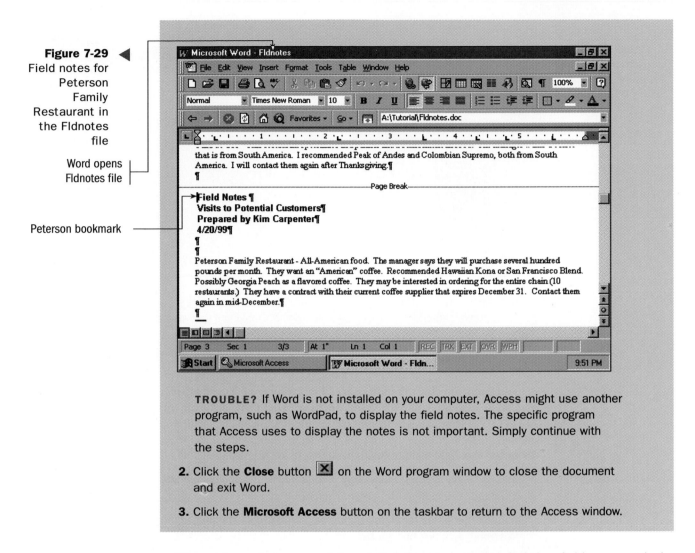

Figure 7-29 ◀
Field notes for
Peterson
Family
Restaurant in
the Fldnotes
file

Word opens
Fldnotes file

Peterson bookmark

> **TROUBLE?** If Word is not installed on your computer, Access might use another program, such as WordPad, to display the field notes. The specific program that Access uses to display the notes is not important. Simply continue with the steps.
>
> 2. Click the **Close** button ⊠ on the Word program window to close the document and exit Word.
>
> 3. Click the **Microsoft Access** button on the taskbar to return to the Access window.

Kim reviews the notes and is satisfied that she can now link her field notes with the Potential Customers data. She asks you to add one more hyperlink field to the Potential Customers table. This new field will contain hyperlinks to World Wide Web pages.

Creating Hyperlinks to World Wide Web Pages

When Kim visited the potential new customers, she learned that some of the restaurants have home pages on the World Wide Web. These pages serve as advertisements for the restaurants. Kim wants you to add a hyperlink field to the Potential Customers table. The field value for each record will be a hyperlink to the particular restaurant's home page.

The field value for the hyperlink is the URL for that Web site. When you click a field value for a record, Access starts the Web browser on your computer and opens the HTML document at that site.

Before you can enter the field values, you must add a new hyperlink field to the Potential Customers table.

To add a new hyperlink field:

> 1. Click the **View** button for Design view ▨ on the Table Datasheet toolbar.
>
> 2. Scroll down the field list to the first blank row, click the **Field Name** text box for the blank row, type **HomePage**, and then press the **Tab** key.
>
> 3. Click the **Data Type** list arrow, and then click **Hyperlink**. See Figure 7-30.

Figure 7-30 ◀
HomePage
hyperlink field
defined

new hyperlink field ──

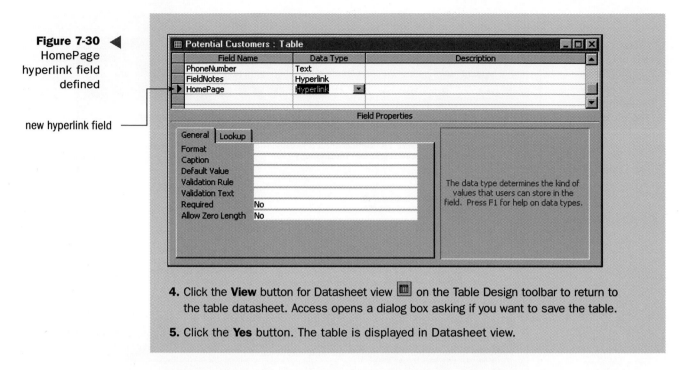

4. Click the **View** button for Datasheet view 🖩 on the Table Design toolbar to return to the table datasheet. Access opens a dialog box asking if you want to save the table.

5. Click the **Yes** button. The table is displayed in Datasheet view.

You can now enter the URLs for the restaurants' home pages. You will not enter actual URLs; instead you will simulate using URLs by entering the names of appropriate HTML files that are stored on your Student Disk.

To enter the field values for hyperlinks to HTML files:

1. Scroll right until the HomePage field is visible, and then click the **HomePage** text box for the Taza de Oro record (record 2).

2. Click the **Insert Hyperlink** button 🖼 on the Table Datasheet toolbar. The Insert Hyperlink dialog box opens.

3. Click the upper **Browse** button. The Link to File dialog box opens.

4. Make sure the Look in list box displays the contents of the Tutorial folder on your Student Disk, click **Taza**, and then click the **OK** button. The Link to File dialog box closes and the name of the Taza file appears in the Link to file or URL text box. See Figure 7-31.

Figure 7-31 ◀
Entering a
hyperlink field
value for the
HTML file

hyperlinked file ──

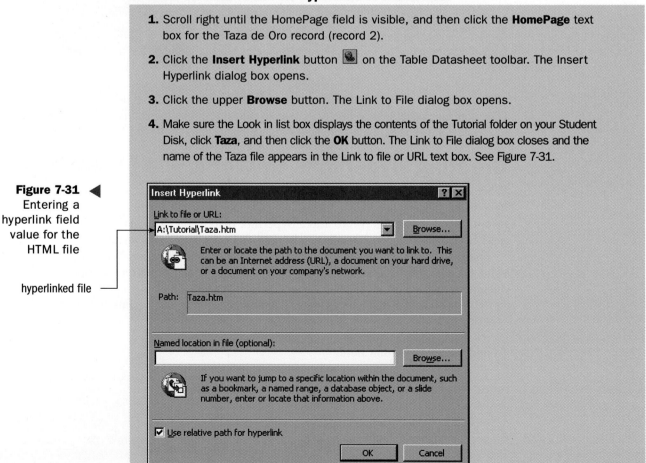

Because you want to view the entire Taza file, not a named location in the file, you do not need to specify a named location.

5. Click the **OK** button to close the Insert Hyperlink dialog box. The hyperlink field value appears in the HomePage field for the second record. See Figure 7-32.

Figure 7-32 ◀
Hyperlink field
value entered
for the
restaurant's
home page

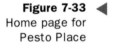

	State	ZipCode	Manager	PhoneNumber	FieldNotes	HomePage
	OH	43603	Mr. Walter Garfield	(419) 336-1899	Fldnotes.doc	
🖉	OH	43560	Ms. Linda Peron	(419) 361-1840	Fldnotes.doc	Taza.htm
	OH	43603	Mr. Thomas Logan	(419) 332-1826		
	MI	48161	Mr. Kyle Dexter	(313) 792-3311		
	IN	46611	Mr. Elmer Peterson	(219) 423-1133	Fldnotes.doc	
	IN	46351	Ms. Penn Suho	(219) 339-6421		
	MI	48446	Mr. Paul Perch	(313) 461-9988		
✱						

new hyperlink field

hyperlink field value

6. Use the same procedure to enter a hyperlink field value for the record for Pesto Place (record 4). Select the HTML file named Pesto as the file to link to.

You can now view the restaurant home pages by clicking the hyperlinks in the HomePage field.

To view the home pages:

1. Click **Pesto.htm** in the HomePage field for record 4. Access starts Internet Explorer and displays the HTML file for Pesto Place's home page. See Figure 7-33.

Figure 7-33 ◀
Home page for
Pesto Place

2. Click the **Close** button ☒ on the Internet Explorer window to close it.

3. Click the **Microsoft Access** button on the taskbar to return to the Access window.

4. Click **Taza.htm** in the HomePage field for record 2. Access starts Internet Explorer and displays the HTML file for Taza de Oro's home page.

5. Click the **Close** button ☒ on the Internet Explorer window to close it.

6. Click the **Microsoft Access** button on the taskbar to return to the Access window.

You can now close the Restaurant database and exit Access. First you'll close the Web toolbar.

7. Click **View** on the menu bar, point to **Toolbars**, and then click **Web**. Access closes the Web toolbar.

8. Click the **Close** button ☒ on the Access program window to close the Restaurant database and to exit Access. You return to the Windows 95 desktop.

Quick Check

1 What types of HTML formats can Access import as table data?

2 How do you specify a named location in a hyperlinked file?

3 What is a bookmark?

4 What is one difference between typing a hyperlink value directly into a field and using the Insert Hyperlink dialog box?

5 What is a URL?

6 How do you view a hyperlink that is named in a hyperlink field?

Kim is pleased with the finished Potential Customers table. She is certain that the link from the table to the document containing her notes will make it much easier for her and others in the Marketing Department to identify and track potential new customers for Valle Coffee.

Tutorial Assignments

Barbara wants you to publish parts of the Products database on the company intranet. She wants to make the Product table data and the Coffee Types report available to company employees on the World Wide Web. She asks you to do the following:

1. Make sure your Student Disk is in the appropriate disk drive, start Access, and then open the Products database located in the TAssign folder on your Student Disk.

2. Use the Publish to the Web Wizard to create a home page:
   a. Save the Product table and the Coffee Types report as HTML files.
   b. Do not use a template for the files.
   c. Choose the static page format for the files.
   d. Publish the files in the TAssign folder on your Student Disk.
   e. Use the Default name for the home page.
   f. Do not save your choices in a profile.

3. Use Internet Explorer to do the following:
   a. Open the Default home page, and then view both the Product table and the Coffee Types report.
   b. Print the Product table HTML file from Internet Explorer.

4. Use the Publish to the Web Wizard to create a home page again:
   a. Save the Special Imports query and the Coffee Types report as HTML files.
   b. Use the Valletbl template for the Special Imports query and the Vallerpt template for the Coffee Types report. Both templates are located in the TAssign folder on your Student Disk.
   c. Choose the static page format for the files.
   d. Publish the files in the TAssign folder on your Student Disk.
   e. Use the name Products for the home page.
   f. Save your choices as a profile named Products Profile.

5. Use Internet Explorer to open the Products home page, and then view both the Special Imports data and the Coffee Types report.

6. Add the record shown in Figure 7-34 to the Product table in the Products database.

Figure 7-34 ◀

ProductCode	CoffeeCode	WeightCode	Price	Decaf
2489	YEMM	6 lb case	68.00	D

7. Use the Publish to the Web Wizard to update the Products home page:
   a. Use the Products Profile to recreate the HTML files.
   b. Use Internet Explorer to open the Products home page, and then view the Special Imports data. Verify that the new record (for ProductCode 2489) has been included in the query results.
   c. Print the Special Imports HTML file from Internet Explorer.

8. View and then print the Coffee Types report HTML file from Internet Explorer.

9. The Importers HTML file on your Student Disk contains a table of coffee importers in the local area. Import the Importers HTML file into the Products database as a new table:
   a. Choose the option for using the column headings as field names in the table.
   b. Let Access assign the primary key.
   c. Name the new table Coffee Importers.
   d. Open the Coffee Importers table, resize all datasheet columns to fit the data, and then print the table.
   e. Close and save the table.

10. Some of the importers have home pages on the World Wide Web. Two of the HTML files for the home pages are stored on your Student Disk. These files are called Wwfoods (the home page for World-Wide Foods) and Johnson (the home page for Johnson Restaurant Supply). Add a hyperlink field called Home Page to the Coffee Importers table. Add hyperlink values for World-Wide Foods (record 3) and Johnson Restaurant Supply (record 5).

11. View the World-Wide Foods home page, and then print the page. View the Johnson Restaurant Supply home page, and then print the page.

12. Close the Products database, and then exit Access.

Case Problems

1. Ashbrook Mall Information Desk Sam Bullard wants to use the mall's computer intranet to publicize job openings at the mall. He wants to put the Job table and Store Jobs report on the intranet as Web pages. He asks you to make the following changes to the MallJobs database:

1. Make sure your Student Disk is in the appropriate disk drive, start Access, and then open the MallJobs database located in the Cases folder on your Student Disk.

2. Use the Publish to the Web Wizard to create a home page:
   a. Save the Job table and the Store Jobs report as HTML files.
   b. Do not use a template for the files.
   c. Choose the static page format for the files.
   d. Publish the files in the Cases folder on your Student Disk.
   e. Use the name MallJobs for the home page.
   f. Do not save your choices in a profile.

3. Use Internet Explorer to do the following:

    a. Open the MallJobs home page, and then view both the Job table and the Store Jobs report.

    b. Print the Job HTML file from Internet Explorer.

4. Use the Publish to the Web Wizard to create a home page again:

    a. Save the Job table and the Store Jobs report as HTML files.

    b. Use the Jobtbl template for the Job table and the Jobsrpt template for the Store Jobs report. Both templates are located in the Cases folder on your Student Disk.

    c. Choose the static page format for the files.

    d. Publish the files in the Cases folder on your Student Disk.

    e. Use the name MallJobs for the home page.

    f. Save your choices as a profile named MallJobs Profile.

5. Use Internet Explorer to open the MallJobs home page, and then view both the Job table and the Store Jobs report.

6. Add the record shown in Figure 7-35 to the Job table in the MallJobs database.

Figure 7-35 ◀

Job	Store	Position	Hours/Week
10010	Big Cookies	Clerk	20-30

7. Use the Publish to the Web Wizard to update the MallJobs home page:

    a. Use the MallJobs Profile to recreate the HTML files.

    b. Use Internet Explorer to open the MallJobs home page, and then view the Job data. Verify that the new record (for Job 10010) has been included in the table.

    c. Print the Job HTML file from Internet Explorer.

8. View and then print the Store Jobs report HTML file from Internet Explorer.

9. The HTML file Wages on your Student Disk contains information about the minimum allowable wages for positions offered by Ashbrook Mall stores. Import the Wages HTML file as an Access table:

    a. Choose the option for using the column headings as field names in the table.

    b. Let Access assign the primary key.

    c. Name the new table Minimum Wages.

    d. Open the Minimum Wages table, resize all datasheet columns to fit the data, and then print the table.

    e. Close and save the table.

10. The file Jobreqs is a Word document containing details about various mall jobs, with bookmarks for each of the jobs. Add a hyperlink field to the Minimum Wages table. Add hyperlink field values for the Baker, Cashier, Clerk and Fry Cook records. The bookmarks are the names of the positions; for example, the bookmark for the Fry Cook position is FryCook.

11. Click the hyperlink for the Clerk job. View the job description in the jobreqs document, and then print the description.

12. Close the MallJobs database, and then exit Access.

2. Professional Litigation User Services Raj Jawahir wants you to integrate the Payments database with the company intranet. He wants to publish the Firm table and the Payments By Account Representative report as Web pages. He asks you to complete the following:

1. Make sure your Student Disk is in the appropriate disk drive, start Access, and then open the Payments database located in the Cases folder on your Student Disk.

Access

2. Use the Publish to the Web Wizard to create a home page:
   a. Save the Firm table and the Payments By Account Representative report as HTML files.
   b. Do not use a template for the files.
   c. Choose the static page format for the files.
   d. Publish the files in the Cases folder on your Student Disk.
   e. Use the Default name for the home page.
   f. Do not save your choices in a profile.

3. Use Internet Explorer to do the following:
   a. Open the Default home page, and then view both the Firm table and the Payments By Account Representative report.
   b. Print the Firm HTML file from Internet Explorer.

4. Use the Publish to the Web Wizard to create a home page again:
   a. Save the Payment Statistics by Date query and the Payments By Account Representative report as HTML files.
   b. Use the PLUStbl template for the Payment Statistics by Date query and the PLUSrpt template for the Payments By Account Representative report. Both templates are located in the Cases folder on your Student Disk.
   c. Choose the static page format for the files.
   d. Publish the files in the Cases folder on your Student Disk.
   e. Use PLUS as the name for the home page.
   f. Save your choices as a profile named PLUS Profile.

5. Use Internet Explorer to open the PLUS home page, and then view both the Payment Statistics by Date data and the Payments By Account Representative report.

6. Add the record shown in Figure 7-36 to the Payment table in the Payments database.

Figure 7-36 ◀

Payment#	Deposit#	FirmName	AmtPaid	DatePaid
10106	117	Ling, Bingham, & Boyer	850.00	20-Jun-99

7. Use the Publish to the Web Wizard to update the PLUS home page:
   a. Use the PLUS Profile to recreate the HTML files.
   b. Use Internet Explorer to open the PLUS home page, and then view the Payment Statistics by Date data. Verify that the new record (for Payment# 10106) has been included in the statistics shown in the query results.
   c. Print the Payment Statistics by Date HTML file from Internet Explorer.

8. View and then print the Payments By Account Representative report HTML file from Internet Explorer.

9. The local bar association maintains a Web site that lists the new legal firms opening in the area. The HTML file Newfirms, which is located in the Cases folder on your Student Disk, contains this data. Import the Newfirms HTML file as an Access table:
   a. Choose the option for using the column headings as field names in the table.
   b. Let Access assign the primary key.
   c. Name the new table Prospects.
   d. Open the Prospects table, resize all datasheet columns to fit the data, and then print the table.
   e. Close and save the table.

10. The firm Dupont Investments has a Web site it uses to advertise its practice. The firm's home page HTML file is named Dupont and is stored in the Cases folder on your Student Disk. Add a hyperlink field to the Prospects table.

Name the field Website. Enter a hyperlink for the Dupont Investments record to the Dupont HTML file on your Student Disk.

11. Click the hyperlink for the Dupont Investments record and view the Dupont HTML file. Print the Web page.

12. Close and save the Payments database, and then exit Access.

3. Best Friends Noah and Sheila Warnick want to publish some of the Walks database data on the office intranet. Specifically, they want to publish the Walker table and the Walkers report as Web pages. They ask you to complete the following:

1. Make sure your Student Disk is in the appropriate disk drive, start Access, and then open the Walks database located in the Cases folder on your Student Disk.

2. Use the Publish to the Web Wizard to create a home page:
   a. Save the Walker table and the Walkers report as HTML files.
   b. Do not use a template for the files.
   c. Choose the static page format for the files.
   d. Publish the files in the Cases folder on your Student Disk.
   e. Use the Default name for the home page.
   f. Do not save your choices in a profile.

3. Use Internet Explorer to do the following:
   a. Open the Default home page, and then view both the Walker table and the Walkers report.
   b. Print the Walker HTML file from Internet Explorer.

4. Use the Publish to the Web Wizard to create a home page again:
   a. Save the Walker Distance query and the Walkers report as HTML files.
   b. Use the Walkstbl template for the Walker Distance query and the Walksrpt template for the Walkers report. Both templates are located in the Cases folder on your Student Disk.
   c. Choose the static page format for the files.
   d. Publish the files in the Cases folder on your Student Disk.
   e. Use the name Walks for the home page.
   f. Save your choices as a profile named Walks Profile.

5. Use Internet Explorer to open the Walks home page, and then view both the Walker Distance data and the Walkers report.

6. Add the record shown in Figure 7-37 to the Walker table in the Walks database.

Figure 7-37 ◄

WalkerID	LastName	FirstName	Phone	Distance
226	Cunningham	Carie	881-3117	2.0

7. Use the Publish to the Web Wizard to update the Walks home page:
   a. Use the Walks Profile to recreate the HTML files.
   b. Use Internet Explorer to open the Walks home page, and then view the Walker Distance data. Verify that the new record (for WalkerID 226) has been included in the query results.
   c. Print the Walker Distance HTML file from Internet Explorer.

8. View and then print the Walkers report HTML file from Internet Explorer.

9. Noah is interested in contacting several local malls to hold "mall walk" events as fundraisers. The file Malls, which is stored in the Cases folder on your Student Disk, is the HTML file from a Web site that publishes a list of local malls and their managers. Import the Malls HTML file as an Access table:
   a. Choose the option for using the column headings as field names in the table.
   b. Let Access assign the primary key.

   c. Name the new table Malls.
   d. Open the Malls table, resize all datasheet columns to fit the data, and then print the table.
   e. Close and save the table.

10. The file Southgat is the HTML file from a Web site for the Southgate Mall. Add a hyperlink field to the Malls table. Name the field Home Pages. Add a hyperlink for the Southgate Mall record to the Southgat HTML file in the Cases folder on your Student Disk.

11. Click the Southgate Mall hyperlink to view the Southgate Mall home page. Print the home page.

12. Close the Walks database, and then exit Access.

4. Lopez Lexus Dealerships Maria and Hector Lopez have established an intranet for their dealerships. They want you to publish some of the Lexus database data as HTML files for their dealers to view. Complete the following:

1. Make sure your Student Disk is in the appropriate disk drive, start Access, and then open the Lexus database located in the Cases folder on your Student Disk.

2. Use the Publish to the Web Wizard to create a home page:
   a. Save the Cars table and the Cars by Model and Year report as HTML files.
   b. Do not use a template for the files.
   c. Choose the static page format for the files.
   d. Publish the files in the Cases folder on your Student Disk.
   e. Use Cars as the name for the home page.
   f. Do not save your choices in a profile.

3. Use Internet Explorer to do the following:
   a. Open the Cars home page, and then view both the Cars table and the Cars by Model and Year report.
   b. Print the Cars HTML file from Internet Explorer.

4. Use the Publish to the Web Wizard to create a home page again:
   a. Save the Car Statistics by Location query and the Cars by Model and Year report as HTML files.
   b. Use the Lopeztbl template for the Car Statistics by Location query and the Lopezrpt template for the Cars by Model and Year report. Both templates are located in the Cases folder on your Student Disk.
   c. Choose the static page format for the files.
   d. Publish the files in the Cases folder on your Student Disk.
   e. Use the name Cars for the home page.
   f. Save your choices as a profile named Lexus Profile.

5. Use Internet Explorer to open the Cars home page, and then view both the Car Statistics by Location data and the Cars by Model and Year report.

6. Add the record shown in Figure 7-38 to the Cars table in the Lexus database.

Figure 7-38 ◀

VehicleID	Manufacturer	Model	Class	Transmission	Year	LocationCode	Cost	SellingPrice
PAJ9B	Lexus	SC400	S3	A4	1999	Amarillo	$37,600.00	$43,000.00

7. Use the Publish to the Web Wizard to update the Cars home page:
   a. Use the Lexus Profile to recreate the HTML files.
   b. Use Internet Explorer to open the Cars home page, and then view the Cars by Model and Year data. Verify that the new record has been included in the report.

   c. Print the Cars by Model and Year HTML file from Internet Explorer.

8. View and then print the Car Statistics by Location HTML file from Internet Explorer.

9. The Mileage HTML file on your Student Disk contains fuel mileage data for Lexus models. Import the Mileage HTML file as a new table in the Lexus database:
   a. Choose the option for using the column headings as field names in the table.
   b. Let Access assign the primary key.
   c. Name the new table Mileage.
   d. Open the Mileage table, resize all datasheet columns to fit the data, and then print the table.
   e. Close and save the table.

10. The Word document named Reviews, which is stored in the Cases folder on your Student Disk, contains a bookmark for each Lexus model. Add a hyperlink field named Reviews to the Mileage table. Add hyperlink field values for each of the records in the table, using the bookmarks to link to the named locations in the Reviews document.

11. Click the hyperlink for the LS400 model. Use the pointer to select the comments for just that model, and then print the selected text. (*Hint:* Use the Print command on the File menu.)

12. Close the Lexus database, and then exit Access.

Answers to Quick Check Questions

SESSION 5.1

1 A Lookup Wizard field lets you select a value from a list of possible values, making data entry easier.

2 the Like comparison operator

3 The asterisk is a wildcard that represents any string of characters in a pattern match query.

4 Use the In comparison operator to define a condition with two or more values.

5 Use the Not logical operator to negate a criterion.

6 when you want the user to be prompted to enter the selection criteria when the query runs

SESSION 5.2

1 A bound control is linked to a field in the underlying table or query; an unbound control is not.

2 Position the pointer anywhere on the border of the control, then drag the control and its attached label box.

3 Right-click the label, click Properties on the shortcut menu, click the Format tab, edit the existing label in the Caption text box or double-click it to select the current value and then type a new caption.

4 Select the control, position the pointer on a sizing handle, and then click and drag the pointer.

5 The Form Header section allows you to add titles, instructions, command buttons, and other information to the top of your form.

6 Open the form in Design view, click the Image button on the toolbox, position the pointer at the location for the upper-left corner of the picture, click the left mouse button, select the picture file, click OK.

SESSION 5.3

1 Open the form in Design view, click the Tab Control button on the toolbox, position the pointer in the form at the location for the upper-left corner of the tab control, click the left mouse button.

2 Click a label, press and hold down the Shift key and click the other labels, click Format, point to Align, click Right.

3 Double-click the subform object.

4 Filter By Form finds records that match multiple selection criteria using the same Access logical and comparison operators that you use in queries.

5 Save the filter as a query, and then apply the query to a form.

6 Opening a query runs the query and displays the results in Datasheet view. Applying a query to a form opens the query and displays the results in the form.

SESSION 6.1

1 The Report Header section appears once at the beginning of a report. The Page Header section appears at the top of each page of a report. The Group Header section appears once at the beginning of a new group of records. The Detail section appears once for each record in the underlying table or query. The Group Footer section appears once at the end of a group of records. The Report Footer section appears once at the end of the report. The Page Footer section appears at the bottom of each page of a report.

2 A custom report is a report you make by modifying a report created by AutoReport or the Report Wizard, or by creating a report from scratch in Design view.

3 The Report window in Design view has many of the same components as the Form window in Design view, including a Properties button, a Field List button, and a Toolbox button on the toolbar. Both windows also have horizontal and vertical rulers, a grid, and a Formatting toolbar. Unlike the Form window in Design view, which initially displays only the Detail section on a blank form, the Report window also displays a Page Header section and a Page Footer section.

4 The Caption property for an object determines the text displayed in the object. You would change the Caption property value for an object if the default value is difficult to read or understand.

5 Click an object, hold down Shift and click the other objects, click Format, point to Align, click Left.

6 Clicking the Zoom button changes the size of the page displayed in Print Preview.

SESSION 6.2

1 a field from the underlying table or query by which records are grouped in a report.

2 Use the Text Box tool to create a text box in a form or report.

3 Type =Date() in the text box.

4 Click Insert, click Page Numbers, specify the format, position, and alignment of the page number, click OK.

5 The Sorting and Grouping button displays the Sorting and Grouping dialog box, which allows you to specify sorting and grouping fields for a report.

6 Place a text box in the Group Footer or Report Footer section. In the text box, enter the expression =Sum([*fieldname*]) where *fieldname* is the name of the field you want to total.

7 Hiding duplicate values makes the report easier to read; duplicate values clutter up the report.

SESSION 6.3

1 You embed or link objects in an Access report to include objects created by other programs, including objects that you cannot create in Access (for example, charts).

2 An embedded object preserves its connection to the program in which it was created. Any changes you make in the object are reflected in the Access embedded file, not in the original file. A linked object preserves its connection to the original source file. Any changes you make in the object are reflected in both the linked file in Access and the original file.

3 OLE stands for Object Linking and Embedding; a program that supports OLE can create objects that can be embedded or linked in another program.

4 Insert the object from a file and select the Link check box.

5 You use the source program in which the object was originally created.

6 Each linked object is updated automatically when the report is opened. To update links manually, click Edit, click OLE/DDE Links, select the link (or links) to update, click Update Now, click Close.

7 Select the table or query in the Database window or open the table or query in Datasheet view, click Tools, point to Office Links, click Analyze It with MS Excel.

SESSION 7.1

1 HTML stands for HyperText Markup Language, the language used to create World Wide Web documents.

2 the collection of HTML documents stored on Web servers linked through the Internet

3 A Web browser is a program used to view HTML documents.

4 A hyperlink links one Web document to another.

5 A template is a file that contains HTML instructions for creating a Web page together with special instructions that tell Access where to place the Access data on the page.

6 You can use a saved profile to recreate HTML documents without having to reenter your choices.

SESSION 7.2

1 Access can import HTML data that is formatted as a table or as a list.

2 In the Insert Hyperlink dialog box, enter the name of the location in the Named location in file text box.

3 A bookmark is a named location in a Microsoft Word document.

4 Typing a hyperlink value directly into a field allows you to specify only the hyperlink address. The Insert Hyperlink dialog box also allows you to specify a named location in the hyperlinked file.

5 URL stands for uniform resource locator; a URL is an Internet address.

6 Click the hyperlink field value to open the hyperlinked document or object.

Microsoft®
Access 97

LEVEL III

TUTORIALS

Read This **Before You Begin**

STUDENT DISKS

To complete Access 97 Tutorials 8–10, you need five Student Disks. Your instructor will either provide you with Student Disks or ask you to make your own.

If you are supposed to make your own Student Disks, you will need five blank, formatted high-density disks. You will need to copy a set of folders from a file server or standalone computer onto your disks. Your instructor will tell you which computer, drive letter, and folders contain the files you need. The following table shows you which folders go on each of your disks, so that you will have enough disk space to complete all the tutorials, Tutorial Assignments, Case Problems, and Additional Cases:

Student Disk	Write this on the disk label	Put these folders on the disk
1	Student Disk 1: Access 97 Tutorials 8–10 Tutorials	Tutorial
2	Student Disk 2: Access 97 Tutorials 8–10 Tutorial Assignments	TAssign
3	Student Disk 3: Access 97 Tutorials 8–10 Case Problems 1 and 2	Cases from Disk 3 folder
4	Student Disk 4: Access 97 Tutorials 8–10 Case Problems 3 and 4	Cases from Disk 4 folder
5	Student Disk 5: Access 97 Additional Cases	AddCases

When you begin each tutorial, be sure you are using the correct Student Disk. See the inside front or inside back cover of this book for more information on Student Disk files, or ask your instructor or technical support person for assistance.

USING YOUR OWN COMPUTER

If you are going to work through Tutorials 8–10 using your own computer, you need:

■ **Computer System** Microsoft Windows 95 or Microsoft Windows NT Workstation 4.0 (or a later version) and Microsoft Access 97 must be installed on your computer. Tutorials 8–10 assume a complete installation of Microsoft Access 97.

■ **Student Disks** Ask your instructor or lab manager for details on how to get the Student Disks. You will not be able to complete the tutorials or end-of-tutorial assignments in this book using your own computer until you have Student Disks. The Student Files may also be obtained electronically over the Internet. See the inside front or inside back cover of this book for more details.

To complete Access 97 Tutorials 8–10, your students must use a set of files on five Student Disks. These files are included in the Instructor's Resource Kit, and they may also be obtained electronically over the Internet. See the inside front or inside back cover of this book for more details. Follow the instructions in the Readme file to copy the files to your server or standalone computer. You can view the Readme file using WordPad.

Once the files are copied, you can make Student Disks for the students yourself, or you can tell students where to find the files so they can make their own Student Disks. Make sure the files get correctly copied onto the Student Disks by following the instructions in the Student Disks section above, which will ensure that students have enough disk space to complete all the tutorials and end-of-tutorial assignments. *At the end of Tutorial 9, instructions are provided for compacting the database students use throughout the tutorials. Encourage students to follow these instructions to make sure that they have sufficient space on their Student Disks, particularly if they are not working from a hard disk or a network.*

COURSE TECHNOLOGY STUDENT FILES

You are granted a license to copy the Student Files to any computer or computer network used by students who have purchased this book.

Using Briefcase Replication, Query Wizards, and Action Queries

Enhancing User Interaction with the Restaurant Database

OBJECTIVES

In this tutorial you will:

■ Use Briefcase replication to create a Design Master and replica of a database

■ Synchronize the Design Master and replica databases

■ Use Query Wizards to create a crosstab query, a find duplicates query, and a find unmatched query

■ Create a top values query

■ Create action queries

■ Join a table using a self-join

■ View SQL query statements

Valle Coffee

CASE

Ten years ago Leonard Valle became president of Algoman Imports, a small distributor of inexpensive coffee beans to supermarkets in western Michigan. Since that time, Leonard has transformed the company into a popular distributor of gourmet coffees to restaurants and offices. He took over company ownership, changed the company name to Valle Coffee, and expanded its market area to include Indiana and Ohio.

Leonard has incorporated the use of computers in all aspects of the business including financial management, inventory, production, and sales. The company has developed the Restaurant database of customer information and uses **Microsoft Access 97** (or simply **Access**) to manage it.

The Restaurant database contains tables, queries, forms, and reports. Barbara Hennessey, office manager, uses the Restaurant database to keep track of invoices sent to customers. She also periodically publishes tables and reports as HTML files on the company intranet to keep others updated on company activity. Kim Carpenter, director of marketing, uses the Restaurant database to keep track of marketing information.

Leonard, Barbara, and Kim have found the Restaurant database to be very useful. They have asked you to continue to enhance the database by creating some more advanced queries. Also, Kim is leaving on a business trip to meet with potential customers. During her trip, she wants to have access to the Restaurant database so that she can record information about new customers immediately if any of the potential customers decide to open accounts with Valle Coffee.

SESSION

8.1

In this session, you will use My Briefcase to create a replica of the Restaurant database. You will make changes to the data in the Briefcase replica and update the Design Master. You will also use Query Wizards to create a crosstab query, a find duplicates query, and a find unmatched query. Finally, you will create a top values query.

Creating a Briefcase Replica of a Database

Kim wants to take a copy of the Restaurant database with her on her business trip. She wants to be sure that while she is away, any changes that she or anyone else makes to the database will be updated, keeping the database accurate and current.

If you simply created a copy of the Restaurant database file and gave it to Kim, her copy would not include any changes made by other Valle Coffee employees while she is away, nor would the changes she makes to her copy of the database be included in the original database. Instead, you'll create a Briefcase replica of the database. The **My Briefcase** feature of Access creates a special copy of a database called a **replica**. When you create a Briefcase replica of a database, the original copy of the database becomes the **Design Master**. The Design Master and all of its replicas are called the **replica set**. Access adds special tables and fields to the Design Master database to keep track of changes made to data and to the design of the database. Anyone using the Design Master can make changes to the design of database tables, queries, and other objects. Any changes in the data or design of database objects in the Design Master can then be automatically updated in the replica. Anyone using a replica of the database can make changes to the data in any of the database tables. A replica prevents the user from changing the structure or the design of an existing table, query, or other database object. Any changes in the data in any replicas can be updated automatically in the Design Master. The process of updating the Design Master and the replicas is called **synchronization**.

REFERENCE window	**CREATING A BRIEFCASE REPLICA OF A DATABASE**
	■ Drag the database file from the desktop into My Briefcase. Access converts the file, adding special tables, fields, and properties, to create the Design Master.
	■ Select the copy you want to make the Design Master, and then click the OK button.

You need to make a replica of the Restaurant database to give to Kim.

To create a replica of the Restaurant database:

1. Make sure you have created your copy of the Access Student Disk, and then place your Student Disk in the appropriate disk drive.

   TROUBLE? If you don't have a Student Disk, you need to get one before you can proceed. Your instructor will either give you one or ask you to make your own. (See your instructor for information.) In either case, be sure you have made a copy of your Student Disk before you begin; in this way, the original Student Disk files will be available on the copied disk in case you need to start over because of an error or problem.

2. On the Windows 95 desktop, use either My Computer or Windows Explorer to open the Tutorial folder on your Student Disk.

3. Drag the Restaurant database file from the Tutorial folder to My Briefcase. Access begins making a replica copy of the Restaurant database and opens a dialog box asking if you want to continue. See Figure 8-1.

Figure 8-1 ◄
First Briefcase
dialog box

My Briefcase ——

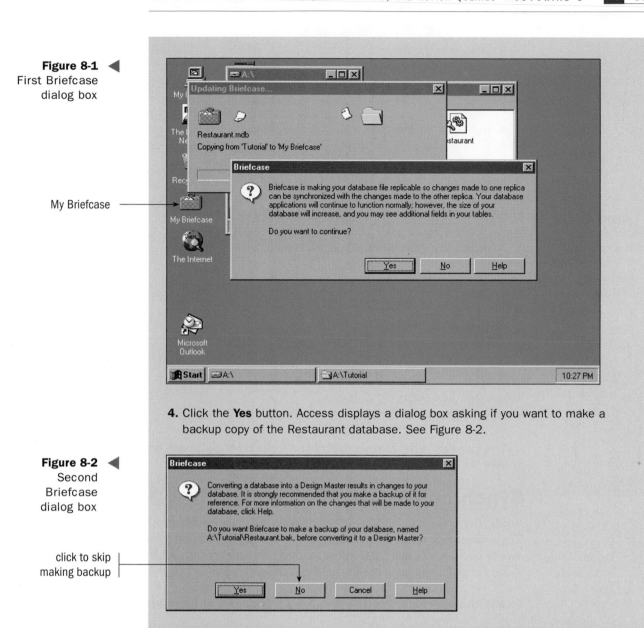

4. Click the **Yes** button. Access displays a dialog box asking if you want to make a backup copy of the Restaurant database. See Figure 8-2.

Figure 8-2 ◄
Second
Briefcase
dialog box

click to skip
making backup

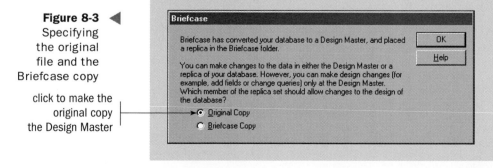

Access can make a backup copy of your database on your Student Disk. This backup can serve as an extra copy of the Restaurant database in case anything goes wrong when Access creates the replica. Your Student Disk does not have enough space for a backup copy of the Restaurant database, so you will not make a backup copy.

5. Click the **No** button. After a few moments, Access displays a dialog box that allows you to choose which copy of the database will become the Design Master and which will be the Briefcase replica. See Figure 8-3.

Figure 8-3 ◄
Specifying
the original
file and the
Briefcase copy

click to make the
original copy
the Design Master

Briefcase

Briefcase has converted your database to a Design Master, and placed a replica in the Briefcase folder.

OK

Help

You can make changes to the data in either the Design Master or a replica of your database. However, you can make design changes (for example, add fields or change queries) only at the Design Master. Which member of the replica set should allow changes to the design of the database?

► ⦿ Original Copy
   ○ Briefcase Copy

6. Make sure the **Original Copy** option button is selected. This will make the Restaurant database on your Student Disk the Design Master.

7. Click the **OK** button. Access completes making the replica of the Restaurant database.

8. Right-click **My Briefcase** to display the shortcut menu, and then click **Open**. My Briefcase contains the replica of the Restaurant database. See Figure 8-4.

   TROUBLE? If you cannot see the Restaurant replica, click View on the menu bar, and then click Details.

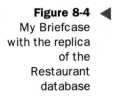

Figure 8-4
My Briefcase with the replica of the Restaurant database

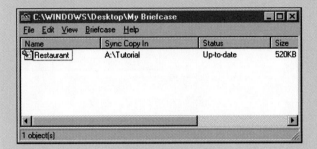

9. Click the **Close** button ☒ on the My Briefcase window to close it.

10. Close any other open windows.

You can now give Kim a copy of the Restaurant database Briefcase replica on a disk to take with her on her trip.

Synchronizing the Replica and the Design Master

While she is on her trip, Kim visits several of the restaurants listed in the Potential Customers table of the Restaurant database. Her visit to Pesto Place is successful, and the owner decides to open an account with Valle Coffee. Kim adds a new record for Pesto Place in the Customer table of the Restaurant database.

To add the new record to the Briefcase replica of the Restaurant database:

1. Start Access. In the Microsoft Access dialog box, make sure the **Open an Existing Database** option button is selected and that **More Files** is highlighted, and then click the **OK** button. Access displays the Open dialog box.

2. Click the **Look in** list arrow, and then click **My Briefcase**.

3. Make sure **Restaurant** is selected in the list box, and then click the **Open** button. Access opens the Restaurant database replica and displays the Database window. See Figure 8-5.

Figure 8-5
Database
window for the
Restaurant
database
replica

indicates an object
in a replica or
Design Master

indicates that this
is a replica copy

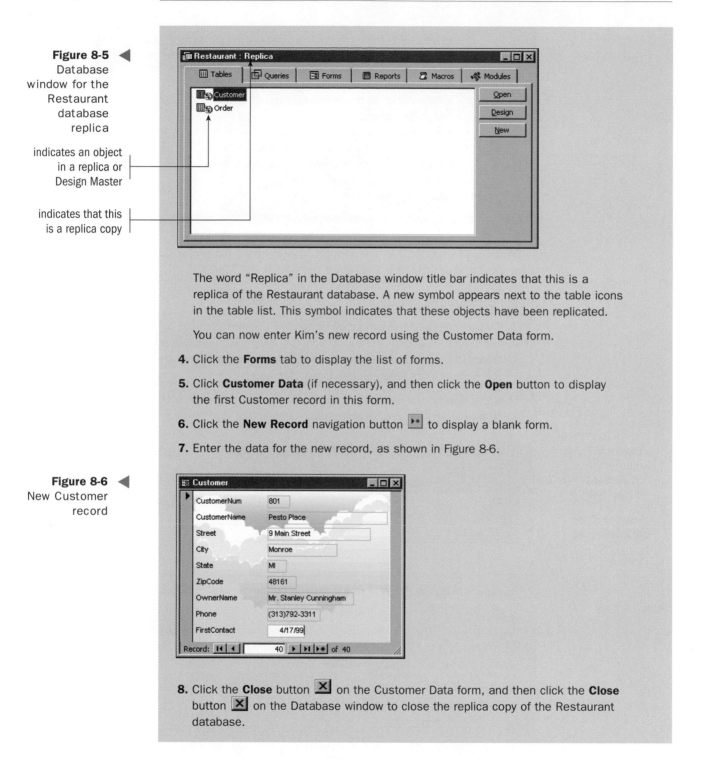

The word "Replica" in the Database window title bar indicates that this is a replica of the Restaurant database. A new symbol appears next to the table icons in the table list. This symbol indicates that these objects have been replicated.

You can now enter Kim's new record using the Customer Data form.

4. Click the **Forms** tab to display the list of forms.

5. Click **Customer Data** (if necessary), and then click the **Open** button to display the first Customer record in this form.

6. Click the **New Record** navigation button ▶* to display a blank form.

7. Enter the data for the new record, as shown in Figure 8-6.

Figure 8-6 ◀
New Customer
record

Customer	
CustomerNum	801
CustomerName	Pesto Place
Street	9 Main Street
City	Monroe
State	MI
ZipCode	48161
OwnerName	Mr. Stanley Cunningham
Phone	(313)792-3311
FirstContact	4/17/99

Record: ◀◀ ◀ 40 ▶ ▶◀ ▶* of 40

8. Click the **Close** button ✕ on the Customer Data form, and then click the **Close** button ✕ on the Database window to close the replica copy of the Restaurant database.

The Briefcase replica of the Restaurant database now contains a new record that is not recorded in the Design Master. When Kim returns from her trip, you can update the Design Master by synchronizing the Design Master and the replica. The synchronizing process compares the Design Master to the replica and checks for any differences. Access updates the Design Master with any changes that have been made to the data in the replica, and updates the replica with any changes that have been made to the data or the design of any database objects in the Design Master. This process ensures that the Design Master and the replica are consistent.

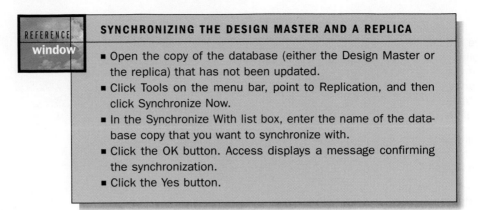

REFERENCE window

SYNCHRONIZING THE DESIGN MASTER AND A REPLICA

- Open the copy of the database (either the Design Master or the replica) that has not been updated.
- Click Tools on the menu bar, point to Replication, and then click Synchronize Now.
- In the Synchronize With list box, enter the name of the database copy that you want to synchronize with.
- Click the OK button. Access displays a message confirming the synchronization.
- Click the Yes button.

You need to synchronize the Design Master of the Restaurant database with the replica Kim used to enter the new Customer record.

To synchronize the Design Master and the replica:

1. Click the **Open Database** button 📂 on the Database toolbar, and then open the Restaurant database (the Design Master) in the Tutorial folder on your Student Disk. Notice that the title bar of the Database window shows that this copy of the Restaurant database is the Design Master.

2. Click **Tools** on the menu bar, point to **Replication**, and then click **Synchronize Now**. The Synchronize Database dialog box opens. See Figure 8-7.

Figure 8-7 ◄
Synchronize Database dialog box

location of the Briefcase replica

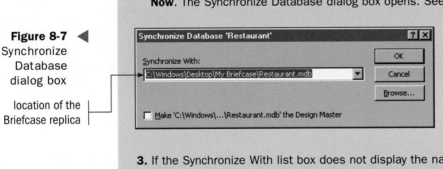

3. If the Synchronize With list box does not display the name of the Restaurant replica in My Briefcase, use the Browse button to select the Restaurant replica in My Briefcase.

   TROUBLE? The path statement in the Synchronize With list box on your screen might not match the one in the figure. Be sure that it is accurate for your system and the location of your database files.

4. Click the **OK** button. After a few seconds Access displays a dialog box indicating that the synchronization is complete.

5. Click the **Yes** button to close and reopen the Restaurant database.

The Design Master and the replica are now synchronized. The new record that Kim added to the replica copy of the Restaurant database has been added to the Design Master. You can now open the Customer table using the Customer Data form and display the new record in the Design Master.

To find and display the new record in the Restaurant table:

1. Click the **Forms** tab to display the list of forms.

2. Click **Customer Data** and then click the **Open** button. Access displays the first Customer record in the form.

3. Click the **Last Record** navigation button ▶| to display the last record. This is the new record that Kim added (see Figure 8-6).

4. Click the **Close** button ☒ on the Form window to close it and return to the Database window.

Now that you have synchronized the databases, you can delete the replica of the Restaurant database in My Briefcase. You can easily create another replica whenever Kim needs to take the database with her on future business trips. Even though you delete the replica of the Restaurant database, the original Design Master of the database remains a Design Master. Because there can be many replicas of a database in a replica set, the Design Master keeps track of any changes you make to the database so that other replicas can be synchronized at any time.

To delete the Briefcase replica of the Restaurant database:

1. Click the **Minimize** button ▬| on the Access window to minimize it.

2. Right-click **My Briefcase** to display the shortcut menu, and then click **Open**. The My Briefcase window opens.

3. Right-click the **Restaurant** database, and then click **Delete**. The Confirm File Delete dialog box opens.

4. Click the **Yes** button to delete the Briefcase replica of the Restaurant database. Windows 95 moves the Briefcase replica of the Restaurant database to the Recycle Bin.

5. Click the **Close** button ☒ on the My Briefcase window to close it.

You are now ready to create queries to provide information for Leonard and Barbara. To do so, you will use different Access Query Wizards.

First, Leonard is interested in learning how much business Valle Coffee is doing in each state. He also wants to know how the total business in each state varies by month. He asks you to create a crosstab query using the Crosstab Query Wizard to provide the information he needs.

Creating a Crosstab Query

A **crosstab query** performs aggregate function calculations on the values of one database field and displays the results in a spreadsheet format. (Recall that aggregate functions perform arithmetic operations on the records in a database.) Figure 8-8 lists the aggregate functions you can use in a crosstab query. A crosstab query can also display one additional aggregate function value that summarizes each row's set of values. The crosstab query uses one or more fields for the row headings on the left and one field for the column headings at the top.

Figure 8-8 ◀
Aggregate
functions
used in
crosstab
queries

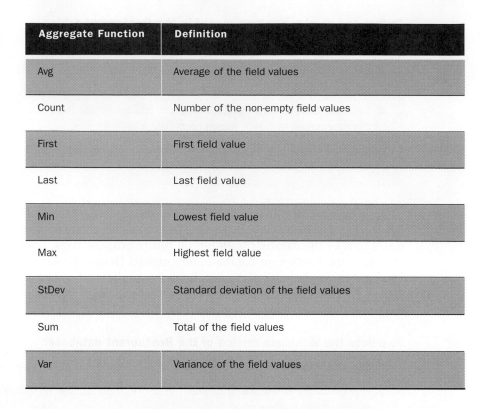

Aggregate Function	Definition
Avg	Average of the field values
Count	Number of the non-empty field values
First	First field value
Last	Last field value
Min	Lowest field value
Max	Highest field value
StDev	Standard deviation of the field values
Sum	Total of the field values
Var	Variance of the field values

Figure 8-9 shows two query results—the first from a select query and the second from a related crosstab query. The title bar indicates the type of query.

Figure 8-9 ◀
Contrasting
a select
query with a
crosstab query

individual MI records

individual
3/15/99 records

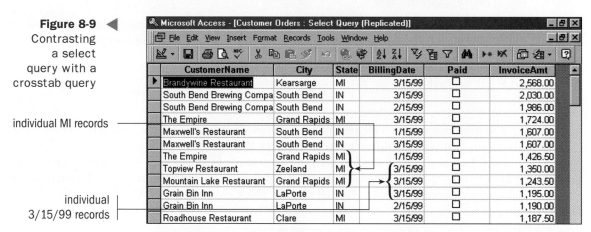

one column for MI

one row for 3/15/99

summarized value

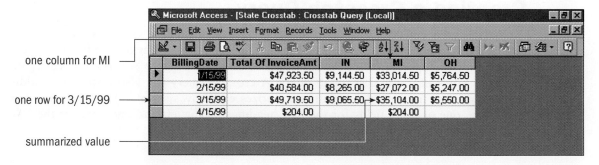

Both queries are based on the Customer Orders query, which joins the Customer and Order tables, but the crosstab query provides more valuable information. For each record in the Customer table, the select query displays the CustomerName, City, and State fields from the Customer table and the BillingDate, Paid, and InvoiceAmt fields from the Order table.

Notice that there are many rows for BillingDate 3/15/99, for example, one row for each invoice sent on that date. Some rows with this BillingDate value might not be currently visible on the screen. On the other hand, the crosstab query displays just one row for 3/15/99. The BillingDate field in the leftmost column identifies each row, and the field values for the State field identify the rightmost columns. The crosstab query uses the Sum aggregate function on the InvoiceAmt field to produce the displayed values in the remainder of the query results. The second column, labeled Total Of InvoiceAmt, represents the total of the InvoiceAmt values for each row.

Using the crosstab query results, Leonard can quickly see the amount of business done each month and the amount of business done in each state.

The quickest way to create a crosstab query is to use the **Crosstab Query Wizard**, which guides you through the steps for creating crosstab queries. You could also change a select query to a crosstab query using the Query Type button on the Query Design toolbar. (Refer to the Help system for more information on creating a crosstab query without using a wizard.)

REFERENCE window

USING THE CROSSTAB QUERY WIZARD

- Click the Queries tab to display the Queries list, and then click the New button.
- Click Crosstab Query Wizard and then click the OK button.
- Complete the wizard dialog boxes to select the table or query on which to base the crosstab query, select the row heading field or fields, select the column heading field or fields, select the calculation field and its aggregate function, and enter a name for the crosstab query.

The crosstab query you will create is like the one shown in Figure 8-9. The crosstab query has the following characteristics:

- The Customer Orders query in the Restaurant database is the basis for the new crosstab query; it includes the CustomerName, City, State, BillingDate, Paid, and InvoiceAmt fields.

- The BillingDate field from the Order table is the leftmost column and identifies each crosstab query row.

- The field values that appear in the Customer table for the State field identify the rightmost columns of the crosstab query.

- The crosstab query applies the Sum aggregate function to the InvoiceAmt field from the Order table and displays the resulting total values in the State columns of the query results. If one state has two or more invoices on the same billing date, then the sum of the invoice amounts appears in the intersecting cell of the query results.

- The total of the InvoiceAmt values appears for each row in a column with the heading Total Of InvoiceAmt.

You are now ready to create the crosstab query based on the Customer Orders query. The crosstab query will show how much business Valle Coffee is doing in each state and how the total business in each state varies by month.

To create the crosstab query using the Crosstab Query Wizard:

1. Click the **Microsoft Access** button on the taskbar, and then click the **Queries** tab to display the Queries list.

2. Click the **New** button to open the New Query dialog box.

3. Click **Crosstab Query Wizard** and then click the **OK** button. The first Crosstab Query Wizard dialog box opens.

4. Click the **Queries** option button to display the list of queries in the Restaurant database, and then click **Customer Orders**. See Figure 8-10.

Figure 8-10 ◀
Choosing the
table or query
for the
crosstab query

Customer Orders
query selected

click to display
queries list

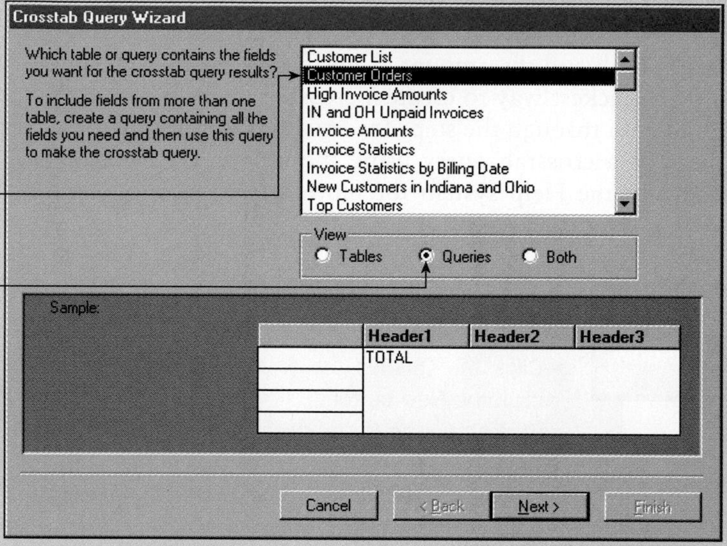

5. Click the **Next** button to display the next Crosstab Query Wizard dialog box, which allows you to choose the field or fields for the row headings. Because Leonard wants the crosstab query to display one row for each BillingDate value, you will select that field for the row headings.

6. In the Available Fields list box, click **BillingDate** and then click the [▸] button to move BillingDate to the Selected Fields list box. When you select a field, Access changes the sample crosstab query in the bottom of the dialog box to illustrate your choice.

7. Click the **Next** button to open the next Crosstab Query Wizard dialog box, in which you select the field values that serve as column headings. Leonard wants to see the invoice amounts by state, so you need to select the State field for the column headings.

8. Click **State** in the list box, and then click the **Next** button.

In the next Crosstab Query Wizard dialog box, you choose the field that will be calculated for each row and column intersection and the function to use for the calculation. The results of the calculation will appear in the row and column intersections of the query results.

9. Click **InvoiceAmt** in the Fields list box, and then click **Sum** in the Functions list box. Be sure that the check box next to **Yes, include row sums** is selected. This option creates a column showing the overall totals for the values in each row of the query results. See Figure 8-11.

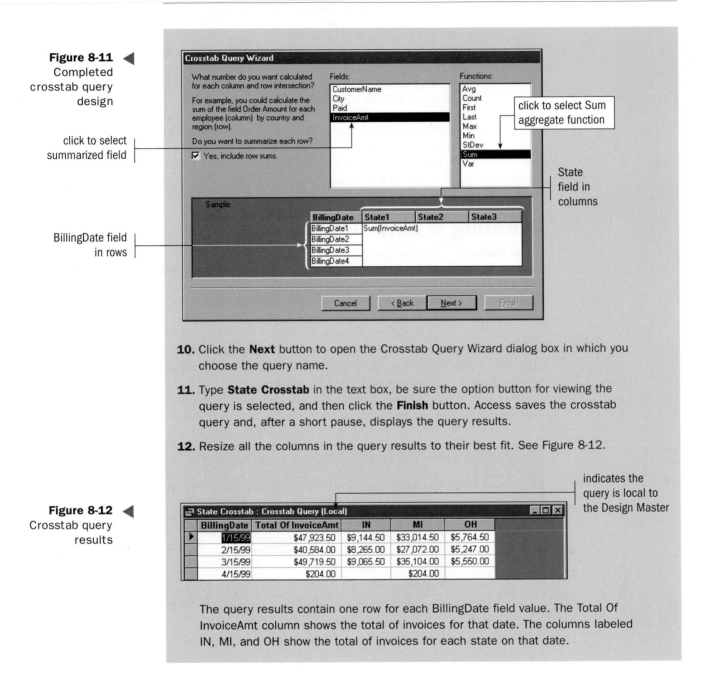

Figure 8-11
Completed
crosstab query
design

click to select
summarized field

BillingDate field
in rows

click to select Sum
aggregate function

State
field in
columns

10. Click the **Next** button to open the Crosstab Query Wizard dialog box in which you choose the query name.

11. Type **State Crosstab** in the text box, be sure the option button for viewing the query is selected, and then click the **Finish** button. Access saves the crosstab query and, after a short pause, displays the query results.

12. Resize all the columns in the query results to their best fit. See Figure 8-12.

Figure 8-12
Crosstab query
results

indicates the
query is local to
the Design Master

State Crosstab : Crosstab Query (Local)

BillingDate	Total Of InvoiceAmt	IN	MI	OH
1/15/99	$47,923.50	$9,144.50	$33,014.50	$5,764.50
2/15/99	$40,584.00	$8,265.00	$27,072.00	$5,247.00
3/15/99	$49,719.50	$9,065.50	$35,104.00	$5,550.00
4/15/99	$204.00		$204.00	

The query results contain one row for each BillingDate field value. The Total Of InvoiceAmt column shows the total of invoices for that date. The columns labeled IN, MI, and OH show the total of invoices for each state on that date.

Notice that the word "Local" in the query results title bar indicates that this is a query that exists in the Design Master only; it is not part of any replica copy of the database.

Because this query shows the total of invoice amounts for each billing date for each state, Leonard can use the information to track the progress of billings in each state. You can now close the completed query results.

To close the query results:

1. Click the **Close** button ☒ on the Query window to close it.

2. Click the **Yes** button to save the changes and return to the Database window.

Access uses unique icons to represent different types of queries. The icon appearing in the Queries list box to the left of the State Crosstab Query is different from the icon for the select and parameter queries. The State Crosstab Query is not marked with the replication symbol because it is local to this copy of the Restaurant database and has not been replicated, as the other queries have been.

Next, Barbara needs some information from the Restaurant database. She is concerned that several customers in Indiana and Ohio have been slow to pay their invoices, and she wants to contact customers who have missed payments. She wants to contact only those customers who consistently don't pay, so she asks you to find out which customers in those states have failed to pay more than one invoice. To find the information Barbara needs, you'll create a find duplicates query.

Creating a Find Duplicates Query

A **find duplicates** query is a select query that locates duplicate records in a table or query. You can create this type of query using the **Find Duplicates Query Wizard**. The query searches for duplicates based on the fields you choose as you answer the wizard's questions. For example, you might want to display all customers who have the same name, all students who have the same phone number, or all products that have the same description. Using this query, you can locate duplicates and avert potential problems (for example, you might have inadvertently assigned two different numbers to the same product), or you can eliminate duplicates that cost money (for example, you could send just one advertising brochure to all the customers having the same address).

You can answer Barbara's request by using the Find Duplicates Query Wizard to display customers who appear more than once in the IN and OH Unpaid Invoices query.

REFERENCE window	USING THE FIND DUPLICATES QUERY WIZARD
	■ Click the Queries tab to display the Queries list, and then click the New button.
	■ Click Find Duplicates Query Wizard, and then click the OK button.
	■ Complete the wizard dialog boxes to select the table or query on which to base the query, select the field or fields to check for duplicate values, select the additional fields to include in the query results, and enter a name for the query.

You can use the Find Duplicates Query Wizard to create and run a new query to check for duplicate customer names in the IN and OH Unpaid Invoices query results.

To create the query using the Find Duplicates Query Wizard:

1. If necessary, click the **Queries** tab to display the Queries list, and then click the **New** button to open the New Query dialog box.

2. Click **Find Duplicates Query Wizard**, and then click the **OK** button. The Find Duplicates Query Wizard dialog box opens.

3. Click the **Queries** option button to display the list of queries, click **IN and OH Unpaid Invoices**, and then click the **Next** button. Access opens the next Find Duplicates Query Wizard dialog box, in which you choose the fields you want checked for duplicate values.

4. In the Available Fields list box, click **CustomerNum** (if necessary), and then click the ⟩ button to select this field to be checked for duplicate values.

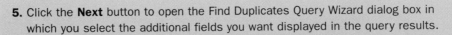

5. Click the **Next** button to open the Find Duplicates Query Wizard dialog box in which you select the additional fields you want displayed in the query results.

   Barbara wants to see the CustomerName and InvoiceAmt fields in the query results so that she can contact these customers about their unpaid invoices.

6. In the Available Fields list box, click **CustomerName**, click the [>] button, click **InvoiceAmt**, and then click the [>] button. Access moves these fields to the Additional query fields list box.

7. Click the **Next** button to open the final Find Duplicates Query Wizard dialog box, in which you enter a name for the query.

8. Type **Late IN and OH Payers** in the text box, be sure the option button for viewing the results is selected, and then click the **Finish** button. Access saves the query and, after a short pause, displays the query results.

9. Resize the query results columns to their best fit. See Figure 8-13. Access displays the records for four customers with more than one unpaid invoice.

Figure 8-13 ◀
Query results
for the Late IN
and OH Payers
query

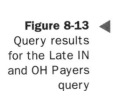

CustomerNum	CustomerName	InvoiceAmt
624	South Bend Brewing Company	2,030.00
624	South Bend Brewing Company	1,986.00
625	Maxwell's Restaurant	1,607.00
625	Maxwell's Restaurant	1,607.00
750	Grain Bin Inn	1,195.00
750	Grain Bin Inn	1,190.00
798	Embers Restaurant	918.00
798	Embers Restaurant	971.00
798	Embers Restaurant	1,004.50

10. Click the **Print** button 🖨 on the Query Datasheet toolbar to print the query results for Barbara.

11. Click the **Save** button 🖫 on the Query Datasheet toolbar to save the query, and then click the **Close** button ☒ on the Query window to close it and return to the Database window.

After you give Barbara the list of late payers, she asks you to find any customers who have never been billed. These are customers who have accounts with Valle Coffee, but who have never placed an order. To create this list, you need to create a find unmatched query.

Creating a Find Unmatched Query

A **find unmatched** query is a select query that finds all the records in a table or query that have no related records in a second table or query. For example, you could display all customers who have not placed orders or all non-degree students who are not currently enrolled in classes. Such a query might help you solicit business from the inactive customers or contact the students to find out their future educational plans. You can use the **Find Unmatched Query Wizard** to create this type of query.

REFERENCE
window

USING THE FIND UNMATCHED QUERY WIZARD

- Click the Queries tab to display the Queries list, and then click the New button.
- Click Find Unmatched Query Wizard, and then click the OK button.
- Complete the wizard dialog boxes to select the table or query on which to base the query, select the table or query that contains the related records, specify the common field in each table or query, select the additional fields to include in the query results, and enter a name for the query.

Barbara wants to know which customers have never been sent an invoice. These customers are inactive, and she will ask Kim to contact them to determine whether they are still interested in ordering from Valle Coffee. Barbara asks you to create a list of any inactive customers. To create this list, you can use the Find Unmatched Query Wizard to display fields from the Customer table, but only when there are no records in the Order table having a matching CustomerNum field value.

To create the query using the Find Unmatched Query Wizard:

1. If necessary, click the **Queries** tab to display the Queries list, and then click the **New** button to open the New Query dialog box.

2. Click **Find Unmatched Query Wizard**, and then click the **OK** button. The first Find Unmatched Query Wizard dialog box opens.

3. Click **Customer** (if necessary) in the list box to select this table. Its records will appear in the query results. Then click the **Next** button to open the dialog box to choose the table that contains the related records.

4. Click **Order** (if necessary) in the list box, and then click the **Next** button to open the next dialog box, in which you choose the common field for both tables. Notice that CustomerNum is highlighted in each list box because it is the common field.

5. Click the ⟨=⟩ button to confirm the common field. The Matching fields text box shows CustomerNum <=> CustomerNum to indicate the common field. See Figure 8-14.

Figure 8-14 ◀
Selecting the common field

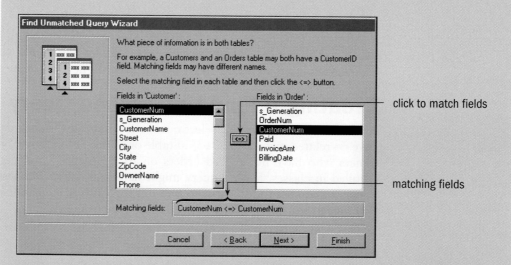

6. Click the **Next** button to open the Find Unmatched Query Wizard dialog box in which you choose the fields you want to see in the query results.

Access

7. Click **CustomerName** and then click the [>] button to select this field. Use the same procedure to select the **OwnerName**, **Phone**, and **FirstContact** fields, and then click the **Next** button to open the final dialog box, in which you enter the query name.

8. Type **Inactive Customers**, make sure the **View the results** option button is selected, and then click the **Finish** button. Access saves the query and, after a short pause, displays the query results. Resize the columns for best fit. See Figure 8-15.

Figure 8-15 ◄
Results of the
Inactive
Customers
query

	CustomerName	OwnerName	Phone	FirstContact
▶	Pesto Place	Mr. Stanley Cunningham	(313)792-3311	4/17/99
✱				

Inactive Customers : Select Query (Local)

The query results include only the record for Pesto Place, the new customer that Kim obtained on her recent trip. No other customers are inactive.

9. Click the **Save** button [🖫] on the Query Datasheet toolbar to save the query design, and then click the **Close** button [✕] on the Query window to close it and return to the Database window.

Barbara now knows that Pesto Place is the only customer who has not placed any orders because it was the only record from the Customer table that did not have a matching record in the Order table. Because Pesto Place is a new customer, Barbara doesn't expect to have an Order record yet, so she does not need to contact Kim about any inactive customers.

Next, Barbara wants to contact those customers who have been placing large orders but who have not paid their invoices. She asks you to create a query to show the largest outstanding invoices. To display the information Barbara wants, you can create a top values query.

Top Values Queries

Whenever you have a query that displays a large group of records, you can limit the number to a more manageable size by showing just the first 10 records, for example. The **Top Values** property for a query lets you limit the number of records in the query results. For the Top Values property, you enter either an integer (such as 10, to show the first 10 records) or a percent (such as 50%, to show the first half).

Suppose you have a select query that displays 45 records. If you want the query results to show only the first five records, you can change the query by entering a Top Values property of either 5 or 10%. If the query contains a sort, Access displays the records sorted in order by the primary sort key. Whenever the last record that Access can display is one of two or more records because they have the same value for the primary sort key, Access displays all the records with matching key values.

REFERENCE
window

CREATING A TOP VALUES QUERY

- Create a select query with the necessary fields and selection criteria.
- Enter the number of records (or percentage of records) you want selected in the Top Values text box on the Query Design toolbar.
- Click the Run button on the Query Design toolbar.

Barbara wants to see the CustomerName, OwnerName, Phone, BillingDate, and InvoiceAmt fields for the 10 largest unpaid invoices. You will create a new query and then use the Top Values property to produce this information for her.

To create the query:

1. From the Queries tab of the Database window, click the **New** button. Make sure that **Design View** is selected, and then click the **OK** button. The Show Table dialog box opens on top of the Query window in Design view.

2. Click **Customer**, click the **Add** button, click **Order**, and then click the **Add** button to add both tables to the Query window. Click the **Close** button to close the Show Table dialog box.

   Now you can add the appropriate fields to the design grid.

3. In the Customer field list, double-click **CustomerName**, double-click **OwnerName**, and then double-click **Phone**, scrolling as necessary, to add these three fields to the design grid.

4. In the Order field list, double-click **Paid**, double-click **InvoiceAmt**, and then double-click **BillingDate**, scrolling as necessary, to add these three fields to the design grid.

5. Click the **Paid Criteria** text box, and then type **=No**. The query will select only unpaid invoices.

   Because all the selected Order records are unpaid, you do not need to show the Paid field values in the query results.

6. Click the **Paid Show** check box to remove the check mark.

7. Scroll right until the InvoiceAmt field is visible, click the right side of the **InvoiceAmt Sort** text box to display the sort order options, and then click **Descending**. The query will display the largest unpaid invoice amounts first.

8. Click the **Run** button [!] on the Query Design toolbar. The query results show the 26 records that represent unpaid invoices. The records appear in descending order sorted by the InvoiceAmt field.

You can now set the Top Values property to limit the query results to the top 10 unpaid invoices, because Barbara wants to focus on the larger outstanding invoices first.

To set the Top Values property of the query:

1. Click the **View** button for Design view [▨] on the Query Datasheet toolbar to switch back to Design view.

2. Double-click the **Top Values** text box on the Query Design toolbar, and then type **10**. See Figure 8-16.

Access

Figure 8-16
Creating the
top values
query

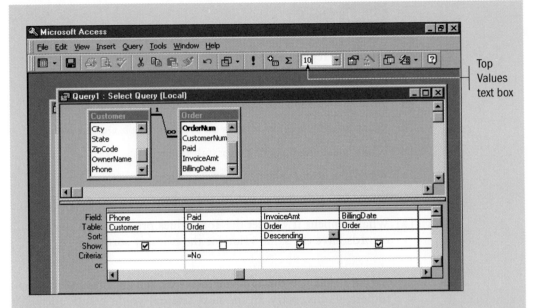

Top
Values
text box

3. Click the **Run** button ! on the Query Design toolbar. Access displays the top 10 largest unpaid invoice records in the query results. See Figure 8-17.

Figure 8-17 ◀
Top values
query results

top 10 records
selected

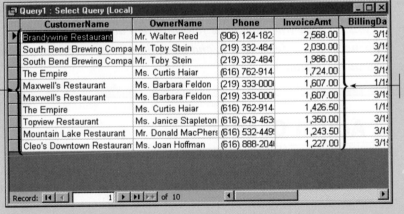

records listed in
descending order
by InvoiceAmt

Barbara asks you to print a copy of the query results so she can contact the customers. Because Barbara will work from the printed results, she does not need you to save the query.

4. Click the **Print** button 🖨 on the Query Datasheet toolbar to print the query results for Barbara.

5. Click the **Close** button ☒ on the Query window, and then click the **No** button when Access asks if you want to save the query changes. Access closes the Query window and returns to the Database window.

1. What is a replica set?

2. How does a Design Master differ from a replica?

3. How can you tell whether the Design Master or a replica copy of a database is open?

4. What does Access do when you synchronize a Design Master and a replica?

5. What is the purpose of a crosstab query?

6. What is a find duplicates query?

7. What does a find unmatched query do?

8. What happens if you set the Top Values property of a query to 2 and the first five records have the same value for the primary sort key?

Barbara will use the information provided by the queries you created to contact customers, as necessary. In the next session, you'll create queries for Leonard and Kim to meet their needs for information about Valle Coffee's restaurant customers.

SESSION 8.2

In this session, you will create four different action queries—a make-table query, an append query, a delete query, and an update query—to change information in the Restaurant database.

Action Queries

Queries can do more than display answers to the questions you ask; they can also perform actions on the data in your database. An **action query** is a query that adds, changes, or deletes multiple table records at one time. For example, if a customer with several unpaid invoices pays all of them at once, Barbara can update all of the customer's Order table records using an action query. Because action queries modify many records in a table at a time, Access allows you to preview the query results before you actually run the query. When the query works correctly, you then save it as an action query.

Access provides four types of action queries: the make-table query, the append query, the delete query, and the update query.

A **make-table query** creates a new table from one or more existing tables. The new table can be an exact copy of the records in an existing table, a subset of the fields and records of an existing table, or a combination of the fields and records from two or more tables. Access does not delete the selected fields and records from the existing tables. You can use make-table queries, for example, to create backup copies of tables or to create customized tables for others to use. The new table reflects data at a point in time; changes made to the underlying tables will not be reflected in the new table. You need to run the make-table query periodically if you want the created table to contain current data.

An **append query** adds records from an existing table or query to the end of another table. For an append query, you choose the fields you want to append from one or more tables or queries; the selected data remains in the original tables. Usually you append records to history tables. A **history table** contains data that is no longer needed for current processing but that might need to be referred to in the future. Tables containing data about cleared bank checks, former employees, inactive customers, and obsolete products are examples of history tables. Because the records you append to a history table are no longer needed for current processing, you can delete the records from the original table.

A **delete query** deletes a group of records from one or more tables. You choose which records you want to delete by entering selection criteria. Deleting records removes them permanently from the database. Quite often, delete queries are run after append queries have added those same records to history tables. This allows you to recapture records from the history tables if they were deleted in error from the original tables.

An **update query** changes selected fields and records in one or more tables. You choose the fields and records you want to change by entering the selection criteria and the update rules. You can use update queries, for example, to increase the salaries of selected employee groups by a specified percent or to change a customer name from one value to another value.

Creating a Make-Table Query

Leonard wants to call some of Valle Coffee's longstanding customers to thank them for their business. He asks you to create a new table containing the CustomerName, OwnerName, and Phone fields from the Customer table records for all customers whose FirstContact date is before January 1, 1992. He wants a new table so he can modify it for notes that he will take when he calls the restaurant owners.

You can create the new table for Leonard by using a make-table query. You can create this query by modifying the Top Customers query already in the Restaurant database. When you use a make-table query, you create a new table. The records in the new table are based on the records in the query's underlying tables. The fields in the new table have the data type and field size of the fields in the query's underlying tables. The new table does not preserve the primary key designation or field properties such as format or lookup properties.

REFERENCE window	CREATING A MAKE-TABLE QUERY
	■ Create a select query with the fields and selection criteria you want in the make-table query.
	■ Click the Run button on the Query Design toolbar to preview the results.
	■ Switch to Design view to make any necessary changes. When the query is correct, click the list arrow for the Query Type button on the Query Design toolbar.
	■ Click Make-Table Query. Access displays the Make Table dialog box.
	■ Type the new table name in the Table Name text box. Make sure the Current Database option button is selected to include the new table in the current database; or, click the Another Database option button and enter the database name in the File Name text box. Then click the OK button.
	■ Click the Run button on the Query Design toolbar.
	■ Click the Yes button to confirm creating the new table.

Now you can create the new table using a make-table query. You'll base the make-table query on the Top Customers query to provide the information Leonard wants in the new table.

To create the make-table query:

1. If you took a break after the previous session, start Access and open the Design Master copy of the Restaurant database in the Tutorial folder on your Student Disk.

2. If necessary, click the **Queries** tab to display the list of queries, click **Top Customers**, and then click the **Design** button. Access opens the Top Customers query in Design view. See Figure 8-18.

Figure 8-18 ◄
Top Customers
query in Design
view

click to select join line ─────

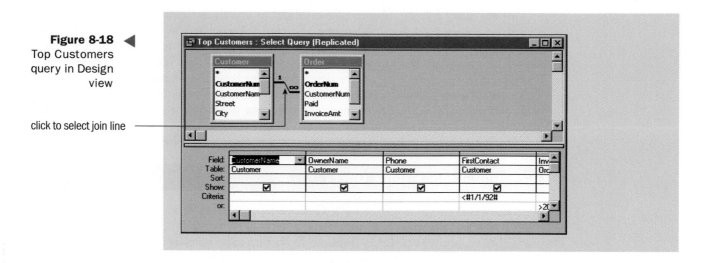

The Top Customers query contains the fields that Leonard wants from the Customer table. However, you do not need the InvoiceAmt field, which comes from the Order table. You will delete the Order table from the query design so that no fields from that table will appear in the query results. At the same time, you will learn how to delete a join line between two tables in a query. Deleting the join line removes the link between the Customer and Order tables for the purposes of this query only; it does not remove the relationship established between the two tables in the Relationships window.

To delete the join line and remove the Order table from the query design:

1. Click the **join line** between the Customer and Order tables, and then press the **Delete** key. The join line disappears. The Customer and Order tables are no longer joined in this query design.

   Because you don't need any fields from the Order table, you can delete the table from the query design.

2. Click anywhere in the Order table field list, and then press the **Delete** key. The Order table field list is removed from the Query window and the InvoiceAmt field is removed from the query design. The query is now ready to be tested. See Figure 8-19.

Figure 8-19 ◄
Modified query
design

Query Type button ─────

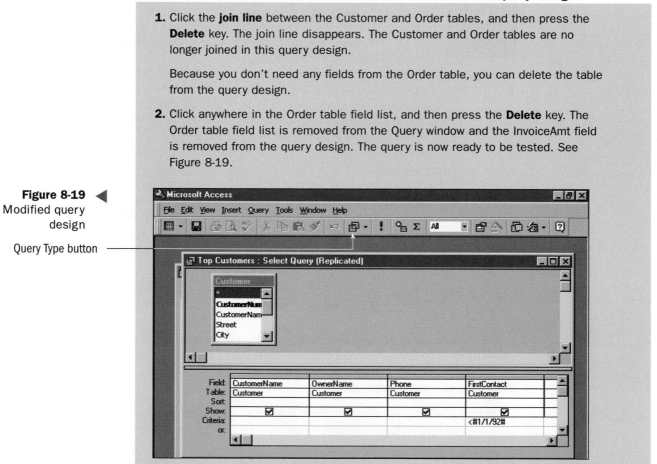

3. Click the **Run** button ⏃ on the Query Design toolbar. The query results show the CustomerName, OwnerName, Phone, and FirstContact fields for customers whose FirstContact field value is before January 1, 1992.

You can verify that the query is correct because the FirstContact field values are displayed. The FirstContact field is not necessary in the new table, so you will exclude this field from the final query design. Then you can change the query to a make-table query.

To delete the field and change the query type:

1. Click the **View** button for Design view ⬚ on the Query Datasheet toolbar to switch back to Design view, and then click the **FirstContact Show** check box to remove the check mark from it. The new table will contain only fields with checked Show boxes. You are now ready to change the query to a make-table query.

2. Click the list arrow for the **Query Type** button ⬚ on the Query Datasheet toolbar, and then click **Make-Table Query**. Access opens the Make Table dialog box, in which you enter the name of the new table. See Figure 8-20.

Figure 8-20 ◄
Make Table
dialog box

enter the new table
name here

3. In the Table Name text box, type **Special Customers**, make sure the **Current Database** option button is selected so that the new table will be included in the Restaurant database, and then click the **OK** button.

Now that you have created and tested the query, you can run it to create the Special Customers table. After you run the query, you can save it.

To run and save the make-table query:

1. Click the **Run** button ⏃ on the Query Design toolbar. Access displays a dialog box indicating that you are about to paste rows into a new table. Because you are running an action query, which alters the contents of the database, Access gives you an opportunity to cancel the operation, if necessary, or to confirm it.

2. Click the **Yes** button. Access closes the dialog box, runs the make-table query to create the Special Customers table, and then displays the Query window in Design view.

3. Click **File** on the menu bar, and then click **Save As/Export**. The Save As dialog box opens.

4. Type **Special Customers Make-Table** in the New Name text box, and then press the **Enter** key to name and save the query.

5. Click the **Close** button ☒ on the Query window to close it and return to the Database window. Notice that the Special Customers Make-Table query appears in the Queries list with a special icon indicating that it is a make-table query.

You can now open the Special Customers table to view the results of the make-table query.

6. Click the **Tables** tab, click **Special Customers** in the Tables list, and then click the **Open** button to view the new table.

7. Resize all columns to their best fit.

The Special Customers table includes the CustomerName, OwnerName, and Phone fields for customers whose FirstContact field value is before January 1, 1992.

8. Click the **Save** button 🖫 on the Table Datasheet toolbar to save the table design changes, and then click the **Close** button ☒ on the Table window to close it and return to the Database window.

Leonard can now use the Special Customers table records when he contacts the customers. He can make changes to the design of the Special Customers table for his own needs without affecting the Customer table in the Restaurant database.

Creating an Append Query

Leonard has decided to expand the list of customers that he will call. He wants to add the CustomerName, OwnerName, and Phone fields for all customers who were first contacted in 1992 to the Special Customers table. He asks you to add these new records. You could make this change by modifying the selection criterion in the Special Customers Make-Table query to select customers with FirstContact field values earlier than 1/1/93. If you ran this modified query, however, you would overwrite the existing Special Customers table with a new table. If Leonard had made any changes to the existing Special Customers records, these changes would also be overwritten.

Instead, you will modify the Special Customers Make-Table query to select only those customers with FirstContact dates in 1992 and change the query to an append query. For the selection criterion, you will use the Between...And operator. When you run this query, the selected records will be appended to the records in the existing Special Customers table.

REFERENCE window

CREATING AN APPEND QUERY

- Create a select query with the necessary fields and selection criteria.
- Click the Run button on the Query Design toolbar to preview the results.
- Switch to Design view to make any necessary changes. When the query is correct, click the list arrow for the Query Type button on the Query Design toolbar.
- Click Append. Access displays the Append dialog box.
- In the Table Name text box, type the name of the table to which you want to append the selected records. Make sure the Current Database option button is selected to append the records to a table in the current database; or, click the Another Database option button and enter the database name in the File Name text box. Then click the OK button.
- Click the Run button on the Query Design toolbar.
- Click the Yes button to confirm appending the records to the table.

You can now modify the Special Customers Make-Table query to create the append query you'll use to include the additional customer data Leonard wants in the Special Customers table.

To create the append query:

1. Click the **Queries** tab, click **Special Customers Make-Table**, and then click the **Design** button to open the query in Design view.

2. Right-click the **FirstContact Criteria** text box, and then click **Cut** on the shortcut menu.

3. In the same Criteria text box, type **Between #1/1/92# And #12/31/92#**. This condition means that the query will select any records with a FirstContact field value between January 1, 1992 and December 31, 1992, inclusive. See Figure 8-21. Notice that only the last part of the criterion is visible.

Figure 8-21 ◀
Changing the
selection
criterion

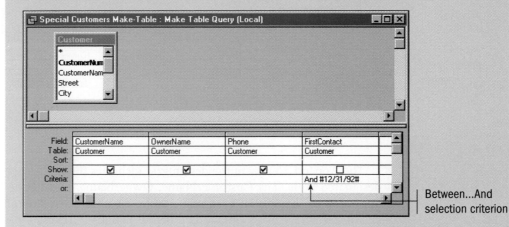

Between...And
selection criterion

Before you can run the query to append the records to the Special Customers table, you have to change it to an append query. It is always a good idea to test an action query before you run it, so you will first change the query to a select query and run it to make sure the correct records are selected. Then you will change it to an append query and run it to append the new records to the Special Customers table.

4. Click the **FirstContact Show** check box to select it. You need to include the FirstContact field values in the query results so that you can verify that the correct records are selected.

5. Click the list arrow for the **Query Type** button 🔲 on the Query Design toolbar, and then click **Select Query**.

6. Click the **Run** button ❗ on the Query Design toolbar. Access runs the query and displays the results. See Figure 8-22.

Figure 8-22 ◀
1992 records
selected

	CustomerName	OwnerName	Phone	FirstContact
▶	Wagon Train Restaurant	Mr. Carl Seaver	(517) 111-5545	5/25/92
	Extra Helpings Restaurant	Ms. Deborah Wolfe	(517) 889-6003	5/25/92
	Mountain Lake Restaurant	Mr. Donald MacPherson	(616) 532-4499	5/25/92
✳				

Special Customers Make-Table : Select Query (Local)

The query shows the three records with a FirstContact field value in 1992. These are the additional records you will append to the Special Customers table. Now that the results show that the query is correct, you can remove the FirstContact field from the results, because you don't want to include it in the append query.

7. Click the **View** button for Design view 🔲 on the Query Datasheet toolbar, and then click the **FirstContact Show** check box to remove the check mark from it. You can now change the query to an append query.

8. Click the list arrow for the **Query Type** button 🔲 on the Query Design toolbar, and then click **Append Query**. Access opens the Append dialog box, in which you enter the name of the table to which you want to append the data.

9. Make sure **Special Customers** appears in the Table Name text box and that the **Current Database** option button is selected, and then click the **OK** button. Access replaces the Show row with the Append To row between the Sort and Criteria rows in the design grid. See Figure 8-23.

Figure 8-23 ◀
Query window
for the append
query

Append To row
inserted

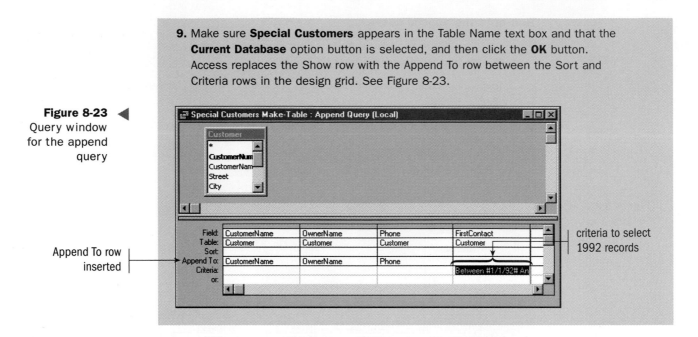

criteria to select
1992 records

The Append To row in the design grid identifies the fields that will be appended to the designated table. The CustomerName, OwnerName, and Phone fields are selected to be appended to the Special Customers table, which already contains these three fields for customers with a FirstContact date before January 1, 1992.

You can now run and then save the append query.

To run and save the append query:

1. Click the **Run** button ![button] on the Query Design toolbar. Access opens a dialog box warning you about the upcoming append operation.

2. Click the **Yes** button to acknowledge the warning. Access closes the dialog box, runs the append query to add the three records to the Special Customers table, and displays the Query window in Design view.

3. Click **File** on the menu bar, and then click **Save As/Export**. The Save As dialog box opens.

4. Type **Special Customers Append** in the New Name text box, and then press the **Enter** key. Access saves the query.

5. Click the **Close** button ![X] on the Query window to close it and return to the Database window.

   Next you'll open the Special Customers table to make sure that the three records were appended to the table.

6. Click the **Tables** tab, click **Special Customers** in the Tables list, and then click the **Open** button to view the modified table.

   The new records have been added to the Special Customers table. Because the Special Customers table does not have a primary key, the new records appear at the end of the table. You could arrange the records in a different order by sorting the records using the Sort Ascending or Sort Descending button.

7. Click the **Close** button ![X] on the Table window to close it and return to the Database window.

Creating a Delete Query

Leonard has contacted all of the customers in the Special Customers table who have phone numbers in the 313 and 517 area codes. He asks you to delete these records from the Special Customers table so that the table contains only records of customers he has not yet contacted. You can either delete the table records individually or create a delete query to remove them.

CREATING A DELETE QUERY

REFERENCE window

- Create a select query with the necessary fields and selection criteria.
- Click the Run button on the Query Design toolbar to preview the results.
- Switch to Design view to make any necessary changes. When the query is correct, click the list arrow for the Query Type button on the Query Design toolbar.
- Click Delete Query. Access replaces the Show and Sort rows with the Delete row.
- Click the Run button on the Query Design toolbar.
- Click the Yes button to confirm deleting the records.

You'll create a delete query to delete the records of all the customers in the Special Customers table who have phone numbers in the 313 and 517 area codes. Because these customers are the only ones who have 313 or 517 area codes, you can create a select query to choose the correct records based on the area code criteria, test the select query, and then change the query to a delete query.

To create the delete query:

1. From the Queries tab of the Database window, click the **New** button to open the New Query dialog box. Make sure that **Design View** is selected, and then click the **OK** button. The Show Table dialog box opens on top of the Query window in Design view.

2. Click **Special Customers** in the Tables list, and then click the **Add** button to add the Special Customers field list to the Query window. Click the **Close** button to close the Show Table dialog box.

3. Double-click the title bar of the Special Customers field list to select all the fields in the table, and then drag the pointer from the highlighted area of the field list to the design grid's first column Field text box. Release the mouse button. Access adds all the fields to the design grid.

4. Click the **Phone Criteria** text box, type **Like "(313)*"**, press the ↓ key, and then type **Like "(517)*"**. Access will select a record only if the Phone field value starts with either (313) or (517).

5. Click the **Run** button ⊞ on the Query Design toolbar. The query results display six records, each one with either a 313 or 517 area code. The query is correct. See Figure 8-24.

Figure 8-24 ◀
Six records to be deleted

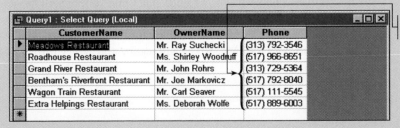

area code is either 313 or 517

TROUBLE? If your query did not select the correct six records, click the View button for Design view ![icon] on the Query Datasheet toolbar, correct the selection criteria as necessary, and then click the Run button ![icon] on the Query Design toolbar.

Now that you have verified that the correct records are selected, you can change the query to a delete query and run it.

6. Click the **View** button for Design view ![icon] on the Query Datasheet toolbar to switch back to Design view, click the list arrow for the **Query Type** button ![icon] on the Query Design toolbar, and then click **Delete Query**. In the design grid, Access replaces the Sort and Show rows with the Delete row. See Figure 8-25.

Figure 8-25 ◀
Design grid for
the delete
query

Delete row inserted ──────→

selection criteria

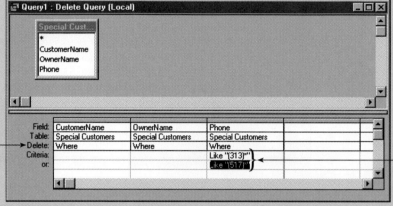

7. Click the **Run** button ![icon] on the Query Design toolbar. Access opens a dialog box warning you about the upcoming delete operation.

8. Click the **Yes** button to close the dialog box and run the delete query. Access still displays the Query window in Design view. Because this query needs to be run only once, you don't have to save it.

9. Click the **Close** button ![icon] on the Query window, and then click the **No** button when Access asks if you want to save the query changes.

You can now open the Special Customers table to verify that the records have been deleted.

10. Click the **Tables** tab, click **Special Customers** in the Tables list, and then click the **Open** button. Access opens the Special Customers table in Datasheet view. Notice that the table now includes only nine records; six records were correctly deleted.

You can now close the Table window.

11. Click the **Close** button ![icon] on the Table window. You return to the Database window.

Kim wants to begin holding annual appreciation dinners for Valle Coffee customers in each state where Valle Coffee does business. She has made arrangements to hold three different dinners—one in Ohio, another in Michigan, and the third in Indiana. Each dinner will be held at a customer's restaurant and all owners of other Valle Coffee customer restaurants in the state will be invited to attend. The Ohio dinner will be held at the Cherry Creek Inn in Toledo. The Michigan dinner will be held at Rosie's Diner in Monroe, and the Indiana dinner will be held at the Embers Restaurant in Goshen. The owners of these restaurants (Mr. Douglas Viereck, Ms. Rosie Finnegan, and Mr. Clifford Merritt) will act as contacts between Kim and the other restaurant owners in the state. They will help handle the necessary travel and accommodation arrangements for the owners coming from out of town.

Kim asks you to add the new contact information to the Restaurant database and then to create a new query that shows which owners will be making arrangements through Mr. Viereck, which through Ms. Finnegan, and which through Mr. Merritt. To produce this information, you'll create an update query.

Creating an Update Query

Recall that an update query changes selected fields and records in one or more tables. In this case, you need to create a new field to contain the contact information for the annual dinners, and then enter the appropriate values in this new field. You could enter the value for every record in the Customer table, but you can accomplish the same thing more quickly and with less chance of error by using an update query to enter the values at one time.

REFERENCE window	CREATING AN UPDATE QUERY
	■ Create a select query with the necessary fields and selection criteria.
	■ Click the Run button on the Query Design toolbar to preview the results.
	■ Switch to Design view to make any necessary changes. When the query is correct, click the list arrow for the Query Type button on the Query Design toolbar.
	■ Click Update Query. Access places the Update To row in the design grid.
	■ Enter the expression for the new value for the update field in the Update To row.
	■ Click the Run button on the Query Design toolbar.
	■ Click the Yes button to confirm updating the records.

First, you will add a field named Contact to the Customer table. This new field will contain either Mr. Viereck's, Ms. Finnegan's, or Mr. Merritt's CustomerNum field value to indicate that this customer is the contact person for the annual dinner being held at their restaurant.

To add the new Contact field to the Customer table:

1. From the Tables tab of the Database window, click **Customer**, and then click the **Design** button. Access opens the Customer table in Design view.

2. Scroll down the field list until a blank row is visible.

3. Click the Field Name text box just below the FirstContact field, type **Contact**, press the **Tab** key twice, and then type **Annual dinner contact for this owner** in the new field's Description text box.

   Because the new field will contain CustomerNum values, which are 3 characters long, you need to change the field size for the new field to 3.

4. Double-click **50** in the Field Size text box, and then type **3**. This completes the addition of the Contact field to the Customer table. See Figure 8-26.

Figure 8-26 ◀
Contact field
added to the
Customer table

new field ─────

Contact field size ─────

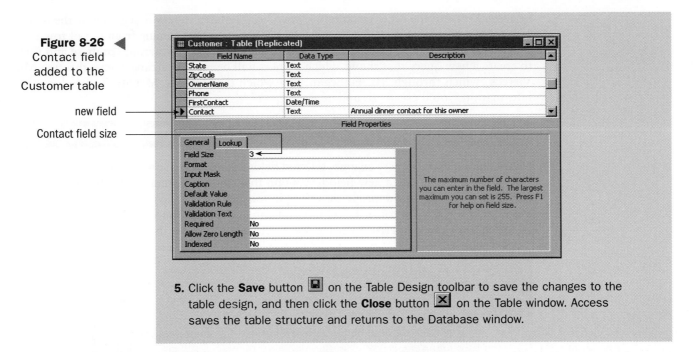

5. Click the **Save** button 🖫 on the Table Design toolbar to save the changes to the table design, and then click the **Close** button ☒ on the Table window. Access saves the table structure and returns to the Database window.

Now you can create an update query to update the Contact field for the records in the Customer table. You'll change the Contact field value to 798 (CustomerNum for Embers Restaurant) for each customer in Indiana, to 800 (CustomerNum for Rosie's Diner) for each customer in Michigan, and to 742 (CustomerNum for the Cherry Creek Inn) for each customer in Ohio. You will not enter Contact values for Embers Restaurant, Rosie's Diner, or Cherry Creek Inn, because the owners of these three restaurants are the three contacts for the dinners.

To create the update query to enter the Contact field values:

1. Click the **Queries** tab to display the Queries list, and then click the **New** button to open the New Query dialog box. Make sure that **Design View** is selected, and then click the **OK** button. The Show Table dialog box opens on top of the Query window in Design view.   •

2. Click **Customer** in the list box, click the **Add** button to add the Customer field list to the Query window, and then click the **Close** button to close the Show Table dialog box.

   You will select the CustomerNum, State, and Contact fields for the query results. The CustomerNum field allows you to exclude the records for the three contact restaurant owners. The State field allows you to select records for customers in a particular state. The Contact field is the field you want to update.

3. In the Customer field list, double-click the **CustomerNum**, **State**, and **Contact** fields to add these fields to the design grid.

   You can now select the records for customers in Indiana and update the Contact field value for those records to 798, the CustomerNum for Embers Restaurant.

4. Click the **State Criteria** text box, and then type **"IN"**. Access will select a record only if the State field value is IN.

5. Click the **CustomerNum Criteria** text box, and then type **Not In ("798","800","742")**. Access will not select the records for the host restaurants.

6. Click the list arrow for the **Query Type** button 🗗 on the Query Design toolbar, and then click **Update Query**. In the design grid, Access replaces the Sort and Show rows with the Update To row.

Access

You tell Access how you want to change a field value for the selected records by entering an expression in the field's Update To text box. An *expression* is a calculation resulting in a single value. You can type a simple expression directly into the Update To text box. If you need help creating a complicated expression, you can create it using the *Expression Builder*, an Access tool that contains an expression box in which the expression is entered, buttons for common operators, and one or more lists of expression elements, such as table and field names. The expression in this case is simple, so you can type it directly in the Update To text box.

7. Click the **Contact Update To** text box, and then type **798**. This is the CustomerNum field value for Embers Restaurant, which is the host restaurant for the dinner in Indiana. See Figure 8-27.

Figure 8-27 ◄
Updating the
Contact field

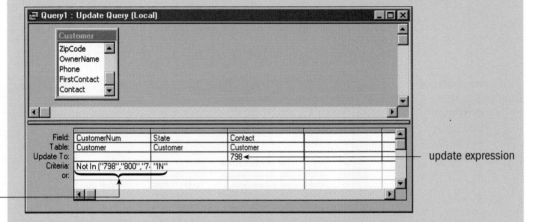

selection criteria

update expression

8. Click the **Run** button on the Query Design toolbar. Access opens a dialog box warning you about the upcoming update operation.

9. Click the **Yes** button to close the dialog box and run the update query. Access updates the Contact field values for the customers in Indiana and leaves the Query window in Design view open.

Now you need to update the Contact field values for customers located in Michigan and Ohio. To do so, you'll modify the criteria for the existing update query twice.

To update the remaining Contact field values:

1. Double-click the entry in the **State Criteria** text box to select it, and then type **"MI"**. Access will select a record only if the State field value is MI.

2. Double-click the entry in the **Contact Update To** text box to select it, and then type **800**. This is the CustomerNum field value for Rosie's Diner, the host restaurant for the dinner in Michigan.

3. Click the **Run** button on the Query Design toolbar. Access opens a dialog box warning you about the upcoming update operation.

4. Click the **Yes** button to close the dialog box and run the update query. Access leaves the Query window in Design view open.

5. Double-click the entry in the **State Criteria** text box, and then type **"OH"**. Access will select a record only if the State field value is OH.

6. Double-click the entry in the **Contact Update To** text box, and then type **742**. This is the CustomerNum field value for Cherry Creek Inn, the host restaurant for the dinner in Ohio.

7. Click the **Run** button 🔘 on the Query Design toolbar, and then click the **Yes** button to confirm running the update query.

You are finished updating the Customer table, so you can close the Query window. Because all the records have been updated, you do not need to save the query.

8. Click the **Close** button ❌ on the Query window to close it, and then click the **No** button when Access asks if you want to save the query changes. Access closes the Query window and returns to the Database window.

Now you can view the Customer table to see the results of the update operation.

To view the updated Customer table:

1. Click the **Tables** tab, click **Customer** in the Tables list, and then click the **Open** button. Access displays the Customer table in Datasheet view.

2. Scroll the datasheet to see the updated Contact field. See Figure 8-28.

Figure 8-28 ◀
Customer table with the updated Contact field values

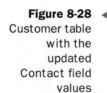

	State	ZipCode	OwnerName	Phone	FirstContact	Contact
▶	MI	48161	Mr. Ray Suchecki	(313) 792-3546	2/28/91	800
	MI	49945	Ms. Doris Reaume	(616) 643-8821	4/3/91	800
	MI	48617	Ms. Shirley Woodruff	(517) 966-8651	4/12/91	800
	MI	49301	Mr. Wayne Bouwman	(616) 888-9827	4/17/91	800
	MI	49063	Mr. John Rohrs	(313) 729-5364	4/20/91	800
	MI	49428	Ms. Michele Yasenak	(616) 111-9148	4/27/91	800
	MI	49031	Mr. Ronald Kooienga	(906) 895-2041	5/1/91	800
	MI	49464	Mr. Donald Bench	(616) 111-3260	5/3/91	800
	MI	49464	Ms. Janice Stapleton	(616) 643-4635	5/11/91	800
	MI	49464	Ms. Joan Hoffman	(616) 888-2046	5/11/91	800
	MI	48653	Mr. Joe Markovicz	(517) 792-8040	5/18/91	800
	MI	49453	Ms. Dawn Parker	(616) 575-6731	5/19/91	800
	MI	48661	Mr. Carl Seaver	(517) 111-5545	5/25/92	800
	MI	48446	Ms. Deborah Wolfe	(517) 889-6003	5/25/92	800
	MI	49571	Mr. Donald MacPherson	(616) 532-4499	5/25/92	800
	MI	49302	Mr. James Cowan	(616) 888-7111	6/2/93	800
	MI	49505	Ms. Rebecca Van Singel	(616) 415-7294	6/12/93	800

Record: ◀ ◀ 1 ▶ ▶l ▶* of 40

updated Contact field values

3. Scroll through the records to see the new values in the Contact field. Notice that there are no values in the Contact field for records 33, 38, and 39 because the owners of these three restaurants are the three contacts for the dinners.

4. Click the **Close** button ❌ on the Table window to close it and return to the Database window.

Quick Check

[1] What is an action query?

[2] What precautions should you take before running an action query?

[3] What is the difference between a make-table query and an append query?

[4] What does a delete query do?

[5] What does an update query do?

[6] How does the design grid change when you create an update query?

[7] What is the Expression Builder?

Now that the contact numbers are in place, you can generate the query that shows the information Kim requested: which restaurant owners will contact Mr. Viereck, which will contact Ms. Finnegan, and which will contact Mr. Merritt. You will create this query in the next session.

SESSION

8.3

In this session, you will learn about the different types of table joins and view the SQL statements Access creates when you design a query.

Joining Tables

You need to create a query to display the new contact relationships in the Customer table. To do so, you'll create a special join using the Customer table. The design of the Restaurant database includes a relationship between the Customer and Order tables using CustomerNum as the common field, which allows you to join the two tables to create a query based on data from both tables. The type of join you have used so far is an inner join, which is one of three available Access joins. The others are the left outer join and the right outer join.

An **inner join** is a join in which Access selects records from two tables only when the records have the same value in the common field that links the tables. For example, in a database containing a table of student information and a table of class information, an inner join would show all students that have a matching class record and all classes that have a matching student record. In the Restaurant database, CustomerNum is the common field for the Customer and Order tables. As shown in Figure 8-29, the results of a query based on an inner join of these two tables include only those records that have a matching CustomerNum value. The record with the CustomerNum 801 in the Customer table is not included in the query results because it fails to match a record with the same CustomerNum value in the Order table. The inner join is the join you ordinarily use whenever you perform a query from more than one table; it is the default join you have used to this point. (The Order record with OrderNum 199 has been added to illustrate the difference in the various types of joins.)

Figure 8-29 ◀
Example of an
inner join

common field

non-matching rows

records that have the
same value in the
common field that
links the tables

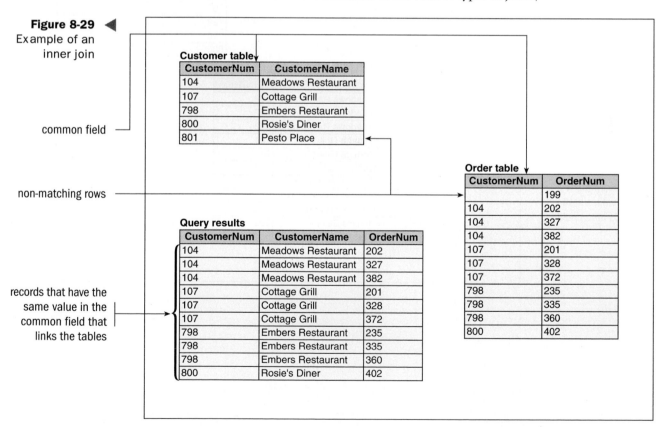

A **left outer join** is a join in which Access selects all records from the first, or left, table and only those records from the second table that have matching common field values. For example, in a database containing a student table and a class table, a left outer join would show all students whether or not the students are enrolled in a class. In the Restaurant database, you would use this kind of join if you wanted to see all records from the Customer table and all matching records from the Order table. Figure 8-30 shows a left outer join for the Customer and Order tables. All records from the Customer table, which is the left table, appear in the query results. Notice that the CustomerNum 801 record appears even though it does not match a record in the Order table.

Figure 8-30 ◀
Example of a
left outer join

common field

non-matching rows

all records from the
first, or left, table and
only those records
from the right table
that have matching
values in the
common field

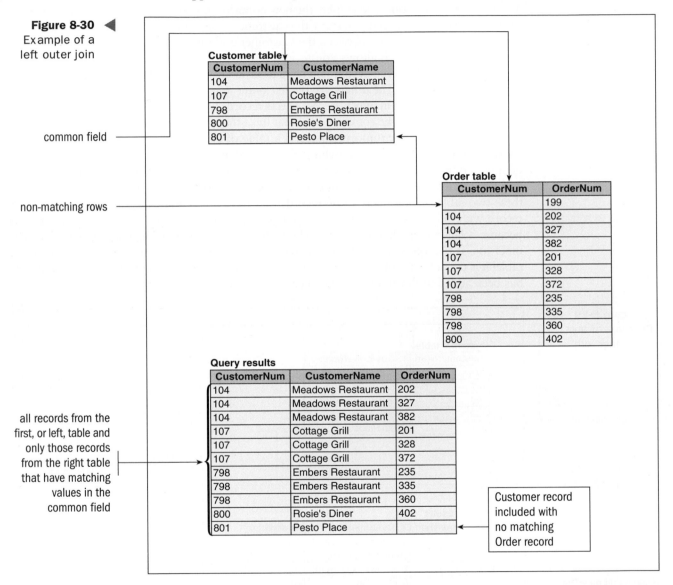

Customer table

CustomerNum	CustomerName
104	Meadows Restaurant
107	Cottage Grill
798	Embers Restaurant
800	Rosie's Diner
801	Pesto Place

Order table

CustomerNum	OrderNum
	199
104	202
104	327
104	382
107	201
107	328
107	372
798	235
798	335
798	360
800	402

Query results

CustomerNum	CustomerName	OrderNum
104	Meadows Restaurant	202
104	Meadows Restaurant	327
104	Meadows Restaurant	382
107	Cottage Grill	201
107	Cottage Grill	328
107	Cottage Grill	372
798	Embers Restaurant	235
798	Embers Restaurant	335
798	Embers Restaurant	360
800	Rosie's Diner	402
801	Pesto Place	

Customer record
included with
no matching
Order record

A **right outer join** is a join in which Access selects all records from the second, or right, table and only those records from the first table that have matching common field values. For example, in a database containing a student table and a class table, a right outer join would show all classes whether or not there are any students enrolled in them. In the Restaurant database, you would use this kind of join if you wanted to see all records from the Order table and all matching records from the Customer table. Figure 8-31 shows a right outer join for the Customer and Order tables. All records from the Order table, which is the right table, appear in the query results. The OrderNum 199 record appears even though it does not match a record in the Customer table. The CustomerNum 801 record in the Customer table does not appear, however, because it does not match a record in the Order table.

Figure 8-31 ◄
Example of a
right outer join

common field

non-matching rows

all records from the
second, or right, table
and only those
records from the left
table that have
matching values in
the common field

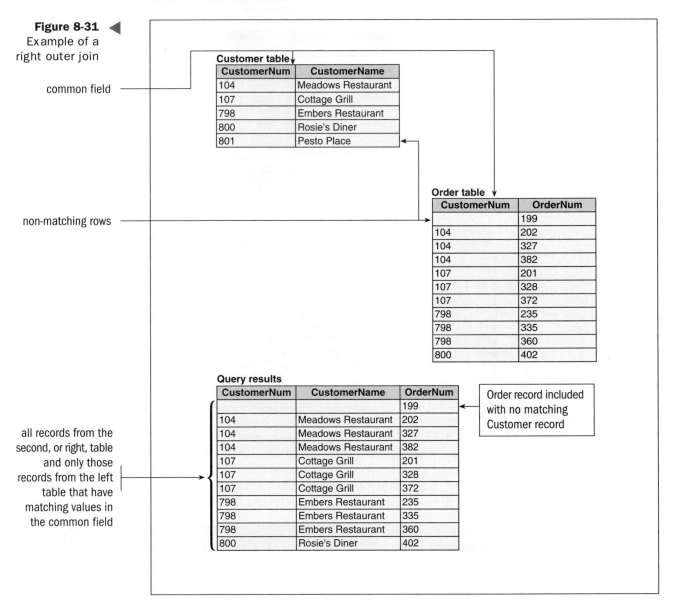

A table can also be joined with itself; this join is called a **self-join**. A self-join can be either an inner or outer join. For example, you would use this kind of join if you wanted to see records from the Customer table together with information about the customers' contacts for the annual dinner. Figure 8-32 shows a self-join for the Customer table. In this case, the self-join is an inner join because records appear in the query results only if the Contact field value matches a CustomerNum field value. To create this self-join, you would add two copies of the Customer table to the Query window in Design view, and then link the Contact field of one Customer table to the CustomerNum field of the other Customer table.

Figure 8-32 ◄
Example
of a self-join

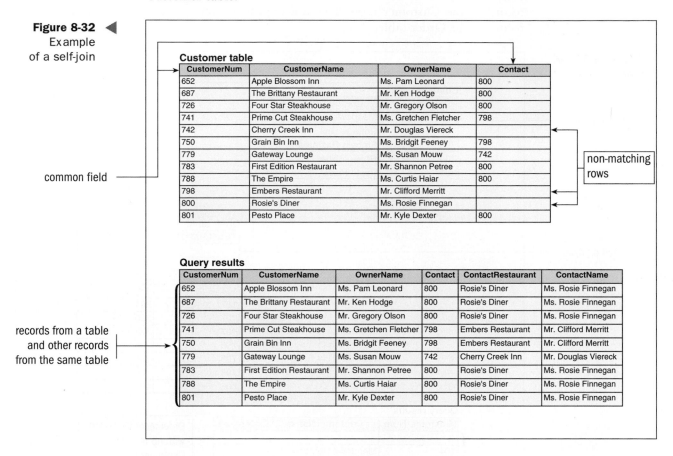

In Figure 8-32, the query results show the record for each customer in the Customer table and the contact information for that customer. The contact information also comes from the Customer table through the Contact field.

To produce the information Kim requested, indicating which restaurant owners will contact which dinner hosts, you need to create a self-join.

Creating a Self-Join

You need to create a query to display the new contact relationships in the Customer table. This query requires a self-join. To create the self-join, you need to add two copies of the Customer field list to the Query window, and then add a join line from the CustomerNum field in one field list to the Contact field in the other. The Contact field is a foreign key that matches the primary key field CustomerNum. You can then create a query that can display Customer information from one table and Contact information from the other table.

REFERENCE window

CREATING A SELF-JOIN

- Click the Queries tab and then click the New button.
- Click Design View and then click the OK button.
- Click the table for the self-join, and then click the Add button. Click the table for the self-join again, and then click the Add button. Click the Close button.
- Click and drag a field from one field list to the related field in the other field list.
- Double-click the join line between the two tables to open the Join Properties dialog box.
- Click the option button for an inner join, a right outer join, or a left outer join, and then click the OK button.
- Select the fields and define the selection criteria and sort options for the query.

Now you'll create the self-join query to determine which restaurant owners will contact which hosts for the annual dinner.

To create the self-join query:

1. If you took a break after the previous session, start Access and open the Restaurant database in the Tutorial folder on your Student Disk.

2. If necessary, click the **Queries** tab to display the list of queries, and then click the **New** button to open the New Query dialog box. Make sure that **Design View** is selected, and then click the **OK** button. The Show Table dialog box opens on top of the Query window in Design view.

3. Click **Customer** and then click the **Add** button.

4. Click the **Add** button again to add a second copy of the Customer field list, and then click the **Close** button. Access identifies the left field list as Customer and the right field list as Customer_1 to distinguish the two copies of the table.

   You will now create a join between the two copies of the Customer table by linking the Contact field in the Customer field list to the CustomerNum field in the Customer_1 field list. The Contact field is a foreign key that matches the primary key field CustomerNum.

5. Scroll the Customer field list until the Contact field is visible. Then click and drag the CustomerNum field from the Customer_1 field list to the Contact field in the Customer field list. Access adds a join line between the two fields. You can verify that this is an inner join query by displaying the Join Properties dialog box.

6. Double-click the **join line** between the two tables to open the Join Properties dialog box. See Figure 8-33.

Figure 8-33 ◀
Join Properties
dialog box

click for inner join

click for right
outer join

click for left outer join

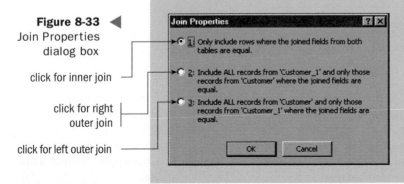

TROUBLE? If double-clicking the join line does not work, click View on the menu bar, and then click Join Properties to open the Join Properties dialog box.

The top option button is selected, indicating that this is an inner join. You would click the middle option button for a right outer join or the bottom option button for a left outer join. Because the inner join is correct, you can cancel the dialog box and then add the necessary fields to the design grid.

7. Click the **Cancel** button and then, scrolling as necessary, double-click the following fields (in order) from the Customer field list: **CustomerNum**, **CustomerName**, **OwnerName**, and **Contact**. Then double-click the following fields (in order) from the Customer_1 field list: **CustomerName** and **OwnerName**.

8. Click the right side of the **CustomerNum Sort** text box, and then click **Ascending** to establish the sort order for the query results.

9. Click the **Run** button 🔲 on the Query Design toolbar. Access displays the query results.

10. Maximize the Query window and then resize the columns in the query results to their best fit. Scroll left until the CustomerNum field is visible. The query results display the records in increasing CustomerNum order and show six fields and 37 records. See Figure 8-34.

Figure 8-34 ◄
Initial self-join
on the
Customer table

fields from the
Customer table

field from the
Customer_1 table

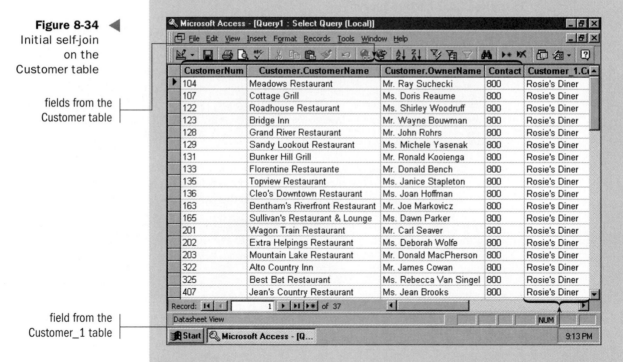

The query results display, in increasing order by CustomerNum, all owners and their contacts, except for the three contact owners, who have null Contact field values.

TROUBLE? If your query results do not match Figure 8-34, click the View button for Design view 🔲 to return to Design view. Review the preceding steps and make any necessary corrections to your query design. Then run the query again.

Access displays 37 of the 40 records from the Customer table; the records for Embers Restaurant, Rosie's Diner, and Cherry Creek Inn have a null Contact field value and, therefore, are not displayed. Four field names in the query results now have prefixes indicating either Customer or Customer_1 to distinguish fields in one table from fields in the other table. For example, the full name of the CustomerName field displayed is Customer.CustomerName, which means the CustomerName field from the Customer (left) table.

Kim asks you to rename some of the fields so that the query results will be easier to read. After you rename the necessary fields, the field names in the query results, from left to right, will be CustomerNum, CustomerName, OwnerName, ContactNum, ContactRestaurant, and ContactName.

To rename the necessary fields:

1. Click the **View** button for Design view 🖾 on the Query Datasheet toolbar to switch back to Design view.

2. Place the insertion point to the left of the first character in the fourth column's Field box, which displays Contact, and then type **ContactNum:**. Be sure the colon is the last character you type. The colon separates the caption for this field from the field name.

   TROUBLE? If Access displays the caption Expr1 for the Contact field, you forgot to enter the colon or you made another error in entering the caption. Edit the text so that it reads ContactNum:Contact.

3. Repeat Step 2 for the fifth column, typing **ContactRestaurant:** before the field name (CustomerName) for that column.

4. Repeat Step 2 for the sixth column, typing **ContactName:** before the field name (OwnerName) for that column.

5. Click the **Run** button 🔣 on the Query Design toolbar. The query results display the new names for the renamed columns.

6. Resize all columns to their best fit. See Figure 8-35.

Figure 8-35 ◀
Final self-join
on the
Customer table

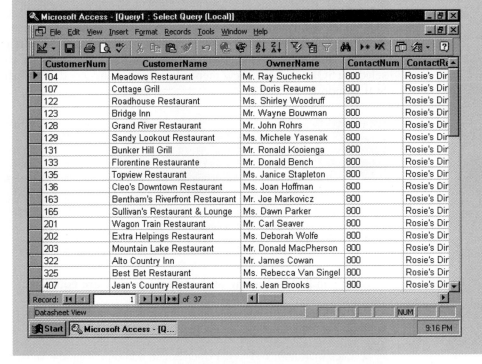

CustomerNum	CustomerName	OwnerName	ContactNum	ContactRe
104	Meadows Restaurant	Mr. Ray Suchecki	800	Rosie's Din
107	Cottage Grill	Ms. Doris Reaume	800	Rosie's Din
122	Roadhouse Restaurant	Ms. Shirley Woodruff	800	Rosie's Din
123	Bridge Inn	Mr. Wayne Bouwman	800	Rosie's Din
128	Grand River Restaurant	Mr. John Rohrs	800	Rosie's Din
129	Sandy Lookout Restaurant	Ms. Michele Yasenak	800	Rosie's Din
131	Bunker Hill Grill	Mr. Ronald Kooienga	800	Rosie's Din
133	Florentine Restaurante	Mr. Donald Bench	800	Rosie's Din
135	Topview Restaurant	Ms. Janice Stapleton	800	Rosie's Din
136	Cleo's Downtown Restaurant	Ms. Joan Hoffman	800	Rosie's Din
163	Bentham's Riverfront Restaurant	Mr. Joe Markovicz	800	Rosie's Din
165	Sullivan's Restaurant & Lounge	Ms. Dawn Parker	800	Rosie's Din
201	Wagon Train Restaurant	Mr. Carl Seaver	800	Rosie's Din
202	Extra Helpings Restaurant	Ms. Deborah Wolfe	800	Rosie's Din
203	Mountain Lake Restaurant	Mr. Donald MacPherson	800	Rosie's Din
322	Alto Country Inn	Mr. James Cowan	800	Rosie's Din
325	Best Bet Restaurant	Ms. Rebecca Van Singel	800	Rosie's Din
407	Jean's Country Restaurant	Ms. Jean Brooks	800	Rosie's Din

You can now give Kim a list of customers and their contacts for the appreciation dinner. Kim can give this list to the restaurant owners so that they can contact Mr. Viereck, Ms. Finnegan, and Mr. Merritt. You are finished with the query, so you can save it as Annual Dinner Contact and then return to the Database window.

To save and close the query:

1. Click **File** on the menu bar, and then click **Save As/Export**. The Save As dialog box opens.

2. In the New Name text box, type **Annual Dinner Contact**, and then press the **Enter** key. Access saves the new self-join query.

3. Click the **Close** button ☒ on the Query window to close it and return to the Database window.

You have now created and saved many queries that Leonard, Barbara, Kim, and others can use to help them manage Valle Coffee's customer and order records. However, if you want to take full advantage of the Access query capabilities, you must learn about the SQL language that Access uses behind the scenes when performing many of its operations. For now, you can familiarize yourself with SQL statements by viewing the corresponding statements for some existing queries.

Introduction to SQL

SQL (Structured Query Language) is a standard language used in querying, updating, and managing relational databases. Every full-featured relational DBMS has its version of the current standard SQL, which is called SQL-92. If you learn SQL for one relational DBMS, it's a relatively easy task to begin using SQL for other relational DBMSs. This is particularly important when you work with two or more relational DBMSs, which is the case in most companies.

Much of what Access accomplishes behind the scenes is done with SQL. Whenever you create a query in Design view, for example, Access automatically constructs an equivalent SQL statement. When you save a query, Access saves the SQL statement version of the query.

When you are working in Design view or viewing the results of a query, you can see the SQL statement that is equivalent to your query by clicking the SQL View button or selecting SQL from the View menu. In response, Access displays the SQL statement in the SQL window.

REFERENCE window

VIEWING AN SQL STATEMENT FOR A QUERY

- Display the query in Design view or Datasheet view.
- Click the list arrow for the View button on the toolbar, and then click SQL View. Access opens the SQL window.
- Use the appropriate View button to return to either Design view or Datasheet view.

Next you'll examine the SQL statements that are equivalent to two existing queries: Customer List and Customer Orders.

To view the SQL statement for the Customer List query:

1. Click **Customer List** in the Queries list, and then click the **Open** button. Access opens the query results in Datasheet view and displays the 40 records from the Customer table. The fields displayed are CustomerNum, CustomerName, City, State, OwnerName, and Phone.

2. Click the list arrow for the **View** button 🖼 on the Query Datasheet toolbar, and then click **SQL View** to open the SQL window. See Figure 8-36.

Figure 8-36 ◄
SQL window for
the Customer
List query

SQL statement ─────

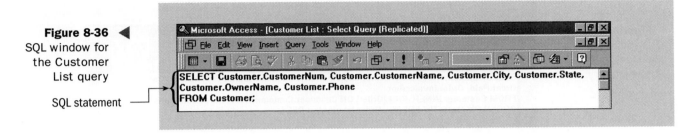

SQL uses the SELECT statement to define what data it retrieves from a database and how it presents the data. For the work you've done so far, the Access menu commands and dialog box options have sufficed. If you learn SQL to the point where you can use it efficiently, you will be able to enter your own SELECT and other SQL statements in the SQL window. You might find if you work with more complicated databases that you need the extra power of the SQL language to implement your database strategies fully.

The rules that SQL uses to construct a statement, similar to the SELECT statement shown in Figure 8-36, are summarized as follows:

- The basic form of an SQL statement is: SELECT-FROM-WHERE-ORDER BY. After SELECT, list the fields you want to display. After FROM, list the tables used in the query. After WHERE, list the selection criteria. After ORDER BY, list the sort keys.

- If a field name includes a space, enclose the field name in brackets.

- Precede a field name with the name of its table. Connect the table name to the field name with a period. For example, you would enter the CustomerNum field in the Customer table as "Customer.CustomerNum."

- Separate field names and table names by commas, and end a statement with a semicolon.

The SQL statement shown in Figure 8-36 selects the Customer.CustomerNum, Customer.CustomerName, Customer.City, Customer.State, Customer.OwnerName, and Customer.Phone fields from the Customer table. The SQL statement does not contain a WHERE clause or an ORDER BY clause, so all records are included in the query results and they are listed in the default order, ascending order by primary key.

You can enter or change SQL statements directly in the SQL window. If you enter an SQL statement and then switch to the Query window in Design view, you will see its equivalent in the design grid.

Next you'll examine the SQL statement for the Customer Orders query.

To view the SQL statement for the Customer Orders query:

1. Click the **Close** button ☒ on the SQL window to close it and return to the Queries tab of the Database window.

2. Click **Customer Orders** in the Queries list, and then click the **Design** button. Access displays the query in Design view. The query selects records from the joined Customer and Order tables in descending order by the Paid field as the primary sort key and in descending order by the InvoiceAmt field as the secondary sort key. The fields displayed are CustomerName, City, and State from the Customer table, and BillingDate, Paid, and InvoiceAmt from the Order table.

3. Click the list arrow for the **View** button ☒ on the Query Design toolbar, and then click **SQL View** to open the SQL window. See Figure 8-37.

Figure 8-37 ◀
SQL window for
the Customer
Orders query

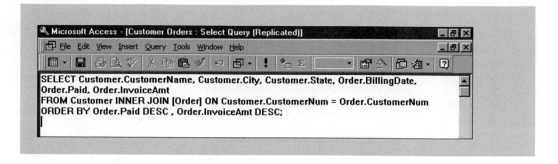

The SELECT statement for this query is similar to the previous one, except for the following added features:

- The ORDER BY clause specifies the sort order for the records.

- The notation DESC indicates a descending sort order. If DESC does not follow a sort key field, then SQL uses an ascending sort order.

- The clause INNER JOIN links the two tables with an inner join. The syntax for this clause is INNER JOIN between the two filenames, followed by ON, and then followed by the names of the field(s) serving as the common field, connected by an equal sign.

The SQL SELECT statements mirror the options you select in Design view. In effect, every choice you make there is reflected as an SQL SELECT statement. Viewing the SQL statements generated from queries that you design is an effective way to learn SQL.

To close the SQL window and exit Access:

1. Click the **Close** button ☒ on the SQL window to return to the Queries tab of the Database window.

2. Click the **Close** button ☒ on the Access window to exit Access.

Quick Check

1 What is the difference between an inner join and an outer join?

2 In what format does Access save a query?

3 What is the basic format of an SQL statement?

4 Figure 8-38 lists the field names from two tables: Telephones and Phone Calls.

Figure 8-38 ◀

Telephones	Phone Calls
Telephone Number	Calling Telephone Number
Billing Name	Called Telephone Number
Billing Address	Call Date
	Call Start Time
	Call End Time
	Billed Telephone Number

a. What is the primary key for each table?
b. What type of relationship exists between the two tables?
c. Is an inner join possible between the two tables? If so, give one example of an inner join.
d. Is either type of outer join possible between the two tables? If so, give one example of an outer join.
e. Is a self-join possible for one of the tables? If so, give one example of a self-join.

You are ready to present your information to Kim so that she can finalize the plans for the appreciation dinner. If you want to pursue SQL further, you can also use the Access Help system to find additional information on SQL.

Tutorial Assignments

The Products database in the TAssign folder on your Student Disk contains information about Valle Coffee products. The Coffee table in the database contains records of the various types of coffee that Valle Coffee sells. The Product table contains pricing information, and the Weight table contains packaging information. The database contains several other objects including queries, forms, and reports. Barbara wants you to make a Briefcase replica of the database for her and to create some new queries. Complete the following:

1. Make sure your Student Disk is in the appropriate disk drive, and then use My Briefcase to create a replica of the Products database. Make the Products database on your Student Disk the Design Master. Do not make a backup of the Products database.

2. Start Access and then open the Products database replica in My Briefcase. Add the record shown in Figure 8-39 to the Coffee table.

Figure 8-39 ◀

CoffeeCode	CoffeeName	CoffeeType	Decaf
VALS	Valle Special Blend	Blended	No

3. Open the Products database on your Student Disk. Synchronize the Design Master of the Products database on your Student Disk with the My Briefcase replica. Open the Coffee table and verify that the new record has been added to the table. Close the Products database, and delete the replica copy in My Briefcase.

4. Create a query based on the Coffee, Product, and Weight tables. Display the CoffeeType, Decaf, and Weight/Size fields in the query results. Print the query results. Save the query as Coffee Types And Weights.

5. Create a crosstab query based on the Coffee Types And Weights query. Use the CoffeeType field values for the row headings and the Decaf field values for the column headings. (Note that the <> symbol is used for the column heading for a null value, in this case, where the Decaf field value is No. The column heading "D" represents a Yes value in the Decaf field.) Use the count of the Weight/Size field as the summarized value. Resize the query results columns to their best fit, and then print the query results. Save the query as Summary Of CoffeeType By Decaf Crosstab.

6. Barbara informs you that coffee prices have increased and Valle Coffee will have to raise the price of its least expensive products. Create an update query that increases the price of all records in the Product table where the Price field value is 7.99. The new price is 8.49. After you run the update query, do not save it.

7. Create a make-table query based on the Coffee table. Select all fields for Decaf coffees. Run the query, saving the results as Decaf Coffees. Close the Query window and do not save the make-table query. Open the Decaf Coffees table and print the table records.

8. Create a delete query that deletes all records from the Decaf Coffees table where the CoffeeType field value is not Flavored. Run the query. Close the Query window and do not save the delete query. Rename the Decaf Coffees table Flavored Decaf Coffees. Open the table and print the table records.

9. Create a find unmatched query that finds all records in the Product table for which there is no matching record in the Flavored Decaf Coffees table. Select all fields from the Product table in the query results. Save the query as Product Without Matching Flavored Decaf Coffees. Print the query results, and then close the Query window.

10. Create a query based on the Flavored Decaf Coffees table and the Product table. Create an outer join between the Flavored Decaf Coffees table and the Product, selecting all records from the Product table and only those records from the Flavored Decaf Coffees table that have matching records. Select the CoffeeCode, CoffeeName, CoffeeType, and ProductCode fields in the query results. Print the query results, and then save the query as Product And Flavored Decaf Coffees Outer Join.

11. Open the Special Imports query and view the SQL statements in the SQL window.

   a. Which tables are used in the query?

   b. Which fields are displayed in the query results?

   c. What type of join is used between the tables?

   d. What selection criteria are used?

   e. How are the query results sorted?

12. Close the SQL window, close the Products database, and then exit Access.

Case Problems

1. Ashbrook Mall Information Desk The Mall Operations Office is responsible for everything that happens in the Ashbrook Mall in Phoenix, Arizona. To maintain a catalog of job openings at the mall stores, Sam Bullard, director of the Mall Operations Office, has created an Access database called MallJobs. Sam asks you to create some new queries for this database. Complete the following:

1. Make sure your Student Disk is in the appropriate disk drive, start Access, and then open the MallJobs database located in the Cases folder on your Student Disk.

2. Create a make-table query based on the Job table. Select all fields for the Salesclerk position. Run the query, saving the results as Salesclerk Jobs. Close the Query window and do not save the make-table query. Open the Salesclerk Jobs table and print the table records.

3. Create a crosstab query based on the Store Jobs query. Use the Location field values for the row headings and the Position field values for the column headings. Use the count of the StoreName field as the summarized value. Resize the columns in the query results to their best fit, and then print the query results. Save the query as Location By Position Crosstab.

4. Create a find unmatched query that finds all records in the Store table for which there is no matching record in the Job table. Select all available fields in the query results. Save the query as Store Without Matching Jobs. Print the query results, and then close the Query window.

5. Open the Clerk Jobs query, and then open the SQL window and view the SQL code that creates the Clerk Jobs query. Answer the following:

   a. Which tables are used in the query?

   b. Which fields are displayed in the query results?

   c. What type of join is used between the tables?

   d. What selection criteria are used?

   e. How are the query results sorted?

EXPLORE

6. Close the MallJobs database. Then make a backup copy of the MallJobs database on a new disk, and use your backup for this exercise.

   a. Place your backup disk in drive A and use My Briefcase to create a Briefcase replica of the MallJobs database. Make your backup the Design Master and make the Briefcase copy the replica. Do not select the option for making a backup copy in My Briefcase.

   b. Open the MallJobs replica database. Create a delete query that deletes all records from the Job table where the Position field value is Salesclerk.

   c. Update the Design Master by synchronizing it with the replica.

   d. Open the Design Master database, open the Job table, and then print the table records.

   e. Close the Design Master database, and then delete the replica copy from My Briefcase.

7. Exit Access.

2. Professional Litigation User Services Professional Litigation User Services (PLUS) creates all types of visual aids for judicial proceedings. To track daily payments received from the firm's clients, Raj Jawahir has created the Payments database. To make the database easier to use, Raj wants several new queries created. To help Raj with the new queries, complete the following:

1. Make sure your Student Disk is in the appropriate disk drive, start Access, and then open the Payments database located in the Cases folder on your Student Disk.

2. Raj has assigned a new PLUS account representative to Sunil Jain's accounts. The new representative is Cathy Cunningham. Create an update query to update the PLUSAcctRep field in the Firm table, updating the PLUSAcctRep field value to Cunningham, Cathy where the current field value is Jain, Sunil.

3. Create a crosstab query based on the Account Representatives query. Use the PLUSAcctRep field values for the row headings and the FirmName field values for the column headings. Use the sum of the AmtPaid field as the summarized value. Save the query as AcctReps By Firm Crosstab. Resize the columns in the query results to their best fit, and then print the query results in landscape orientation.

4. Create a make-table query based on the Payment table. Select all fields for payments before June 10, 1999. Run the query, saving the results as Early June Payments. Close the Query window and do not save the make-table query. Open the Early June Payments table and print the table records.

5. Create an append query to select all records from the Payments table where the DatePaid field value is between June 10, 1999 and June 14, 1999 and append them to the Early June Payments table. After you run the query, close the Query window and do not save the append query. Open the Early June Payments table and print the table records.

6. Create a delete query to delete all records from the Early June Payments table where the AmtPaid is less than $1000.00. Run the query. Close the Query window and do not save the delete query. Rename the Early June Payments table as Large Early June Payments. Open the table and print the table records.

7. Create a query based on the Payment table. Display the Payment#, Firm# and AmtPaid fields in the query results. Sort the query results in descending order by the AmtPaid field. Use the Top Values property to select the top 5% of records based on the AmtPaid field. Print the query results. Do not save the query.

Access

EXPLORE

8. Create an outer join from the Firm table to the Large Early June Payments table. Display the Firm#, FirmName, PLUSAcctRep fields from the Firm table and the AmtPaid field from the Large Early June Payments table. Select all records from the Firm table and any matching records from the Large Early June Payments table. Run the query and print the query results. Do not save the query.

9. Close the PLUS database and then exit Access.

3. Best Friends Best Friends is a not-for-profit organization that trains hearing and service dogs for people with disabilities. To raise funds, Best Friends periodically sponsors Walk-A-Thons. These fundraisers have been so popular that Noah and Sheila Warnick, the founders of Best Friends, have created the Walks database to keep track of walkers and their pledges. The Walks database has been a useful tool for Noah and Sheila. Now, they need several new queries to provide them with better information. You'll help them create these queries by completing the following:

1. Make sure your Student Disk is in the appropriate disk drive, start Access, and then open the Walks database in the Cases folder on your Student Disk.

2. Create an update query to select all records in the Walker table where the Distance field value is greater than 2.6. Update the Distance field value to 3.0. Do not save the query.

3. Create a find unmatched query to select all records in the Walker table for which there are no matching records in the Pledge table. Select the WalkerID, LastName, and FirstName fields for display in the query results and save the query as Walker Without Matching Pledge. Run the query and print the query results.

4. Open the Walker Distance query in Design view and sort the query results in ascending order by Distance. Use the Top Values property to select the top 5 records. Run the query and print the query results. Why does the query select records with the smallest Distance values? Why does the query select more than 5 records? Save the query as Short Walks.

5. Switch to SQL view to view the SQL statements that create the Short Walks query. What SQL phrase is used to select the top 5 records? Close the Short Walks query.

6. Create a make-table query based on the Difference query. Select records where the PerMile field value is greater than 0. Run the query and save the results to a table called PerMile Pledge. Close the query, but do not save the query design. Open the PerMile Pledge table and print the records.

EXPLORE

7. Close the Walks database. Then make a backup copy of the Walks database on a new disk, and use your backup for this exercise.

   a. Place your backup disk in drive A, and use My Briefcase to create a Briefcase replica of the Walks database. Make your backup the Design Master and make the Briefcase copy the replica. Do not select the option for making a backup copy in My Briefcase.

   b. Open the replica copy of the Walks database, and then open the Walker table. Change the phone number for Kim Shah to 723-5778.

   c. Synchronize the Design Master of the Walks database on your Student Disk with the My Briefcase replica. Open the Design Master of the Walks database and verify that the change you made in the replica copy is reflected in the Design Master.

   d. Close the Design Master database, and then delete the replica copy of the Walks database from My Briefcase.

8. Exit Access.

4. Lopez Lexus Dealerships Maria and Hector Lopez own a chain of Lexus dealerships throughout Texas. They have used a computer in their business for several years to handle their payroll and normal accounting functions. To keep track of their car inventory, they have developed the Lexus database. The database has three tables: Cars, Locations, and Mileage. The Cars table contains data about each car in the inventory. The Locations table contains data about each of the Lopez dealership lots. The Mileage table contains data about mileage of each of the Lexus models in stock. Maria and Hector have also created queries, forms, and reports to make the database easy to use. They ask you to create a Briefcase replica of the Lexus database and to create some new queries. To create the replica and the queries, you will complete the following:

1. Make sure your Student Disk is in the appropriate disk drive, start Access, and then open the Lexus database in the Cases folder on your Student Disk.

2. Create a query using the Cars and Locations tables. Select the Model and Cost fields from the Cars table. Select the LocationName field from the Locations table. Save the query as Models By Location.

3. Create a crosstab query named Car Inventory Crosstab that is based on the Models By Location query. Base the row headings on the LocationName field, the column headings on the Model field, and the numbers in the middle on the sum of the Cost field. Do not calculate a summary for each row. Save the query as Models By Location Crosstab. Resize the columns in the query results to their best fit, and then print the query results.

4. Create a top values query based on the Cars table. Select all fields in the table. The query should sort the records in descending order by SellingPrice and select the 10 most expensive cars. Save the query as Most Expensive Cars. Print the query results.

5. Lopez Lexus Dealerships is having a sale on GS300 model cars. The selling price is reduced by $1000. Create an update query to reduce the SellingPrice for all GS300 model cars. Use the Expression Builder to create the expression [SellingPrice]-1000 as the update value. (*Hint:* Read the Help topic Expression Builder to learn more about the Expression Builder.) Run the query and do not save the query. Open the Cars table and print the table records.

6. Create a find duplicates query based on the Cars table. Select the LocationCode as the field that might contain duplicates. Select all other fields as additional fields in the query results. Save the query as Find Duplicate Locations. Run the query and print the query results.

7. Close the Lexus database. Then make a backup copy of the Lexus database on a new disk, and use your backup for this exercise.

   a. Place your backup disk in drive A and use My Briefcase to create a Briefcase replica of the Lexus database. Make your backup the Design Master and make the Briefcase copy the replica. Do not select the option for making a backup copy in My Briefcase.

   b. Open the replica copy of the Lexus database, and then open the Locations table. Change the name of the manager at the San Antonio location to Hunsley, Betsey.

   c. Open the Cars table and delete the record for the car with VehicleID 888TL.

   d. Synchronize the Design Master of the Lexus database on your Student Disk with the My Briefcase replica. Open the Design Master of the Lexus database and verify that the changes you made in the replica copy are reflected in the Design Master.

   e. Close the Design Master database, and then delete the replica copy of the Lexus database from My Briefcase.

8. Exit Access.

Automating Tasks with Macros

Creating a Switchboard to Work with the Restaurant Database

CASE

Valle Coffee

At a recent office automation conference, Leonard saw several database applications developed by database designers. The designers' applications used several advanced Access features to automate and control how a user interacts with Access. These features allowed the designers to create a custom user interface for a database. This interface made it much easier for inexperienced users to access the database, and it minimized the chance that an unauthorized user could change the design of any database objects.

Leonard would like a similar user interface for the Restaurant database. He would like the interface to display a list of available forms, queries, and reports in the database that the user can select by clicking a command button. This interface will make it much easier for the employees of Valle Coffee to use the Restaurant database, and it will reduce the chance that database users will make undesirable changes to the design of the database objects.

SESSION

9.1

In this session, you will design a graphical user interface for the Restaurant database. You will create, test, run, and save macros. You will also create a new table and its associated queries.

Designing a User Interface

A **user interface** is what you see and how you communicate with a computer program. Not too long ago, most users communicated with a program by typing in words that issued commands. You had to remember these commands, which were part of a command language. Most of the programs developed for today's popular operating environments, such as Microsoft Windows 95, provide graphical user interfaces. A **graphical user interface (GUI)** (pronounced "gooey") displays windows, menu bars, pull-down menus, dialog boxes, and graphical pictures, called **icons**, which you use to communicate with the program. Microsoft Windows 95 programs use a similar visual interface, so once you learn one Windows 95 program, you can easily learn another. Overall, a GUI benefits a user by simplifying work, improving productivity, and decreasing errors.

Leonard wants to provide an easier way to work with the Restaurant database. The type of user interface you need for working with a database is called a switchboard.

Introduction to Switchboards

A **switchboard** is a form that appears when you open a database and that provides controlled access to the database's tables, forms, queries, and reports. When a user opens the database, Access displays a switchboard from which the user can choose an option. When you create a switchboard, you are essentially creating a new interface, and it's up to you to decide what options you want to give the user. Figure 9-1 shows the finished Restaurant Database switchboard, which you will create.

Figure 9-1
Restaurant
Database
switchboard

custom menu bar

custom toolbar

graphic image

command buttons

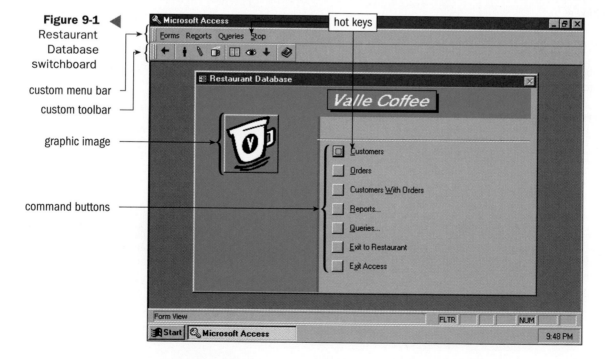

A typical switchboard provides the following:

- Command buttons for all the options available to the user. In the switchboard shown in Figure 9-1, for example, you can click command buttons to open one of three forms (Customers, Orders, or Customers With Orders), to open lists of available reports or queries, to exit from the switchboard and return to the Database window for the Restaurant database, or to exit Access. When a selected form, query list, or report list is closed, Access redisplays the switchboard, allowing you to choose the next option. In other words, you start and end with the switchboard and navigate between options from the switchboard.

- A custom menu bar, which allows you to choose menu options as an alternative to clicking command buttons.

- A custom toolbar. You can use standard Access toolbar buttons or create your own buttons. You can also change the icon on the face of a button to another icon or to text.

- **Shortcut keys** (or **hot keys**), which are underlined letters in each menu name and on each command button option. You can use shortcut keys by holding down the Alt key while pressing the underlined letter to make a selection, instead of clicking a command button, menu option, or toolbar button.

- Text boxes and graphic images that provide identification and visual appeal. The display of a small number of attractively designed graphic images and text boxes can help users understand the switchboard's functions, but keep in mind that too many can be confusing or distracting.

A switchboard gives an attractive look to a user interface, but there are two more important reasons to use a switchboard instead of the Database window to work with a database. First, a switchboard lets you customize the organization of the user interface. Second, a switchboard prevents users from changing the design of tables, forms, queries, and reports. By hiding the Database window and using a custom menu bar and toolbar, you limit users to just those database features you want them to use. If you do not include any menu, toolbar, or command button options that let users open database objects in Design view, users cannot inadvertently change the design of the database.

The Restaurant Database switchboard contains seven command buttons, each of which has an attached command. When the user clicks a command button, Access executes the command for that button. The first three command buttons are attached to commands that open one of three forms (Customers, Orders, or Customers With Orders). The next two command buttons open dialog boxes that contain lists of available reports or queries. The sixth command button allows you to exit from the switchboard and return to the Database window for the Restaurant database. Finally, the last command button closes the Restaurant Database switchboard and exits Access.

Dialog Boxes

Two command buttons on the Restaurant Database switchboard, the Reports and Queries buttons, include ellipses following the button names. As you know from your work in Windows, these ellipses signify that a dialog box containing additional options opens when you click that command button. To display the list of available reports and queries and their options, you will design two custom dialog boxes. A **custom dialog box** is a form that resembles a dialog box, both in appearance and function. You use a custom dialog box to ask for user input, selection, or confirmation before an action is performed, such as opening the results of a query or printing a report. Figure 9-2 shows the finished dialog boxes for the Restaurant database user interface.

Figure 9-2 ◀
Reports
dialog box
and **Queries**
dialog box

opens Print
Preview window

prints report

closes dialog box

opens Print
Preview window

opens query results
in Datasheet view

closes dialog box

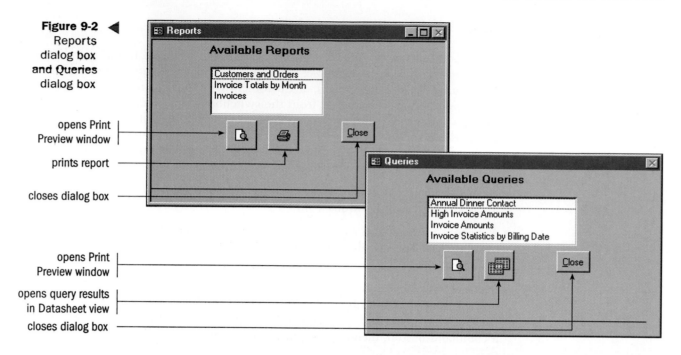

Both dialog boxes contain list boxes that display the queries and reports available for selection. The dialog boxes also contain several command buttons. Command buttons can contain text, standard graphic images available from Access, or graphic images you supply, to indicate their functions. Clicking the Close command button on either dialog box returns you to the switchboard. The other command buttons contain graphic images to identify their functions. Each dialog box has a command button on the left with the icon of a magnifying glass over a piece of paper. This is the same icon shown on the Print Preview button. Just as the Print Preview button opens the Print Preview window, these command buttons open the Print Preview window for the selected query or report. The Reports dialog box also includes a command button for printing the selected report, and the Queries dialog box includes a command button for displaying the results of the selected query in Datasheet view.

Introduction to Macros

The command buttons and custom dialog boxes on the Restaurant Database switchboard gain their power from macros—and from Visual Basic code. A **macro** is a command or a series of commands you want Access to perform automatically for you. Macros automate repetitive tasks, such as opening forms, printing reports, and running queries. Each command in a macro is called an action. An **action** is an instruction to Access to perform an operation, such as opening a form or displaying a report in the Print Preview window. For example, clicking the Orders command button on the Restaurant Database switchboard causes Access to perform a macro containing the action that opens the Order Data form.

Access lets you automate most tasks using either macros or Visual Basic, the programming language for Microsoft applications. As a beginner, you will find it easier to write macros than to create programs using Visual Basic. With macros, you simply select a series of actions from a list so that the macro does what you want it to do. To use Visual Basic you need to understand the Visual Basic command language well enough to be able to write your own code. Visual Basic does provide advantages over macros, including better error-handling capabilities, and it makes your application easier to change. Macros, however, are useful for small applications and for simple tasks, such as opening and closing objects. Additionally, you cannot use Visual Basic and must use macros when assigning actions to a specific key or key combination, and when opening an application in a special way, such as displaying a switchboard.

Before you begin creating the Restaurant Database switchboard, Leonard suggests that you gain some experience with macros by creating a few practice macros first.

Creating Macros

You create macros in the Macro window, which you display from the Macros tab of the Database window.

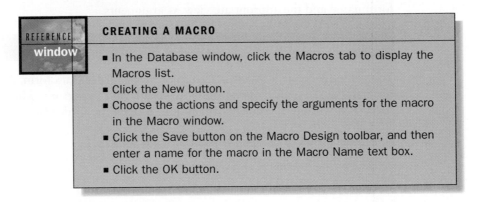

REFERENCE window

CREATING A MACRO

- In the Database window, click the Macros tab to display the Macros list.
- Click the New button.
- Choose the actions and specify the arguments for the macro in the Macro window.
- Click the Save button on the Macro Design toolbar, and then enter a name for the macro in the Macro Name text box.
- Click the OK button.

You'll practice working with macros by first creating a simple macro that will open the Order Data form in the Restaurant database. To begin, you need to open the Macro window.

To open the Macro window:

1. Place your Student Disk in the appropriate disk drive, start Access, and then open the Restaurant database in the Tutorial folder on your Student Disk.

2. Click the **Macros** tab in the Database window to display the Macros list. The list is empty because the database currently contains no macros.

3. Click the **New** button. Access opens the Macro window. See Figure 9-3.

Figure 9-3 ◀
Macro window

Macro Design toolbar —

Macro window —

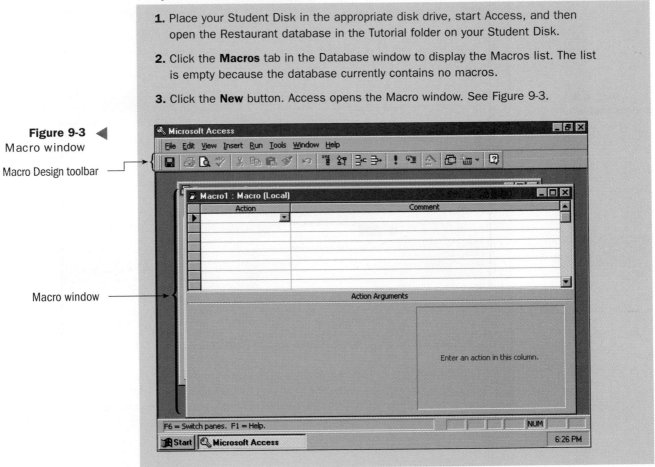

In the Macro window you create and modify macros. Both the menu bar and toolbar for the Macro window have options that are specifically related to macros. The Macro window also includes an **Action column,** in which you enter the action you want Access to perform, and a **Comment column,** in which you enter optional comments to document the specific action.

When you choose the first action for your macro, Access displays a hint for the current macro property in the lower panel of the Macro window on the right. On the left, Access lists the arguments associated with the action you choose. **Arguments** are additional facts Access needs to execute an action. The action for opening a form, for example, needs the form name and the appropriate view as arguments.

Choosing Actions for a Macro

You can now create a simple macro to open the Order Data form. Access provides actions for many of the typical operations you would want to perform while working with a database. You will use the OpenForm action to open the Order Data form.

To create a macro to open the Order Data form:

1. Click the **Action** list arrow in the first row.

2. Scroll down the list, and then click **OpenForm**. Access closes the list box, displays OpenForm as the first action, and displays six arguments for this action in the lower panel.

3. Press the **Tab** key, and then type **Open the Order Data form** in the Comment text box.

   Next, you will specify the argument for the action. The argument for this action is the name of the form that Access opens when the OpenForm action is performed.

4. In the Action Arguments panel of the Macro window, click the right side of the **Form Name** text box to display the list of forms, and then click **Order Data**. See Figure 9-4.

Figure 9-4 ◄
OpenForm
action

action ──────

comment ──────

arguments ──────

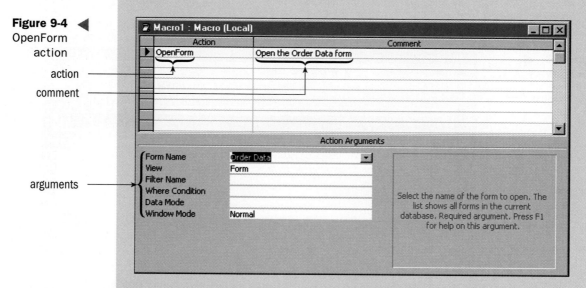

For now, you don't need to change any other argument. When you run the macro, Access will open the Order Data form in Form view, display the form without using a filter or special condition, and allow edits or changes to the data. Now you can save the macro as Open Practice.

5. Click the **Save** button 🖫 on the Macro Design toolbar.

6. Type **Open Practice** in the Macro Name text box, and then press the **Enter** key. Access closes the dialog box and saves the macro.

Access

Running a Macro

After creating a macro, you need to run it to make sure that it works correctly. You can run a macro in three different ways:

- In the Macro window, click the Run button on the Macro Design toolbar.

- Click Tools on the menu bar, click Run Macro, scroll through the Macro Name list box, click the macro name, and then click the OK button.

- In the Database window, click the Macros tab, click the macro name, and then click the Run button.

You will use the first method to run the macro you just created and saved. If you had not already saved the macro, Access would tell you to save the macro before you could run it.

To run the Open Practice macro:

1. Click the **Run** button on the Macro Design toolbar. Access opens the Order Data form in Form view. See Figure 9-5.

Figure 9-5
Using a macro to open the Order Data form

Order Data form in Form view

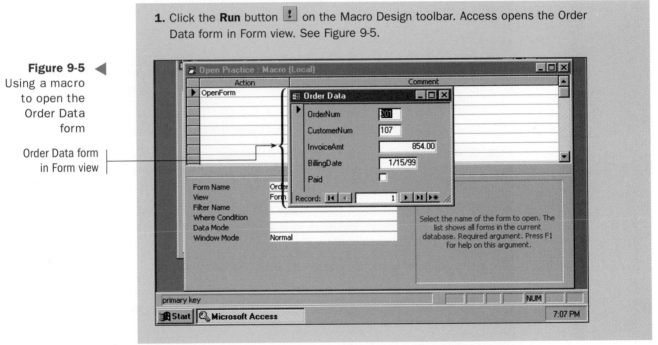

Access executes the macro by opening the Order Data form in Form view. You could now work with the fields and records of the Order Data form. This first macro is not very sophisticated; it involves only one action. However, it illustrates how to create and use a macro.

Adding Actions to a Macro

To practice creating a macro with more than one action, you can add a few actions to the Open Practice macro. Before the OpenForm action, you will add the Hourglass and Beep actions. The **Hourglass action** displays an hourglass pointer while the macro is being executed, and the **Beep action** sounds a beep tone through the computer's speaker. Because the Hourglass and Beep action names are self-descriptive, you do not need to add comments to document them. Following the OpenForm action, you will add actions to open the Invoice Statistics by Billing Date query, perform the Beep action, close the Invoice Statistics by Billing Date query, close the Order Data form, and then perform the Beep action a final time.

To add the actions to the Open Practice macro:

1. Click the **Close** button ☒ on the Form window to close it and return to the Macro window.

2. Right-click the row selector for the first row in the Macro window to open the shortcut menu, and then click **Insert Rows**. Access inserts a blank row above the OpenForm action. Repeat this step to insert a second blank row above the OpenForm action.

   First you'll add the Hourglass action so that the hourglass pointer will appear when you run the macro. Then you'll add the Beep action.

3. Click the right side of the first row's **Action** text box, scroll down the list, and then click **Hourglass**. The default value for the Hourglass On argument is Yes. This is the value you want, so you are done adding the first action.

4. Click the right side of the second row's **Action** text box, and then click **Beep**. The Beep action has no arguments, so you are done adding this action.

   You need to add the Beep action two more times, so that the beep will sound after you open the query and after you close the query and the form. The easiest way to add this action twice is to copy and paste it.

5. Right-click the row selector for the second row, click **Copy** on the shortcut menu, right-click the row selector for the fifth row, click **Paste**, right-click the row selector for the eighth row, and then click **Paste**. Access adds the Beep action to the fifth and eighth rows.

   Next, in the fourth row, you need to add the action for opening the query.

6. Click the right side of the fourth row's **Action** text box, scroll down the list, click **OpenQuery**, press the **Tab** key, and then type **Open the Invoice Statistics by Billing Date query** in the Comment text box.

7. Click the right side of the **Query Name** text box in the Action Arguments panel, and then click **Invoice Statistics by Billing Date**. This specifies the query that you want the action to open.

   Next you need to add the action for closing the query.

8. Click the right side of the sixth row's **Action** text box, click **Close**, press the **Tab** key, and then type **Close the Invoice Statistics by Billing Date query** in the Comment text box.

   For this action, you need to specify two arguments: the type of object to close and the name of the specific object to close.

9. Click the right side of the **Object Type** text box in the Action Arguments panel, and then click **Query**. Click the right side of the **Object Name** text box, and then click **Invoice Statistics by Billing Date**.

   Finally, you need to add the Close action to close the Order Data form.

10. Click the right side of the seventh row's **Action** text box, click **Close**, press the **Tab** key, and then type **Close the Order Data form** in the Comment text box.

11. Click the right side of the **Object Type** text box in the Action Arguments panel, and then click **Form**. Click the right side of the **Object Name** text box, and then click **Order Data**. You have finished adding the actions to the macro. See Figure 9-6.

Access

Figure 9-6
Macro with
multiple
actions

Single Step button

macro now contains
eight actions

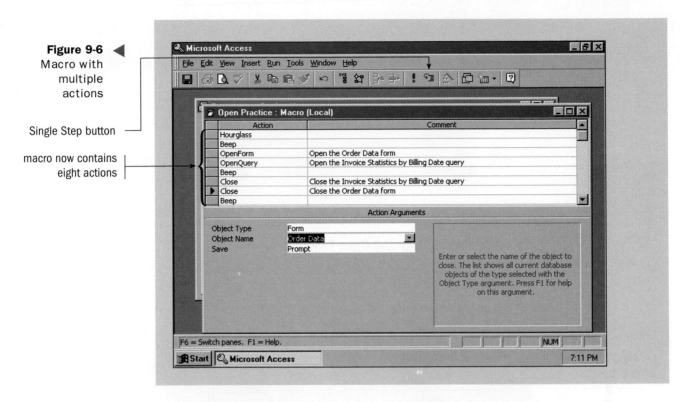

Now you can execute the macro, again using the Run button on the toolbar. When you do, you'll be prompted to save the modified macro.

To run and save the macro:

1. Click the **Run** button 🔳 on the Macro Design toolbar. A dialog box asks if you want to save the macro.

2. Click the **Yes** button. Access closes the dialog box, saves the macro, and executes the macro.

Depending on the speed of your computer, the Form and Query windows might open and close too quickly to be seen clearly, but you should be able to hear the three beeps distinctly and see the hourglass pointer.

TROUBLE? If you hear only two beeps, your computer probably executed the macro so quickly that the last two beeps occurred very close together and sounded like one beep.

Because a macro often runs too quickly for you to check all the actions it performs, Access allows you to run through a macro one step at a time.

Single-Stepping a Macro

Single-stepping executes a macro one action at a time, pausing between actions. You use single-stepping to make sure you have placed actions in the right order and with the right arguments. If you have problems with a macro, you can use single-stepping to find the cause of the problems and to determine their proper corrections. The Single Step button on the Macro Design toolbar (see Figure 9-6) is a toggle you use to turn single-stepping on and off. Once you turn on single-stepping, it stays on for all macros until you turn it off.

SINGLE-STEPPING A MACRO

- In the Macro window, click the Single Step button on the Macro Design toolbar.
- Click the Run button on the Macro Design toolbar.
- In the Macro Single Step dialog box, click the Step button to execute the next action, click the Halt button to stop the macro, or click the Continue button to execute all remaining actions in the macro and turn off single-stepping.

To get a clearer view of the Open Practice macro's actions, you can single-step through it.

To single-step through the Open Practice macro:

1. Click the **Single Step** button on the Macro Design toolbar to turn on single-stepping.

2. Click the **Run** button on the Macro Design toolbar. The Macro Single Step dialog box opens. See Figure 9-7.

Figure 9-7 ◀
Macro Single
Step dialog box

information about
the current macro
and action

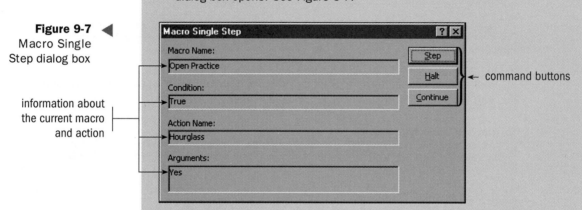

command buttons ←

When you single-step through a macro, Access displays the Macro Single Step dialog box before performing each action. This dialog box shows the macro name and the action's condition, name, and arguments. The action will be executed or not executed, depending on whether the condition is true or false. The three command buttons let you step one action at a time through the macro, halt the macro and return to the Macro window, or continue by executing all remaining actions without pause. Note that single-stepping is turned off if you click the Continue button.

3. Click the **Step** button. Access runs the first action (Hourglass) and shows the macro's second action in the Macro Single Step dialog box. Because the Hourglass action changes the pointer to an hourglass for the duration of the macro, you can see the hourglass pointer if you move the pointer outside the Macro Single Step dialog box.

4. Click the **Step** button. Access runs the second action by sounding a beep and shows the macro's third action.

5. Click the **Step** button six more times, making sure you read the Macro Single Step dialog box carefully and observe the windows opening and closing on the screen after each click. The Macro Single Step dialog box closes automatically after the last macro action is completed.

6. Click the **Close** button on the Macro window to close it and return to the Database window.

Adding Actions by Dragging

Another way to add an action to a macro is by dragging an object from the Database window to a new row in the Macro window. When you do so, Access adds the action that is appropriate and specifies default argument values for the action. Figure 9-8 describes the effect of dragging each of the six Access objects to a new row in the Macro window. For example, dragging a table creates an OpenTable action that opens the table in Datasheet view and permits editing or updating. To use this dragging technique, be sure that the Macro and Database windows are both visible. You can move the two windows until you see all the critical components of each window, or use the Tile Horizontally or Tile Vertically command on the Window menu.

Figure 9-8 ◀
Actions created
by dragging
objects from
the Database
window

Object Dragged	Action Created	Arguments and Their Default Values
Table	OpenTable	View: Datasheet Data Mode: Edit
Query	OpenQuery	View: Datasheet Data Mode: Edit
Form	OpenForm	View: Form Data Mode: none Filter Name: none Where Condition: none Window Mode: Normal
Report	OpenReport	View: Print Filter Name: none Where Condition: none
Macro	RunMacro	Repeat Count: none Repeat Expression: none
Module	OpenModule	Procedure Name: none

REFERENCE
window

CREATING AN ACTION BY DRAGGING

- Open the Macro window and the Database window.
- Drag a database object from the Database window to an Action text box in the Macro window. Access adds the action that is appropriate for the macro and sets the arguments to their default values.

To continue practicing working with macros, you'll create a new macro named More Practice, and you'll use the dragging technique to add an action that opens the Customer Data form.

To create the new macro and add an action using the dragging method:

1. Click the **New** button to open the Macro window.

2. Click **Window** on the menu bar, and then click **Tile Vertically** to tile the Macro window and the Database window. See Figure 9-9.

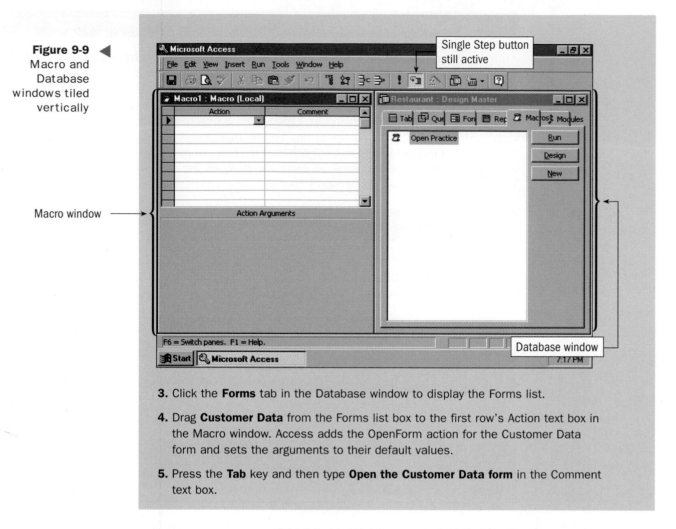

Figure 9-9
Macro and
Database
windows tiled
vertically

Macro window

3. Click the **Forms** tab in the Database window to display the Forms list.

4. Drag **Customer Data** from the Forms list box to the first row's Action text box in the Macro window. Access adds the OpenForm action for the Customer Data form and sets the arguments to their default values.

5. Press the **Tab** key and then type **Open the Customer Data form** in the Comment text box.

Next you will add the MsgBox action to the macro to open a dialog box containing an informational message. Before adding this action, Leonard suggests that you first use the Access Help system to learn more about macros and actions in general and the MsgBox action in particular.

Using Help to Learn About Macros and Actions

When you create Access macros, you need to know about the available actions and their arguments. Access provides 48 actions for use in macros grouped under five categories. Actions in the "Data in forms and reports" category move the focus from one record to another record. **Focus** refers to the record and control that is currently active and awaiting user action. For example, a field has the focus when it is highlighted or when the insertion point is positioned in it, and a command button has the focus when a dotted box appears around its label.

Actions in the "Execution" category either start or stop tasks. Actions in the "Import/export" category transfer data between the active database and other applications. Actions in the "Object manipulation" category open, close, size, and otherwise act upon Access objects. The "Miscellaneous" category contains actions that inform the user (Echo, Hourglass, MsgBox, SetWarnings, and ShowToolbar), emit a sound (Beep), send keystrokes (SendKeys), and create a custom menu bar (AddMenu, SetMenuItem).

Do not be concerned about learning all 48 actions. You will rarely need to use more than a dozen actions in most database applications. In this tutorial and the next, you will gain experience with several macro actions. Because there are so many, it is difficult to remember them all. Fortunately, the Access Help system is a complete and convenient reference for macros and actions. The Access Help system contains, in a single reference

Access

source with one index, all the information you need and is available to answer your questions while you are working with Access. You can even print more complicated topics for study away from the computer.

You'll use the Access Help system to learn more about the MsgBox action.

To use Help to learn about the MsgBox action:

1. Click **Help** on the menu bar, and then click **Contents and Index** to open the Access Help window.

2. If necessary, click the **Index** tab to display the Index page.

3. Type **actions** in the upper text box. The Index page displays a list of index entries associated with actions.

4. Click **reference topics** and then click the **Display** button. Access opens the Actions Grouped by Task topic, which is a complete list of the 48 actions. See Figure 9-10.

Figure 9-10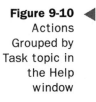
Actions
Grouped by
Task topic in
the Help
window

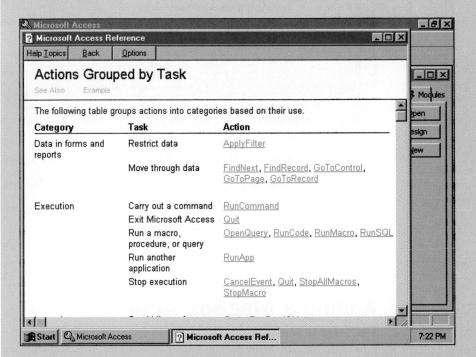

Next, you'll display the MsgBox Action topic and then print it. You can then refer to this information to complete the macro you are creating.

5. Scroll down the Actions Grouped by Task topic window to the Miscellaneous category, and then click **MsgBox**. Access opens the MsgBox Action topic. See Figure 9-11.

Figure 9-11 ◀
MsgBox Action
topic in the
Help window

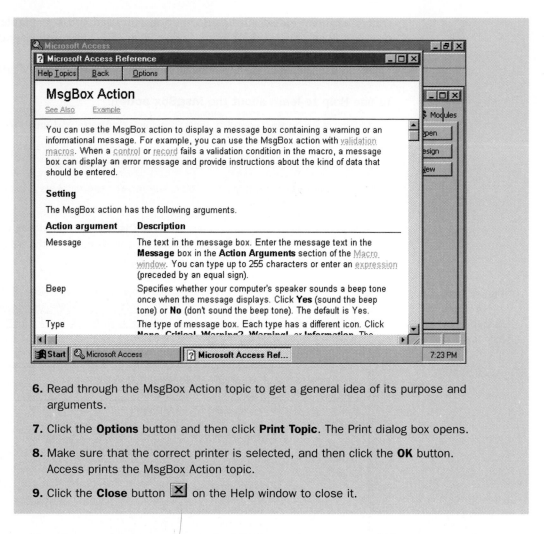

6. Read through the MsgBox Action topic to get a general idea of its purpose and arguments.

7. Click the **Options** button and then click **Print Topic**. The Print dialog box opens.

8. Make sure that the correct printer is selected, and then click the **OK** button. Access prints the MsgBox Action topic.

9. Click the **Close** button [X] on the Help window to close it.

Now that you know more about the MsgBox action, you can add it to your practice macro.

Adding a MsgBox Action

The **MsgBox action** causes Access to open a dialog box that remains on the screen until you click the OK button. The macro containing this action does not proceed to the next action until you click the OK button, so when you add this action to your More Practice macro, you'll have as much time as you need to look at the opened Customer Data form.

The MsgBox action requires four arguments: Message, Beep, Type, and Title, as described in the MsgBox Action Help topic. You will provide the following action arguments for the MsgBox action in your macro:

- Message: Click OK to resume the macro. This is the text that will appear in the message box when it is displayed.

- Beep: No. This means that no beep will sound when the message box is opened.

- Type: Information. This argument determines which icon appears in the message box. The information icon indicates that this message is for information only, as opposed to a warning that an irreversible action will take place.

- Title: Message Box Practice. This title will appear in the message box title bar.

As you move from one macro argument to the next in the Macro window, Access changes the description that appears to the right of the argument text boxes. The description is a brief explanation of the current macro argument. If you need a more detailed explanation, press the F1 key. When you are working with the MsgBox action in the

Macro window and press the F1 key, for example, the Access Help system opens the MsgBox Action topic. This is the same topic you saw using the Access Help system.

To add a MsgBox action to the macro:

1. Click the right side of the second row's **Action** text box, scroll down, and then click **MsgBox**.

2. Press the **Tab** key and then type **Display a practice message box** in the Comment text box.

3. Click the **Message** text box, and then type **Click OK to resume the macro**. This text will appear in the message box when you run the macro.

4. Click the right side of the **Beep** text box, and then click **No**.

5. Click the right side of the **Type** text box, and then click **Information**. This argument specifies that the message box will be an informational one as opposed to a warning.

6. Click the **Title** text box, and then type **Message Box Practice**.

The macro now contains two actions: the first action opens the Customer Data form, and the second action displays an informational message box. To complete the macro, you need to add the Close action for the Customer Data form. Once again you can drag the Customer Data form from the Database window, but this time you'll do so to specify the Close action's arguments.

To set the Close action's arguments using the dragging method:

1. Click the right side of the third row's **Action** text box, and then click **Close**.

2. Press the **Tab** key, and then type **Close the Customer Data form** in the Comment text box.

3. Drag **Customer Data** from the Forms list in the Database window to the Object Name text box in the Macro window. When you release the mouse button in the Object Name text box, Access automatically sets the Object Type argument to Form and the Object Name argument to Customer Data. See Figure 9-12.

Figure 9-12 ◄
Macro window
with action
arguments set
by dragging

Close action
specified

Object Name text box

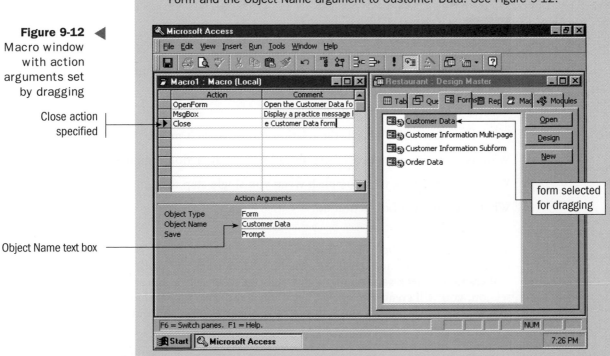

Because the macro is now complete, you need to run it to be sure it is correct. Before you do, you'll save the macro with the name More Practice.

To save and run the macro:

1. If the Single Step button ▣ on the Macro Design toolbar is selected, click it to deselect it.

2. Click the **Save** button 🖫 on the Macro Design toolbar to save the macro. The Save As dialog box opens.

3. Type **More Practice** in the Macro Name text box, and then press the **Enter** key. Access saves the macro.

4. Click the **Run** button ❗ on the Macro Design toolbar. Access runs the first two macro actions by opening the message box after opening the Customer Data form. See Figure 9-13.

Figure 9-13 ◀
Running
the MsgBox
macro action

information icon

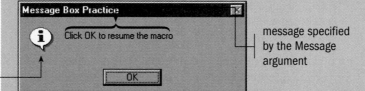

message specified
by the Message
argument

Notice that the text you entered for the Message argument appears above the OK button. Also, notice the icon with the letter "i" to the left of the message box text. This icon indicates an informational message box.

5. Click the **OK** button. Access closes the dialog box, runs the last macro action by closing the Customer Data form, and displays the Macro window.

6. Click the **Close** button ✕ on the Macro window to close it and return to the Database window.

TROUBLE? If you accidentally clicked the Close button on the Database window and closed the Restaurant database, simply reopen the Restaurant database.

Quick Check

[1] Give a definition of a switchboard, describe its significant features, and provide two reasons for using one.

[2] What is a hot key and how do you use it?

[3] What is a macro and what is the relationship between a macro and an action?

[4] What is an action argument? Give an example of an action argument.

[5] What are you trying to accomplish when you single-step through a macro?

[6] What does the MsgBox action do?

You have now finished practicing with macros and are ready to create the macros you need for the Restaurant Database switchboard and dialog boxes. In the next session, you will create the necessary dialog boxes and place command buttons on them. In the final session, you will create the switchboard form and the macros that will be attached to the dialog box command buttons and the switchboard command buttons.

SESSION

9.2

In this session you will create a new table and associated queries to create the lists of reports and queries displayed in the dialog boxes. Then you will create and test the dialog boxes containing command buttons.

Planning the User Interface

There are many steps necessary to create the user interface for the Restaurant database. You will create forms for the switchboard and the two dialog boxes, build a custom menu bar, and create a custom toolbar. In addition, each dialog box will contain a list of available objects (reports or queries). To make these lists available to the dialog boxes when they open, you will create a special table, called ObjectNames, that contains the names of all the available reports and queries. Using the table, you will then create two queries. One query will select all report names in alphabetical order, and the other query will select all query names in alphabetical order. When the Reports Dialog Box is opened, it will run the report names query and display the query results in a list box. The user will then be able to select from the list of report names to view or print a report. Similarly, when the Queries Dialog Box is opened, it will run the query names query and display the list of available queries in a list box. The user will then be able to select a query to run or preview.

Figure 9-14 shows the objects you will create and their names.

Figure 9-14 ◀
Objects to be created for the Restaurant database user interface

Object	Object Name
Switchboard form	Switchboard
Queries dialog box	Queries Dialog Box
Reports dialog box	Reports Dialog Box
Custom menu bar	Restaurant Menu
Custom toolbar	Restaurant
Query and report names table	ObjectNames
Query names query	QueryNames
Report names query	ReportNames

Creating the ObjectNames Table and Its Queries

The switchboard command buttons run macros to do the following: display three forms (Customers, Orders, and Customers With Orders), display two dialog boxes (one for reports and one for queries), exit the switchboard, and exit Access, as shown in Figure 9-15.

Figure 9-15 ◀
Command
buttons on the
switchboard

open forms ——————

open dialog boxes ——————

exit switchboard ——————

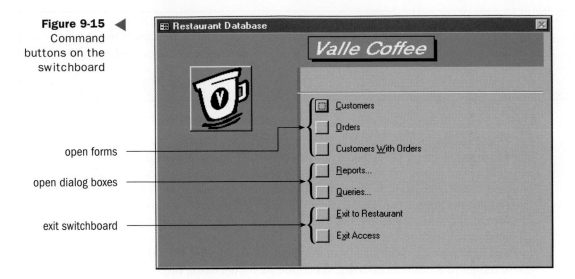

To test the switchboard design, the forms and dialog boxes must be available. You have some work to do before creating the switchboard. Because you have already created the three forms, your next task is to create the dialog boxes for the switchboard. In addition, each dialog box will use a query to select and display the names of the available reports or queries. One query will select the report names; the other query will select the query names. You need to create the table and queries before you can create the dialog boxes.

Creating the ObjectNames Table Structure

Your first step is to create the table containing the report and query names. The table design consists of the following three fields:

- ObjectId is an AutoNumber field that serves as the table's primary key.

- ObjectType is a one-character Text field with two valid field values: Q for query and R for report.

- ObjectName is a 35-character Text field that will contain the report and query names as field values.

You'll begin by creating the ObjectNames table.

To create the ObjectNames table:

1. If you took a break after the previous session, start Access and open the Restaurant database in the Tutorial folder on your Student Disk.

2. If necessary, reposition and resize the Database window so that all tabs are completely visible.

3. Click the **Tables** tab to display the Tables list, and then click the **New** button. The New Table dialog box opens.

4. Click **Design View** and then click the **OK** button. Access opens the Table window in Design view. Now you can define the three fields for the table.

5. Type **ObjectID** in the Field Name text box, press the **Tab** key, type **a** (for AutoNumber) in the Data Type text box, press the **Tab** key, type **primary key** in the Description text box, and then press the **Tab** key. The definition of the first field is complete.

6. Type **ObjectType** in the Field Name text box, press the **Tab** key twice, and then type **Q for a query, R for a report** in the Description text box.

To complete the second field's definition, you must set the field properties. You will set the Field Size property value to 1 because the ObjectType field will contain a single character, Q (for Query) or R (for Report). To prevent any user from entering a value other than Q or R, you will also set the Validation Rule property value. The **Validation Rule** property value specifies the valid values that can be entered in a field. You will also enter a Validation Text property value. The **Validation Text** property value will be displayed in a dialog box if the user enters an invalid value (in this case, a value other than Q or R).

To complete the ObjectNames table structure definition:

1. Double-click **50** in the Field Size text box, and then type **1**.

   To make sure that the only values entered in the ObjectType field are Q or R (for Query or Report), you'll specify a list of valid values in the Validation Rule text box.

2. Click the **Validation Rule** text box, and then type **Q Or R**.

   The Validation Text text box allows you to specify a message that will be displayed if the user enters a value not listed in the Validation Rule text box.

3. Click the **Validation Text** text box, and then type **Must be Q or R**. The second field is now defined.

   You can now enter the definition of the third field.

4. Click the third row's **Field Name** text box, type **ObjectName**, press the **Tab** key twice, double-click **50** in the Field Size text box, and then type **35**.

   The third field is defined, and you can now specify ObjectID as the table's primary key.

5. Click the row selector for the **ObjectID** field to highlight the row, and then click the **Primary Key** button on the Table Design toolbar. Access places the primary key field symbol in the row selector for the ObjectID field. See Figure 9-16.

Figure 9-16 ◀
Structure of the
ObjectNames
table

primary key
indicator

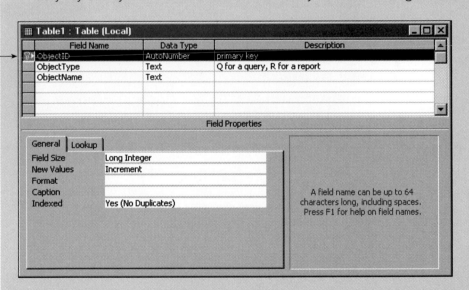

6. Click the **Save** button on the Table Design toolbar. Access opens the dialog box to save the table.

7. Type **ObjectNames** in the Table Name text box, and then press the **Enter** key. Access saves the new table structure

8. Click the **View** button for Datasheet view on the Table Design toolbar. Access displays the table in Datasheet view.

Adding Records to the ObjectNames Table

You can now add the necessary records to the ObjectNames table. Each record will identify a report or a query that Leonard wants to make available through the Restaurant Database switchboard. The ObjectType field value identifies the object as a report or a query. The ObjectName field contains the name of the report or the query. You do not need to enter a field value for the ObjectID field, because it is an AutoNumber field that Access automatically controls.

You can now add the records to the table.

To add the records to the ObjectNames table:

1. Press the **Tab** key, type **R**, press the **Tab** key, type **Customers and Orders**, and then press the **Tab** key. The first record is added to the table.

2. Enter the remaining six records shown in Figure 9-17. Resize the widths of all three datasheet columns to their best fit. Take a moment to check the values you entered and correct any that do not appear exactly as shown in Figure 9-17. Capitalization and spelling are important because these object names will appear in the dialog boxes. In the next tutorial, you will create the Visual Basic code that will use the ObjectName values to open the appropriate database objects.

Figure 9-17 ◀
Completed datasheet for the ObjectNames table

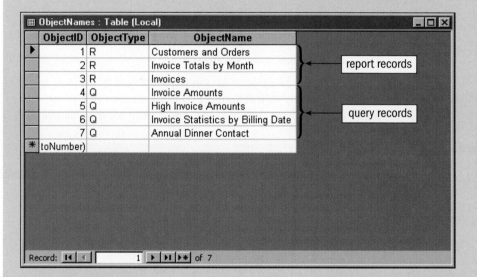

The records in Figure 9-17 contain the names of the reports and queries that Leonard wants to make available to users of the Restaurant Database switchboard. When a user clicks the Reports command button on the switchboard, the Reports Dialog Box will display the list of report names in the ObjectNames table. Similarly, when a user clicks the Queries command button on the switchboard, the Queries Dialog Box will display the list of query names.

3. Click the **Save** button 🖫 on the Table Datasheet toolbar, and then click the **Close** button ⊠ on the Table window to close it and return to the Database window.

Now that you have created the ObjectNames table, you can create the two new queries. These queries will select either the report names or the query names from the ObjectNames table so that they can be displayed in the appropriate dialog boxes.

Creating the Queries

Both queries you need to create are based on the ObjectNames table. Each query selects the ObjectType and ObjectName fields and performs an ascending sort using the ObjectName field. One query, which you will call QueryNames, selects only query object records. These records will appear in the list box of the Queries Dialog Box so that a user can choose a particular query to run. The second query, which you will call ReportNames, selects only report object records. These records will appear in the list box of the Reports Dialog Box, so that a user can choose a particular report to view or print.

First, you'll create the QueryNames query.

To create the QueryNames query:

1. Click the **Queries** tab to display the Queries list, and then click the **New** button. The New Query dialog box opens.

2. Make sure that **Design View** is selected, and then click the **OK** button. The Show Table dialog box opens on top of the Query window in Design view.

3. Click **ObjectNames** in the Tables list, click the **Add** button to add the ObjectNames table to the Query window, and then click the **Close** button to close the Show Table dialog box.

4. Click and drag the **ObjectType** field from the ObjectNames field list to the first column in the design grid. Access adds the ObjectType field to the design grid.

5. Click and drag the **ObjectName** field from the ObjectNames field list to the second column in the design grid. Access adds the ObjectName field to the design grid.

6. Click the **Criteria** text box for the ObjectType field, and then type **Q** to select just the query object records.

7. Click the right side of the **Sort** text box for the ObjectName field, and then click **Ascending** to produce an ascending sort based on the ObjectName field.

8. Click the **Run** button ⬍ on the Query Design toolbar. Access displays the query results. See Figure 9-18. Make sure you have spelled each query name correctly.

Figure 9-18 ◀
Queries
from the
ObjectNames
table

queries displayed in
ascending order

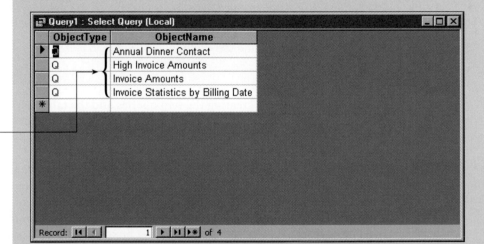

TROUBLE? If you haven't spelled each name correctly, make the corrections now in the query datasheet.

9. Click the **View** button for Design view 📐 on the Query Datasheet toolbar to switch back to Design view.

10. Click the **Save** button 🖫 on the Query Design toolbar, type **QueryNames** in the Query Name text box, and then press the **Enter** key. Access saves the QueryNames query.

The QueryNames query selects the ObjectName field values for the queries in the ObjectNames table. These query names will appear in the list of available queries when the Queries Dialog Box is open. The user will then be able to select the appropriate query to run.

You can now modify the QueryNames query to create the query that will list the report names. You'll simply change the Q in the Criteria text box for the ObjectType field to an R, run the query to test it, and then save it as ReportNames.

To create the ReportNames query:

1. Double-click the **Q** in the Criteria text box for the ObjectType field, and then type **R**. The query will display the report objects in ascending order.

2. Click the **Run** button 🛗 on the Query Design toolbar. Access displays the query results. See Figure 9-19. Be sure you have spelled each report name correctly.

Figure 9-19 ◀
Reports
from the
ObjectNames
table

reports displayed in
ascending order

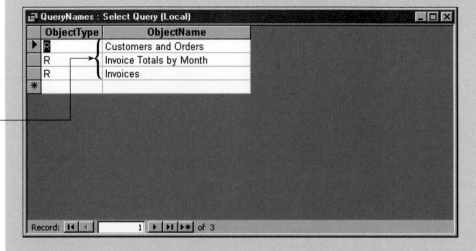

TROUBLE? If you haven't spelled each name correctly, make the corrections now in the query datasheet.

3. Click **File** on the menu bar, click **Save As/Export**, select **Query** in "QueryNames" in the New Name text box, type **Report** to change the name to ReportNames, and then press the **Enter** key. Access saves the query as ReportNames.

4. Click the **Close** button ⊠ on the Table window to close it and return to the Database window.

You have completed creating the two queries and the table for the Restaurant Database switchboard. When the switchboard interface is completed, the user will be able to display the Reports Dialog Box, which will show a list of available reports for viewing or printing. If Leonard wants to change the list of available reports, you simply need to add or delete report records in the ObjectNames table. These changes will automatically be reflected when the Reports Dialog Box is displayed. Similarly, the Queries Dialog Box will show a list of available queries for viewing. If Leonard wants to change the list of available queries, you simply need to add or delete query records in the ObjectNames table.

Your next step is to create the two dialog boxes. The results of the queries you just created will appear in list boxes in the two dialog boxes for the switchboard.

Creating Dialog Boxes

You will first create the Reports Dialog Box form and then create the Queries Dialog Box by modifying the Reports Dialog Box. The queries based on the ObjectNames table supply the values that appear in the list boxes in the dialog boxes. Figure 9-20 shows how the list will look in each dialog box.

Figure 9-20
Lists in the
Reports Dialog
Box and
Queries
Dialog Box

list from
ReportNames query

list from
QueryNames query

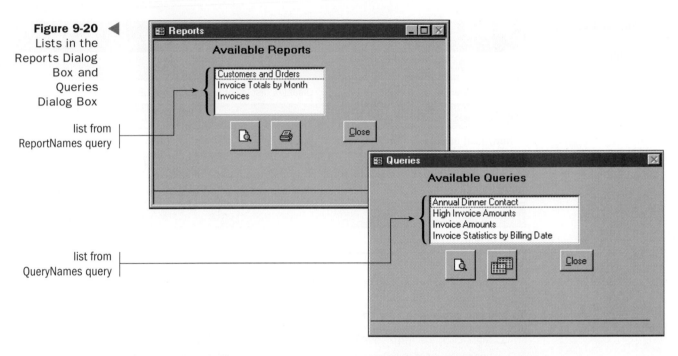

Both dialog boxes will look and work in the same way. Double-clicking a report or query name will open that report or query in Print Preview, as will clicking a report or query name and then clicking the command button that contains the Print Preview icon. Clicking a report name and then clicking the command button with the printer icon will print that report. Clicking a query name and then clicking the command button with the datasheet icon will display that query's results. Clicking the Close button will close the dialog box and activate the switchboard. The underlined letter "C" in the two Close command buttons identifies the button's hot key. Pressing Alt + C will close the dialog box, just as clicking the Close command button will.

Creating the Reports Dialog Box

To create the Reports Dialog Box, you'll begin by creating a blank form based on the ReportNames query.

To create the Reports Dialog Box form:

1. Click the **Forms** tab to display the Forms list, and then click the **New** button. The New Form dialog box opens.

2. Make sure that **Design View** is selected, click the list arrow for choosing the table or query for the form, click **ReportNames**, and then click the **OK** button. Access opens the Form window in Design view.

Before adding any controls to the form, you need to set the overall form properties so that the form matches Leonard's design. You will set the Caption property to Reports, which will appear in the title bar for the form. You will also set the Shortcut Menu, Record Selectors, Navigation Buttons, and Close Button properties to No, because Leonard doesn't want the form to include these elements. You will set the Auto Resize property to No so that Access will not resize the form when it is opened, maintaining a consistent form size. Also, Leonard does not want users to be able to open the form in Design view, so you will set the Modal property to Yes. Finally, after you have completed the design of the form, you will set the Border Style property to Dialog so that the form will be similar to a dialog box in that users will not be able to resize the form using the pointer. The property settings you will use are shown in Figure 9-21.

Figure 9-21 ◀
Form
properties

Property	Setting	Function
Caption	Reports	Value appears in the form's title bar
Shortcut Menu	No	Disables display of shortcut if the user right-clicks the form
Record Selectors	No	Disables display of record selectors
Navigation Buttons	No	Disables display of navigation buttons
Auto Resize	No	Opens a form in the last saved size
Modal	Yes	Prevents users from opening the form in Design view
Border Style	Dialog	Prevents users from resizing the form
Close Button	No	Disables display of the Close button

Working from this list, you can use the property sheet to set the form properties.

To set the properties for the form:

1. Right-click the form selector, which is the gray box immediately to the left of the horizontal ruler in the Form window, and then click **Properties** to open the property sheet for the form.

2. If necessary, click the **All** tab to display the All page of the property sheet.

   You can now set the Caption property for the form. The Caption property value will appear in the title bar when the form is displayed.

3. Click the **Caption** text box, and then type **Reports**.

   Next, you'll set the Record Selectors property so that record selectors will not be displayed on the form. Because the form does not display any records, there's no need to include selectors for them.

4. Scroll down until the Record Selectors property is visible, click the right side of the **Record Selectors** text box, and then click **No**.

   Now, set the remaining form properties.

5. Continue scrolling and set the **Navigation Buttons** property to **No**, set the **Auto Resize** property to **No**, set the **Modal** property to **Yes**, set the **Close Button** property to **No**, and then set the **Shortcut Menu** property to **No**.

6. Click the **Close** button ☒ on the property sheet to close it.

7. Click the **Save** button 🖫 on the Form Design toolbar, type **Reports Dialog Box** in the Form Name text box, and then press the **Enter** key. Access saves the form and displays the title in the title bar.

Now that you have set all the properties for the form, you can add a label and a list box to the form, using the Control Wizards tool for the list box. The label will identify the dialog box for the user, and the list box will display the list of reports from which to choose.

Adding a List Box to a Form

A **list box** is a control that displays a list of values. The list box in the Reports Dialog Box will display the list of reports that the user can view or print. Clicking the name of a report will select the report name. The user will then be able to click one of the command buttons to view or print the report. Double-clicking a report name in the list box will open the report in the Print Preview window.

REFERENCE window

ADDING A LIST BOX TO A FORM USING CONTROL WIZARDS

- If necessary, click the Control Wizards tool on the toolbox so that it is selected.
- Click the List Box tool on the toolbox.
- Position the pointer where you want the list box to appear in the form, and then click the left mouse button.
- Complete the List Box Wizard dialog boxes to choose the source of the list, select the fields to appear in the list box, size the columns, select the field that will provide the data for the field in the main form, choose to remember the value for later use or store it in a field, and enter the value to appear in the list box label.

First you'll add the label "Available Reports" to the form. Then you'll add the list box to display the list of reports from which to choose.

To add the label to the form:

1. If the toolbox is not displayed, click the **Toolbox** button 🛠 on the Form Design toolbar.

2. If necessary, drag the toolbox to the right side of the Form window, and then click the **Label** tool 〔Aa〕 on the toolbox.

3. Position the pointer ⁺A in the top line of grid dots at the ¾-inch mark on the horizontal ruler, and then click the left mouse button.

4. Type **Available Reports** and then press the **Enter** key.

   Leonard wants the label to stand out more, so you'll change the label's font size from the default of 8 to 10, make the label boldface, and then resize the label box.

5. Click the **Font Size** list arrow on the Formatting toolbar, click **10**, and then click the **Bold** button 〔B〕 on the Formatting toolbar.

6. Click **Format** on the menu bar, point to **Size**, and then click **To Fit**.

Now you can add the list box to the form. To do so, you'll use the List Box Wizard.

To add the list box to the form:

1. If the Control Wizards tool is not selected, click the **Control Wizards** tool 〔⬚〕 on the toolbox.

2. Click the **List Box** tool 〔▦〕 on the toolbox, position the pointer ⁺▦ two grid dots below the left edge of the Available Reports text box, and then click the left mouse button. After a few seconds, Access opens the first List Box Wizard dialog box.

   The ReportNames query will supply the values for the list box, so you want the list box to look up values from the ReportNames query.

3. Make sure the option button for looking up values in a table or query is selected, and then click the **Next** button. The next List Box Wizard dialog box opens.

4. Click the **Queries** option button, scroll the list box, click **ReportNames**, and then click the **Next** button.

   The ObjectName field contains the report names that you want to appear in the list box, so you need to select this field.

5. Click **ObjectName** in the Available Fields list to select it, and then click the ▸ button to move it to the Selected Fields list. Then click the **Next** button.

6. Double-click the right edge of the column selector to get the best column fit, and then click the **Next** button.

   In this dialog box, you can instruct Access to remember the selected value in the list box for later use (that is, when the user clicks a command button) or enter the selected value as a field value in a record. You want Access to remember the value for later use.

7. Make sure the option button for remembering the value for later use is selected, and then click the **Next** button. The final List Box Wizard dialog box opens.

   Leonard's design does not show a label for the list box, so you will delete the default label later. Because you will delete the label box attached to the list box, you do not need to change the label name.

8. Click the **Finish** button. Access closes the final List Box Wizard dialog box and displays the completed list box in the form's Detail section. See Figure 9-22.

Figure 9-22 ◀
Form design after adding the label and the list box

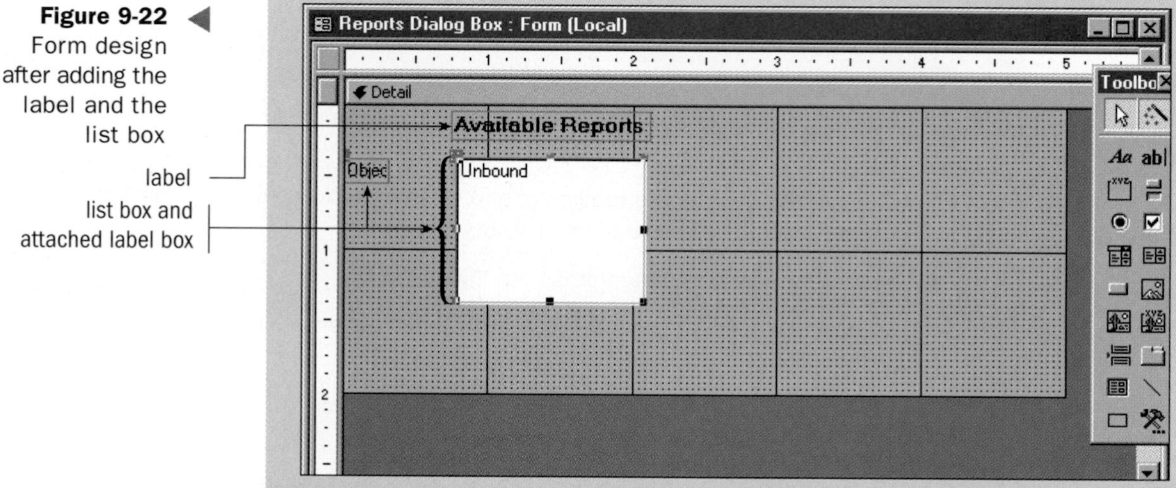

label

list box and attached label box

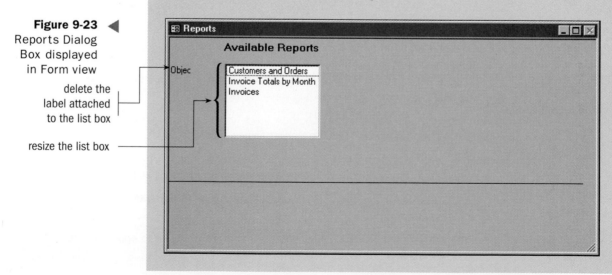

You can now save the form and then check your progress by switching to Form view.

9. Click the **Save** button 🖫 on the Form Design toolbar to save the form.

10. Click the **View** button for Form view 🖩 on the Form Design toolbar. Access displays the form in Form view. See Figure 9-23.

Figure 9-23 ◀
Reports Dialog Box displayed in Form view

delete the label attached to the list box

resize the list box

After viewing the form, Leonard asks you to make two changes to it before adding the command buttons. Because the form already includes the label "Available Reports," the label attached to the list box is unnecessary. Leonard asks you to delete this label. He'd also like you to resize the list box so that it will accommodate the list of reports better.

To delete the label attached to the list box and resize the list box:

1. Click the **View** button for Design view [icon] on the Form View toolbar to switch to Design view.

2. Right-click the label box for the attached label to open the shortcut menu, and then click **Cut** to delete the label box.

3. Click the list box to select it.

4. Drag the bottom border up to the row of grid dots at the 1-inch mark on the vertical ruler, and then drag the right border to the right until it lines up with the 2¼-inch mark on the horizontal ruler.

5. Click the **Save** button [icon] on the Form Design toolbar to save the form.

Adding a Command Button to a Form

Next you need to add the Print Preview command button to the form. A macro cannot handle the complex interaction that is involved in the actions of selecting a report or query in a list box and clicking a command button. This task requires Visual Basic code. So, the Print Preview and Print command buttons and the list box will be attached to Visual Basic code instead of macros.

In the next steps, you will add the Print Preview command button to the form. You can add a command button to a form by directly placing the button on the form or by using the Control Wizards tool. If you use the Control Wizards tool, you can attach a standard Access action (such as opening a specific report or closing a window) or a macro to the button. You cannot use a standard Access action for this command button, because the report you want to open will depend on the report the user has selected in the list box. Instead, you will add the command button directly to the form now and attach Visual Basic code to it in the next tutorial.

To add the Print Preview command button to the form:

1. Click the **Control Wizards** tool [icon] on the toolbox to deselect it.

2. Click the **Command Button** tool [icon] on the toolbox, position the pointer [icon] just below the list box and at the 1-inch mark on the horizontal ruler, and then click the left mouse button. Access adds a command button to the form.

3. Right-click the command button, and then click **Properties** on the shortcut menu to open the property sheet.

    TROUBLE? If the property sheet is covering the form, drag it out of the way.

    You can now change the picture that appears on the command button to the Print Preview picture, the same picture that appears on the Print Preview button on the standard toolbar.

4. Click the **All** tab in the property sheet (if necessary), click the **Picture** text box, and then click the **build** button [icon] that appears next to the text box. Access opens the Picture Builder dialog box, which provides a list of all the available pictures you can add to a command button.

5. Scroll through the Available Pictures list box, and then click **Preview Document**. Access shows the picture on the command button in the Sample box.

6. Click the **OK** button. Access closes the Picture Builder dialog box, resizes the command button, and places the picture on the command button.

Instead of repeating the steps to add the command button for printing, you can copy the first command button and paste it in the Detail section. After moving the copied button into position, you can change the picture on it to show the printer icon.

To create the Print command button on the form:

1. Right-click the command button, and then click **Copy** on the shortcut menu.

2. Click **Edit** on the menu bar, and then click **Paste**. Access adds a copy of the command button to the Detail section.

3. Move the new command button into position to the right of the original command button. See Figure 9-24.

Figure 9-24 ◄
Adding a copy of the command button

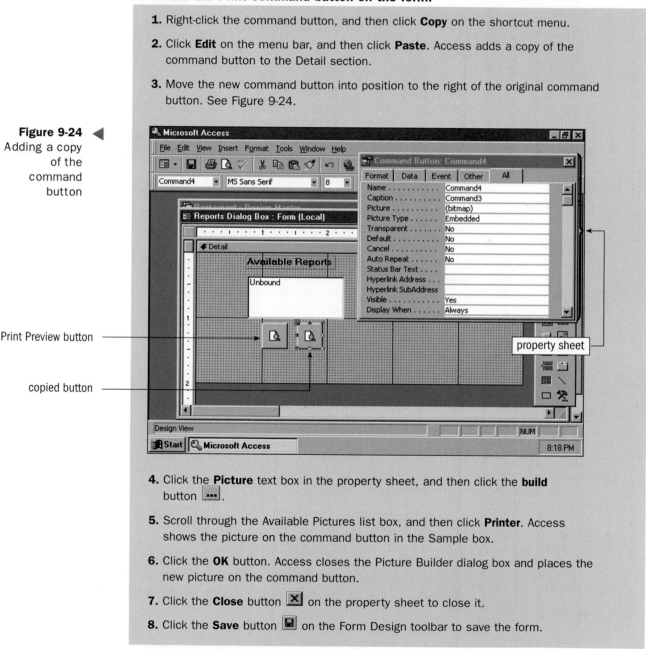

Print Preview button

copied button

property sheet

4. Click the **Picture** text box in the property sheet, and then click the **build** button 〔...〕.

5. Scroll through the Available Pictures list box, and then click **Printer**. Access shows the picture on the command button in the Sample box.

6. Click the **OK** button. Access closes the Picture Builder dialog box and places the new picture on the command button.

7. Click the **Close** button ☒ on the property sheet to close it.

8. Click the **Save** button 🖫 on the Form Design toolbar to save the form.

You can now add the final command button using Control Wizards. This button will close the dialog box when the user clicks it.

REFERENCE window

ADDING A COMMAND BUTTON TO A FORM USING CONTROL WIZARDS

- If necessary, click the Control Wizards tool on the toolbox so that it is selected.
- Click the Command Button tool on the toolbox.
- Place the pointer in the form where you want the command button to appear, and then click the left mouse button.
- Complete the Command Button Wizard dialog boxes to select the action category and the action for the command button, enter the text for the command button, define a hot key, and enter a name for the button.

To define the Close button, you can use the Control Wizards tool because the tool automatically attaches the correct Visual Basic code (for closing the dialog box) to the command button. Standard operations, such as opening and closing forms, are good candidates for using the Control Wizards tool. Leonard also wants a user to be able to close the dialog box using a keyboard combination, so you will specify the letter "C" as the hot key for the Close button. To underline the letter C and make it the hot key, you need to enter &Close as the Caption property value for the command button control on the form. Placing an ampersand (&) to the left of a character in a caption underlines the character on the open form and makes it that control's hot key. Note that any character, not just the first, can be specified as the hot key.

To add the Close command button using the Control Wizards tool:

1. Click the **Control Wizards** tool ⬚ on the toolbox to select it.

2. Click the **Command Button** tool ⬚ on the toolbox, position the pointer ⁺⬚ just below the list box and at the 2½-inch mark on the horizontal ruler, and then click the mouse button. Access adds a command button to the form and, after a few seconds, opens the first Command Button Wizard dialog box. The Sample box shows how the command button will appear. See Figure 9-25.

Figure 9-25 ◀
First Command
Button Wizard
dialog box

sample button

Categories list

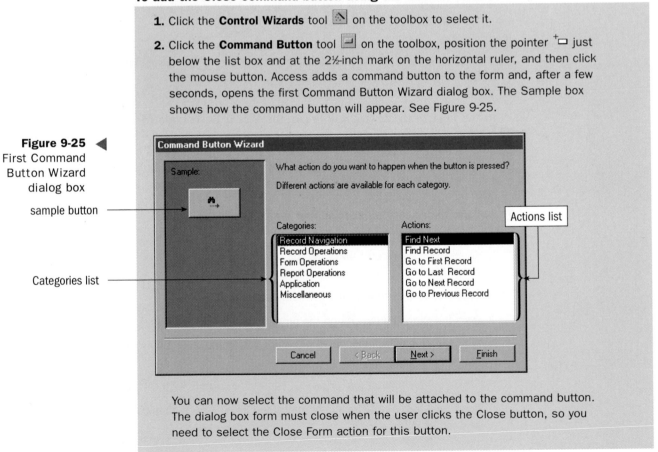

You can now select the command that will be attached to the command button. The dialog box form must close when the user clicks the Close button, so you need to select the Close Form action for this button.

3. Click **Form Operations** in the Categories list box, click **Close Form** in the Actions list box, and then click the **Next** button. Access opens the next Command Button Wizard dialog box, in which you specify the text or picture you want to appear on the button. In this case, Leonard wants the button to display the word "Close," with the letter "C" identified as the hot key.

4. Click the **Text** option button, select **Close Form** in the text box, and then type **&Close**. See Figure 9-26.

Figure 9-26 ◄
Specifying the
text on the
command
button

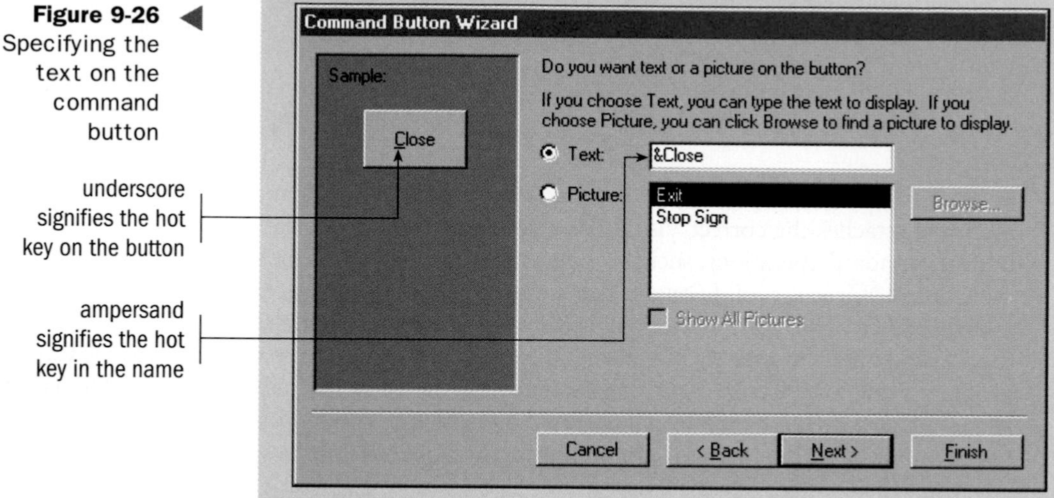

underscore
signifies the hot
key on the button

ampersand
signifies the hot
key in the name

5. Click the **Next** button. Access opens the next Command Button Wizard dialog box, in which you enter a name for the button.

6. Type **Close** in the text box, and then click the **Finish** button. Access closes the final Command Button Wizard dialog box and shows the new command button on the form.

In the next tutorial, you will create the Visual Basic code for the command buttons. This code will define what Access should do when a user clicks each button. The Visual Basic code you will create later will need to refer to the list box control, so now you will enter the name ReportList Control for the list box control. You will also resize the form and set the form's Border Style property to Dialog, according to Leonard's design.

To set the necessary properties and resize the form:

1. Right-click the list box control, and then click **Properties** to open the property sheet. If necessary, scroll to the top of the property sheet, and double-click the **Name** text box to select the current value for this property.

2. Type **ReportList Control** and then press the **Enter** key.

3. Click the **Close** button ☒ on the property sheet to close it.

4. Drag the right edge of the form's Detail section to the 3½-inch mark on the horizontal ruler.

5. Click the **View** button for Form view ▤ on the Form Design toolbar.

6. Resize the form until it is approximately the same size as the form in Figure 9-27. See Figure 9-27.

Figure 9-27 ◀
Resized form

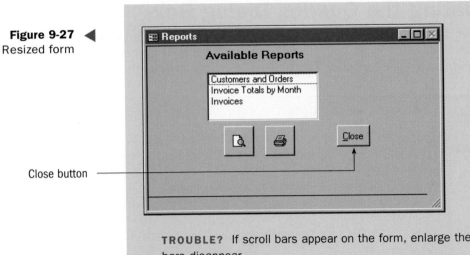

Close button ——————

TROUBLE? If scroll bars appear on the form, enlarge the form until the scroll bars disappear.

7. Click the **Save** button 🖫 on the Form View toolbar, and then click the **View** button for Design view 🖾 on the Form View toolbar to switch back to Design view.

You can now set the form's Border Style property to Dialog. This will prevent the user from resizing the form.

8. In the Form window, right-click the form selector, click **Properties** to display the property sheet, and then click the **All** tab. Scroll down the property sheet, click the right side of the **Border Style** text box, and then click **Dialog**.

9. Click the **Close** button 🗙 on the property sheet to close it, and then click the **Save** button 🖫 on the Form Design toolbar.

10. Click the **Close** button 🗙 on the Form window to close it and return to the Database window.

You can now test the form by opening it in Form view. Clicking the Print Preview command button, clicking the Print command button, or double-clicking a report name in the list box should have no effect, because you have not yet written the Visual Basic code for these actions. However, you will be able to click the Close button or press Alt + C to close the form.

To test the form's design:

1. Click **Reports Dialog Box** in the Forms list, if necessary, and then click the **Open** button. Access opens the form in Form view.

   TROUBLE? If the form is not the correct size or if scroll bars appear on the form, switch to Design view and set the form's Border Style property to Sizable. Switch back to Form view and resize the form. Save the form changes, switch to Design view, set the form's Border Style property to Dialog, and then save the form again. Close the Form window, and then repeat Step 1.

2. Double-click any report name in the list, click the **Print Preview** command button, and then click the **Print** command button. Each double-click or click moves the focus but does not execute any other action. Recall that "focus" refers to the record and control that is currently active and awaiting user action.

3. Either click the **Close** button or press the **Alt + C** keys. Access closes the form and returns to the Database window.

You have finished the initial work on the Reports Dialog Box. Your next task is to create the Queries Dialog Box.

Creating the Queries Dialog Box

Because the forms for the two dialog boxes are so similar, you can start to create the Queries Dialog Box by making a copy of the form for the Reports Dialog Box. Then you can modify the Queries Dialog Box to work correctly with the list of available queries.

REFERENCE window

COPYING AN OBJECT IN THE SAME DATABASE

- In the Database window, click the appropriate tab, and then right-click the name of the object you want to copy to display the shortcut menu.
- Click Copy to copy the object to the Clipboard.
- Position the pointer in an empty area of the list, and then right-click to display the shortcut menu.
- Click Paste, type the new object name, and then press the Enter key.

You will copy the Reports Dialog Box form to the Clipboard and paste it in the Forms list, renaming it as Queries Dialog Box.

To copy the form in the same database:

1. Right-click **Reports Dialog Box** in the Forms list, and then click **Copy**. Access copies the form to the Clipboard.

2. Position the pointer in an empty area of the Forms list, and then right-click to display the shortcut menu.

3. Click **Paste**. The Paste As dialog box opens.

4. Type **Queries Dialog Box** in the Form Name text box, and then press the **Enter** key. Access creates a new form with the name Queries Dialog Box, which is a copy of the Reports Dialog Box form.

Now, you will open the Queries Dialog Box in Design view and change the form's design so that it matches Leonard's design. Specifically, you will:

- Change the form's Record Source property to QueryNames, and change the Caption property to Queries.

- Change the label above the list to Available Queries.

- Change the Row Source property for the list box to the QueryNames query.

- Change the icon on the middle command button to the Query Datasheet icon.

To change the properties of the copied form to create the Queries Dialog Box:

1. Click **Queries Dialog Box** in the Forms list, and then click the **Design** button.

2. Right-click the form selector, and then click **Properties** to open the property sheet for the form.

3. Make sure the **Record Source** text box is selected in the property sheet, click the **Record Source** list arrow, and then click **QueryNames**.

4. Double-click the entry in the Caption text box, and then type **Queries**.

   Now you can change the label on the form to Available Queries.

5. Click the label box above the list box to open the property sheet for the label.

Access

6. Select **Reports** in the Caption text box, and then type **Queries**.

The Visual Basic code you will create later will need to refer to the list box control, so you'll enter the name QueryList Control for the list box control.

7. Click the list box in the form's Detail section, select **Report** in the Name text box in the property sheet, and then type **Query**. The entry in the Name text box is now QueryList Control.

The Row Source text box contains the SQL statement SELECT DISTINCTROW [ReportNames].[ObjectName] FROM [ReportNames], which selects the ObjectName field from the ReportNames query to display the names in the list box. You will edit this to select the ObjectName field from the QueryNames query instead, so that the list of queries will appear in the list box.

8. Click the **Row Source** text box. Press the → key until [ReportNames] appears, select **Report**, type **Query** so that the text now reads [QueryNames]; again, press the → key until [ReportNames] appears, select **Report**, type **Query** so that the text now reads [QueryNames], and then press the **Enter** key.

Next, you'll change the picture on the middle command button to show the standard Access icon for query results displayed in Datasheet view. When the user clicks this button, Access will run the query and display the query results in Datasheet view.

9. Click the **Print** command button to display the property sheet for this button. In the property sheet, click the **Picture** text box, and then click the **build** button ... to open the Picture Builder dialog box.

10. Scroll through the Available Pictures list, click **MS Access Query**, and then click the **OK** button. Access closes the Picture Builder dialog box and places the new picture on the command button.

11. Click the **Save** button 🖫 on the Form Design toolbar, and then click the **Close** button ✕ on the property sheet to close it.

Now you can view your changes to the form in Form view.

12. Click the **View** button for Form view 🖩 on the Form Design toolbar. Access displays the form in Form view. See Figure 9-28.

Figure 9-28 ◀
Queries
Dialog Box
displayed in
Form view

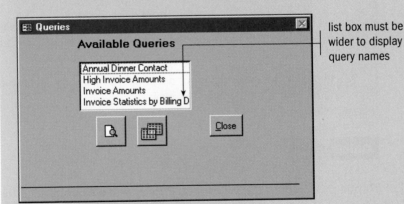

list box must be wider to display query names

The list box is not wide enough to display the complete query names. You need to increase the width of the list box so that the complete query names will be displayed.

To resize the list box:

1. Click the **View** button for Design view 🖾 on the Form View toolbar to switch back to Design view.

2. Click the list box, position the pointer on the middle right sizing handle and, when the pointer changes to ↔, drag the right border of the list box to the right to the 2¾-inch mark on the horizontal ruler.

   TROUBLE? If you moved the list box instead of resizing it, click Edit on the menu bar, click Undo Move, and then repeat Step 2.

3. Click the **View** button for Form view 🖩 on the Form Design toolbar to redisplay the form in Form view.

4. Click the **Save** button 🖫 on the Form View toolbar to save the form's design.

5. Click the **Close** button ⊠ on the Form window to close it.

Leonard wants to view the completed Queries Dialog Box. So, you'll test the form for the Queries Dialog Box in the same way that you tested the form for the Reports Dialog Box.

To test the design of the Queries Dialog Box:

1. Click **Queries Dialog Box** in the Forms list (if necessary), and then click the **Open** button. Access displays the dialog box in Form view. See Figure 9-29.

Figure 9-29 ◀
Copied form
with completed
changes

resized list box ——

Print Preview button ——

Query Datasheet
button |

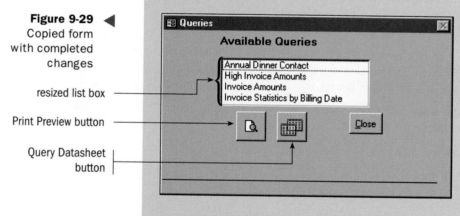

2. Double-click any query name in the list box, click the **Print Preview** command button, and then click the **Query Datasheet** command button. Each click or double-click moves the focus but does not execute any other actions.

3. Either click the **Close** button or press the **Alt + C** keys. Access closes the form and returns to the Database window.

Quick **Check**

1 Define the Validation Rule property and give an example of when you would use it.

2 Define the Validation Text property and give an example of when you would use it.

3 What is the purpose of setting a form's Border Style property value to Dialog?

4 What is a list box control?

5 How do you change the picture on a command button?

6 How do you copy an object in a database?

You have now created the table containing the names of the reports and queries that will be available from the switchboard. You also created two queries to select report names or query names for the dialog box list boxes, and you created two dialog boxes (Reports and Queries) for the Restaurant Database switchboard. Your next task is to create the form for the switchboard itself and the macros for the switchboard and dialog boxes command buttons. You'll create these objects in the next session.

SESSION

9.3

In this session, you will create a macro group that will be associated with buttons on the switchboard. You will also use the Switchboard Manager to create a switchboard form for the Restaurant Database switchboard.

Creating a Switchboard

Recall that a switchboard is a form that provides controlled access to a database's tables, forms, queries, and reports. You need to create the switchboard form that will serve as the primary user interface for the Restaurant database. Figure 9-30 shows the finished Restaurant Database switchboard form.

Figure 9-30 ◄
Restaurant
Database
switchboard
form

graphic image

command buttons

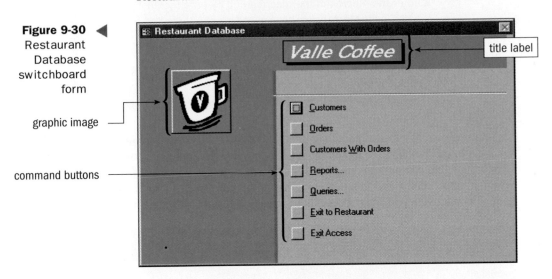

Leonard has the following design specifications for the Restaurant Database switchboard:

- The form will not include Minimize, Restore, or Close buttons, scroll bars, navigation buttons, record selectors, or sizing buttons; the form cannot be resized.

- A picture of the Valle Coffee cup will appear in the left section of the form.

- The picture of the Valle Coffee cup will have the raised special effect applied to it.

- The command buttons will all be the same size.

- Macros will be attached to each command button to specify the actions that Access should take when the command button is clicked.

Your first step in creating the switchboard is to create the macros you need to attach to the seven command buttons on the switchboard form.

Creating the Macro Group

Instead of creating seven separate macros, one for each command button, you will place the seven macros in a macro group. A **macro group** is a macro that contains other macros. Macro groups allow you to consolidate related macros and provide a way to manage large numbers of macros.

To create a macro group, you use the same Macro window you used to create a single macro. Recall that when you worked with the Macro window earlier in this tutorial, you entered actions in the Action column and comments in the Comment column. Now, you'll add a third column, the Macro Name column, which lets you distinguish macros in your macro group. Because a macro can contain many actions, the macro name tells Access where the macro begins. First you'll name one macro and list the actions for that macro. Then you'll name the second macro, list the actions for the second macro, and so on. You can define the macros in any order, and you can group as many macros as you want in the Macro window.

REFERENCE window

CREATING A MACRO GROUP

- In the Database window, click the Macros tab, and then click the New button.
- Click the Macro Names button on the Macro Design toolbar.
- Enter the macros in the macro group by entering each macro name in the Macro Name column and the corresponding action(s) in the Action column.
- Click the Save button on the Macro Design toolbar, enter the macro group name in the Macro Name text box, and then click the OK button.

You will use the name Switchboard Macros for the macro group. Figure 9-31 shows the names and actions for the seven macros in the macro group. For example, the Customers macro will execute the OpenForm action to open the Customer Data form when a user clicks the Customers button on the switchboard. Notice that both the ExitToRestaurant and ExitAccess macros each contain two actions.

Figure 9-31 ◄
Macros and actions in the Switchboard Macros macro group

Macro Name	Actions	Form Name
Customers	OpenForm	Customer Data
Orders	OpenForm	Order Data
CustomersWithOrders	OpenForm	Customer Information Multi-page
Reports	OpenForm	Reports Dialog Box
Queries	OpenForm	Queries Dialog Box
ExitToRestaurant	Close SendKeys	Switchboard
ExitAccess	Close Quit	Switchboard

Next, you'll create the Switchboard Macros macro group for the seven command buttons on the switchboard form. First you'll start a new macro, enter two of the macros (ExitAccess and Customers), and then save the macro group.

To create the macro group:

1. If you took a break after the previous session, start Access and open the Restaurant database in the Tutorial folder on your Student Disk.

2. In the Database window, click the **Macros** tab, and then click the **New** button. The Macro window opens. Click the **Maximize** button ▢ to maximize the Macro window.

3. Click the **Macro Names** button on the Macro Design toolbar. Access adds the Macro Name column to the left of the Action column. See Figure 9-32.

Figure 9-32 ◀
Macro Name
column added
to the Macro
window

Macro Names button

Macro Name column

Action column

Comment column

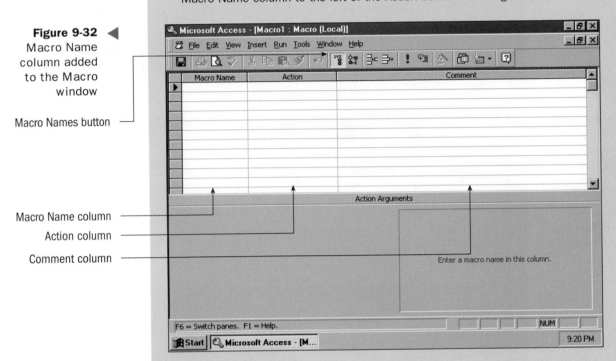

You enter the name of the macro in the Macro Name column. In the Action column, you enter the action or actions for the macro, placing each action on a separate row when the macro contains multiple actions. In the Comment column, you enter text describing the purpose of each action in the macro. The end of the macro is signified by an empty line in the Action column or by a new name in the Macro Name column.

Now you'll enter the ExitAccess macro and its two actions: the Close action to close the switchboard form and the Quit action to exit Access.

4. Type **ExitAccess**, press the **Tab** key, click the **Action** list arrow, click **Close**, press the **Tab** key, and then type **Close Switchboard**.

You need to specify the arguments for the Close action. In the Object Type text box, you specify the type of object to close, in this case, a form. In the Object Name text box, you specify which object to close. Even though you haven't created the Switchboard form yet, you can specify it as the object to close.

5. In the Action Arguments panel, click the right side of the **Object Type** text box, and then click **Form**. Click the **Object Name** text box, and then type **Switchboard**. This completes the first action for the first macro. Now you need to define the second action for this macro, which will exit the Access program.

6. Click the right side of the second row's **Action** text box, scroll through the list, and then click **Quit**. This completes the first macro, which contains two actions: the first to close the switchboard form and the second to exit Access. These two actions will occur when a user clicks the Exit Access button on the switchboard.

Next, you'll define the second macro, Customers, which will open the Customer Data form.

7. Click the third row's **Macro Name** text box, type **Customers**, press the **Tab** key, click the list arrow, scroll through the list, click **OpenForm**, press the **Tab** key, and then type **Open Customer Data form**.

Now you need to specify the name of the form to open.

8. In the Action Arguments panel, click the right side of the **Form Name** text box, and then click **Customer Data**. This completes the second macro, which contains one action.

9. Click the **Save** button 🖫 on the Macro Design toolbar, type **Switchboard Macros** in the Macro Name text box, and then press the **Enter** key. See Figure 9-33.

Figure 9-33
Two macros in the macro group

macro group name

macro with two actions

macro with one action

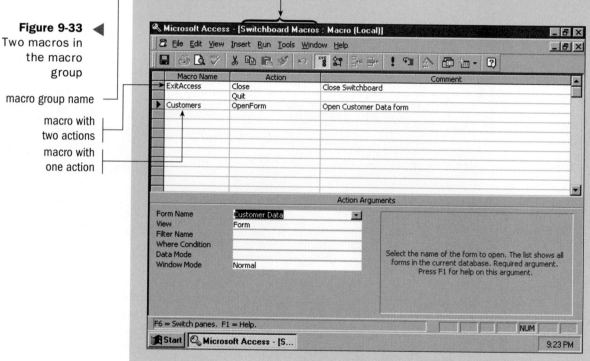

The macro name, which appears in the Macro window title bar, is Switchboard Macros. This is also the name of the macro group, because the Switchboard Macros macro comprises more than one macro. The first macro in the macro group is ExitAccess, and the second macro in the macro group is Customers. A macro in a macro group starts in the row containing the macro name and continues until the next macro name or until a blank row.

When Access executes the ExitAccess macro, it runs the Close action, and then runs the Quit action, and then ends. The Customers macro begins with the OpenForm action and then ends when it reaches the end of the macro group.

Now you can complete the macro group by entering the remaining five macros—one to open the Order Data form, one to open the Customer Information Multi-page form, one to open the Reports Dialog Box form, one to open the Queries Dialog Box form, and the last one to close the switchboard and return to the Database window of the Restaurant database.

To finish creating the macro group:

1. Click the next row's **Macro Name** text box, type **Orders**, press the **Tab** key, click the **Action** list arrow, scroll through the list, click **OpenForm**, press the **Tab** key, and then type **Open Order Data form**.

2. In the Action Arguments panel, click the **Form Name** text box, click the list arrow, and then click **Order Data**. This completes the third macro, which contains one action to open the Order Data form.

3. Click the next row's **Macro Name** text box, type **CustomersWithOrders**, press the **Tab** key, click the **Action** list arrow, click **OpenForm**, press the **Tab** key, and then type **Open Customer Information Multi-page form**.

4. In the Action Arguments panel, click the **Form Name** text box, click the list arrow, and then click **Customer Information Multi-page**. This completes the fourth macro, which contains one action to open the Customer Information Multi-page form.

5. Click the next row's **Macro Name** text box, type **Reports**, press the **Tab** key, click the **Action** list arrow, click **OpenForm**, press the **Tab** key, and then type **Open Reports Dialog Box**.

6. In the Action Arguments panel, click the **Form Name** text box, click the list arrow, and then click **Reports Dialog Box**. This completes the fifth macro, which contains one action to open the Reports Dialog Box.

7. Click the next row's **Macro Name** text box, type **Queries**, press the **Tab** key, click the **Action** list arrow, click **OpenForm**, press the **Tab** key, and then type **Open Queries Dialog Box**.

8. In the Action Arguments panel, click the **Form Name** text box, click the list arrow, and then click **Queries Dialog Box**. This completes the sixth macro, which contains one action to open the Queries Dialog Box.

   The final macro you need to define is the ExitToRestaurant macro, which will execute two actions: the Close action to close the switchboard and the *SendKeys* action, which simulates keystrokes. In this macro, you will use the SendKeys action to simulate pressing the F11 key, which activates the Database window, because Leonard wants users to return to the Database window after closing the switchboard.

9. Click the next row's **Macro Name** text box, type **ExitToRestaurant**, press the **Tab** key, click the **Action** list arrow, click **Close**, press the **Tab** key, and then type **Close Switchboard**.

10. In the Action Arguments panel, click the **Object Type** text box, click the list arrow, click **Form**, click the **Object Name** text box, type **Switchboard**, and then press the **Enter** key.

11. Click the right side of the next row's **Action** text box, scroll the list, click **SendKeys**, press the **Tab** key, and then type **Activate Database window**.

    For the SendKeys action, you need to specify the Keystrokes argument value {F11}, which is the same as pressing the F11 key, so that the action will return to the Database window after closing the switchboard form.

12. In the Action Arguments panel, click the **Keystrokes** text box, and then type **{F11}**. Be sure to type the braces but not the period. This completes the second of two actions for the final macro. See Figure 9-34.

Figure 9-34 ◄
Completed
macro group
containing
seven macros

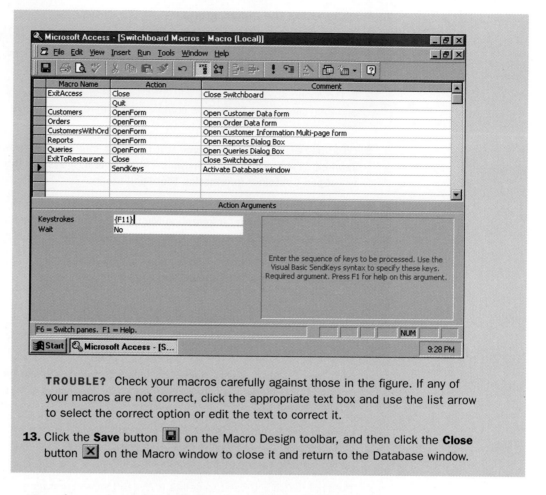

TROUBLE? Check your macros carefully against those in the figure. If any of your macros are not correct, click the appropriate text box and use the list arrow to select the correct option or edit the text to correct it.

13. Click the **Save** button 🖫 on the Macro Design toolbar, and then click the **Close** button ⊠ on the Macro window to close it and return to the Database window.

Now that you've defined all the macros that will execute the necessary actions for the command buttons on the switchboard, you can create the form for the switchboard.

Creating the Switchboard Form

To create the switchboard, you use the Access Switchboard Manager. The **Switchboard Manager** is a Microsoft Access add-in tool that helps you create and customize a switchboard. When you use the Switchboard Manager, you specify the command buttons that are to appear on the switchboard. For each button, you identify the command to be carried out when the button is clicked. The Switchboard Manager automatically attaches the command to the OnClick property for that command button; this property specifies the action to take when the command button is clicked. Some commands require one or more arguments, which you can specify as well. When you complete the switchboard design, the Switchboard Manager creates a form for your switchboard with the default name Switchboard. The Switchboard Manager also creates a table, called **Switchboard Items**, which contains records describing the command buttons on the switchboard.

The Switchboard Manager allows you to create only one switchboard for a database, but the switchboard can contain many pages. Only one of the switchboard pages can be designated as the default page. The **default page** is the switchboard page that will appear when you open the switchboard form. You can place a command button on the default page to open other switchboard pages.

You will use the Switchboard Manager to create the switchboard form for the Restaurant database. Review the design of the form shown in Figure 9-30. Notice that each command button has an associated hot key, signified by the underlined character in the button label. As you use the Switchboard Manager to create the form, you'll place the appropriate command buttons on the switchboard, define the hot keys, and associate the corresponding macros from the Switchboard Macros macro group with the buttons.

To create the switchboard form:

1. Click **Tools** on the menu bar, point to **Add-Ins**, and then click **Switchboard Manager**. Access displays a dialog box asking if you want to create a switchboard.

   TROUBLE? If you do not see the Switchboard Manager in the Add-Ins list, it might not be installed on your computer. See your instructor or technical support person for assistance.

2. Click the **Yes** button. The Switchboard Manager dialog box opens. See Figure 9-35.

Figure 9-35 ◀
Switchboard
Manager
dialog box

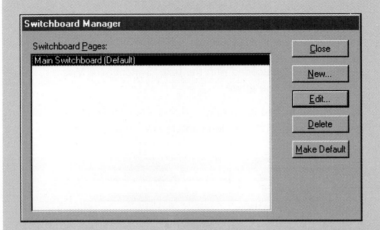

In the Switchboard Manager dialog box, the Switchboard Pages list highlights the Main Switchboard page, which is the default page. You need to edit this page to change its name to Restaurant Database and to add the command buttons to it.

3. Click the **Edit** button. The Edit Switchboard Page dialog box opens. This dialog box allows you to specify the name for the switchboard page and to add command buttons to the page.

4. Select the current entry in the Switchboard Name text box (Main Switchboard), and then type **Restaurant Database**. See Figure 9-36.

Figure 9-36 ◀
Edit
Switchboard
Page
dialog box

name of
switchboard

place command
buttons here

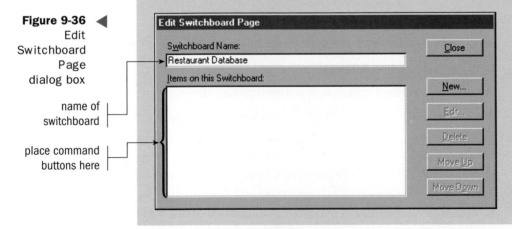

You can now add command buttons for each of the macros in the Switchboard Macros macro group. Each command button will carry out the actions in its associated macro when the command button is clicked.

To add the first command button to the switchboard page:

1. Click the **New** button. The Edit Switchboard Item dialog box opens.

   The first button you will add is the Customers button, which will open the Customer Data form. According to Leonard's design, the hot key for this button is C.

2. In the Text box, type **&Customers**. This text will appear to the right of the command button. Recall that the ampersand (&) creates the hot key.

Next, you need to specify the command that will be executed when the user clicks the button. In this case, you want Access to run the Customers macro, which displays the Customer Data form. This macro is part of the Switchboard Macros group.

3. Click the **Command** list arrow, and then click **Run Macro**. The third text box in the Edit Switchboard Item dialog box now displays the label "Macro." In this text box you need to specify the macro that should be run when the button is clicked. When you click the Macro list arrow, you see a list of all the macros defined for the database. The names of all the macros that are part of the macro group you created are preceded with the text "Switchboard Macros" to identify them as belonging to the group.

4. Click the **Macro** list arrow, and then click **Switchboard Macros.Customers**. The first command button definition is now complete. See Figure 9-37.

Figure 9-37 ◀
Edit
Switchboard
Item dialog box

name of button on
the switchboard

action executed when
the button is clicked

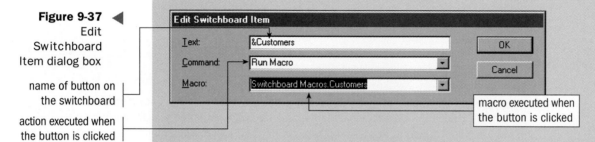

macro executed when
the button is clicked

5. Click the **OK** button. The Switchboard Manager returns to the Edit Switchboard Page dialog box. Notice that the Items on this Switchboard list now shows the Customers command button.

Now you can add the remaining command buttons to the switchboard.

To add the other six buttons to the switchboard form:

1. Click the **New** button. The Edit Switchboard Item dialog box opens.

2. In the Text box, type **&Orders**.

3. Click the **Command** list arrow, and then click **Run Macro**.

4. Click the **Macro** list arrow, and then click **Switchboard Macros.Orders**.

5. Click the **OK** button. The definition of the second command button, Orders, is now complete. When clicked, the button will run the Orders macro in the Switchboard Macros macro group, which opens the Order Data form in Form view.

6. Repeat Steps 1 through 5 to define the **Customers &With Orders** command button. Specify the macro **Switchboard Macros.CustomersWithOrders** as the macro to be run.

The next command button you need to define is the button for opening the Reports Dialog Box. According to Leonard's design, the name of this button includes the ellipses after the word "Reports" to signify that a dialog box will open when you click the button.

7. Repeat Steps 1 through 5 to define the **&Reports...** command button (be sure to include the ellipses in the button name). Specify the macro **Switchboard Macros.Reports** as the macro to be run.

8. Repeat Steps 1 through 5 to define the **&Queries...** command button (be sure to include the ellipses in the button name). Specify the macro **Switchboard Macros.Queries** as the macro to be run.

9. Repeat Steps 1 through 5 to define the **&Exit to Restaurant** command button. Specify the macro **Switchboard Macros.ExitToRestaurant** as the macro to be run.

10. Repeat Steps 1 through 5 to define the **E&xit Access** command button. Specify the macro **Switchboard Macros.ExitAccess** as the macro to be run. The switchboard design now contains all the necessary command buttons. See Figure 9-38.

Figure 9-38 ◀
Completed Edit
Switchboard
Page
dialog box

seven command
buttons added

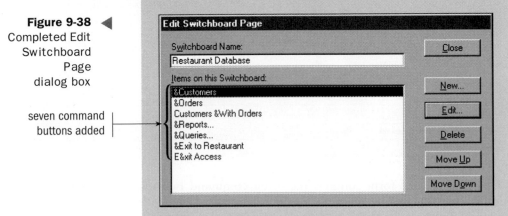

TROUBLE? Compare your Edit Switchboard Page dialog box with Figure 9-38. If any of your command buttons are incorrect, click the button name and then click the Edit button. Make the necessary changes and then click the OK button to return to the dialog box.

You are finished using the Switchboard Manager, so you can now exit the Switchboard Manager and view the new switchboard.

To exit the Switchboard Manager and view the Switchboard form:

1. Click the **Close** button to close the Edit Switchboard Page dialog box.

2. Click the **Close** button to close the Switchboard Manager dialog box and return to the Database window.

3. Click the **Restore** button 🗗 on the Database window to restore it.

4. If necessary, click the **Forms** tab to display the Forms list.

5. Click **Switchboard** and then click the **Open** button. Access opens the Switchboard form. See Figure 9-39.

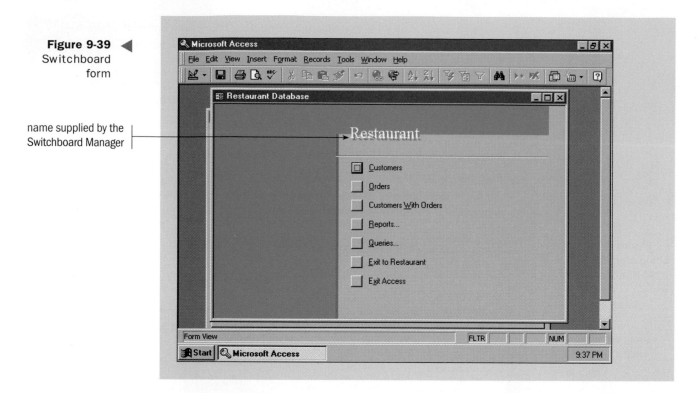

Figure 9-39 ◄
Switchboard
form

name supplied by the
Switchboard Manager

The Switchboard form contains the seven command buttons you defined using the Switchboard Manager. Each command button has an attached label displaying the button name. The underscore in the button name indicates the hot key for that button. The name "Restaurant" appears in white text in a label above the buttons; this label was supplied automatically by the Switchboard Manager. Behind the Restaurant label is another copy of the Restaurant label displaying the text in gray letters, creating a shadow effect. The large green areas on the switchboard are green colored rectangles placed in the form design by the Switchboard Manager.

Overall, Leonard is pleased with the appearance of the Switchboard form, but there are some changes he would like you to make. Before you make these changes, you will test some of the command buttons to make sure that they work properly.

To test the command buttons:

1. Click the **Customers** command button. Access displays the record for the Meadows Restaurant in the Customer Data form in Form view.

2. Click the **Close** button ⊠ on the Form window to close it and return to the switchboard.

3. Press and hold the **Alt** key, and then press **O**. Access opens the Order Data form and displays the first Order record.

4. Click the **Close** button ⊠ on the Form window to close it and return to the switchboard.

5. Click the **Reports** command button. Access opens the Reports Dialog Box.

6. Click the **Close** button to return to the switchboard.

Leonard wants you to make some changes to the design of the switchboard. He likes the layout of the buttons, but he wants you to make sure that the form always appears the same size on the screen. He also wants you to remove the Restaurant label above the buttons and add a new label, Valle Coffee, and a graphic image of the Valle Coffee cup.

Because the switchboard is a form, you can make these changes in Design view. However, you need to be careful not to make any changes to the command buttons that would affect the actions and macros associated with them. Such changes should only be made through the Switchboard Manager. If you were to change the definitions of any of the command buttons in Design view, the Switchboard Manager would not be able to make the necessary updates and the switchboard would not function correctly.

Next, you'll delete the Restaurant label, place the new label "Valle Coffee" on the form, and add the graphic image of the Valle Coffee cup.

To modify the switchboard:

1. Click the **View** button for Design view 🖳 on the Form View toolbar. Access displays the Switchboard form in Design view.

2. Right-click the **Restaurant** label above the command buttons to open the shortcut menu, and then click **Cut**. The label is deleted. Notice that there is a second Restaurant label now visible. This label appeared as the shadow of the first label in the switchboard.

3. Right-click the **Restaurant** label above the command buttons to open the shortcut menu, and then click **Cut**. The second label is deleted.

   You can now add the Valle Coffee label in the green area above the command buttons.

4. If the toolbox is not displayed, click the **Toolbox** button 🛠 on the Form Design toolbar.

5. Click the **Label** tool 🄰🄰 on the toolbox, position the pointer ⁺A at the top of the form directly below the 2-inch mark on the horizontal ruler, and then click the mouse button to place the label box.

6. Type **Valle Coffee** and then press the **Enter** key.

   Leonard wants the title to stand out, so he asks you to format it in bold and italics, increase its font size, change its font color to yellow, and apply the shadowed special effect to the title.

7. Click the **Bold** button **B** on the Form Design toolbar, click the **Italic** button *I* on the Form Design toolbar, click the **Font Size** list arrow on the Formatting toolbar, and then click **18**.

8. Click **Format** on the menu bar, point to **Size**, and then click **To Fit**. Access resizes the label box to display the entire label.

9. Click the list arrow for the **Font/Fore Color** button 🄰 on the Formatting toolbar to display the palette of available colors.

10. Click the bright yellow color box (the third button in the fourth row). The Valle Coffee label now appears bright yellow.

11. Click the list arrow for the **Special Effect** button ⊟ on the Formatting toolbar, and then click the **Shadowed** button ⊟.

Now you'll add the picture of the Valle Coffee cup to the form. After you do, you'll apply the raised special effect to the picture to enhance it.

To add the Valle Coffee cup picture to the form:

1. Click the **Image** button 🖾 on the toolbox, position the pointer ⁺🖾 at the ½-inch mark on the vertical ruler and the ½-inch mark on the horizontal ruler, and then click the mouse button to place the graphic image. The Insert Picture dialog box opens.

2. In the Look in list box, select the Tutorial folder on your Student Disk, click **ValleCup** in the file list, and then click the **OK** button. Access inserts the ValleCup graphic image in the form.

3. Click the list arrow for the **Special Effect** button ▣ on the Formatting toolbar, and then click the **Raised** button ▣. The raised effect is applied to the button. You've finished making the necessary changes to the layout of the Switchboard form. See Figure 9-40.

Figure 9-40 ◄
Modified
Switchboard
form layout

new label ——

graphic image
inserted

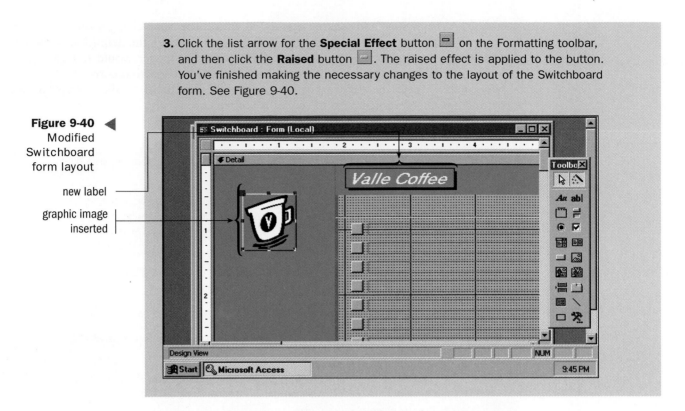

Now you can change the form properties so that the form will be correctly sized and positioned on the screen.

To change the Switchboard form properties:

1. Click the **Close** button ☒ on the toolbox to close it.

2. Right-click the form selector, and then click **Properties** to display the property sheet for the form.

First you'll set the Auto Resize property to No so that Access will not resize the form when it is opened.

3. Click the **Format** tab, click the right side of the **Auto Resize** text box, and then click **No**.

Now you'll set the Border Style property to Dialog to prevent users from resizing the form.

4. Click the right side of the **Border Style** text box, and then click **Dialog**.

Setting the Close Button property to No disables the Close button in the title bar of the form. You'll disable this button because Leonard wants users to close the form by clicking the Exit to Restaurant or Exit Access command buttons.

5. Click the right side of the **Close Button** text box, and then click **No**.

6. Click the **Close** button ☒ on the property sheet.

7. Click the **Save** button 🖫 to save the switchboard design.

8. Click the **Close** button ☒ on the Form window to close it and return to the Database window.

Leonard wants to view the modified switchboard, so you'll open the switchboard in Form view to see its appearance.

To view the switchboard:

1. Click **Switchboard** to select it (if necessary), and then click the **Open** button. The switchboard is displayed in Form view. See Figure 9-41.

Figure 9-41 ◀
Modified switchboard in Form view

graphic image ——

| Restaurant Database |
| Valle Coffee   new label |
| □ Customers |
| □ Orders |
| □ Customers With Orders |
| □ Reports... |
| □ Queries... |
| □ Exit to Restaurant |
| □ Exit Access |

2. Click the **Exit to Restaurant** button. Access closes the switchboard and returns to the Database window.

3. Click the **Close** button ⊠ on the Database window to close the database.

To make sure that you have sufficient space on your Student Disk to complete the next tutorial, you might want to compact the Restaurant database now, particularly if you are not working from a hard disk or a network.

To compact the Restaurant database:

1. Click **Tools** on the menu bar, point to **Database Utilities**, and then click **Compact Database**. The Database to Compact From dialog box opens.

2. Make sure Tutorial appears in the Look in list box, click **Restaurant** in the list box, and then click the **Compact** button. The Compact Database Into dialog box opens. Your Student Disk does not have enough space for you to place the copy of the compacted database on it, so you need to compact the database into a file on the desktop.

3. Type **Restaurant** in the File name text box, click the **Save in** list arrow, click **Desktop**, and then click the **Save** button.

4. Click the **Close** button ⊠ on the Access window to exit Access and display the desktop. Notice that an icon for the compacted Restaurant database file now appears on the desktop.

   Next you'll use My Computer to copy the compacted Restaurant database file from the desktop to your Student Disk to replace the version currently on your disk.

5. Open the My Computer window, and then open the disk drive containing your Student Disk.

6. Drag the icon for the compacted Restaurant database from the desktop to the Tutorial folder on your Student Disk in My Computer, and then click the **Yes** button when asked if you want to replace the existing file. Your Student Disk now contains the compacted Restaurant database.

7. Close any open windows.

Quick Check

1   What are two reasons for using macro groups?

2   What does the SendKeys action do?

3   What is the Switchboard Manager?

4   When using the Command Button Wizard, how do you define a hot key for a command button?

5   How do you specify that a form is a dialog box?

6   What are two special effects you can use for a control?

Leonard's design for the Restaurant database user interface also includes a custom menu bar and a custom toolbar. In the next tutorial, you'll add these features to the switchboard and create the necessary Visual Basic code for the dialog box command buttons.

Tutorial Assignments

Barbara wants you to create a switchboard interface for the Products database. You can create the interface by completing the following steps:

1. Make sure your Student Disk is in the appropriate disk drive, start Access, and then open the Products database in the TAssign folder on your Student Disk.

2. Create a table called ReportNames. The table should contain one 25-character text field named Report. Enter the names of the two reports that will be available from your switchboard: Coffee Types and Coffee Type Chart. Save the table.

3. Design and create a dialog box form named Reports Dialog Box that has the following components and characteristics:

   a. The text "Print Reports" appears in the title bar.

   b. A list box displays all the report names contained in the ReportNames table.

   c. The text "Reports Available" appears as a heading above the list box.

   d. Two command buttons appear below the list box. The left command button displays the Print Preview icon, and the right command button displays the word "Close" with the letter "C" underlined.

   e. Double-clicking a report name has the same effect as clicking the left command button. Both events cause Access to display the Print Preview window for the selected report. (You will add the Visual Basic code for these events in the next tutorial. For now, double-clicking or clicking should cause no action to occur.)

   f. Clicking the Close command button causes Access to close the dialog box.

4. Design and create a switchboard form named Switchboard. Use Figure 9-42 as a guide in designing the switchboard.

Figure 9-42 ◀

title label

white background
color

graphic image

command buttons

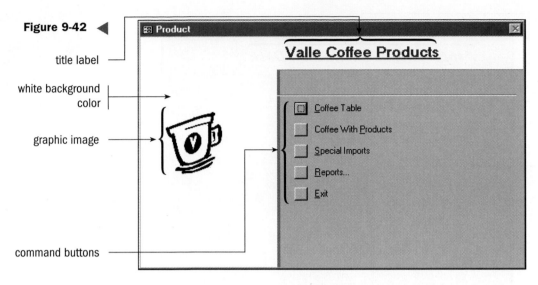

5. Specify "Product" as the name to appear in the title bar. Delete the default label in the form and place a label at the top center of the switchboard. The label should read "Valle Coffee Products."

6. Place five command buttons on the switchboard. The command buttons perform these actions: open the Coffee table, open the Enhanced Coffee Multipage form, open the Special Imports form, open the Reports Dialog Box form, and close the switchboard and activate the Database window.

7. Create a macro group named Switchboard Macros for the command buttons.

8. Set the background color and visual effects for the switchboard and its components, as shown in Figure 9-42, and then size and position the switchboard in Form view to match the figure.

9. Save and close the Switchboard form, and then exit Access.

Case Problems

1. Ashbrook Mall Information Desk Sam Bullard wants the MallJobs database to have an interface that is easy to use. He asks you to create a switchboard interface for the MallJobs database by completing the following:

1. Make sure your Student Disk is in the appropriate disk drive, start Access, and then open the MallJobs database in the Cases folder on your Student Disk.

2. Design and create a switchboard form named Switchboard. Use Figure 9-43 as a guide in designing the switchboard.

Figure 9-43 ◀

title label ―

yellow background color

command buttons

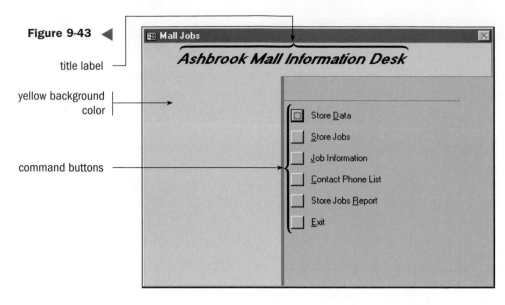

3. Specify "Mall Jobs" as the name to appear in the title bar. Delete the default label in the form and place a label at the top center of the switchboard. The label should read "Ashbrook Mall Information Desk."

4. Place six command buttons on the switchboard. The command buttons perform these actions: open the Store Data form, open the Store Jobs form, open the Job Information Multi-page form, open the Contact Phone List query results, open the Store Jobs report in the Print Preview window, and close the switchboard and activate the Database window.

5. Create a macro group named Switchboard Macros for the command buttons.

6. Set the background color and visual effects for the switchboard and its components, as shown in Figure 9-43, and then size and position the switchboard in Form view to match the figure.

7. Save and close the Switchboard form, and then exit Access.

2. Professional Litigation User Services To make the Payments database easier to use, Raj Jawahir wants you to create a switchboard interface for it. To create the interface, you will complete the following:

1. Make sure your Student Disk is in the appropriate disk drive, start Access, and then open the Payments database in the Cases folder on your Student Disk.

2. Design and create a switchboard form named Switchboard. Use Figure 9-44 as a guide in designing the switchboard.

Figure 9-44 ◀

title label colored purple

white background color

graphic image

label colored purple

command buttons

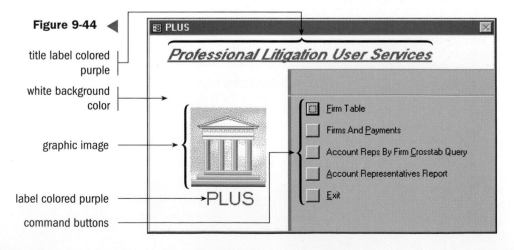

Access

3. Specify "PLUS" as the name to appear in the title bar. Delete the default label in the form and place a label at the top center of the switchboard. The label should read "Professional Litigation User Services." Set the label's color to purple.

4. Add the PLUS graphic image from the Cases folder of your Student Disk to the appropriate position on the switchboard.

5. Add the label PLUS below the graphic image and set the label's color to purple.

6. Place five command buttons on the switchboard. The command buttons perform these actions: open the Firm table, open the Enhanced Firm Multi-page form, open the AcctReps By Firm Crosstab query, open the Payments By Account Representative report in the Print Preview window, and close the switchboard and activate the Database window.

7. Create a macro group named Switchboard Macros for the command buttons.

8. Set the background color and visual effects for the switchboard and its components, as shown in Figure 9-44, and then size and position the switchboard in Form view to match the figure.

9. Save and close the Switchboard form, and then exit Access.

3. Best Friends Noah and Sheila Warnick, the founders of Best Friends, want to have an interface for the Walks database that is easier to use. They ask you to create a switchboard interface for the database by completing the following:

1. Make sure your Student Disk is in the appropriate disk drive, start Access, and then open the Walks database in the Cases folder on your Student Disk.

2. Design and create a switchboard form named Switchboard. Use Figure 9-45 as a guide in designing the switchboard.

Figure 9-45 ◀

labels
rectangle object
command buttons
blue background color
form resized

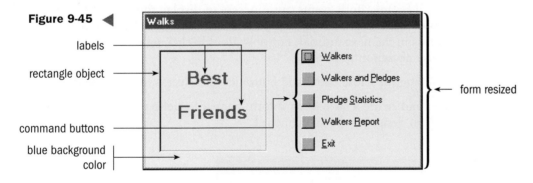

3. Specify "Walks" as the name to appear in the title bar.

4. Delete the default label in the form and place two labels at the left of the switchboard. The first label should read "Best" and the second label "Friends" (see Figure 9-45).

5. Place five command buttons on the switchboard. The command buttons perform these actions: open the Walker form, open the Enhanced Walker Information Multi-page form, open the Pledge Statistics By Walker query, open the Walkers report in the Print Preview window, and close the switchboard and activate the Database window.

6. Create a macro group named Switchboard Macros for the command buttons.

7. Set the background color and visual effects for the switchboard and its components, as shown in Figure 9-45, and then size and position the switchboard in Form view to match the figure. (*Hint:* Delete the rectangle objects on the Switchboard form before setting the Detail section Back Color property.)

8. Save and close the Switchboard form, and then exit Access.

4. Lopez Lexus Dealerships Marie and Hector Lopez want you to create a friendly user interface for the Lexus database. They ask you to create a switchboard for the Lexus database by completing the following:

1. Make sure your Student Disk is in the appropriate disk drive, start Access, and then open the Lexus database in the Cases folder on your Student Disk.

2. Create a table called ReportNames. The table should contain one 30-character text field named Report. Enter the names of the two reports that will be available from your switchboard: Cars By Model And Year, and Model Pie Chart. Save the table.

3. Design and create a dialog box form named Reports Dialog Box that has the following components and characteristics.

   a. The text "Print Reports" appears in the title bar.

   b. A list box displays all the report names contained in the ReportNames table.

   c. The text "Reports Available" appears as a heading above the list box.

   d. Two command buttons appear below the list box. The left command button displays the Print Preview icon, and the right command button displays the word "Close" with the letter "C" underlined.

   e. Double-clicking a report name has the same effect as clicking the left command button. Both events cause Access to display the Print Preview window for the selected report. (You will add the Visual Basic code for these events in the next tutorial. For now, double-clicking or clicking should cause no action to occur.)

   f. Clicking the Close command button causes Access to close the dialog box.

4. Design and create a switchboard form named Switchboard. Use Figure 9-46 as a guide in designing the switchboard.

Figure 9-46 ◀

title label

yellow background color

labels

command buttons

blue background color

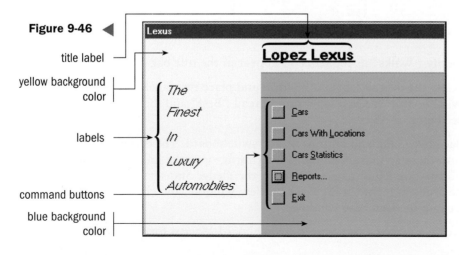

5. Specify "Lexus" as the name to appear in the title bar. Delete the default label in the form and place a label at the top center of the switchboard. The label should read "Lopez Lexus."

6. On the left side of the form, enter the labels indicated in the figure.

7. Place five command buttons on the switchboard. The command buttons perform these actions: open the Cars table, open the Enhanced Locations Information Multi-page form, open the Car Statistics By Location query results, open the Reports Dialog Box, and close the switchboard and activate the Database window.

8. Create a macro group named Switchboard Macros for the command buttons.

9. Set the background colors and visual effects for the switchboard and its components, as shown in Figure 9-46, and then size and position the switchboard in Form view to match the figure.

10. Save and close the Switchboard form, and then exit Access.

Creating Custom Toolbars and Menus and Writing Visual Basic Code

Completing the Restaurant Database Switchboard

Valle Coffee

CASE

Leonard reviews your progress in developing the graphical user interface for the Restaurant database. So far, you have created the switchboard that contains command buttons for opening forms, displaying dialog boxes, and exiting the switchboard. You have created a macro group that contains the macros attached to the command buttons on the switchboard. You have also created two dialog boxes—one for displaying the list of available reports and another for displaying the list of available queries.

Leonard's design for the Restaurant database user interface includes several other features. Leonard wants the standard toolbar and the standard menu bar replaced with a custom toolbar and a custom menu bar. The custom toolbar will contain buttons that perform the same operations as the command buttons on the switchboard and an extra button that allows the user to open the Access Help window. The custom menu bar will contain menu choices that perform the same operations as the command buttons on the switchboard. You will create the custom toolbar and the custom menu bar in this tutorial.

You'll also complete the user interface by modifying the Reports Dialog Box and the Queries Dialog Box so that their command buttons carry out the appropriate operations, and by modifying the Customer Data and Order Data forms to make data entry easier and to highlight important information on the forms. To make these modifications, you will write Visual Basic code to perform the necessary operations and attach the code to the appropriate event properties for the buttons and forms.

Finally, you will set the startup options for the Switchboard form so that it opens automatically when a user opens the Restaurant database.

SESSION

10.1

In this session, you will create a custom toolbar from a macro group and modify the custom toolbar. You will attach the custom toolbar to a form and then test the toolbar. Then you will create a custom menu bar and attach it to the same form.

Creating a Custom Toolbar

Leonard wants the Restaurant Database switchboard to include a custom toolbar. The toolbar will provide users with an alternate way of performing the operations available in the switchboard. Each toolbar button will be attached to a macro. When the user clicks a toolbar button, the corresponding macro responds and takes the appropriate action (for example, it opens a form).

You can attach a custom toolbar to a form or report so that Access displays the custom toolbar only when the attached form or report is displayed. Alternatively, a custom toolbar can be **global**, so that Access displays it in all windows of your application. You can position, or **float**, a toolbar anywhere on the screen. In this way, toolbars are similar to the toolbox. In any Access window you can also display two or more toolbars on the screen.

You can create a custom toolbar in three ways:

- Customize a standard Access toolbar, called a **built-in toolbar**, by replacing standard toolbar buttons with ones you choose (or create from scratch).

- Create a custom toolbar from macros.

- Create a custom toolbar with Visual Basic code. This type of toolbar is called a **command bar**.

Because you have already created the macros in the Switchboard Macros macro group, you can create a custom toolbar from these macros. Recall that the Switchboard Macros macro group contains seven macros that open the Customer Data form, open the Order Data form, open the Customer Information Multi-page form, open the Reports Dialog Box, open the Queries Dialog Box, close the Switchboard form and return to the Database window, and close the Switchboard form and exit Access.

You will name the toolbar Restaurant and attach it to the Switchboard form so that when the form is open, the Restaurant toolbar will replace the built-in Form View toolbar and will be the only toolbar on the screen. In all other situations, the built-in Access toolbars appear. The Restaurant toolbar will contain eight buttons that will provide an alternative way to perform the switchboard operations:

- The first button on the left will exit Access.

- The next three buttons will be grouped together, and each will open one of the three forms that make up the user interface.

- Three more buttons will, respectively, open the Reports Dialog Box, open the Queries Dialog Box, and exit to the Restaurant database.

- A button at the far right will open the Access Help system.

Creating the Toolbar from Macros

You'll create the Restaurant toolbar by using a macro tool that automatically creates a toolbar from a macro group. A toolbar button will be created for each macro in the group.

REFERENCE window

CREATING A CUSTOM TOOLBAR FROM A MACRO GROUP

- Click the Macros tab in the Database window, and then click the macro that contains the macro group.
- Click Tools on the menu bar, click Macro, and then click Create Toolbar from Macro. Access creates a toolbar containing one button for each macro in the macro group.

Your first step is to create a new toolbar with the name Restaurant.

To create the Restaurant toolbar:

1. Place your Student Disk in the appropriate disk drive, start Access, and then open the Restaurant database in the Tutorial folder on your Student Disk.

2. Click the **Macros** tab (if necessary) to display the Macros list, and then click **Switchboard Macros** to select it. This is the macro group you created in the previous tutorial.

3. Click **Tools** on the menu bar, point to **Macro**, and then click **Create Toolbar from Macro**. Access creates a new toolbar with the name Switchboard Macros. See Figure 10-1.

Figure 10-1 ◄
Switchboard
Macros toolbar

custom toolbar ───→

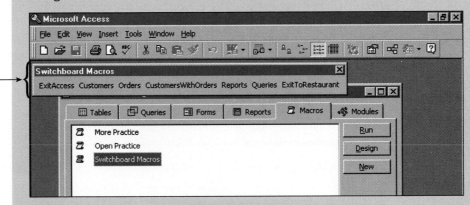

TROUBLE? If the new toolbar is not completely visible on the screen, click the toolbar title and drag the toolbar so that it is positioned like the one in Figure 10-1.

The new toolbar contains seven buttons, one for each macro in the Switchboard Macros macro group. Each button displays the name of the macro to which it is attached. Clicking a button will cause the macro to execute; for example, clicking the Customers button will open the Customer Data form.

The new toolbar has the name Switchboard Macros in its title bar, but Leonard wants the toolbar to be named "Restaurant." You can easily modify the toolbar to change the toolbar name. Also, although the macro names indicate the functions of the buttons, Leonard wants the toolbar for the Restaurant Database switchboard to display icons, just as the built-in toolbars do.

To make the changes Leonard wants to the toolbar, you'll use the Customize dialog box.

To open the Customize dialog box:

1. Right-click the **Switchboard Macros** toolbar to display the shortcut menu, and then click **Customize**. The Customize dialog box opens.

2. If necessary, click the **Toolbars** tab to display the Toolbars page. See Figure 10-2.

Figure 10-2 ◀
Customize
dialog box

list of existing
toolbars

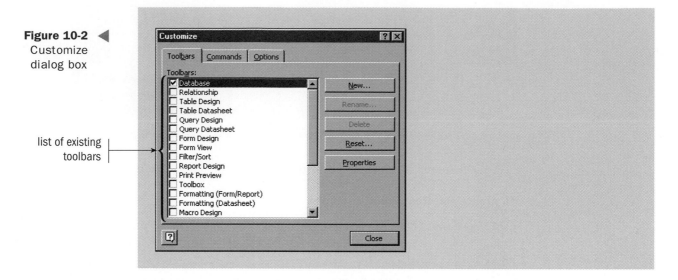

The Customize dialog box allows you to create a new toolbar from scratch or to modify or delete an existing toolbar. The Toolbars page displays a list of existing toolbars with a check mark next to the toolbar name if the toolbar is currently displayed. The Commands page allows you to add new buttons to a toolbar or to modify the meaning of existing buttons on a toolbar. The Options page allows you to specify the size of the icons displayed and whether ToolTips are displayed when the user points to a toolbar button. You can customize any Access built-in or custom toolbar using the Customize dialog box.

You are now ready to make the necessary changes to the custom toolbar. You'll begin by changing the toolbar title to "Restaurant."

To change the toolbar title:

1. Scroll down the Toolbars list until Switchboard Macros is visible, and then click **Switchboard Macros** (not the check box) to select it.

2. Click the **Properties** button. The Toolbar Properties dialog box opens. See Figure 10-3.

Figure 10-3 ◀
Toolbar
Properties
dialog box

enter toolbar
name here

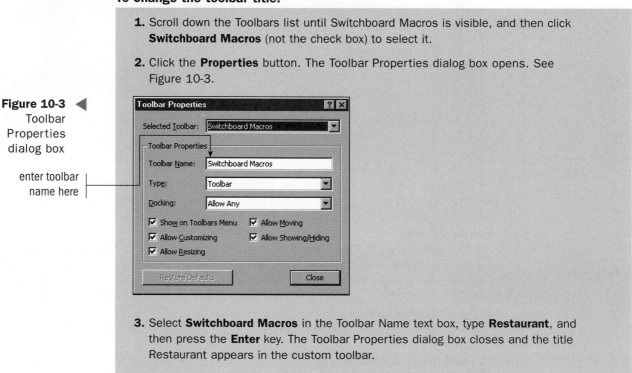

3. Select **Switchboard Macros** in the Toolbar Name text box, type **Restaurant**, and then press the **Enter** key. The Toolbar Properties dialog box closes and the title Restaurant appears in the custom toolbar.

You can now change the buttons to show icons (images) instead of words. This will make the toolbar more consistent with the built-in toolbars.

To display icons on the custom toolbar buttons:

1. Right-click the **ExitAccess** button on the Restaurant toolbar to display the short-cut menu, and then point to **Change Button Image**. Access displays the palette of custom button images. See Figure 10-4.

Figure 10-4 ◀
Custom button images

Pencil image

Coffee Cup image

Left Arrow image

Open Page image

Standing Figure image

Eye image

Down Arrow image

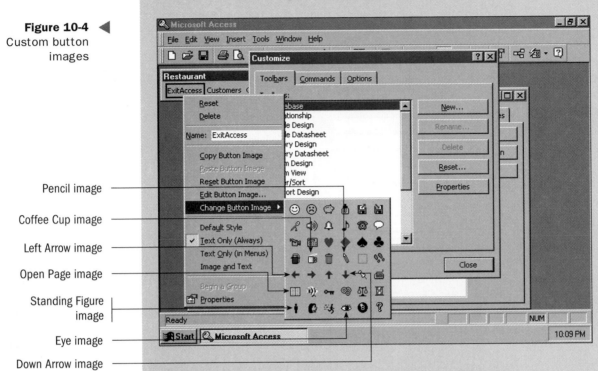

Leonard has chosen the Left Arrow image for the ExitAccess button, so you will select that image from the palette of custom button images.

2. Click the **Left Arrow** image ⬅. The ExitAccess button now displays the left arrow icon together with the label ExitAccess. You need to change the style of the button so that it displays only the icon, not the label.

3. Right-click the **ExitAccess** button to display the shortcut menu, and then click **Default Style**. The button now appears with only the left arrow icon. See Figure 10-5.

Figure 10-5 ◀
Modified ExitAccess toolbar button

new button image

The toolbar button now displays the left arrow icon and no label. If you place the pointer over the button, a ToolTip appears displaying the name of the attached macro, in this case ExitAccess. Leonard asks you to modify the ToolTip so that it displays complete words (Exit Access, in this case), making the ToolTip easier to read.

4. Right-click the **ExitAccess** button to display the shortcut menu, and then click **Properties**. The Restaurant Control Properties dialog box opens. See Figure 10-6.

Figure 10-6 ◀
Restaurant
Control
Properties
dialog box

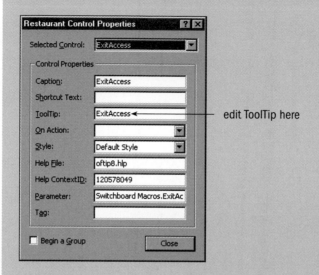

edit ToolTip here

The ToolTip text box determines what text is displayed when the pointer is positioned over the toolbar button.

5. Place the insertion point between the **t** and the **A** in ExitAccess in the ToolTip text box, and then press the **spacebar**. The ToolTip now reads Exit Access.

6. Press the **Enter** key. The Restaurant Control Properties dialog box closes, and the ToolTip for the button is changed. Note that you cannot display ToolTips for the toolbar buttons while the Customize dialog box is open; you'll check the ToolTips later, after you've finished customizing the toolbar.

Now you can modify the other six buttons on the custom toolbar to display the images Leonard wants.

7. Repeat Steps 1 through 6 to modify each of the other buttons on the custom toolbar. For the Customers button, choose the **Standing Figure** image 🧍 and do not change the ToolTip. For the Orders button, choose the **Pencil** image ✏️ and do not change the ToolTip. For the CustomersWithOrders button, use the **Coffee Cup** image ☕ and change the ToolTip to **Customers With Orders**. For the Reports button, choose the **Open Page** image 🗐 and do not change the ToolTip. For the Queries button, choose the **Eye** image 👁️ and do not change the ToolTip. Finally, for the ExitToRestaurant button, choose the **Down Arrow** image ⬇️ and change the ToolTip to **Exit to Restaurant**. (Refer to Figure 10-4 for the correct images to choose.) See Figure 10-7.

Figure 10-7 ◀
Modified
Restaurant
toolbar

toolbar with images
on buttons

TROUBLE? You might need to move the Restaurant toolbar or the Customize dialog box so that the Restaurant toolbar is not obscured.

After looking at the new toolbar, Leonard asks whether you can visually separate the three form buttons (Customers, Orders, and Customers With Orders) from the other buttons on the toolbar. This design is also consistent with the built-in toolbars, many of which include vertical lines to visually group related buttons together on the toolbar. He also reminds you that the interface design shows a Help button on the custom toolbar, which should also be visually separated from the other buttons. You can make these changes now.

To group the toolbar buttons and add a Help button:

1. Right-click the **Customers** button 🔼 on the Restaurant toolbar, and then click **Begin a Group**. Access places a vertical dividing line between the Exit Access button and the Customers button on the Restaurant toolbar.

2. Right-click the **Reports** button 🔲 on the Restaurant toolbar, and then click **Begin a Group**. Access places a dividing line between the Customers With Orders button and the Reports button.

   To add the Help button, you can simply add a copy of an existing Help button from the Access standard toolbar buttons. These buttons are available on the Commands tab of the Customize dialog box.

3. Click the **Commands** tab in the Customize dialog box.

4. In the Categories list box, click **Window and Help** to display the list of standard window and help buttons. See Figure 10-8.

Figure 10-8 ◀
Window and
Help buttons

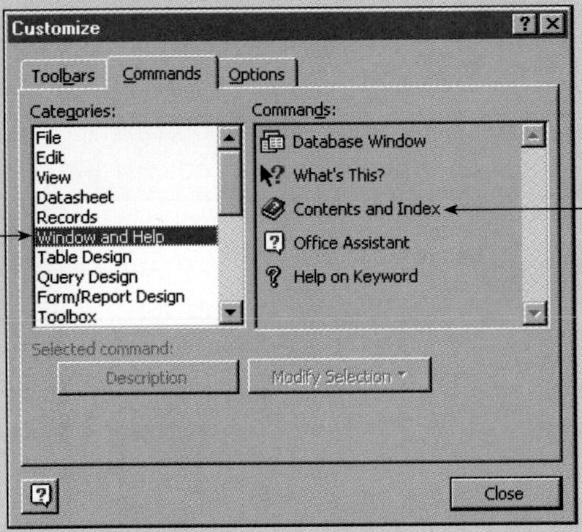

selected category ⟶

Contents and Index
command

5. Click the **Contents and Index** button 🖋 in the Commands list, and then drag it to the right edge of the Restaurant toolbar. When a large I-beam appears at the right edge of the toolbar, release the mouse button. Access places a copy of the Contents and Index button on the Restaurant toolbar.

   The Contents and Index button will appear on the Restaurant toolbar whenever it is displayed. You will be able to click the Contents and Index button and the effect will be the same as if you had chosen the Contents and Index command from the Help menu.

6. Right-click the **Contents and Index** button 🖋 on the Restaurant toolbar, and then click **Begin a Group**. Access adds the dividing line to the left of the Contents and Index button.

   Now you can change the ToolTip for the Contents and Index button to "Help." This is the ToolTip that will appear when the user places the pointer on the button.

7. Right-click the **Contents and Index** button 🖋 on the Restaurant toolbar, and then click **Properties**. The Restaurant Control Properties dialog box opens.

8. Select the text in the ToolTip text box, type **Help**, and then press the **Enter** key. The Restaurant Control Properties dialog box closes.

You have finished modifying the custom toolbar, so you can close the Customize dialog box.

9. Click the **Close** button in the Customize dialog box to close it.

Leonard wants to have the Restaurant toolbar appear at the top of the Access window, as the standard toolbar does. When a toolbar is attached to the top, bottom, or side of an Access window, its title bar disappears and a move handle appears at the left end or the top of the toolbar. When a toolbar is in this position, it is called a **docked** toolbar. A toolbar that is not attached to the top, bottom, or side of an Access window is called a **floating** toolbar. A floating toolbar, such as the Restaurant toolbar, displays a title bar. Leonard's design shows the Restaurant toolbar docked at the top of the Access window. You can dock a toolbar by simply moving it into the docked position.

To dock the Restaurant toolbar at the top of the Access window:

1. Click the **Restaurant** toolbar title bar and drag the Restaurant toolbar up until it is overlapping the Database toolbar and its shape changes to an elongated rectangle, and then release the mouse button. Access docks the Restaurant toolbar below the Database toolbar at the top of the Access window. See Figure 10-9.

Figure 10-9 ◀
Custom toolbar docked below the Database toolbar

move handle

toolbar docked

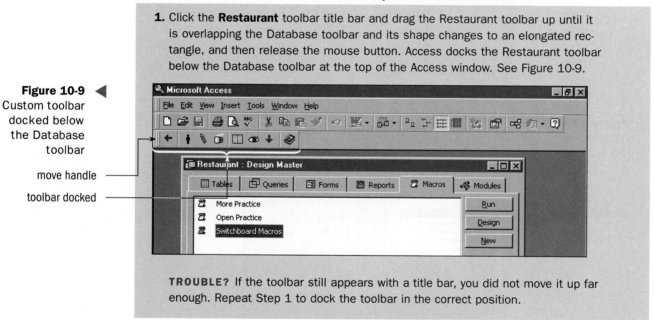

TROUBLE? If the toolbar still appears with a title bar, you did not move it up far enough. Repeat Step 1 to dock the toolbar in the correct position.

The custom toolbar is complete. You can now specify when you want Access to show and hide the custom toolbar.

Attaching a Custom Toolbar to a Form

When a user opens the Restaurant Database switchboard, Leonard wants only the Restaurant toolbar to appear; the Form View toolbar should be hidden. Leonard does not want the user to display the Restaurant toolbar at other times (by selecting it from the Toolbars submenu of the View menu), nor does he want it to appear by default on other windows. To control the display of the toolbar, you can attach the custom toolbar to the Switchboard form so that the custom toolbar will appear whenever the Switchboard form is opened. Then you can change the custom toolbar properties so that it does not appear on the Toolbars submenu. Finally, you can hide the custom toolbar so that it does not appear by default on other windows.

To attach the Restaurant toolbar to the Switchboard form:

1. Click the **Forms** tab in the Database window (if necessary), click **Switchboard**, and then click the **Design** button. Access displays the form in Design view.

2. Click the form selector to display the properties for the form in the property sheet.

TROUBLE? If the property sheet is not open, right-click the form selector, and then click Properties on the shortcut menu.

The form's Toolbar property specifies the name of the toolbar that will appear when the form is open.

3. Click the **All** tab in the property sheet (if necessary), scroll the properties list, click the right side of the **Toolbar** text box, and then click **Restaurant**.

4. Click the **Save** button 🖫 on the Form Design toolbar to save the design changes, and then click the **Close** button ☒ on the property sheet to close it.

5. Close the Form window to return to the Database window.

6. Make sure **Switchboard** is selected, and then click the **Open** button to open the Switchboard form in Form view. See Figure 10-10.

Figure 10-10 ◀
Switchboard
form with the
custom toolbar

custom toolbar

Switchboard form

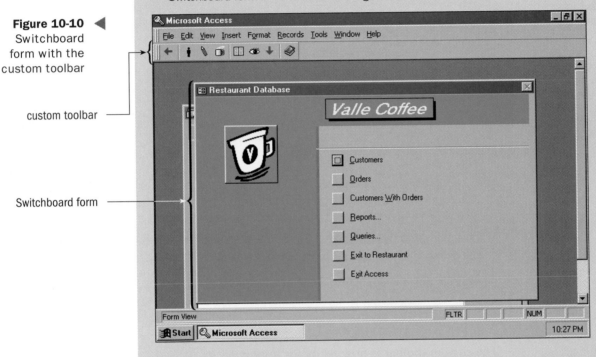

TROUBLE? If your toolbar is not in the same location as the one in the figure, use either the toolbar's move handle (see Figure 10-9) or its title bar to reposition the toolbar to the correct location.

Access opens the Switchboard form and displays the custom toolbar in place of the built-in Form View toolbar. The custom toolbar, therefore, is properly attached to the Switchboard form.

Attaching the Restaurant toolbar to the Switchboard form means that the toolbar will appear whenever the Switchboard form is open. Leonard does not want the Restaurant toolbar to appear when the Switchboard form is not open. You can now customize the Restaurant toolbar so that it does not appear by default in the Database window. You can also change the Restaurant toolbar properties so that it does not appear as an option on the Toolbars submenu of the View menu. This will prevent users from displaying the custom toolbar when the Switchboard form is not open.

To hide the toolbar and change the toolbar properties:

1. Click the **Down Arrow** button 🔽 on the Restaurant toolbar to close the Switchboard form and return to the Database window. The Switchboard form closes but the Restaurant toolbar remains on the screen.

2. Right-click the **Restaurant** toolbar to open the shortcut menu, and then click **Customize**. Access opens the Customize dialog box.

3. Click the **Toolbars** tab, scroll the toolbars list, and then click the **Restaurant** check box. The Restaurant toolbar disappears. In the future, it will not appear in the Restaurant Database window by default.

   You can now change the Restaurant toolbar properties so that it does not appear on the Toolbars submenu of the View menu.

4. Click the **Properties** button. The Toolbar Properties dialog box opens. See Figure 10-11.

Figure 10-11 ◀
Specifying the properties for the Restaurant toolbar

deselect to remove from Toolbars submenu

deselect to prevent customizing

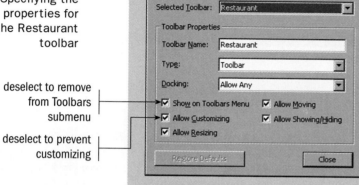

5. Click the **Show on Toolbars Menu** check box to remove the check mark. The Restaurant toolbar will not appear on the Toolbars submenu of the View menu. This will prevent users from displaying the toolbar by selecting it from this menu.

6. Click the **Allow Customizing** check box to remove the check mark. This prevents users from changing the custom toolbar.

7. Click the **Close** button in the Toolbar Properties dialog box.

8. Click the **Close** button in the Customize dialog box.

The custom toolbar is now ready for testing.

Testing a Custom Toolbar

To test the custom toolbar, you will open the Switchboard form and confirm that the custom toolbar is displayed when the form is opened. Then you'll place the pointer on each button and verify that its ToolTip is correct. Finally, you'll click each button to test that the proper response occurs.

To test the custom toolbar:

1. In the Forms list, click **Switchboard** and then click the **Open** button. Access opens the Switchboard form and displays the Restaurant toolbar.

2. Place the pointer on each toolbar button and verify that the correct ToolTip appears.

3. Click the **Customers** button [i] on the Restaurant toolbar to open the Customer Data form, and then click the **Close** button [X] on the Form window to close it.

4. Repeat Step 3 for the Orders button [≡] and the Customers With Orders [▦] button on the Restaurant toolbar to view these two forms.

5. Click the **Reports** button on the Restaurant toolbar to open the Reports Dialog Box, and then click the **Close** button to return to the Switchboard form.

6. Repeat Step 5 for the **Queries** button on the Restaurant toolbar.

7. Click the **Help** button on the Restaurant toolbar to open the Access Help window, and then click the **Close** button on the Help window to close it.

8. Click the **Exit to Restaurant** button on the Restaurant toolbar. Access closes the Switchboard form and returns to the Database window.

9. Click the **Open** button to open the Switchboard form in Form view again.

10. Click the **Exit Access** button on the Restaurant toolbar. Access closes all windows and exits.

You have completed the custom toolbar and you can now create the custom menu bar for the Restaurant Database switchboard.

Planning a Custom Menu Bar

Leonard has designed a custom menu bar to be used with the Restaurant Database switchboard. The custom menu bar has menu options for the different operations available in the user interface. The menu options provide users with an alternative method for performing the available operations. Figure 10-12 shows Leonard's plan for the menus and menu items.

Figure 10-12 ◀
Leonard's design for the custom menu bar

drop-down menus

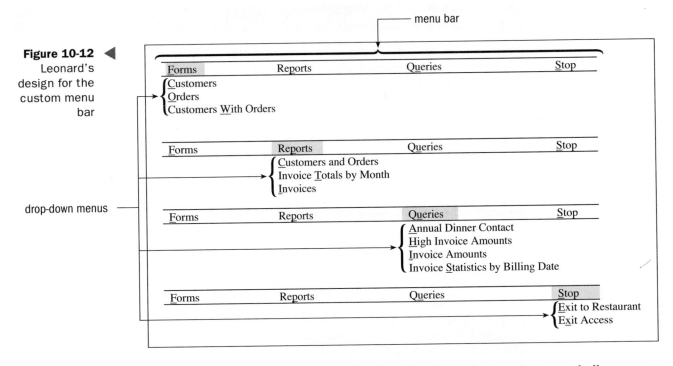

In Access, a **menu bar** is a type of toolbar that displays menu choices and allows you to use hot keys to activate them. A **custom menu bar** is a menu bar you create for an application. Custom menu bars are similar to standard Access menu bars, which are called **built-in menu bars**, in the following ways:

■ A custom menu bar appears immediately below the title bar, replacing the built-in menu bar.

■ A custom menu bar contains one or more menu names. The menu names on Leonard's custom menu bar are Forms, Reports, Queries, and Stop.

- A list of menu item names, which are usually the names of commands, appears in a drop-down menu when you click a menu name on the menu bar. The menu item names for the Forms menu are Customers, Orders, and Customers With Orders.

- Each menu name has an underlined letter that identifies the hot key to the menu. Pressing Alt + F, for example, opens the Forms menu to display the three menu items (the three different forms you can open).

- Each menu item name has an underlined letter that identifies the hot key for selecting that option. Pressing the W key when the Forms menu is open, for example, opens the Customers With Orders form.

- A hot key can apply to only one active control or menu choice on the screen. You cannot assign a hot key to a custom menu bar choice if it is already used on the switchboard or other control. When a menu is displayed, hot keys apply only to the available menu items.

You create a custom menu bar in much the same way as you create any custom toolbar: you place command buttons on the custom menu bar. One command you will use is the New Menu command, which displays a list of menu items associated with that menu name. When the user clicks a menu name or menu item, Access responds by carrying out the appropriate command (for example, it opens a form). You can attach a custom menu bar to a form or report so that Access displays the custom menu bar only when the attached form or report is displayed. Alternatively, your custom menu bar can be global, so that Access displays the custom menu bar in all windows of your application.

Creating a Custom Menu Bar

When you created the Restaurant custom toolbar, you created the toolbar from the macros in the Switchboard Macros macro group. You could do the same for the custom menu bar; Access would create a custom menu bar with menu names for each of the macros in the Switchboard Macros macro group. However, you would then have to modify the custom menu bar in several ways to make it consistent with Leonard's custom menu bar design. For example, you would have to associate most of the macros with menu items on submenus rather than with the menu names on the custom menu bar. It is simpler to create the custom menu bar directly using the Customize dialog box.

To create the custom menu bar:

1. Start Access and open the Restaurant database.

2. Right-click the **Database** toolbar, and then click **Customize**. The Customize dialog box opens.

3. Click the **New** button to display the New Toolbar dialog box, type **Restaurant Menu** in the Toolbar name text box, and then press the **Enter** key. Access displays a new toolbar in front of the Customize dialog box. See Figure 10-13.

Access

Figure 10-13 ◀
New custom
toolbar for the
menu bar

custom menu bar ——

new toolbar now
listed

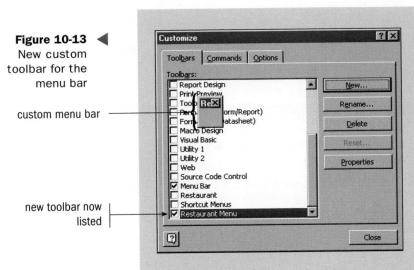

4. Drag the new custom toolbar to the left side of the screen. This will prevent the Customize dialog box from obscuring the custom toolbar as you work with it.

5. Click the **Properties** button to display the Toolbar Properties dialog box.

6. Click the **Type** list arrow, and then click **Menu Bar**. The toolbar is now a custom menu bar.

7. Click the **Close** button in the Toolbar Properties dialog box. The Toolbar Properties dialog box closes and the Customize dialog box appears.

You can now add the commands for the menu names to the custom menu bar. Each command is a New Menu command, which will display a submenu when the user clicks it. You will also rename the New Menu commands to display the appropriate labels, according to Leonard's design.

To add the commands to the custom menu bar:

1. Click the **Commands** tab, scroll the Categories list box, and then click **New Menu**. Access displays New Menu in the Commands list box. See Figure 10-14. The small arrow at the right of the New Menu command indicates that a submenu will appear for this command on the menu bar.

Figure 10-14 ◀
New Menu
command in
the Commands
list box

New Menu command ——

New Menu category ——

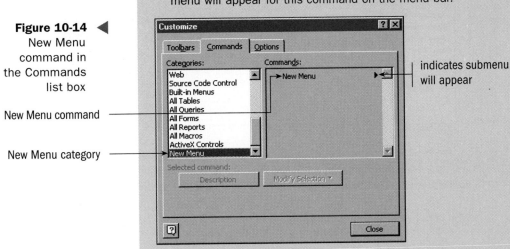

indicates submenu
will appear

2. Click and drag the **New Menu** command to the custom menu bar and release the mouse button. Access adds a menu button labeled New Menu.

3. Right-click the **New Menu** button to display the shortcut menu.

According to Leonard's design, the first menu on the menu bar is Forms, with F as the hot key, so the name of this menu should be &Forms.

4. Select the current entry (New Menu) in the Name text box, and then type **&Forms**. Recall that the & creates a hot key. See Figure 10-15.

Figure 10-15 ◀
Changing the
menu name

new menu button
name

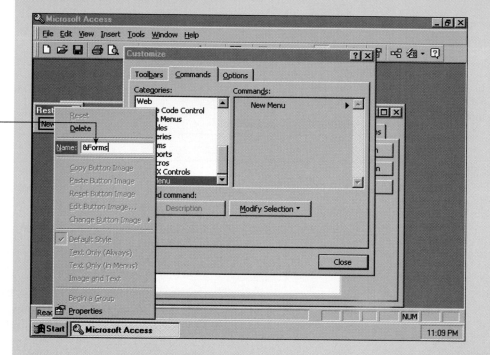

5. Press the **Enter** key. The shortcut menu closes and Access displays the new menu name in the menu bar. See Figure 10-16.

Figure 10-16 ◀
New menu
name in the
menu bar

renamed menu
button

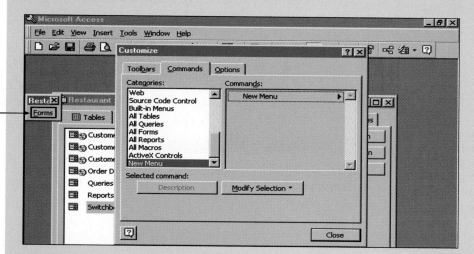

6. Repeat Steps 2 through 5 to add three more New Menu buttons to the custom menu bar. Change the names for the menus (from left to right) to **Re&ports**, **Q&ueries**, and **&Stop**. You might need to move the Customize dialog box to the right side of the screen so it does not obscure the custom menu bar. When you are finished, your screen should look like Figure 10-17.

Figure 10-17 ◀
Custom menu
bar with four
menu names

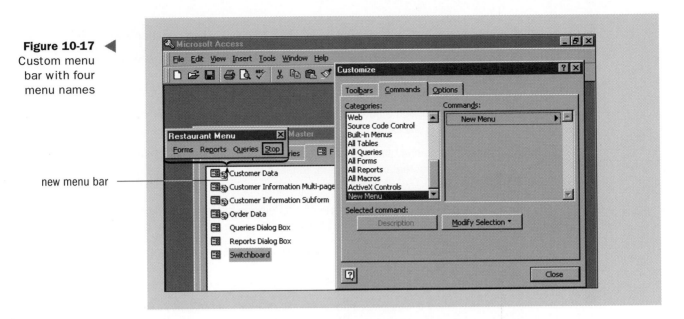

new menu bar

You can now add the menu items that will appear when the user clicks one of the menus on the custom menu bar. First you will add the menu items for displaying the three forms to the Forms menu.

To add the menu items to the Forms menu:

1. In the Categories list box of the Customize dialog box, click **All Forms**. The Commands list box now displays a list of all the forms in the Restaurant database.

2. Click and drag **Customer Data** until the pointer is on the Forms menu name on the Restaurant Menu toolbar. Access displays a submenu box below the Forms menu button. Move the pointer to the submenu box and release the mouse button to place the Customer Data form in the submenu box. See Figure 10-18.

Figure 10-18 ◀
Placing the
command in
the submenu
box

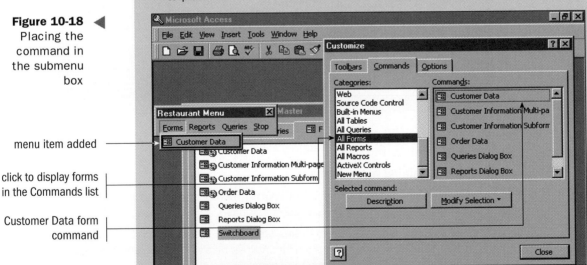

menu item added

click to display forms
in the Commands list

Customer Data form
command

TROUBLE? If the Customer Data form button appears on the menu bar and not in the submenu box, click and drag the Customer Data form button until it is on the Forms menu name, and then move the pointer to the submenu box and release the mouse button to place the Customer Data form in the submenu box.

You can now change the name of the new menu item to &Customers. This makes "C" the hot key for this menu item.

3. Right-click the **Customer Data** menu item to display the shortcut menu.

4. Select the current entry in the Name text box, type **&Customers**, and then press the **Enter** key.

The name of the menu item is now Customers, and the letter "C" is the hot key. Next, you will add a button for the Order Data form to the same submenu, change the name of the button to Orders, and make O the hot key for this menu item.

5. In the Commands list box, click **Order Data** and drag it to the Forms submenu below the Customers menu item. Release the mouse button. Access adds the Order Data item to the submenu.

6. Right-click the **Order Data** menu item to display the shortcut menu, select the current entry in the Name text box, type **&Orders**, and then press the **Enter** key.

7. In the Commands list box, click **Customer Information Multi-page** and drag it to the Forms submenu below the Orders item. Release the mouse button. Access adds the Customer Information Multi-page item to the submenu.

8. Right-click the **Customer Information Multi-page** menu item to display the shortcut menu, select the current entry in the Name text box, type **Customers &With Orders**, and then press the **Enter** key. See Figure 10-19.

Figure 10-19 ◄
Completed
Forms menu

three menu items
added

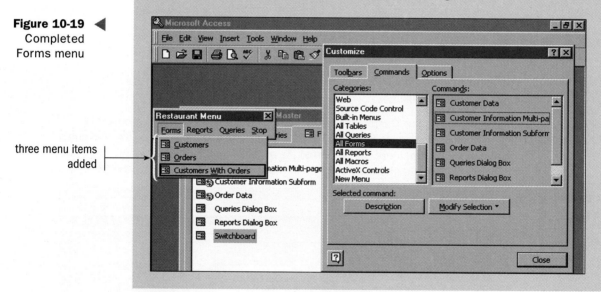

You can now add the menu items to the remaining menus on the Restaurant Menu bar.

To add the remaining menu items:

1. In the Categories list box, click **All Reports**. The Commands list box displays a list of all the reports in the Restaurant database.

2. Click and drag **Customers and Orders** until the pointer is on the Reports menu name on the Restaurant Menu toolbar. Access displays a submenu box below the Reports menu button. Move the pointer to the submenu box and release the mouse button to place the Customers and Orders report in the submenu box.

You can now edit the name for this menu item to specify "C" as the hot key.

3. Right-click the **Customers and Orders** menu item to display the shortcut menu, position the insertion point to the left of the "C" in the Name text box, type **&**, and then press the **Enter** key.

4. In the Commands list box, click **Invoice Totals by Month** and drag it to the Reports submenu below the Customers and Orders menu item. Release the mouse button. Access adds the Invoice Totals by Month item to the submenu.

5. Right-click the **Invoice Totals by Month** menu item to display the shortcut menu, and then edit the name of this item to **Invoice &Totals by Month**.

6. Repeat Steps 4 and 5 to add the Invoices item to the Reports submenu. Edit the name of the Invoices report to **&Invoices**.

7. Click **All Queries** in the Categories list box, and then add the following items (in order) to the Queries submenu: **Annual Dinner Contact**, **High Invoice Amounts**, **Invoice Amounts**, and **Invoice Statistics by Billing Date**. Edit the names of the query menu items to **&Annual Dinner Contact**, **&High Invoice Amounts**, **&Invoice Amounts**, and **Invoice &Statistics by Billing Date**, respectively.

8. Click **All Macros** in the Categories list box, and then add the following items (in order) to the Stop submenu: **Switchboard Macros.ExitToRestaurant** and **Switchboard Macros.ExitAccess**. Edit the names of the macro items to **&Exit to Restaurant** and **E&xit Access**, respectively.

The custom menu bar is complete. The next step is to dock the custom menu bar above the Database toolbar. Then you can change the custom menu bar's properties, as you did with the custom toolbar, so that it does not appear in the Database window by default and so that users cannot customize it.

To dock the custom menu bar and set its properties:

1. Drag the custom menu bar up until it is between the Database menu bar and the Database toolbar, and then release the mouse button. Access docks the custom menu bar between the Database menu bar and the Database toolbar. See Figure 10-20.

Figure 10-20 ◀
Docking
the custom
menu bar

custom menu bar
docked between the
Database menu bar
and Database toolbar

You can now remove the Restaurant Menu bar from the list of menu bars displayed by default in the Database window.

2. Click the **Toolbars** tab in the Customize dialog box, scroll the toolbars list, and then click the **Restaurant Menu** check box to remove the check mark. The Restaurant Menu bar disappears.

3. Click the **Properties** button to open the Toolbar Properties dialog box.

4. Click the **Allow Customizing** check box to remove the check mark. Access will not allow users to customize the Restaurant Menu bar.

5. Click the **Close** button to close the Toolbar Properties dialog box.

6. Click the **Close** button to close the Customize dialog box.

Now you can attach the custom menu bar to the Switchboard form in Design view. The Restaurant Menu bar, like the Restaurant toolbar you created earlier, will appear only when the Switchboard form is open. Users cannot display this menu bar at any other time. The Restaurant Menu bar, the Restaurant toolbar, and the Switchboard form are the three visual components of Leonard's design for the Restaurant database graphical user interface.

To attach the custom menu bar to the Switchboard form:

1. Click the **Forms** tab, click **Switchboard**, and then click the **Design** button. Access opens the Switchboard form in Design view.

2. Right-click the form selector to open the shortcut menu, and then click **Properties** to open the property sheet.

3. Click the **All** tab in the property sheet (if necessary), scroll down and click the right side of the **Menu Bar** text box, and then click **Restaurant Menu** in the list. This attaches the Restaurant Menu bar to the Switchboard form. When the Switchboard form is opened, it will automatically display the Restaurant Menu bar.

4. Click the **Save** button 🔲 on the Form Design toolbar to save the changes, and then click the **Close** button ✖ on the property sheet to close it.

5. Click the **Close** button ✖ on the Form Design window to close it and return to the Database window.

6. Click the **Open** button to open the Switchboard form in Form view. See Figure 10-21.

Figure 10-21 ◄
Custom menu
bar with the
Switchboard
form

custom menu bar

custom toolbar

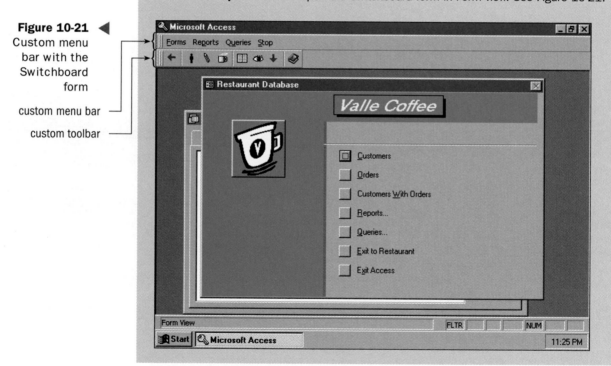

When the Switchboard form opens, the visual components of the Restaurant database graphical user interface are displayed. The Restaurant Menu bar and the Restaurant toolbar appear at the top of the screen, and the Switchboard form is displayed at the center of the screen. The standard menu bar and toolbar are not displayed.

Next, you need to test all the buttons on the menu bar to make sure they work correctly.

Testing the Custom Menu Bar

To test each menu, you click each menu name and verify that the drop-down menu opens in response. To test keyboard access to the menus, you press the Alt key and the underlined menu character to open a drop-down menu, and then press the Esc key to close the drop-down menu. In a similar way, you test the mouse and keyboard access to the menu items on each drop-down menu. For keyboard access to the menu items, you simply press the underlined character (you do not have to also press the Alt key). You will test the Exit Access menu item last, because it closes the Restaurant database and exits Access.

To test the custom menu bar:

1. Click the **Forms** menu to verify that the drop-down menu appears. Move the pointer over the other menu names, in turn, from left to right, to verify that each drop-down menu appears.

2. Press the **Esc** key to close the displayed drop-down menu.

3. Press **Alt + F** to display the Forms drop-down menu, and then press the **Esc** key to close the drop-down menu.

   TROUBLE? If the hot key for a menu or menu item is a capital letter, you do not have to press the Shift key as well to execute the hot key combination; you simply press the key for the underlined letter.

4. Repeat Step 3 for the underlined character in each of the other three menu names.

5. Click **Forms** to display its drop-down menu, and then either click **Customers** or press **C** to open the Customer Data form. Click the **Close** button ⊠ on the Form window to close it. Repeat this step for each of the other two menu items on the Forms menu.

   TROUBLE? If you are tempted to skip these testing steps, remember that there are many points in the menu-building process at which things can go wrong. If other users will be using your switchboard, you should be sure to test every part of it.

6. Click **Reports** to display its drop-down menu, and then either click **Customers and Orders** or press **C** to open the **Customers and Orders** report in Print Preview. Click the **Close** button ⊠ on the Report window to close it. Repeat this step for each of the other two menu items on the Reports menu.

7. Click **Queries** to display its drop-down menu, and then either click **Annual Dinner Contact** or press **A** to open the Annual Dinner Contact query results in Datasheet view. Click the **Close** button ⊠ on the Query window to close it. Repeat this step for each of the other three menu items on the Queries menu.

8. Click **Stop** to display its drop-down menu, and then either click **Exit to Restaurant** or press **E**. Access closes the Switchboard form and returns to the Database window.

9. Click the **Open** button to open the Switchboard form in Form view.

10. Click **Stop** on the menu bar, and then either click **Exit Access** or press **X**. Access closes all windows and exits.

Quick Check

1 What is the difference between a built-in toolbar, a custom toolbar, and a command bar?

2 How can you change the image on a toolbar button?

3 How do you attach a toolbar to a form?

4 How do you remove a toolbar from the Toolbars submenu of the View menu?

5 What is a global custom menu bar?

6 What are the rules for determining hot keys in a menu?

You have now completed the custom toolbar and custom menu bar for the Restaurant database user interface. When you resume the tutorial, you will complete the user interface using Visual Basic.

SESSION

10.2

In this session you will learn about Visual Basic functions, subprocedures, and modules. You will create and test a function in a standard module. Then you will create, compile, and test an event procedure.

Introduction to Visual Basic

You are ready to finish the graphical user interface for the Restaurant database. Your next task is to refine the user interface further by adding a function to help with the capitalization of data entered in the Customer Data form. Leonard wants to make sure that all values entered in the State field for this form appear in uppercase letters, and he asks you to modify the form so that it will automatically convert any lowercase letters entered in this field to uppercase. To accomplish this, you will use Visual Basic.

Visual Basic is the programming language provided with Access. The process of writing Visual Basic instructions is called **coding**. You write Visual Basic instructions, called **statements**, to respond to events that occur with the objects in a database. A language such as Visual Basic is, therefore, called both an **event-driven language** and an **object-oriented language**. Your experience with macros, which are also event-driven and object-oriented, should facilitate your learning of Visual Basic. You can do almost anything with Visual Basic that you can do with macros, but Visual Basic gives you more control over commands and objects than you have with macros. For example, with Visual Basic you can create your own functions to perform special calculations. You can also change an object's properties dynamically; for example, Visual Basic code can change the color on a form when the user enters a specific field value.

Events

An **event** occurs when the user takes some action, such as clicking a button using the mouse or pressing a key to choose an option. In your work with Access, you've initiated hundreds of events on forms, controls, records, and reports. For example, three form events are: Open, which occurs when you open a form; Activate, which occurs when the form becomes the active window; and Close, which occurs when you close a form and it is removed from the screen. Each event has an associated event property. An **event property** specifies how an object responds when an event occurs. For example, each form has OnOpen, OnActivate, and OnClose event properties associated with the Open, Activate, and Close events, respectively.

Event properties appear in the property sheet when you create forms and reports. Unlike most properties you've used before in property sheets, event properties do not have an initial value. If an event property contains no value, it means the event property has not been set. In this case Access takes no special action when the associated event occurs. For example, if a form's OnOpen event property is not set and you open the form, then the Open event occurs (the form opens), and no special action occurs. You can set an event property value to a macro name, and Access will execute the macro when the event occurs. For example, you could write a macro that automatically highlights a particular field in a form. You can also create a group of statements using Visual Basic code and set the event property value to the name of that group of statements. Access will then execute the group of statements, or procedure, when the event occurs. Such a procedure is called an **event procedure**.

Access has 43 events and 43 associated event properties. As with actions, you do not need to learn all 43 events. You will gain experience with several event properties in this text, and if you need information on other event properties, you can use the Help system as a reference tool.

You'll use Help to review two particularly useful Help topics on events.

To review the Help topics for events:

1. If you took a break after the previous session, start Access and open the Restaurant database in the Tutorial folder on your Student Disk.

2. Click **Help** on the menu bar, and then click **Contents and Index** to open the Access Help window.

3. If necessary, click the **Index** tab, and then type **events** in the upper text box.

4. Click the **listed alphabetically** subtopic under events, and then click the **Display** button. The Help window displays the list of events and event properties. Scroll down the list to view the available events.

5. Click the **Help Topics** button to return to the Access Help window Index page.

6. Click the **order of** subtopic, and then click the **Display** button. Access displays a Help window describing the order in which events occur. Review the contents of this window.

7. Click the **Close** button [X] on the Help window to close it and return to the Database window.

Procedures

When you work with Visual Basic, you code a group of statements and then attach the group to the event property of an object. Access then executes, or **calls**, these statements every time the event occurs for that object. Each group of statements is called a **procedure**. The two types of procedures are functions and subprocedures, or subroutines.

- A **function** is a procedure that performs operations, returns a value, can accept input values, and can be used in expressions (recall that an expression is a calculation resulting in a single value). For example, some of the Restaurant database queries use built-in functions provided with Access (Sum, Count, and Avg) to calculate a sum, a record count, and an average. To meet Leonard's request, you will create a function named CapAll by entering the appropriate Visual Basic statements. The CapAll function will accept the value entered in a field—in this case, the State field—as an input value, capitalize all characters of the field value, and then return the changed field value.

- A **subprocedure**, or **subroutine**, performs operations and can accept input values but does not return a value and cannot be used in expressions. In the next session, you will create a subprocedure that displays a message on the Order Data form only when the data for an unpaid invoice is displayed in the form.

Modules

You store a group of related procedures together in a **module**. Figure 10-22 shows the structure of a typical module.

Figure 10-22 ◀
Structure of a
Visual Basic
module and its
procedures

Declarations section

procedures

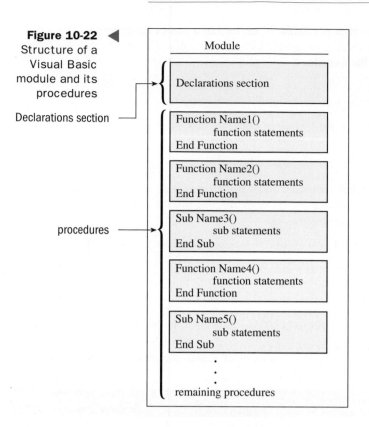

Each module starts with a **Declarations section**, which contains statements that apply to all procedures in the module. One or more procedures, which follow the Declarations section, constitute the rest of the module. A module is either standard or it is contained in a form or report.

- A **standard module** is a separate database object that is stored in memory with other database objects when you open the database. You can use the procedures in standard modules from anywhere in a database, even from procedures in other modules. A procedure that can be used by more than one object is called a **public** procedure. For example, the CapAll function that you will create capitalizes all letters in the value passed to it. Although you are creating this function specifically to work with the State field value, you will place it in a standard module and make it public. You could then use the CapAll function for any object in the database. All standard modules are listed on the Modules tab of the Database window.

- Access automatically creates a form module for each form and a report module for each report. Also called **class modules**, each form or report module contains event procedures. Event procedures are **local**, or **private**, which means that they cannot be used outside the form or report. Unlike standard modules, a class module is stored with its form or report and is loaded into memory only when you open the form or report.

Using Help and Sample Applications

The most difficult part of becoming proficient with Access is learning how to code effective Visual Basic procedures. Visual Basic is a powerful programming language containing hundreds of statements and built-in functions, along with hundreds of event properties, object properties, and built-in procedures. Deciding when and how to use each Visual Basic feature can be intimidating to programming novices and even experts. Fortunately, you can perform many fundamental operations without using Visual Basic by setting control properties and by using macros, as you have done in previous tutorials.

When you use Visual Basic to create new procedures, you can take advantage of the excellent Access Help system as a reference tool. Two particularly useful Help topics are

"Visual Basic code" and "event procedures." You can also find help for every Visual Basic statement, function, and property; most of these topics have a corresponding example that displays sample Visual Basic code. If you find sample code similar to what you need, you can simply copy the statements to the Windows Clipboard, paste them into a procedure in your own database, and modify the statements to work for your special case.

Another source for sample Visual Basic code is the set of sample databases that comes with Access. Three databases appear in the Samples subdirectory provided with Access: the Northwind database, the Orders database, and the Solutions database. Each database has a variety of simple and complex examples of Visual Basic procedures. You can view the effects of these procedures by using them in the sample databases. Microsoft encourages you to copy and use the proven procedures in the sample databases as a way to learn Visual Basic more quickly.

Creating Functions in a Standard Module

Leonard asks whether you can create a Visual Basic procedure for the Customer Data form that will automatically convert the values entered in the State field to uppercase. That is, if a user enters "mi" for the state, the Visual Basic procedure should automatically convert it to "MI." Leonard feels that this will make data entry easier and reduce the number of data entry errors. Users might not always be consistent about capitalizing entries in the State field, and using this function to check entries and capitalize them will ensure consistency.

To accomplish this, you will first create a simple function, called CapAll, that accepts a **string** (text) input value and returns that string with all letters converted to uppercase. You create the function by typing the function statements in the Module window. Then you will create an event procedure that calls the CapAll function whenever the user enters a value in the State field in the Customer Data form.

Whenever a user enters or changes a field value in a control on a form, Access automatically triggers the **AfterUpdate event**, which, by default, simply accepts the new or changed entry. However, you can set the AfterUpdate event property of a field to a specific event procedure in order to have something else happen when a user enters or changes the field value. In this case, you need to set the State field's AfterUpdate event property to [Event Procedure], and then code an event procedure to call the CapAll function. This will cause the entry in the State field to be converted to uppercase letters.

The CapAll function will be used with the Customer Data form, so you could add it to the class module for that form. The function would then be private; that is, it could not be used in other forms or database objects. However, the CapAll function might be useful with other forms, such as the Customer Information Multi-page form. Because you might use the function in other forms in the Restaurant database, you'll place it in a new standard module called Restaurant Functions. Generally, when a procedure is entered in a standard module, it is public; that is, it can be used in event procedures by any object in the database.

To create a new standard module, you begin by opening the Module window.

	CREATING A NEW STANDARD MODULE
REFERENCE window	■ In the Database window, click the Modules tab to open the Modules list.
	■ Click the New button. Access opens the Module window, in which you create a new module.

To create a new standard module:

1. Click the **Modules** tab and then click the **New** button. Access opens the Module window.

2. Click the **Maximize** button on the Module window. See Figure 10-23.

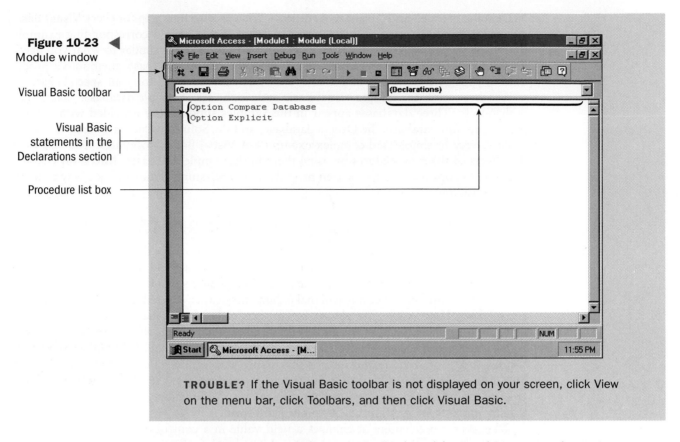

Figure 10-23 ◀
Module window

Visual Basic toolbar —

Visual Basic
statements in the
Declarations section

Procedure list box —

TROUBLE? If the Visual Basic toolbar is not displayed on your screen, click View on the menu bar, click Toolbars, and then click Visual Basic.

You use the Module window to create and modify Visual Basic procedures. Access automatically includes the Option Compare statement in the Declarations section of a new module, followed by a method specifying the technique Access uses when it executes Option Compare. The Option Compare statement designates the technique Access uses to compare and sort text data. The default method "Database," shown in Figure 10-23, means that Access compares and sorts letters in normal alphabetical order, using the language settings specified for Access running on your computer.

The second statement, Option Explicit, states that any variable that is used in the module must be explicitly declared in the module. A **variable** is a named location in memory that can contain a value. If you use a variable in the module, you must explicitly declare it in the Declarations section or in the function definition where the variable is used. For example, if you wanted to use a variable called CustomerCount to store the number of customers in the Customer table, you would declare it with the statement:

Dim CustomerCount as Integer

The CapAll function is a simple function that does not require any variables, so you do not need to declare any variables in the function definition.

Creating a Function

Each function begins with a Function statement and ends with an End Function statement. Access visually separates each function in the Module window with a horizontal line. You can view a function's statements by selecting the function name from the Procedure list box. The CapAll function begins with the statement "Function CapAll (FValue)" on the line below the Option Explicit statement. CapAll is the function name and FValue is used as a placeholder for the input value in the function definition. When the user enters a value for the State field in the Customer Data form, that value will be passed to the CapAll function and substituted for FValue in the function definition. A placeholder like FValue is called a **parameter**. The value passed to the function and used in place of the parameter when the function is executed is called an **argument** (similar to an action in a macro). In other words, the value passed to the function is the argument and it is assigned to the parameter named FValue.

All Visual Basic function names, subprocedure names, and variable names you create must conform to the following rules:

- They must begin with a letter.

- They cannot exceed 255 characters.

- They can include letters, numbers, and the underscore character (_). The space, period (.), exclamation mark (!), or the characters @, &, $, # cannot be used.

- They cannot contain reserved words, such as Function, Sub, and Option, that the language uses for its regular statements. Use the Access Help topic "reserved words" to see a list of reserved words.

- They cannot be keywords such as If, Open, or Print. Use the Access Help topic "keywords" to see the categories of keywords.

- They must be unique; that is, you can't declare two variables with the same name within the same procedure.

You will enter the CapAll function in the Module window and then test it. Then you'll attach it to an event procedure for the Customer Data form. As you enter the statements for the CapAll function in the Module window, remember that capitalization is important in all statements (except comments). You can start entering the CapAll function now.

To start a new function:

1. With the insertion point on the line below the Option Explicit statement, type **Function CapAll (FValue)** and then press the **Enter** key. Access displays a dividing line that visually separates the new function from the Declarations section. See Figure 10-24.

Figure 10-24 ◀
Starting a new
function

dividing line ⎯⎯⎯⎯

entered statement ⎯⎯⎯⎯

statement
automatically entered

function name in the
Procedure list box

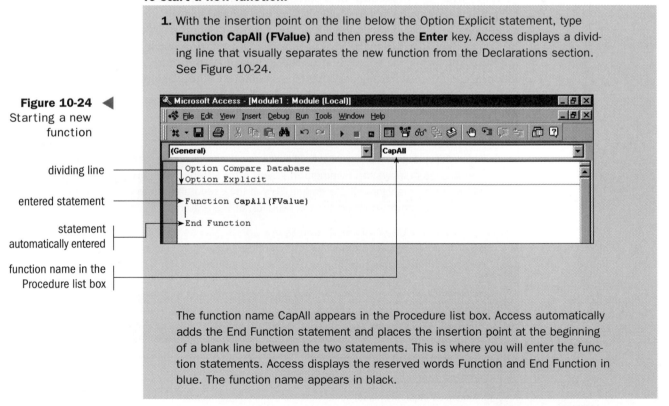

The function name CapAll appears in the Procedure list box. Access automatically adds the End Function statement and places the insertion point at the beginning of a blank line between the two statements. This is where you will enter the function statements. Access displays the reserved words Function and End Function in blue. The function name appears in black.

The CapAll function will consist of a single executable statement, called an assignment statement, which you will place between the Function and End Function statements. An **assignment statement** assigns the value of an expression to a variable or function. Associated with a variable or function is its name, which must follow the Visual Basic naming rules. The general format of an assignment statement is "variable name = expression." You need to enter the following assignment statement: CapAll = UCase(FValue).

Here, the name of the function, CapAll, is the variable name in the statement, and UCase(FValue) is the expression.

The expression in the assignment statement uses a built-in Access function named UCase. The **UCase function** accepts a single string argument as input, converts the value of the argument to uppercase, and then returns the converted value. The assignment statement assigns the converted value to the CapAll function. Figure 10-25 illustrates this process.

Figure 10-25 ◀
Evaluation of
the assignment
statement

argument supplied
to the function

value assigned
to CapAll

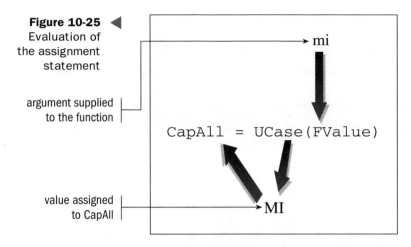

Before entering the assignment statement, you will add a comment line to explain the procedure's purpose. You can include comments anywhere in a Visual Basic procedure to describe what the procedure or a statement does. This makes it easier to remember the purpose of statements in your code. It is a good idea to include frequent comments in your code to make it easier for anyone reading it to understand it. You begin a comment with the word Rem (for "Remark") or with a single quotation mark ('). Visual Basic ignores anything following the word Rem or the single quotation mark on a line. Also, you will indent these lines; indenting statements is a common practice to make code easier to read.

To add comments and statements to the function:

1. Press the **Tab** key to indent the line.

2. Type **'Capitalize all letters of a field value**, and then press the **Enter** key. Notice that Access displays the comment in green. After entering the comment line, you can enter the assignment statement. This is the executable statement in the function that performs the actual conversion of the argument to uppercase.

3. Type **CapAll = UCase(FValue)**. See Figure 10-26. Access assists you as you enter statements. For example, when you type UCase(, Access displays a reminder that UCase accepts a single string argument.

Figure 10-26 ◀
CapAll function
in the Module
window

Debug
Window
button

parameter

comment

assignment
statement

```
Option Compare Database
Option Explicit

Function CapAll(FValue)
    'Capitalize all letters of a field value
    CapAll = UCase(FValue)
End Function
```

Access scans each statement for errors when you press the Enter key or change the focus to another statement. Because the function is complete and you want Access to scan for errors, you can move the insertion point to another line.

4. Press the ↓ key to move the insertion point to the next line. Because Access finds no errors, the insertion point continues to blink in the last line.

TROUBLE? If Access finds an error in the assignment statement, it highlights the error in red and opens a dialog box with a message describing the nature of the error. Click the OK button and change the highlighted error by comparing each character you entered against what you should have entered. Then repeat Step 4 so that Access again scans the statement for errors.

You have finished entering the function, so you can save it before continuing with your work.

Saving a Module

When you click the Save button in the Module window, Access saves the module and its procedures. If you are entering a long procedure, it is a good idea to save your work periodically.

To save the module:

1. Click the **Save** button 💾 on the Visual Basic toolbar, type **Restaurant Functions** in the Module Name text box, and then press the **Enter** key. Access saves the module and places the new module name in the title bar.

Before making the changes to the Customer Data form so that the CapAll function automatically acts on every entry in the State field, you can test the function using the Debug window.

Testing a Procedure in the Debug Window

Even the simplest procedure can contain errors. Be sure to test each procedure thoroughly to ensure it does exactly what you expect it to do in all situations. When working in the Module window, you can use the **Debug window** to test Visual Basic procedures. In the Debug window, you can enter different values to test the procedure you just entered. To test a procedure, use the keyword "Print" or a question mark (?), followed by the procedure name and the value you want to test in parentheses. For example, to test the CapAll function in the Debug window using the test word "mi," type "?CapAll ("mi")" and press the Enter key. Access executes the function and prints the value returned by the function (you expect it to return "MI"). Note that you must enclose a string of characters within quotation marks.

REFERENCE
window

TESTING A PROCEDURE IN THE DEBUG WINDOW

- In the Module window, click the Debug Window button on the Visual Basic toolbar to open the Debug window.
- Type a question mark (?), the procedure name, and the procedure's arguments in parentheses.
- Press the Enter key.

Now you can use the Debug window to test the CapAll function.

To test the function in the Debug window:

1. Click the **Debug Window** button 🖼 on the Visual Basic toolbar. Access opens the Debug window on top of the Module window and places the insertion point inside the window.

The Debug window contains two panes. The upper pane has two tabs. The Locals tab allows you to display the name, type, and current value of all variables in a procedure. The Watch tab allows you to view the values of specific variables in a procedure. The lower pane in the Debug window is called the *immediate pane.* It allows you to run individual lines of Visual Basic code for debugging (testing). You will use the immediate pane to test the CapAll function.

2. Type **?CapAll("mi")** and then press the **Enter** key. Access executes the function and prints the function result, MI, on the next line. See Figure 10-27.

Figure 10-27 ◄
Function
executed in the
Debug window

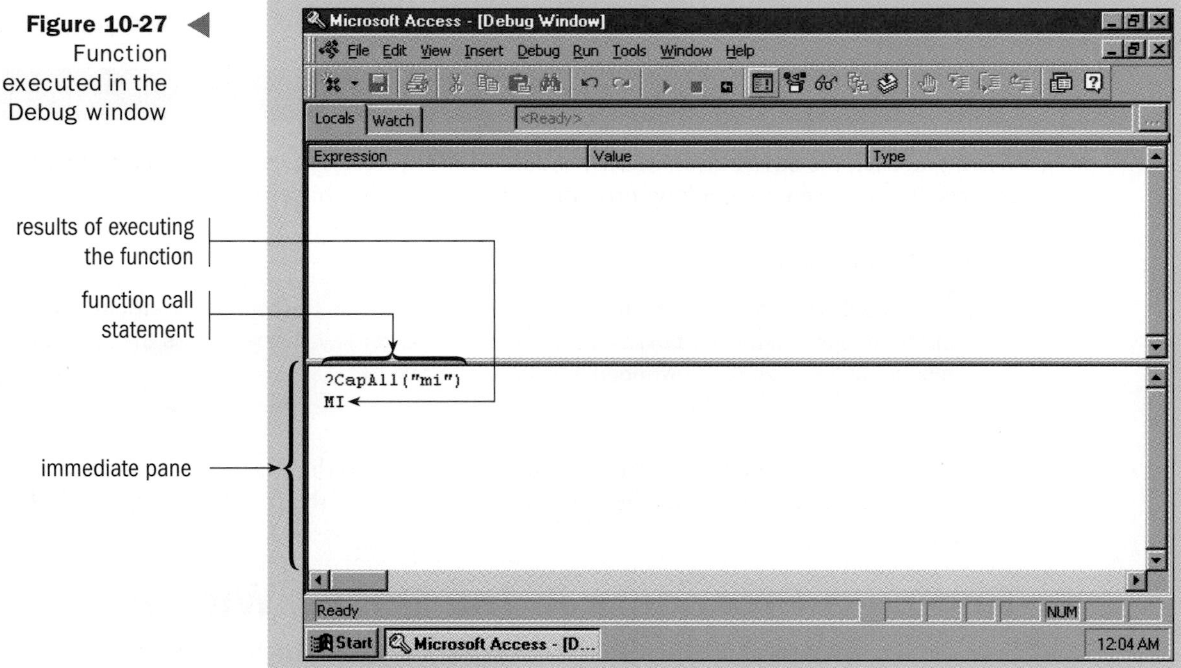

results of executing
the function

function call
statement

immediate pane

TROUBLE? If Access displays a dialog box with an error message, click the Debug button on the dialog box and correct the error in the Module window. If the function does not produce the correct output (MI), close the Debug window and then correct the CapAll function statements. Then repeat Steps 1 and 2.

To test the CapAll function further, you can enter several other test values, retyping the entire statement each time. Instead, you can select the current test value, type another value, and then press the Enter key.

To continue testing the function in the Debug window:

1. Select the characters **mi** in the first line of the Debug window.

2. Type **oH** and then press the **Enter** key. Access executes the function and prints the function result, OH, on the next line.

3. Repeat Steps 1 and 2 two more times, using **In** and then **MI** as the test values. Access prints the correct values, IN and MI.

4. Click the **Close** button ⊠ on the Debug window to close it, and then click the **Close** button ⊠ on the Module window to return to the Database window.

Your initial test of the CapAll function is successful. Next you will modify the Customer Data form to call the CapAll function for the State field.

Creating an Event Procedure

Recall that Access automatically creates a form module for each form and a report module for each report. When you add a procedure to one of these modules, Access stores the procedure with the form or report and treats the procedure as a private procedure that can be used with that form or report only. Each of these procedures is called an event procedure; Access runs a procedure when a specific event occurs.

Now that you have created the CapAll function as a public procedure in the standard module, you can create an event procedure for the Customer Data form to call the CapAll function for the State field's AfterUpdate event. Whenever a user enters or changes a State field value, the AfterUpdate event occurs and Access runs your event procedure.

What exactly happens when Access calls a procedure? There is an interaction between the calling statement and the function statements as represented by a series of steps. Figure 10-28 shows the process for the CapAll procedure.

Figure 10-28 ◀
Process of
executing a
function

function call

Step 7

Step 2

function called

Step 5

Step 4

Step 3

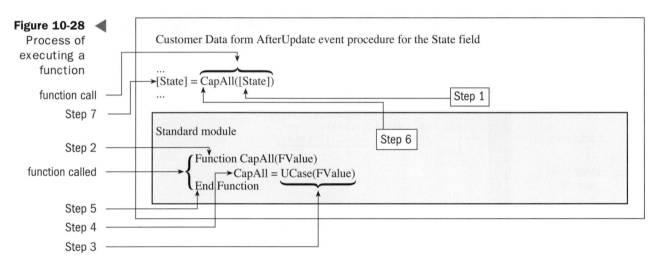

The steps in Figure 10-28 are numbered in the order in which they occur as Access processes the statement and the function. Access goes through the following steps:

- Step 1. The call to the function CapAll passes the value of the argument [State]. This is the value of the State field that is entered by the user.

- Step 2. The function CapAll begins, and the argument FValue receives the value of [State].

- Step 3. FValue is changed to uppercase.

- Step 4. The value of CapAll is set equal to the results of Step 3.

- Step 5. The function CapAll ends.

- Step 6. The value of CapAll is returned to the point of the call to the function.

- Step 7. The value of [State] is set equal to the returned value of CapAll.

Although it looks complicated, the general function process is simple—a statement contains a function call; when the statement is executed, Access performs the function call, executes the function, returns a single value back to the original statement, and completes that statement's execution. Study the steps in Figure 10-28 and trace their execution until you understand the complete process.

Designing an Event Procedure

Whenever a user enters a new value or modifies an existing value in the State field of the Customer Data form, Leonard wants Access to execute the CapAll function to ensure that all State field values appear in uppercase. After a user changes a State field value, the AfterUpdate event automatically occurs. You can set the AfterUpdate event property to run a macro, call a built-in Access function, or execute an event procedure. Because you want to call your user-defined function from within the event procedure, you will set the AfterUpdate event property to [Event Procedure].

All event procedures are subprocedures. Access automatically adds the Sub and End Sub statements to an event procedure. All you need to do is place the statements between the Sub and End Sub statements. Figure 10-29 shows the completed event procedure. The following text describes the parts of the procedure.

Figure 10-29 ◀
AfterUpdate
event
procedure for
the State field

comment

If statement

assignment
statement

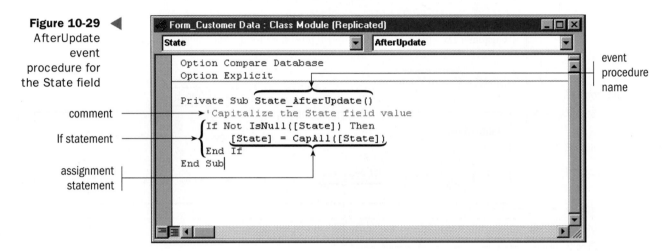

event
procedure
name

Access names each event procedure in a standard way: name of the control, an underscore (_), and the event name. No parameters are passed to an event procedure, so Access places nothing in the parentheses following the name of the subprocedure. If the name of the control contains spaces, Access substitutes underscores for the spaces in the event procedure name.

A user might delete an existing State field value, so that it contains no value, or becomes **null**. In this case, calling the function accomplishes nothing. The procedure is designed to call the CapAll function only when a user changes the State field to a value that is not null. The If statement screens out the null values. In its simplest form, an **If statement** executes one of two groups of statements based on a condition, similar to common English usage. For example, consider the English statements, "If I work the night shift, then I'll earn extra spending money. Otherwise, I'll go to the movies and I'll dip into my savings." In these sentences, the two groups of statements come before and after the "otherwise," based on the condition, "if I work the night shift." The first group of statements consists of the clause "I'll earn extra spending money." This is called the **true-statement group** because it is what happens if the condition ("I work the night shift") is true. The second group of statements contains "I'll go to the movies and I'll dip into my savings." This is called the **false-statement group** because it is what happens if the condition is false. Visual Basic uses the keyword If to precede the condition. The keyword Then precedes the true-statement group and the keyword Else precedes the false-statement group. The general syntax, or valid form, of a Visual Basic If statement is:

```
If condition Then
        true-statement group
[Else
        false-statement group]
End If
```

Access executes the true-statement group when the condition is true and the false-statement group when the condition is false. Bracketed portions of a statement's syntax are optional parts of the statement. Therefore, you must omit the Else and its related false-statement group when you want Access to execute a group of statements only when the condition is true.

In Figure 10-29, the If statement uses the Access **IsNull function**, which returns True when the State field value is null and False when it is not null. The Not is the same logical operator you've used before to negate an expression. So, Access executes the statement "[State] = CapAll([State])" only when the State field value is not null.

You are ready to make your changes to the Customer Data form.

Adding an Event Procedure

To add an event procedure for the State field's AfterUpdate event property, you need to open the Customer Data form in Design view.

REFERENCE window

ADDING AN EVENT PROCEDURE

- Open the form or report in Design view, open the property sheet, and then select the control whose event property you want to set.
- Set the appropriate event property to [Event Procedure], and then click the build button.
- Enter the subprocedure statements in the Module window.
- Compile the procedure, fix any statement errors, and then save the event procedure.

You can now add the event procedure to the Customer Data form.

To add the event procedure:

1. Click the **Forms** tab, click **Customer Data**, and then click the **Design** button to open the Customer Data form in Design view.

2. Click the **Restore** button on the Form window.

3. Right-click the field-value text box for the **State** field to display the shortcut menu, and then click **Properties** to open the property sheet.

4. Click the **Event** tab. Access shows only the event properties in the property sheet. These properties determine what happens when an event occurs while the Customer Data form is displayed. For example, the On Click event for the State field control specifies what Access should do when the user clicks the State field control. You need to set the After Update property.

5. Click the right side of the **After Update** text box, click **[Event Procedure]**, and then click the **build** button to the right of the AfterUpdate property. Access opens the Module window, which contains the Private Sub and End Sub statements. See Figure 10-30.

Figure 10-30 ◄
Initial event
procedure in
the Module
window

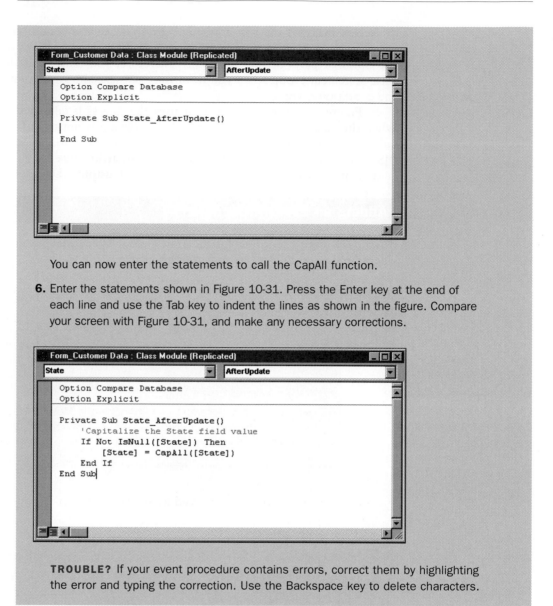

You can now enter the statements to call the CapAll function.

6. Enter the statements shown in Figure 10-31. Press the Enter key at the end of
each line and use the Tab key to indent the lines as shown in the figure. Compare
your screen with Figure 10-31, and make any necessary corrections.

Figure 10-31 ◄
Completed
event
procedure

TROUBLE? If your event procedure contains errors, correct them by highlighting
the error and typing the correction. Use the Backspace key to delete characters.

Before saving the event procedure, you must compile the procedure so that Access can
run it.

Compiling a Procedure

Access cannot execute the Visual Basic statements you enter in a procedure without compiling them first. **Compiling** a procedure checks the procedure for syntax errors. A **syntax
error** is a violation of the Visual Basic rules for statements. If Access finds a syntax error,
it displays a dialog box describing the error and displays the statement with the error in
red. If there are no syntax errors in the code, Access translates Visual Basic statements
into a form Access can execute.

When you run a procedure for the first time, Access compiles it for you automatically
and opens a dialog box only if it finds syntax errors in the procedure. If it finds an error,
Access does not translate the procedure statements. If no errors are detected, Access translates the procedure and does not display a confirmation. You can also compile a procedure
at any point as you enter it. Just click the Compile Loaded Modules button on the toolbar.
In response, Access compiles the procedure and all other procedures in all modules in the
database. Access does not, however, compile class modules for closed forms and reports.

You can now compile the event procedure and save the class module for the Customer
Data form.

To compile the event procedure and save the class module:

1. Click the **Compile Loaded Modules** button 🗐 on the Visual Basic toolbar. Access compiles the class module for the Customer Data form.

   TROUBLE? If Access identifies any errors in your code, correct the errors and repeat Step 1.

2. Click the **Save** button 🖫 on the Visual Basic toolbar.

3. Click the **Close** button ☒ on the Module window to close it, and then click the **Close** button ☒ on the property sheet to close it.

4. Click the **Close** button ☒ on the Form window to return to the Database window.

You have created the function and the event procedure and have set the event property. You can now test the event procedure to make sure it works correctly.

Testing an Event Procedure

You need to display the Customer Data form in Form view and test the State field's event procedure by entering a few different test State field values in the first record of the form. Moving the focus to another control on the form or to another record triggers the AfterUpdate event for the State field and executes the attached event procedure.

To test the event procedure:

1. Make sure **Customer Data** is selected in the Forms list in the Database window, and then click the **Open** button.

2. Select the **State** field value (MI), type **mi** in the State text box, and then press the **Enter** key. Access executes the AfterUpdate event procedure for the State field and changes the State field value to "MI." See Figure 10-32.

Figure 10-32 ◀
Customer Data form after executing the event procedure

```
┌─ Customer ──────────────────────── _□✕ ┐
│ ▯  CustomerNum     104                   │
│    CustomerName    Meadows Restaurant    │
│    Street          Pond Hill Road        │
│    City            Monroe                │
│    State           MI        ◀───────────┼── capitalized State
│    ZipCode         48161                 │      field value
│    OwnerName       Mr. Ray Suchecki      │
│    Phone           (313) 792-3546        │
│    FirstContact    2/28/91               │
│ Record: ◀◀ ◀     1  ▶ ▶▶ ▶✳ of 40       │
└──────────────────────────────────────────┘
```

3. Repeat Step 2 three more times, entering **Mi**, then **ml**, and finally **MI** in the State field box. Access displays the correct value "MI" each time.

4. Click the **Close** button ☒ on the Form window to return to the Database window.

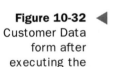 **Quick** Check

1. Why is Visual Basic called an event-driven, object-oriented language?

2. What are the differences between a function and a subprocedure?

3. What are the two different types of modules?

4 What is an event procedure?

5 What can you accomplish in the Debug window?

6 What does Access do when you compile a procedure?

You have completed the CapAll function. In the next session, you'll create a similar, but more complicated, function for the Customer Name field in the Customer Data form.

SESSION

10.3

In this session, you will add a second function to a standard module. You will write the function in Visual Basic, compile it, and then call the function from an event procedure.

Adding a Second Function to a Standard Module

Leonard wants to make it easier for users to enter a customer's name when using the Customer Data form, so he asks you to create a second function that will automatically correct the case of letters entered in the CustomerName field. This function, called CapAllFirst, will capitalize the first letter of each word in the field and change all other letters to lowercase. The function will be used by an event procedure attached to the AfterUpdate event for the CustomerName field. When a user enters or edits a customer name in the Customer Data form, the event procedure will use the CapAllFirst function to correct any capitalization errors in the CustomerName field value. For example, if the user enters "meadOWs reStaurant" as the CustomerName field value, the event procedure will use the CapAllFirst function to correct the field value to "Meadows Restaurant."

The Design of the CapAllFirst Function

Figure 10-33 shows the CapAllFirst function that you will create. You've already seen several of the statements in this function in your work with the CapAll function. Except for the function name, the Function and End Function statements are the same. The next two lines of the function are comments; these comments are specific to the CapAllFirst function. You'll learn about each new statement as you enter it to code this procedure.

Figure 10-33 ◀
CapAllFirst
function

parameter —

function name —

comments —

define variables —

assign initial values
to variables —

loop to capitalize the
first letter in each
word and convert
other letters to
lowercase —

assigns modified
argument value to
CapAllFirst —

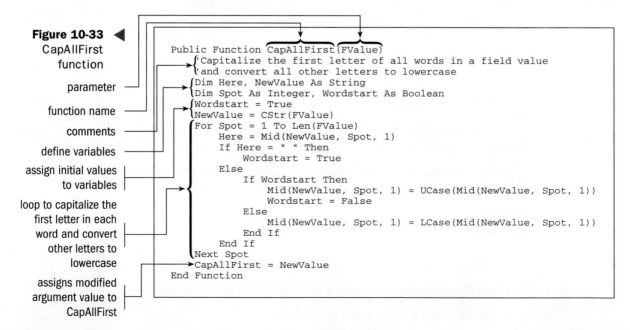

```
Public Function CapAllFirst(FValue)
    'Capitalize the first letter of all words in a field value
    'and convert all other letters to lowercase
    Dim Here, NewValue As String
    Dim Spot As Integer, Wordstart As Boolean
    Wordstart = True
    NewValue = CStr(FValue)
    For Spot = 1 To Len(FValue)
        Here = Mid(NewValue, Spot, 1)
        If Here = " " Then
            Wordstart = True
        Else
            If Wordstart Then
                Mid(NewValue, Spot, 1) = UCase(Mid(NewValue, Spot, 1))
                Wordstart = False
            Else
                Mid(NewValue, Spot, 1) = LCase(Mid(NewValue, Spot, 1))
            End If
        End If
    Next Spot
    CapAllFirst = NewValue
End Function
```

Access

The CapAllFirst function has a single parameter, called FValue. When the CapAllFirst function is called by the AfterUpdate event procedure for the CustomerName field, the CustomerName field value entered by the user is passed to the function, and this value is used in place of FValue when CapAllFirst is executed. So, the CustomerName field value is the argument passed to the function.

The CapAllFirst function capitalizes the first letter in each word of the argument and converts all other letters to lowercase. You will learn about the function in detail as you enter the function statements in the following steps. Basically, the function works by examining the argument, character by character. Whenever a space is encountered, the function "knows" that the next letter encountered should be capitalized, because a space immediately precedes the first letter of a word. When the next letter is found, it is capitalized. After the entire argument has been examined, the modified argument is returned to the event procedure that called the function.

Creating a Second Function

You need to add the CapAllFirst function to the Restaurant Functions module, which is a standard module. This will make the CapAllFirst function available for use with any object in the Restaurant database. Once you have added the function to the Restaurant Functions module, you will be able to attach it to an event procedure for the AfterUpdate event of the CustomerName field in the Customer Data form.

REFERENCE window

ADDING A NEW PROCEDURE TO A STANDARD MODULE

- In the Database window, click the Modules tab, click the module name, and then click the Design button.
- In the Module window, click the list arrow for the Insert Module button on the Visual Basic toolbar, and then click Procedure.
- Type the new procedure name, click the Sub or Function option button, and then click the OK button.
- Enter the new procedure, and then click the Compile Loaded Modules button on the Visual Basic toolbar.
- Click the Save button on the Visual Basic toolbar.

As you enter the statements in the following steps, refer to Figure 10-33 to verify that you are entering the statements correctly. You'll begin by adding the descriptive comments to the function.

To begin creating the CapAllFirst function and add the comments:

1. If you took a break after the previous session, start Access and open the Restaurant database in the Tutorial folder on your Student Disk.

2. Click the **Modules** tab, click the **Design** button, and then click the **Maximize** button on the Module window.

3. Click the list arrow for the **Insert Module** button on the Visual Basic toolbar, and then click **Procedure** to open the Insert Procedure dialog box.

   This dialog box allows you to name the new procedure and define its type and scope. The new procedure can be a subprocedure, a function, or a new property definition for an existing object. The scope of the new procedure can be either public or private. The new procedure you will create is a function, and you want it to be public so that you can use it in an event procedure for the Customer Data form.

4. Type **CapAllFirst** in the Name text box, make sure the **Function** and **Public** option buttons are selected, and then click the **OK** button. Access starts a new procedure named CapAllFirst and displays the Function and End Function statements in the Module window. See Figure 10-34.

Figure 10-34 ◀
CapAllFirst
function
started in the
Module window

existing CapAll
function

new CapAllFirst
function started

place parameter
FValue here

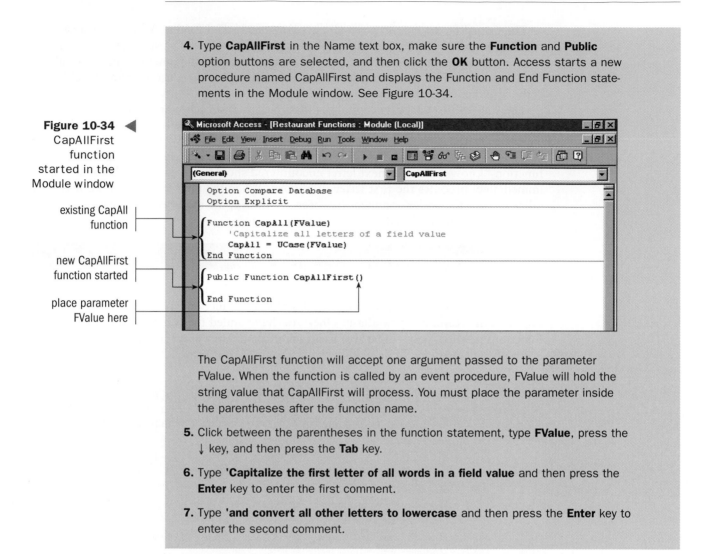

```
Microsoft Access - [Restaurant Functions : Module [Local]]
File  Edit  View  Insert  Debug  Run  Tools  Window  Help

(General)                                    CapAllFirst

Option Compare Database
Option Explicit

Function CapAll(FValue)
    'Capitalize all letters of a field value
    CapAll = UCase(FValue)
End Function

Public Function CapAllFirst()

End Function
```

The CapAllFirst function will accept one argument passed to the parameter FValue. When the function is called by an event procedure, FValue will hold the string value that CapAllFirst will process. You must place the parameter inside the parentheses after the function name.

5. Click between the parentheses in the function statement, type **FValue**, press the ↓ key, and then press the **Tab** key.

6. Type **'Capitalize the first letter of all words in a field value** and then press the **Enter** key to enter the first comment.

7. Type **'and convert all other letters to lowercase** and then press the **Enter** key to enter the second comment.

The next two lines of the CapAllFirst function declare the variables that are used in the function. The **Dim statement** is used to declare variables in a procedure. The variables in the CapAllFirst function are Here, NewValue, Spot, and Wordstart. (You'll see what these variables do in a moment.) Each variable is assigned an associated data type. Figure 10-35 shows the primary data types for Visual Basic variables.

Figure 10-35
Visual Basic
data types

Data Type	Stores
Boolean	True/False values
Currency	Currency values
Date	Date and time values
Double	Non-integer values, from $-1.79769313486231*10^{308}$ to $-4.09460645841247*10^{-324}$ for negative values, from $4.09460645841247*10^{-324}$ to $1.79769313486231*10^{308}$ for positive values, and 0
Integer	Integer values, -32768 to 32767
Long	Integer values, -2,147,483,648 to 2,147,483,647
Single	Non-integer values, $-3.402823*10^{38}$ to $-1.401298*10^{-45}$ for negative values, from $1.401298*10^{-45}$ to $3.402823*10^{38}$ for positive values, and 0
String	Text values up to 2 billion characters in length
Variant	Any data type

You specify the data type for a variable by following the variable name with the word "As" and the data type. In the CapAllFirst function, for example, the two variables Here and NewValue are string variables. The **String type** is the equivalent of the Access Text data type. Spot is an integer variable, and Wordstart is a Boolean variable. The **Boolean type** is the equivalent of the Yes/No type used to define the data type of a table record field. The Boolean type can take one of two values: True or False. If a module does not include the Option Explicit statement in the Declarations section and you create a variable without specifying a data type, Visual Basic assigns the Variant data type to the variable. The **Variant data type** is the default data type, and a variant variable can store any value.

The variable Here is a string variable that will temporarily hold a copy of the character that is being examined. The variable NewValue is a string that holds a copy of the argument. The first character in each word of NewValue is converted to uppercase as the function executes. Spot is an integer that is used as a counter to keep track of which character is being examined. Spot counts from 1 to the number of characters in the argument. Finally, WordStart is a Boolean variable that records whether the next letter should be capitalized. When WordStart is True, the next letter encountered in the argument should be capitalized. When WordStart is False, the next letter is not capitalized.

You can enter the Dim statements to declare the variables now.

To enter the Dim statements:

1. With the insertion point positioned on the line below the second comment line, type **Dim Here, NewValue As String** and then press the **Enter** key.

2. Type **Dim Spot As Integer, Wordstart As Boolean** and then press the **Enter** key.

The next two lines of the CapAllFirst function assign WordStart and NewValue their initial values. WordStart is initialized to True because the next letter encountered (the first letter in the argument) should be capitalized. The next line uses the **CStr function** to convert the value of the parameter FValue, which has the variant data type, to a string and assigns this converted value to the variable NewValue. Because CapAllFirst is a public function, a value of any type could be passed to FValue when the function is called. The CStr function ensures that the value in FValue is converted to a string. This must happen because the value in FValue is assigned to NewValue, which must contain a string.

You can enter the initial assignment statements now.

To enter the initial assignment statements:

1. Type **Wordstart = True** and then press the **Enter** key.

2. Type **NewValue = CStr(FValue)** and then press the **Enter** key.

The main body of the CapAllFirst function consists of a group of statements that are executed repeatedly to examine and process each character in NewValue (the CustomerName value entered by the user). A group of statements executed repeatedly is called a **loop**. The statement For Spot = 1 To Len(FValue) marks the beginning of the loop, and the statement Next Spot marks the end of the loop. The group of statements between the For and Next statements is called the **loop body**.

The For statement establishes how many times to repeat the loop body. In this case, the For statement uses the variable Spot as a counter to keep track of how many times to repeat the loop body. The For Spot = 1 To Len(FValue) statement in the CapAllFirst function sets the starting value of Spot, which is an integer variable, to 1 and the ending value of Spot to Len(FValue). The **Len function** returns the number of characters in a string. For example, if FValue is the string "Restaurant Name," Len(FValue) returns 15 as the number of characters, including spaces. In this case, the statements in the loop will be executed 15 times.

Then Access executes the loop body, ending with the statement before the Next Spot statement. After reaching the Next Spot statement, Access adds 1 to Spot, goes back to the For statement, and compares the value of Spot to Len(FValue). If Spot is less than or equal to Len(FValue), which means that there are still more characters to check and determine if any should be capitalized, Access executes the loop statements again, reaches the Next Spot statement, and repeats the cycle. When Spot becomes greater than Len(FValue), which means that there are no more characters to check in the field entry, Access terminates the loop and executes the statement following the Next Spot statement.

The loop body is executed once for each value of Spot, that is, once for each character in NewValue. The statement Here = Mid(NewValue, Spot, 1) uses the built-in **Mid function** to copy a single character, as specified by the argument "1" in the statement, from NewValue and store it in Here. The character selected is indicated by the value of Spot. So, if the current value of Spot is 3, then the third character in NewValue is copied into Here. For example, if the user enters Pesto Place in the CustomerName field of the Customer Data form, and Spot equals 3, the value of "s" is assigned to the variable Here so that the function can determine if "s" needs to be capitalized.

The next statement is an If statement that decides which operations to perform depending on the value of Here. If Here is a space, then the value of WordStart is set to True (indicating that the next letter encountered should be capitalized) and the Else part of the If statement is skipped. If Here is not a space, then the current character is a letter that might need to be capitalized. A second If statement checks to see if WordStart is True. If WordStart is True, then the next statement uses the UCase function to convert Here to uppercase and assigns it to the appropriate position in NewValue. If WordStart is not True, then the next statement uses the LCase function to convert Here to lowercase and assigns it to the appropriate position in NewValue. The UCase and LCase functions have no effect on characters that are not letters.

When the loop body has finished processing the current character, the Next Spot statement increments Spot and returns control to the For Spot = 1 to Len(NewValue) statement. If Spot is less than or equal to the length of NewValue, the loop body is executed again, processing the next character in NewValue.

When the loop has processed the last character in NewValue, the loop ends and control is passed to the statement following the Next Spot statement. NewValue now has the first letter of each word capitalized and all other letters converted to lowercase.

You can enter the statements for the loop in the Module window now.

To enter the loop statements in the CapAllFirst function:

1. Type **For Spot = 1 To Len(FValue)** and then press the **Enter** key.

2. Enter the remaining loop statements, ending with the statement Next Spot, as shown in Figure 10-36. Be sure to use the Tab key to indent as necessary. Recall that pressing Backspace moves the insertion point one tab stop to the left. When you are finished, your screen should look like Figure 10-36.

Figure 10-36 ◄
After entering
the loop
statements in
the CapAllFirst
function

loop statements

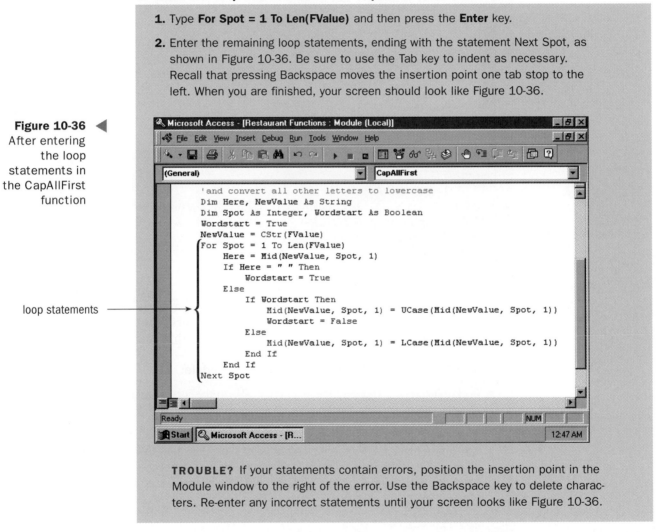

TROUBLE? If your statements contain errors, position the insertion point in the Module window to the right of the error. Use the Backspace key to delete characters. Re-enter any incorrect statements until your screen looks like Figure 10-36.

When the loop ends, NewValue capitalizes the first letter of each word and converts all other letters to lowercase. The final step in the CapAllFirst function assigns the NewValue to CapAllFirst, to be returned to the event procedure that called the CapAllFirst function. In the case of the Customer Data form, the CustomerName field's event procedure will call the CapAllFirst function, which will return the customer name with the correct capitalization. You can enter this final statement now.

To enter the final statement:

1. Type **CapAllFirst = NewValue** and then press the ↓ key. See Figure 10-37.

Figure 10-37 ◀
Completed
CapAllFirst
function

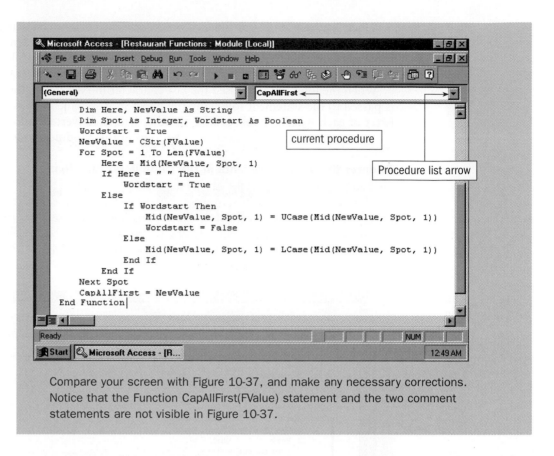

Compare your screen with Figure 10-37, and make any necessary corrections. Notice that the Function CapAllFirst(FValue) statement and the two comment statements are not visible in Figure 10-37.

You are now ready to compile and save the Restaurant Functions module, which now contains the CapAllFirst function. Recall that compiling a module checks all procedures in the module for syntax errors and alerts you to any errors found. If no errors are found, the module will automatically be translated into a form that Access can execute.

To compile and save the Restaurant Functions module:

1. Click the **Compile Loaded Modules** button 📘 on the Visual Basic toolbar to compile the CapAllFirst function.

   TROUBLE? If Access finds an error, it highlights the error and opens a dialog box with a message describing the nature of the error. Click the OK button and change the statement contained in the highlighted area by comparing each character you entered to what should be entered. Then repeat Step 1.

2. Click the **Save** button 💾 on the Visual Basic toolbar to save the Restaurant Functions module.

The Module window now contains the Declarations section of the Restaurant Functions module, the CapAll function, and the CapAllFirst function. You can view each procedure in a module by clicking the Procedure list arrow and selecting a procedure.

To view the procedures in the Restaurant Functions module:

1. Click the **Procedure** list arrow, and then click **CapAll**. Access displays the CapAll function and displays CapAll in the Procedure text box.

2. Click the **Procedure** list arrow, and then click **(Declarations)**. Access displays the module's Declarations section.

3. Click the **Procedure** list arrow, and then click **CapAllFirst** to display the top of the CapAllFirst function.

4. Click the **Close** button ☒ on the Module window to return to the maximized Database window.

Creating a Second Event Procedure

Leonard wants all names entered by users in the CustomerName field of the Customer Data form to be correct. That means that each word in the customer name must begin with a capital letter and all other letters must be lowercase. To ensure that this happens, you will open the Customer Data form in Design view, and then add an event procedure for the CustomerName field's AfterUpdate event property. Recall that the AfterUpdate property determines the actions Access will take after the user has entered or edited the specified field value. The event procedure will be executed whenever the user updates the value in the CustomerName field. The new event procedure is similar to the event procedure for the State field in the Customer Data form, which changes all values for that field to uppercase.

To add the event procedure for the CustomerName field in the Customer Data form:

1. Click the **Forms** tab, click **Customer Data**, and then click the **Design** button to display the form in Design view.

2. Right-click the **CustomerName** field-value text box to display the shortcut menu, and then click **Properties** to open the property sheet.

3. If necessary, click the **Event** tab of the property sheet.

4. Click the right side of the **After Update** text box, click **[Event Procedure]**, and then click the **build** button ⋯ to the right of the AfterUpdate property. Access opens the Module window, which is maximized and contains the Private Sub and End Sub statements. Notice that the Module window also contains the event procedure for the AfterUpdate property of the State field, which you created earlier.

5. Press the **Tab** key, and then type the subprocedure statements exactly as shown in Figure 10-38.

Figure 10-38 ◄
Event
procedure
for the
CustomerName
field

new event
procedure for the
CustomerName field

existing event
procedure for the
State field

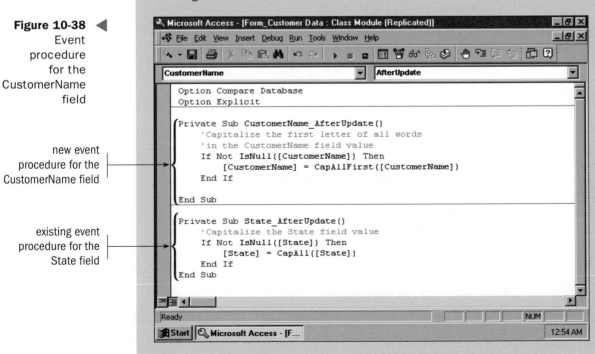

The CustomerName field AfterUpdate event procedure works in a similar way as the State field AfterUpdate event procedure. If the CustomerName field is not null (empty), then the CustomerName field value is passed to the CapAllFirst function. The CapAllFirst function capitalizes the first letter of each word in the CustomerName field value, converts all other letters to lowercase, and then returns the value to the event procedure. The event procedure assignment statement then assigns the converted value to the CustomerName field.

6. Click the **Compile Loaded Modules** button 🖫 on the Visual Basic toolbar, and then click the **Save** button 🖫 on the Visual Basic toolbar.

7. Click the **Close** button ⊠ on the Module window, and then click the **Close** button ⊠ on the property sheet.

8. Click the **Restore** button 🗗 on the Form window, and then click the **Close** button ⊠ on the Form window to return to the Database window.

You have entered the function and the event procedure and have set the event property. You can now test the event procedure. To do so, you'll open the Customer Data form in Form view and test the CustomerName field's event procedure by entering different CustomerName field values.

To test the new event procedure:

1. Make sure **Customer Data** is selected in the Forms list, and then click the **Open** button to open the form in Form view.

2. Click the **Last Record** button ▶❘ to display the record for the Pesto Place restaurant.

3. Select the value in the CustomerName text box, type **test restaurant name**, and then press the **Enter** key. Access executes the AfterUpdate event procedure for the CustomerName field and changes the CustomerName field value to "Test Restaurant Name."

4. Press the ↑ key to highlight the CustomerName field value.

5. Repeat Steps 3 and 4 two more times, entering **sECond test nAme** (correctly changed to "Second Test Name"), and then entering **pesto place** (correctly changed to "Pesto Place").

6. Click the **Close** button ⊠ on the Form window to return to the Database window.

Quick Check

1. What does the UCase function do?

2. What is the purpose of a Dim statement?

3. How many times would the following loop be executed?
   For MyCounter = 2 To 11

4. What is the Boolean data type?

5. What is the String data type?

6. What does the CStr function do?

Now that you've finished coding the functions to facilitate using the Customer Data form, you're ready to put the finishing touches on the Restaurant database user interface, which you'll do in the next session.

SESSION

10.4

In this session, you will learn how to hide text and change color in a form during the execution of a procedure. You will also create event procedures for two dialog boxes. Finally, you will set the Restaurant database startup options.

Hiding Text and Changing Display Color

Barbara wants you to add a message to the Order Data form that will remind users when an invoice is unpaid. Access will display the message, in red, only when the invoice is unpaid. Also, Access will display the value in the InvoiceAmt text box in red for unpaid invoices and in black for paid invoices. The red display will help to draw attention to those invoices that have not yet been paid. See Figure 10-39.

Figure 10-39 ◄
Order Data
form with the
unpaid
message

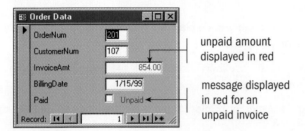

unpaid amount
displayed in red

message displayed
in red for an
unpaid invoice

The Visible property determines when Access displays a control. Access displays a control when its Visible property is True, which is the default, and hides the control when its Visible property is False. A field's Fore Color property determines the field's foreground color. In the Order Data form, you will add a label to the right of the Paid check box. The text "Unpaid" will be displayed in red letters. Because Barbara wants the text to appear only when the Paid column has the value No, you will change the label's Visible property during execution. You will also change the foreground color of the InvoiceAmt field to red for unpaid invoices and to black for paid invoices.

Because the change to the Visible property takes place during execution, you will add code to the Current event procedure in the Order Data form. The **Current event** occurs every time Access displays a new record in a form. To set a property in a Visual Basic statement, you enter the object name followed by the property name, separating the two with a period. For example, if the label name for the message is UnpaidMsg, then "[UnpaidMsg].Visible = False" hides the label on the form.

To add the Current event procedure to the Order Data form:

1. If you took a break after the previous session, start Access and open the Restaurant database in the Tutorial folder on your Student Disk.

2. If necessary, click the **Forms** tab to display the Forms list, click **Order Data**, and then click the **Design** button to open the Order Data form in Design view. Click the **Maximize** button 🔲 on the Form window.

3. If necessary, click the **Toolbox** button 🛠 on the Form Design toolbar to open the toolbox, and then click the **Label** tool **Aa** on the toolbox.

4. Position the pointer ⁺A in the grid dots to the right of the Paid field-value check box, click the left mouse button, type **Unpaid**, and then press the **Enter** key. See Figure 10-40.

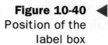
Figure 10-40 ◀
Position of the
label box

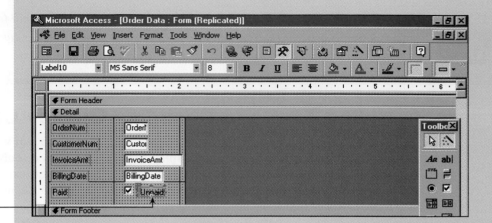

new label box ——

5. Right-click the new label to display the shortcut menu, and then click **Properties** to open the property sheet.

6. Click the **All** tab, if necessary, double-click the value in the **Name** text box, and then type **UnpaidMsg**.

You can now set the Fore Color property for the label so that the message is displayed in red.

7. Scroll the property sheet, click the **Fore Color** text box, and then click the **build** button ⌐···⌐. Access displays the Color dialog box. Click the **red color box** (the first color box in the second row of Basic Colors), and then click the **OK** button. Access places the code for red (255) in the Fore Color property value. Access also changes the foreground color of the label box to red.

You can now enter the event procedure for the form's On Current event. This event procedure will be executed whenever the Order Data form is displayed (current) on the screen.

8. Click the form selector, scroll the property sheet, click the right side of the **On Current** text box, click **[Event Procedure]**, and then click the **build** button ⌐···⌐. Access opens the Module window, displaying the Sub and End Sub statements.

9. Press the **Tab** key, and then type the subprocedure statements exactly as shown in Figure 10-41.

Figure 10-41
Current event
procedure for
the Order Data
form

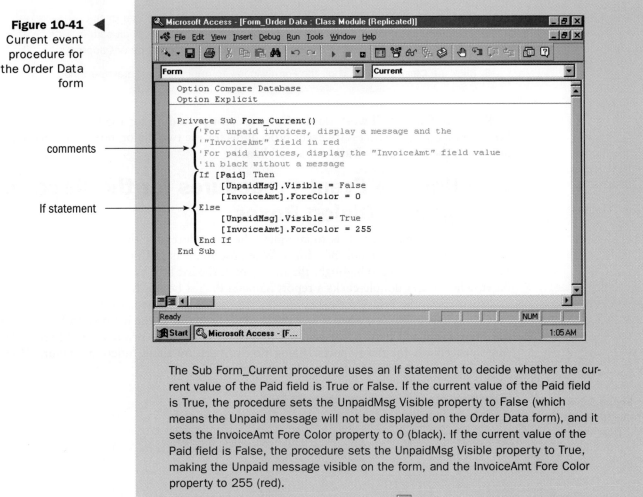

comments

If statement

The Sub Form_Current procedure uses an If statement to decide whether the current value of the Paid field is True or False. If the current value of the Paid field is True, the procedure sets the UnpaidMsg Visible property to False (which means the Unpaid message will not be displayed on the Order Data form), and it sets the InvoiceAmt Fore Color property to 0 (black). If the current value of the Paid field is False, the procedure sets the UnpaidMsg Visible property to True, making the Unpaid message visible on the form, and the InvoiceAmt Fore Color property to 255 (red).

10. Click the **Compile Loaded Modules** button 🖉 on the Visual Basic toolbar, and then click the **Save** button 🖫 on the Visual Basic toolbar.

11. Click the **Close** button ☒ on the Module window, and then click the **Close** button ☒ on the property sheet. Click the **Restore** button 🗗 on the Form window, and then click the **Close** button ☒ on the Form window to return to the Database window.

Now you can test the Current event procedure for the Order Data form.

To test the Current event procedure for the Order Data form:

1. Make sure **Order Data** is selected in the Forms list, and then click the **Open** button to display the Order Data form in Form view. Access displays the first record for OrderNum 201, which is unpaid. The message "Unpaid" appears in red, as does the Amount value 854.00.

TROUBLE? If Access displays a dialog box indicating a run-time error, Access could not execute the event procedure. Click the Debug button on the dialog box. Access displays the event procedure in the Module window and highlights the line containing the error. Check the statements carefully to make sure that they are exactly like those in Figure 10-41. Compile the module, save the module, and then close the Module window. Then repeat Step 1.

> **2.** Click the **Next Record** button several times to make sure that each unpaid order's message and InvoiceAmt value appear in red, and that each paid order's InvoiceAmt value appears in black and the Unpaid message does not appear.
>
> **3.** Click the **Close** button on the Form window to return to the Database window.

You have finished all work on the Current event procedure for the Order Data form. Next you'll create the necessary event procedures for the two dialog boxes that are available from the Restaurant Database switchboard.

Creating the Event Procedures for the Reports and Queries Dialog Boxes

Your last programming task is to complete the procedures for the Reports Dialog Box form and the Queries Dialog Box form. When the Reports Dialog Box form first opens, Leonard wants Access to highlight the first item in the list box by placing the focus on it. Next, when a user double-clicks a report name in the list box or highlights a report name and then clicks the Print Preview command button, that report is displayed in the Print Preview window. Finally, when a user selects a report name in the list box and then clicks the Print command button, the selected report is immediately printed. You'll create the three procedures for the Reports Dialog Box to perform these functions. Figure 10-42 shows the procedure names for the three functions.

Figure 10-42 ◄
Reports Dialog
Box form's
procedures

Function
PreviewReport

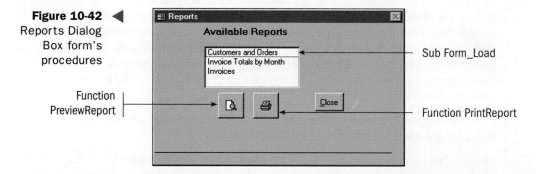

Sub Form_Load

Function PrintReport

Coding the Load Event Procedure for the Reports Dialog Box

When a user opens the Reports Dialog Box form, Leonard wants Access to place the focus on the top report in the list box automatically. To accomplish this, you need to specify the form's Load event. Figure 10-43 shows the code for the form's Load event.

Figure 10-43 ◀
Load event
procedure for
the Reports
Dialog Box
form

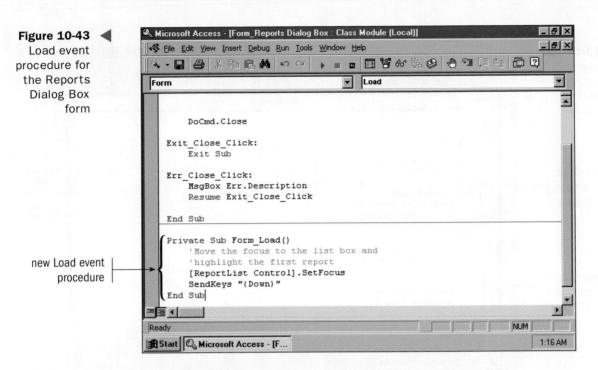

new Load event
procedure

The **Load event** occurs when Access opens a form. Anything you specify for this event will happen whenever the form is opened. **SetFocus** is a method that moves the focus to the specified object or control. A **method** is an action that operates on specific objects or controls. The statement [ReportList Control].SetFocus moves the focus to the ReportList Control, which is the name for the form's list box, but does not set the focus to any specific report name. The SendKeys "{Down}" statement sends the down arrow keystroke to the list box; Access highlights the top report in the list box in response to this statement. The end result of these statements is that when the user opens the dialog box, the top report is highlighted and has the focus.

Now you'll open the Reports Dialog Box form in Design view and create the Load event procedure.

To add the Load event procedure for the Reports Dialog Box form:

1. Click the **Forms** tab (if necessary), click **Reports Dialog Box** in the Forms list, click the **Design** button to open the Reports Dialog Box in Design view, and then maximize the Form window.

2. Right-click the form selector to display the shortcut menu, and then click **Properties** to open the property sheet.

3. Click the **Event** tab (if necessary), scroll the property sheet, click the right side of the **On Load** text box, click **[Event Procedure]**, and then click the **build** button ▣. Access opens the Module window, displaying the Sub and End Sub statements. The Module window also displays the Visual Basic code for other events for the Reports Dialog Box form. These event procedures are automatically created by Access when you design the form.

4. Press the **Tab** key, and then type the subprocedure statements as shown in Figure 10-44.

Figure 10-44 ◄
Load event
procedure
entered in the
Module window

existing Visual Basic
code in the class
module

completed Load
event procedure

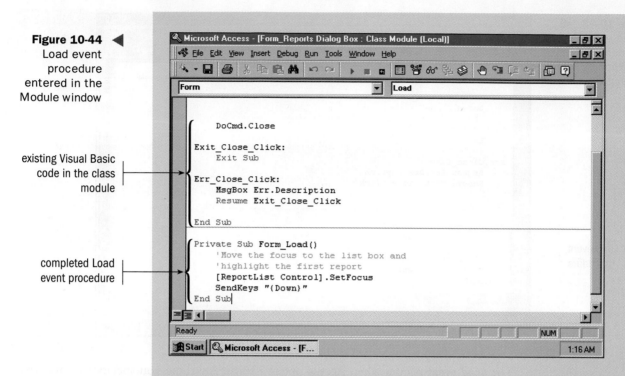

The word "Private" in the first line of the function definition indicates that this function can be used only in the class module for this form. Form_Load indicates that this function is the event procedure for the Load event.

5. Click the **Compile Loaded Modules** button 🖺 on the Visual Basic toolbar, and then click the **Save** button 🖫 on the Visual Basic toolbar.

6. Close the Module window and then close the property sheet.

7. Click the **Close** button ☒ on the Form window to return to the Database window.

   Next you'll test the procedure by opening the Reports Dialog Box in Form view and verifying that the first report in the list box is selected.

8. Make sure **Reports Dialog Box** is selected in the Forms list in the Database window, and then click the **Open** button to display the form in Form view. Notice that the top report in the list box is selected.

   TROUBLE? If the top report in the list box is not highlighted, you probably did not use the curly braces ({}) in the SendKeys statement. Click the View button for Design view 🖾 and then display the properties list for the form. Click the On Load event text box, click the build button 📖, and then correct the event procedure. Then repeat Steps 6 through 8.

9. Click the **Close** button on the dialog box to close it and return to the Database window.

You have finished your work with the Load event procedure for the Reports Dialog Box form. Next, you need to create the form's PreviewReport and PrintReport functions.

Coding the PreviewReport and PrintReport Functions for the Reports Dialog Box

Double-clicking a report name in the list box or selecting a report name and then clicking the Print Preview command button must open that report in the Print Preview window. Selecting a report name in the list box and then clicking the Print command button must immediately print that report. Figure 10-45 shows the code to handle these processes.

Figure 10-45 ◄
PreviewReport
and
PrintReport
functions for
the Reports
Dialog Box
form

Insert Procedure
button

PreviewReport
function

PrintReport function

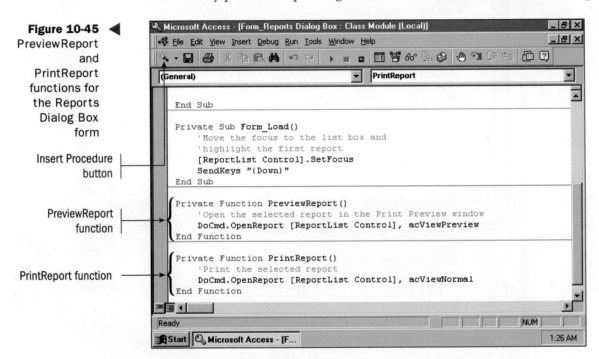

A Visual Basic **DoCmd statement** executes an action in a function. You use the DoCmd statements in these functions to run the OpenReport action. The parameter choices for the selected report of [ReportList Control] in the OpenReport action are: acViewPreview to open the Print Preview window, acViewNormal to print the report, and acViewDesign to display the report in Design view. Because the OpenReport action and its parameter values acViewPreview, acViewNormal, and acViewDesign are standard features of Access, you do not have to define them in a Dim statement as you do for variables you create.

Next you'll open the Reports Dialog Box form in Design view, create the two functions, and attach the functions to the appropriate control properties.

To add the two functions to the Reports Dialog Box form:

1. Click the **Design** button to display the form in Design view, and then click the **Code** button 🖺 on the Form Design toolbar to open the Module window for the form's class module.

2. Click the list arrow for the **Insert Module** button 🗷 on the Visual Basic toolbar, and then click **Procedure**. The Insert Procedure dialog box opens.

3. Type **PreviewReport** in the Name text box, make sure the **Function** option button is selected, click the **Private** option button, and then click the **OK** button. Access displays the Function and End Function statements for a new procedure.

4. Press the **Tab** key, and then type the statements for the PreviewReport function exactly as shown in Figure 10-46.

Figure 10-46 ◀
PreviewReport
function for the
Reports Dialog
Box form

completed
PreviewReport
function

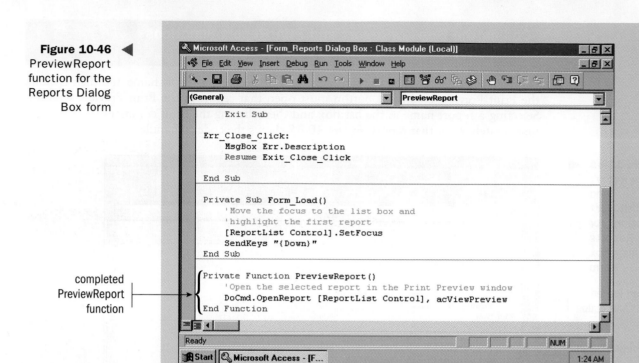

Now you'll enter the function for printing a report.

5. Click the **Save** button 🖫 on the Visual Basic toolbar, and then click the **Insert Procedure** button ⬛ on the Visual Basic toolbar.

6. Type **PrintReport** in the Name text box, make sure the **Function** option button is selected, click the **Private** option button, and then click the **OK** button.

7. Press the **Tab** key, and then type the statements for the PrintReport function exactly as shown in Figure 10-47.

Figure 10-47 ◀
PrintReport
function for the
Reports Dialog
Box form

completed
PrintReport function

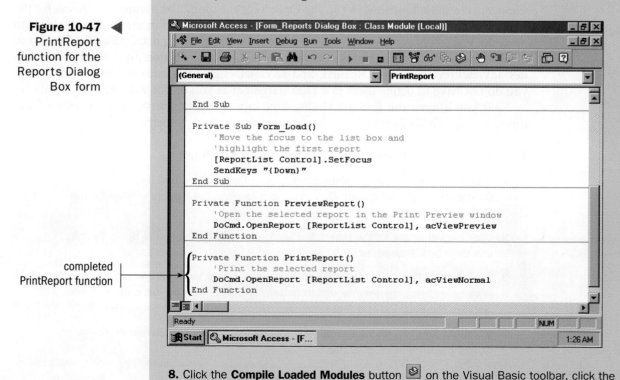

8. Click the **Compile Loaded Modules** button 🔳 on the Visual Basic toolbar, click the **Save** button 🖫 on the Visual Basic toolbar, and then close the Module window.

Next you need to attach the appropriate event procedure to the correct properties for the form objects.

To specify the event procedures for the properties:

1. Right-click the form's list box (the box containing the word "Unbound") to display the shortcut menu, and then click **Properties** to open the property sheet.

2. Make sure the **Event** tab is selected, scroll the property sheet as necessary, click the **On Dbl Click** text box, and then type **=PreviewReport()**. This specifies that Access will execute the event procedure for previewing a report whenever a user double-clicks a report name in the list box.

3. Click the form's **Print Preview command button**, click the property sheet's **On Click** text box, and then type **=PreviewReport()**. This specifies that Access will execute the event procedure for previewing a report whenever a user selects a report name and then clicks the Print Preview command button.

4. Click the form's **Print command button**, click the property sheet's **On Click** text box, and then type **=PrintReport()**. This specifies that Access will execute the event procedure for printing a report whenever a user selects a report name and then clicks the Print command button.

5. Click the **Save** button 🖫 on the Form Design toolbar to save the form changes, close the property sheet, and then click the **Close** button ✕ on the Form window to return to the Database window.

6. Restore the Database window.

You can now test the changes you made to the Reports Dialog Box form.

To test the changes to the Reports Dialog Box form:

1. Make sure **Reports Dialog Box** is selected in the Forms list in the Database window, and then click the **Open** button to display the form in Form view.

2. Double-click each of the report names, in turn, in the list box to verify that the correct report opens in Print Preview. From the Print Preview window, click the **Close** button each time to return to the dialog box in Form view.

3. Click a report name in the list box, and then click the **Print Preview command button** to verify that the correct report opens in the Print Preview window. From the Print Preview window, click the **Close** button to return to the dialog box in Form view.

4. Repeat Step 3 for each report name in the form's list box.

5. Click a report name in the list box, and then click the **Print command button** to verify that the correct report prints.

6. Repeat Step 5 for each report name in the form's list box.

7. Click the **Close** button on the dialog box to close it and return to the Database window.

Completing the Queries Dialog Box

The event procedures you will create for the Queries Dialog Box form are similar to the ones you created for the Reports Dialog Box. You will create an event procedure for the Queries Dialog Box Load event and two functions. The first function, called PreviewQuery, will display the selected query results in Print Preview and will be attached to the control properties for the query names and the Print Preview command button on the Queries Dialog Box. In this way, the query results will be displayed in Print Preview whenever a user double-clicks a query name in the list box or clicks a query name and then clicks the Print Preview command button. The second function, called DisplayQuery, will display the query results in Datasheet view and will be attached to the On Click control property for the Query Datasheet command button on the Queries Dialog Box.

You'll start by adding the Load event procedure for the Queries Dialog Box.

To add the Load event procedure for the Queries Dialog Box form:

1. Click **Queries Dialog Box** in the Forms list, and then click the **Design** button to open the Queries Dialog Box form in Design view.

2. Right-click the form selector to display the shortcut menu, and then click **Properties** to open the property sheet.

3. Make sure the **Event** tab is selected, scroll the property sheet, click the right side of the **On Load** text box, click **[Event Procedure]**, and then click the **build** button 	. Access opens the Module window, displaying the Sub and End Sub statements.

4. Press the **Tab** key, and then type the subprocedure statements as shown in Figure 10-48.

Figure 10-48 ◀
Load event procedure for the Queries Dialog Box form

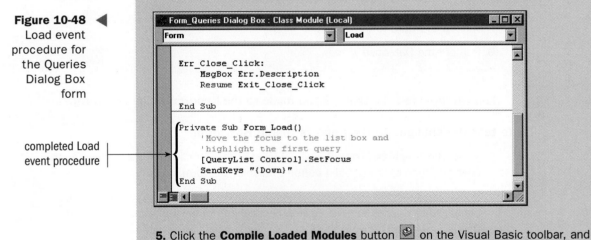

completed Load event procedure

5. Click the **Compile Loaded Modules** button 	 on the Visual Basic toolbar, and then click the **Save** button 	 on the Visual Basic toolbar.

You have finished coding the Load event procedure for the Queries Dialog Box form. Next, you'll create the form's PreviewQuery and DisplayQuery functions.

To add the two functions to the Queries Dialog Box form:

1. Click the **Insert Procedure** button 	 on the Visual Basic toolbar. The Insert Procedure dialog box opens.

2. Type **PreviewQuery** in the Name text box, make sure the **Function** option button is selected, click the **Private** option button, and then click the **OK** button. Access displays the Function and End Function statements for a new procedure.

3. Press the **Tab** key, and then type the statements for the PreviewQuery function exactly as shown in Figure 10-49.

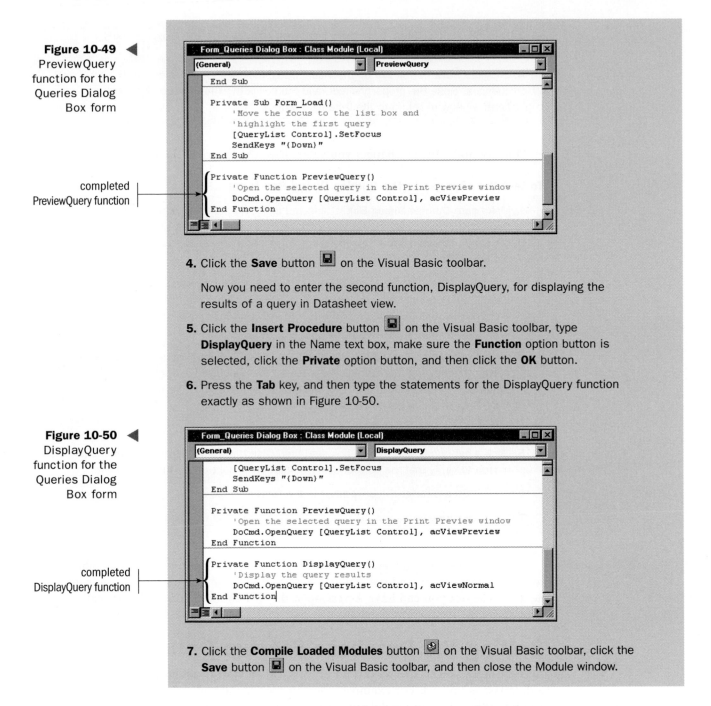

Figure 10-49 ◄
PreviewQuery
function for the
Queries Dialog
Box form

completed
PreviewQuery function

Figure 10-50 ◄
DisplayQuery
function for the
Queries Dialog
Box form

completed
DisplayQuery function

4. Click the **Save** button 🖫 on the Visual Basic toolbar.

Now you need to enter the second function, DisplayQuery, for displaying the results of a query in Datasheet view.

5. Click the **Insert Procedure** button 🖫 on the Visual Basic toolbar, type **DisplayQuery** in the Name text box, make sure the **Function** option button is selected, click the **Private** option button, and then click the **OK** button.

6. Press the **Tab** key, and then type the statements for the DisplayQuery function exactly as shown in Figure 10-50.

7. Click the **Compile Loaded Modules** button 🖫 on the Visual Basic toolbar, click the **Save** button 🖫 on the Visual Basic toolbar, and then close the Module window.

Now you can attach these functions to the appropriate events for the form's controls. First, you will attach the PreviewQuery function to the On Dbl Click event for the list box so that the query is displayed in Print Preview when the user double-clicks a query name in the list box. Then you will attach the PreviewQuery to the Print Preview command button and attach the DisplayQuery function to the Query Datasheet command button.

To attach the functions to the form's controls:

1. Click the form's list box, scroll the property sheet as necessary, click the **On Dbl Click** text box, and then type **=PreviewQuery()**.

2. Click the form's **Print Preview command button**, click the property sheet's **On Click** text box, and then type **=PreviewQuery()**.

3. Click the form's **Query Datasheet command button**, click the property sheet's **On Click** text box, and then type **=DisplayQuery()**.

4. Click the **Save** button 🖫 on the Visual Basic toolbar to save all the form changes, close the property sheet, and then click the **Close** button ⊠ on the Form window to return to the Database window.

You can now test the changes you've made to the Queries Dialog Box form.

To test the changes to the Queries Dialog Box form:

1. Make sure **Queries Dialog Box** is selected in the Forms list, and then click the **Open** button to display the form in Form view. Notice that the first query in the list box is selected because you set the form's Load event procedure to highlight the first query.

2. Double-click each of the query names, in turn, in the list box to verify that the correct query results are displayed in Print Preview. From the Print Preview window, click the **Close** button on the Print Preview toolbar each time to return to the dialog box in Form view.

3. Click a query name in the list box, and then click the **Print Preview command button** to verify that the correct query results are displayed in Print Preview. From the Print Preview window, click the **Close** button on the Print Preview toolbar to return to the dialog box in Form view.

4. Repeat Step 3 for each query name in the form's list box.

5. Click a query name in the list box, and then click the **Query Datasheet command button** to verify that the correct query results are displayed in Datasheet view.

6. Repeat Step 5 for each query name in the form's list box.

7. Click the **Close** button on the dialog box to return to the Database window.

Leonard stops by and views your results. He is very pleased with the switchboard, the toolbar, the menu bar, and the dialog boxes. As a final enhancement to the user interface, he asks whether you can have Access open the Switchboard form automatically when a user opens the Restaurant database.

Setting the Database Startup Options

Access allows you to specify certain actions, called **startup options**, that take place when a database is opened. For example, you can specify the name that appears in the Access window title bar, specify a default custom menu bar to replace the standard menu bar, or specify a form that is automatically displayed. If you want to bypass the startup options, you can press and hold the Shift key when you open the database.

Leonard wants users to be able to open the Restaurant database and have the switchboard appear automatically. This way, users won't need to use the Forms list to access the Switchboard form.

SETTING THE DATABASE STARTUP OPTIONS

- Click Tools on the menu bar, and then click Startup to open the Startup dialog box.
- Specify the startup options, and then click the OK button. The options will be in effect the next time the database is opened.

You need to set the Restaurant database startup options so that the switchboard appears automatically when the database is opened, and so that the Database window is hidden from view.

To change the Restaurant database startup options:

1. Click **Tools** on the menu bar, and then click **Startup**. The Startup dialog box opens. See Figure 10-51.

Figure 10-51 ◀
Startup
dialog box

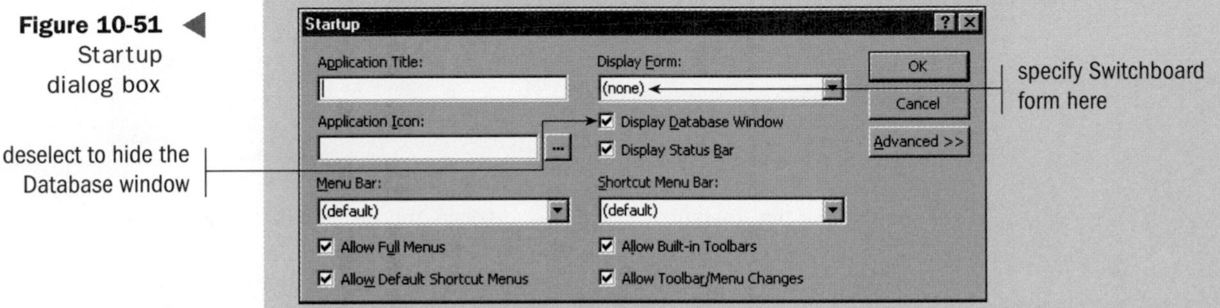

deselect to hide the
Database window

specify Switchboard
form here

2. Click the **Display Form** list arrow, scroll down the list, and then click **Switchboard**. This setting specifies that the Switchboard form will be displayed upon startup.

3. Click the **Display Database Window** check box to remove the check mark. This setting specifies that the Database window will not be displayed upon startup.

4. Click the **OK** button to close the Startup dialog box.

To test the startup options, you need to close and then open the Restaurant database.

To test the startup options:

1. Click the **Close** button [X] on the Database window to close the Restaurant database.

2. Click **File** on the menu bar, and then click **1 A:\Tutorial\Restaurant** to open the Restaurant database. See Figure 10-52.

   TROUBLE? The path might be different in your menu option, depending on the location of your Student Disk.

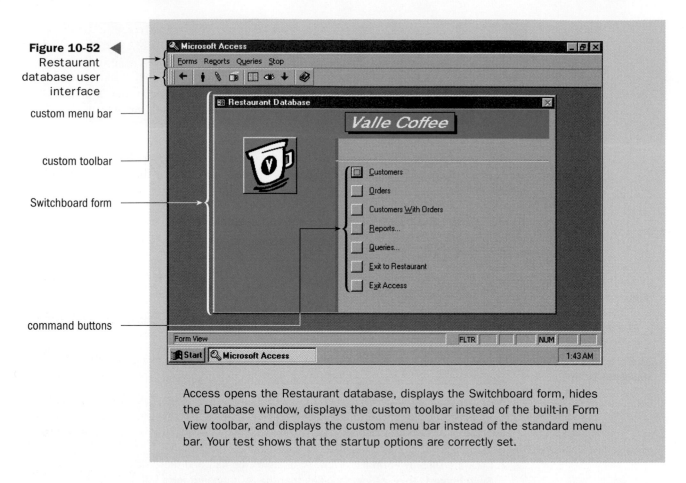

Figure 10-52
Restaurant
database user
interface

custom menu bar

custom toolbar

Switchboard form

command buttons

Access opens the Restaurant database, displays the Switchboard form, hides the Database window, displays the custom toolbar instead of the built-in Form View toolbar, and displays the custom menu bar instead of the standard menu bar. Your test shows that the startup options are correctly set.

Now you can make one final test of the Restaurant database user interface. When you finish your final testing, you can exit Access.

To test the features of the Restaurant database user interface:

1. Make one final pass through all the menu, toolbar, and command button options to verify that all features work properly on the Restaurant database user interface.

2. Click the **Exit Access** button on the Restaurant Database switchboard as your last test to close the form, close the Restaurant database, and exit Access.

Quick Check

1 What does the Visible property determine?

2 When does the Current event occur?

3 What is a method?

4 What is the purpose of the DoCmd statement in Visual Basic?

5 What is a startup option?

6 How do you display a form automatically when a database opens?

The Restaurant database user interface is complete. Leonard reviews the final interface with Barbara and Kim, and they all agree that the interface will give them controlled, easy access to the database's forms, queries, and reports. After working with the interface and making any final adjustments, they can use the Switchboard Manager to remove the Exit to Restaurant command button from the Switchboard form. In this way, the Restaurant Database switchboard will be the only interface that users will see when they work with the Restaurant database.

Tutorial Assignments

Barbara asks you to complete the switchboard interface for the Products database. You can complete it by doing the following:

1. Make sure your Student Disk is in the appropriate disk drive, start Access, and then open the Products database in the TAssign folder on your Student Disk.

2. For the Switchboard form, design and create a custom toolbar and a custom menu bar with the following characteristics:

   a. Enter the name "Product" for the custom toolbar and the name "Product Menu" for the custom menu bar.

   b. Display the custom menu bar and the custom toolbar only when the Switchboard form has the focus.

   c. Place six buttons on the custom toolbar to perform the following operations: open the Coffee table, open the Enhanced Coffee Multi-page form, open the Special Imports form, open the Coffee Types report, open the Coffee Type Chart report, close the switchboard.

   d. Create a custom menu bar with four menu buttons. The first button contains a menu item for opening the Coffee table. The second button contains menu items for opening the Enhanced Coffee Multi-page form and opening the Special Imports form. The third button contains a menu item for opening the Reports Dialog Box. The fourth button contains a menu item for closing the Switchboard form. Allow both mouse and keyboard selection for menu buttons and menu items.

3. Complete the Reports Dialog Box design by doing the following:

   a. Create a Load event procedure that moves the focus to the Coffee Types report name in the list box when the Reports Dialog Box form is opened.

   b. Create a PreviewReport function to open a report in Print Preview.

   c. Attach the PreviewReport function to the On Dbl Click property for the Reports Dialog Box form list box.

   d. Attach the PreviewReport function also to the On Click property for the Print Preview command button on the Reports Dialog Box form.

4. Modify the Enhanced Coffee Multi-page form to display the Coffee Type field value in red when the value is "Flavored" and in black otherwise. Test the modified form.

5. Set the startup options to hide the Database window and open the Switchboard form whenever you open the Products database.

6. Test the custom menu bar, the custom toolbar, and the startup options.

7. Close the switchboard and exit Access.

Case Problems

1. Ashbrook Mall Information Desk Sam Bullard asks you to complete the switchboard interface for the MallJobs database. You can complete it by doing the following:

1. Make sure your Student Disk is in the appropriate disk drive, start Access, and then open the MallJobs database in the Cases folder on your Student Disk.

2. For the Switchboard form, design and create a custom toolbar and a custom menu bar with the following characteristics:

   a. Enter the name "MallJobs" for the custom toolbar and the name "MallJobs Menu" for the custom menu bar.

   b. Display the custom menu bar and the custom toolbar only when the Switchboard form has the focus.

   c. Place six buttons on the custom toolbar to perform the following operations: open the Store Data form, open the Store Jobs form, open the Job Information Multi-page form, open the Contact Phone List query, open the Store Jobs report, close the switchboard.

   d. Create a custom menu bar with four menu buttons. The first button contains menu items for opening the Store Data form, opening the Store Jobs form, and opening the Job Information Multi-page form. The second button contains a menu item for opening the Contact Phone List query. The third button contains a menu item for opening the Store Jobs report. The fourth button contains a menu item for closing the Switchboard form. Allow both mouse and keyboard selection for menu buttons and menu items.

3. Modify the Job Information Multi-page form to display a label next to the Position field-value text box. The label should be visible when the Position field value is "Assistant Manager" and hidden otherwise. The label should display the message "Management Position!" in red when it is visible.

4. Set the startup options to hide the Database window and open the Switchboard form whenever you open the MallJobs database.

5. Test the custom menu bar, the custom toolbar, and the startup options.

6. Close the switchboard and exit Access.

2. Professional Litigation User Services Raj Jawahir asks you to complete the switchboard interface for the Payments database. You can complete it by doing the following:

1. Make sure your Student Disk is in the appropriate disk drive, start Access, and then open the Payments database in the Cases folder on your Student Disk.

2. For the Switchboard form, design and create a custom toolbar and a custom menu bar with the following characteristics:

   a. Enter the name "Payments" for the custom toolbar and the name "Payments Menu" for the custom menu bar.

   b. Display the custom menu bar and the custom toolbar only when the Switchboard form has the focus.

   c. Place five buttons on the custom toolbar to perform the following operations: open the Firm table, open the Enhanced Firm Multi-page form, open the AcctReps By Firm Crosstab query, open the Payments by Account Representative report, close the switchboard.

d. Create a custom menu bar with three menu buttons. The first button contains menu items for opening the Firm table, opening the Enhanced Firm Multi-page form, and opening the AcctReps By Firm Crosstab query. The second button contains a menu item for opening the Payments by Account Representative report. The third button contains a menu item for closing the Switchboard form. Allow both mouse and keyboard selection for menu buttons and menu items.

3. Cathy Cunningham and David Abelson are partners at Professional Litigation User Services. Add the message "Partner's Account" to the Enhanced Firm Multi-page form so that the message appears next to the PLUSAcctRep field. Use the Fore Color value of red, and make the font bold. Display the message only when the PLUSAcctRep field value is "Cunningham, Cathy" or "Abelson, David."

4. Set the startup options to hide the Database window and open the Switchboard form whenever you open the Payments database.

5. Test the custom menu bar, the custom toolbar, and the startup options.

6. Close the switchboard and exit Access.

3. Best Friends Noah and Sheila Warnick ask you to complete the switchboard interface for the Walks database. You can complete it by doing the following:

1. Make sure your Student Disk is in the appropriate disk drive, start Access, and then open the Walks database in the Cases folder on your Student Disk.

2. For the Switchboard form, design and create a custom toolbar and a custom menu bar with the following characteristics:

   a. Enter the name "Walks" for the custom toolbar and the name "Walks Menu" for the custom menu bar.

   b. Display the custom menu bar and the custom toolbar only when the Switchboard form has the focus.

   c. Place five buttons on the custom toolbar to perform the following operations: open the Walker form, open the Enhanced Walker Information Multi-page form, open the Pledge Statistics By Walker query, open the Walkers report, close the switchboard.

   d. Create a custom menu bar with four menu buttons. The first button contains menu items for opening the Walker form and opening the Enhanced Walker Information Multi-page form. The second button contains a menu item for opening the Pledge Statistics By Walker query. The third button contains a menu item for opening the Walkers report. The fourth button contains a menu item for closing the Switchboard form. Allow both mouse and keyboard selection for menu buttons and menu items.

3. Modify the Enhanced Walker Information Multi-page form to display the message "Long Distance" in yellow. Display the message next to the Distance field when the Distance field value is greater than 2.5. Do not display the message otherwise. Test the modified form.

4. Set the startup options to hide the Database window and open the Switchboard form whenever you open the Walks database.

5. Test the custom menu bar, the custom toolbar, and the startup options.

6. Close the switchboard and exit Access.

4. Lopez Lexus Dealerships Hector and Maria Lopez ask you to complete the switchboard interface for the Lexus database. You can complete it by doing the following:

1. Make sure your Student Disk is in the appropriate disk drive, start Access, and then open the Lexus database in the Cases folder on your Student Disk.

2. For the Switchboard form, design and create a custom toolbar and a custom menu bar with the following characteristics:

    a. Enter the name "Lexus" for the custom toolbar and the name "Lexus Menu" for the custom menu bar.

    b. Display the custom menu bar and the custom toolbar only when the Switchboard form has the focus.

    c. Place six buttons on the custom toolbar to perform the following operations: open the Cars table, open the Enhanced Locations Information Multi-page form, open the Car Statistics By Location query, open the Cars By Model And Year report, open the Model Pie Chart report, close the switchboard.

    d. Create a custom menu bar with five menu buttons. The first button contains a menu item for opening the Cars table. The second button contains a menu item for opening the Enhanced Locations Information Multi-page form. The third button contains a menu item for opening the Car Statistics By Location query. The fourth button contains menu items for opening the Cars By Model And Year report and opening the Model Pie Chart report. The fifth button contains a menu item for closing the Switchboard form. Allow both mouse and keyboard selection for menu buttons and menu items.

3. Soon Hong has been honored as "Manager of the Year" by Lopez Lexus Dealerships. Add the message "Manager of the Year!" to the Enhanced Locations Information form. Use the Fore Color value of red, and make the font 14-point bold. Display the message only when the ManagerName field value is "Hong, Soon."

4. Set the startup options to hide the Database window and open the Switchboard form whenever you open the Lexus database.

5. Test the custom menu bar, the custom toolbar, and the startup options.

6. Close the switchboard and exit Access.

Answers to Quick Check Questions

SESSION 8.1

1 When you create a Briefcase replica of a database, the Design Master and all of its replicas are called the replica set.

2 Anyone using the Design Master can make changes to the design of database tables, queries, and other objects. A replica prevents the user from changing the structure or the design of an existing table, query, or other database object.

3 A Design Master displays the words "Design Master" in the Database window title bar. A replica displays the word "Replica" in the Database window title bar.

4 The synchronizing process compares the Design Master to the replica and checks for any differences. Access updates the Design Master with any changes that have been made to the data in the replica, and updates the replica with any changes that have been made to the data or to the design of any database objects in the Design Master.

5 A crosstab query performs aggregate function calculations on the values of one database field and displays the results in a spreadsheet format.

6 A find duplicates query is a select query that locates duplicate records in a table or query.

7 A find unmatched query is a select query that finds all the records in a table or query that have no related records in a second table or query.

8 Access displays the first five records.

SESSION 8.2

1 An action query is a query that adds, changes, or deletes multiple table records at one time.

2 You should preview the query results before running an action query.

3 A make-table query creates a new table from one or more existing tables. An append query adds records from an existing table or query to the end of another table.

4 A delete query deletes a group of records from one or more tables.

5 An update query changes selected field values in one or more tables.

6 Access places the Update To row in the design grid.

7 The Expression Builder is an Access tool that contains an expression box in which the expression is entered, buttons for common operators, and one or more lists of expression elements, such as table and field names.

SESSION 8.3

1 An inner join selects records from two tables when they have matching values in the common field(s). An outer join selects all records from one table and records from a second table whose common field value(s) match records in the first table.

2 Access saves a query in its SQL format.

3 The basic format of an SQL statement is SELECT-FROM-WHERE-ORDER BY. The SELECT clause identifies the fields selected; the FROM clause specifies the table from which the fields are selected; the WHERE clause specifies the selection criteria; and the ORDER BY clause specifies the sort sequence.

4 a. The primary key for the Telephones table is Telephone Number. There is no single field that serves as the primary key for the Phone Calls table. A primary key can be constructed using a combination of the Calling Telephone Number, Call Date, and Call Start Time fields.

   b. There is a one-to-many relationship between the primary Telephones table and the related Phone Calls table.

   c. Yes, an inner join is possible. Examples use these fields: Telephone Number and Calling Telephone Number; Telephone Number and Called Telephone Number; Telephone Number and Billed Telephone Number.

   d. Yes. Assume that the primary keys are defined as in Quick Check 4-a and that Telephones is the left table. Examples of a left outer-join use these common fields: Telephone Number and Calling Telephone Number; Telephone Number and Called Telephone Number; Telephone Number and Billed Telephone Number.

   e. No, a self-join is not possible for either of these tables.

SESSION 9.1

1 A switchboard is a form that appears when you open a database and that provides controlled access to the database's tables, forms, queries, and reports. A typical switchboard provides command buttons, a custom menu bar, a custom toolbar, shortcut keys, text boxes, and graphic images that provide identification and visual appeal. A switchboard lets you customize the organization of the user interface, and a switchboard prevents users from changing the design of tables, forms, queries, and reports.

2 A hot key is an underlined letter in a menu name, a menu item, a toolbar button, or a command button option that provides a keyboard shortcut to a common operation. You can use shortcut keys by holding down the Alt key while pressing the underlined letter to make a selection, instead of clicking a command button, menu option, or toolbar button.

3 A macro is a command or a series of commands you want Access to perform automatically for you. Each command in a macro is called an action.

4 Action arguments are additional facts Access needs to execute an action. The action for opening a form, for example, needs the form name and the appropriate view as arguments.

5 Single-stepping executes a macro one action at a time, pausing between actions. You use single-stepping to make sure you have placed actions in the right order and with the right arguments to ensure that the macro works correctly.

6 The MsgBox action causes Access to open a dialog box that remains on the screen until you click the OK button.

SESSION 9.2

1 The Validation Rule property specifies the valid values that can be entered in a field. For example you could use this property to specify that only positive numeric values can be entered in a numeric field.

2 The Validation Text property value will be displayed in a message dialog box if the user enters an invalid value. For example you could display the message "Must be a positive value" if the user enters a value less than or equal to zero.

3 When a form's Border Style property value is Dialog, the form will be similar to a dialog box in that users will not be able to resize the form using the pointer.

4 A list box is a control that displays a list of values.

5 Open the property sheet for the command button in Design view. Click the All tab in the property sheet, click the Picture text box, and then click the build button. Select the picture from the Picture Builder dialog box.

6 Right-click the object, click Copy on the shortcut menu, click Edit on the menu bar, and then click Paste.

SESSION 9.3

1 Macro groups allow you to consolidate related macros and provide a way to manage large numbers of macros.

2 The SendKeys action simulates keystrokes in a macro.

3 The Switchboard Manager is a Microsoft Access add-in tool that helps you create and customize a switchboard.

4 In the Command Button Wizard dialog box, enter an ampersand (&) to the left of the hot key character to create the hot key.

5 Open the form in Design view, open the form's property sheet, and then set the Border Style property to Dialog.

6 Shadowed and raised are two special effects you can use for a control.

SESSION 10.1

1 A built-in toolbar is a standard Access toolbar. A custom toolbar is a toolbar you create from scratch or by modifying a built-in toolbar. A command bar is a custom toolbar created with Visual Basic.

2 With the Customize dialog box open, right-click the toolbar button to display the shortcut menu, and then point to Change Button Image. Select the image from the palette of custom button images.

3 Display the form in Design view, open the form's property sheet, click the right side of the Toolbar text box, and then select the toolbar.

4 In the Toolbar Properties dialog box, click the Show on Toolbars Menu check box to remove the check mark.

5 A global custom menu bar is displayed in all windows of your application.

6 A hot key can apply to only one active control or menu choice on the screen. When a menu is displayed, hot keys apply only to the available menu items.

SESSION 10.2

1 Visual Basic statements respond to events that occur with the objects in a database.

2 A function is a procedure that performs operations, returns a value, can accept input values, and can be used in expressions. A subprocedure, or subroutine, performs operations and can accept input values but does not return a value and cannot be used in expressions.

3 A standard module is a separate database object that is stored in memory with other database objects when you open the database. A class module is associated with a specific database object, such as a form or report.

4 An event procedure is a procedure that runs when a specific event occurs.

5 When working in the Module window, you can use the Debug window to test Visual Basic procedures while you are coding them.

6 Access checks the procedure for syntax errors. If no syntax errors are found, Access translates the procedure into executable form.

SESSION 10.3

1 The UCase function converts its argument to uppercase letters. It has no effect on characters that are not letters.

2 A Dim statement is used to declare variables and their types.

3 The loop would be executed 10 times.

4 The Boolean data type is the Visual Basic equivalent of the Yes/No data type.

5 The String data type is the Visual Basic equivalent of the Text data type.

6 The CStr function converts its argument to a String data type.

SESSION 10.4

1 The Visible property determines when Access displays a control.

2 The Current event occurs every time Access displays a new record in a form.

3 A method is an action that operates on specific objects or controls.

4 A Visual Basic DoCmd statement executes an action in a function.

5 A startup option is an action that takes place when a database is opened.

6 In the Startup dialog box, click the Display Form list arrow, and then select the form.

Company Financial Information by FINSTAT Inc.

OBJECTIVES

In this case you will:

- Change field properties

- Add a table to a database and define relationships between tables

- Create select, parameter, and crosstab queries

- Create a form using the Form Wizard

- Create custom forms

- Create custom reports

- Prepare a chart

- Design and create a switchboard

- Add macros and event procedures

CASE

FINSTAT Inc.

When Pat Mitchell graduated from a prestigious business college, she had her pick of job offers. Employers could see from her internship record and her grades that she was a bright, ambitious worker who would be an asset to their company. Pat had always dreamed of being her own boss, however, so after careful market analysis and planning she founded FINSTAT Inc., an electronic information service that markets financial information to its clients. Since the time Pat started her company, competing vendors have appeared on the market offering similar databases of financial information.

Pat and her team of financial analysts are now realizing that to remain competitive, their products must supply current and complete data. Also their clients must be able to access the data effortlessly and with as many options as possible. Pat decides to take the current databases she has and upgrade them with ease of use in mind. Her most successful database contains recent financial statement data on several of the leading U.S. corporations. She starts her new campaign by reorganizing the financial statement information to make it more accessible, and then designing an interface that is easier for clients to use.

Pat's corporation database currently consists of two tables, Company and Finance. Figure AC-1 shows the structure of the Company table, which stores general data about each company. The Company table contains an ID number and name for each company, a code classifying the company's industry, and a symbol that uniquely identifies the company on the stock exchange and in financial publications.

Figure AC-1 ◄
Structure of the
Company table

Field Name	Data Type	Properties
CompanyID	Text	Field Size—3
		Caption—Company ID
Company Name	Text	Field Size—30
		Caption—Company Name
Industry	Text	Field Size—2
Symbol	Text	Field Size—6

Figure AC-2 shows the structure of the Finance table, which tracks the yearly financial data for each company. The Finance table contains the same ID numbers used in the Company table and contains additional data on the sales, assets, and profits for each company for a given year, 1994 or later.

Figure AC-2 ◄
Structure of the
Finance table

Field Name	Data Type	Properties
CompanyID	Text	Field Size—3
		Caption—Company ID
Year	Number	Field Size—Integer
		Decimal Places–Auto
Sales	Currency	Description—Rounded to the nearest million
		Decimal Places—0
Assets	Currency	Description—Rounded to the nearest million
		Decimal Places—0
Profits	Currency	Description—Rounded to the nearest million
		Decimal Places—0

Pat wants to create a new customized version of the database so that clients can choose information more easily. She formulates the following plan: she will modify the field properties in the Company and Finance tables, add a table for industry codes and descriptions, define relationships for the three tables, and create and save four queries. She will then create the form shown in Figure AC-3 using the Form Wizard. This new form will make it easier for both her own staff and her clients to add current financial data to the database.

Figure AC-3 ◄
Company
Finances form
created by the
Form Wizard

fields from the
Company table

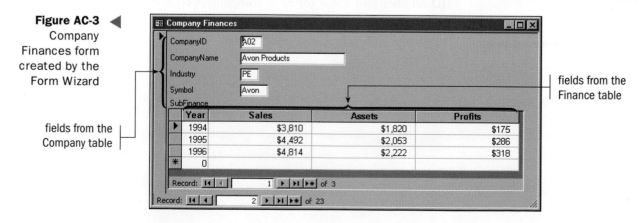

fields from the
Finance table

Pat plans to create a custom form, shown in Figure AC-4, that uses all three tables to display a company's financial information, a year at a time. Calculations are included on this form for the company's rate of return and profit margin.

Figure AC-4 ◀
Annual
Financials
form

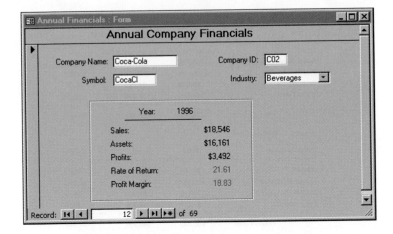

Next, Pat plans to create two reports that are easy to generate and are of presentation quality. The first report, shown in Figure AC-5, groups companies by industry and provides industry and overall totals.

Figure AC-5 ◀
Custom
Industry
1996 report
(page 1)

FINSTAT

Financial Analysis for 1996

Figures rounded to the nearest million

Industry: Apparel

Company Name	Sales	Assets	Profits
Liz Claiborne	$2,217	$1,382	$155
Nike	$6,471	$3,952	$553
Reebok International	$3,483	$1,786	$139
Fruit of the Loom	$2,447	$2,547	$151
Industry Total:	$14,618	$9,667	$998

Industry: Beverages

Company Name	Sales	Assets	Profits
Coca-Cola	$18,546	$16,161	$3,492
PepsiCo	$31,645	$24,512	$1,149
Anheuser-Busch	$10,884	$10,464	$1,190
Industry Total:	$61,075	$51,137	$5,831

Industry: Cars & Trucks

Company Name	Sales	Assets	Profits
Chrysler	$61,397	$56,184	$3,529
Ford Motor	$146,991	$262,867	$4,446
General Motors	$168,369	$222,142	$4,963
Industry Total:	$376,757	$541,193	$12,938

Industry: Chemicals

Company Name	Sales	Assets	Profits
Monsanto	$9,262	$11,191	$385
du Pont	$39,689	$37,987	$3,636
Dow Chemical	$20,053	$24,673	$1,907
Industry Total:	$69,004	$73,851	$5,928

Industry: Discount Retailing

Company Name	Sales	Assets	Profits
Kmart	$31,437	$14,286	($220)
J.C. Penney	$23,649	$22,088	$565

Figure AC-5 ◀
Custom
Industry 1996
report (page 2)

FINSTAT

Financial Analysis for 1996

Figures rounded to the nearest million

Sears, Roebuck	$38,236	$36,167	$1,271
Wal-Mart Stores	$106,147	$39,501	$3,056
Toys "R" US	$9,932	$8,023	$427
Home Depot	$19,535	$9,342	$938
Industry Total:	$228,936	$129,407	$6,037

Industry: Personal Care

Company Name	Sales	Assets	Profits
Gillette	$9,698	$10,435	$949
Procter & Gamble	$35,284	$27,730	$3,046
Colgate-Palmolive	$8,749	$7,902	$635
Avon Products	$4,814	$2,222	$318
Industry Total:	$58,545	$48,289	$4,948
Industry Total:	$808,935	$853,544	$36,680

The second report, shown in Figure AC-6, summarizes sales, assets, and profits by industry.

Figure AC-6 ◀
Custom
Industry 1996
Summary
report

Industry Summary for 1996

Figures rounded to the nearest million

Industry	Sales	Assets	Profits
Apparel	$14,618	$9,667	$998
Beverages	$61,075	$51,137	$5,831
Cars & Trucks	$376,757	$541,193	$12,938
Chemicals	$69,004	$73,851	$5,928
Discount Retailing	$228,936	$129,407	$6,037
Personal Care	$58,545	$48,289	$4,948
Grand Total:	$808,935	$853,544	$36,680

After creating a crosstab query showing the profits by company name and by year, and a bar chart showing average sales and average profits by year, Pat plans to design and create a switchboard, set the startup options, and create an event procedure for one of the new forms. Figure AC-7 shows the finished switchboard.

Figure AC-7 ◄
FINSTAT
Database
switchboard

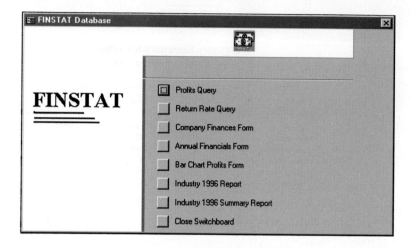

Complete the following to create the customized database:

1. Make sure you have created your copy of the Access Student Disk, place your Student Disk in the appropriate drive, start Access, and then open the Finstat database in the AddCases folder on your Student Disk.

2. Review the Company and Finance tables to become familiar with their structures and datasheet contents. If you are unfamiliar with any property setting, use the Access Help system for an explanation of that property.

3. For the Company table, make CompanyName a required field and make CompanyID the primary key. For the Finance table, add a validation rule for the Year field to allow values greater than or equal to 1994, add an appropriate validation text message, and make the combination of CompanyID and Year the primary key. Finally, define a one-to-many relationship between the primary Company table and the related Finance table using CompanyID as the common field and enforcing referential integrity.

4. The Company table contains the Industry field, which stores a two-character industry code. The acceptable industry codes and associated industry descriptions are: AP (Apparel), BV (Beverages), CA (Cars & Trucks), CH (Chemicals), DI (Discount Retailing), PE (Personal Care). Design and create a new table to store the industry codes and industry descriptions, using the field names Industry and IndustryDesc and making Industry the primary key. Name this table Industry and add the six industry records to the table. Define a one-to-many relationship between the primary Industry table and the related Company table using the two-character industry code as the common field and enforcing referential integrity. Print the six records from the Industry table.

5. Change the Industry field in the Company table to a Lookup Wizard field. Display the IndustryDesc field from the Industry table.

6. Create and save a query named Profits that displays the CompanyID, CompanyName, Year, IndustryDesc, Sales, and Profits fields for all companies with sales above 4000 and profits above 300. Print the query results in ascending order by Profits.

7. For all companies, create a query to display the CompanyName, Sales, Assets, Profits, and RateofReturn for the year 1996. Calculate RateofReturn by dividing Profits by Assets. Format RateofReturn as a percent with one decimal place. Print the query results in descending order by RateofReturn, and then save the query as Return Rate.

8. For all companies, create a query to display the CompanyID, CompanyName, Industry, Symbol, Year, Sales, Assets, Profits, RateofReturn, and ProfitMargin. Calculate RateofReturn by dividing Profits by Assets and then multiplying by 100. Calculate ProfitMargin by dividing Profits by Sales and then multiplying by 100. For both RateofReturn and ProfitMargin, use a fixed format with two decimal places. Print the query results in ascending order by CompanyName as the primary sort key and Year as the secondary sort key, and then save the query as Company Data.

9. Create and save a parameter query named Profits Parameter that displays the CompanyName, Symbol, Sales, Assets, Profits, and Industry fields for companies during 1996 in a selected industry (use Industry as the parameter). Print the query results in ascending order by Profits using the parameter value PE.

10. Use the Form Wizard to create the form shown in Figure AC-3. Use the Company and Finance tables. Save the subform as SubFinance, and save the main/subform form as Company Finances. Print the first record.

11. Create the custom form shown in Figure AC-4 and save it as Annual Financials. Use the Company Data query as the basis for the form. Position the label boxes and text boxes as shown in Figure AC-4, and draw a rectangle around the financial information. Set the Back Style property to Transparent and the Special Effect property to Flat to remove the boxes from the financial text boxes. Print the first and last records of the custom form.

12. Create a query using the Company, Finance, and Industry tables to select all the financial records for the year 1996. Refer to Figure AC-5 to determine which fields to include in the query and which fields to use as sort keys. Save the query as Industry 1996. Then create the custom report shown in Figure AC-5, using the Industry 1996 query as the basis for the report. Save the report as Industry 1996, and then print the report. (*Note:* The FINSTAT logo at the top of the report is stored as Finlogo.bmp in the AddCases folder on your Student Disk.)

13. Create the Industry Summary for 1996 report shown in Figure AC-6. Base the report on the Industry 1996 query. Save the report as Industry 1996 Summary. Print the report. (*Hint*: Use the report from Step 12 as a guide, but include only summary information for this report.)

14. Create a crosstab query showing the profits by industry by year. Base the query on the Company Data query. Save the query as Profit Crosstab, and then print the query results.

15. Create a form with a bar chart showing profits by industry by year for all industries. Base the chart form on the Profit Crosstab query. Add appropriate titles and a legend. Save the form as Bar Chart Profits, and then print the form.

16. Design and create a switchboard, using Figure AC-7 as a model, and save it as Switchboard. Provide the wording for the title bar and a heading at the top center of the switchboard. Add the Finmoney.bmp graphic image from your Student Disk to the location shown on the switchboard in the figure. On the switchboard, place eight command buttons to perform the following actions:

   - Open the Profits query

   - Open the Return Rate query

   - Open the Company Finances form

   - Open the Annual Financials form

   - Open the Bar Chart Profits form

   - Open the Industry 1996 report

   - Open the Industry 1996 Summary report

   - Close the switchboard and activate the Database window

   Create a macro group for these command buttons. Use appropriate background and foreground colors and visual effects for the switchboard and its components, and size and position the switchboard in Form view. Test the switchboard.

17. Set the startup options to hide the Database window and open the Switchboard form whenever the Finstat database is opened.

18. For the Annual Financials form, display the RateofReturn field value with a Fore Color value of red when the field value is over 10 and with the default black color otherwise. Similarly, display the ProfitMargin field value with a Fore Color value of red when the field value is over 10 and with the default black color otherwise. Test the form.

Customer Orders
for Pet Provisions

OBJECTIVES

In this case you will:

- Create select queries

- Create a form using the Form Wizard

- Create custom forms

- Create custom reports

- Design and create a switchboard

CASE

Pet Provisions

Pet Provisions, started by Manny Cordova in 1993, sells pet food and pet supplies to pet shops around the world. His company has enjoyed steady annual increases in sales, but profits have lagged behind. Manny asks his office manager, Kerri Jackson, to tighten the company's collection methods as a first step in improving profits.

Currently the office maintains an Access database named Pet that contains information on its customers. After looking over the database, Kerri realizes that there is no easy way to tell which client accounts are paid in full and which have outstanding balances. She decides to create the necessary forms, queries, and reports to automate the collection process. Her work will include creating an invoice report that she can automatically generate to send to any client with an outstanding balance.

Kerri uses the Pet database as the starting point for her work. Among the tables in the Pet database are the Customer and Order tables. Figure AC-8 shows the structure for the Customer table, which contains one record for each customer. CustomerNum is the primary key for the table, which has 26 customer records. The other fields in the table are CustomerName, Street, City, State/Prov, Zip/PostalCode, Country, Phone, and FirstContact.

Figure AC-8 ◀
Structure of the
Customer table

Field Name	Data Type	Properties
CustomerNum	Number	Primary Key
		Field Size—Integer
		Format—Fixed
		Decimal Places—0
		Caption—Customer Num
		Required—Yes
CustomerName	Text	Field Size—35
		Caption—Customer Name
Street	Text	Field Size—30
City	Text	Field Size—20
State/Prov	Text	Field Size—20
Zip/PostalCode	Text	Field Size—10
		Caption—Zip/Postal Code
Country	Text	Field Size—20
Phone	Text	Field Size—15
FirstContact	Date/Time	Format—m/d/yy
		Caption—First Contact

Figure AC-9 shows the structure for the Order table, which contains one record for each customer order. OrderNum is the table's primary key. CustomerNum is a foreign key in the Order table, and the Customer table will have a one-to-many relationship with the Order table.

Figure AC-9 ◄
Structure of the
Order table

Field Name	Data Type	Properties
OrderNum	Number	Primary Key Field Size—Integer Format—Fixed Decimal Places—O Caption—Order Num Required—Yes
CustomerNum	Number	Field Size—Integer Format—Fixed Decimal Places—O Caption—Customer Num Required—Yes Foreign Key
SaleDate	Date/Time	Format—m/d/yy Caption—Sale Date
ShipVia	Text	Field Size—7 Caption—Ship Via
TotalInvoice	Number	Field Size—Double Format—Standard Decimal Places—2 Caption—Total Invoice
AmountPaid	Number	Field Size—Double Format—Standard Decimal Places—2 Caption—Amount Paid
PayMethod	Text	Field Size—5 Caption—Pay Method

Kerri plans to create special queries, forms, and reports to help her analyze the 144 orders in the Order table. One of the special forms, shown in Figure AC-10, displays all orders for a customer along with totals for the customer's invoices, amount paid, and amount owed.

Figure AC-10 ◄
Customer With
Orders form

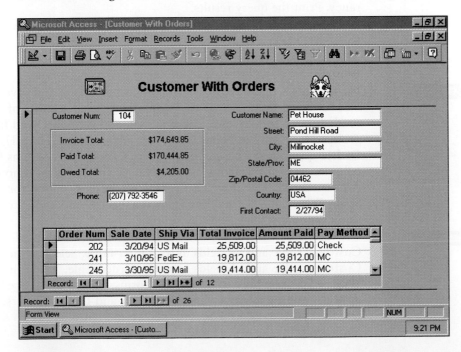

Kerri also wants to create a special report, shown in Figure AC-11, that she can send to customers owing money to Pet Provisions.

Figure AC-11 ◀
Custom
Customer
Statement
report

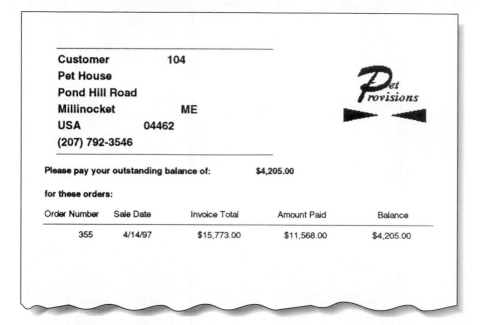

Complete the following to analyze profits at Pet Provisions:

1. Make sure you have created your copy of the Access Student Disk, place your Student Disk in the appropriate drive, start Access, and then open the Pet database in the AddCases folder on your Student Disk.

2. Review the Customer and Order tables to become familiar with their structures and datasheet contents. If you are unfamiliar with any property settings, use the Access Help system for an explanation of that property.

3. Define a one-to-many relationship between the primary Customer table and the related Order table.

4. Create and save a query named Order Totals that displays the grand total number of orders and grand totals for the TotalInvoice, AmountPaid, and AmountOwed fields. AmountOwed, a calculated field, is the difference between the TotalInvoice and AmountPaid fields. Format the fields as currency. Print the query results.

5. For all orders that have not been paid in full, create a query to display the CustomerName, Phone, SaleDate, TotalInvoice, AmountPaid, and AmountOwed. Print the query results in descending order by AmountOwed, and then save the query as Open Orders.

6. For all orders that have not been paid in full, create and save a query named Owed By Customer that displays the total number of orders and totals for the TotalInvoice, AmountPaid, and AmountOwed fields, grouped by CustomerName. Print the query results. (*Hint:* Use the Open Orders query as the basis for this query.) The query contains four columns to be displayed: CustomerName, TotalInvoice, AmountPaid, and AmountOwed. The query also contains a second column for AmountPaid. Select Where as the Total line value for this column and enter the selection criterion in the Criteria text box.

7. Use the Form Wizard to create linked forms to maintain all fields in the Customer table and all fields in the Order table. Select all fields from the Customer table and all fields from the Order table. When the Form Wizard asks you how to display the forms, choose the Linked forms option. Save the forms as Customer Data and Linked Orders, respectively. Use the forms to add the records shown in Figure AC-12 to the tables, and then print the new records from each table.

Figure AC-12 ◄
New Customer
and Order
records

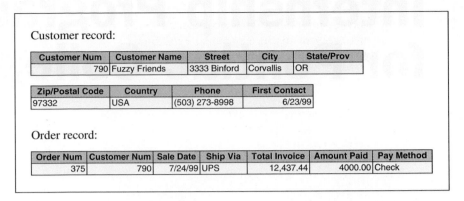

Customer record:

Customer Num	Customer Name	Street	City	State/Prov
790	Fuzzy Friends	3333 Binford	Corvallis	OR

Zip/Postal Code	Country	Phone	First Contact
97332	USA	(503) 273-8998	6/23/99

Order record:

Order Num	Customer Num	Sale Date	Ship Via	Total Invoice	Amount Paid	Pay Method
375	790	7/24/99	UPS	12,437.44	4000.00	Check

8. Create and save two queries that will be used with the form shown in Figure AC-10. For the first query, use the Order table to display totals for the TotalInvoice, AmountPaid, and AmountOwed fields, grouping by CustomerNum and using the column names Invoice Total, Paid Total, and Owed Total, respectively. Save the query as Customer Order Totals, and then print the query results. For the second query, use the Customer Order Totals query and the Customer table; display the CustomerNum, InvoiceTotal, PaidTotal, OwedTotal, CustomerName, Street, City, State/Prov, Zip/Postal Code, Country, Phone, and FirstContact fields; and sort in ascending order by CustomerNum. Save the query as Customer With Totals, and then print the query results.

9. Create the custom form shown in Figure AC-10 and save it as Customer With Orders. Create an initial approximation of the form using the Customer With Totals query for the main form. Using the Subform/Subreport tool on the toolbox, create a subform based on the Order table, and place it on the form as shown in the figure. Select all the fields from the Customer table and all the fields from the Order table except CustomerNum. Save the subform as SubOrder. Then change the form so that it looks similar to the form shown in Figure AC-10. Use the Flat Special Effect property value, the Transparent Border Style property value, and the Transparent Back Style property value to remove the boxes from the three text boxes between the Customer Num and Phone boxes. Print the first record of the custom form. (*Note:* The images that appear on the top of the form are stored as Petfish.bmp and Petdog.bmp on your Student Disk.)

10. Create and save a query named For Special Report that selects customers who owe money to Pet Provisions and the unpaid orders for these customers. Refer to Figure AC-11 to determine which fields to include in the query. (*Hint:* Use the Customer With Totals query and the Order table to create this query; create a join line between the CustomerNum fields; and sort in ascending order by CustomerNum as the primary sort key and OrderNum as the secondary sort key.) Then create the custom report shown in Figure AC-11, using the For Special Report query as the basis for the report. Include a Group Header section based on CustomerNum, and place orders in the Detail section. Set the Force New Page property in the Group Header section to the value "Before Section" so that one customer statement is printed per page. Save the report as Customer Statement, and then print pages 6 through 8 of the report. (*Note:* The logo in the upper-right corner of the report is stored as Petlogo.bmp on your Student Disk.)

11. Design and create a switchboard and save the form as Pet Provisions Switchboard. Place command buttons on the switchboard to coordinate the running of two forms (Customer Data and Customer With Orders), three queries (Open Orders, Order Totals, and Owed By Customer), and one report (Customer Statement). Also provide a command button to close the switchboard and return to the Database window. Test the switchboard.

Internship Program for Pontiac College

In this case you will:

- Design a database and draw its entity-relationship diagram

- Create the tables and relationships for the database

- Create forms to maintain the database

- Design and enter test data for the database

- Create queries and reports from the database

- Design and create a switchboard

CASE

Pontiac College

Pontiac College provides students with opportunities for professional development and field study through its internship program, which is administered by the Office of Internships and Field Experience. Students complement their courses with a structured training experience provided by qualified professionals in selected fields. Internships are offered in many different areas, including law, counseling, government, administration, public relations, communications, health care, computer programming, and marketing.

Anjali Bhavnani has just been hired as Pontiac College's new Internship Coordinator. She is eager to make information about the sponsoring agencies, potential internships, and current student interns more readily available to her office and to the students who qualify for the program. Anjali's most ambitious project is to develop a computerized database for the internship program to help meet these goals.

Instead of visually scanning all internship possibilities, Anjali, her staff, and interested students will be able to select internships of specific interest to them. The new database will allow potential interns to view only the internships that meet the criteria they specify. Anjali asks Roula Mendes, an information systems major working in the Office of Internships and Field Experience, to help the office develop a computerized database system for the internship program.

Anjali first outlines the steps in the internship program process for Roula:

- Identify and document the available internships

- Arrange for student intern placements

- Assign and track student interns

As the first step in the internship program process, Anjali receives a letter or phone call from a potential sponsoring agency. After some discussions, a sponsoring agency proposes an internship possibility and fills out the Agency/Internship Information form, shown in Figure AC-13. (Anjali's office currently maintains this form on a word processor.)

Figure AC-13 ◀
Agency/
Internship
Information
form

Many agencies offer more than one type of internship possibility. For each possible internship, the agency fills out a separate form and assigns one person as the contact for all internship questions and problems. In addition, each internship lists a supervisor who will work with the student intern. The internship remains active until the agency notifies the Office of Internships and Field Experience that the internship is filled or no longer available.

Anjali assigns a three-digit Agency ID to each new agency and a four-digit Internship ID to each new internship. These are sequential numbers. She also classifies each internship into a category that helps students identify internships that are related to their major or interests. For example, a student might be interested in health care, accounting, social service, or advertising.

A copy of each Agency/Internship Information form is placed in reference books in the Office of Internships and Field Experience. Students browse through these books to find internships that are of interest to them. If an internship interests a student, the student copies the information about the internship and contacts the sponsoring agency directly to request an interview.

When a student gets an internship, the student and agency establish a Learning Contract, outlining the goals to be accomplished during the internship. The student then fills out the Student Internship form, shown in Figure AC-14, to provide basic information on the student for the office files.

Figure AC-14 ◄
Student
Internship form

Anjali enters the Internship ID and year on the Student Internship form and checks the term for the internship. Next, a clerk enters information from the form into a word processor to prepare lists of current interns and internships, and then places the form in a binder.

Anjali and Roula determine that getting these two forms into an Access database is their first priority, and then they will work on creating several new reports. The first report, the design of which is shown in Figure AC-15, lists all student interns alphabetically by last name for a selected term. In order to identify the student interns who should be included in the report, the system prompts the user for the term and year.

Figure AC-15 ◄
Student Interns
report design

A second new report lists all agencies in the database alphabetically by agency name. Figure AC-16 shows the design of this report.

Figure AC-16 ◀
Internship
Agencies
report design

```
<today's date>                    Internship Agencies                        Page x


Agency Name             Department              Contact                 Phone
X_____X  X_____X  X_____X  X_____X
X_____X  X_____X  X_____X  X_____X
X_____X  X_____X  X_____X  X_____X
X_____X  X_____X  X_____X  X_____X


                                  End of Report
```

The Internship by Category report, the design of which is shown in Figure AC-17, lists internships grouped by category. The staff will use this report when talking with students about the internship program.

Figure AC-17 ◀
Internship by
Category
report design

```
<today's date>                 Internship by Category                      Page x


Category x_____ x
Internship ID        Internship Title         Internship Description
XXXX                 X_____X  X_____X
                                      X_____X
                                      X_____X
XXXX                 X_____X  X_____X
XXXX                 X_____X  X_____X
                                      X_____X


Category x_____ x
Internship ID        Internship Title         Internship Description
XXXX                 X_____X  X_____X
XXXX                 X_____X  X_____X
                                      X_____X
                                      X_____X


                                 End of Report
```

At the end of an internship, the intern's supervisor evaluates the intern's work experience, using an evaluation form mailed from the Office of Internships and Field Experience. Anjali needs mailing labels addressed to the supervisor of each intern for the current term and year. The mailing labels should contain the supervisor's name on the first line; the agency name on the second line; the agency's street on the third line; and the agency's city, state, and zip code on the fourth line.

Complete the following to create the complete database system:

1. Read the appendix entitled "Relational Databases and Database Design."

2. Identify each entity (relation) in the database for the internship system.

3. Draw an entity-relationship diagram showing the entities and the relationships between the entities.

4. Design the database for the internship system. For each relation, list the fields and their attributes, such as data types, field sizes, and validation rules. Place the set of relations in third normal form and identify all primary, alternate, and foreign keys.

5. Create the database structure using Access and the database name Intern. Be sure to define relationships between appropriate tables.

6. Create and save forms to maintain data on agencies, internships, student interns, and any other entity in your database structure. The forms should be used to view, add, edit, and delete records in the database.

7. Create test data for each table in the database and add the test data, using the forms you created in Step 6.

8. Create and save the Student Interns report, Internship Agencies report, Internship by Category report, and mailing labels report. The layouts shown in Figures 15 through 17 are guides—improve them as you see fit.

9. Design, create, and save a form that a student can use to view internships for a selected category. Display one internship at a time on the screen. For each internship, display the category, internship ID, title, description of duties, orientation and training, academic background, agency name, department, agency address, contact name, and contact phone. Provide an option to print the internship displayed on the screen. (*Note*: The AddCases folder on your Student Disk contains two graphic images, Intmatch.bmp and Inttrack.bmp, which you can include on this form.)

10. Design, create, and save a switchboard to coordinate the running of the internship system. (*Note*: The AddCases folder on your Student Disk contains two graphic images, named Intmatch.bmp and Inttrack.bmp, which you can include on the switchboard if you want.)

11. Test all the features of the internship system.

Relational Databases
and Database Design

A P P E N D I X

Relational Databases and Database Design

In this section you will:

- Learn the characteristics of a relation

- Learn about primary, candidate, alternate, foreign, and composite keys

- Study one-to-one, one-to-many, and many-to-many relationships

- Learn to describe relations and relationships with entity-relationship diagrams and with a shorthand method

- Study database integrity constraints for primary keys, referential integrity, and domains

- Learn about determinants, functional dependencies, anomalies, and normalization

This appendix introduces you to the basics of database design. Before trying to master this material, be sure you have an understanding of the following concepts: data, information, field, field value, record, table, relational database, common fields, database management system (DBMS), and relational database management system.

Relations

A relational database stores its data in tables. A **table** is a two-dimensional structure made up of rows and columns. The terms table, row, and column are the popular names for the more formal terms **relation** (table), **tuple** (row), and **attribute** (column), as shown in Figure AP-1.

Figure AP-1 ◄
A relation consisting of tuples and attributes

tblClient

ClientID	ClientName	VetID
2173	Barbara Hennessey	27
4519	Vernon Noordsy	31
8005	Sandra Amidon	27
8112	Helen Wandzell	24

← tuples (rows)

attributes (columns)

The tblClient table shown in Figure AP-1 is an example of a relation, a two-dimensional structure with the following characteristics:

- Each row is unique. Because no two rows are the same, you can easily locate and update specific data. For example, you can locate the row for Client ID 8005 and change the Client Name value, Sandra Amidon, or the Vet ID value, 27.

- The order of the rows is unimportant. You can add or view rows in any order. For example, you can view the rows in Client Name order instead of Client ID order.

- Each table entry contains a single value. At the intersection of each row and column, you cannot have more than one value. For example, each row in Figure AP-1 contains one Client ID, one Client Name, and one Vet ID.

- The order of the columns is unimportant. You can add or view columns in any order.

- Each column has a unique name called the **attribute name**. The attribute name allows you to access a specific column without needing to know its position within the relation.

- The entries in a column are from the same domain. A **domain** is a set of values from which one or more columns draw their actual values. A domain can be broad, such as "all legitimate names of people" for the Client Name column, or narrow, such as "24, 27, or 31" for the Vet ID column. The domain of "all legitimate dates" could be shared by the Birth Date, Start Date, and Last Pay Date columns in a company's employee relation.

- The columns in a relation describe, or are characteristics of, an entity. An **entity** is a person, place, object, event, or idea for which you want to store and process data. For example, Client ID, Client Name, and Vet ID are characteristics of the clients of a pet-sitting company. The tblClient relation represents the client entity and its characteristics. That is, the sets of values in the rows of the tblClient relation describe the different clients of the company. The tblClient relation includes only characteristics of a client. Other relations would exist for the company's other entities. For example, a tblPet relation might describe the clients' pets and a tblEmployee relation might describe the company's employees.

Knowing the characteristics of a relation leads directly to a definition of a relational database. A **relational database** is a collection of relations.

Keys

Primary keys ensure that each row in a relation is unique. A **primary key** is an attribute, or a collection of attributes, whose values uniquely identify each row in a relation. In addition to being *unique*, a primary key must be *minimal* (that is, contain no unnecessary extra attributes) and must not change in value. For example, in Figure AP-2 the tblState relation contains one record per state and uses State Abbrev as its primary key.

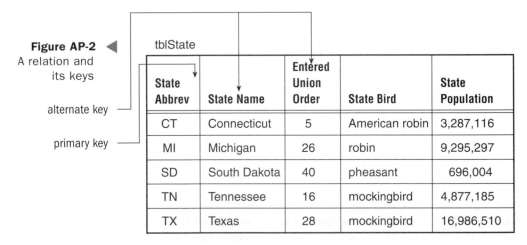

Figure AP-2
A relation and
its keys

alternate key

primary key

tblState

State Abbrev	State Name	Entered Union Order	State Bird	State Population
CT	Connecticut	5	American robin	3,287,116
MI	Michigan	26	robin	9,295,297
SD	South Dakota	40	pheasant	696,004
TN	Tennessee	16	mockingbird	4,877,185
TX	Texas	28	mockingbird	16,986,510

Could any other attribute, or collection of attributes, be the primary key of the tblState relation?

- Could State Bird serve as the primary key? No, because the column does not have unique values (for example, the mockingbird is the state bird of more than one state).

- Could State Population serve as the primary key? No, because the column values change periodically and are not guaranteed to be unique.

- Could State Abbrev and State Name together serve as the primary key? No, because the combination is not minimal. Something less, State Abbrev by itself, can serve as the primary key.

- Could State Name serve as the primary key? Yes, because the column has unique values. In a similar way, you could select Entered Union Order as the primary key for the tblState relation. One attribute, or collection of attributes, that can serve as a primary key is called a **candidate key**. The candidate keys for the tblState relation are State Abbrev, State Name, and Entered Union Order. You choose one of the candidate keys to be the primary key, and the remaining candidate keys are called alternate keys.

Figure AP-3 shows a tblCity relation containing the attributes State Abbrev, City Name, and City Population.

Figure AP-3
A relation with
a composite
key

primary key

tblCity

State Abbrev	City Name	City Population
CT	Hartford	139,739
CT	Madison	14,031
CT	Portland	8,418
MI	Lansing	127,321
SD	Madison	6,257
SD	Pierre	12,906
TN	Nashville	488,374
TX	Austin	465,622
TX	Portland	12,224

What is the primary key for the tblCity relation? The values for City Population periodically change and are not guaranteed to be unique, so City Population cannot be the primary key. Because the values for each of the other two columns are not unique, State Abbrev alone cannot be the primary key and neither can City Name (for example, there are two Madisons and two Portlands). The primary key is the combination of State Abbrev and City Name. Both attributes together are needed to identify, uniquely and minimally, each row in the tblCity relation. A multiple-attribute primary key is also called a **composite key** or a **concatenated key**.

The State Abbrev attribute in the tblCity relation is also a foreign key. A **foreign key** is an attribute, or a collection of attributes, in one relation whose values must match the values of the primary key of some relation. As shown in Figure AP-4, the values in the tblCity relation's State Abbrev column match the values in the tblState relation's State Abbrev column. Thus, State Abbrev, the primary key of the tblState relation, is a foreign key in the tblCity relation. Although the attribute name State Abbrev is the same in both relations, the names could be different. Most people give the same name to an attribute stored in two or more tables to broadcast clearly they are really the same attribute.

Figure AP-4 ◀
State Abbrev as a primary key (tbleState relation) and a foreign key (tblCity relation)

tblState

State Abbrev	StateName	Entered Union Order	StateBird	State Population
CT	Connecticut	5	American robin	3,287,116
MI	Michigan	26	robin	9,295,297
SD	South Dakota	40	pheasant	696,004
TN	Tennessee	16	mockingbird	4,877,185
TX	Texas	28	mockingbird	16,986,510

primary key

primary key

tblCity

foreign key

State Abbrev	CityName	City Population
CT	Hartford	139,739
CT	Madison	14,031
CT	Portland	8,418
MI	Lansing	127,321
SD	Madison	6,257
SD	Pierre	12,906
TN	Nashville	488,374
TX	Austin	465,622
TX	Portland	12,224

A **nonkey attribute** is an attribute that is not part of the primary key. In the two relations shown in Figure AP-4, all attributes are nonkey attributes except State Abbrev in the tblState and tblCity relations and City Name in the tblCity relation. *Key* is an ambiguous word because it can refer to a primary, candidate, alternate, or foreign key. When the word key appears alone, however, it means primary key and the definition for a nonkey attribute consequently makes sense.

Relationships

The tblCapital relation, shown in Figure AP-5, has one row for each state capital. The Capital Name and State Abbrev attributes are candidate keys; selecting Capital Name as the primary key makes State Abbrev an alternate key. The State Abbrev attribute in the tblCapital relation is also a foreign key, because its values match the values in the tblState relation's State Abbrev column.

Figure AP-5
A one-to-one
relationship

tblState

primary key →

State Abbrev	StateName	Entered Union Order	StateBird	State Population
CT	Connecticut	5	American robin	3,287,116
MI	Michigan	26	robin	9,295,297
SD	South Dakota	40	pheasant	696,004
TN	Tennessee	16	mockingbird	4,877,185
TX	Texas	28	mockingbird	16,986,510

foreign key ————

tblCaptial

primary key →

Capital Name	State Abbrev	Year Designated	Phone Area Code	Capital Population
Austin	TX	1845	512	465,622
Hartford	CT	1662	203	139,739
Lansing	MI	1847	517	127,321
Nashville	TN	1843	615	488,374
Pierre	SD	1889	605	12,906

One-to-One

The tblState and tblCapital relations, shown in Figure AP-5, have a one-to-one relationship. A **one-to-one relationship** (abbreviated 1:1) exists between two relations when each row in one relation has at most one matching row in the other relation. State Abbrev, which is a foreign key in the tblCapital relation and the primary key in the tblState relation, is the common field that ties together the rows of each relation.

Should the tblState and tblCapital relations be combined into one relation? Although the two relations in any 1:1 relationship can be combined into one relation, each relation describes different entities and should usually be kept separate.

One-to-Many

The tblState and tblCity relations, shown once again in Figure AP-6, have a one-to-many relationship. A **one-to-many relationship** (abbreviated 1:M) exists between two relations when one row in the first relation matches many rows in the second relation and one row in the second relation matches only one row in the first relation. Many can mean zero rows, one row, or two or more rows. State Abbrev, which is a foreign key in the tblCity relation and the primary key in the tblState relation, is the common field that ties together the rows of each relation.

Figure AP-6 ◀
A one-to-many
relationship

primary key ─────

tblState

State Abbrev	StateName	Entered Union Order	StateBird	State Population
CT	Connecticut	5	American robin	3,287,116
MI	Michigan	26	robin	9,295,297
SD	South Dakota	40	pheasant	696,004
TN	Tennessee	16	mockingbird	4,877,185
TX	Texas	28	mockingbird	16,986,510

primary key ─────

tblCity

foreign key ─────

State Abbrev	CityName	City Population
CT	Hartford	139,739
CT	Madison	14,031
CT	Portland	8,418
MI	Lansing	127,321
SD	Madison	6,257
SD	Pierre	12,906
TN	Nashville	488,374
TX	Austin	465,622
TX	Portland	12,224

Many-to-Many

In Figure AP-7, the tblState relation with a primary key of State Abbrev and the tblCrop relation with a primary key of Crop Name have a many-to-many relationship. A **many-to-many relationship** (abbreviated as M:N) exists between two relations when one row in the first relation matches many rows in the second relation and one row in the second relation matches many rows in the first relation. You form a many-to-many relationship between two relations indirectly by adding a third relation that has the primary keys of the M:N relations as its primary key. The original relations now each have a 1:M relationship with the new relation. The State Abbrev and Crop Name attributes represent the primary key of the tblProduction relation that is shown in Figure AP-7. State Abbrev, which is a foreign key in the tblProduction relation and the primary key in the tblState relation, is the common field that ties together the rows of the tblState and tblProduction relations. Likewise, Crop Name is the common field for the tblCrop and tblProduction relations.

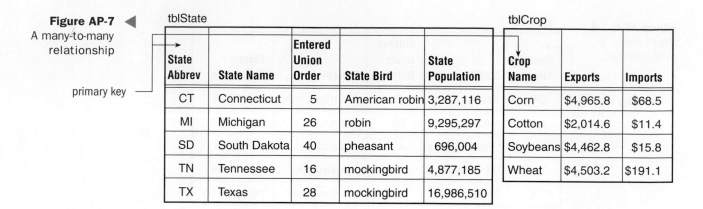

Figure AP-7
A many-to-many relationship

primary key

tblState

State Abbrev	State Name	Entered Union Order	State Bird	State Population
CT	Connecticut	5	American robin	3,287,116
MI	Michigan	26	robin	9,295,297
SD	South Dakota	40	pheasant	696,004
TN	Tennessee	16	mockingbird	4,877,185
TX	Texas	28	mockingbird	16,986,510

tblCrop

Crop Name	Exports	Imports
Corn	$4,965.8	$68.5
Cotton	$2,014.6	$11.4
Soybeans	$4,462.8	$15.8
Wheat	$4,503.2	$191.1

primary key

foreign key

tblProduction

State Abbrev	Crop Name	Quantity
MI	Corn	241,500
MI	Soybeans	47,520
MI	Wheat	35,280
SD	Corn	377,200
SD	Soybeans	63,000
SD	Wheat	119,590
TN	Corn	79,360
TN	Soybeans	33,250
TN	Wheat	13,440
TX	Corn	202,500
TX	Cotton	3,322
TX	Soybeans	12,870
TX	Wheat	129,200

Entity Subtype

Figure AP-8 shows a special type of one-to-one relationship. The tblShipping relation's primary key is State Abbrev and contains one row for each state having an ocean shoreline. Because not all states have an ocean shoreline, the tblShipping relation has fewer rows than the tblState relation. However, each row in the tblShipping relation has a matching row in the tblState relation with State Abbrev serving as the common field; State Abbrev is the primary key in the tblState relation and is a foreign key in the tblShipping relation.

Figure AP-8
An entity
subtype

primary key

tblStat

State Abbrev	State Name	Entered Union Order	State Bird	State Population
CT	Connecticut	5	American robin	3,287,116
MI	Michigan	26	robin	9,295,297
SD	South Dakota	40	pheasant	696,004
TN	Tennessee	16	mockingbird	4,877,185
TX	Texas	28	mockingbird	16,986,510

primary key

foreign key

tblShipping

State Abbrev	Ocean Shoreline	Export Tonnage	Import Tonnage
CT	618	3,377,466	2,118,494
TX	3,359	45,980,912	109,400,314

The tblShipping relation, in this situation, is called an **entity subtype**, a relation whose primary key is a foreign key to a second relation and whose attributes are additional attributes for the second relation. You can create an entity subtype when a relation has attributes that could have null values. A **null value** is the absence of a value. A null value is not blank, nor zero, nor any other value. You give a null value to an attribute when you do not know its value or when a value does not apply. For example, instead of using the tblShipping relation, you could store the Ocean Shoreline, Export Tonnage, and Import Tonnage attributes in the tblState relation and allow them to be null for states not having an ocean shoreline. You should be aware that database experts are currently debating the validity of the use of nulls in relational databases and many experts insist that you should never use nulls. Part of this warning against nulls is based on the inconsistent way different relational DBMSs treat nulls and part is due to the lack of a firm theoretical foundation for how to use nulls. In any case, entity subtypes are an alternative to the use of nulls.

Entity-Relationship Diagrams

A common shorthand method for describing relations is to write the relation name followed by its attributes in parentheses, underlining the attributes that represent the primary key and identifying the foreign keys for a relation immediately after the relation. Using this method, the relations that appear in Figures AP-5 through AP-8 are described in the following way:

tblState (<u>State Abbrev</u>, State Name, Entered Union Order, State Bird, State Population)
tblCapital (<u>Capital Name</u>, State Abbrev, Year Designated, Phone Area Code, Capital Population)
    Foreign key: State Abbrev to tblState relation
tblCity (<u>State Abbrev</u>, <u>City Name</u>, City Population)
    Foreign key: State Abbrev to tblState relation
tblCrop (<u>Crop Name</u>, Exports, Imports)
tblProduction (<u>StateAbbrev</u>, <u>Crop Name</u>, Quantity)
    Foreign key: State Abbrev to tblState relation
    Foreign key: Crop Name to tblCrop relation
tblShipping (<u>State Abbrev</u>, Ocean Shoreline, Export Tonnage, Import Tonnage)
    Foreign key: State Abbrev to tblState relation

Another popular way to describe relations *and their relationships* is with entity-relationship diagrams. An **entity-relationship diagram (ERD)** graphically shows a database's entities and the relationships among the entities. In an entity-relationship diagram, an entity and a relation are equivalent. Figure AP-9 shows an entity-relationship diagram for the relations that appear in Figures AP-5 through AP-8.

Figure AP-9 ◄
An entity-relationship diagram

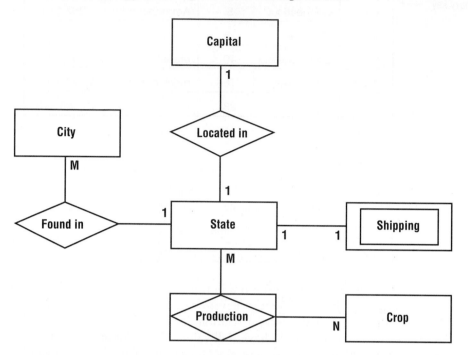

Entity-relationship diagrams have the following characteristics:

■ Entities, or relations, appear in rectangles and relationships appear in diamonds. The entity name appears inside the rectangle and a verb describing the relationship appears inside the diamond. For example, the City rectangle is connected to the State rectangle by the FOUND IN diamond and is read: "a city is found in a state."

■ The 1 by the State entity and the M by the City entity identify a 1:M relationship between these two entities. In a similar manner, an M:N relationship exists between the State and Crop entities and 1:1 relationships exist between the State and Capital entities and between the State and Shipping entities.

■ A diamond inside a rectangle defines a composite entity. A **composite entity** is a relationship that has the characteristics of an entity. For example, Production connects the State and Crop entities in an M:N relationship and acts as an entity by containing the Quantity attribute, along with the composite key of the State Abbrev and Crop Name attributes.

■ An entity subtype appears in a double rectangle and is connected without an intervening diamond directly to its related entity, State.

You can also show attributes in an ERD by placing each individual attribute in a bubble connected to its entity or relationship. However, typical ERDs have large numbers of entities and relationships, so including the attributes might confuse rather than clarify the ERD.

Integrity Constraints

A database has **integrity** if its data follows certain rules, known as **integrity constraints**. The ideal is to have the DBMS enforce all integrity constraints. If a DBMS can enforce some integrity constraints but not others, the other integrity constraints must be enforced by other programs or by the people who use the DBMS. Integrity constraints can be divided into three groups: primary key constraints, referential integrity, and domain integrity constraints.

- One primary key constraint is inherent in the definition of a primary key, which says that the primary key must be unique. The **entity integrity constraint** says that the primary key cannot be null. For a composite key, none of the individual attributes can be null. The uniqueness and nonnull properties of a primary key ensure that you can reference any data value in a database by supplying its table name, attribute name, and primary key value.

- Foreign keys provide the mechanism for forming a relationship between two tables, and referential integrity ensures that only valid relationships exist. **Referential integrity** is the constraint specifying that each nonnull foreign key must match a primary key value in the related relation. Specifically, referential integrity means that you cannot add a row with an unmatched foreign key value. Referential integrity also means that you cannot change or delete the related primary key value and leave the foreign key orphaned. In some relational DBMSs, if you try to change or delete a primary key value, you can specify one of these options: restricted, cascades, or nullifies. If you specify **restricted**, the DBMS updates or deletes the value only if there are no matching foreign key values. If you choose **cascades** and then change a primary key value, the DBMS changes the matching foreign keys to the new primary key value, or, if you delete a primary key value, the DBMS also deletes the matching foreign-key rows. If you choose **nullifies** and then change or delete a primary key value, the DBMS sets all matching foreign keys to null.

- A domain is a set of values from which one or more columns draw their actual values. **Domain integrity constraints** are the rules you specify for an attribute. By choosing a data type for an attribute, you impose a constraint on the set of values allowed for the attribute. You can create specific validation rules for an attribute to limit its domain further. As you make an attribute's domain definition more precise, you exclude more and more unacceptable values for an attribute. For example, in the tblState relation you could define the domain for the Entered Union Order attribute to be a unique integer between 1 and 50 and the domain for the State Bird attribute to be any name containing 25 or fewer characters.

Dependencies and Determinants

Relations are related to other relations. Attributes are also related to other attributes. Consider the tblStateCrop relation shown in Figure AP-10. Its description is:

tblStateCrop (<u>State Abbrev</u>, <u>Crop Name</u>, State Bird, Bird Scientific Name, State Population, Exports, Quantity)

Figure AP-10 ◄
A relation
combining
several
attributes from
the tblState,
tblCrop, and
tblProduction
relations

null value ─────

primary key ─────

tblStateCrop

State Abbrev	Crop Name	State Bird	Bird Scientific Name	State Population	Exports	Quantity
CT	Corn	American robin	Planesticus migratorius	3,287,116	$4,965.8	
MI	Corn	robin	Planesticus migratorius	9,295,297	$4,965.8	241,500
MI	Soybeans	robin	Planesticus migratorius	9,295,297	$4,462.8	47,520
MI	Wheat	robin	Planesticus migratorius	9,295,297	$4,503.2	35,280
SD	Corn	pheasant	Phasianus colchicus	696,004	$4,965.8	277,200
SD	Soybeans	pheasant	Phasianus colchicus	696,004	$4,462.8	63,000
SD	Wheat	pheasant	Phasianus colchicus	696,004	$4,503.2	119,590
TN	Corn	mockingbird	Mimus polyglottos	4,977,185	$4,965.8	79,360
TN	Soybeans	mockingbird	Mimus polyglottos	4,977,185	$4,462.8	33,250
TN	Wheat	mockingbird	Mimus polyglottos	4,977,185	$4,503.2	13,440
TX	Corn	mockingbird	Mimus polyglottos	16,986,510	$4,965.8	202,500
TX	Cotton	mockingbird	Mimus polyglottos	16,986,510	$2,014.6	3,322
TX	Soybeans	mockingbird	Mimus polyglottos	16,986,510	$4,462.8	12,870
TX	Wheat	mockingbird	Mimus polyglottos	16,986,510	$4,503.2	129,200

The tblStateCrop relation combines several attributes from the tblState, tblCrop, and tblProduction relations that appeared in Figure AP-7. The State Abbrev, State Bird, and State Population attributes are from the tblState relation. The Crop Name and Exports attributes are from the tblCrop relation. The State Abbrev, Crop Name, and Quantity attributes are from the tblProduction relation. The Bird Scientific Name attribute is a new attribute for the tblStateCrop relation, whose primary key is the combination of the State Abbrev and Crop Name attributes.

Notice the null value in the Quantity attribute for the state of Connecticut (State Abbrev CT). If you look back to Figure AP-7, you can see that there were no entries for Quantity for the state of Connecticut, which is why Quantity is null in the tblStateCrop table. However, note that Crop Name requires an entry because it is part of the composite key for the relation. If you want the state of CT to be in the relation, you need to assign a dummy Crop Name for the CT entry, in this case, Corn.

In the tblStateCrop relation, each attribute is related to other attributes. For example, a value for State Abbrev determines the value of State Population, and a value for State Population depends on the value of State Abbrev. In database discussions, the word functionally is used, as in: "State Abbrev functionally determines State Population" and "State Population is functionally dependent on State Abbrev." In this case, State Abbrev is called a determinant. A **determinant** is an attribute, or a collection of attributes, whose values determine the values of another attribute. We also state that an attribute is functionally dependent on another attribute (or collection of attributes) if that other attribute is a determinant for it.

You can graphically show a relation's functional dependencies and determinants in a bubble diagram. Bubble diagrams are also called data model diagrams and functional dependency diagrams. Figure AP-11 shows the bubble diagram for the tblStateCrop relation.

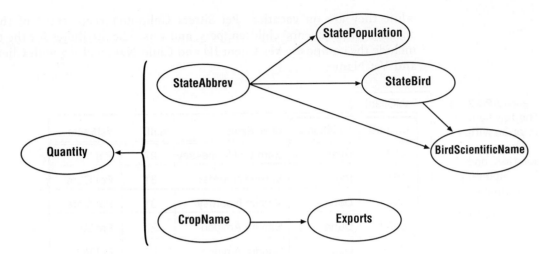

- State Abbrev is a determinant for State Population, State Bird, and Bird Scientific Name.

- Crop Name is a determinant for Exports.

- Quantity is functionally dependent on State Abbrev and Crop Name together.

- State Bird is a determinant for Bird Scientific Name.

Only Quantity is functionally dependent on the relation's full primary key, State Abbrev and Crop Name. State Population, State Bird, and Bird Scientific Name have partial dependencies, because they are functionally dependent on State Abbrev, which is part of the primary key. A **partial dependency** is a functional dependency on part of the primary key, instead of the entire primary key. Does another partial dependency exist in the tblStateCrop relation? Yes, Exports has a partial dependency on Crop Name.

Because State Abbrev is a determinant of both State Bird and Bird Scientific Name, and State Bird is a determinant of Bird Scientific Name, State Bird and Bird Scientific Name have a transitive dependency. A **transitive dependency** is a functional dependency between two nonkey attributes, which are both dependent on a third attribute.

How do you know which functional dependencies exist among a collection of attributes, and how do you recognize partial and transitive dependencies? The answers lie with the questions you ask as you gather the requirements for a database application. For each attribute and entity, you must gain an accurate understanding of its meaning and relationships in the context of the application. **Semantic object modeling** is an entire area of study within the database field devoted to the meanings and relationships of data.

Anomalies

When you use a DBMS, you are more likely to get results you can trust if you create your relations carefully. For example, problems might occur with relations that have partial and transitive dependencies, whereas you won't have as much trouble if you ensure that your relations include only attributes that are directly related to each other. Also, when you remove data redundancy from a relation, you improve that relation. **Data redundancy** occurs when you store the same data in more than one place.

The problems caused by data redundancy and by partial and transitive dependencies are called **anomalies**, because they are undesirable irregularities of relations. Anomalies are of three types: insertion, deletion, and update.

To examine the effects of these anomalies, consider the tblClient relation that is shown in Figure AP-12. The tblClient relation represents part of the database for Pet Sitters Unlimited, which is a company providing pet-sitting services for homeowners while they are on vacation. Pet Sitters Unlimited keeps track of the data about its clients and the clients' children, pets, and vets. The attributes for the tblClient relation include the composite key Client ID and Child Name, along with Client Name, Vet ID, and Vet Name.

Figure AP-12
The tblClient relation with insertion, deletion, and update anomalies

primary key

tblClient

ClientID	ChildName	ClientName	VetID	VetName
2173	Ryan	Barbara Hennessey	27	Pet Vet
4519	Pat	Vernon Noordsy	31	Pet Care
4519	Dana	Vernon Noordsy	31	Pet Care
8005	Dana	Sandra Amidon	27	Pet Vet
8005	Dani	Sandra Amidon	27	Pet Vet
8112	Pat	Helen Wandzell	24	Pets R Us

- An **insertion anomaly** occurs when you cannot add a row to a relation because you do not know the entire primary key value. For example, you cannot add the new client Cathy Corbett with a Client ID of 3322 to the tblClient relation when you do not know her children's names. Entity integrity prevents you from leaving any part of a primary key null. Because Child Name is part of the primary key, you cannot leave it null. To add the new client, your only option is to make up a Child Name, even if the client does not have children. This solution misrepresents the facts and is unacceptable, if a better approach is available.

- A **deletion anomaly** occurs when you delete data from a relation and unintentionally lose other critical data. For example, if you delete Client ID 8112 because Helen Wandzell is no longer a client, you also lose the only instance of Vet ID 24 in the database. Thus, you no longer know that Vet ID 24 is Pets R Us.

- An **update anomaly** occurs when you change one attribute value and either the DBMS must make more than one change to the database or else the database ends up containing inconsistent data. For example, if you change the Client Name, Vet ID, or Vet Name for Client ID 4519, the DBMS must change multiple rows of the tblClient relation. If the DBMS fails to change all the rows, the Client Name, Vet ID, or Vet Name now has two different values in the database and is inconsistent.

Normalization

Database design is the process of determining the precise relations needed for a given collection of attributes and placing those attributes into the correct relations. Crucial to good database design is understanding the functional dependencies of all attributes; recognizing the anomalies caused by data redundancy, partial dependencies, and transitive dependencies when they exist; and knowing how to eliminate the anomalies.

The process of identifying and eliminating anomalies is called **normalization**. Using normalization, you start with a collection of relations, apply sets of rules to eliminate anomalies, and produce a new collection of problem-free relations. The sets of rules are called **normal forms**. Of special interest for our purposes are the first three normal forms: first normal form, second normal form, and third normal form. First normal form improves the design of your relations, second normal form improves the first normal form design, and third normal form applies even more stringent rules to produce an even better design.

First Normal Form

Consider the tblClient relation shown in Figure AP-13. For each client, the relation contains Client ID, which is the primary key; the client's name and children's names; the ID and name of the client's vet; and the ID, name, and type of each client's pets. For example, Barbara Hennessey has no children and three pets, Vernon Noordsy has two children and one pet, Sandra Amidon has two children and two pets, and Helen Wandzell has one child and one pet. Because each entry in a relation must contain a single value, the structure shown in Figure AP-13 does not meet the requirements for a relation, therefore it is called an **unnormalized relation**. Child Name, which can have more than one value, is called a **repeating group**. The set of attributes that includes Pet ID, Pet Name, and Pet Type is a second repeating group in the structure.

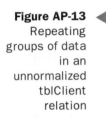

Figure AP-13
Repeating groups of data in an unnormalized tblClient relation

repeating group

tblClient

ClientID	ClientName	ChildName	VetID	VetName	PetID	PetName	PetType
2173	Barabara Hennessey		27	Pet Vet	1 2 4	Sam Hoober Sam	Bird Dog Hamster
4519	Vernon Noordsy	Pat Dana	31	Pet Care	2	Charlie	Cat
8005	Sandra Amidon	Dana Dani	27	Pet Vet	1 2	Beefer Kirby	Dog Cat
8112	Helen Wandzell	Pat	24	Pets R Us	3	Kirby	Dog

First normal form addresses this repeating-group situation. A relation is in **first normal form (1NF)** if it does not contain repeating groups. To remove a repeating group and convert to first normal form, you expand the primary key to include the primary key of the repeating group. You must perform this step carefully, however. If the unnormalized relation has independent repeating groups, you must perform the conversion step separately for each.

The repeating group of Child Name is independent from the repeating group of Pet ID, Pet Name, and Pet Type. That is, the number and names of a client's children are independent of the number, names, and types of a client's pets. Performing the conversion step to each independent repeating group produces the two 1NF relations shown in Figure AP-14.

Figure AP-14 ◀
After
conversion to
1NF

primary key ⎯

tblChild

ClientID	ChildName	ClientName	VetID	VetName
4519	Pat	Vernon Noordsy	31	Pet Care
4519	Dana	Vernon Noordsy	31	Pet Care
8005	Dana	Sandra Amidon	27	Pet Vet
8005	Dani	Sandra Amidon	27	Pet Vet
8112	Pat	Helen Wandzell	24	Pets R Us

primary key ⎯

tblClient

ClientID	PetID	ClientName	VetID	VetName	PetName	PetType
2173	1	Barbara Hennessey	27	Pet Vet	Sam	Bird
2173	2	Barbara Hennessey	27	Pet Vet	Hoober	Dog
2173	4	Barbara Hennessey	27	Pet Vet	Sam	Hamster
4519	2	Vernon Noordsy	31	Pet Care	Charlie	Cat
8005	1	Sandra Amidon	27	Pet Vet	Beefer	Dog
8005	2	Sandra Amidon	27	Pet Vet	Kirby	Cat
8112	3	Helen Wandzell	24	Pets R Us	Kirby	Dog

The alternative way to describe the 1NF relations is:

tblChild (<u>Client ID</u>, <u>Child Name</u>, Client Name, Vet ID, Vet Name)

tblClient (<u>Client ID</u>, <u>Pet ID</u>, Client Name, Vet ID, Vet Name, Pet Name, Pet Type)

tblChild and tblClient are now true relations and both have composite keys. Both relations, however, suffer from insertion, deletion, and update anomalies. (Find examples of the three anomalies in both relations.) In the tblChild and tblClient relations, Client ID is a determinant for Client Name, Vet ID, and Vet Name, so partial dependencies exist in both relations. It is these partial dependencies that cause the anomalies in the two relations, and second normal form addresses the partial-dependency problem.

Second Normal Form

A relation in 1NF is in **second normal form (2NF)** if it does not contain any partial dependencies. To remove partial dependencies from a relation and convert it to second normal form, you perform two steps. First, identify the functional dependencies for every attribute in the relation. Second, if necessary, create new relations and place each attribute in a relation, so that the attribute is functionally dependent on the entire primary key. If you need to create new relations, restrict them to ones with a primary key that is a subset of the original composite key. Note that partial dependencies occur only when you have a composite key; a relation in first normal form with a single-attribute primary key is automatically in second normal form.

Figure AP-15 shows the functional dependencies for the 1NF tblChild and tblClient relations.

Figure AP-15 ◀
A bubble
diagram for the
1NF tblChild
and the
tblClient
relations

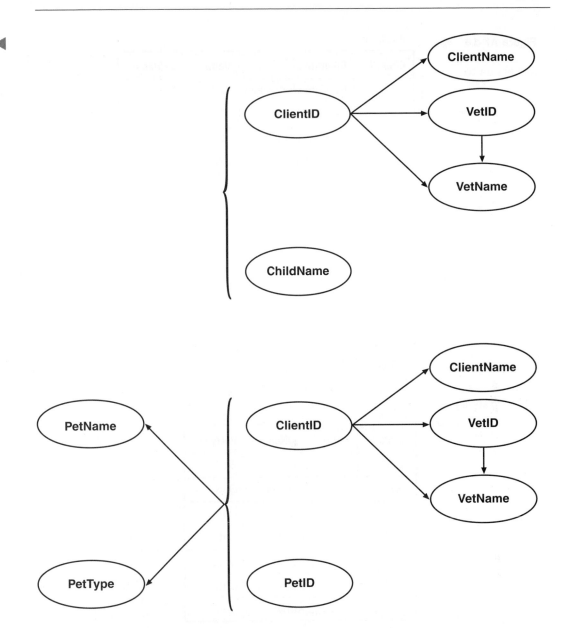

Client ID is a determinant for Client Name, Vet ID, and Vet Name in both relations. The composite key Client ID and Pet ID is a determinant for Pet Name and Pet Type. Child Name is not a determinant, nor is Pet ID. Is the composite key of Client ID and Child Name a determinant? No, it is not a determinant. What happens, however, if you do not have a relation with this composite key? You lose the names of the children of each client. You need to retain this composite key in a relation to preserve the important 1:M attribute relationship between Client ID and Child Name. Performing the second conversion step produces the three 2NF relations shown in Figure AP-16.

Figure AP-16 ◀

After conversion to 2NF

primary key ———

tblClient

ClientID	ClientName	VetID	VetName
2173	Barbara Hennessey	27	Pet Vet
4519	Vernon Noordsy	31	Pet Care
8005	Sandra Amidon	27	Pet Vet
8112	Helen Wandzell	24	Pets R Us

primary key ———

tblChild

ClientID	ChildName
4519	Pat
4519	Dana
8005	Dana
8005	Dani
8112	Pat

primary key ———

tblPet

ClientID	PetID	PetName	PetType
2173	1	Sam	Bird
2173	2	Hoober	Dog
2173	4	Sam	Hamster
4519	2	Charlie	Cat
8005	1	Beefer	Dog
8005	2	Kirby	Cat
8112	3	Kirby	Dog

The alternative way to describe the 2NF relations is:
tblClient (<u>Client ID</u>, Client Name, Vet ID, Vet Name)
tblChild (<u>Client ID</u>, <u>Child Name</u>)
    Foreign key: Client ID to tblClient relation
tblPet (<u>Client ID</u>, <u>Pet ID</u>, Pet Name, Pet Type)
    Foreign key: Client ID to tblClient relation
All three relations are in second normal form. Do anomalies still exist? The tblChild and tblPet relations show no anomalies, but tblClient suffers from anomalies caused by the transitive dependency between Vet ID and Vet Name. (Find examples of the three anomalies caused by the transitive dependency.) You can see the transitive dependency in the bubble diagram shown in Figure AP-15; Vet ID is a determinant for Vet Name and Client ID is a determinant for Vet ID and Vet Name. Third normal form addresses the transitive-dependency problem.

Third Normal Form

A relation in 2NF is in **third normal form (3NF)** if every determinant is a candidate key. This definition for 3NF is referred to as **Boyce-Codd normal form (BCNF)** and is an improvement over the original version of 3NF.

To convert a relation to third normal form, remove the attributes that depend on the non-candidate-key determinant and place them into a new relation with the determinant as the primary key. For the tblClient relation, you remove Vet Name from the relation, create a new tblVet relation, place Vet Name in the tblVet relation, and then make Vet ID the primary key of the tblVet relation. Note that only Vet Name is removed from the tblClient relation; Vet ID remains as a foreign key in the tblClient relation. Figure AP-17 shows the database design for the four 3NF relations.

Figure AP-17 ◀
After conversion to 3NF

primary key

tblVet

VetID	VetName
24	Pets R Us
27	Pet Vet
31	Pet Care

primary key

tblClient

ClientID	ClientName	VetID
2173	Barbara Hennessey	27
4519	Vernon Noordsy	31
8005	Sandra Amidon	27
8112	Helen Wandzell	24

primary key

tblChild

ClientID	ChildName
4519	Pat
4519	Dana
8005	Dana
8005	Dani
8112	Pat

primary key

tblPet

ClientID	PetID	PetName	PetType
2173	1	Sam	Bird
2173	2	Hoober	Dog
2173	4	Sam	Hamster
4519	2	Charlie	Cat
8005	1	Beefer	Dog
8005	2	Kirby	Cat
8112	3	Kirby	Dog

The alternative way to describe the 3NF relations is:

tblVet (<u>Vet ID</u>, Vet Name)

tblClient (<u>Client ID</u>, Client Name, Vet ID)
Foreign key: Vet ID to tblVet relation

tblChild (<u>Client ID</u>, <u>Child Name</u>)
Foreign key: Client ID to tblClient relation

tblPet (<u>Client ID</u>, <u>Pet ID</u>, Pet Name, Pet Type)
Foreign key: Client ID to tblClient relation

The four relations have no anomalies, because you have eliminated all the data redundancy, partial dependencies, and transitive dependencies. Normalization provides the framework for eliminating anomalies and delivering an optimal database design, which you should always strive to achieve. You should be aware, however, that experts often denormalize relations to improve database performance—specifically, to decrease the time it takes the database to respond to a user's commands and requests. When you denormalize a relation, you reintroduce redundancy to the relation. At the same time, you reintroduce anomalies. Thus, improving performance exposes a database to potential integrity problems. Only database experts should denormalize relations, but even experts first complete the normalization of their relations.

Questions

1. What are the formal names for a table, for a row, and for a column?
2. What is a domain?
3. What is an entity?
4. What is the relationship between a primary key and a candidate key?
5. What is a composite key?
6. What is a foreign key?
7. Look for an example of a one-to-one relationship, an example of a one-to-many relationship, and an example of a many-to-many relationship in a newspaper, magazine, book, or everyday situation you encounter. For each one, name the entities and select the primary and foreign keys.
8. When do you use an entity subtype?
9. What is a composite entity in an entity-relationship diagram?
10. What is the entity integrity constraint?
11. What is referential integrity?
12. What does the cascades option, which is used with referential integrity, accomplish?
13. What are partial and transitive dependencies?
14. What three types of anomalies can be exhibited by a relation, and what problems do they cause?
15. Figure AP-18 shows the tblVet, tblClient, and tblChild relations with primary keys Vet ID, Client ID, and both Client ID and Child Name, respectively. Which two integrity constraints do these relations violate and why?

Figure AP-18 ◀

tblVet

VetID	VetName
24	Pets R Us
27	Pet Vet
31	Pet Care

tblClient

ClientID	ClientName	VetID
2173	Barbara Hennessey	27
4519	Vernon Noordsy	31
8005	Sandra Amidon	37
8112	Helen Wandzell	24

tblChild

ClientID	ChildName
4519	Pat
4519	Dana
8005	
8005	Dani
8112	Pat

16. The tblState and tblCapital relations, shown in Figure AP-5, are described as follows:

    tblState (State Abbrev, State Name, Entered Union Order, State Bird, State Population)

    tblCapital (Capital Name, State Abbrev, Year Designated, Phone Area Code, Capital Population)

    Foreign key: State Abbrev to tblState relation

    Add the attribute County Name for the county or counties containing the state capital to this database, justify where you placed it (that is, in an existing relation or in a new one), and draw the entity–relationship diagram for all the entities. The counties for the state capitals shown in Figure AP-5 are Travis and Williamson counties for Austin TX; Hartford county for Hartford CT; Clinton, Eaton, and Ingham counties for Lansing MI; Davidson county for Nashville TN; Hughes county for Pierre SD.

17. Suppose you have a relation for a dance studio. The attributes are dancer's identification number, dancer's name, dancer's address, dancer's telephone number, class identification number, day that the class meets, time that the class meets, instructor name, and instructor identification number. Assume that each dancer takes one class, each class meets only once a week and has one instructor, and each instructor can teach more than one class. In what normal form is the relation currently, given the following shorthand description?

    tblDancer (<u>Dancer ID</u>, Dancer Name, Dancer Addr, Dancer Phone, Class ID, Class Day, Class Time, Instr Name, Instr ID)

    Convert this relation to 3NF and then draw an entity–relationship diagram for this database.

18. Store the following attributes for a library database: Author Code, Author Name, Book Title, Borrower Address, Borrower Name, Borrower Card Number, Copies Of Book, ISBN (International Standard Book Number), Loan Date, Publisher Code, Publisher Name, and Publisher Address. A one-to-many relationship exists between publishers and books. Many-to-many relationships exist between authors and books and between borrowers and books.

    a. Name the entities for the library database.

    b. Create the relations for the library database and describe them using the shorthand method. Be sure the relations are in third normal form.

    c. Draw an entity–relationship diagram for the library database.

Relational Databases and Database Design Index

Microsoft Access 97 **Index**

If you are using this text as part of our Custom Edition Program, you will find entries in the Index and Task Reference that do not apply to your custom tutorials.

TASK	PAGE #	RECOMMENDED METHOD
Character, delete	WIN95 33	Press Backspace
Check box, de-select	WIN95 21	Click the check box again, or tab to option, press Spacebar
Check box, select	WIN95 21	Click the checkbox, or tab to option, press Spacebar
Detailed file list, view	WIN95 45	From My Computer, click View, Details
Disk, copy your	WIN95 50	Place disk in drive A:, from My Computer click 3½ Floppy (A:) , click File, Copy Disk, Start
Disk, format	WIN95 30	Click My Computer , click 3½ Floppy (A:) , press Enter, click File click Format, click Start
Drop-down list, display	WIN95 20	Click ▼
File, copy	WIN95 47	From My Computer, right-click the file, drag to the new location, press C
File, delete	WIN95 49	From My Computer, click the file, press Delete, click Yes
File, move	WIN95 48	From My Computer, use the left mouse button to drag the file to the desired folder or drive
File, open	WIN95 37	Click 📂
File, print	WIN95 39	Click 🖨
File, print preview	WIN95 39	Click 🔍
File, rename	WIN95 49	From My Computer, click the file, click File, click Rename, type new name, press Enter
File, save	WIN95 35	Click 💾
Folder, create	WIN95 46	From My Computer, click File, New, Folder
Help topic, display	WIN95 23	From the Help Contents window, click the topic, then click Open
Help topic, open	WIN95 23	From the Help Contents window, click the book, then click Display
Help, start	WIN95 21	Click 🏁 Start , then click Help
Icon, open	WIN95 43	Click the icon, then press Enter or double-click the icon
Icons, view large	WIN95 45	From My Computer, click View, Large Icons
Insertion point, move	WIN95 34	Click the desired location in the document; use arrow keys
List box, scroll	WIN95 20	Click ▲ or ▼, or drag the scroll box
Menu option, select	WIN95 17	Click the menu option
Menu, open	WIN95 17	Click the menu option

If you are using this text as part of our Custom Edition Program, you will find entries in the Index and Task Reference that do not apply to your custom tutorials.

Windows 95 Brief **Task Reference**

TASK	PAGE #	RECOMMENDED METHOD
Program, quit	WIN95 10	Click ❎ or Alt+F4
Program, start	WIN95 9	Click the Start button, point to Programs, point to the program option, click the program
Radio button, de-select	WIN95 21	Click a different radio button
Radio button, select	WIN95 21	Click the radio button
Start menu, display	WIN95 9	Ctrl+Esc
Student data disk, create	WIN95 41	Click **Start**, click Programs, CTI Win95, Windows 95 Brief, Make Windows 95 Student Disk, press Enter
Text, select	WIN95 34	Drag the pointer over the text
Tooltip, display	WIN95 19	Position pointer over the tool
Window, change size	WIN95 17	Drag ◢
Window, close	WIN95 10	Click ❎ or Ctrl+F4
Window, maximize	WIN95 17	Click ⬜
Window, minimize	WIN95 15	Click ▬
Window, move	WIN95 17	Drag the title bar
Window, redisplay	WIN95 16	Click the taskbar button
Window, restore	WIN95 16	Click ❐
Window, switch	WIN95 12	Click the taskbar button of the program, or Alt+Tab
Windows 95, shut down	WIN95 12	Click **Start**, click Shut Down, Click Yes
Windows 95, start	WIN95 5	Turn on the computer

Microsoft Access 97 **Task Reference**

TASK	PAGE #	RECOMMENDED METHOD
Access, exit	A 1.13	Click ⊠ on the program window
Access, start	A 1.7	Click Start, point to Programs, click Microsoft Access
Action, add by dragging	A 9.11	See Reference Window: Creating an Action by Dragging
Action, add to macro	A 9.7	In the Macro window, click the Action list arrow, click the action
Aggregate functions, use	A 3.31	Display the query in Design view, click Σ
And operator, enter in selection criteria	A 5.12	Enter selection criteria in the same Criteria row in the design grid
Append query, create	A 8.24	See Reference Window: Creating an Append Query
AutoForm, create	A 1.16	Click the Forms tab, click New, click an AutoForm Wizard, choose the table or query for the form, click OK
AutoFormat, change	A 4.4	See Reference Window: Changing a Form's AutoFormat
AutoReport, create	A 1.21	Click the Reports tab, click New, click an AutoReport Wizard, choose the table or query for the form, click OK
Briefcase replica, create	A 8.4	See Reference Window: Creating a Briefcase Replica of a Database
Calculated field, add to a query	A 3.28	See Reference Window: Using Expression Builder
Caption, change for a label	A 5.24	Right-click the label, click Properties, click the Format tab, edit the label in the Caption text box
Chart, edit	A 6.35	Double-click the chart object
Chart, embed in a report	A 6.33	See Reference Window: Embedding a Chart in a Report
Chart Wizard, activate	A 6.34	Click the Reports tab, click New, click Chart Wizard, select the table or query, click OK
Color, add to a form control	A 5.32	Select the control, click the Fill/Back Color list arrow, click the color box you want
Column, adjust width of	A 3.21	Double-click the right border of the column heading
Command button, add to a form	A 9.29	Click ▢ on the toolbox, position the pointer in the form, click the left mouse button
Command button, add to a form using Control Wizards	A 9.29	See Reference Window: Adding a Command Button to a Form Using Control Wizards
Control, move	A 5.23	Select the control, click the control's move handle, drag the control to its new position
Control, resize	A 5.26	Select the control, click and drag a sizing handle, release the mouse button
Crosstab query, create	A 8.11	See Reference Window: Using the Crosstab Query Wizard

If you are using this text as part of our Custom Edition Program, you will find entries in the Index and Task Reference that do not apply to your custom tutorials.

Microsoft Access 97 **Task Reference**

TASK	PAGE #	RECOMMENDED METHOD
Data, find	A 4.7	See Reference Window: Finding Data
Data, group in a report	A 6.24	See Reference Window: Sorting and Grouping Data in a Report
Data, sort in a report	A 6.24	See Reference Window: Sorting and Grouping Data in a Report
Database, compact	A 4.28	See Reference Window: Compacting a Database
Datasheet view, switch to	A 2.14	Click [icon]
Date, add to a report	A 6.16	See Reference Window: Adding the Date to a Report
Debug window, open	A 10.27	Click [icon] on the Visual Basic toolbar
Delete query, create	A 8.27	See Reference Window: Creating a Delete Query
Design Master and replica, synchronize	A 8.8	See Reference Window: Synchronizing the Design Master and a Replica
Design view, switch to	A 2.18	Click [icon]
Dialog box, create	A 9.32	Display the form in Design view, open the form's property sheet, set the Border Style property to Dialog
Duplicate values, hide	A 6.30	Right-click the field's text box, click Properties, click the right side of the Hide Duplicates text box, click Yes
Event procedure, add	A 10.31	See Reference Window: Adding an Event Procedure
Field, add	A 2.19	See Reference Window: Adding a Field Between Two Existing Fields
Field, add to a form or report	A 5.21	Drag the field from the field list to the form or report in Design view
Field, define	A 2.8	See Reference Window: Defining a Field in a Table
Field, delete	A 2.18	Display the table in Design view, right-click the field's row selector, click Delete Rows
Field, move	A 2.19	Display the table in Design view, click the field's row selector, drag the field with the pointer
Filter, save as a query	A 5.46	Click [icon], enter the query name
Filter, saved as a query, apply	A 5.46	See Reference Window: Applying a Filter that Was Saved as a Query
Filter By Form, activate	A 5.43	Click [icon]
Filter By Form, create	A 5.43	See Reference Window: Selecting Records Using Filter By Form
Filter By Selection, activate	A 3.16	Select the field value, click [icon]

Microsoft Access 97 **Task Reference**

Microsoft Access 97 **Task Reference**

TASK	PAGE #	RECOMMENDED METHOD
Macro, create	A 9.5	See Reference Window: Creating a Macro
Macro, run from the Database window	A 9.7	Click the Macros tab, click the macro, click the Run button
Macro, run from the Macro window	A 9.7	Click ⚡ on the Macro Design toolbar; or click Tools, click Run Macro, select the macro from the list, click OK
Macro, single-step	A 9.10	See Reference Window: Single-Stepping a Macro
Macro group, create	A 9.36	See Reference Window: Creating a Macro Group
Make-table query, create	A 8.21	See Reference Window: Creating a Make-Table Query
Menu bar, attach to a form	A 10.18	Display the form in Design view, open the form's property sheet, click the right side of the Menu Bar text box, click the menu bar
Menu bar, create	A 10.12	Create a custom toolbar, right-click the toolbar, click Properties, click the Type list arrow, click Menu Bar
Menu item, add to a menu bar	A 10.15	With the Customize dialog box open, click the Commands tab, click the New Menu category, drag New Menu to the menu bar, release the mouse button
Module, compile	A 10.40	Click 📦 on the Visual Basic toolbar
Module, create	A 10.23	See Reference Window: Creating a New Standard Module
Module, save	A 10.27	Click 💾 on the Visual Basic toolbar, enter the module name, press Enter
Object, embedded or linked, edit	A 6.35	Double-click the object
Object, embedded or linked, update manually	A 6.43	Click Edit, click OLE/DDE Links, select the object, click Update Now
Object, link in a report	A 6.40	Click 🖼, click and drag the pointer to create a box for the linked object, click Create from File, specify the file containing the object, click Link, click OK
Objects, align	A 5.36	Select the objects, right-click a selected object, point to Align, and then click the alignment you want
Objects, save in an HTML file	A 7.4	See Reference Window: Saving Access Objects in an HTML File
Office Assistant, use to get Help	A 1.18	See Reference Window: Using the Office Assistant
Or operator, enter in selection criteria	A 5.12	Enter selection criteria in the Criteria and or rows in the design grid
Overall totals, calculate in a report	A 6.26	See Reference Window: Calculating Totals in a Report
Page numbers, add to a report	A 6.18	Click the section to contain page numbers, click Insert, click Page Numbers, select formatting options, click OK

Microsoft Access 97 **Task Reference**

TASK	PAGE #	RECOMMENDED METHOD
Parameter query, create	A 5.14	See Reference Window: Creating a Parameter Query
Picture, add to a form	A 5.30	Click ▣, click the left mouse button to place an outline in the form, click the name of the picture file, click OK
Picture, change on a command button	A 9.27	Open the property sheet for the command button, click the Picture text box, click ▦, select the picture, click OK
Picture, insert on a report	A 4.24	Click Insert on the menu bar, click Picture, select the picture file, click OK
Primary key, specify	A 2.12	See Reference Window: Specifying a Primary Key for a Table
Procedure, create	A 10.35	See Reference Window: Adding a New Procedure to a Standard Module
Procedure, test in the Debug window	A 10.27	See Reference Window: Testing a Procedure in the Debug Window
Profile, create	A 7.11	In the final Publish to the Web Wizard dialog box, click the check box to save a profile, enter a name for the profile
Profile, use	A 7.14	In the first Publish to the Web Wizard dialog box, select the profile to use
Publish to the Web Wizard, activate	A 7.5	Click File, click Save As HTML
Query, define	A 3.3	Click the Queries tab, click New, click Design View, click OK
Query, export as an Excel worksheet	A 6.45	Click Tools, point to Office Links, click Analyze It with MS Excel
Query, run	A 3.5	Click ▯
Query results, sort	A 3.14	See Reference Window: Sorting a Query Datasheet
Record, add a new one	A 1.12	Click ▶*
Record, delete	A 2.25	Right-click the record's row selector, click Delete Record, click Yes
Record, move to first	A 1.12	Click ◀◀
Record, move to last	A 1.12	Click ▶▶
Record, move to next	A 1.12	Click ▶
Record, move to previous	A 1.12	Click ◀
Record, move to a specific one	A 1.12	Type the record number in the Specific Record box, press Enter
Records, redisplay all after filter	A 3.17	Click ▽
Relationship, define between two tables	A 3.8	Click ▦

Microsoft Access 97 **Task Reference**

TASK	PAGE #	RECOMMENDED METHOD
Report, custom, create	A 6.6	Click the Reports tab, click New, click Design View, select the table or query for the report, click OK
Report, preview	A 6.14	Click
Report Footer, add	A 6.20	Click View, click Report Header/Footer
Report Footer, remove	A 6.20	Click and drag the bottom edge of the footer up until the section area disappears
Report Header, add	A 6.20	Click View, click Report Header/Footer
Report Header, remove	A 6.20	Click and drag the bottom edge of the header up until the section area disappears
Report Wizard, activate	A 4.17	Click the Reports tab, click New, click Report Wizard, choose the table or query for the report, click OK
Self-join, create	A 8.37	See Reference Window: Creating a Self-Join
Sort, specify ascending	A 3.12	Click
Sort, specify descending	A 3.12	Click
Special effect, create	A 9.45	Select the object, click the list arrow for , click the special effect
SQL statement, view	A 8.40	See Reference Window: Viewing an SQL Statement for a Query
Startup options, set	A 10.55	See Reference Window: Setting the Database Startup Options
Subform/Subreport Wizard, activate	A 5.38	Make sure is selected, click , click at the upper-left corner for the subform
Submenu, add to a menu bar	A 10.11	With the Customize dialog box open, click the Commands tab, drag the button from the Categories list to the menu choice then to the submenu box, release the mouse button
Switchboard Manager, activate	A 9.41	Click Tools, point to Add-Ins, click Switchboard Manager
Tab control, add to a form	A 5.35	Click , click at the upper-left corner for the tab control
Table, create	A 2.6	Click the Tables tab, click New, click Design View, click OK
Table, export as an Excel worksheet	A 6.45	Click Tools, point to Office Links, click Analyze It with MS Excel
Table, open	A 1.11	Click the Tables tab, click the table name, click Open
Table, print	A 1.13	Click
Table structure, save	A 2.13	See Reference Window: Saving a Table Structure
Template, use	A 7.10	Select HTML template in the Publish to the Web Wizard dialog box

Microsoft Access 97 **Task Reference**